W9-BBJ-401

Oakstone Legal & Business Publishing, Inc.
6801 Cahaba Valley Road
Birmingham, Alabama 35242-2627

For editorial inquiries contact:
Oakstone Legal & Business Publishing
175 Strafford Avenue, Building 4, Suite 140
Wayne, Pennsylvania 19087

First edition 1984
Nineteenth edition 2002
Printed in the United States of America

The Library of Congress has catalogued this book as follows:

Library of Congress Cataloging-in-Publication Data
Students with disabilities and special education. 19th ed.
p. cm.
Includes index.
ISBN 1-931200-17-3

1. Special education—Law and legislation—United States. 2. Handicapped children—Education—Law and legislation—United States. I. Oakstone Publishing (Birmingham, Ala.)

LC4031.5875 1999
371.91'0973—dc20

Library of Congress Catalog Card Number: 93-13784

ISBN 1-931200-17-3
ISSN 1076-0911

Other Titles Published by Oakstone Publishing:

Deskbook Encyclopedia of American School Law
Private School Law in America
Higher Education Law in America
U.S. Supreme Court Education Cases
Deskbook Encyclopedia of American Insurance Law
Deskbook Encyclopedia of Public Employment Law
U.S. Supreme Court Employment Cases
Deskbook Encyclopedia of Employment Law
Statutes, Regulations and Case Law Protecting Individuals with Disabilities
Federal Laws Prohibiting Employment Discrimination

TABLE OF CONTENTS

CHAPTER THREE
IDEA Procedural Safeguards

CHAPTER FOUR
Private School Tuition

TABLE OF CONTENTS

CHAPTER FIVE
Related Services

CHAPTER SIX
School Liability

TABLE OF CONTENTS

CHAPTER SEVEN
Employment

CHAPTER EIGHT
School District Operations

TABLE OF CONTENTS

CHAPTER NINE
Discrimination

REFERENCE SECTION

INTRODUCTION

Federal law requires that school districts provide each child with a disability a free appropriate education. This volume has been published in response to the need of school administrators and others involved in providing special education services to have a reference available when confronted with any of the multitude of problems in the special education area. The 19th Edition continues to group cases by subject matter and contains the full text of the Individuals with Disabilities Education Act Amendments of 1997, and the final text of the Part 300 federal regulations governing the education of children with disabilities. The full legal citation is given for each reported case, and all cases have been indexed and placed in a Table of Cases following the Table of Contents.

Although the IDEA has undergone several major amendments — from the EHA to the EAHCA to the HCPA and finally to the IDEA — the book generally uses the abbreviation "IDEA" in place of the others for ease of readability and textual flow.

The intent of this volume is to provide professional educators and lawyers with access to important case, statutory and regulatory law in the field of special education and disabled student rights.

Patricia Grzywacz Walsh, Esq.
Editorial Director
Oakstone Legal & Business Publishing

ABOUT THE EDITORS

Patricia Grzywacz Walsh is the Editorial Director of Oakstone Legal and Business Publishing's Education and Employment Newsletters. She is the co-author of the *Deskbook Encyclopedia of American School Law*. Ms. Walsh graduated from Widener University School of Law and received her undergraduate degree from Villanova University. Prior to joining Oakstone, she was the Managing Editor of the *Individuals with Disabilities Education Law Report®* and authored the *1999 Special Educator Deskbook*, both published by LRP Publications. She is admitted to the Pennsylvania and New Jersey bars.

Steve McEllistrem is an editorial director of Oakstone Legal & Business Publishing, Inc. He co-authored the deskbook *Statutes, Regulations and Case Law Protecting Individuals with Disabilities* and is a former editor of *Special Education Law Update*. He graduated *cum laude* from William Mitchell College of Law and received his undergraduate degree from the University of Minnesota. Mr. McEllistrem is admitted to the Minnesota Bar.

James A. Roth is the editor of *Special Education Law Update* and *Legal Notes for Education*. He is a co-author of the *Deskbook Encyclopedia of American School Law* and adjunct program assistant professor at St. Mary's University (MN). He is a graduate of the University of Minnesota and William Mitchell College of Law. Mr. Roth is admitted to the Minnesota Bar.

How to Use Your Deskbook

We have designed ***Students with Disabilities and Special Education*** in an accessible format for both attorneys and non-attorneys to use as a research and reference tool toward the prevention of legal problems.

Research Tool

As a research tool, our deskbook allows you to conduct research on two different levels—by topics or cases.

Topic Research

- If you have a general interest in a particular **topic** area, our **table of contents** provides descriptive chapter headings containing detailed subheadings from each chapter.

  - For your convenience, we have included the chapter table of contents at the beginning of each chapter.

Example:

For more information on the implementation of IEPs, the table of contents indicates that a discussion of that topic takes place in Chapter One, under Individualized Education Programs on page 59:

How to Use Your Deskbook

- ♦ If you have a specific interest in a particular **issue**, our comprehensive **index** collects all of the relevant page references to particular issues.

> **Example:**
> For more information on related services, the index provides references to all of the cases dealing with related services including those cases dealing with medical services:
>
> → Related services
> for private school students, 5, 205-212
> generally, 6-7, 205-221
> home schooled students, 212-213
> medical services, 7, 20, 221-226
> occupational therapy and rehabilitation services, 215-217
> sign language interpreters, 10-11, 19, 201, 213-214, 209-211
> transition services, 214-215
> transportation, 226-230, 374
> Religious schools, 201-204

Case Research

- ♦ If you know the **name** of a particular case, our **table of cases** will allow you to quickly reference the location of the case.

> **Example:**
> If someone mentioned a case named *Glass v. Hillsboro School District 1J,* looking in the table of cases, which has been arranged alphabetically, the case would be located under section G, on pg. 162.
>
> **G**
>
> Girty v. School District of Valley Grove, 85
> Glass et al. v. Hillsboro School District 1J, 370
> → Glass v. Hillsboro School District 1J, 162
> Glendale Unified School District v. Almasi, 57
> Goleta Union Elementary School District v. Ordway, 292

✓ Each of the cases summarized in the deskbook also contains the case citation which will allow you to access the full text of the case if you would like to learn more about it. *See: How to Read a Case Citation, p. 669.*

- If your interest lies in cases from a **particular state**, our **table of cases by state** will identify the cases from your state and direct you to their page numbers.

> **Example:**
> If cases from Massachusetts were of interest, the table of cases by state, arranged alphabetically, would list all of the case summaries contained in the deskbook from "Massachusetts."
>
> **MASSACHUSETTS**
>
> Andrew S. v. School Comm. of Town of Greenfield, 297
> Arunim D. by Ashim D. v. Foxborough Pub. Schools, 272
> Booker v. City of Boston et al., 262
> Burlington School Comm. v. Dep't of Educ. of Massachusetts, 18, 184
> City of Worcester v. Governor, 345
> Commonwealth of Massachusetts v. Buccella, 354

✓ Remember, the judicial system has two court systems—state and federal court—which generally function independently from each other. *See: The Judicial System, p. 665.* We have included the federal court cases in the table of cases by state according to the state in which the court resides. However, federal court decisions often impact other federal courts within that particular circuit. Therefore, it may be helpful to review cases from all of the states contained in a particular circuit.

Reference Tool

As a reference tool, we have highlighted important resources which provide the framework for many legal issues.

- If you would like to see specific wording of the **Individuals with Disabilities Education Act Amendments of 1997**, refer to **Appendix A**.

- If you have questions about the **Federal Regulations Implementing the 1997 IDEA Amendments**, we have included the appropriate text in one convenient location, **Appendix B**.

If you develop a particular interest in an area of the law and would like to learn more about it, we have included several tools to guide you in your research.

How to Use Your Deskbook

- If you would like to review the **Table of Special Education Cases Decided by the U.S. Supreme Court** in a particular subject matter area, our topical list of U.S. Supreme Court case citations located in **Appendix C** will be helpful.

We hope you benefit from the use of ***Students with Disabilities and Special Education.*** If you have any questions about how to use the deskbook, please contact Oakstone Publishing at 800-365-4900.

TABLE OF CASES

TABLE OF CASES

C

D

E

F

G

N

O

P

R

S

T

TABLE OF CASES BY STATE

FLORIDA

GEORGIA

HAWAII

ILLINOIS

INDIANA

IOWA

KANSAS

KENTUCKY

LOUISIANA

TABLE OF CASES BY STATE

MAINE

MARYLAND

MASSACHUSETTS

MICHIGAN

TABLE OF CASES BY STATE

MINNESOTA

MISSISSIPPI

MISSOURI

MONTANA

NEBRASKA

NEVADA

NEW HAMPSHIRE

NEW JERSEY

NEW MEXICO

NEW YORK

NORTH CAROLINA

OHIO

OKLAHOMA

OREGON

PENNSYLVANIA

PUERTO RICO

RHODE ISLAND

SOUTH CAROLINA

SOUTH DAKOTA

TENNESSEE

TEXAS

TABLE OF CASES BY STATE

UTAH

VERMONT

VIRGINIA

WASHINGTON

WEST VIRGINIA

WISCONSIN

WYOMING

CHAPTER ONE

The Individuals with Disabilities Education Act

I. THE INDIVIDUALS WITH DISABILITIES EDUCATION ACT

Most of the summaries in this volume describe cases filed under the Individuals with Disabilities Education Act (IDEA), 20 U.S.C. § 1400 et seq. *In 1997, Congress passed Public Law 105–17, known as the Individuals with Disabilities Education Act Amendments of 1997. The amendments include local educational agency eligibility rules, a revised state funding formula based on a state's child population and child poverty level, detailed requirements for individualized education programs and special education evaluations, specific requirements concerning placement in the least restrictive appropriate environment, procedures for mediation of special education disputes, and other measures to ensure compliance with state and federal laws. In March of 1999, the U.S. Department of Education released the IDEA 1997 implementing regulations.*

A. Background

The IDEA was originally passed as the Education of the Handicapped Act of 1970 (EHA). It was intended to assist the states in providing a free appropriate public education to children with disabilities by establishing minimum requirements with which the states had to comply in order to receive federal financial assistance. The EHA was a congressional response to findings that children with disabilities historically received inadequate educational services, were improperly identified and evaluated, and were often needlessly segregated and excluded from regular school populations. Congress amended the EHA in 1975 with the Education for All Handicapped Children Act (EAHCA) (P.L. 94–142), which contains many of the most important legal protections of the legislation now known as the IDEA. The passage of the EAHCA resulted in thousands of administrative challenges and EAHCA lawsuits filed by disabled students and their parents, forcing states, local education agencies, and school districts to bring themselves into compliance with the new federal law.

The Handicapped Children's Protection Act of 1986 (HCPA) (P.L. 99–372), further amended the EHA by specifically authorizing awards of attorney's fees to the families of students with disabilities who prevailed in EHA lawsuits. The HCPA also expressly allowed disabled students to cumulate their available remedies under § 504 of the Rehabilitation Act of 1973 (29 U.S.C. § 794) and 42 U.S.C. § 1983. The HCPA is found in the present IDEA at 20 U.S.C. § 1415(i)(3) and § 1415(*l*). In 1990, Congress passed the amendment renaming the legislation the Individuals with Disabilities Education Act (IDEA) (P.L. 102–119), and added specific clauses to abrogate sovereign immunity and authorize remedies under both legal and equitable theories (20 U.S.C. § 1403). In 1994, Congress amended the IDEA as part of the Improving America's Schools Act of 1994, P.L. 103–382, Title III, Amendments to Other Acts, Part A §§ 311–315. The 1994 amendments include language that permits interim placements of up to 45 days for students with disabilities who have brought a weapon to school. The interim placement must be made by the student's IEP team. If the student's parent requests a due process hearing, the student must remain in the interim placement during the pendency of any IDEA proceeding, unless the parents and local educational agency otherwise agree. As noted in the **Introduction**, this volume relies on the abbreviation "IDEA" in reference to the various acts and amendments that make up this federal law.

The IDEA requires states and local educational agencies to meet minimum federal special education standards. Although states remain the entities that directly receive IDEA funds, local educational agency eligibility is now explicitly addressed in 20 U.S.C. § 1413, as amended by the 1997 IDEA Amendments. Local educational agencies (LEAs) must comply with state policies, procedures and programs as specified by new 20 U.S.C. § 1413. Although the 1997 IDEA Amendments impose certain restrictions on the expenditure of IDEA funds at local levels, LEAs are permitted to design and implement school-based improvement plans to improve educational and transitional results for students with disabilities. LEAs may also use up to five percent of their IDEA grants to develop coordinated services systems for students with disabilities and their families and may establish school-based improvement plans designed to improve educational and transitional results for students with disabilities. Failure to comply with the congressional directives contained in the IDEA may result in a state's retention and use of payments that would otherwise have been available to the LEA. States also bear the risk of losing federal funding eligibility for non-compliance with IDEA requirements, as set forth in 20 U.S.C. §§ 1412 and 1415.

State eligibility requirements under the IDEA now appear in 20 U.S.C. § 1412. While retaining much of the state eligibility requirements of former 20 U.S.C. § 1413, 20 U.S.C. § 1412 specifically details state requirements in several areas. These include more explicit requirements for the provision of a free appropriate education, the state's child find obligation, development of individualized education programs, procedural safeguards, evaluations and student transition from early intervention programs. The 1997 IDEA Amendments emphasize the designing of a free appropriate public education to meet the unique needs of students with disabilities, in order to prepare them for employment and independent living. A multidisciplinary team must consider a number of special factors to the extent applicable to the student. The focus of the IEP must be on access to general curriculum and the IEP must explain the extent to which a student will not be participating with nondisabled students. An IEP must include a statement of any modifications that are required to enable a student to participate in an assessment. A student's IEP must establish benchmarks or short-term objectives. 20 U.S.C. § 1414(d). The IDEA's triennial reevaluation requirement has been modified to allow evaluation teams to forego testing where new information is not needed to assist in a placement decision. 20 U.S.C. § 1414(c)(4). The 1997 Amendments require state and local educational agencies receiving IDEA assistance to offer parents voluntary mediation, with the states being required to establish an informal mediation procedure and to make mediation available whenever a due process hearing is requested.

Some of the most important sections of the IDEA Amendments of 1997 concern student discipline and **the requirement that a free appropriate public education be made available to all students with disabilities, including those who have been suspended or expelled from school**. 20 U.S.C. § 1415(k). The Amendments provide that certain students with disabilities can be removed from the classroom and placed in an alternative educational setting for an additional 45 days over the 10-day limit for carrying or possessing firearms, or for having, using, soliciting the sale of, or selling, medication or illegal drugs at school or school functions. A hearing officer may also order a change in placement if there is substantial evidence that maintenance of the current placement is substantially likely to result in injury to the student or others. Under the final regulations published by the U.S. Secretary of Education in 1999, school officials can request an expedited due process hearing where they believe that a student's current placement poses a risk of harm to the student or others. Under the regulations, misbehaving students would continue to receive services in alternative educational settings.

The 1997 IDEA Amendments require an IEP team to review whether the student's inappropriate action was a manifestation of the disability. The student's placement may then be changed, with the consent of the parents, if the behavior is the result of the disability. A primary change in the 1997 Amendments relating to the expulsion or suspension of students with disabilities is the explicit statement, already recognized by several courts, that **students with disabilities may properly be disciplined in the same manner as students without disabilities if the behavior giving rise to the discipline is not a manifestation of the student's disability**. The 1997 Amendments provide for an immediate appeal to a hearing officer if the parents disagree with the determination or the changed educational placement. A due process hearing is allowed if the parents are in disagreement with the decision.

◆ The U.S. Court of Appeals, Seventh Circuit, has considered the 1997 IDEA Amendments with regard to student discipline, although it refused to give them retroactive application. In *Doe v. Bd. of Educ. of Oak Park and River Forest High School Dist. 200*, 115 F.3d 1273 (7th Cir.1997), the court held that the amendments did not apply to the suspension of an Illinois high school freshman with a learning disability accused of marijuana possession at a school dance. The school board suspended him for ten days, held a multidisciplinary conference, and then determined that his misconduct was unrelated to his learning disability. It voted to expel the student for the rest of the semester, a decision that was affirmed by a federal district court. The Seventh Circuit held that the pre-1997 IDEA did not require the provision of educational services to a student expelled for misconduct unrelated to a disability. The IDEA stay put provision was inapplicable since the school board had determined that the student's disabilities had nothing to do with his marijuana possession. The court affirmed the judgment for the board and denied the family's request for a rehearing, acknowledging that **the IDEA Amendments of 1997 mandate that a FAPE be made available to all students with disabilities, including those who have been suspended or expelled from school**. Since the misconduct had occurred prior to the effective date of the Amendments, the court held them inapplicable. For a further summary of this case, see Chapter Two.

The 1997 IDEA Amendments impose new limits on the availability of reimbursement for private school costs for parents who initiate a private school placement without public school approval. Parents of students who previously received special education and related services from a public agency may obtain reimbursement for private school tuition where they unilaterally make a private school placement, if a court or hearing officer finds that the agency has failed to make a free appropriate public education available. 20 U.S.C. § 1412 (a)(10)(C)(iii). However, parents must promptly notify public school agencies of the decision to remove a student. Public agencies may now reduce or deny reimbursement to parents of a child placed in a private school without agency consent or referral if the parents fail to give at least 10 days' notice of the intended placement, if the child was not made available for an assessment and evaluation before the child's removal from public school, or if a judge so rules. The Eighth Circuit has held that parents now have no individual right under the IDEA to specific special education and related services. *Peter v. Wedl*, 155 F.3d 992, 998 (8th Cir.1998). LEAs are not required by the IDEA to use federal funds to pay for the private school costs of a student with disabilities if they have made a free appropriate public education available to the student.

- On-site related services may be provided to students attending private schools, including those with a religious affiliation, to the extent consistent with the law. In *Cefalu v. East Baton Rouge Parish School Bd.*, 117 F.3d 231 (5th Cir.1997), the U.S. Court of Appeals, Fifth Circuit, considered the impact of the 1997 IDEA Amendments in a case involving a Louisiana student with hearing impairments who attended a parochial school and requested on-site sign language interpretation services from the board of the school district in which he resided. The board refused to provide the services and the student's parents appealed to a federal district court, which granted their summary judgment motion. The Fifth Circuit issued a decision that was favorable to the student in some respects, but then granted petitions for rehearing by the parties. At the court's request, the U.S. Department of Education submitted a brief to the court, in which it observed that federal IDEA funding only covers a small fraction of the cost of special education services at the local level, and that school districts pay the remainder from state and local sources. The court accepted the department's argument that the IDEA does not require school districts to expend non-IDEA funds for students voluntarily enrolled in private schools. An LEA's obligation is to make a free appropriate public education available to all disabled students and to provide a proportionate share of IDEA funds to students enrolled in private schools. **The IDEA Amendments of 1997 specify that an educational agency need only provide students enrolled in private schools with a proportionate share of IDEA funds. Because the district had offered the student an appropriate public school IEP, it was not required to provide him with an on-site interpreter**, and the court reversed the judgment.

For additional cases involving the impact of the 1997 IDEA Amendments and corresponding implementing regulations on the provision of services to voluntarily enrolled private school students with disabilities, see Chapter 5, Section A.

Amended 20 U.S.C. § 1415(i) allows for a reduction in attorney's fees awards whenever a court finds that a parent has unreasonably protracted the final resolution of an IDEA dispute, the amount of attorney's fees is unreasonable or excessive, or the attorney representing a parent has failed to provide the school district with appropriate information. State and local educational agencies may also be penalized for unreasonably protracting the final resolution of an IDEA action. The 1997 Amendments transferred the Early Intervention Program from IDEA Part H to Part C. Statutory changes include the addition of two sections relating to the provision of early intervention services in natural environments. Each state system must establish procedures to ensure that early intervention services are provided to students in natural environments to the maximum extent appropriate. 20 U.S.C. § 1432(4)(g). States are required to develop written policies and procedures for submission to the Department of Education as part of each state's funding application. Each individualized family service plan must contain a statement of the natural environments in which services will be provided, and justification for providing services that will not occur in natural environments. 20 U.S.C. § 1436(d)(5). The 1997 IDEA Amendments revise the program for infants and toddlers with disabilities, and replace current provisions for training personnel to educate students with disabilities.

B. Overview

The IDEA provides state and local educational agencies with the opportunity to receive federal funds for the education of students with disabilities. States and LEAs must have in place a number of statutory policies and procedures in order to ensure the receipt of IDEA funds. State and local agencies are required under 20 U.S.C. § 1414(a) to conduct a full and individual evaluation to determine the educational needs of resident students. If parents refuse to give consent for such evaluations, the agency may pursue available mediation and due process procedures. As discussed in Section V, below, the IDEA requires educational agencies to provide students with certain procedural protections, the most important of which is the development of an individualized education program (IEP). The IEP constitutes a written statement of each special education student's present level of educational performance, including how the disability affects the student's involvement and progress in the general curriculum, a statement of annual goals including benchmarks or short-term objectives, and a statement of the special education and related services that will be provided to the student. Special education and related services must be provided so that the student may advance appropriately toward annual goals, be involved and progress in the general curriculum, participate in extracurricular and nonacademic activities, and participate with nondisabled students to the maximum extent appropriate.

IEPs must be reviewed at least annually to evaluate whether the educational agency is providing the student with a free appropriate public education. An important IDEA goal is to integrate students with disabilities into regular classrooms to the extent appropriate for the student and others. An IEP must be in effect for each student with a disability in an educational agency's jurisdiction at the beginning of each school year. 20 U.S.C. § 1414(d)(2)(A). The IDEA includes sections describing additional requirements for students with disabilities ages three through five, alternative educational placements and requirements for students with disabilities who have been convicted as adults and incarcerated in adult prisons.

"Special education" means specially designed instruction, at no cost to parents or guardians, to meet the unique needs of a child with a disability, including classroom instruction, home instruction, and instruction in other settings such as hospitals and institutions. 20 U.S.C. § 1401(25). The IDEA defines a child with a disability at 20 U.S.C. § 1401(3) as a child "(i) with mental retardation, hearing impairments (including deafness), speech or language impairments, visual impairments (including blindness), serious emotional disturbance (... referred to as 'emotional disturbance'), orthopedic impairments, autism, traumatic brain injury, other health impairments, or specific learning disabilities; and (ii) who, by reason thereof, need special education and related services." Local educational agencies must provide all children with disabilities with a free appropriate public education, which means "special education and related services that—(A) have been provided at public expense, under public supervision and direction, and without charge; (B) meet the standards of the State educational agency; (C) include an appropriate preschool, elementary, or secondary school education in the State involved; and (D) are provided in conformity with the individualized education program required under section 1414(d)." 20 U.S.C. § 1401(8).

Related services are an important part of an educational agency's obligation to students with disabilities. Such services make access to education possible for students with disabilities. The IDEA defines related services as "transportation, and such developmental, corrective, and other supportive services (including speech-language pathology and audiology services, psychological services, physical and occupational therapy, recreation, including therapeutic recreation, social work services, counseling services, including rehabilitation counseling, orientation and mobility services, and medical services, except that such medical services shall be for diagnostic and evaluation purposes only) as may be required to assist a child with a disability to benefit from special education, and includes the early identification and assessment of disabling conditions in children." 20 U.S.C. § 1401(22). Although excluded from the definition of related services, medical services needed by a child for diagnostic and evaluative purposes must be provided free of charge. See *Darlene L. v. Illinois State Bd. of Educ.*, 568 F.Supp. 1340 (N.D.Ill. 1983). Also, if certain services, like catheterization and tracheostomy suctioning, do not require a physician to perform them, they will not be excluded medical services, and school districts will have to provide them where necessary to enable the student to learn. See *Irving Indep. School Dist. v. Tatro*, and *Cedar Rapids Community School Dist. v. Garret F.*, Chapter Five, Section III.

The IDEA contains mandatory procedures designed to safeguard the rights of students with disabilities. The general procedural requirements remain in 20 U.S.C. § 1415. Under the 1997 IDEA Amendments, state eligibility is described in 20 U.S.C. § 1412, while local eligibility rules appear in 20 U.S.C. § 1413. Procedures for evaluations, eligibility determinations, individualized education programs and placement are now located in 20 U.S.C. § 1414. IDEA safeguards emphasize, among other things, notice to parents and an opportunity for parental participation in the development of a child's special education program. Significantly, 20 U.S.C. § 1415 requires that parents have an opportunity to examine their child's records, and "to participate in meetings with respect to the identification, evaluation, and educational placement of the child, and the provision of a free appropriate public education" to the child. Parents are entitled to obtain an independent evaluation of their children and to receive prior written notice whenever an educational agency proposes to initiate or change, or refuses to initiate or change, the education of the child, and where the identification, evaluation or placement of the child, or the provision of a FAPE to the child is at issue.

Parents who disagree with an educational agency's proposed IEP or a proposal to change a placement have the right to receive an impartial hearing before a hearing officer who is neither an employee of the school district nor of the state education department. 20 U.S.C. § 1415(f). Under revised 20 U.S.C. § 1415(d), states and LEAs that receive IDEA funds must ensure that a mediation process is available to allow parties to resolve special education disputes. The parents or the school may appeal unfavorable hearing decisions to the state education department after the exhaustion of available administrative procedures. A lawsuit may be commenced by an aggrieved party in either state or federal court after a decision has been reached by the state education agency. The IDEA stay put requirement, now found at 20 U.S.C. § 1415(j), is a frequently-litigated provision requiring the maintenance of a student's current educational placement pending any IDEA proceeding, unless the parties agree otherwise. See Chapter Two, Section III, Part B for cases interpreting the stay put requirement. The Supreme Court has held that the indefinite suspension of a student with a disability violates the stay put provision. See *Honig v. Doe*, Chapter Two, Section IV.

◆ A federal court of appeals held in 1989 that **the IDEA was enacted to ensure that all children with disabilities, even those with severe disabilities, receive a FAPE.** The case involved a New Hampshire student who was multiply disabled and profoundly mentally retarded. His mother attempted to obtain appropriate education for him but the school district stated that because of the student's severe disability, he would not gain educational benefits and was therefore not entitled to special education. The New Hampshire Department of Education ordered a special education placement, but the district again declined to place the student. A hearing officer found for the student, but a federal district court ruled that the student was not capable of benefiting from special education services and therefore the district was not obligated to provide educational services. On appeal, the U.S. Court of Appeals, First Circuit, held that the IDEA was intended to ensure that all children with disabilities receive a free appropriate education regardless of the severity of the disability. Severely disabled students have priority under the act. The student was multiply disabled and entitled to a FAPE. The appeals court reversed and remanded the case for determination of a suitable IEP and damages. The student was entitled to an interim special education placement until a final IEP was developed. *Timothy W. v. Rochester, N.H., School Dist.*, 875 F.2d 954 (1st Cir.1989).

◆ Achievement alone does not determine eligibility. The parents of an Illinois elementary school student with speech impairments due to small nodules on his vocal cords sought speech therapy services. The school rejected the parents' request for weekly speech therapy, stating that the student's impairments did not interfere with his academic performance. A hearing officer agreed with the parents that **the student's disability required special education services despite his competent level of academic achievement.** The district was ordered to provide the student with weekly speech therapy. A level II hearing officer reversed, and the parents appealed to a federal court.

The court considered the district's argument that the IDEA does not require a school district to provide special education to students whose disabilities do not affect their academic achievement. The court analyzed federal regulations published under the IDEA that state **academic achievement may be a component of an eligibility determination, but may not form the sole basis for the determination.** School districts must rely upon professional opinions that include other factors. For students with speech impairments, they must also consider linguistic competence and performance. No single factor could be relied upon in making an eligibility determination, and the level II hearing officer had erroneously done so. The court reinstated the original hearing officer's decision. The court also ordered the district to reimburse the parents for private speech therapy services provided through the date of the court order. *Mary P. v. Illinois State Bd. of Educ.*, 919 F.Supp. 1173 (N.D.Ill.1996).

◆ The IDEA was enacted to vindicate the rights of disabled students, not to provide a general forum for federal claims. A three-year-old Pennsylvania child suffered severe head injuries in a traffic accident. As a result, she required special education services. After making initial payments for educational services, the family's insurer refused to provide further benefits. The parents sued the insurance company in a federal district court. The insurer then filed a third-party complaint against the student's school district under the IDEA. The insurer alleged that the district was primarily responsible for providing special education services. **The district court ruled that the IDEA did not provide general jurisdiction for special education issues in federal courts.** Federal regulations under the statute stated that insurers were not relieved from paying for services to students with disabilities. Accordingly, **the insurer had no standing to bring an IDEA lawsuit against the school district**, and the court dismissed the insurer's complaint. *Gehman v. Prudential Property and Cas. Ins. Co.*, 702 F.Supp. 1192 (E.D.Pa.1989).

C. Organization of this Book

The subject matter of cases in special education overlaps, perhaps more than in other areas of the law. For example, a case that primarily involves a placement dispute may also contain important information in other subject matter areas such as procedures, private school tuition reimbursement, related services and attorney's fees. Many lawsuits filed under the IDEA include causes of action under other federal statutes such as the Americans with Disabilities Act, 42 U.S.C. § 12101 *et seq.*, the Rehabilitation Act of 1973 (29 U.S.C. § 701 *et seq.*) and 42 U.S.C. § 1983. Accordingly, the concerned professional will want to become familiar with all of the cases in this volume. Although some cases appear in more than one chapter of the book because they concern multiple subject matters, the cases have generally been categorized according to the subject matter of the court's most significant holding. IDEA cases make up most of the first seven chapters of this volume.

Unlike the IDEA, which mandates special education standards and procedures, § 504 of the Rehabilitation Act of 1973 emphasizes employment training and habilitation for individuals with disabilities. It contains an antidiscrimination provision that prohibits entities that receive federal funds from discriminating against individuals with disabilities in their programs or services. 29 U.S.C. § 794. Since all school districts, states and educational agencies receive federal funds, § 504 complaints are commonly filed by students seeking educational benefits, by individuals seeking employment or benefits from educational agencies, and by employees claiming employment discrimination on the basis of disability. Whereas courts are permitted to award damages under § 504, claims for monetary damage awards under the IDEA have been dismissed by several courts despite the apparently permissive language of 20 U.S.C. § 1403(b).

For employment discrimination cases under § 504, see Chapter Seven, Section II, subsection A. For § 504 cases involving complaints by students for failure to provide them with reasonable accommodations, see Chapter Nine, Section I, subsection A. Because many students combine IDEA complaints with § 504 claims, references to the Rehabilitation Act appear in other chapters as well.

For the same reason, Chapters Eight and Nine contain some cases with IDEA aspects. The Americans with Disabilities Act of 1990 (ADA) is another important federal statute utilized by individuals with disabilities in discrimination complaints. Although based upon the antidiscrimination principles of § 504 of the Rehabilitation Act and its regulations, the ADA's application extends to many public and private entities without restriction to recipients of federal funding. For employment discrimination cases under the ADA, see Chapter Seven, Section II, subsection A. For ADA cases involving complaints by students for failure to provide reasonable accommodation, see Chapter Nine, Section I, subsection B.

II. MINIMUM IDEA STANDARDS UNDER *BOARD OF EDUCATION V. ROWLEY*

The IDEA and its regulations focus on procedural requirements and delegate substantive educational issues to the states and their local educational agencies. However, the IDEA has been interpreted by the U.S. Supreme Court as establishing a minimum "floor of educational opportunity" that requires educational agencies to provide educational benefits that are reasonably calculated to enable students with disabilities to receive a free appropriate public education. States may voluntarily establish their own higher standards as New Jersey, North Carolina, California and Massachusetts have done. According to the U.S. Supreme Court, the IDEA was not enacted to maximize the potential of students with disabilities, but rather to open the door of educational opportunity. The Supreme Court's decision in Bd. of Educ. v. Rowley, *458 U.S. 176, 102 S.Ct. 3034, 73 L.Ed.2d 690 (1982) discusses the substantive requirements of the IDEA.*

◆ The parents of an eight-year-old New York student with profound hearing impairments disagreed with their local education board over the student's need for a sign language interpreter during academic classes. They insisted that the tutoring and hearing aid provided by the school district were insufficient, even though the student performed better than average and advanced educationally. The parents argued that because of the disparity between her achievement and her potential, she was not receiving a FAPE under the IDEA (then known as the EHA). The state commissioner of education affirmed an independent hearing examiner's decision that found the interpreter unnecessary because the student was achieving educationally, academically and socially without this service. **A federal district court held that because of the disparity between the student's achievement and her potential, she was not receiving a FAPE**. The U.S. Court of Appeals for the Second Circuit affirmed and the U.S. Supreme Court granted review.

The Court observed that in passing the IDEA, "Congress sought primarily to make public education available to [children with disabilities]. But in seeking to provide such access to public education, Congress did not impose upon the States any greater substantive educational standard than would be necessary to make such access meaningful." According to the Court, the IDEA imposed no requirement on states to provide equal educational opportunities and Congress recognized that educational opportunity differs among students of varying abilities. Because of the "wide spectrum" of abilities, the Court refused to establish a test to determine the adequacy of educational benefits provided by schools under the IDEA. Instead of imposing a general rule, the Court held:

> **Insofar as a State is required to provide a handicapped child with a "free appropriate public education," we hold that it satisfies this requirement by providing personalized instruction with sufficient support services to permit the child to benefit educationally from that instruction.** Such instruction and services must be provided at public expense, must meet the State's educational standards, must approximate the grade levels used in the State's regular education, and must comport with the child's IEP. In addition, the IEP, and therefore the personalized instruction, should be formulated in accordance with the requirements of the Act and, if the child is being educated in the regular classrooms of the public education system, should be **reasonably calculated to enable the child to achieve passing marks and advance from grade to grade.**

The Court ruled that the school board was not required to provide a sign language interpreter. The IDEA required only the development of an IEP that was reasonably calculated to enable the disabled student to derive some educational benefit. The act was not meant to guarantee a particular level of education. **The IDEA created a minimum floor for the provision of special education services but did not require states to maximize the potential of each disabled child.** In this case, the child was advancing through school easily and was not entitled to an interpreter, despite evidence that this would remedy the disparity between her achievement and her potential. *Board of Education v. Rowley,* 458 U.S. 176, 102 S.Ct. 3034, 73 L.Ed.2d 690 (1982).

Bd. of Educ. v. Rowley *remains a primary source of authority for interpreting the IDEA and is still relied upon by state and federal courts. The following cases concern the special education standards and policies cited in* Rowley.

♦ A California student was on a home/hospital instruction plan during the 1994-95 school year. However, **his school district did not provide him with instruction from a teacher with a special education credential** until March. For the first three months of the school year, the district provided him with a regular education teacher, and for the next two months, it did not provide any teacher. The next year, the district placed the student in a class for students with serious emotional disturbance, even though he was not seriously emotionally disturbed. After the conclusion of an administrative action, a federal district court awarded the student compensatory education and his parents reimbursement for various expenses.

The district appealed to the U.S. Court of Appeals for the Ninth Circuit, which observed that the IDEA requires educational agencies provide eligible students with instruction in the least restrictive possible environment. Improper placement in the seriously emotionally disturbed classroom violated the IDEA's least restrictive environment requirement. **The district's failure to provide the student any special education services for a significant part of a school year meant that it did not provide services that were reasonably calculated to provide the student with educational benefits.** The IDEA requires districts to provide qualified students with access to specialized instruction and related services. The district fell below the minimum "basic floor of opportunity" by failing to provide access to a special education teacher. Parents have an equitable right to reimbursement for the cost of compensatory education when a school district fails to provide a student with a FAPE. Despite the parents' repeated requests for services, the student had not graduated with his class and did not perform at his grade level while in school. Although he had now left school, he was entitled to an award of compensatory education. The court affirmed the district court order awarding the parents reimbursement for certain costs and attorneys' fees. *Everett v. Santa Barbara High School District*, 28 Fed.Appx. 683 (9th Cir. 2002) (unpublished).

◆ After a parent became concerned about her son's low standardized test scores; the student's school district subsequently determined that the student had learning disabilities. An IEP was proposed calling for a regular education placement with supplementary services, modified instruction and one-on-one time with a special education teacher. After meeting with district officials, the parents stated their intent to place the student in a private summer school program. At the beginning of the next school year, the district agreed to modify the IEP to include many recommendations from the private school. Despite the modifications, the parents withdrew the student from district schools in favor of a home-school program. The parents then requested a due process hearing. **A state due process hearing panel disregarded the parents' argument that it should apply Missouri's special education standards, which require the maximization of a student's capabilities.** The panel noted that the IDEA does not require that a program maximize a student's potential or provide students with the best education possible. According to the panel, the district had developed an IEP that was carefully tailored to the student's needs, substantially adequate and reasonably calculated to provide him with educational benefit. The parents appealed, and a state trial court held that the panel had correctly applied IDEA standards, not the maximizing standard of Missouri law.

The parents further appealed to the Missouri Court of Appeals, which explained that the IDEA's requirement that education agencies provide a FAPE has been described by the U.S. Supreme Court in *Rowley*, above, as establishing only a "basic floor of opportunity" for students with disabilities. However, the *Rowley* standard could not be read as imposing any particular substantive educational requirement upon the states. To the contrary, the IDEA requires each state to provide instruction and services to students with disabilities that meet the state's educational standards. While the IDEA sets the minimum standard for a state special education program, a state legislature may require a higher standard. **The court found that Missouri Stat. § 162.670 declared it the state's policy to provide special education services "sufficient to meet the needs and maximize the capabilities" of students with disabilities.** Missouri's maximizing standard was higher than that of the IDEA, and the court held that the maximizing language of the statute was not idle verbiage or superfluous language. The court rejected the reasoning of the U.S. Court of Appeals for the Eighth Circuit, which held in an earlier case that Missouri's maximizing language should not be construed as imposing a higher standard on Missouri schools than the IDEA. The trial court decision was reversed and remanded. *Lagares v. Camdenton R-III School District*, 68 S.W.3d 518 (Mo. Ct. App. 2001).

◆ A California school district proposed placing a student with cerebral palsy, hydrocephalus, seizure disorder, cortical visual impairment and other disabilities in a pre-kindergarten special day program for orthopedically handicapped students. The parents agreed to the placement and indicated their assent to the same program for the next school year. However, they advised the school district that the student would be attending a private program during the summer. That fall, the parents asked the district to place the student in the private program. The district declined, and the parents unilaterally placed him in the private program. During the summer of 1998, the student's IEP team decided to continue offering an early childhood education special day placement with related services. The parents again requested that he be placed in the private program, and formally requested retroactive reimbursement for the prior year's tuition. They also requested a due process hearing. **The hearing officer found that the district had offered to provide the student with a FAPE for both of the school years in question and was not required to reimburse the family**. The district's failure to provide a written offer of placement for the second year did not constitute a violation of IDEA procedures.

On appeal to a federal district court, the court noted that the hearing officer had properly evaluated the district's proposed IEPs under the *Rowley* standard. For the 1997–1998 school year, the hearing officer held that the district had devised a program designed to meet the student's intense needs with a pre-kindergarten special day class for orthopedically handicapped students and an array of related services. The parents had signed and accepted the 1997–1998 IEP and only disagreed with it in the fall. All of the student's areas of need were addressed in the IEP, and the parents' disagreement with the use of augmentative communication devices and music were educational policy choices that were inappropriate for review by a court. Although the parents argued that the student had made only trivial progress toward his IEP goals, the evidence indicated that his progress was more than minimal, given the seriousness of his disabilities. **The IDEA does not require school districts to maximize the potential of a student, but only requires the provision of meaningful educational benefits.** The court found that the district placement would have allowed the student to gain educational benefit both school years. Since the district had offered the student a FAPE, the parents were not entitled to reimbursement. The court agreed that the district's failure to provide the family with a formal written placement for the 1998–1999 school year did not result in a significant procedural violation. Only procedural violations that result in a loss of educational opportunities have been deemed by the courts to create a denial of FAPE. Since the district's actions in this case did not rise to this level, the court affirmed the administrative decision in favor of the district. *Fermin v. San Mateo-Foster City School District*, No. C 99-3376 SI, 2000 U.S. Dist. Lexis 11328 (N.D. Cal. 2000).

◆ A Michigan student was diagnosed as autistic and received services in a trainable mentally impaired classroom operated by an educational services agency. The agency discontinued the program, and for two subsequent years the student was placed in a cross-categorical program. During this time period, the parents and school district could not agree on an appropriate placement. The parties eventually agreed on a placement within another school district, but the offer was withdrawn. The parents requested a due process hearing. The agency special education coordinator notified the parents that the district would offer the student a program equivalent to that offered at the other district, and that an IEP calling for placement within the district would be finalized. The action was taken without the parents' involvement, and they argued to the hearing officer that this constituted a violation of the IDEA. An administrative hearing officer agreed with the parents, and ordered the district to reconvene an IEP committee. A state review officer reversed the local hearing officer's decision, finding the proposed district placement provided the student with a FAPE. **The parents commenced a federal district court action against the district, alleging violations of the IDEA, Rehabilitation Act, Americans with Disabilities Act, and state and federal civil rights laws**. The court held that the school system had violated IDEA procedures by unilaterally determining the student's placement. It ordered the district to reconvene an IEP committee meeting within 30 days. The meeting took place and the parties agreed on a new program. The court then held that the district's procedural violations did not deprive the student of a FAPE because the eventual placement was reasonably calculated to provide him with educational benefits.

The parents appealed to the U.S. Court of Appeals for the Sixth Circuit, which observed that a school district's failure to abide by IDEA procedures does not by itself require a finding of substantive failure to provide a FAPE. The parents asserted that Michigan special education standards requiring school boards to maximize the potential of each student with disabilities should be read into the IDEA definition of educational benefits. According to the circuit court, states may voluntarily impose higher standards on schools than those imposed by the IDEA. However, **"maximum potential" was not well defined in Michigan law and did not necessarily mean the best education possible**. Interpretation of state law was best left to state officials, and the court required only that the student receive a FAPE that was reasonably calculated to provide educational benefits. The district court had correctly found that the program proposed by the school district was reasonably calculated to provide the student with educational benefits. The program was designed for educable mentally impaired students and provided him with a full-time aide, along with other services. The circuit court affirmed the district court judgment on the IDEA issue and held that because there was no IDEA violation, the Rehabilitation Act and ADA claims failed. Since there had been no failure by the school district to provide the student with a FAPE and there was no state law or civil rights violation, the panel affirmed the district court judgment. *Soraruf v. Pinckney Comm. Schools*, 208 F.3d 215 (6th Cir. 2000).

◆ Although a student struggled in his public school placement, he did not initially qualify for special education services. His parents obtained an independent evaluation and learned that the student had dyslexia and attention deficit disorder and enrolled him in a private school for second grade. The student returned to the public school system before the end of the year and was eventually referred to an admission, review and dismissal committee, which identified reading and language deficiencies. The ARD committee recommended 10 hours per week in a reading and language resource room with an hour of weekly speech therapy. The student continued to experience some difficulties in grade four and received extended-year services and 25 hours of compensatory speech therapy. His parents objected to the district's failure to implement certain IEP modifications and agreed to services in alphabetic phonics. **A hearing officer found that the district failed to consistently or appropriately implement the IEP**. The parties then failed to agree upon an IEP for the student's seventh grade year and the parents withdrew him from public school in favor of a private placement.

The school district appealed to a federal district court, which granted its motion for summary judgment, finding that the student showed improvement and received educational benefit during the disputed time period. The court dismissed the parents' counterclaim for private school compensatory services reimbursement, and the parents appealed to the Fifth Circuit, which initially noted that **under *Rowley*, an IEP need not maximize a student's educational potential; it must only be designed to meet the student's unique needs and provide the student with a basic floor of opportunity to receive educational benefits**. The court also discussed the test for appropriateness of an IEP from *Cypress-Fairbanks Indep. School Dist. v. Michael F.*, 118 F.3d 245 (5th Cir. 1997), which included assessment of whether education is provided in a coordinated and collaborative manner by key stakeholders and indicates that the student is receiving positive academic and nonacademic benefits. According to the circuit court, the district court properly determined that any shortcomings in the school district's implementation of the IEP were remedied by the compensatory services it offered, and the student received educational benefits. A student challenging the adequacy of an IEP must demonstrate more than a minimal failure to implement all elements of an IEP and must demonstrate that school authorities failed to implement substantial or significant IEP provisions. **It was unnecessary for the student to improve in every academic area in order to receive educational benefit from his IEP**, and the district court properly held that the student received a FAPE in his public school placement. The parents' claim for private school reimbursement was rejected and the circuit court affirmed judgment for the school district. *Houston Indep. School Dist. v. Bobby R.*, 200 F.3d 341 (5th Cir. 2000).

◆ A New Jersey student whose intelligence was at the ninety-fifth percentile had very low test scores. During the third grade, the school's child study team noted the discrepancy between the student's test scores and his abilities, but refused to assign a learning disabled designation. Four years later, the CST agreed to classify the student as perceptually impaired and devised an IEP including Orton Gillingham instruction in reading and spelling, with resource center instruction in three other subjects. The student made only minimal progress through grade eight and the CST proposed an IEP that called for placement in a resource center. The student's parent requested a due process hearing and requested a private school placement. **A state administrative law judge held that the IEP proposed by the school district was inappropriate and ordered it to pay the student's tuition at a private school**. However, the administrative judge denied the parents' request for reimbursement for non-tuition related expenses. The district appealed to a federal district court and the parents counterclaimed for compensatory education and non-tuition expenses.

The district court reversed the administrative decision concerning denial of FAPE, finding that the IDEA requires only that an IEP provide a student with more than a trivial educational benefit. It also reversed the order requiring tuition reimbursement in view of evidence that the student could remain in a public school placement. It affirmed the administrative judgment rejecting the parents' claim for compensatory education. The court also denied the parents' request for expenses and costs, and awarded summary judgment to the school district on the parents' claims for damages under 42 U.S.C. § 1983 and § 504 of the Rehabilitation Act. The parents appealed to the Third Circuit, which rejected the district court's analysis of minimal standards for FAPE under the IDEA. The circuit court held that **the IDEA calls for more than a trivial educational benefit and requires a satisfactory IEP to provide significant learning and confer meaningful benefit**. That part of the district court judgment was vacated and remanded for further consideration, as was the question of the student's entitlement to a private school placement. On remand, the district court was to determine whether the district knew or should have known whether the student was receiving an appropriate education. The court also reversed the district court order denying the family's request for fees and costs, and reinstated its § 504 claim and the claim for IDEA damages under § 1983. *Ridgewood Bd. of Educ. v. N.E.*, 172 F.3d 238 (3d Cir.1999).

◆ The parents of a child identified as autistic determined that the child would benefit most from a 40-hour per week, Lovaas-type program of discrete trial training. Members of the individual family service plan team sought to include other available methodologies in the child's program, and the parties began to dispute the frequency and level of services. The county educational service district rejected the parents' request for an extension in services to 40 hours per week of DTT. The parties ultimately agreed on a program of 12.5 hours of weekly early intervention services. The parents voluntarily supplemented this with more intensive home services and private tutoring. They approved the IFSP and did not seek reimbursement for supplemental services. The parents also approved the county's decision to reduce the hours of weekly services for the child to 7.5 hours during the summer to accommodate vacation schedules. After noting increasingly aggressive behavior by the child, the parents sought additional training for staff in more intensive instruction methods. Staff failed to attend a training session, and **the parents initiated an administrative proceeding against the county, asserting that it failed to provide appropriate early intervention services.** A hearing officer held for the county and a federal district court affirmed. The parents then appealed to the Ninth Circuit.

The circuit court observed that the IDEA requires that each infant or toddler with a disability and their family receive an IFSP, and that each state provide appropriate early intervention services, including a timely, comprehensive evaluation. **As in the case of K-12 students, infants and toddlers are not entitled to early intervention programs that maximize their potential. States are only obligated to provide the basic floor of opportunity through the IFSP.** The district court had applied an improper standard by failing to simply ask whether the child's progress had been adequate and whether the IFSP was appropriately designed and implemented. Courts must look to IFSP goals as of the time of implementation, and ask whether the methods were reasonably calculated to confer meaningful educational benefit on the child. The district court had instead speculated that it was impossible to determine whether the child received meaningful benefit in view of his participation in home tutoring. The Ninth Circuit agreed with the hearing officer's conclusion that the IFSP was sufficient to confer meaningful benefit. There was no error in the district court's conclusion that the family was not entitled to reimbursement for the child's school year programming. The reduction in services had erroneously been made in consideration of staff vacation schedules. Although a reduction in hours that is linked with developmental goals is permissible, this one was not. As a result, the parents were entitled to reimbursement for their expenses in obtaining appropriate services and tutoring during the summer. Parental consent to the reduction in services was irrelevant and did not bar the claim for reimbursement. The court remanded the case to the district court for a more specific determination of the entitlement to reimbursement for the summer services. *Adams v. State of Oregon*, 195 F.3d 1141 (9th Cir. 1999).

◆ A Massachusetts student suffered from Atypical Pervasive Developmental Disorder and received special education from his school district. By the time he reached his junior year of high school, all his academic courses were mainstream classes. His parents sought to have him go through graduation ceremonies with his classmates the following year while remaining at the school for an additional year of transition services, even though district policy did not allow non-graduating students to participate in graduation activities. The parents rejected the proposed IEP for the next year and unilaterally enrolled the student in a private residential school. They then sought tuition reimbursement.

A hearing officer found that **the school district's IEP had been reasonably calculated to provide the student with the maximum possible educational benefit in the least restrictive setting, as required by Massachusetts law**. A federal magistrate judge affirmed that decision, and the parents appealed to the U.S. District Court for the District of Massachusetts. The court found that although the Magistrate judge had improperly failed to differentiate the more stringent state standard from the less stringent federal mandate, the school district had met its responsibility to maximize the student's educational development. **The parents' expectation that the district would be able to mold their son into a responsible and independent individual capable of interacting with the social world around him was unreasonable given the student's innate disabilities**. Because the district had provided for the student's maximum possible development, the court affirmed the decisions denying reimbursement. *Frank S. v. School Committee of Dennis-Yarmouth Regional School Dist.*, 26 F.Supp.2d 219 (D. Mass. 1998).

◆ A moderately mentally retarded California student spent time in special education classes while her parents attempted to have her placed in full-time regular education classes. Although the district created an IEP and eventually proposed part-time placement in regular classes for all academic subjects, her parents sought a full-time regular education placement. After this request was denied, they enrolled her in a private school in regular classes, and appealed the placement decision. A hearing officer held for the student and ordered the school district to place her in regular classes with appropriate support services. The district appealed to a federal district court. **The IDEA requires LEAs to provide students with disabilities an appropriate education in the least restrictive appropriate environment (LRE).** Four factors must be considered in determining the LRE: educational benefits, nonacademic benefits, effect on the teacher and other children, and cost. The student met the educational benefit requirement through progress in her IEP goals and objectives and her increased motivation to learn. She could also derive benefits from language and behavior models. Nonacademic benefits were evidenced in her improved self-confidence, excitement about school and development of friendships. The student did not present a discipline problem and did not distract the other students, and the cost of full-time regular class enrollment would not increase beyond the funding needed for special education. **The court held that the student must be placed full-time in regular classes with support services.** *Bd. of Educ., Sacramento City Unif. School Dist. v. Holland*, 786 F.Supp. 874 (E.D.Cal.1992).

III. U.S. SUPREME COURT CASES

The following brief summaries provide an overview of important IDEA cases decided by the U.S. Supreme Court. For the full summary of each case and other cases dealing with issues in the subject matter of the Supreme Court's case, please refer to the chapter and section indicated.

◆ The U.S. Supreme Court held that a New York statute which created a special school district for a religious community (which had been incorporated as a village) had to be struck down as violative of the Establishment Clause. **The special school district exceeded the bounds of religious neutrality required by the Constitution.** *Bd. of Educ. of Kiryas Joel Village School Dist. v. Grumet*, 512 U.S. 687, 114 S.Ct. 2481, 129 L.Ed.2d 546 (1994). See Chapter Eight, Section I.

◆ The parents of a learning disabled Massachusetts student were found by the Court to have violated the IDEA's stay put provision by unilaterally enrolling him in a private school. Because the proposed IEP had been appropriate, the parents were not entitled to tuition reimbursement and other costs. The Court, however, noted that in some situations parents could be reimbursed even though they unilaterally placed a student in a private school where a court later held that the proposed IEP was educationally inappropriate. **Parents who unilaterally changed their children's placement did so at their own risk, because if (as in this case) the proposed IEP was appropriate, the parents had to pay the private school costs.** *Burlington School Comm. v. Dept. of Educ. of Massachusetts*, 471 U.S. 359, 105 S.Ct. 1996, 85 L.Ed.2d 385 (1985). See Chapter Four, Section I.

◆ The Court held that the failure of a school district to propose an appropriate IEP and placement for a learning disabled South Carolina student justified an award of private school tuition reimbursement by the district, even though the private school was not approved by the state of South Carolina. This was because the private school placement was appropriate and because South Carolina did not publish a list of approved schools. The IDEA requirement to provide a free appropriate public education did not apply to parental placements. **To recover private school tuition costs, parents must show that the placement proposed by the school district violates the IDEA, and that the private school placement is appropriate under the act**. Federal courts have broad discretion in granting relief under the IDEA, and may reduce tuition reimbursement awards found to be unreasonably expensive. The Court upheld the lower court decisions in favor of the parents. *Florence County School Dist. Four v. Carter*, 510 U.S. 7, 114 S.Ct. 361, 126 L.Ed.2d 284 (1993). See Chapter Four, Section I.

◆ **The Establishment Clause of the First Amendment did not prohibit a public school district from providing a sign language interpreter to an Arizona student who attended a parochial school**. According to the Court, the provision of the interpreter was a neutral service that provided only an indirect economic benefit to the parochial school. *Zobrest v. Catalina Foothills School Dist.,* 509 U.S. 1, 113 S.Ct. 2462, 125 L.Ed.2d 1 (1993). See Chapter Four, Section II.

◆ The Court held that Congress did not intend that the IDEA permit monetary damage awards against states in actions brought in federal courts under the doctrine of sovereign immunity. This permitted the Commonwealth of Pennsylvania to avoid liability in an IDEA damage suit brought by a learning disabled student. [In 1990, Congress passed an amendment abrogating sovereign immunity (20 U.S.C. § 1403) in IDEA cases and authorizing both equitable (injunctive and declaratory) and legal (damage award) remedies under the IDEA.] *Dellmuth v. Muth,* 491 U.S. 223, 109 S.Ct. 2397, 105 L.Ed.2d 181 (1989). For a full discussion of sovereign immunity issues, see Chapter Six, Section I.

◆ The suspension or expulsion of a special education student constitutes a change of placement under the IDEA, according to the 1988 decision, *Honig v. Doe*. School authorities may not unilaterally exclude a child from classes pending administrative proceedings. However, **the IDEA's stay put provision** (20 U.S.C. § 1415(e)(3), now § 1415(j)) **did not prevent school districts from imposing temporary suspensions of ten school days or less** upon students who present a threat of harm to other persons. *Honig v. Doe*, 484 U.S. 305, 108 S.Ct. 592, 98 L.Ed.2d 686 (1988). The 1997 Amendments address suspensions for disciplinary reasons in 20 U.S.C. § 1415(k) and allow removal from class for up to 55 days in certain circumstances. See Chapter Two, Section IV.

◆ **A Texas school district was required to provide catheterization services for a disabled student while she attended school because it was a "supportive service" (related service) under the IDEA**, 20 U.S.C. § 1401(22). The Court held that the student's parents were also entitled to receive their attorney's fees under § 504 of the Rehabilitation Act. *Irving Independent School Dist. v. Tatro*, 468 U.S. 883, 104 S.Ct. 3371, 82 L.Ed.2d 664 (1984). See Chapter Five, Section III.

◆ The Supreme Court held that an Iowa school district had to provide a quadriplegic student with a full-time aide to assure his meaningful access to education under the IDEA. The Court determined that **providing an aide amounted to a necessary related service, and not an excluded medical service.** Using a "bright-line" rule, the Court limited medical services to those provided by a physician. *Cedar Rapids Community School Dist. v. Garret F.*, 526 U.S. 66, 119 S.Ct. 992, 143 L.Ed.2d 154 (1999). See Chapter Five, Section II.

◆ A disabled Rhode Island student was not entitled to recover attorney's fees despite prevailing in an IDEA lawsuit against his school district in *Smith v. Robinson*. The Court ruled that there was no evidence that the school district had violated any of the student's procedural safeguards under the IDEA. Congress responded to the *Smith* decision by passing the Handicapped Children's Protection Act of 1986 (P.L. 99–372), which **specifically authorized attorney's fee awards to students with disabilities who prevailed in IDEA lawsuits.** The same legislation provided that disabled students may cumulate available remedies under § 504 of the Rehabilitation Act (29 U.S.C. § 794) and 42 U.S.C. § 1983. See 20 U.S.C. § 1415(i)(3) and § 1415(l). *Smith v. Robinson*, 468 U.S. 992, 104 S.Ct. 3457, 82 L.Ed.2d 746 (1984). Because the Handicapped Children's Protection Act of 1986 substantially overruled *Smith v. Robinson*, there is no further summary of the case in this volume.

IV. IDENTIFICATION AND EVALUATION

The IDEA requires each state and LEA to conduct a full and individual evaluation before the initial provision of special education and related services to resident students with disabilities. See 20 U.S.C. § 1414(a)(1)(A). Each state must also demonstrate that each resident student with a disability is identified, located and evaluated under 20 U.S.C. § 1412(a)(3)(c), and is provided with an IEP that meets IDEA requirements described at 20 U.S.C. § 1414(d). LEAs must comply with the notice and procedural requirements of 20 U.S.C. § 1414(b). The IDEA's triennial reevaluation requirement was modified by the 1997 Amendments to allow evaluation teams to forego testing where new information is unnecessary to assist in a placement decision.

A. Educational Agency Obligations

◆ A Tennessee student with learning disabilities and an emotional disturbance never attended public schools in his district of residence. His parents enrolled him in a private Connecticut school with a curriculum designed for students with learning disabilities. They did not contact the district before making the placement or request an evaluation. When the family requested an evaluation over a year later, the district took more than six months to complete it. The evaluation was hampered by the student's absence from the district and by delays in obtaining information. During a meeting to discuss the student's educational program, his father expressed his intention to keep his son in the Connecticut facility for the rest of the school year and did not complain about the lengthy evaluation process.

The district certified the student for special education and proposed a public school placement. **The parents commenced an IDEA action against the district, asserting** they were entitled to reimbursement and claiming **that the district had an insufficient child find plan**.

A federal district court found that the district's plan called for the dissemination of information to all area private schools, day-care centers, nursery schools, hospitals and other places where medical professionals were likely to encounter children with special education requirements. The district also made public service announcements in the local media and conducted an outreach program. The district court decision was appealed to the U.S. Court of Appeals for the Sixth Circuit, which remanded the case for a trial. On remand, the district court found that the school district had made adequate child find efforts and denied the parents' request for private school tuition reimbursement. The parents appealed to the Sixth Circuit again, which observed that they had never contacted the district about their son's placement before seeking reimbursement. **The district's publicity campaign fulfilled its child find duties. The IDEA's child find obligation requires districts to ensure that students in need of special education are identified and served. It does not require districts to pursue the parents of private school students who do not act upon available information**. Although the student's evaluation took six months to complete, the parents were not entitled to reimbursement on that basis. The court affirmed the district court judgment. *Doe v. Metropolitan Nashville Public Schools*, 9 Fed.Appx. 453 (6th Cir. 2001).

◆ Near the end of a private school student's kindergarten year, her parents met with the principal of a public school and toured various classes. They voiced their concerns about a public school placement for the child, as she had a learning disability, and enrolled her in another private school. The following year, they obtained an evaluation recommending that the student be placed at a different private school. The parents notified the school district of the evaluation and explained that they were interested in a placement at the recommended private school. A district special education committee drafted an IEP but never completed it. The parents rejected the draft and requested transportation to the private school. The district agreed. The parents moved out of the school district prior to the end of the school year. The parents requested a due process hearing. **A hearing officer held that the district was negligent in its child-find duties under the IDEA, failed to notify the parents of their due process rights or identify public school facilities available to the student**. Further, the district did not evaluate the student or prepare a complete and accurate IEP for her. The hearing officer approved the private school placement and held that the district must reimburse the parents for its costs up to the time they moved. A state review officer agreed that the district did not provide the student with a FAPE because of its failure to evaluate her. Although he approved of the placement selected by the parents, he denied the award of tuition reimbursement because he found that the parents had no intention of enrolling their daughter in public schools.

The parents appealed to a federal district court, which observed that tuition reimbursement may be awarded where a district fails to provide a student with a FAPE and the placement selected by the parents is appropriate to the student's needs. There was ample evidence in this case that **the district had failed to provide the student with a FAPE**. The court focused on whether it was fair to award the parents tuition reimbursement in view of all the relevant factors. **While the parents had made statements indicating an interest in the private school placement, they should not be blamed for the district's failure to perform its child-find obligations.** The district had never advised the parents of their due process rights or explained what public-school facilities were available in the district. The review officer had improperly set aside the hearing officer's decision awarding them tuition reimbursement, as the district had failed to contact them and advise them of appropriate procedures. The district's conduct amounted to gross violations of special education due process procedures. The district did not act reasonably in many respects. Because the parents had been reasonable and the district should not be rewarded for failing to comply with the IDEA, the court reinstated the award of tuition reimbursement and approved an award of attorneys' fees. *Wolfe et al. v. Taconic-Hills Central School District*, 167 F.Supp.2d 530 (N.D.N.Y. 2001).

◆ A student had over 150 absences and numerous behavioral referrals during her sophomore year of high school. The student had a problematic relationship with her mother and exhibited signs of drug use. A school support team began an initial evaluation for special education and a social worker urged the student's parents to have her tested for drug use late in her junior year. Two days later, the mother confronted the student about drug use and the student responded by threatening to kill her mother. The student was hospitalized and tested positive for marijuana. She underwent a special education evaluation that resulted in her classification as emotionally impaired. She spent time in a juvenile detention center but eventually completed a residential program at another hospital during the summer. She received tutoring and graduated the following spring. **Her parents filed an administrative action against state education officials seeking reimbursement for the hospitalization costs**, characterizing them as IDEA related services. A hearing officer concluded that the costs were reimbursable and awarded the parents $7,713.

The Hawaii education department appealed to a federal district court, which stated that under the IDEA, medical services are subject to parental reimbursement as "related services" if they are for diagnostic and evaluation purposes. **The IDEA's affirmative duty to identify, locate and evaluate children with disabilities in the state applied to all students suspected of being disabled, even those who advanced from grade to grade.** The child-find duty required the identification and evaluation of students within a reasonable time after school officials were on notice of behavior that was likely to indicate a disability. The IDEA states that a state or local education agency is deemed to have knowledge that a child has a disability if behavior or performance demonstrates the need for special education and related services. The hearing officer found reason to suspect that the student was disabled and that she might need special education services to address her emotional impairment as early as the beginning of her junior year. She was absent from school 79 times and had many behavior referrals the previous year. The court rejected the state's argument that the student's graduation under the IEP it eventually developed satisfied its obligation to provide a FAPE. The student's receipt of some educational benefit was not determinative, because instruction was not provided under an appropriate IEP, despite numerous warning signs, before the end of her junior year. The state had a reason to suspect that the student had a disability and that special education and related services might be necessary. It violated the IDEA's child-find provisions by failing to evaluate her earlier. The services provided at the hospital were diagnostic and for evaluation. While they had been precipitated by a crisis, her disability might never have been addressed and she might not have ever received IDEA services if not for her hospitalization. The student's parents were entitled to reimbursement for her hospitalization costs. *Department of Education, State of Hawaii v. Cari Rae S.*, 158 F.Supp.2d 1190 (D. Haw. 2001).

◆ Until the fifth grade, a student received special education services, but that year a multidisciplinary team report stated that she had no disability. While a sixth-grade team report determined that she was disabled by an "other health impairment," there was no physician documentation detailing her current health status, as required by Nebraska law. The student advanced to high school and school officials concluded that she was not eligible for special education services. **When the student's grades dropped in the seventh grade, her parents questioned the lack of special education services**. Although they signed a release allowing the school to inspect her medical records, they provided outdated information to the school. The student claimed that her band teacher called her "stupid", "retarded" and "dumb" on a daily basis and threw a notebook at her. She stated that he told her "she could no longer play in the band because she was too stupid and that he did not have to teach students like her." The parents met with school officials, including the band teacher. She was removed from band class and assigned to a music appreciation class taught by the same teacher. The student's grades continued to drop and she was placed in a home-school program. The parents sued the district and officials, including the band teacher, in federal district court for claims arising under the IDEA, ADA, and Section 504 of the Rehabilitation Act. They also sought monetary damages under 42 U.S.C. § 1983. The court awarded summary judgment to the district and officials; the parents appealed to the Eighth Circuit.

According to the circuit court, the district followed appropriate procedures to determine whether the student was entitled to receive special education services. **School officials lacked the required reports to verify her current health status and concluded that she did not qualify for special education services**. While the district was required to provide written notice that the student would not receive special education, the parents did not appropriately respond to its requests for current information. The district performed its obligation to identify and evaluate the student, and there was no IDEA violation. The court rejected the family's equal-protection claim for removal from the band class, finding no constitutional rights violation. The ADA and Section 504 claims failed because the parents could not rely on past diagnoses of impairment to support a claim of actual disability. The student's impairments were only moderately limiting, and she was not disabled within the meaning of either act. Although the band teacher's conduct was "unprofessional, intemperate and unworthy of one entrusted with the responsibility of educating students," it did not support an intentional infliction of emotional distress claim. The court affirmed the judgment. *Costello v. Mitchell Public School District 79*, 266 F.3d 916 (8th Cir. 2001).

◆ While in grade ten at a parochial school, a student experienced behavior problems, but continued to receive above average grades. The parents decided to transfer the student to a public school for eleventh grade. The family returned intake forms to the new school asserting that the student had never been in any special classes or accelerated programs. The family hired a private counselor who determined that the student had depression, but did not allow school employees access to this information. In February of the student's eleventh grade year, the family enrolled him in an out-of-state residential treatment program. After six months, the family asked the district to evaluate the student. The school district sought to have the student's private school records transferred, but the family failed to do so until almost one year later. In the meantime, the district sought and received time extensions from the state education department that relieved the district of its state law obligation to perform an evaluation within 90 days. By the time the records were forwarded to the district, the student had withdrawn himself from the residential school. After an administrative hearing, **a hearing officer held that the school district had reason to know that the student was eligible for evaluation and that he was a student with emotional disabilities who needed special education**. The private school provided the student with an appropriate educational program and educational benefits, and the district was ordered to reimburse the family in excess of $84,000. A review officer reversed, finding the hearing officer's findings were unsupported by the record.

The family appealed to a federal district court, which first held that where a state utilizes a two-tiered hearing process, only the final decision is entitled to deference. **The court agreed with the review officer that the district had no reasonable cause to suspect that the student had exceptional educational needs. There was no violation of the IDEA's child find obligation and no evidence that district screening policies were deficient**. The most serious problems experienced by the student, falling asleep and receiving lower grades, did not indicate a disability and the father had denied that they were caused by a disability. The student passed all but one of his classes and was receiving some educational benefit. The district had not committed any procedural violations and demonstrated good faith. District employees had no reasonable cause to suspect that the student was emotionally disabled or required special education. He was removed from district schools before the pre-referral screening process was complete, and the family had resisted early screening efforts. The court held that the family had a strictly financial motive for seeking an emotionally disturbed classification and had blocked the district's good faith efforts to evaluate the student. The school district was awarded summary judgment in its favor. *Hoffman v. East Troy Community School Dist.*, 38 F.Supp.2d 750 (E.D. Wis. 1999).

◆ A special education student's parents received an exemption from the state's compulsory attendance law by providing him with home education services. **The local school district denied their request for speech therapy services under a district policy stating that home-schooled students "do not have access to**

instruction and/or ancillary services with the public schools." The school administration explained that the policy complied with Nevada law and suggested that the parents either seek an exception from the school board or enroll the student in the district. The parents instead filed a complaint against the school district with the state department of education, which the department denied on the basis of a 1992 Office of Special Education Programs policy letter declaring that states have discretion to determine whether or not home education qualifies as a private school or facility that implicates IDEA coverage. The parents then sued the school district in a federal district court, alleging that its policy violated the IDEA and the Equal Protection Clause of the 14th Amendment. They sought a declaration that the student was entitled to speech therapy services, reimbursement for private speech costs that they had incurred and an award of attorneys' fees.

The district court awarded summary judgment to the school district and the parents appealed to the Ninth Circuit, which observed that the Nevada legislature had amended the law after the commencement of the action to require the provision of special education and related services to home-educated children. The school district conceded that it was presently required to provide speech therapy to the student. The circuit court remanded the question of the parents' entitlement to a declaratory judgment based on the intervening change in Nevada law. In examining the parent's request for reimbursement of their speech therapy costs and attorneys' fees, the court noted that nothing in the IDEA requires the provision of services to children who are not enrolled in a school. The court found that neither the IDEA nor its regulations define the term "private school or facility." By contrast, pre-1999 Nevada law defined private schools as private education institutions, and specifically excluded homes in which instruction was offered to children who were excluded from the compulsory attendance law under the home education exception. The court declined the parents' invitation to create its own definition of "private school," and held that the states were permitted to determine whether home education should be considered an IDEA-qualifying "private school or facility." Nevada's pre-1999 definition of private school coincided with common definitions, and was consistent with the authoritative guidance of the OSEP policy letter. Moreover, **the school district had offered the student a free appropriate education in its schools and nothing in the IDEA required it to provide services to children whose parents reject an offer of education but fail to enroll them in any "school," as defined by the state**. The state's former policy did not violate the student's due process or equal protection rights as it was permissible for the state to attach conditions to the receipt of benefits and limit the receipt of benefits in order to limit scarce resources. The court affirmed the district court judgment for the school district. *Hooks v. Clark County School Dist.*, 228 F.3d 1036 (9th Cir. 2000).

◆ After moving from Florida to Alabama, a student's grades dropped and she experienced significant turmoil personally and socially. During the ninth grade, the student began receiving psychotherapy for depression, family conflict and acting-out behavior. She continued to perform below her ability in classes, but did not show outward signs of depression at school. After an alleged rape at school, the student was placed in a home instruction program. An evaluation around this time noted the student's "conflictual and intense relationship with her mother," symptoms of post-traumatic stress disorder and attention deficit disorder, but found no formal learning disability. The evaluator recommended medication and therapy. After the student was asked to leave a private day school because of inappropriate behavior, her parents began a home-school program. This program was unsuccessful. A psychologist determined that the student had possible bi-polar symptoms, oppositional-defiant disorder, a history of ADHD and depression. The psychologist's recommendations did not include a referral for special education. The student's mother contacted the district's special education director for information. The director did not refer the student for an evaluation or provide any information about IDEA rights. The parents eventually placed the student in a residential psychiatric hospital and sought an IEP. The district did not develop an IEP or evaluate the student. The student received no academic credit for the school year and her parents enrolled her in a Maine residential facility. She remained there for three years and graduated. Once the parents requested district funding for the residential placement, the district evaluated the student for special education. The district evaluation conflicted with a report obtained by the parents and the Maine school's psychologist, who stated that the student was emotionally disturbed. **The district convened a multidisciplinary eligibility committee, which determined that the student was ineligible for special education and related services**. The parents commenced a due process request and a hearing officer held for the district, finding that the student was not disabled under the IDEA and that the district's failure to provide IDEA notices was harmless. Because the student was ineligible for special education, the hearing officer held that the family was not entitled to reimbursement.

The parents appealed to a federal district court, which noted that it had to determine whether the student was "emotionally disturbed" as defined by the IDEA and state and federal special education regulations. The IDEA defines "student with a disability" as one who has been evaluated as within one of the categories of disability, and who "needs special education and related services." Federal regulations at 34 CFR Part 300.26(b)(3) specify that a student with a disability is one who must have specially designed instruction in order to have access to and benefit from the general educational curriculum. The court held that the evidence indicated that the student had been accessing and benefiting from the general educational curriculum until she stopped attending. While her grades slipped prior to the rape incident, she attended school regularly, earned passing grades, and participated in extracurricular activities. The student's home behavior problems and family conflicts were not reflected in her school behavior. Her therapist did not identify her as being in need of special education services during her time in the Alabama school. **As there was no evidence that the student required specially designed instruction to access and benefit from the general curriculum, she was not in need of special education and related services**. Although the court was critical of the school district's lack of responsiveness to the family's requests for assistance, its mistakes did not support a finding of eligibility. Numerous other court decisions have emphasized that **a student's home behavior does not confer IDEA eligibility to students with emotional or behavioral problems that are not primarily manifested at school**. Experts who evaluated the student identified her family as the source of her emotional difficulties, and the decision to place the student in the Maine school was motivated largely by her parents' inability to care for her at home. The court affirmed the decision for the school district with regard to the eligibility and reimbursement issues, ruling that the IDEA does not permit a finding of entitlement to special education when a student has not demonstrated an inability to learn in public schools. The student did not exhibit one or more of the five characteristics of emotional disturbance described in Alabama special education regulations. The court refused to impose liability on the district for IDEA procedural violations, despite evidence that school authorities were unresponsive and failed to offer assistance to the family. The court granted judgment to the district and officials. *Katherine S. v. Umbach*, No. CIV.A. 00-T-982-E, 2002 WL 226697 (M.D.Ala. 2002).

◆ During an honors student's 10th grade year, his father contacted school officials, expressing concern about his son's emotional problems and drug use and asking them for assistance. Prior to the father's request, the student was diagnosed with ADHD, bipolar disorder, obsessive-compulsive disorder and marijuana abuse. The following year, he became chronically truant and was hospitalized. Physicians who treated him noted his daily marijuana use and recommended placement in a therapeutic boarding school. The parents placed the student in a Connecticut therapeutic school, where he received treatment for his emotional problems. However, he continued to use marijuana and inhalants and was transferred to a residential drug treatment program in Utah. His behavior soon improved and he returned to the Connecticut school, where he completed 11th grade. The student re-enrolled in his public school for grade 12. **The parents requested an IDEA due process hearing, arguing that their request for assistance with identification of the student's problems created a duty on the school district to make an special education eligibility determination.** Moreover, they argued that the district's failure to make an eligibility determination denied the student a FAPE.

An administrative law judge agreed with the parents, finding that school officials' failure to identify the student as having a disability amounted to a procedural violation of the IDEA. The ALJ based this finding on the student's negative behavioral changes and academic decline. Because the district violated IDEA procedures, the ALJ found it fundamentally unfair to require the student to prove that he had a disability as a prerequisite to an award of tuition reimbursement for the Connecticut placement. The ALJ also held that the Connecticut placement was appropriate for the student under the IDEA. The school district appealed to the U.S. District Court for the District of Maryland, which reversed the administrative decision. According to the district court, the ALJ had improperly held that a procedural violation alone can create a duty on the school district to reimburse the parents for the cost of private school tuition. **The district court** also **found that the student's behavior problems resulted not from an educational disability but from social maladjustment, as evidenced by his history of drug abuse. The student was not disabled under the IDEA** and the school district was entitled to summary judgment. The parents appealed to the Fourth Circuit, which affirmed the order for summary judgment in a brief, unpublished memorandum decision that stated only that its decision was based on the reasoning of the district court. *Board of Education of Frederick County, Maryland v. JD III et al.*, 232 F.3d 886 (4th Cir. 2000).

◆ An eighth grader was expelled from her Christian school and her parents enrolled her in another private school and requested special education assistance from their school district. The district considered an IEP and reviewed conflicting test results. The district's psychologist concluded that while the student was impulsive, manipulative and oppositional to authority figures, she was not seriously emotionally disturbed and had the potential to control her behavior. Approximately four months later, the team determined that the student was not eligible for special education services. The student was then examined by three mental health specialists, each of whom reached different conclusions regarding an appropriate diagnosis. None of the specialists ruled out ADHD. **The parents commenced an administrative action against the school district, seeking certification of the student as disabled, along with reimbursement for the costs of the second private school**. An ALJ held that the student was not eligible for special education and related services because she did not meet the criteria for other health impairment, serious emotional disturbance or learning disabilities. The parents appealed to a federal district court. Before the court ruled on the case, the student was expelled from her private school and her parents enrolled her in district schools. The IEP team then determined that she was eligible for special education as emotionally disturbed with a learning disability.

In considering the case, the court initially determined that the student was entitled to present evidence of treatment that had taken place after the conclusion of the administrative hearing for the limited purpose of determining whether she was disabled at the time of the hearing. The court found that Tennessee special education regulations require that an IEP team find a student eligible for special education where she has mental or physical impairments that require special education and related services in order to be educated within the regular school program. Similarly, the IDEA states that in order to be classified as a child with disabilities, the student must need special education and related services. The parents argued that the student qualified for special education as either having "other health impairments" due to ADHD, or as having a serious emotional disturbance. The court agreed, ruling that the ALJ's decision was incorrect in view of additional evidence obtained after the hearing. Although the evidence was "murky and conflicting," it indicated that the student had an emotional disturbance, as defined by the IDEA. The court relied on the testimony of one specialist who concluded that the student's behavior was actually related to an underlying emotional disorder. The court found the specialist's testimony indicative of emotional disturbance that had occurred over an extended time period. **Because the student's behavior adversely affected her educational performance to the point she was unable to remain in school, even thought her grades were satisfactory and she had made reasonable progress in school, she was eligible for special education services due to an emotional disturbance**. The court held that the parents were entitled to tuition reimbursement during the time the district disputed the student's eligibility. There was no evidence that the district intended to offer the student special education services or otherwise accommodate her behavior through a Section 504 plan. Because the private school offered a highly structured environment, the parents had little choice but to select it to gain educational benefits for the student. *Johnson v. Metro Davidson County School System*, 108 F.Supp.2d 906 (M.D. Tenn. 2000).

◆ After a hazing incident at a private school, a student enrolled in public school where he received poor grades and did not interact well with other students. School officials repeatedly asked the student's mother for permission to evaluate him for special education. She provided written authorization for an evaluation but withdrew her consent at the initial evaluation session. The mother also refused to provide school officials with requested medical records. A pediatric neurologist examined the student and advised school representatives that he had no learning disability. The school implemented a general education intervention plan for the student. The following year, the student entered high school and school officials initially believed that he might be eligible for special education services. However, **the student's mother advised them that he was not experiencing academic problems and was not disabled**. The student played on the basketball team, developed friendships, and made the honor roll. The following year, the student's mother declined an offer to have the student placed in a special study hall because of his middle school performance. Later in the year, he was cut from the junior varsity basketball team and was repeatedly late for geometry class. After being reprimanded for frequent tardiness, school officials withdrew the student from his geometry class. Two days later, the mother asserted that the student had a disability and consented to an evaluation. However, she refused to sign an evaluation consent form and again refused to provide supporting medical records.

The mother commenced a federal district court action that was dismissed for failure to exhaust administrative remedies. She initiated administrative proceedings, and a hearing officer determined that the school system had not failed to identify the student as eligible for special education. **The hearing officer found that school officials had made every effort to assist the student and gain parental permission to evaluate him**. The school system did not violate the student's rights under § 504 of the Rehabilitation Act by applying the tardiness policy to him and cutting him from the basketball team. The state board of special education appeals affirmed the hearing officer's decision, and a federal district court awarded summary judgment to the school system. The parents appealed to the U.S. Court of Appeals for the Seventh Circuit, which agreed with the hearing officer's findings that, in view of the student's improved academic performance, the neurologist's diagnosis, and the mother's resistance to the performing of an evaluation, the school system did not fail to identify the student as requiring special education services. Because Indiana special education regulations require written parental consent before the performance of any evaluation, there was no merit to the mother's claim that the system was responsible for evaluating and identifying the student over her objection. There was also no merit to the student's § 504 claims, since there was evidence that the decisions to enforce the tardiness policy and cut him from the basketball team were non-discriminatory. The court affirmed the judgment for the school system. *P.J. v. Eagle-Union Comm. School Corp.*, 202 F.3d 274 (7th Cir. 1999).

◆ A Virginia student attended public schools through grade six and progressed in regular education programs. He was placed by his parents in a private school from seventh to ninth grade and received no special education services there. He then returned to the public school system and obtained passing grades in tenth grade, maintaining positive relationships with teachers and peers. However, in eleventh grade, **the student was arrested and sentenced to probation for criminal activities and began to regularly use marijuana and alcohol. The school disciplined him for frequent absenteeism, fighting and breaking school rules.** He failed three of seven courses for the year, and his parents enrolled him in a private residential school. They sought tuition reimbursement from the school board, asserting that the student had a serious emotional disturbance as defined by the IDEA regulations. The district refused the request, and the parents asked for a due process hearing. The hearing officer found the student seriously emotionally disturbed and eligible for special education services. A state level review officer reversed the decision, and the parents appealed to a Virginia federal district court.

The court affirmed the state review officer's decision and refused to allow testimony by the student's psychiatrist. The parents appealed to the U.S. Court of Appeals, Fourth Circuit, which stated that **the evidence in this case indicated that the student had committed juvenile delinquent acts that demonstrated social maladjustment and not serious emotional disturbance. Unlike persons with serious emotional disturbance, the student was in complete control of his actions.** He did not have an inability to learn, build or maintain satisfactory personal relationships or have a general pervasive mood of unhappiness or depression or fears associated with personal or school problems. IDEA regulations specifically exclude social maladjustment from the definition of serious emotional disturbance. It was not unjust to exclude testimony by the psychiatrist since the parents had apparently refrained from presenting his testimony to the local hearing officer in a strategic decision. The court affirmed the judgment for the school board. *Springer v. Fairfax County School Bd.*, 134 F.3d 659 (4th Cir.1998).

◆ A New York student who was classified as speech impaired received special education services through her fourth grade year. She was placed in a remedial reading program through grade seven, then promoted to ninth grade despite failing multiple subjects in grades seven and eight. She then began to experience behavior problems, and was hospitalized for depression. The student's emotional and behavioral problems resumed after she returned to school and she was again hospitalized. Her family placed her in a residential treatment and educational facility in Connecticut. She was then diagnosed as having conduct disorder, and later, oppositional defiant disorder. The student's parents sought payment for the private placement from the school district. **The district's committee on special education formally determined that the student was ineligible for special education services under the IDEA, but recommended referral for services under § 504 of the Rehabilitation Act**. The family rejected a public school educational plan proposed by the § 504 committee and enrolled the student in a private program where she showed behavioral and academic progress. The family commenced administrative proceedings against the school committee, which resulted in affirmation of the school committee's determination that the student had no disability under the IDEA. The family appealed the final administrative order to a federal district court, which vacated the administrative findings and held that the student was emotionally disturbed, as defined under state and IDEA regulations. The court ordered the school committee to reimburse the family for the costs of the private placement.

The school committee appealed to the U.S. Court of Appeals, Second Circuit, which held that the student had been deprived of appropriate IDEA services due to the school committee's erroneous attempts to classify her. Evidence indicated that the student had demonstrated an inability to learn that could not be explained solely by intellectual, sensory or health factors. This included her repetition of a grade, her receipt of special education services through fourth grade and her failure of multiple subjects in higher grades. There was also evidence that she improved in academic settings that addressed her emotional and behavioral problems. **Because the student's academic problems resulted at least in part from her emotional problems, and most of her medical evaluations indicated symptoms of depression that endured for several years, the district court had properly deemed her eligible for IDEA services due to a serious emotional disturbance.** The court affirmed the judgment for the family. *Muller on Behalf of Muller v. Committee on Special Education of East Islip Union Free School Dist.*, 145 F.3d 95 (2d Cir.1998).

- A group of Chicago public school students with disabilities and their parents initiated a federal district court action against the City of Chicago Board of Education (CBE), Illinois State Board of Education (ISBE) and certain education officials, seeking declaratory and injunctive relief to correct systemic failures by the CBE and ISBE. The complaint alleged that the education boards and officials had failed to educate students with disabilities in the least restrictive educational environment as required by the IDEA. The court denied dismissal motions filed by the boards and officials. After five years of negotiations, the students and parents reached a settlement with the CBE requiring it to comply with the IDEA's least restrictive educational environment mandate within eight years. However, no settlement was reached with the ISBE, and the court conducted a trial concerning its statutory responsibility to ensure local compliance with the IDEA.

The court found that placement decisions in Chicago public schools continued to be based on a student's individual needs and that the obsolete method of associating students with particular disabilities persisted, partly as a result of the ISBE's pre-1990 special education regulations. **The ISBE had failed to meet its statutory responsibilities to ensure local compliance with the IDEA** and had apparently impeded progress by disregarding its duties. **It was permissible for a court to find a state educational agency responsible for a school district's systemic failures, and since the ISBE had accepted federal funding under the IDEA, it was the party responsible for ensuring local compliance.** The court directed the ISBE to submit a comprehensive compliance plan for court approval in specific areas. These included placement decisions based upon individual needs, local violations to be identified and corrected, teacher certification standards, and state funding formulas. *Corey H. v. Bd. of Educ. of City of Chicago*, 995 F.Supp. 900 (N.D.Ill.1998).

◆ A New Jersey first grade student exhibited behavior problems and was identified as potentially having attention deficit disorder, but the school district did not refer him for an evaluation or special education services. The school district and the student's mother engaged in a long dispute before agreeing to obtain an independent evaluation of the student. Although the child study team agreed that he had attention deficit disorder/hyperactivity disorder (ADHD), the student was performing at or above his grade level so the team resisted making a special education placement. The parties reached a settlement after attending an administrative hearing, at which the evaluator determined that the student had Tourette's syndrome and a severe obsessive-compulsive disorder as well as ADHD. The district again resisted making a special education placement and further hearings were held. When the mother brought constitutional and state law claims against the district, a New Jersey federal court determined that the parties' settlement agreement barred her claims for money damages. She appealed to the U.S. Court of Appeals, Third Circuit.

The court observed that **the IDEA requires each school district to identify, locate and evaluate resident students with disabilities within a reasonable time**. It had been inappropriate for the district court to dismiss the mother's claims when factual issues existed concerning the parties' intentions in reaching the settlement agreement. It did not appear that the parties contemplated settling her claims for monetary damages. While the IDEA had no specific language authorizing an award of damages, the court held that money damages could be recovered under the IDEA through the use of 42 U.S.C. § 1983. The district court had inappropriately dismissed the damage claims under both statutes, and the court of appeals remanded them for further consideration. **The district court would have to reconsider the district's delays in evaluating the student and denying the requests for special education services**. The constitutional and state law claims had also been improperly dismissed. *W.B. v. Matula*, 67 F.3d 484 (3d Cir.1995).

◆ In 1969, California education officials implemented **standardized IQ testing for determining appropriate placements for educable mentally retarded (EMR) students.** Within two years of the commencement of standardized testing, a class representing African-American students filed a lawsuit in federal court, claiming that their overrepresentation in EMR classrooms and the standardized testing violated the IDEA and Title VI of the Civil Rights Act of 1964. In 1979, the district court issued an injunction banning the use of IQ tests for evaluating EMR students and for students who attended classes that were the substantial equivalent of EMR classes. The parties then reached a settlement agreement that abolished the EMR category and **banned the use of standardized tests to evaluate African-American students for any special education assessment**. This resulted in a 1986 modification of the 1979 injunction.

Years later, another group of African-American students petitioned the district court for an order to vacate the 1986 modification because they wanted to take IQ tests. The district court consolidated the case with the original action and vacated the 1986 modification, awarding summary judgment to the students seeking to be tested. Members of the original plaintiff class and the state superintendent of public instruction appealed the summary judgment order to the

U.S. Court of Appeals, Ninth Circuit. The court of appeals affirmed the district court's decision to vacate the 1986 modification and reinstate the original order. It also affirmed the order for further proceedings to determine whether all special education classes were substantially equivalent to the EMR designation and whether IQ tests were effective in placing African-American students. The new class of plaintiffs should not be bound by the prior judgment because its members had not been adequately represented by the original class. **The 1986 ban on all IQ tests expanded the scope of the original injunction and was unsupported by the original factual findings. These findings pertained only in the context of EMR placements**. *Crawford v. Honig*, 37 F.3d 485 (9th Cir.1994).

B. Independent Evaluations

◆ A Pennsylvania special education student, his mother and a brother lived in a townhouse during the week and spent some weekends and holidays with the father in their house in another district. After the student was hospitalized twice, the district stated that the family had never established residency and refused to pay for the private school recommended by two experts. The student's parents unilaterally enrolled him in a private school for students with learning disabilities. An administrative board agreed with the district that the townhouse was a temporary residence that was established for convenience and not intended to be a primary residence. However, a Pennsylvania trial court found that the student's residence was the place of his physical presence. The commonwealth court adopted the trial court's decision in favor of the family. *Thane v. Cumberland Valley School Dist.*, 724 A.2d 978 (Pa.Commw.Ct.1999).

A hearing officer also found that the district failed to provide a FAPE to the student. The district appealed to an appeals panel, which affirmed the hearing officer's order. The case reached the commonwealth court, which held that the district had a duty to implement the IEP created by the student's former district. The IEP proposed by the district failed to meet state and federal standards because it was vague, did not address the student's behavioral disorders and contained immeasurable standards. The district had also committed procedural irregularities and had failed to staff the student's multidisciplinary team with a certified school psychologist. The student was entitled to receive private school tuition reimbursement because of the district's failure to provide him with a FAPE. **He was** also **entitled to part of the cost of an independent evaluation, due to the district's failure to obtain a certified school psychologist and because it relied on the independent evaluation when preparing the IEP**. *Cumberland Valley School Dist. v. Lynn T.,* 725 A.2d 215 (Pa.Commw.Ct.1999).

◆ A Georgia public school student performed well during his first two years of elementary school, achieving average or better grades. However, during his third year, he began to receive failing grades as a result of incomplete homework and class assignments. The student's mother discussed his continuing difficulties and the school began to conduct some informal testing. **The mother** also **had the student evaluated by a private neuropsychologist, who determined that the student had no specific learning disability or attention deficit disorder** that would make him eligible for special education services. The mother verbally relayed this information to school officials but did not give them a copy of the report. The student continued to fail his academic classes, and the parents enrolled him in a private academy. **Another test by the neuropsychologist determined that the student had a specific learning disability**, and the parents requested a due process hearing, asserting that the school had violated the IDEA by failing to identify his disability and provide him with an adequate education. The hearing officer held that the school district did not violate the IDEA; however, it should have referred the student to its formal special education screening team when he continued to fail his classes. The hearing officer ordered the district to devise an IEP for the student, but the parents refused to attend the meeting and appealed to a federal district court.

The court found no evidence that the district had failed to maintain adequate testing and screening practices, observing that the student's standard tests had not revealed significant deficiencies. Although the mother asserted that school officials had failed in their duty to refer her son to a multi-disciplinary team for evaluation, there was no evidence that school officials had ignored clear signs of a learning disability or ADD, and no evidence that they had violated the duty to identify him as having a disability. The court rejected the hearing officer's determination that the student was entitled to special education services, but affirmed the ruling that the school district had not violated IDEA procedural protections. It granted the district's dismissal motion. *Clay T. v. Walton County School Dist.*, 952 F.Supp. 817 (M.D.Ga.1997).

◆ An Indiana student with mental retardation, attention deficit hyperactivity disorder, leukemia and a history of acute seizures attended public schools and received special education services. His parents disputed an IEP requiring him to attend special education classes for almost the full day. When his seizure activity worsened and his behavior problems increased, the student was withdrawn from school and received homebound instruction. **The student's doctor placed him on an experimental drug to control the seizures and recommended that he resume school** with individualized instruction, a full-time aide and increased supervision. When the school IEP case review team convened prior to the following school year, **team members stated that a reevaluation of the student by the school was required prior to the creation of an IEP**. The parents rejected the request and refused to attend a later IEP meeting. They requested a due process hearing with the state department of education, seeking a specific placement for the student and reimbursement for an independent evaluation. The hearing officer ordered a reevaluation, and the parents appealed to the state board of special education appeals. The board affirmed the hearing officer's decision, and its decision was affirmed by a federal court. The parents appealed to the U.S. Court of Appeals, Seventh Circuit.

The court considered an IDEA regulation that requires a reevaluation at least every three years and upon request by a parent or teacher. Other federal circuit courts have held that the regulation gives a school district the right to conduct a triennial reevaluation by personnel it selects. In this case, **the student's condition had changed since his last day of school attendance, and the district had a right to conduct a reevaluation**. Indiana special education regulations permitted reevaluation without parental consent in the absence of a request for a hearing on the issue. Because the parents had requested a due process hearing on the issue of placement, and not reevaluation, the district court judgment was affirmed. *Johnson by Johnson v. Duneland School Corp.*, 92 F.3d 554 (7th Cir.1996).

◆ A 13-year-old Washington, D.C. student with behavior problems was admitted to a psychiatric hospital. Her parents requested an evaluation by the District of Columbia Public Schools, and provided the DCPS with an independent psychiatric evaluation and a discharge summary from the hospital. DCPS took no action, and the parents requested a due process hearing. The hearing officer held for the parents and ordered DCPS to evaluate the student. DCPS then notified the parents of its intent to conduct a clinical interview, obtain a social history and perform classroom observations. **The parents demanded information about the clinical interview**, which DCPS failed to provide. In the meantime, the parents enrolled the student in a private residential special education program. At a second hearing, the hearing officer held that although a private placement was appropriate, the parents were not entitled to tuition reimbursement because they had wrongfully withheld their consent for a DCPS assessment, and their refusal to allow the clinical interview rendered DCPS unable to fulfill its statutory obligations. A federal court affirmed the hearing officer's decision, and the parents appealed to the U.S. Court of Appeals, District of Columbia Circuit.

On appeal, the parents argued that DCPS had no right to examine the student when an independent evaluation already existed. DCPS asserted an absolute right to conduct its own evaluation of the student. The court found that both parties had overstated their legal positions, and that a fact issue existed concerning whether each had performed its statutory obligations. The IDEA does not require local education agencies to conduct their own psychological tests, but simply requires an evaluation to be performed by a knowledgeable person. **Although the parents were entitled to a response to their inquiry about the composition of the clinical interview, they could not unreasonably withhold their consent from DCPS to evaluate and place the student**. The matter was remanded to the district court. *Holland v. Dist. of Columbia*, 71 F.3d 417 (D.C.Cir.1995).

◆ An Iowa student with Down's syndrome attended regular kindergarten classes in a public school with modifications, related services and a teacher's aide. He experienced behavior problems and his parents scheduled an independent education evaluation at a university hospital. **The evaluation cost over $7,000 and the family's private health insurance carrier paid $6,500 of this amount. Because this payment reduced the amount of the student's lifetime maximum benefits under the policy, the family sought reimbursement** from the state department of education, local school district and area education association. They also sought reimbursement for their transportation and meal expenses. An administrative law judge ordered the district and area educational association to reimburse the parents for their actual expenses, including transportation and meals. The parents and educational association reached a settlement under which the association paid the parents $3,500, which was then paid to the insurer. With respect to the remaining defendants, the administrative law judge declared that the claim for reimbursement based on reduction in available lifetime benefits was speculative. The parents appealed to an Iowa federal court.

The court observed that the IDEA requires educational agencies to provide an independent educational evaluation at public expense. The parents' failure to notify the district prior to obtaining the evaluation was not fatal to their claim. The court noted that a 1980 notice of interpretation by the U.S. Secretary of Education declared that **a decrease in available lifetime benefits under an insurance policy constitutes a financial loss to parents that prohibits an agency from compelling the parents to file an insurance claim where financial loss poses a realistic threat**. The administrative law judge had failed to consider this notice and had improperly held that the reduction in lifetime benefits was speculative. The parents were entitled to recover the balance paid by their insurer plus their attorney's fees and costs. The court also ordered the parents to pay this sum over to their insurer. *Raymond S. v. Ramirez*, 918 F.Supp. 1280 (N.D.Iowa 1996).

V. INDIVIDUALIZED EDUCATION PROGRAMS

An individualized education program (IEP) is a written statement for each student with a disability that describes the student's present levels of educational performance, progress in the general curriculum, services to be provided, annual goals and complies with many other statutory requirements. The specific requirements for IEPs are now found at 20 U.S.C. § 1414(d). Many of the issues presented in this section of the book are more fully discussed in the closely related area of placement, found in Chapter Two.

A. Generally

Each IEP includes statements of annual goals, including benchmarks or short-term objectives, related to meeting the student's needs that result from the student's disability, to enable involvement and progress in the general curriculum. ***IEPs include a statement of the special education and related services to be provided to the student and a statement of the program modifications to be furnished****, which will allow the student to advance appropriately toward attaining the annual goals, and be involved and progress in the general curriculum and participate with other students. Each IEP must explain the extent to which a student will not participate with nondisabled students in regular classes and a statement of any individual modifications that are needed for the student to participate in state or local student achievement assessments. For students age 14 and over, a statement of the student's necessary transition services under the applicable components of an IEP focusing on courses of study must be included. For those over 16, a statement of necessary transition services must be included which may describe interagency responsibilities. Beginning at least one year before the student reaches the age of majority under state law, the IEP must include a statement that the student has been advised of IDEA rights that will transfer to the student upon the attainment of the age of majority.*

The composition of an IEP team is described at 20 U.S.C. § 1414(d)(1)(B). IEP teams include the student's parents, at least one of the student's regular education teachers, at least one special education teacher of the student, and a local educational agency representative who is qualified to provide or supervise the provision of specially designed instruction to meet the unique needs of the student and who is knowledgeable about the general curriculum and local agency's resources.

◆ The parents of a student with cerebral palsy, scoliosis and learning disabilities sought the assistance of an aide for toileting. They further requested a due process hearing to contest the lack of accessible facilities at his school. The hearing was continued to allow time for the parties to revise the student's IEP. The hearing officer determined that the school board had provided the student with a FAPE. The decision was affirmed by a state-level review panel, which held that the board provided the student with educational benefits and a FAPE. The panel found that the parents' concerns about a lavatory aide had been addressed and that accessibility problems did not deprive the student of educational services. It also approved the student's IEP, encouraging the board to complete his transition plan as soon as possible. **The family appealed to a federal district court, asserting that the board did not provide the student with transition services, that his IEPs and transition plans were deficient, that he received no educational benefit from his current program** and that the administrative proceedings were not impartial.

The court rejected the family's argument that the board violated IDEA procedural requirements for transition services. While the review panel indicated concern that a transition plan be finished as soon as possible, there was insufficient evidence that the IEP was procedurally deficient. The board had discussed transition services in the student's reports and evaluations, outlined desirable adult outcomes for him, and listed school and family action steps. The board had contacted appropriate state and local agencies to assist with transition services, and the family's expert conceded that the student was receiving appropriate transition services. The family had been provided with the opportunity for meaningful participation in the decision-making process. The court also disagreed with the family's claim that the IEP was substantively deficient. The IEP had been formulated to enable the student to receive educational benefits. The court found that **the student's IEP was appropriately individualized on the basis of his assessment and performance. The IEP accounted for his particular academic and vocational needs, and identified and addressed his special needs**, including toileting assistance. His program was administered in the least restrictive environment, as he attended mainstream classes and ate in the cafeteria with other students. The court found that the student's program resulted in positive academic and nonacademic benefits, and his evaluation report explained that he had progressed in his IEP goals, along with raising his grades in six areas. For these reasons, the court affirmed the administrative decision. *Pace v. Bogalusa City School Board*, 137 F.Supp.2d 711 (E.D. La. 2001).

◆ A visually impaired student's IEP called for her placement in an alternative setting, occupational and physical therapy, adaptive physical education, and extensive modifications. A transition plan was also developed. The student's mother approved the IEP and transition plan, but soon requested a due process hearing. An independent hearing officer held the IEP inadequate for failing to specify therapy and adaptive physical education with particularity. **The IHO also faulted the IEP for not describing "the appropriate program for the child during each minute of the day"** and ordered the parties to revise the IEP. The district appealed to a state review panel, which agreed with the IHO's order to convene an IEP meeting to address related services. However, the panel disagreed with the IHO's finding that the IEP and related services were inadequate. The parties created a new IEP within 30 days, but the student's mother commenced a federal district court action against the school district, asserting IDEA violations.

The court noted that the IEP and its developmental processes were not ideal. However, minor procedural inadequacies did not result in loss of educational opportunity. School personnel adequately complied with requirements to provide occupational and physical therapy and adaptive physical education. The court disagreed with the IHO's finding that the IEP lacked sufficient particularity regarding services. The IEP stated the duration and scheduling of the services for the entire school year. **It was not necessary for the IEP to "account for each minute of each day." Each IEP is individualized to the needs of each disabled student and the failure to account for every minute in the school day did not result in the loss of educational opportunity.** The court found evidence that the IEP contained proper goals, and that the student was receiving instruction in areas of need. The administrative record did not support the mother's claim that no transition services were being provided and the district satisfied its procedural responsibilities for transition services. The court determined the IEP was reasonably calculated to provide the student with educational benefit. It was appropriately individualized, administered in the least restrictive environment, provided in a coordinated and collaborative manner by key educational stakeholders and demonstrated positive academic and non-academic benefits. There was no testimony that the student was not receiving educational benefit and while the IEP was not optimal, it was specifically designed to meet her unique needs and satisfied the IDEA's requirements. The court affirmed the review panel's decision and dismissed the mother's appeal. *Barber v. Bogalusa City School Bd.*, No. CIV. A. 98-1333, 2001 WL 667829 (E.D.La. 2001).

◆ During an Indiana student's junior year at a Christian school, he experienced severe allergies and depression that affected his school performance. Prior to enrolling in the Christian school, the student had received special education services from his school district due to his history of anxiety, distractibility, and ADHD. The student's mother requested special education services from a county special education cooperative, and the student returned to district schools before the end of the year. He received special education services only three percent of the time and also received home instruction. A conference committee approved of a residential placement for the student's senior year, noting that he was profoundly depressed and unable to function in a traditional school environment. The state education department agreed to fund his placement in a California private school, which he attended for six months. He then demanded to attend a Massachusetts school. **The student, who was then 18 years old, soon rejected the Massachusetts school, and the district complied with his request to return to the public school he formerly attended.** After the student returned to the Indiana public high school for his second senior year, his father died suddenly. His conference committee recommended homebound instruction and family counseling. The student rejected district efforts to perform a vocational rehabilitation evaluation. A few weeks before he completed his graduation requirements and received a regular diploma, his mother requested a due process hearing. Several days after the student graduated, the hearing officer deemed the case moot.

The student commenced a federal district court action against the school district, special education cooperative and school officials, alleging violations of Section 504 of the Rehabilitation Act, 42 U.S.C. § 1983, the ADA, the Equal Protection Clause and indirect violations of the IDEA. He sought compensatory education and damages for denial of a FAPE under Section 504 and the IDEA. The court applied the IDEA's legal analysis to the student's ADA and Section 504 claims. His Section 1983 claim was derivative of IDEA standards, and the equal protection claim also resembled an IDEA claim. The court rejected the district's argument that the case should be dismissed as moot because the student was now 24 years old and had graduated. He sought compensatory relief for past violations and neither his age nor his graduation mooted his claims. Graduation does not equate with the provision of a FAPE. The student argued that his return to the high school for his second senior year came under an IEP that dramatically reduced his special education services. The court found that higher rates of special education had been rejected as overly restrictive. There was no basis for finding the student's program inappropriate. The death of his father resulted in significant and unforeseen changes in circumstances. **When the IEP became unworkable, the district took necessary action in less than one month. An IEP prepared shortly before the father's death was not procedurally defective. The IEP drafted in response to the father's death showed consideration for less restrictive options than homebound instruction**. The student had agreed with the program at the time and stated that his goal was to graduate as soon as possible. The IEP also addressed the student's increased emotional problems from the loss of his father. The court found no evidence that the student's graduation had been a sham to get rid of him. He earned the number of required credits and learned what was required. The district had opened the door of educational opportunity for the student and there was no evidence that a certificate and continuing services was a better option than graduation. The court awarded summary judgment to the district, cooperative and school officials. *Brett v. Goshen Community School Corp.*, 161 F.Supp.2d 930 (N.D. Ind. 2001).

◆ After a family moved to North Carolina to take advantage of TEACCH programming for their autistic child, the parents obtained homebound Lovaas therapy for him. The parents and the district were unable to agree on an IEP for several school years. During this period, the parents consistently sought funding for the student's Lovaas program. The district proposed placement in a preschool classroom for 22 hours per week, along with extended school year or in-home services three times per week. The parents rejected this offer, but some six months later signed an IEP calling for one and one-half hours of direct special education and speech therapy. During the 1996-97 school year, the child attended a private preschool with a Lovaas therapist, along with receiving 20 hours per week of home Lovaas therapy. After the parents again sought reimbursement, an IEP meeting was held. The parents presented a draft IEP calling for Lovaas therapy, while the district offered to place the child in a TEACCH preschool setting with speech and occupational therapy, then proposed placing him in kindergarten for the 1997-98 school year. In response to the parents' attempt to have the child declassified as a disabled student, the district conducted a reevaluation, and found that he no longer qualified for special education. When the district denied the parents' renewed request for reimbursement, the parents filed a request for due process. **The parents brought two experts to the hearing that had never seen the child's IEPs or evaluations. The administrative law judge found the experts unable to render opinions** on the IEPs. The ALJ determined that the parents had requested funding for Lovaas therapy, but never challenged the child's IEPs. They also did not commence due process proceedings within the 60-day statute of limitations. Therefore, the ALJ dismissed the case.

A state review officer affirmed the decision, and the parents appealed to a federal district court. The court held the action was time-barred, but the Fourth Circuit reversed on grounds that the district did not sufficiently advise the parents about commencement of the 60-day limitations period. The district court reviewed the administrative record and recited the ALJ's findings concerning the inability of the parents to challenge the district's IEPs with competent expert evidence. The parents never sought reimbursement for the 1995-96 school year, and did not contact the district at all until March 1996. Reimbursement is barred when parents unilaterally arrange for private educational services without notifying the district of dissatisfaction with an IEP. There was no authority for reimbursing parents for their expenses prior to the development of an IEP. While the Fourth Circuit held that the district failed to provide due process notice to the parents, the court stated that this procedural violation did not result in a duty of reimbursement for Lovaas therapy during the 1996-97 school year. **The parents had no expert witness who could show that the IEP for that year was insufficient. Because they could not counter the district's evidence that it had created an appropriate IEP for 1996-97, the district was awarded summary judgment**. *M.E. and P.E. on behalf of their son, C.E. v. Bd. of Educ. for Buncome County*, 186 F.Supp.2d 630 (W.D.N.C. 2002).

◆ A West Virginia school board and the parents of a student with autism had a longstanding dispute over the student's educational program. The parents filed due process proceedings to force the district to pay for the student's in-home Lovaas program. The proceedings resulted in an administrative decision in favor of the parents, and a state court decision in favor of the parents. At an IEP meeting held after the court decision was issued, the parties couldn't agree on an IEP and the parents continued the home program. The student began attending kindergarten classes when he reached age five, but after two weeks his parents withdrew him from school to continue the home program. The student's IEP did not incorporate the home-based program. The next academic year, the student attended kindergarten under a modified IEP that did not incorporate the supplemental home-based Lovaas program. Although the student continued to attend kindergarten throughout the school year, the parents provided him with weekly home supplemental Lovaas training. The student made significant progress during the school year, which led to the initiation of new administrative proceedings over the supplemental home-based program. The parents sought reimbursement for the costs of the program, claiming that it was necessary for the student to attain a FAPE. **A hearing officer agreed with the parents that the IEPs devised by the school board were inadequate and that the home-based Lovaas program was necessary for the student to obtain a FAPE**. The hearing officer ordered the school district to reimburse the parents for costs related to the home program.

The board challenged the administrative decision in a federal district court, which noted that the Supreme Court decision in *Bd. of Educ. v. Rowley*, 458 U.S. 176 (1982), sets a minimal standard for the appropriateness of an IEP, finding only that the IEP must be reasonably calculated to confer some educational benefit on the student. In the public school context, a student receives sufficient educational benefit if the IEP is reasonably calculated to enable the student to achieve passing marks and advance in grade. **The court found that regular grading and advancement systems, while generally useful as guideposts for the courts, are not as useful in the context of a student with autism or similar disability. In this case, because of the student's autism, the concept of "educational benefit" embraced non-traditional areas essential to continuing the child's education, along with academics**. The court found that the board had not met its burden of proving that the proposed IEPs were adequate. In examining the disputed IEPs, the court noted that the school district's witnesses gave testimony that was conclusory in nature and some witnesses conceded that the IEPs were inadequate in the absence of a home program. The family's witnesses provided clear testimony that the student required a home-based Lovaas program in view of his academic, behavioral and social deficiencies. Since the board failed to meet its burden of showing that the IEPs were reasonably calculated to provide the student with a FAPE, the court found it in violation of the IDEA. If the parents could show in further proceedings that the home-based program was reasonably calculated to provide the student with a FAPE, they would be entitled to reimbursement for the costs of the program. *Board of Education of County of Kanawha v. Michael M.*, 95 F.Supp.2d 600 (S.D. W.Va. 2000).

◆ When a preschool student was three years old, his parents started a home-based discrete trial training (DTT) program and notified the district that he had autism. A psychologist selected by the parents submitted a written proposal for a DTT program including staff training at an IEP conference. The meeting was taped but never written into a formal IEP. The district's director of special education drafted a new proposal calling for placement in a mainstream kindergarten class, without DTT. At the next IEP conference, the parents objected to the proposed mainstream placement. They then initiated due process proceedings against the district. A local hearing officer decided for the parents, holding that the taped proposal was an IEP that should have been implemented and that the parents were entitled to reimbursement for their DTT expenses. **A state hearing review officer reversed the decision, finding that the oral proposal was not an IEP and that the written one was valid and provided a FAPE designed to maximize the student's potential. The order denied the parents' request for reimbursement**, and they appealed. A district court granted the school district's motion for summary judgment, holding that the district had conducted a proper evaluation of the student and proposed an IEP designed to address his needs and attain his maximum potential as required by state law. Because the IEP was appropriate, the court affirmed the decision not to award the parents reimbursement.

The parents appealed to the Sixth Circuit, which described the appropriate standard of review in special education cases arising under the IDEA. The court stated that if IDEA procedural requirements are met, greater deference is given to a district's placement decision. According to the court, the IDEA's requirement that the courts give "due weight" to administrative decisions means that courts should defer to administrative findings only when educational expertise is relevant and the decision is reasonable. There was no merit to the parents' argument that the taped IEP proceeding was a final IEP. State and federal laws indicate that an IEP is a written document, and there had been no writing in this case until the second IEP meeting. The parents were not entitled by law to attend the staff meetings occurring between the two IEP meetings, and staff members were entitled to discuss the student's IEP outside the presence of the parents. The district was not required to conduct a comprehensive evaluation at the time of the second IEP, since the parents' unilateral decision to decrease his school participation in favor of increased use of DTT did not amount to a change in placement. There was no statutory time limit for the district to recertify the student's autism diagnosis and any delay identified by the parents did not substantively deprive the student of appropriate services. **The IEP prepared by the school district took into account the unique needs of the student, set out his goals and included detailed daily schedules addressing each goal**. His program included group instruction and one-to-one therapy. The court affirmed the district court's finding that the IEP was developed specifically to accommodate the student. Because the IEP offered the student a FAPE, the remaining state and federal claims were properly dismissed. *Burilovich v. Bd. of Educ. of Lincoln Consol. Schools*, 208 F.3d 560 (6th Cir. 2000).

◆ A Texas student was diagnosed as having a learning disability and attention deficit disorder in sixth grade but was later classified as seriously emotionally disturbed. A school counselor reported that the student's emotional problems arose from her poor relationship with her mother. The student began failing classes, ran away from home, and refused to return home after being located. Her parents enrolled her at a Maine residential school specializing in students with behavioral impairments. The parents sought to recover the costs of the private placement from the school district. **The district refused to pay for the placement and instead devised an IEP recommending a psychological evaluation and a behavior management plan**. The parents requested a due process hearing. An administrative hearing officer determined that the district had not prepared an adequate IEP for the student because it did not recognized her SED. He ordered the district to provide the student with weekly therapy. However, because the Maine school was not the least restrictive environment, he denied the request for reimbursement.

The parents appealed to the U.S. District Court for the Western District of Texas. The court evaluated the IEP proposed by the school district under the four-part test described by the U.S. Court of Appeals, Fifth Circuit, in *Cypress-Fairbanks Indep. School Dist. v. Michael F.*, 118 F.3d 245 (5th Cir.1997). According to *Cypress-Fairbanks*, four factors can indicate whether an IEP is reasonably calculated to provide meaningful education benefit to a student under the IDEA. The four factors are: 1) The program is individualized on the basis of the student's assessment and performance; 2) it is administered in the least restrictive environment; 3) the services are provided in a coordinated and collaborative manner by key personnel; and 4) positive academic and non-academic benefits are demonstrated. Applying the *Cypress-Fairbanks* factors, the court held that the district IEP provided the student with a FAPE. **There was no evidence that the IEP was not individually tailored, and the student's school behavior did not put school personnel on notice of the serious emotional problems she experienced at home.** The residential facility was more restrictive than a placement in district schools. Key personnel were actively involved in the student's case and her academic failure was in large part attributable to her refusal to do homework. The district program assured that the student would receive educational benefits and the court entered judgment for the district. *Sylvie M. v. Bd. of Educ. of Dripping Springs Indep. School Dist.,* 48 F.Supp.2d 681 (W.D.Tex.1999).

◆ A Minnesota student with dyslexia performed in the third grade range in several subjects during her fourth grade year in public school. Three years later, her broad reading, broad written language and writing skills remained in the third grade range as she prepared to enter seventh grade. She then received extended year services from the school district during the summer months, including one-to-one tutoring under the Orton-Gillingham instructional method. The student's mother requested continuation of the Orton-Gillingham method for the following school year, but the district declined to include it in the student's IEP. Instead, **it stated that her teachers should be free to select from a variety of teaching methodologies, including Orton-Gillingham**. It also claimed that the student did not require exclusive one-to-one tutoring and that attendance in pull-out classes of three to five students at a similar level were appropriate for her. The mother rejected the proposed IEP and requested a due process hearing. A hearing officer held that the proposed IEP was adequate, and a state review officer agreed, finding no substantive violations of the IDEA.

The student's mother filed a federal court action against the school district, state education board and other state agencies, asserting IDEA violations and other state and federal claims. The court severed the IDEA claims and awarded judgment to the district and state agencies. The mother appealed to the U.S. Court of Appeals, Eighth Circuit, which noted that despite the lack of grade-level achievement by the student in many critical skill areas, the IDEA does not require the best possible education or the achievement of outstanding results. As long as a student is benefiting from her education, there is no IDEA violation. **Educators are entitled to determine appropriate methodologies for carrying out IEPs that provide appropriate educational benefits**. The court affirmed the lower court's decision. *E.S. v. Indep. School Dist. No. 196*, 135 F.3d 566 (8th Cir.1998).

B. Appropriateness of IEP

◆ After a Pennsylvania toddler with cerebral palsy and hearing loss was identified with developmental delays, her parents contacted their county mental health and retardation agency for early intervention services. The county developed an individualized family service plan that was modified several times, eventually calling for 24.25 hours of weekly physical, speech and occupational therapy and special instruction. The parents requested additional weekly therapy, expressing a preference for Lovaas early intervention training. **The county declined the request for Lovaas programming, and the parents hired a therapist to provide the services in a home program for more than two months**. They requested a due process hearing to recover their costs, but an administrative hearing officer upheld the county's IFSP.

The parents appealed to the Pennsylvania Commonwealth Court, which initially determined that it had never before considered a claim for reimbursement of therapy costs arising under Part C of the IDEA pertaining to special education for infants and toddlers. It found that **the appropriate way to evaluate such claims was to determine whether the IFSP was appropriate to a student's unique needs. Where an IFSP provided for multiple types of developmental services, each of them had to be likely to produce meaningful progress**. The court found evidence that the student had progressed after receiving the private Lovaas training along with her IFSP services. However, the record did not indicate that she made progress solely from her IFSP services. The county presented evidence that the student was making meaningful progress from physical therapy, but failed to show that she did so from occupational and speech therapy and special instruction. With the exception of physical therapy, the court found that the county failed to prove that the IFSP services it provided to the student produced meaningful progress toward her goals. Although the student was no longer eligible to receive services under Part C, the parents' claim for reimbursement for the private Lovaas training they arranged was not moot. According to the court, when a county fails to provide adequate services for a child, the IDEA authorizes a court to grant such relief it deems appropriate. In this case, it was appropriate to reimburse the family for the cost of the supplemental Lovaas services. The court found that the hearing officer's decision was erroneous and remanded the case for calculation of the family's actual costs. *De Mora v. Department of Public Welfare*, 768 A.2d 904 (Pa.Commw.Ct.2001).

◆ A New Hampshire student was classified as learning disabled. He also had a history of attention and emotional difficulties, low self-esteem, poor impulse control and other behavior problems. During elementary school he attended a variety of placements, including a private school that lacked a special education program and a public school. In the middle of the student's fourth grade year, the parents decided to place the student in a private school because of his home behavior. During the summer, the student was hospitalized twice for suicidal ideation, homicidal threats and physical and verbal abuse. After his discharge, the parents enrolled him in a private school and urged the district to change the student's classification to seriously emotionally disturbed. While the district evaluated this request, the student was asked to leave the private school. He was placed in a public school special education classroom. The district rejected a classification of seriously emotionally disturbed, since the student's emotional problems did not interfere with his educational performance. After the student threatened suicide while away from school and was suspended, his parents placed him in a private tutorial program. He was removed from the private program and instructed individually. The parents obtained an evaluation indicating that the student was seriously emotionally disturbed, other health impaired and multiple handicapped. **The district again rejected additional classifications or codings, observing that the student's attention and emotional issues were adequately addressed in the classroom or did not interfere with his education.** The district denied the parents' request for extended school-year programming, and recommended placement in a self-contained, highly structured, alternative-learning team program. The parents rejected a proposed IEP and requested a due process hearing, seeking reimbursement for private school costs. The hearing officer ordered a final IEP and placement meeting, at which the team approved an IEP similar to the one it had proposed earlier.

The hearing officer held that there were no substantive or procedural deficiencies in the proposed IEP and that tuition reimbursement was inappropriate. The parents appealed to a federal district court, which observed that the IDEA does not require that students be classified by their disability. The hearing officer discounted testimony by the parents' expert about placements that he had never observed personally and found that his testimony was influenced by inappropriate factors. The court accepted the hearing officer's credibility findings. The court disagreed with the parents' assertion that a school-wide discipline system incorporated into the student's IEP was inappropriate. Testimony indicated that his behavior improved through a similar program used at home. **The student did not experience the violent, out-of-control problems at school that he demonstrated at home, and the district was not responsible for his home behavior**. His behavior problems occurred while he was on a reduced schedule and during summer vacation, continuing through to his tutorial placement. The **district's proposal for an alternative-school placement provided a mainstream setting that was the student's least restrictive appropriate environment**. He was not likely to suffer harm or regression sufficient to require extended-year programming. The student was not entitled to an award of compensatory education. Because the district's IEP proposals were appropriate, the district was entitled to judgment and the parents were not entitled to reimbursement for unilaterally placing him in the tutorial program. *J.W. ex rel. K.W. v. Contoocook Valley School District*, 154 F.Supp.2d 217 (D.N.H. 2001).

◆ A Delaware student with a learning disability received special education services from preschool on. The student started his education in only special education classes, but was eventually integrated into regular classrooms with resource room instruction. His IEPs were expanded over a four-year period to include various related services and assistive technology. The student's parents had concerns about his progress and obtained an evaluation. The evaluator's suggestions were implemented, but the parents continued to have concerns, which they expressed at an IEP meeting. A second IEP meeting was cancelled by the parents pending further evaluation. The district advised the parents that not all IEP team members could attend a rescheduled meeting in the middle of the summer. The meeting went forward and **the district presented a draft IEP calling for an integrated classroom placement. The parents requested a due process hearing, seeking a residential placement**. The school conducted an IEP team meeting, which the parents declined to attend. The team met in the parents' absence and ratified the proposal calling for an integrated classroom placement with accommodations. A hearing panel held that the IEP was reasonably calculated to provide the student with meaningful educational benefits, and the parents appealed to a federal district court.

The court considered summary judgment motions by the parties, and observed that the proper inquiry under the IDEA was not whether a program actually provided meaningful benefit, but whether the proposed IEP was reasonably calculated to provide such benefit at the time it was proposed. The case was unusual because the proposed IEP was discussed over a six-month time period and was not formally adopted until after the start of a school year. Because the parents had asked to reschedule the second team meeting, it would be unfair to evaluate the IEP as drafted at the start of the process. The proper time frame to consider was the date when the IEP was finally approved. The court held that the IEP was reasonably calculated to provide the student with meaningful educational benefit. **There was ample evidence that the student was progressing in math, reading and writing, and evidence that he would continue making meaningful progress under the proposed IEP**. The integrated classroom approach was consistent with his need for continuity across subject areas. He would receive instruction with nondisabled students and one-to-one tutoring. While the IEP was far from perfect, there were no procedural defects that denied the student a FAPE. The inadequacy of annual goals was mitigated by other portions of the IEP. Although the IEP's evaluative criteria were somewhat subjective, they were sufficient. The IEP did not have to adapt concepts from the writing intervention program or describe how assistive technology would be used to achieve goals. The court refused to award compensatory education, as any procedural flaws did not deprive the student of educational opportunity or hamper his parents' participation in the development of an IEP. The court awarded judgment to the state and school district. *Coale v. State Department of Education*, 162 F.Supp.2d 316 (D. Del. 2001).

◆ A New York student was classified as learning disabled in second grade and received special education services. During the ninth-grade, his parents became concerned about his progress and disagreed with the school district's testing and evaluation methods. After an emergency IEP meeting, the parents disputed several aspects of the student's IEP, and several modifications were made to his mainstream education program. The parents removed the student from public school and placed him in a private school, where he remained through grade 11. An IEP meeting was held after the unilateral placement, at which the district agreed to add an hour to the student's weekly resource room time. The district added goals of reading decoding, word recognition and comprehension, and revised the student's annual goals and short-term objectives for writing. The parents commenced an administrative proceeding against the district seeking tuition reimbursement, but an impartial hearing officer held that the district had offered the student an appropriate program for ninth grade. **The hearing officer found that the district IEP offered the student substantially the same academic program in which he had made progress the prior school year**. The parents appealed to a state review officer, who noted that the IEP could have provided more detail, but held that this defect did not invalidate the IEP. The review officer affirmed and the parents appealed.

The federal district court noted that the state review officer had thoroughly reviewed the student's recent IEPs and evaluations. The student's achievements were substantial and he obtained good grades and test scores. The court found that the review officer had reviewed each of the factors normally required in an IEP and determined that **the IEP satisfied IDEA requirements**. There was evidence that **the IEP stated the student's present level of educational performance and his annual goals, including short-term instructional objectives. It further specified the educational services to be provided, and the extent to which he would be able to participate in regular education programs**. Moreover, the IEP stated the objective criteria, evaluation procedures and schedules for determining whether his instructional objectives were being archived. The court found no reason to set aside the review officer's decision. The school district had offered the student a FAPE, and it was therefore unnecessary to consider the appropriateness of the private school placement and whether the parents were entitled to reimbursement. *Protano v. Valley Central School District*, No. 00 CV 3789(CM), 2001 WL 209935 (S.D.N.Y. 2001).

- After attending a private school, a student returned to public schools and his grades initially improved during the sixth grade. In grade seven, his grades dropped sharply and he often failed to complete assignments. After being identified as academically gifted, the student was diagnosed with a learning disability that primarily affected his writing skills. The district agreed to implement certain accommodations for the student. The parties then met to discuss an IEP, which was never completed due to disagreements. The student's parent filed a complaint with the state department of public instruction and office for civil rights, asserting that the system failed to identify her son as having a disability and had mishandled the IEP process. A state investigation indicated no failure by the school system to comply with state or federal law. The student's performance deteriorated in grade eight, which resulted in further modifications to his IEP. Despite continued problems, the student passed the eighth grade. The mother requested a due process hearing, asserting that the school system failed to appropriately implement the student's IEPs. **The administrative law judge ruled that the school failed to provide a FAPE, and did not consistently implement the student's IEPs. A hearing review officer reversed** that decision based on his findings that the school system had timely identified the student's learning disability and that the IEPs were reasonably calculated to provide him with a FAPE. A federal district court affirmed the review officer's decision and the mother appealed to the U.S. Court of Appeals for the Fourth Circuit.

The court held that the IDEA requires that an IEP contain statutorily specified elements and be reasonably calculated to enable the student to receive passing grades and advance in school. The administrative hearing officer's decision was entitled to little or no deference because there had been no independent evaluation or analysis of the case. There was no merit to the assertion that the district court had improperly failed to give deference to the initial administrative decision in favor of the review officer's decision. The court found that the student had been evaluated by seven different evaluators and that four of them recommended the minimization of writing. The school system followed these recommendations by providing for reduced handwriting through the use of computers and tape recorders. It also modified tests, provided additional time, and otherwise attempted to minimize the effect of the student's handwriting deficiency on his academic performance. The student's performance improved during his eighth grade year, and while he continued to struggle academically, his failure to turn in assignments and make up missed examinations was a continuing factor. The court found that the student's IEPs contained specific goals and a means to assess his performance. **Any deficiency in the IEPs did not deny the student a FAPE or diminish his opportunity to achieve his full potential as required by North Carolina law**, therefore, the circuit court affirmed the judgment in favor of the school system. *D.B. v. Craven County Bd. of Educ.*, 210 F.3d 360 (4th Cir. 2000).

♦ A Michigan student showed signs of a disability and his parents contacted the school district for services. The student was placed in a preprimary impaired program. When the student failed to progress, the parents arranged for a home Lovaas-type program. The parents approved of an IEP developed by the district that placed the student in a four-hour program, five days per week and reduced his participation in one-on-one home therapy. **When the parties failed to agree on changing the student's IEP, the parents requested a due process hearing** and withdrew the student from school. A hearing officer agreed with the parents that the student was entitled to one-on-one, discrete trial training and extended school year services. He ordered the district to reimburse the parents for a substantial part of the amount they spent on the home program and the psychologist. **A state hearing review officer reversed, finding that the IEP proposed by the school district was adequate**, and ruling that the hearing officer had improperly allocated the burden of proof to the school district. The parents appealed to a federal district court, which referred the case to a magistrate judge. The magistrate judge submitted a report and recommendation approving of summary judgment for the school district, and the court adopted the report.

The family appealed to the Sixth Circuit, which reviewed the initial administrative decision and found that despite evidence of an academic dispute over the Lovaas approach, the hearing officer had relied heavily on the opinion of the parents' expert, who had recommended the Lovaas methodology. The hearing officer had identified certain procedural deficiencies in the formulation of the IEP, but no procedural or substantive violations of the IDEA. The magistrate judge had appropriately noted the existence of a substantial dispute over methodology. The circuit court found no error in the magistrate judge's decision finding the IEP appropriate. **The IEP team could have appropriately chosen to implement only a part of the discrete trial training program recommended by the parents' psychologist**. Moreover, the team was familiar with the student and with available options for the IEP. The district had provided the student with a FAPE. The court then evaluated the IEP under Michigan's special education law, which requires the design of an IEP that maximizes the potential for a student with disabilities. Noting that the maximum potential standard has not been well defined, the court nonetheless found that the Michigan standard does not require "a model education" that adopts the most sophisticated methods available. The family was not entitled to prescribe or require a specific methodology under the facts of this case. The magistrate judge had correctly found the existence of a dispute in the educational and medical fields about autism. **The IEP satisfied the requirements of Michigan law, because it was adequate and sufficient to provide the student a FAPE that offered to meet and develop his maximum potential, in light of his abilities and needs**. The circuit court affirmed the decision for the school board. *Renner v. Bd. of Educ. of Pub. Schools of City of Ann Arbor*, 185 F.3d 635 (6th Cir.1999).

◆ An Ohio school district evaluated a student during her kindergarten year and found that she had speech and language disabilities. During the next three years, the parties agreed on IEPs calling for speech and language therapy and tutoring, but the student's standardized test scores declined. She became overwhelmed with her homework in the third grade and was unable to complete her assignments. Although her standardized test scores continued to decline and her vocabulary and total reading ability regressed to mid-first grade level, she received satisfactory grades. Her parents requested that the district test her for learning disabilities. The school district proposed private tutoring and enrollment in a summer reading program. However, the district failed to test the student for learning disabilities prior to the end of the school year and did not admit her into special reading programs in the fall. The parents obtained a private evaluation indicating that the student required multi-sensory instruction. They asked the district to waive special education testing and allow their daughter into appropriate programs. When the district did not grant the waiver, the parents unilaterally placed the student in a private school. A multi-factored examination conducted by the district after the start of the next school year indicated that the student had a specific learning disability. The parents agreed to delay an IEP meeting until the end of the school year, and the student continued to attend the private school.

When the parties met to discuss an IEP at the end of the year, the district asserted that it no longer had an obligation to prepare an IEP since the student had attended the private school that year. The parties met again after district personnel realized that the IDEA required the preparation of an IEP despite the student's private school attendance. However, the parents rejected the district's proposed IEP because it included no means of objectively measuring her progress. They re-enrolled the student in the private school and sought reimbursement of their expenses for both years. A hearing officer awarded reimbursement to the parents, holding that **the district had failed to provide the student with an appropriate IEP and had ignored indications of her learning disability**. A state-level review officer upheld the order for reimbursement of tuition for the second year, but held that the claim for the first year of private school tuition was time-barred. The parties appealed to a federal district court, which affirmed the review officer's decision.

The case then reached the Sixth Circuit, which noted that the parents had failed to appeal the initial administrative decision until 78 days after the ruling. Because Ohio has a 45-day statute of limitations that specifically applies to IDEA and analogous state law actions, the tuition claim for the first year was barred. However, **the school district's appeal of the order for reimbursement for the second year was meritless, since the IEP prepared for that year did not provide appropriate objective criteria for measuring the student's progress as required by the IDEA**. The district's assertion that the IDEA's mainstreaming requirement barred the tuition reimbursement claim was incorrect. The IDEA requires that students with disabilities participate in the same activities as students without disabilities to the maximum extent appropriate, but does not require leaving a student in an inappropriate mainstream setting. *Cleveland Heights-University Heights City School Dist. v. Boss*, 144 F.3d 391 (6th Cir.1998).

C. Procedural Violations

◆ Although a school district concluded a preschool age child with autism was eligible for special education; it failed to provide the parents with notice of IDEA parental rights at that time. The parents did not attend the student's first IEP meeting, but eventually signed an IEP and attested to the receipt of an "Advisement of Parental Rights" form. The district did not implement the IEP for three months. During the next school year, the district formulated a new IEP that reduced the level of services provided to the student, which the mother signed. The parents unilaterally removed the student from public schools and placed him in a private Lovaas, applied behavioral analysis program. Over a year later, they learned that they had the right to bring a due process proceeding to contest their son's IEP. Their request for a hearing was made nearly two years after the unilateral placement. **A hearing officer found that the district had failed to notify the parents of their right to a hearing and engaged in a pattern and practice of failing to follow IDEA procedures**. It awarded almost $118,000 to the parents for educational expenses. The district appealed to a state review officer, who affirmed the local hearing officer's decision but held that a Virginia statute barred reimbursement prior to the date of the family's request for a due process hearing. A federal district court held that the parents were relieved of the limitation statute for all but six months of the period for which they sought reimbursement, because the district had kept them ignorant of their hearing rights.

The school district appealed to the Fourth Circuit, which first held that the district court had properly found that the district's failure to inform the parents of their due process rights deprived them of the opportunity to seek a hearing. No statute of limitations applied until the date they first learned that the district had a duty to inform them of their rights. The parents' claims were viable because they did not learn about these rights until at least a year after they removed their son from public schools. **The Fourth Circuit agreed with the district court's finding that the repeated failure by school officials to provide the parents with notice of their hearing rights amounted to the failure to provide the student with a FAPE**. Even though the parents had signed a form acknowledging receipt of notice of their IDEA hearing rights, they testified consistently and persuasively that they had never seen the parental rights form or otherwise received notice of their right to a due process hearing. Even the parental signatures on IEP documents did not demonstrate that they had notice of their rights. The court affirmed the reimbursement award, noting the evidence indicated Lovaas therapy was appropriate and benefited the student. *Jaynes v. Newport News School Bd.*, 13 Fed.Appx. 166 (4th Cir. 2001).

◆ A student who was diagnosed with ADHD and pervasive developmental disorder was unilaterally enrolled by his parents in a private school. The parents sought reimbursement for the private school tuition from their school district. The district denied the request and sought to place the student in public school special education classes. The parents rejected the district's proposed placement for the 1998-1999 school year in favor of a private school. The district ultimately failed to propose an IEP for the student until June 1999, when the school year was nearly over. The school district applied the June 1999 IEP to the 1999-2000 school year. The parents commenced an administrative action against the district, seeking tuition reimbursement for both school years. **An administrative law judge held the parents primarily responsible for the delay in preparing an IEP and found that the district had attempted to prepare one in good faith**. According to the ALJ, the district's procedural failure to provide an IEP for the student at the beginning of the 1998-99 school year did not deny him a FAPE. The tuition reimbursement claim was denied for both school years.

On appeal by the parents, **a federal district court found that the district's failure to prepare an IEP for the student prior to the start of a school year was a serious violation of the IDEA for which tuition reimbursement was an appropriate remedy**. The ALJ had improperly focused her analysis on the parents' conduct, instead of the district's clear obligations under 20 U.S.C. § 1414(a)(5) to develop an IEP by the beginning of the 1998-99 school year and to provide him with a FAPE. The district's procedural violations were not merely technical, according to the court. Courts have repeatedly rejected the argument that parental delays justify clear-cut violations of the IDEA. The parents did not act in bad faith and did not make delays until after the district had violated its duty to prepare an IEP by the start of the 1998-99 school year. The ALJ's decision put the onus on the parents to monitor and police the development of an IEP, which was improper. Federal regulations provide guidance for school districts to proceed with the development of an IEP when parents are unwilling or unable to participate in IEP meetings. 34 C.F.R. Part 300.345. There was no evidence that the district had availed itself of this procedure or considered an interim placement or IEP. The court found the private school selected by the parents was appropriate, since the student showed improvement during his time there. The parents were awarded reimbursement for the 1998-99 school year. However, the 1999-2000 IEP was appropriate and the district committed no procedural violations when creating it. The court found no reason to disturb the administrative decision denying reimbursement for that year. *Justin G. v. Board of Education of Montgomery County*, 148 F.Supp.2d 576 (D. Md. 2001).

◆ Each year through grade five, the parents of a middle school student with learning disabilities approved the proposed district IEP. For that year, the school provided the student with two hours of daily special education services plus one-half hour per week of speech services, with the rest of the day spent in regular education classes. The district then reverted to a pull-out teaching method. The student's mother was not present at the student's annual IEP review, but later signed the IEP and gave her permission to implement a new IEP calling for a "self-contained" placement. The student's parents unilaterally removed him from district schools at the start of the next school year in favor of a private school. They commenced due process proceedings against the district, seeking tuition reimbursement. The district initiated an evaluation of the student and held an IEP meeting, even though the parents stated that he would remain in the private school. The parents did not sign the IEP, and private school staff did not attend the IEP meeting. The team considered information from the private school that indicated the student had regressed in reading, written language and math during his year there. A local hearing officer held that the district provided a FAPE to the student and denied the parents' request for tuition. However, **a state-level review officer determined that procedural violations by the district invalidated the student's proposed IEPs for a two-year period and that the IEPs were inappropriate**. The officer awarded tuition reimbursement to the parents, and the district appealed to a Virginia trial court, which held that the district had offered the student FAPE and that the procedures it utilized did not prevent him from receiving educational benefit.

The student appealed to the Virginia Court of Appeals, which stated that procedural violations of the IDEA may constitute a failure to provide a FAPE under certain circumstances. **An IEP will not be set aside unless there is some rational basis to believe that procedural inadequacies compromised the student's right to FAPE, seriously hampered parental participation, or caused a deprivation in educational benefits.** The court found that procedural inadequacies in this case did not prevent the parents from participating in the development of the student's IEP and did not result in a loss of FAPE. The change in teaching method did not invalidate the IEP and was not a change in services. A change in methodology was within the district's authority. There was no procedural violation in failing to inform the parents in the change in instructional method and failing to amend the IEP. The mother's absence from an IEP meeting did not invalidate the IEP, and her failure to attend the meeting was not attributable to the district. While the district had failed to prepare an IEP until after the start of the student's second year in the private school, there was no resulting loss of educational opportunity, since the parents had stated they would not accept a public placement. The IEP team had sufficient current information to develop an appropriate IEP. According to the court, the district's use of a draft IEP to start the meeting was allowed. The court rejected the parents' other arguments based on the substantive provisions of the district's IEP. Evidence indicated that the student would have benefited from the IEP in the less restrictive environment. The student had a severe learning disability and although he was not progressing at the same rate as his peers, his progress was real and measurable. The court affirmed the decision for the school district. *White v. School Board of Henrico County*, 549 S.E.2d 16 (Va. Ct. App. 2001).

◆ The parents of a three-year-old student with autism sought to include a home-based program of applied behavior assessment in his IEP. **At a school committee on preschool special education meeting to consider the request, the committee chair stated that the question would be resolved by vote of the**

committee. A dispute arose over who was eligible to participate in the voting. School representatives asserted that only the parents and district members should participate. The parents argued that recent amendments to the IDEA allowed other members with knowledge and special expertise about their son to vote. The school district's attorney recommended that all members in attendance vote. When all votes were counted, seven of 12 members voted for the applied behavior assessment program. When non-school members were excluded, the request to include an ABA program was defeated four votes to two. The school district accepted the committee chair's recommendation to exclude the ABA program from the student's IEP and the parents commenced administrative proceedings. A hearing officer agreed with the parents that under the amended IDEA, an IEP team included those "who have knowledge or special expertise regarding the child." Since the six excluded team members clearly possessed necessary knowledge or expertise regarding the student, their votes should have been considered. A state review officer affirmed the hearing officer's decision and the district appealed to a state trial court. The court affirmed the administrative decision.

The district appealed to the New York Supreme Court, Appellate Division, which declined to answer the district's question concerning the appropriateness of resolving placement issues by voting as untimely. The court observed that although the state education department later expressed disapproval of the practice, **no federal law or regulation made it inappropriate to establish an IEP by voting. The administrative decisions approving the inclusion of all IEP team members in the voting were appropriate** under the amended IDEA, even though New York had not amended its special education law at the time of the meeting. The district had notice of the IDEA amendments, which expanded the composition of IEP teams to include individuals with knowledge or special expertise regarding the student. The court rejected the district's argument that individuals had to be affiliated with a school district in order to qualify as IEP team members. Neither state nor federal law created any such requirement. The district did not claim that the six team members whose votes it sought to exclude lacked necessary expertise, and their votes should have been considered. The court explained that its decision was limited, and cautioned that it not be interpreted to suggest that IEP impasses be resolved through majority vote. It held that only if a district determines to resolve an IEP impasse by a vote, it must allow all members to vote. The court affirmed the trial court decision. *Sackets Harbor Central School District v. Munoz*, 725 N.Y.S.2d 119 (N.Y. App. Div. 2001).

♦ A Nevada student was placed in her school district's early childhood program before her third birthday after a psychologist determined that she had moderately low communication and daily-living skills. The next year, two school psychologists evaluated the student, reaching mixed conclusions. **One of the psychologists determined that she was "severely autistic," but this finding was not communicated to the parents**. A district eligibility team found that the student was eligible for special education because of her language, cognitive, self-help, social and emotional needs. The district denied a request by the student's mother for copies of her daughter's assessment reports, instead sending her a two-page summary. After the family moved to California, the student was diagnosed as autistic and began an in-home intervention program using discrete trial training. During a review of the student's California IEP, the parents obtained the child's records from Nevada. They learned of the earlier evaluation indicating severe autism and noted that this finding had not been included in the summary. The parents requested a due process hearing in Nevada. A hearing officer determined that the student was misidentified as developmentally delayed and denied FAPE. A state review officer reversed, overturning the credibility determinations of several witnesses.

The parents appealed to a federal district court, which affirmed the state review officer's decision, and then sought review by the Ninth Circuit. The court observed that autism is a little-understood condition whose early diagnosis is critical to treatment. Research indicated that without early identification and diagnosis, children with autism are unable to benefit from educational services. The circuit court held that a final state administrative decision is entitled to due weight, unless a credibility determination is at issue. A hearing officer who reviews live testimony firsthand is in the best position to determine credibility. The court noted that **the right to examine all records relating to a child and to participate in meetings to identify, evaluate and place a child is guaranteed to parents by the IDEA. Districts are specifically required to give parents a copy of their procedural safeguards as well as a copy of the evaluation report** and documentation regarding the determination of eligibility. The district in this case did not provide the parents with copies of reports indicating the possibility of autism or the need for further evaluation, resulting in a blatant violation of the IDEA. The information withheld from the parents would have changed the educational approach employed for the student by increasing individualized speech therapy and possibly beginning discrete trial training much sooner. By failing to disclose the student's full records upon request, the district denied a FAPE to the student. The appeals court reversed the district court's decision. *Amanda J. v. Clark County School District et al.*, 267 F.3d 877 (9th Cir. 2001).

◆ A student who was diagnosed with attention-deficit hyperactivity disorder, oppositional defiant disorder and depression attended private schools until the fifth grade. An evaluation team concluded the student was eligible for "severe behavior handicap" services. **Although the parties arranged for a meeting to discuss the evaluation and possible placements, they never met at an IEP team meeting, and a formal IEP was never prepared**. The district proposed an internal placement, which the parents rejected. The parents located a residential placement in a Connecticut school that had a "psychiatrically oriented" program. A school district official faxed them a draft IEP proposing the placement they had already rejected and that required them to pay for costs over their insurance coverage. The parents enrolled the student in the residential school without informing the school district. They requested a due process hearing midway through the student's seventh-grade year, seeking reimbursement. A hearing officer held that the while the district did not hold an IEP conference, it could provide the student with a FAPE, and therefore, was not liable for tuition reimbursement. The family was not responsible for paying for any services under the proposed IEP, since the resulting reduction in their lifetime medical insurance coverage would deprive the student of FAPE. A review officer dismissed the case, and the parents appealed to a federal district court. The school district moved for dismissal based on the parents' failure to request a due process hearing prior to making the residential placement. The court then issued an opinion affirming the hearing officer's decision. Both parties appealed to the U.S. Court of Appeals for the Sixth Circuit.

The circuit court concluded that **the district violated IDEA regulations requiring school districts to convene an IEP meeting within 30 calendar days of the determination that a student requires special education and related services.** It had also violated Ohio administrative regulations requiring IEP conferences as soon as possible after officials initially suspect that a student has a disability. A formal IEP meeting was never held, and no IEP was produced. The court rejected the district's assertion that it had failed to convene an IEP meeting because of the parents' lack of cooperation. IDEA regulations do not require that parents agree to a proposed placement before an IEP meeting can be held, but expressly provide for the development of an IEP without parental involvement if they refuse to participate. The court concluded that **because the district never held an IEP meeting, the parents were denied any meaningful opportunity to participate in the IEP process. The lack of an IEP for the student during a full school year denied him access to specialized instruction and related services.** The draft IEP prepared by the district could not be considered an IEP, as it did not meet IDEA statutory and regulatory requirements. The district had not even offered a free program, as the draft IEP asserted that it would only pay for costs beyond the parents' insurance coverage. Since the district had defaulted on its obligations and the private school was a proper placement under the IDEA, the parents were entitled to reimbursement. On remand, the district court was directed to address the appropriate level of reimbursement. *Knable ex rel. Knable v. Bexley City School District*, 238 F.3d 755 (6th Cir. 2001).

◆ **A Maine school district placed a six-year-old with autism in a mainstream kindergarten class for the morning, with 12.5 hours of applied behavioral analysis therapy in the afternoon.** However, the district provided the student only four hours of ABA therapy per week and he began to disrupt classes and kick, pinch and grab his educational technician. At a meeting, the parents and district agreed that the student should work one-to-one with the technician, but she became frustrated and resigned. The district had not trained any other personnel in ABA therapy. An emergency IEP team meeting was called, and the parties agreed that the student should remain home until a new technician could be hired. The district unsuccessfully tried to hire a new technician. Another IEP meeting was convened, at which the district special education director presented the parents with a revised IEP calling for the student's placement in a self-contained special education program operated by a nonprofit mental health agency. The agency did not offer ABA therapy and did not typically provide students with one-to-one educational technicians. No evaluation was made of the student to support the placement there and no input was sought from the parents, who rejected the proposal, requested a due process hearing and enrolled the student in a home-based ABA program. The hearing officer held that the placement suggested by the district violated the student's right to receive a FAPE in the least restrictive environment, and ordered the reinstitution of the prior year's IEP. The district was also ordered to train a second educational technician in ABA therapy and provide the student with two months of compensatory education.

The district commenced a federal district court action challenging the administrative decision. The court referred the case to a federal magistrate judge, who issued a recommendation affirming the administrative order. The magistrate agreed with the hearing officer's findings that the proposed IEP violated IDEA procedural requirements because it bore no relation to any diagnostic information that would support a change in placement. The decision to revise the IEP was based solely on administrative convenience to the school district and violated the student's right to receive a FAPE. The magistrate rejected the district's attempt to cast the parents' insistence on ABA therapy as a dispute based on competing educational methodologies. District procedural violations had deprived the student of an appropriate placement. The district had never considered whether its proposed placement was appropriate for the student's unique needs. The hearing officer had correctly held that **the IEP violated the IDEA because the IEP team did not determine whether the placement it proposed was capable of conferring any meaningful educational benefits upon the student. The placement served the district's administrative convenience, without regard to the student's needs**. The magistrate recommended affirmation of the recommendation to award the student compensatory education. *Sanford School Committee v. Mr. and Mrs. L.*, No. CIV. 00-CV113 PH, 2001 WL 103544 (D. Me. 2001).

◆ An IEP meeting was held to determine an educational program for a three-year-old California student with a genetic condition that caused delays in all areas of development. The student's mother declined to sign the resulting IEP and the meeting reconvened some months later. The school district then offered the parent a choice of placements. The mother signed the IEP and consented to placement in a full-inclusion public preschool program with individual speech and language therapy, physical therapy and three monthly sessions of occupational therapy. The placement lasted only a few months. The mother then requested a due process hearing because she felt that the student was regressing and that her IEP goals and objectives were not being met. The student continued to receive occupational and physical therapy in the interim, but the district rejected a recommendation by the student's therapist to increase her occupational therapy. The reason stated was the mother's failure to abide by a settlement agreement arising from the due process hearing. The mother failed to attend an IEP meeting scheduled as a result of the due process proceeding. Instead, she unilaterally enrolled the student in a private preschool program for typically developing students that was not certified for special education. She did not inform the district of her placement decision until the following month, even though the parties met at an IEP meeting to discuss goals and objectives and determine a placement for the school year. The IEP called for individual and group speech and language therapy, occupational therapy once per week, physical therapy twice per week, and reimbursement for the mother's transportation costs to therapy sessions. **The placement listed suggestions or offers for three programs and noted the**

placement selected by the mother, but did not include an offer to fund it. The mother did not approve of any of the proposed placements. She consented to the implementation of the therapy provisions of the IEP, except for the occupational therapy evaluations. She began paying for additional occupational therapy sessions and requested a due process hearing challenging the district's IEP and the proposed level of district funded occupational therapy. The hearing officer held that two sessions of weekly occupational therapy were appropriate. She also held that the mother was entitled to reimbursement for the costs of the private preschool and transportation. Only one of the programs offered by the district was appropriate, according to the hearing officer. The multiple offerings failed to make a legally sufficient placement offer and denied the student a FAPE.

The district appealed the administrative decision to a federal district court, asserting that the mother's conduct required the denial of all reimbursement. The court upheld the hearing officer's decision regarding the additional weekly session of occupational therapy in light of the student's extensive needs. The court also agreed with the administrative findings that the mother was entitled to reimbursement for the cost of occupational therapy, transportation and parking because the additional sessions she had obtained for her daughter were necessary and the denial of additional sessions amounted to the deprivation of FAPE. The court refused to disturb the hearing officer's findings concerning the district's procedural violations of the IDEA. Although one of the placements identified in the IEP was appropriate and satisfied IDEA substantive requirements, **the district's failure to present one coherent written placement offer violated the IDEA**. Parents had no expertise in evaluating educational programs and the district was required to select an appropriate placement designed to meet the unique needs of a student. In this case, the multiple placement offerings required the parent to ferret out the only appropriate one identified by the district. **While discussion of possible placements during an IEP meeting was appropriate, the district could not abdicate its responsibility to make a specific offer by making a parent choose among several placements**. This procedural violation resulted in the denial of a FAPE. Even though the preschool chosen by the parent was not certified for special education, the student participated in mainstreaming and age-appropriate activities that benefited her educationally. The court affirmed the hearing officer's decision that the district was required to reimburse the mother for tuition, and rejected the district's claim that her conduct required the denial of all reimbursement. Although the IDEA emphasizes parental involvement and the mother had the right to be an aggressive advocate, her withholding of relevant information justified a reduction in the amount of reimbursement she claimed. The court affirmed the hearing officer's decision. *Glendale Unified School District v. Almasi*, 122 F.Supp.2d 1093 (C.D. Cal. 2000).

◆ Among other disabilities, a Vermont student had a severe language disorder. Although she was mainstreamed into some regular classes while in junior high school, she received extensive special education in speech and language. Her school district refused to address the mother's objections to the size of the school, complexity of the classes and lack of coordination among teachers. Her mother asked the district to consider a private school placement but it refused and developed an IEP without her participation and in the absence of the student's teachers. The IEP lacked a language development program and the mother rejected it, requesting reevaluation and a private school placement. After the district denied the requests, **the mother placed the student at a private residential school.** In a due process hearing, her request for tuition reimbursement was denied. The district then failed to adopt an IEP for the next three years. The mother sued the district for tuition reimbursement in the U.S. District Court for the District of Vermont.

The court found that **the school district had violated IDEA procedural requirements by failing to inform the mother of her rights, excluding her from IEP meetings, failing to conduct an evaluation and failing to adopt a formal IEP for over three years**. The court also found that draft IEPs prepared by the district failed to address the student's severe language problems, omitted goals and objectives from previous IEPs and did not consider the effect of the complex high school environment on the student. The private school placement selected by the mother was appropriate. Because the district had violated IDEA procedures and substantive requirements, and the district had failed to propose any nonresidential alternatives, **the court awarded tuition reimbursement**. *Briere v. Fair Haven Grade School Dist.*, 948 F.Supp. 1242 (D.Vt.1996).

◆ A 16-year-old New York student with multiple disabilities received special education services from a public school district. After he exhibited behavioral problems during the summer, his parents placed him in a psychiatric hospital. Upon his discharge, the district decided to place the student in public school special education classes, which was contrary to the parents' request for a residential placement. He was hospitalized again for setting fires and committing assault. The district again recommended placement in special education classes and the parents requested a hearing. However, **the county social services department obtained an order from a New York family court placing the student in a residential facility and requiring the parents to pay the department $1,200 in monthly maintenance**. The hearing officer determined that the proposed IEP was deficient, but denied the parents' request for tuition reimbursement. A state level review officer affirmed the decision, observing that the family court had placed the student in the residence and that the proposed IEP was appropriate. The parents appealed to a New York federal court.

The county department of social services, school district and New York State Education Department moved to dismiss the lawsuit. The court granted the school district's motion to dismiss all the claims because the academic year was over. The court refused to grant the department of social services' motion to dismiss the lawsuit, as there was a question of whether the family court order violated the IDEA. **If the order required the parents to contribute to maintenance costs for a placement that was educational in nature, it violated the IDEA. On the other hand, if the placement resulted from juvenile delinquency proceedings based on the student's behavior and was unrelated to educational needs, the placement would not violate the IDEA**. The court also denied the state education department's dismissal motion in order to further consider whether state policies allowed county social service boards to seek maintenance from parents for educational placements. The court dismissed the claim that the education department violated the parents' rights under 42 U.S.C. § 1983. *King v. Pine Plains Central School Dist.*, 918 F.Supp. 772 (S.D.N.Y.1996).

D. Implementation of IEPs

◆ **The IEP for a seven-year-old kindergarten student with cerebral palsy, hydrocephalus and a seizure disorder called for a full-time aide to assist him**. At the conclusion of the school year, the district transferred the student to another school and contracted with a health-services employer for temporary employees to serve as aides. These employees frequently arrived after school commenced, left before school was dismissed or did not show up at all. The school sometimes assigned first-grade students to accompany the student to his locker. On one such occasion, the student was knocked down by other students and hit his head on the floor, shattering a shunt that had been implanted in his head. As a result, he was hospitalized for three weeks. The state education department conducted an investigation into a complaint made by the student's mother that alleged the district failed to implement the student's IEP and did not provide him with an aide on a consistent basis. A department official was unable to determine whether the district had complied with the IEP. The family requested a due process hearing, which resulted in an administrative law judge's decision that the district did not deprive the student of a FAPE.

The student then sued the district and state education department in a federal district court, which noted that his IEP called for a program aide to assist him each day he attended school. The IEP also included the goal of safe independent mobility in the school environment. The court refused to dismiss the education department from the case, holding that it had failed to fulfill its obligations under the IDEA when its official made her "non-conclusion." If the department truly had insufficient evidence to make a determination, it was bound to continue its investigation until it found such information. Instead, it had issued a decision without reaching any legal conclusion. The IDEA did not permit the department to "merely throw up its bureaucratic hands." The inclusion of an aide was a significant element of the student's IEP and made it possible for him to receive education in a general education setting. The administrative law judge's contradictory findings did not support a conclusion that the IEP was properly implemented because no aide was present at the start of the school year and aides were frequently late or absent. The district was unable to rely on claims that it made a "good faith effort" to comply with the IDEA. It was bound to provide the services actually listed in the IEP. **The district had violated the IDEA and even though there was evidence the student was progressing educationally, this could not be used to insulate the district from adequately implementing his IEP. The school had no discretion to decline to implement the IEP or to unilaterally decide that a listed service not be provided**. The administrative decision was not supported by substantial evidence and the court ordered the district to re-enroll the student in his former school with appropriate implementation of his IEP. *Manalansan v. Board of Education of Baltimore City*, No. Civ. A.MD 01-312, 2001 WL 939699 (D. Md. 2001).

◆ **After a 22-year-old student with autism completed his final year of attendance at district schools, he filed an administrative complaint, alleging the district failed to implement his IEPs throughout his high school career**. During the administrative hearing, the hearing officer took judicial notice of the 12 prior proceedings involving the student and the district. The hearing officer held that the school committee had implemented and complied with the student's IEPs. The family appealed to the U.S. District Court for the District of Massachusetts, arguing that the student did not receive any significant benefit from his entire four-year high school program, and seeking five years of compensatory education plus punitive damages of $100,000. The court agreed with the administrative hearing officer's decision to disregard all claims other than those based on the student's final year of school.

Although the administrative decision had not been issued within 45 days as required by federal regulations, the court found no prejudice to the student, because the delay did not deprive him of any benefits or remedies to which he was entitled. The court held that **when evaluating a claim of failure to implement a student's IEP, it must be determined whether the alleged failure to implement has deprived the student of the entitlement to a FAPE** as required by state and federal law. The court stated that a school district fails to implement a student's IEP when 1) the failure to implement is complete, 2) there is a variance from the program described in the IEP that deprives the student of FAPE, and 3) the student does not make progress toward IEP goals. Applying this three-part framework to the facts of the case, the court found that the district had not completely failed to implement the IEPs, and found no support for the student's claim that he was not making progress toward his IEP goals. It further rejected the assertion that the IDEA requires the complete realization of all IEP goals, even under the strict requirements of Massachusetts special education law. The services offered by the school district provided the student with a FAPE, and the school committee was entitled to summary judgment. *Ross v. Framingham School Comm.*, 44 F.Supp.2d 104 (D.Mass.1999).

E. Transfer Students

◆ A student attended a private special education school under an IEP formulated by the District of Columbia Public Schools, when the student's family moved to Pennsylvania and his new school district proposed placing him in a learning support or combined learning/emotional support program. The family rejected these proposals and unilaterally enrolled the student in a private school. He remained there for 41 days before the family moved to New Jersey. The student's parents commenced Pennsylvania due process proceedings, seeking tuition reimbursement. The hearing officer held that because state standards differ, the adoption of an IEP from another state would require the receiving state to approve of standards that would not necessarily be applicable under the receiving state's standards. The parents appealed to a federal district court, which reviewed the U.S. Department of Education's Office of Special Education Programs (OSEP) Policy Memorandum 96-5 for guidance. **The court agreed with the school district and hearing officer that a receiving school district is not required to accept an IEP drafted by a district in another state pending an appeal**

involving an intrastate transfer. The Washington IEP was presumably based on local standards that did not necessarily comply with Pennsylvania special education standards. The court agreed with the OSEP policy memorandum that there is a distinction between intrastate and interstate transfers and held that the Pennsylvania district was not compelled to accept the Washington IEP.

The family appealed to the U.S. Court of Appeals for the Third Circuit, arguing that the OSEP policy memorandum was not entitled to deference because it conflicted with the IDEA stay-put provision and Pennsylvania special education regulations. The circuit court observed that the stay-put provision does not specifically address student transfers between states. The policy memorandum and district court judgment were both based on sound reasoning, since the IDEA recognizes the traditional role of the states to determine their own educational standards. Under the IDEA, provision of a FAPE requires that special education and related services meet the standards of the state educational agency and that states have special education policies, procedures and programs consistent with their own standards. **The circuit court found it unlikely that Congress intended the stay-put provision to require a state to implement an IEP established in another state without first considering consistency with its own policies**. Where a parent unilaterally removes a student from a placement determined under state procedures, the stay-put provision is inoperative until the parties reach a new agreement. The Third Circuit held that the stay-put provision is inapplicable when a parent removes a student from an existing placement in favor of another placement not assigned through state procedures. Because the student was without a "then current educational placement" in Pennsylvania, he was not entitled to stay-put protection. Moreover, **whenever a student moves into a new state, the receiving state is not obligated to automatically effectuate a prior IEP from another state, and parents maintain the risk of unilateral private school placements**. Pennsylvania special education regulations did not create any contrary rule and were silent on the subject of accepting IEPs devised in other states, and the court affirmed the district court's decision that the school district was not required to preserve a private school placement for the student on the basis of the IEP prepared in Washington, D.C. The school district took no action to alter or deny the student's right to a FAPE, and the court affirmed the summary judgment order for the district. *Michael C. v. Radnor Township School Dist.*, 202 F.3d 642 (3d Cir. 2000).

♦ A profoundly deaf student with a cochlear implant attended a private school in Missouri that practiced oral education, pursuant to an IEP developed for him by his school district. The district completed another IEP for the student shortly before he and his family moved to Minnesota. **The student's parents contacted Minnesota school officials and explained that they had located a private Minnesota school similar to the Missouri one, and that they wanted their son placed there**. The Minnesota district sought to assess the student and proposed placing him in its "Early Childhood Special Education" classroom. The parents rejected the proposal and informed the district that they intended to enroll their son in the Minnesota private school. A private assessment recommended placing the student in a cued speech program, which was not offered by the Minnesota private school. The district developed an IEP calling for the student's placement in a district classroom with six or seven other students. He would receive one-on-one time with a speech pathologist, ECSE teacher and two paraprofessionals. The IEP also called for one-on-one time with a speech language pathologist or teacher of the deaf and hard of hearing. The parents rejected the proposal and commenced an administrative due process proceeding. An independent hearing officer made detailed factual findings and held that the district IEP offered the student a FAPE. The IHO ordered the implementation of the proposed IEP in a district school. On appeal, a state hearing review officer reversed, finding the district failed to show that its placement proposal was appropriate for the student's audiological needs. The review officer nonetheless found that the parents did not show that the private placement was appropriate, and they appealed to a federal district court.

The court rejected the parents' assertion that the district was required to accept the IEP developed for the student by the Missouri school district. They did not establish that the Missouri IEP was consistent with Minnesota policies and mandates. **The district was under no obligation to automatically adopt an IEP from another state, as Congress left the primary responsibility for providing a free appropriate public education under the IDEA to the states themselves**. The IHO had considered evidence that the district could provide modifications to meet the student's audiological needs. The review officer had improperly reweighed this evidence when finding the proposed IEP inappropriate. The district had the necessary information to modify the student's ECSE classroom and was willing to undertake those modifications. The court found it irrelevant that the private school classrooms might be quieter than the ECSE classroom. The district's willingness to make the necessary modifications to allow the student to hear in the ECSE classroom indicated that he could receive educational benefits there. The court entered an order that reinstated the IHO's decision. *Grafe et al. v. Independent School District No. 834*, No. CIV.00-1690 (MJD/JGL), 2001 WL 1631455 (D. Minn. 2001).

- A student with autism moved with his family from Georgia to Florida. The Florida school district received copies of the student's Georgia IEP. Instead of implementing the Georgia IEP, as the parents wished, the school board advised the family that additional evaluations were required before a permanent IEP could be adopted. **It placed the student under an interim IEP pending a placement within six months**, as required by the Florida Administrative Code. The board conducted several evaluations to create a permanent IEP, but the parents objected and requested an independent evaluation. The board determined that the student met the criteria for its program for students with autism and should receive speech and occupational therapy. However, the parents refused to consent to the IEP until the completion of the independent evaluation and removed the student from the school district. They filed an administrative complaint against the district, challenging its use of the interim IEP. The hearing officer held that the IEP was appropriate, that the district had performed adequate evaluations for developing a permanent IEP, that the student had received a free appropriate public education, and that the family had suffered no harm due to any defective notices by the board.

The parents appealed to a federal district court, seeking monetary damages, but the court affirmed the hearing officer's decision. **It rejected the parent's**

equal protection argument that the administrative code's allowance of up to six months for school districts to formulate a permanent IEP for students moving to Florida from other states treated such students less favorably that disabled students transferring between in-state schools. In those cases, districts are required to formulate a new IEP within 30 days. Because the IDEA requires only the provision of an education meeting the standards of the state educational agency, the administrative code did not violate federal law. The six-month time frame allowed school districts the necessary time to gather evaluation information and determine a student's eligibility for Florida programs. The court dismissed the Rehabilitation Act claim, since it duplicated the IDEA claim. The U.S. Court of Appeals, Eleventh Circuit, accepted the parents' petition for review. In a memorandum decision, it adopted the summary judgment order for the school board. *Weiss v. School Bd. of Hillsborough County*, 141 F.3d 990 (11th Cir.1998).

VI. GRADUATION

◆ **A group of students with learning disabilities claimed that a California High School Exit Exam (CAHSEE) administration planned for March 2002 violated their rights under the IDEA and its regulations. They asserted that there was no alternate assessment and no provision for required accommodations** to learning disabled test-takers. The students sued the state education department in a federal district court, which considered their motion for a preliminary injunction that would prevent the March 2002 CAHSEE administration. The court observed that the students had either IEPs or Section 504 plans. Regulations published under the IDEA require each IEP to address state wide assessments such as the CAHSEE. Each IEP must specify any individual modifications in the administration of state or district-wide assessments that are needed to allow the student's participation. The court rejected the state's argument that the students lacked standing to bring the action, noting that they did not have to take and fail a defective exam before filing suit. The students had a statutory right under the IDEA to meaningfully participate in the CAHSEE and could vindicate it through a private right of action. Because they were challenging a policy or practice of general applicability, it was unnecessary to bring an administrative action before proceeding in court. There was evidence that some students were unable to meaningfully access the CAHSEE, regardless of accommodations. The court held that for these students, the CAHSEE would be an invalid measurement of academic achievement. While some students were incapable of mastering the CAHSEE's content, they were still entitled to a valid assessment of their capabilities. The court held that the state's waiver policy was unlikely to satisfy IDEA requirements for alternate assessment because under the current system, school districts applied for waivers. Because the system allowed for waivers only when a student achieved the equivalent of a passing CAHSEE score, the waiver policy was meaningless. The court held that the students were entitled to receive accommodations during the state-wide examination, finding persuasive a memorandum from the U.S. Department of Education' s Office of Special Education Programs that suggested "appropriate accommodation" under the IDEA meant "necessary to access the test." Appropriate accommodation for the CAHSEE meant "any accommodation necessary to render a student's score on the CAHSEE a meaningful measure of that student's academic achievement." The determination of specific appropriate accommodations for each student was best left to the IEP and Section 504 processes. While the students were entitled to accommodations on the CAHSEE, the court ruled that they did not show a likelihood of success on the merits of their other claims. Halting the March 2002 CAHSEE administration would impose significant hardship on the state. The public interest was best served by allowing students with learning disabilities to use the accommodations set forth in their IEPs and Section 504 plans. **Students whose IEPs or 504 plans did not specifically address the CAHSEE could take the test with any accommodations for standardized testing or general classroom testing described in their IEP or 504 plans. Students whose IEPs or 504 plans specified alternate assessments in lieu of the CAHSEE were entitled to take alternate assessments.** The court ordered the state to develop an alternate assessment and ordered all school districts in the state to provide a notice to parents of children with IEPs or 504 plans of their rights under the court order. *Chapman v. California Dept. of Educ.*, No. C 01-01780 CRB (N.D.Cal. 2002).

♦ **A group of Indiana students with disabilities asserted that the state violated student due process rights by imposing a graduation qualification examination** (GQE) **as a condition of high school graduation beginning in the 1999-2000 school year**. Students with disabilities were previously exempt from the exam and they claimed they received no instruction in the material being tested. **A second subclass of students claimed that they were denied testing accommodations and adaptations** in violation of the IDEA. They alleged the state denied them permission to use many of the accommodations specified in their IEPs. A state trial court refused to certify one subclass for failing to first exhaust available administrative remedies and rejected a proposal for certification of all students claiming denial of appropriate accommodations. On appeal, the Indiana Appellate Court reversed and remanded the trial court judgment. On remand, the trial court again entered judgment for the state, and the students appealed.

The court of appeals observed that the GQE is part of the Indiana Statewide Testing for Educational Progress program applicable to all Indiana students. Prior to the change in the law requiring students to pass the GQE in order to graduate, students with disabilities could graduate if they satisfied their IEP requirements, without regard to standardized testing. The court agreed with the students that they had property interests in the award of a diploma if they met graduation requirements. This interest was protected by the right to due process, including adequate notice of the examination and exposure to the material being tested. **The state had provided school districts with at least five years' notice about the GQE and the students learned of it at least three years in advance**. The trial court did not erroneously find that this notice to students was adequate, in view of the multiple, free opportunities they received for remediation and retaking the GQE, if necessary. The trial court had permissibly found that the students were exposed to the curriculum tested on the GQE. School systems were required to align their curriculum with state standards as of 1996. The appeals court agreed with the trial court that the proper remedy for failing to teach students the subjects tested on the GQE was remediation, not the award of diplomas. It stated that **the IDEA does not require specific results such as the award of a diploma, but instead mandates that students with disabilities receive access to specialized and individualized educational services**. Denying diplomas to these students did not violate the IDEA's FAPE requirement. **The state did not violate the IDEA by failing to honor accommodations specified in IEPs that would affect the validity of test results**. It permitted some accommodations, only prohibiting accommodations such as reading aloud questions that were designed to measure reading comprehension or allowing students unlimited testing time. In a 1997 case involving the Alabama exit examination, the U.S. Department of Education's Office of Civil Rights determined that states can properly require students to take reading comprehension tests without providing them readers. Accordingly, the Indiana court held that the state was not required to provide the accommodations specified in student IEPs during the GQE. It affirmed the trial court judgment. *Rene et al. v. Reed*, 751 N.E.2d 736 (Ind. App. Ct. 2001).

◆ At the beginning of his senior year, a student requested a due process hearing, claiming that his school district denied him a FAPE by devising an IEP for him that did not identify his weakness in typing and did not provide modifications for two classes. A hearing officer held that the IEP was appropriate, and that decision was affirmed on appeal. The student did not appeal this decision, **but just before his last day of school, he requested another due process hearing**. The district determined that he graduated before the second request for due process was received and was not entitled to any relief under the IDEA. A hearing officer held that he lacked jurisdiction to hold another hearing and an appeals officer affirmed. This time, the student appealed to a federal district court, which held that the administrative decisions were correct.

On appeal to the U.S. Court of Appeals for the 10th Circuit, the court held that **if a student graduates from high school and does not contest the validity of the graduation, the case is moot**. This rule does not apply to cases in which graduated former students seek compensatory relief. The student in this case raised some issues that could be construed as contesting the appropriateness of his graduation. However, this was tempered by evidence that he was prepared for graduation and actually sought to graduate at the end of his senior year. The student claimed that the district should have provided him with formal notification of his impending graduation and an "exit IEP meeting." He asserted that the district was required to evaluate him prior to any determination that he was no longer eligible for special education services. While IDEA regulations provide that graduation with a regular diploma is a change of placement requiring prior notice, the student did not claim that the lack of notice rendered his graduation invalid. By failing to directly challenge the validity of his graduation, the student conceded that he suffered no harm and the administrative officers had no jurisdiction over the case. At best, the failure to provide the student with a formal written notice of graduation was a harmless technical procedural defect. The IDEA does not specify an "exit IEP meeting," and IDEA regulations at 34 C.F.R. Part 300.534, provide that an evaluation is not required before the termination of educational benefits due to graduation with a regular diploma. There was no substantive educational deprivation for which compensatory relief was available. He did not show that he was unqualified to graduate. The school district did not violate the student's rights by failing to specify certain accommodations in his high-school IEP. The district's obligation to the student ceased upon his graduation with a regular diploma. **At the time he submitted his request for a second hearing, he had completed his graduation requirements and was no longer entitled to IDEA protections and benefits, including a hearing.** The court upheld the administrative decisions. *T.S. v. Independent School District No. 54*, 265 F.3d 1090 (10th Cir. 2001).

◆ An 18-year-old with cerebral palsy reported to school officials that her mother was abusing her. The student was then placed in protective custody pending a court determination of her competency. The school scheduled an IEP meeting to consider the student's placement for the following school year, without providing notice to her mother. The district denied the mother's request to attend the meeting. **School officials consulted with a social worker and determined that it was in the student's best interest to graduate early.** She agreed to the graduation decision. The district never notified the mother of the graduation decision. The student later agreed to return to her mother, and then filed a complaint against the district with the state department of education, alleging her graduation was rushed. The complaint was rejected. The mother commenced a federal district court action against the school district, school officials, the state Department of Human Services and several of its employees, asserting that she had been deprived of adequate notice of the graduation decision in violation of the IDEA, Section 504 and the ADA. She also sought monetary damages for civil rights violations under 42 U.S.C. § 1983. The court dismissed the IDEA claim on the grounds that it was not timely filed, and the Section 504 and ADA claims because of the failure to show bad faith or gross misjudgment.

The mother appealed to the Eighth Circuit, which held that the school district's failure to provide her with notice of her child's graduation was a violation of the IDEA. State and federal law required the education of students with disabilities until the age of 21 or the completion of a secondary education program. The pre-1997 version of the IDEA applied to this case, since the protective order and graduation had occurred in 1995. Under the pre-1997 version of the statute, there was no language providing for the transfer of parental rights to a student with disabilities. Accordingly, the mother retained her parental rights under the IDEA despite the court order. **The district's failure to provide the mother with written notice of the graduation decision violated the IDEA, as the student was under 21 years old and had not completed the state's secondary education program at the time the graduation decision was made.** The panel rejected the defendants' assertion that the IDEA claim was barred for failure to timely file the action, finding the district court erroneously applied a 30-day limitations period. The Eighth Circuit reversed that part of the district court judgment. Although the district court had improperly dismissed the Section 1983 claim for compensatory education, there was no merit to the mother's claim for monetary damages under Section 1983. The Eighth Circuit held that general and punitive damages are unavailable in a Section 1983 claim based on alleged IDEA violations. The district court had correctly dismissed the Section 504 and ADA claims, since there was no showing that any of the defendants had acted in bad faith or with gross misjudgment. The case was remanded to determine the nature and extent of a compensatory education award. *Birmingham v. Omaha School District*, 220 F.3d 850 (8th Cir. 2000).

◆ A student with autism resided in the Unorganized Territories of Maine, which has no public schools. The local education agency funded his placement in a private school where he received special education services. In the spring of the year in which the student turned 19, his pupil evaluation team recommended that he graduate with his class. **His parents challenged the recommendation and requested a due process hearing.** The hearing officer determined that the agency's decision did not deprive the student of a free appropriate public education. The agency sent the student a diploma and the parent appealed to the U.S. District Court for the District of Maine.

The court considered the parents' motion for a preliminary order requiring the agency to maintain the student's placement pending consideration of the case under the IDEA's stay put provision, 20 U.S.C. § 1415(j). The court rejected the parents' argument that the stay put provision operates as an automatic stay, compelling the agency to maintain the student's placement at the private school. It agreed with the agency that parents must make the traditional four-part showing required when any party petitions a court for preliminary relief: likelihood of success on the merits of the claim, the potential for irreparable harm if the relief is denied, the balance of hardships between the parties, and the public interest. However, the burden of establishing these four elements rested on the agency, because it was the party seeking to modify the student's existing placement. The court found the hearing officer's decision ambiguous because although it approved the agency's decision to allow graduation, it did not specify the student's current educational placement, referring only to the date of his last IEP. According to the court, in the absence of detailed administrative findings, the student's current educational placement was the one described in his last IEP. The parents had objected to the agency's decision to graduate the student while he was still attending the private school and the court interpreted the hearing officer's ambiguity in their favor. The court further held that **graduation constitutes a change in placement for purposes of the stay put provision**. Because the agency failed to prove the four required elements for preliminary relief and thus failed to overcome the strong preference for preservation of the educational status quo, the court held that the student should remain in his private school placement under the previous year's IEP, pending further proceedings. *Bell et al. v. Education in the Unorganized Territories et al.*, 2000 WL 1855096 (D. Me. 2000).

◆ A 20-year-old student with Down's syndrome and mental retardation received instruction in a learning support environment for two-thirds of the school day under an IEP. His parents requested the school IEP team allow him to participate in graduation ceremonies at the end of the school year, even though he would not graduate at that time. **The district refused the request, observing that while the student had sufficient academic credits for graduation, he**

had not completed his special education program and was not yet eligible for a diploma. The parents requested a due process hearing, arguing that the student was entitled to have his diploma "banked" and should be allowed to participate in graduation ceremonies. A hearing officer upheld the district policy requiring the completion of all local and state graduation requirements, including completion of the IEP, before participation in graduation ceremonies. An appeals panel reversed and ordered the district to allow the student to participate in the 1999-2000 graduation ceremonies.

The district appealed to the Pennsylvania Commonwealth Court, arguing that it was vested with discretion to develop its own criteria for student participation in graduation ceremonies, and that its decision to exclude the student for failing to meet his IEP requirements was a valid exercise of its discretion. The court agreed, observing that the state general assembly vested local districts with the authority to establish graduation requirements and confer diplomas upon those who completed the requirements. **Any ceremony celebrating the completion of these requirements, and the decision to award a diploma, was within the local district's basic educational policy discretion.** The school district in this case had a policy requiring that a student first complete an appropriate instructional program before receiving a diploma. The family did not dispute that the student was not yet eligible to receive a diploma, and the appeals panel had improperly found the district policy void for vagueness. The IDEA requires education agencies to provide an IEP for qualified students in order to ensure the delivery of an appropriate education. **The district's policy did not violate the IDEA, which does not grant students the right to participate in graduation ceremonies without meeting IEP requirements**. The IDEA gives students with disabilities the right to an IEP, not a right to graduate with their peers. The court reversed the appeals panel's decision. *Woodland Hills School Dist. v. S.F.*, 747 A.2d 433 (Pa. Commw. Ct. 2000).

CHAPTER TWO

Placement

I. PLACEMENT IN SPECIAL EDUCATION PROGRAMS

The IDEA requires local education agencies to provide students with disabilities in the jurisdiction with an appropriate program of special education and related services that is individualized and reasonably calculated to confer educational benefits. The placement must also take into consideration the least restrictive appropriate environment to maximize the student's contact with regular education students. The placement must comply with state educational standards, which in some cases exceed the IDEA minimum standard, and the agency may be required to locate and pay for a private school placement if it is necessary for the student to realize educational benefits.

A. Educational Benefit Generally

◆ The kindergarten IEP for a student with autism called for 20 percent of her day in regular education. While her instruction included numerous methods of teaching, it relied most heavily on the Treatment and Education of Autistic and

Related Communication Handicapped Children (TEACCH) method. The student continued to attend a mix of regular and special education classes in subsequent years, with instruction in a curriculum that was primarily based on TEACCH methodology. During the student's second-grade year, her parents requested district funding for a 40-hour-per-week home Lovaas program. The district denied this request, along with the parents' request for funding of a summer Lovaas program. The student's third-grade program called for 25.5 hours of weekly applied behavioral analysis, including 12.5 hours of discrete trial training. Although the student made considerable progress during the third grade, **the parents** requested a due process hearing, **seeking a 40-hour program of weekly individual direct instruction to be administered year-round, staffed by personnel trained in discrete trial methods, and one-to-one supervision of the student at all times**. The parents further sought tuition reimbursement for the costs of summer programs and home programs. An administrative law judge ruled that the claims arising more than two years prior to the parents' request for administrative review were barred by Oregon's two-year limitation on actions. The remaining IEPs were found adequate to provide the student with a FAPE.

The parents appealed to a federal district court, which agreed that the appropriate limitations period was two years. The court found that while Lovaas programming benefits some students, its general applicability to all students with autism remains unclear. The district had included methods of direct teaching in the student's program and her teacher regularly used drills during the school day. The court held that **the district's TEACCH-based methodology was reasonably calculated to provide the student with some educational benefit**. There was substantial evidence to support a TEACCH-based curriculum. It was not the court's role to make a determination of appropriate methodology, since this is an area within the expertise of schools and their experts. **Since the school had provided the student with access to specialized instruction and related services that were individually designed to provide her with educational benefits, the district did not deny her a FAPE**. While affirming the ALJ's decision in favor of the district, the court held that the failure to include a knowledgeable district representative as part of the student's second-grade IEP team was a procedural violation of the IDEA that denied the parents an opportunity to meaningfully participate in the IEP process and deprived the student of educational opportunity. The remaining IEPs under consideration were reasonably calculated to confer meaningful educational benefit and did not deprive the student of a FAPE. *Pitchford v. Salem-Keizer School District No. 24J*, 155 F.Supp.2d 1213 (D. Or. 2001).

◆ When a student with significant learning disabilities was in the eighth grade, her parents and local school system met to develop her IEP for the ninth grade and to determine an appropriate placement. For the first eight years of school, the student was enrolled in a private school, and **the parents wanted her placed in an out-of-state residential school. The district recommended the student be placed in a non-residential public school in a fundamental life skills program**. The parents rejected the district placement offer and enrolled their daughter in the residential school. At due process, an ALJ upheld the proposed district placement and denied the parents' request for tuition reimbursement. He determined that there had been no procedural violations of the IDEA and that the district's placement proposal afforded the student the opportunity to receive a FAPE. The parents then commenced a federal district court action against the school district for IDEA violations, adding claims under Section 504 of the Rehabilitation Act and seeking an award of monetary damages under 42 U.S.C. § 1983.

The court referred the case to a federal magistrate judge, who considered the district's motion for summary judgment. The magistrate observed that the IDEA does not guarantee each student will receive an ideal educational opportunity. Moreover, administrative decisions under the IDEA are presumed to be valid. In this case, the only procedural error alleged was that the hearing officer had improperly imposed the burden of proof on the parents. The magistrate found this argument meritless, ruling that while the allocation of the burden of proof may determine the outcome in certain cases, it did not affect the outcome of this case. **The district proved by a preponderance of evidence that its placement recommendation for the student's first year in high school would provide her with a FAPE**. Educators at the student's private school agreed that she needed fundamental skills instruction to prepare her for everyday life and that it would be difficult for her to attend a diploma-track program. The student failed Maryland's functional math, reading and writing examinations, fortifying the ALJ's decision that the placement recommendation of fundamental skills instruction was suited to her needs. School officials strongly believed that a residential placement was unnecessary because the student did not require that restrictive a placement. The magistrate held that the fundamental life skills curriculum at the public school would provide the student with educational benefit. The administrative decision was affirmed. Because the parents' IDEA claim failed, the closely related Section 504 and Section 1983 claims also failed. *Steinberg v. Weast*, 132 F.Supp.2d 343 (D. Md. 2001).

◆ A placement team designed an IEP for a preschooler with autism that called for his placement in a self-contained classroom with physical, occupational and speech therapy. The parents initially accepted the IEP, but eventually decided to fund a home-based Lovaas program. **The district rejected the parents' claim for funding of the home-based program, but offered to substantially modify the student's IEP by increasing his time in the self-contained classroom with placement in a reverse mainstream classroom**. The district also offered one-on-one training in school and an additional classroom aide. The parents agreed to implement the proposed IEP on days that the student would attend school. The parties were unable to agree on a new IEP, with the parents arguing for a Lovaas program and the district claiming that the student required interaction with nondisabled peers. The parents eventually requested a formal hearing, at which an administrative panel upheld the IEP, but found it should include 10 hours of weekly home-based therapy. The parents appealed to a federal district court, which concluded that the district IEP was appropriate. The court awarded summary judgment to the school district and the parents appealed to the Eighth Circuit.

First, the Eighth Circuit noted that the standard for reviewing an IEP under the IDEA is whether it offers instruction and related services that are reasonably calculated to provide the student with educational benefits. There was no merit to the parents' assertion that Missouri state law created a higher standard than that contained in the IDEA. The circuit court then rejected the parents' claim that the student was entitled to receive 40 hours per week of one-to-one Lovaas instruction. In this case, the district court had made extensive factual findings. **There was ample evidence that the student had made progress in his initial district program and that the district had made substantial modifications to his plan under the guidance of an autism expert**. The court found evidence that the student's social skills suffered during the time he was in private therapy and the supplemental one-to-one program offered by the district had proven effective. Although the IDEA created an interactive process to determine a student's IEP, it did not empower parents to make unilateral placement decisions. The student had received a FAPE, and the circuit court affirmed the district court judgment for the school district. *Gill v. Columbia 93 School District*, 217 F.3d 1027 (8th Cir. 2000).

- A Tennessee school system proposed a placement calling for six hours of daily instruction three times per week in a special education classroom, use of an auditory trainer, classroom assistance by a deaf educator, weekly speech/language therapy, and periodic audiology and occupational therapy evaluations for a student with a hearing impairment and dyspraxia. **The parents objected to the proposed special education classroom on the grounds that it was not suitable for a student with hearing impairments** and that the teacher had little experience. The parents filed an administrative complaint, seeking reimbursement for the costs of a private program they enrolled the student in. An ALJ ordered the school system to provide necessary related services, including modification of the proposed classroom and to provide qualified professionals to appropriately address his hearing, speech and language impairments. In addition to requiring the school system to devise an appropriate IEP, the ALJ awarded the parents tuition reimbursement for the cost of educating the student at a private hearing and speech facility for 15 months. The school system appealed to a state trial court, which affirmed. The Tennessee Court of Appeals remanded, and the trial court again entered judgment for the parents. On appeal, the court of appeals vacated the judgment and remanded to the ALJ for supplemental findings of fact and conclusions of law. The ALJ entered a revised final order in favor of the parents and the trial court affirmed, awarding the parents tuition reimbursement and attorneys' fees. The school system then filed a second appeal.

The court agreed with the administrative finding that the IEP proposed by the school system was inappropriate for the student and that the private hearing and speech facility represented an appropriate placement. School witnesses admitted the failure of the school system to modify the proposed classroom. They testified that the classroom had a comprehensive development curriculum designed for special education students, and did not emphasize speech and language for students with hearing impairments or dyspraxia. The school witnesses also admitted that the special education classroom teacher had no formal training or certification in deaf education or speech/language pathology. Evidence presented by the parents indicated that the student required an acoustically treated classroom with minimal visual distraction and a curriculum that consistently emphasized and reinforced speech and language development. The court observed that the hearing and speech facility was appropriate and affirmed the award of tuition reimbursement. The administrative order required the school system to provide important services that exceeded the level of services it had proposed. The award of attorneys' fees was also justified since the parents were prevailing parties and the system had failed to offer any evidence that the amount claimed was unreasonable or unsupported. However, the parents were not entitled to an award of prejudgment interest on the amounts approved by the court, since the school system had reasonably disputed its obligations to the student under federal law. The court affirmed the judgment for the parents. *Wilson County School System v. Clifton*, 41 S.W.3d 645 (Tenn. App. Ct. 2000).

◆ Prior to her third birthday, an Illinois student who demonstrated autistic-like behaviors was identified as having moderate global development delay, secondary to seizure disorder with developmental language disorder and suspected oral apraxia. She was found eligible for special education and attended public schools. **A program prepared for her just before she turned nine called for her placement in a program for students with severe cognitive/health impairments**. The program included various related services and extended year services. Her parents objected to the continued public school placement and requested a due process hearing. At mediation, the parties agreed on another public school placement pending further proceedings. A hearing officer then considered the family's claims that the school board failed to fully implement the student's IEP, failed to provide a safe classroom and transportation, failed to provide professional nursing services and failed to document daily school activities. **The parents sought placement in a therapeutic day school**. The hearing officer held that the educational program prepared by the board was appropriate and that adequate medical and transportation services were available for the student at her new school. Because the public school placement was appropriate and the therapeutic day placement was not the least restrictive available setting for the student, the hearing officer upheld the IEP. A second-level hearing officer affirmed, finding that the board provided the student with a FAPE in the LRE.

The parents petitioned a U.S. district court for review of the final administrative decision. The court noted that the student's public school teachers were appropriately certified, and that she was making progress toward her current IEP goals. The IEPs prepared by the board at each of her last two schools had been calculated to provide her with educational benefits. Because of her health and cognitive impairments, her progress would be very slow and the disparity between her abilities and those of her peers would increase over time. **The court stated that it was unable to require a school district to do more than follow IDEA procedures and develop an IEP that was reasonably calculated to enable a student to receive educational benefits**. The board had placed the student in the least restrictive appropriate environment, in contrast to the placement preferred by the parents, which provided for no interaction with nondisabled students. The administrative hearing officers had correctly found that the IEPs were reasonably calculated to provide the student with a FAPE, and the court held that the board did not violate the IDEA. *M.T. ex rel. D.T. v. Board* *of Educ. of City of Chicago*, No. 98 C 2914, 2000 U.S. Dist. Lexis 10590 (N.D. Ill. 2000).

◆ When a student with hypotonic and autistic behaviors and a developmental disability was 15 months old, her parents enrolled her in First Steps, a program operated by the Missouri Department of Mental Health. According to the parents, she made significant progress in her gross motor skills in the program, but no significant improvement in fine motor skills. The parents were dissatisfied with her progress and enrolled her in an intensive, home-based program of individualized therapy for 12 hours a day. The home program was offered by the Institutes for the Achievement of Human Potential. They requested district funding for the program when the student turned three. The district prepared a proposed IEP calling for instruction in a classroom with developmentally disabled students, as well as some non-disabled students, supplemented by individualized speech, occupational and physical therapy. **The parents' proposal for in-home individualized training was discussed at an IEP meeting, but ultimately rejected because of the lack of interaction with other students.** The parents left the meeting before it ended. The district sent the parents a letter stating its decision to place the student as described in the proposed IEP, including a notice of their procedural rights. After a failed attempt at mediation, the parents initiated due process proceedings at which they challenged the proposed IEP and expressly waived any argument based on IDEA procedural violations. They appealed to a federal district court, which reversed the hearing panel's decision, finding that they intended only to waive procedural technicalities in the form of notices, and not all claims based on procedural issues. The district court further held that the school district's proposal called for traditional therapies resembling those employed with little success in the First Steps Program. Reasoning that the student could not receive educational benefit from the proposed IEP, the court ordered the district to reimburse the parents for tuition at the Institutes, with an award of attorneys' fees and costs.

The school district appealed to the Eighth Circuit, which held that the parents had waived all procedural claims during the administrative proceedings and received a meaningful opportunity to participate in the development of the IEP. According to the court, a procedural error did not occur when district personnel brought a draft of the proposed IEP to the meeting. Under 34 C.F.R. Part 300, Appendix C, a school district may come to an IEP meeting with proposals, as long as parents are informed that they are merely recommendations for review and discussion. The parents admitted that they came to the meeting with the expectation that the district would approve of their request for funding of the home-based program. By abruptly leaving the meeting, they had truncated their own procedural rights to participate in the IEP development process. The school district considered the parents' proposal but rejected it because it did not provide for sufficient interaction with peers. The district court had improperly evaluated the proposed IEP by comparing it to the First Steps Program. The student's gross motor skills had improved in the First Steps Program and the district proposal significantly expanded the time she would spend in therapy. Although the programs employed similar methodologies, the school's plan called for different techniques, instructors and therapists. **The district court improperly rejected the significant educational expertise of school authorities when it reversed the hearing panel decision, and should have accepted testimony that the proposed IEP was reasonably calculated to provide the student with a FAPE.** The court reversed the district court's decision. *Blackmon v. Springfield R-XII School Dist.*, 198 F.3d 648 (8th Cir. 1999).

- A Kansas student with hearing impairments participated in a public school program that included both regular class and resource room attendance. Her father obtained an evaluation that recommended she avoid mainstreaming in favor of an intensive, individualized reading instruction program. The private school accepted the student for the following school term and the father asked the school district to pay for her attendance there. The school district held an IEP meeting that resulted in a recommendation that the student remain in her public school placement, but otherwise followed the recommendations of the private school. The father disagreed with the IEP and withdrew her from the school system. He requested a due process hearing that resulted in an administrative decision for the school district. **The hearing officer held that Kansas law creates no greater duty to educate a disabled student than that created by the IDEA.** The IEPs proposed by the district set forth adequate goals and evaluative criteria for the student and the student had been provided with a FAPE.

A review officer reversed the decision with respect to the annual goals and objectives of the IEPs and remanded the case. The father appealed to a federal district court, which granted the school district's summary judgment motion. On appeal, the Tenth Circuit held that Kansas's educational standards were no higher than the minimum established by the IDEA. There was no merit to the argument that state statutory language required school districts to maximize each student's potential. The court discussed IEP requirements in general, and held that they need not provide the detail found in monthly instructional plans. The goals stated in the IEPs in this case contained sufficient criteria for evaluating the student's general progress toward her goals. **The record supported the finding that the IEPs called for an adequate educational program that, while not optimal, conferred some educational benefits and satisfied the minimal requirements of state and federal law**. The fact that the student made better progress at the private school did not affect this conclusion, and the court affirmed the judgment for the school district. *O'Toole v. Olathe Dist. Schools Unif. School Dist. No. 233*, 144 F.3d 692 (10th Cir.1998).

- A Missouri school district imposed discipline on a student for possession of a controlled substance found in his locker. The discovery occurred just prior to a meeting concerning a initial language skills evaluation. An IEP meeting was conducted and the team determined that the substance possession offense was a manifestation of his disability. **The team opted to impose alternative disciplinary measures, and added behavior and language goals to his IEP** It suspended discipline if the student consented to a drug screening. At a subsequent IEP meeting, the student's mother requested that his IEP reflect medical conditions including Tourette's Syndrome and attention deficit disorder. When the district did not do so, the family unilaterally enrolled the student in a private school that did not offer speech services, even though he was identified as having a speech impairment. They requested a due process hearing under state special education law, after which a panel of hearing officers issued a decision for the school district. A state-level review officer upheld the decision, and the parents appealed to the U.S. Court of Appeals for the Eastern District of Missouri. They included claims arising under the U.S. Constitution and § 504 of the Rehabilitation Act.

The court found that the student had received passing grades in his public school classes, had friends there and had received necessary modifications to his curriculum. **The school district had prepared an IEP for him that was designed to meet his specific educational needs and he had been successful in his public school program.** The proposed IEP offered the student personalized instruction with support services sufficient to allow him to benefit from his instructional program and receive passing grades. The district and state education department had fulfilled their IDEA obligations to him and were entitled to summary judgment on the IDEA claims. The court also awarded summary judgment to the school district on the student's claim for due process and equal protection violations. Since the district and education department had fulfilled their IDEA obligations to the student, no constitutional violations could have occurred. The court found the student's § 504 and state law claims meritless and awarded summary judgment to the district. *Breen by and through Breen v. St. Charles R-IV School Dist.*, 2 F.Supp.2d 1214 (E.D.Mo.1997).

◆ A New York preschool student was identified with autistic symptoms and his parents enrolled him in a home-based program in which he received 40 hours per week of one-on-one instruction using the applied behavioral analysis method. His parents applied to their school district of residence for public preschool educational services. Following an evaluation and assessment by a multi-disciplinary team, the school district recommended placement in a private nursery school for autistic children. **The proposed placement called for 25 hours of applied behavioral analysis instruction**, which the parents believed would be contingent on funding. The school district relied on evaluators who believed that the home-based program, in which the student was showing remarkable progress, was impossible under state law. The student's father requested a due process hearing at which he alleged that the proposed placement violated state and federal law. The hearing officer upheld the proposed IEP, and a state review officer affirmed the decision. The father appealed to the U.S. District Court for the Southern District of New York.

The court found substantial evidence that the 40-hour intensive one-on-one applied behavioral analysis program was appropriate since it was supported by a psychological and behavioral evaluation and a neuropsychological evaluation of the student. There was also evidence that the 25 hours of instruction proposed by the school district would not be intensive and would therefore be inappropriate. **The court rejected the school district's assertion that the home-based placement violated the IDEA.** Some students with disabilities must be educated in segregated facilities because of their disruptive behavior or because the gains from inclusive instruction may be marginal. The court reversed the administrative decisions, ruling that the IEP proposed by the district was not calculated to provide educational benefits to the student. It granted the father's summary judgment motion. *Mr. X v. New York State Educ. Dept.*, 975 F.Supp. 546 (S.D.N.Y.1997).

◆ A Texas preschooler with profound hearing loss in both ears was enrolled in the total communication program of her local school district. The program included sign language instruction in which the parents participated. The student received a cochlear implant and made significant progress in speech development. She was then placed in a self-contained classroom with four other preschool students, where she received instruction from a teacher certified in speech methodology and therapy as well as deaf education. The student also received weekly individual speech therapy. Despite the progress made by the student, she began to prefer sign language over speech. **The student's father determined that he did not want her using sign language, fearing that she would become part of "the deaf subculture." He requested that she be placed in an aural/oral program without use of sign language**, along with one hour per day of individual speech therapy and auditory training. The student's teachers voiced concern about immediate transition from the total communication program to an aural/oral program, and the school placement committee promised to provide an aural/oral program the following school year. The father nonetheless called for a due process hearing under the IDEA and placed his daughter in a private school. The hearing officer determined that the school district had provided the student with a FAPE and the parents appealed to the U.S. District Court for the Southern District of Texas.

The court determined that overwhelming evidence indicated that the student had received a FAPE from the school district. **Her improvement in speech and auditory skills resulted as much from her public school instruction as from that received from the private school**. The IEP developed by the school district had been reasonably calculated to enable the student to receive educational benefits and the father's fears were unjustified. Parents who made private placements on their own initiative did so at their own risk, and the school district was not required to reimburse the student's parents for tuition. *Bonnie Ann F. by John R.F. v. Calallen Indep. School Dist.*, 835 F.Supp. 340 (S.D.Tex.1993).

B. Neighborhood Placement

◆ Two mentally retarded women were voluntarily admitted to a Georgia state hospital for psychiatric treatment. Their doctors eventually determined that the women's needs could be met in community-based treatment programs, however, they remained institutionalized. **The women sued various state officials under 42 U.S.C. 1983 and Title II of the ADA, challenging their continued confinement in a segregated environment**. A federal district court held that the state's failure to place the women in a community-based treatment program violated Title II, and the U.S. Court of Appeals, Eleventh Circuit, affirmed. The circuit court remanded the case for a reassessment of the state's "cost-based" defense, wherein the state had argued that inadequate funding, not discrimination, accounted for the continued institutionalization of the women. It stated that a cost justification would fail unless the state could prove that requiring it to spend additional funds to provide integrated placements would fundamentally alter its services.

On review by the U.S. Supreme Court, the court initially noted that the unjustified isolation of disabled individuals is properly considered discrimination based on disability. However, it then held that the circuit court's remand was too restrictive. If the state could show that, in the allocation of available resources, immediate relief for the women would be inequitable, given the state's responsibility for many persons with mental disabilities, it would have to be allowed some leeway in placing the women outside the institution. In the court's opinion, **community settings are required when the state's treatment professionals have determined a community placement is appropriate, the affected persons do not oppose the transfer, and the placement can be reasonably accommodated, taking into account the resources available to the state and the needs of others with mental disabilities**. *Olmstead v. L.C.*, 527 U.S. 581, 119 S.Ct. 2176, 144 L.Ed.2d 540 (1999).

◆ An 11-year-old Rhode Island student had a respiratory condition that required the use of a tracheal tube for breathing and the presence of a full-time nurse. His parents met with school district representatives to discuss an appropriate IEP. The parties agreed to an acceptable program, but **the parents objected to implementation of the program at the location designated by the school district, which was a school located three miles away**. They argued that the district should reassign its only full-time nurse from that school to the student's neighborhood school. They claimed that attendance at the neighborhood school would facilitate his development and provide him with an opportunity to form friendships with peers beyond the school day. The parents asserted that the school district's plan was to eventually place the student in a self-contained special education classroom and remove him from regular classes, observing that the neighborhood school did not have a self-contained special education classroom. They filed an administrative appeal, and a hearing officer upheld the proposed IEP. When the decision was affirmed by a review officer, the parents appealed to the U.S. District Court for the District of Rhode Island.

The court refused to second-guess the school district's deployment of its only full-time nurse and rejected the parents' claim that she should be transferred to the neighborhood school. **The need to respond to a possible medical emergency overcame the IDEA's presumption in favor of a neighborhood school placement** in this case, and the court affirmed the administrative decisions. The parents appealed to the U.S. Court of Appeals, First Circuit, which noted that the site selected by the school district was only three miles from the student's home and was readily accessible to the student. The district's obligation to provide the student with a FAPE did not require an optimal placement or a change in district staffing decisions. The court affirmed the district court judgment. *Kevin G. by Robert G. v. Cranston School Comm.*, 130 F.3d 481 (1st Cir.1997).

◆ A trainable mentally impaired Michigan student achieved at the first grade level as she entered seventh grade. Her middle school IEP team recommended three hours of cross-categorical basic special education classes at a particular school in the district, with mainstreaming for most classes. The student's mother disputed the recommendation, arguing for placement in regular education classes at the middle school closest to her home. After an unsuccessful trial placement at the neighborhood school, the mother requested a due process hearing. The hearing officer agreed with the school district that the neighborhood school placement was inappropriate because the student was not achieving in her regular education classes. The mother appealed to a state review officer, who affirmed the local hearing officer's decision.

On further review, a federal district court determined that while the IDEA does not expressly require placement as close as possible to the student's home, an IDEA regulation calls for neighborhood placement to be a consideration. However, **neighborhood school placement is not mandatory, and is only one relevant factor in the placement decision process**. In this case, the student was gaining nothing from the mainstreaming component of her IEP, and the educational program component identified by the IEP team as most beneficial for her was unavailable at the neighborhood school. The court therefore granted the school district's summary judgment motion. The mother appealed to the U.S. Court of Appeals, Sixth Circuit, which adopted the district court decision as its own in affirming the judgment for the school district. *Hudson v. Bloomfield Hills Pub. Schools*, 108 F.3d 112 (6th Cir.1997).

C. Mainstreaming

1. Appropriateness

◆ An Illinois student with a rare neurodevelopmental disorder known as Rett Syndrome, which is characterized as a form of autism, was placed in a regular kindergarten class at the insistence of her parents. By second grade, her IEP team recommended placing her in an Educational Life Skills program, where she would spend most school days in a segregated classroom. The parents rejected this offer and demanded a due process hearing. A hearing officer held the district's proposal appropriate, and the parents appealed to a federal district court. The court held that **while the IDEA requires schools to maximize interactions between students with disabilities and their non-disabled peers to the greatest extent possible, this does not override a district's primary obligation to provide educational benefits to students**. There was evidence that the student would gain nothing from attending regular classes. At the age of 13, her motor skills were similar to an infant's, her cognitive skills were in the one- to six-year-old range, and she communicated primarily by eye gaze. She was unable to participate in class lectures and discussions and according to the court was effectively segregated from her classmates by the use of "special education in a regular classroom." The court found that the district's efforts in developing an IEP for the student were reasonable, and the Educational Life Skills program placement was appropriate. The court noted that there are circumstances where mainstreaming in regular education classes is inappropriate, and that this was one of those cases, as the student would not benefit from a regular education placement, despite the district's efforts. Her interactions with regular students were limited in the classroom, she was frequently absent, and transportation and toileting issues made it more appropriate for her to be placed in a self-contained classroom. The court awarded judgment to the school district. *Beth B. v. Van Clay*, No. 00 C 4771, 2001 WL 1095026 (N.D. Ill. 2001).

◆ A Michigan student with Down syndrome was placed in a regular education kindergarten classroom for half of each school day and received special education services in a categorical classroom for the other half of the day under an IEP devised by the Holt Public Schools. Her parents sought to place her in a general education setting in their neighborhood school but the district refused. The parents requested a due process hearing, seeking placement at the neighborhood school. During this time, they paid for a laboratory school placement. At an IEP meeting held before the hearing, the parties agreed to a half-day program of regular education kindergarten classes with special instruction and ancillary and related services. The parents requested another due process hearing to contest the location of the placement. The hearing officer in the first action issued a decision in favor of the Holt school district and ordered that the student be placed in a categorical classroom that was not located in the neighborhood school. The parents appealed to a review officer, who affirmed the categorical classroom placement. The parents commenced a federal court action against Holt. The student was accepted into a full-day program operated by the East Lansing Public Schools and the parents soon disagreed with representatives of that district about the student's IEP. The parents commenced due process proceedings against East Lansing, but before a hearing was held, the court issued a preliminary order determining that the student's stay put placement pending the outcome of IDEA proceedings was the full-day kindergarten program offered by East Lansing. **The hearing officer in the East Lansing action then upheld the proposed IEP, concluding that the split placement represented the LRE for the student**. The parents appealed, and a state hearing review officer reversed, concluding that the student should be placed in a full-day general education classroom with support services.

East Lansing appealed to a federal district court, which held that under the circumstances, the IDEA required placement of the student at her neighborhood school. There was no merit to the parents' procedural violation claims. They waived these claims when they agreed to incorporate the student's triennial evaluation results into any future IEP. However, **the court agreed with the parents that the student's IEP goals could be met in a general education setting**. The special education director at Holt Public Schools had admitted this, and **it was unnecessary to place the student in a more restrictive setting simply because it was considered academically superior**. The hearing and review officers had incorrectly found that the student required placement in a categorical classroom. The review officer in the East Lansing action failed to apply the factors used by courts for evaluating cases under the LRE requirement. There was no evidence that she would not benefit from the neighborhood school placement. Moreover, special education classes could be provided to her in the neighborhood school, and there was no evidence that she would be a disruptive force in regular education classes. The maximum potential standard of Michigan special education law did not warrant departure from the IDEA's presumption in favor of placement in the LRE. The court reversed the administrative decision in the Holt action and affirmed part of the East Lansing decision, vacating the requirement that East Lansing provide the student with a teacher consultant with an endorsement for teaching mentally impaired students. *McLaughlin v. Board of Education of Holt Public Schools*, 133 F.Supp.2d 994 (W.D. Mich. 2001).

◆ A New Jersey student was identified as preschool handicapped when she was three years old. Her parents rejected a school district proposal to place her in a regular kindergarten program. The following year, **the school district did not offer to place the student in a regular classroom, instead proposing a half-day integrated preschool class with a half day in the school resource room**. The parents rejected the placement offer and placed the student in a non-accredited private daycare center. When the parents sought payment of the student's private preschool tuition by the school board, plus supplemental on-site special education services, the board initiated due process proceedings, seeking approval of the proposed IEP. An ALJ held that the placement offered by the school district satisfied IDEA requirements and that the board was not compelled to fund the private placement. The parents appealed. A federal district court held that the board had offered an appropriate education to the student that offered more than a trivial educational benefit, and that the proposed classroom setting constituted the student's LRE.

The parents appealed to the Third Circuit, which determined that the district court had applied the improper standard for assessing an IEP. Instead of determining whether an IEP was sufficient to confer trivial educational benefits on a student, courts must inquire into whether the IEP would confer meaningful educational benefits. This error was harmless under the facts of this case, since there was ample evidence that the school board satisfied the more stringent "meaningful educational benefit" standard. The evidence indicated that the student would benefit from resource room work in the areas of communication and motor skills, the small class size, the presence of a full time aide and supplemental staff and the on-site child study team. Although the district court had correctly determined that the IEP proposed by the school district satisfied IDEA requirements, it did not adequately investigate potential alternative placements, as required by *Oberti v. Board of Education of Clementon School District*, 995 F.2d 1204 (3d Cir. 1993). Under *Oberti*, **courts evaluating a student's least restrictive placement must consider the steps taken by the school district to accommodate the student in regular classrooms, the student's ability to receive educational benefits in a regular classroom and the effect of the student's presence on others in the classroom**. The integrated classroom offered by the school district was more restrictive than a fully mainstreamed preschool class. Since there was no evidence that the student could not receive educational benefits in a regular classroom, the district court had erroneously failed to inquire into alternative settings, and this part of the decision was remanded for further proceedings. The court rejected the parents' argument that the school board should be responsible for their tuition payments for the private preschool. Since the school was not an eligible placement under state regulations, the board was not required to consider it. The court affirmed the district court decision with respect to the appropriateness of the IEP, and vacated the portion of the decision that found that the integrated classroom was the student's LRE. *T.R. v. Kingwood Township Board of Education*, 205 F.3d 572 (3d Cir. 2000).

◆ A 13-year-old Pennsylvania student with a learning disability and speech and language impairments attended summer kindergarten in the public school system, but then began attending private schools. After some time, his mother made a formal written request to the school district for additional testing. **The district conducted the testing and prepared an IEP calling for a regular school placement with supplemental and supportive intervention, and speech, language and learning support**. The parents rejected the district's proposal and filed an administrative complaint against the district, seeking placement at a specific private school. After a due process hearing, a local hearing officer held that the proposed IEP was inappropriate and that the district was required to reimburse the parents for part of the cost of the student's private school tuition and related transportation. The parties appealed unfavorable aspects of the administrative decision to a state appeals panel.

The panel held for the school district and the parents appealed to a federal district court, which noted that the school selected by the parents was not a special education institution. There was also no evidence that the school made up for any element of programming identified by the parents as being deficient in the district IEP. The only apparent difference between the education offered by the private school and public school placement was the lower student/teacher ratio offered by the private school. The IDEA states a strong preference for integrating children with disabilities in regular classrooms. **The student possessed the skills required to gain meaningful educational benefit from his regular school placement. Anything other than a regular classroom placement would have violated the IDEA mainstreaming preference**, and the parents failed to show what additional benefits were available to the student at the private school. The court granted the school district's motion for disposition on the administrative record. *Robert M. v. Hickok*, No. CIV.A. 98-4682, 2000 U.S. Dist. Lexis 6292 (E.D. Pa. 2000).

◆ The parents of a preschool student with Down's Syndrome enrolled him in a private preschool with nondisabled students when he was two years old. They asked their home school district to evaluate him for special education services. The district held a multidisciplinary conference and prepared an IEP calling for the student's placement in another district's segregated program, since it had no program in its own schools for students with disabilities. **The parents rejected this program and requested that the district establish its own program that would allow the student to attend classes with nondisabled students**. In response to the parents' request, the district proposed that the student attend a program for at-risk students located in a district school. The parents rejected the proposal and requested a due process hearing. A hearing officer held that the at-risk program was appropriate, but ordered the school district to fund the student's private school attendance up to the point at which the at-risk placement was first offered. The parties appealed to a state review officer, who held that both placements proposed by the district were inappropriate and therefore, the district was required to pay the private school costs. A federal district court affirmed and the school district appealed.

The Seventh Circuit reviewed the mainstreaming provisions of the IDEA and its regulations, and noted their strong preference in favor of inclusive placements.

The IDEA regulations state that students are to be educated in the school that they would otherwise attend in the absence of a disability, unless the IEP requires some other placement. The court affirmed the district court and review officer's findings that the placements offered by the district did not satisfy the LRE requirement and did not meet the student's unique needs. The court also adopted the district court finding that the private preschool selected by the parents was appropriate and afforded the student opportunities to interact with nondisabled students. The court affirmed the judgment for the family. *Bd. of Educ. of LaGrange School Dist. No. 105 v. Illinois State Bd. of Educ.*, 184 F.3d 912 (7th Cir.1999).

◆ An eleven-year-old student with autism was unable to speak and had severe communication and behavior problems. When the student's family moved to Virginia, he was enrolled in a public school system. **After an initial placement in regular education classrooms, the school district proposed a self-contained classroom for academic instruction and speech, with regular education for art, music, physical education and recess.** His parents rejected the placement proposal, and the school district initiated due process proceedings. A local hearing officer upheld the proposed IEP because of the student's behavior problems and the lack of academic benefits he received in regular education classes. A state level review officer affirmed this decision, and the student's parents appealed to the U.S. District Court for the Eastern District of Virginia. The court reversed the administrative decision based upon the IDEA's strong presumption in favor of mainstreaming.

The school district appealed to the U.S. Court of Appeals, Fourth Circuit, which found that the district court had improperly substituted its judgment for that of the administrative hearing officer. **The district court had disregarded overwhelming evidence that the student made no academic progress in regular classes and that separate, one-on-one instruction was appropriate for him.** The IDEA establishes a presumption in favor of inclusion in regular education classes, but explicitly states that inclusion is inappropriate when the nature or severity of the disability prevents satisfactory progress in regular classes. Because the district court had improperly disregarded substantial evidence of the student's behavior problems and had substituted its judgment for that of public school administrators, the court reversed and remanded the decision. *Hartmann v. Loudoun County Bd. of Educ.*, 118 F.3d 996 (4th Cir.1997).

◆ An eleven-year-old California student with an IQ of 44 attended special education classes in her public school district. Her parents requested full-time placement in regular classes. The school district rejected this request and proposed special education instruction in academic classes and regular classes in nonacademic subjects and activities. The parents enrolled the student in regular classes at a private school and requested a hearing before a state hearing officer. The hearing officer found that the district had failed to comply with the IDEA's mainstreaming requirement, that **the student had benefited from her placement in regular classes at the private school and that she was not too disruptive to attend regular classes in public school**. The hearing officer ruled that the district had overstated the cost of placing the student in regular classes and ordered the district to place her in a regular classroom with support services. The U.S. District Court for the Eastern District of California affirmed the hearing officer's decision, and the district appealed to the U.S. Court of Appeals, Ninth Circuit.

On appeal, the district argued that the student was too severely disabled to benefit from a full-time regular education placement. The parents argued that the student was learning social and academic skills in regular classes and would not benefit from special education. **The court determined that the hearing officer and district court had properly considered the applicable factors in their decisions to mainstream the student. These included the educational benefits of full-time placement in a regular class, the nonacademic benefits, the effect of placement on other students in the regular class, and the cost.** The evidence indicated that the student could benefit educationally from regular classes without being too disruptive and that the district had overstated the cost of such a placement. The court of appeals affirmed the district court's judgment in favor of the parents. *Sacramento City Unif. School Dist. v. Rachel H.*, 14 F.3d 1398 (9th Cir.1994).

2. Services and Aids

- For the sixth grade, a Pennsylvania school district proposed placing a student with an IQ of 36 in a part-time life-skills support placement for academic subjects and a school in another district for nonacademic subjects. Before this time, **the student was placed in a regular education classroom while receiving special education instruction from an aide**. The student's parents objected to the recommendation and requested a due process hearing. The hearing officer held that the district's proposal did not comply with the IDEA, as the student was not instructed in an inclusive manner and the district had not planned to integrate his IEP goals into his regular education instruction and activities. According to the hearing officer, the student's regular education teachers were not trained in inclusion and did not consult with special-education teachers. The student's aide lacked adequate training. The hearing officer ordered the district to provide the student's program in an inclusive setting and provide staff training on inclusion. The district appealed to an appeals panel, which reversed, finding that the regular sixth-grade curriculum exceeded the student's ability level to the point that it could not be modified for him.

The parents appealed to a federal district court, which considered the case under the framework devised by the Third Circuit in *Oberti v. Board of Education of the Borough of Clementon School District*, below. The court found that **the school district was required to make reasonable efforts to accommodate the student in a regular education setting. It was required to consider a range of supplemental aids and services and to make efforts to modify the regular education program to accommodate his needs**. The district had failed to give the requisite consideration to the student in this case. The district had assigned all responsibility for the student's education to his aide, rather than his teachers. Teachers received no special-education training or support and were not in a position to modify the curriculum or mainstream the student into their classes.

The student's aide only received a "crash course in special ed." While the student was placed in regular classes, the school did not meaningfully attempt to instruct him as inclusively as required by the IDEA. Citing *Oberti*, the court observed, "mainstreaming requires far more than the physical placement of a disabled student in a regular education classroom." The district also failed to provide supplementary aids and services to the student. In the court's view, the appeals panel erroneously focused on the gap between the student's ability and the demands of the regular sixth-grade curriculum, not the district's efforts to include him. The panel decision was reversed, and the district was ordered to develop an IEP after considering the full range of available supplementary aides and services. *Girty v. School District of Valley Grove*, 163 F.Supp.2d 527 (W.D. Pa. 2001).

◆ A child with Down's syndrome was placed in segregated special education classes by a New Jersey school district. The child's parents disagreed with the placement and requested an IDEA hearing. As the result of a mediated settlement with the child's parents, **the school district agreed to consider future mainstreaming possibilities, but placed the child in another special education class in which he demonstrated behavior problems**. A second due process hearing resulted in a decision favorable to the school district, based upon a finding by the hearing officer that the student's disruptive behavior prevented him from obtaining any meaningful educational benefit in regular classes. The student's parents appealed the hearing officer's decision to the U.S. District Court for the District of New Jersey, which reversed the hearing officer's decision. The school board appealed to the U.S. Court of Appeals, Third Circuit. The court of appeals observed that the student could be educated in a regular classroom with the use of appropriate supplementary aids and services. Integrating the student into regular classes would enable him to improve his social skills by interacting with nondisabled students. **The school district had taken no meaningful steps to integrate the student into regular classrooms and the student's alleged behavior problems may have been exacerbated by the school district's failure to provide appropriate aids and services**. The district court's decision was affirmed. *Oberti v. Bd. of Educ. of Borough of Clementon School Dist.*, 995 F.2d 1204 (3d Cir.1993).

D. Private School Placement

◆ The parents of a student with disabilities challenged the placement of their son in a public school program through an administrative hearing. As relief, the parents sought reimbursement for the costs of a private school they enrolled the student in. **A hearing officer determined that the district provided the student with a program that met the IDEA's substantive requirements**, as it offered the student a FAPE. The parents appealed to a federal district court, which affirmed the decision, finding that the student had made steady academic progress in a district placement that provided for his unique emotional needs.

On appeal to the Ninth Circuit, the parents argued that they were entitled to reimbursement for a private assessment and schooling. The court stated that the district had acted in compliance with a state policy encouraging less drastic intervention before placing a student in special education programs. This policy, as stated in Section 56303 of the California Education Code, weighed heavily in IDEA decisions. Under the circumstances, **the court found that the district's provision of special education to the student and refusal to pay for the private school did not deny him a FAPE**. The court noted that both the district court and the hearing officer found the district program complied with the IDEA. It deferred to conclusions by the hearing officer and district court that the student's placement allowed him to make progress and satisfied his emotional needs. Because the district did not deny the student a FAPE, the court denied the parents' request for reimbursement. *Johnson v. Upland Unified School District*, 26 Fed.Appx. 689 (9th Cir. 2002).

◆ Vermont law permits school districts that do not maintain a public high school to pay tuition on behalf of resident students at approved public or independent high schools. The majority of high school students residing in the St. Johnsbury School District attend St. Johnsbury Academy. The academy maintains programs for students with disabilities, including a resource room and an individualized services program. In order to attend the resource room program and regular academic classes, the school requires students to perform at least at a fifth-grade level. A St. Johnsbury student with cerebral palsy, a learning impairment and a visual deficit completed eighth grade in the public middle school, where he was mainstreamed for some academic classes. **He was admitted to the academy, but denied permission to attend mainstream academic classes because he did not read at a fifth-grade level.** His parent refused to send him to the academy as an ISP student, since his IEP for grade nine called for regular education placement in English and social studies. The district offered an alternative placement, which the parent rejected. The parent decided instead to re-enroll the student as an eighth grader, and initiated a due process complaint against the academy and district. A hearing officer ordered the district to "influence the Academy to change" its performance policy, finding that the IDEA and Section 504 required the academy to accept the student into mainstream academic classes. The academy commenced an IDEA action against the student and school district in a federal district court. The student filed a counterclaim against the academy and added additional claims against the district under the IDEA and Section 504. The district court ordered the academy to admit the student into the two specified mainstream academic classes. It later issued a written opinion holding that the fifth-grade-level performance requirement violated the LRE requirement, as well as Section 504.

The academy appealed to the Second Circuit, which first held that even though the student was now 22, the case presented a live controversy and was not moot. Under the IDEA, a student is entitled to a FAPE through the age of 21, unless this is contrary to state law. In states such as Vermont, where students are entitled to services "through twenty-one years of age," this means until a student's 22nd birthday. The court agreed with the academy that its performance requirement was not directly subject to IDEA standards. It relied on a 1989 Office for Special Education Programs policy letter interpreting the general standards under the IDEA for private schools serving eligible students with disabilities. The letter stated that private schools are not bound by the same admission and discipline policies applicable to public schools. The court held that **the IDEA and**

its regulations apply only to state and local agencies, and expressly contemplate that federal IEP and LRE requirements will be enforced by a public agency when it places a student in a private school. Even when a private school conducts and revises IEPs, the public agency remains responsible for IDEA compliance. The student had no IDEA cause of action against the academy and the district court had improperly found that it was a local education agency under the IDEA. The Second Circuit held that a local education agency is by definition a public entity, and must be an agency, as opposed to a school. The circuit court vacated the district court's order, noting that the student might still have IDEA claims against the district and state education department. The academy also prevailed in its Section 504 appeal, since its performance requirement was a legitimate academic policy with respect to all students, regardless of disability. Further, the court noted that Section 504 does not require institutions to lower their academic standards. *St. Johnsbury Academy v. D.H.*, 240 F.3d 163 (2d Cir. 2001).

◆ A 19-year-old student with mental, hearing, speech and language impairments functioned at the level of a two or three-year-old. The student attended a private school at her parents' expense for seven years. The parents then presented her for enrollment in the school district, which agreed to pay her tuition at the private school during a one-year evaluation period. A placement recommendation calling for a public school placement at a school employing a total communication program was made. Although the placement was segregated, it emphasized vocational training and community involvement and provided mainstreaming opportunities. **The parents objected to the placement and requested a due process hearing, at which they sought continued funding of the private school placement and retroactive tuition reimbursement for the previous seven years**. A hearing officer held for the school district, finding that the proposed total communication program afforded her with a FAPE in the least restrictive setting. He also ruled that the request for retroactive tuition reimbursement was untimely. A second-level hearing officer affirmed the decision, and the parents appealed to a federal district court.

The parents first argued that the district failed to comply with procedural requirements by taking 270 days to develop an IEP, instead of the 60 days specified by the IDEA. The court observed that the parents fully participated in the one-year evaluation plan as members of the IEP team, and that the team had recommended continuation of the private placement to accurately assess the student's needs. The parents did not object to the evaluation method until the district reached a conclusion with which they disagreed. **The court held that the IDEA does not require the best placement possible, or the one preferred by a student's parents. It agreed with the school district that the student required a total communication program to develop her communication skills. The placement proposed by the district addressed this objective and also offered training in appropriate vocational and independent living skills**. Although the private school offered more mainstreaming opportunities, the IDEA does not require students to sacrifice educational opportunities in favor of mainstreaming. The private school did not offer a total communication program, and the court found that the IEP team's decision was entitled to deference. The court also upheld the administrative determination that the tuition reimbursement claim was barred by Illinois limitation statutes. *Heather S. v. Niles Township High School Dist.,* 1999 U.S. Dist. LEXIS 18628 (N.D. Ill. 1999).

◆ A Massachusetts student with Schizotypical personality disorder attended public school from kindergarten through grade eight, except for fourth grade. During seventh grade, his parents obtained an independent evaluation, stating that he required placement with peers who were not overly aggressive. They considered returning him to a parochial school. **The school district refused to consider the parochial school as a placement, since the school integrated Christian doctrine throughout its program and did not offer special education services.** The district notified the parents that a behavior-based program would be appropriate and the parties agreed that the student would remain in public school special education programs with mainstreaming, an individual aide, resource room services and psychological counseling. Although the district agreed to seek a day school program outside the district for the following school year, it failed to implement the agreement, and failed to develop an IEP for the student's eighth grade year. The student's parents unilaterally placed him in the parochial school and requested tuition reimbursement. The school district denied the parents' request for tuition reimbursement and subsequently developed two IEPs calling for an out of district placement. While declining any tuition reimbursement for the parochial school, it designated the school as the student's placement in IEP documents. The parents initiated a due process hearing in which they sought tuition reimbursement. A hearing officer determined that reimbursement was prohibited by the state and federal constitutions due to the school's sectarian nature.

The parents appealed to the U.S. District Court for the District of Massachusetts, which noted that **the school district had never challenged the parents' placement decision and had led them to believe it was seeking tuition reimbursement from the state education department**. The district had failed to propose a placement for the student's eighth grade year and while the parochial school lacked a formal special education program, it satisfied his unique needs. The low student/teacher ratio and supportive environment with appropriate peers addressed the student's vulnerability and educational needs. **The school committee had designated the facility as the location of the student's placement in two IEPs and could not now assert that it was inappropriate**. The court found that the placement was reasonably calculated to enable the student to receive educational benefits and that the school committee had failed to provide him with an appropriate placement. The request for reimbursement did not violate the U.S. Constitution or the Anti-Aid Amendment to the Massachusetts Constitution because payment went directly to the parents and had no purpose or effect of founding, maintaining or aiding the parochial school. The court awarded summary judgment to the parents. *Matthew J. v. Massachusetts Dept. of Educ.*, 989 F.Supp. 380 (D.Mass.1998).

◆ A Maryland student with learning disabilities attended a private day school through the eighth grade. His parents then requested an evaluation for special education services from the Baltimore City Public Schools (BCPS). **BCPS failed to develop an IEP for the student and the parents unilaterally enrolled him**

in a private Connecticut residential school. The parents challenged the IEP later developed by the school district for a public school placement. The parties settled the dispute under an agreement by which BCPS agreed to pay a statutory portion of private school tuition as described in the Maryland Education Code. The code provides for shared state and local funding of approved private school placements, but only where there has been compliance with specific procedures including approval of the placement by local and state coordinating councils. **The state of Maryland refused to pay a portion of the private school's cost because BCPS agreed to the placement without first obtaining the approval of the state coordinating council.** The parents filed an administrative challenge with a state board, asserting that the state's refusal to consider the application amounted to denial of the claim. The board determined that the state had committed procedural violations that denied the student a free appropriate public education. It held that the state was responsible for its portion of the private school placement costs.

The parents then filed a federal district court action for enforcement against BCPS, the state school superintendent and the state education department. The court granted dismissal motions by the education officials and BCPS, and the parents appealed to the U.S. Court of Appeals, Fourth Circuit. The court agreed with the state hearing board that the IDEA applied to the dispute. **Because the IDEA places the ultimate responsibility upon the state education agency to ensure local education agency compliance with the IDEA, the state could not avoid its share of liability if the district court held on remand that relief was appropriate. Either or both the state and BCPS could be held liable for the failure to provide a student with a FAPE.** However, the court rejected the parents' assertion that procedural errors alone justified finding that the student had been deprived of a free appropriate public education. The court vacated and remanded the case to the district court. *Gadsby by Gadsby v. Grasmick*, 109 F.3d 940 (4th Cir.1997).

E. Residential School Placement

1. Appropriateness

- An Illinois student who was disruptive and frequently truant became a serious disciplinary problem. A psychologist determined that the student did not have a learning disability but suffered from depression, accompanied by substance abuse and a conduct disorder. **The student's mother objected to a proposal by the school district for the resumption of his placement in a therapeutic day school. Upon the boy's release from jail, she unilaterally placed him in a Maine residential school** and requested reimbursement. School officials refused the request, and the mother commenced an administrative proceeding. A hearing officer ordered the district to pay for the residential placement. The district appealed and a review officer reversed. A federal district court reversed the review officer's decision and the school district appealed to the Seventh Circuit.

The court noted that the review officer had found no evidence the Maine facility provided a superior educational placement to that of the therapeutic day school. The review officer had properly determined that the IDEA does not require a school district to pay for the confinement of a truant student. The district court had improperly rejected the review officer's determination that the Maine residential school did not provide a FAPE to the student. The Maine school did not provide the student with psychological services, and did not offer treatment for his depression or conduct disorder. The court characterized the school as "a jail substitute." According to the court, the only difference between the therapeutic day school and the Maine school was its residential character. Moreover, the district court was obligated to defer to the review officer's decision, since he was presumed to have superior competence to that of federal courts in resolving educational policy matters. The court stated that the student's problems were primarily the result of improper socialization, as he had the intelligence to perform well in school and had no cognitive defects or disorders. **Residential placement was improper where it was not a necessary predicate for learning or where medical, social or emotional problems were separate from the learning process**. The court stated that the residential placement was appropriate for the student "only if confinement is a related service" under the IDEA. Since it was obviously not, the district court erroneously reversed the review officer's decision. *Dale M. v. Board of Education of Bradley Bourbonnais High School District No. 307*, 237 F.3d 813 (7th Cir. 2001).

◆ A student who was seriously impaired in all areas of functioning and classified as autistic was placed by his Florida school district in a day program for exceptional children. For the next three years, the student attended an autism program with family counseling and in-home behavioral counseling under IEPs. However, the parties could not agree on an appropriate placement the following school year. **The parents insisted that the student attend a particular residential school, while school representatives argued that residential placement was unnecessary**. The parents rejected the school's proposal and requested a due process hearing. A hearing officer found the IEP for that year inappropriate because it failed to provide the student a FAPE. However, the officer disagreed with the parents' assertion that a residential placement was necessary. The parents appealed to a federal district court, which determined the contested IEP was appropriate and that a residential placement was not required.

The parents appealed to the 11th Circuit, which first held that a party challenging an IEP bears the burden of showing why the educational setting established by the IEP is inappropriate. This was primarily because great deference must be paid to educators. Since the parents were challenging the adequacy of the IEP, the burden rested on them. **The court found that when the student arrived at the school he was largely uncontrollable and unable to establish relationships. There was evidence that under his current IEP, he progressed** in 26 out of 27 areas and learned skills that could be displayed across settings. Although the parents presented expert testimony that the student received no educational benefits during the school year in question, their witnesses had performed only limited observations and relied on the parents' statements. The district court had discredited one of these experts, who stated that an appropriate education is more than making measurable and adequate classroom gains. The court observed that generalization across settings is not required to show educational benefit. Since the student benefited from his district placement, the residential placement sought by the parents was not warranted. The trial court's decision in favor of the district was upheld. *Devine v. Indian River County School Board*, 249 F.3d 1289 (11th Cir. 2001).

◆ A high school student was diagnosed with generalized anxiety and depressive disorders and a nonverbal learning disability. His school district committee on special education recommended a residential placement, but the school board rejected the recommendation. The board later rejected a second CSE's recommendation for a residential placement, and the parents requested a due process hearing. The parties reached a settlement under which the district agreed to actively seek out a residential placement for the student. The district also agreed to provide him with an appropriate educational program until he earned a high school diploma, or at least through the 2001 school year. The district was unable to find a residential school that would accept the student, but paid his mother's expenses to evaluate the Learning Resource Center at Mitchell College in Connecticut. The college accepted the student, but the district was unable to get approval for state funding of this placement, as the state education department found that the college was a post-secondary institution that was not approved as a secondary special education school. The district asserted that it was unable to find another residential placement and the parents requested another due process hearing, claiming the district violated the terms of the settlement. **The hearing officer issued a decision finding that the district had failed to provide the student with a FAPE and that the college placement was authorized by the IDEA.** She also found that the student was entitled to an award of compensatory education beyond the age of 21 and placement at Mitchell under the agreement. The district appealed to a state review officer, but no decision was issued within the 30-day time frame required by IDEA regulations.

The parents petitioned a federal district court for an order requiring the district to comply with the hearing officer's decision and prohibiting review of that decision pending trial. They also asserted claims under Section 504 of the Rehabilitation Act and the Americans with Disabilities Act, and sought compensatory damages of $500,000 and attorneys' fees. The district asserted that the parents failed to exhaust their available administrative remedies, and claimed that the state should be joined in the action, since its permission was required in order to fund the placement selected by the parents. The court rejected these arguments, ruling that it would be unfair to allow the education department to drag out the administrative process, then claim the delay barred a federal lawsuit. The state was not a necessary party to the action, since the state interest in approving private schools must yield to a student's entitlement to a FAPE. **Although no other court has approved of IDEA funding for college tuition, and the IDEA does not expressly forbid college coursework as a form of compensatory education, the fact that Mitchell was a college did not mean that it could not provide the student with the services he required to obtain a high school diploma.** The school district had been "less than fully cooperative" in determining the student's educational needs and was at least partly to blame for the inability to locate a residential placement. The court, therefore, rejected the district's claim that the parents were not entitled to their requested order. The court found no reason to expect that the state review officer's decision would reach a conclusion contrary to that reached by the hearing officer, and the parents were entitled to an order implementing the hearing officer's decision pending further proceedings. *Sabatini v. Corning-Painted Post Area School Dist.*, 78 F.Supp.2d 138 (W.D.N.Y. 2000).

◆ **A California county filed a state court action to recover retroactive and future child support from the mother of a special education student with a severe emotional disturbance who was attending a private residential facility after becoming a ward of the court**. The mother asserted that she was not required to pay for a residential educational placement since the IDEA mandates the provision of a FAPE to all students with disabilities. The court ordered the mother to reimburse the county for its past expenditures of almost $7,000, representing the time the student was first placed in a non-secure facility until 25 days after the entry of judgment. However, the court denied any award of future costs, and specifically found that the student was entitled to a FAPE.

The county appealed to a state court of appeal, which observed that the student was placed under an IEP, but was failing his high school classes and had a long history of emotional concerns. There was evidence that the student required a residential placement due to several school suspensions, incidents of violence and inappropriate behavior at school, and his SED. Although the juvenile court placement had come as the result of a credit card theft, it was undisputed that the residential placement had been certified by the county mental health department and was in compliance with the student's IEP. **The appeals court held that the IDEA prohibited the state and its local agencies from requiring the parent to pay for the costs of the student's placement under an IEP, since he was entitled to a FAPE. The student could not function in a normal school setting and was entitled to a residential placement**. Enforcement of a state law requiring a parent to pay such costs in contravention of the IDEA would violate the Supremacy Clause of the federal constitution. The trial court had correctly denied the award of any future costs against the parent, but had improperly awarded the county its past residential placement costs. Although programs arising under Title IV of the Social Security Act require the states to attempt to collect funds expended for the support of children under the Aid for Families with Dependent Children program and similar federally-funded programs, the court refused to allow this mandate to supercede the IDEA mandate requiring the provision of a FAPE to all disabled students. The parent was required to fulfill her state law obligation to reimburse the county for any costs it incurred when the student was not placed pursuant to an IEP. The court reversed the reimbursement order and remanded the case to the superior court for further proceedings. *County of Los Angeles v. Smith*, 74 Cal.App.4th 500 (Cal. App. 1999).

◆ The parent of a 16-year-old student with a chromosomal defect sought a residential placement for the student within four months of her enrollment in a New Jersey school district. The student had an IQ of approximately 36 and was classified as trainable mentally retarded. **The school district proposed an IEP calling for placement in a TMR program** with speech therapy and other related services, **but rejected the parent's request for residential placement**. It also rejected her request for an extended summer program, and she requested a due process hearing to challenge the decisions. An administrative law judge determined that a residential placement was appropriate and found that the district's proposed IEP did not include required annual goals, specific measurable objectives and evaluation criteria that were related to the student's goals and objectives. The school district appealed to a federal district court and the student's parent moved for an order affirming the administrative ruling, plus an award of attorney's fees. The court considered the motion along with the district's motion for judgment.

The court found that the administrative law judge had inappropriately adopted the proposal for a residential placement suggested by the parent's expert witness. The IDEA only requires schools to provide disabled students with access to an appropriate education. It does not mandate that states maximize the educational potential of such students. The court determined that the student in this case would receive some meaningful educational benefit from the public school placement proposed by the school district. **The residential placement urged by the parent did not satisfy the IDEA's strong preference for placement in the least restrictive appropriate educational environment.** The administrative decision failed to address several factors identified by federal courts when considering the issue of residential placement. The court held that the proposed IEP met the IDEA's substantive requirements. Although agreeing with the administrative finding that there had been procedural violations by the school district, the court held that the district had responded appropriately when it learned of the deficiencies and that the student was not entitled to compensatory education or an award of attorney's fees. *D.B. v. Ocean Township Bd. of Educ.*, 985 F.Supp. 457 (D.N.J.1997).

◆ A 20-year-old Connecticut student had language and learning disabilities with conduct disorder, ADD and multiple personality disorder. After he was charged with the sexual assault of several young boys, the Connecticut Department of Children and Families (DCF) accepted responsibility for his non-educational residential placement. The student's school district funded the special education component. After he was observed inappropriately touching other students, his placement team recommended moving him to a more restrictive hospital setting in order to address his multiple personality disorder and avoid contact with younger students. He was then placed in a residential treatment program operated by DCF where his special education services were reduced. The placement team determined that the student had sufficient credits to graduate, although he had not achieved high school competency in any subject area. **The student requested a placement review hearing, at which a hearing officer determined that the school district had erroneously issued him a high school diploma, due to its failure to establish appropriate graduation requirements.** She issued an order incorporating an agreement under which the school district agreed to provide educational and treatment services to the student until age 21. The state Department of Mental Health (DMH) refused to provide him with a community-based residential treatment program and the hearing officer ruled that she had no authority to order it to provide one. The relief ordered was limited to two years of compensatory education and a transition program.

The student appealed to a federal district court, claiming entitlement to a community-based residential placement. The court found that the hearing officer had properly refrained from exercising jurisdiction over the DMH, since it was a non-educational agency. However, the district court had the power to issue appropriate orders relating to a student's special education or related services, and DMH was an appropriate party. DMH had no power to invoke the IDEA's stay put provision, since this protection was available only to parents and students. **The hearing officer had properly held that the school district failed to provide the student with an adequate transition plan. Because he was a danger to himself and the community, he was appropriately placed in a community-based residential program with counseling and psychological services.** He was entitled to instruction in the acquisition of community and daily living skills. Interagency agreements require a local educational agency to pay for or provide services that a non-educational agency fails to pay for or provide. The LEA may later seek reimbursement from the non-educational agency. The school district in this case remained primarily responsible for ensuring that the student received special education and related services during the pendency of the proceedings and was required to prepare an IEP with appropriate transition services. The placement team was to determine an appropriate residential placement, which would continue during the two-year compensatory education period. *J.B. v. Killingly Bd. of Educ.*, 990 F.Supp. 57 (D.Conn.1997).

◆ A Connecticut student had serious social and emotional problems including hyperactivity, inability to interact with others and lack of self-confidence. **Although she was in the average intelligence range, she failed to progress academically and met only four of 32 objectives stated in her IEP.** A public school evaluator recommended placement in a residential facility, but the board refused the recommendation. However, the placement was arranged through the state Department of Child and Youth Services. The student attended the residential facility, where her academic and social skills improved. However, the school board maintained that the placement was non-academic and was made necessary by the student's mother's manipulative behavior. The mother requested a due process hearing to obtain complete funding for the placement, resulting in a decision favorable to the school board. The U.S. District Court for the District of Connecticut reversed the hearing officer's decision and granted the mother's summary judgment motion. The board appealed to the U.S. Court of Appeals, Second Circuit.

The court observed that, **notwithstanding the non-academic reasons for the residential placement, the student had failed to progress in her public school placement and the school board had failed to take action to remedy her serious academic regression.** The residential placement was necessary to enable the student to obtain academic benefits, and it was appropriate for the board to fund the non-educational portion of the residential placement despite the other factors that were present in the decision to place her there. The other factors did not relieve the school district of its obligation to pay for a necessary academic program, and the court affirmed the district court decision. *Mrs. B. v. Milford Bd. of Educ.*, 103 F.3d 1114 (2d Cir.1997).

◆ A 13-year-old student with profound deafness moved from Idaho to a small town in Arizona. The Arizona school district contacted his previous district in Idaho and relied in part on his records there in making a placement decision. **The Arizona district determined that it did not have the resources to provide the student with a full-day immersion program in American sign language,** which was identified as an educational requirement. **It therefore determined that the student should be placed at the Arizona School for the Deaf and Blind,** a residential facility located 280 miles away. The student's parents argued that the placement selected by the district failed to consider the continuum of alternative placements required by the IDEA and failed to comply with the IDEA's mainstreaming requirement. When the parents insisted on mainstreaming the student at district schools, the district's special education coordinator initiated an impartial IDEA hearing at which the hearing officer agreed that the student should be placed at ASDB. The Arizona Department of Education affirmed the hearing officer's decision, and the parents appealed to the U.S. Court of Appeals, Ninth Circuit.

The court stated that it had been appropriate for the district to rely on the student's Idaho IEPs in reaching its decision. The district had considered alternative placements and reasonably concluded that mainstreaming did not allow the student to receive educational benefits. **The student had only primitive communication skills and he could not receive educational benefits in a regular classroom until he acquired greater communication skills. Because ASDB was the closest facility at which the student could obtain the services he required, it was appropriate** under IDEA regulations at 34 CFR § 300.552(a)(3). Since the school district had complied with the IDEA in developing an IEP that was reasonably calculated to confer educational benefits, the court of appeals affirmed the judgment for the school district. *Poolaw v. Bishop*, 67 F.3d 830 (9th Cir.1995).

2. Behavioral/Emotional Problems

◆ Prior to moving from one Minnesota school district to another, a student with emotional and behavioral disorders was placed in a self-contained classroom, where she repeatedly exhibited inappropriate behavior. In non-school settings she used alcohol and illegal drugs, was promiscuous, ran away, and was hospitalized three times. Her mother's attempts to secure a residential placement at district expense were unsuccessful. The new school district initially placed the student in a self-contained classroom for students with emotional and behavioral problems. After three days, she was suspended for inappropriate behavior and stopped attending school. District staff members sought a residential placement through a state juvenile court order, but the court refused to order a residential placement. **The student's mother continued to seek a residential placement, even locating an Idaho facility, but the district only offered placement in the previous self-contained program or a day treatment program.** The district eventually agreed to pay only the educational portion of the Idaho placement. An independent evaluator diagnosed the student with a conduct disorder and strongly recommended placement in a secure facility. The mother commenced due process proceedings, seeking district funding of the Idaho placement. A hearing officer ordered the district to provide the student with a residential placement and compensatory education. A hearing review officer affirmed the decision and the district appealed to a federal district court. The court affirmed the award of compensatory education but reversed the administrative decisions concerning the need for a residential placement.

The mother appealed to the Eighth Circuit, which stated that if a student cannot reasonably be expected to benefit from instruction in a less restrictive setting, residential placement is educationally necessary, and the state must pay for it. The court rejected the district's argument that the case was moot because the family had by then moved into another school district. She sought a compensatory remedy that did not depend on any present or future obligation to develop an IEP. While the district court had focused on the student's "unwillingness" to attend school or comply with her IEP, the Eighth Circuit found that a student with an emotional disturbance is prevented from normal responses. According to the court, suspension or expulsion is not normally the appropriate response to the behavior problems of students whose disability is manifested by disruptive conduct. Instead, the IEP team should address the behavior in the first place. The student was entitled to a residential placement based on evidence that her behavior and attendance problems were a result of her emotional disturbance. **Because the evidence did not indicate that the student's behavior problems could be separated from the learning process, she would not receive educational benefit until her behavior was addressed**. The student's psychologist, the evaluator and both hearing officers concluded that a residential placement was necessary, and there was compelling evidence that she would leave any treatment facility unless she was confined. The court reversed the judgment and remanded the case to the district court for consideration of an appropriate remedy. *Indep. School Dist. No. 284 v. A.C.*, 258 F.3d 769 (8th Cir. 2001).

◆ A 17-year-old student with autism had a history of temper tantrums at home. He attended a residential school in Boston for nine years, demonstrating some progress. **His parents sought approval for the Boston placement, or placement in a comparable residential facility**, from the Puerto Rico Department of Education. They expressed concern for their safety at home and asserted that the department was required to pay for a residential placement as part of its obligation to provide the student with a FAPE. The department proposed an IEP that did not call for a residential placement, and the parents commenced administrative proceedings. An administrative hearing officer held that the proposed IEP was sufficient under the IDEA, but ordered the department to include additional services. The parents appealed to a federal district court, which heard conflicting testimony concerning the student's need for a residential placement. It affirmed the IEP but ordered the inclusion of some services intended to facilitate his transition into Puerto Rico schools.

The parents appealed to the First Circuit, arguing that the district court did not take into account the student's past behavioral difficulties at home by allowing a non-residential placement. The court observed that there are no clear lines between a student's educational needs and social problems at home. It stated, "typically, an IEP in cases where the student's disability is this serious (and requires such a degree of structure) must address such problems in some fashion, even if they do not warrant residential placement." The district court had correctly analyzed the case by considering whether the proposed IEP provided educational benefit to the student. The circuit court noted its decision in *Abrahamson v. Hershman*, 701 F.2d 223 (1983), which held that **the IDEA does not require a residential program to remedy a poor home setting**. Contrary to the parents' argument, the district court had given due consideration to the student's problems at home and ordered the department to change his IEP to address them. The district court order directed the department to expand his IEP to include further services and training for the parents to help manage his home behavior. There was support for the district court's finding that the student's home behavior could be effectively managed through the amended IEP, and the First Circuit found no error by the district court in this respect. In affirming the judgment for the department, the court urged the parties to cooperate and collaborate in the future. *Gonzalez v. Puerto Rico Dept. of Educ.*, 254 F.3d 350 (1st Cir. 2001).

◆ During a five-year period, an Illinois school district prepared 14 IEPs for a student with a behavioral/emotional disorder and other impairments who functioned at a first- or second-grade level. Each IEP had the basic goals of appropriate behavior and a functional level of understanding. The student attended a series of therapeutic day school programs in which she bit, slapped and punched staff members. She also engaged in screaming episodes, indecent exposure, profanity, provocation of other students and destruction of property. **The school district recommended placement in a Wisconsin residential treatment center, but the student's mother disagreed** with the recommendation and requested a due process hearing. The student began attending the residential facility, but after less than two months, her mother brought her home. She then attended another therapeutic day school where she was soon arrested after being restrained for throwing a book and ripping up a teacher's papers. The student later attacked a bus driver and her mother withheld her from school. A hearing officer considered testimony from the school district that the student required a residential placement in order to have any chance of receiving a FAPE, and determined that a residential placement was required. The family's requests for placement in a program for students with communications disorders, compensatory education and attorneys' fees were denied.

The family appealed to a federal district court, which found that while the IDEA contains a well-established preference for educating students with disabilities along with nondisabled peers, this can be inappropriate if it deprives a student of minimum educational opportunities. The court rejected the family's assertion that the Illinois Probate Act prohibited a residential placement order in the absence of an order by a state court judge. The IDEA does not require states to offer probate services for students with disabilities at public expense and, in any event, the family had refused to make a residential placement. The court noted that each educator familiar with the student had testified unequivocally that she needed a residential placement. Her IEP goals focused on controlling behavior, accepting responsibility for her actions, remaining seated without disturbing others and respecting other students and their property. The student's academic objectives remained rudimentary and focused on everyday tasks, indicating that her misconduct interfered with her academic progress. Educators testified that her behavioral gains at school were washed away at home. **The structure, positive reinforcement and peer interaction of a residential placement was required in order for the student to progress**, in spite of the family's assertion that it was not the LRE. Limitations on the mother's ability to communicate with the residential school were necessary in view of her past record of frequent, negative discussions with staff and the student's ability to manipulate her mother. The court found that the district had complied with the IDEA and was entitled to summary judgment. *Reed v. Lincoln-Way Community High School District No. 210*, No. 98 C 4934, 2000 U.S. Dist. Lexis 7402 (N.D. Ill. 2000).

◆ The mother of an elementary school student with attention deficit disorder, aggressive behavior disorder and a learning disability decided to home school him during the third grade. In response to the student's increasingly violent behavior the following year, **a school team meeting was held, at which the mother sought a residential placement. The school offered to return the student to his previous public school alternative program with related services**. Although the mother initially consented to the arrangement, the student threatened suicide when he learned that he would be returning to the school. The mother then placed the student in a highly structured Massachusetts residential facility. When an agreement was not reached regarding the student's placement, the mother initiated due process proceedings. The hearing officer held that the district failed to follow IDEA procedures, failed to timely refer the student for special education services, and developed inappropriate IEPs for several school years. The district appealed to a federal district court.

The court assigned the case to a federal magistrate judge, who noted the administrative hearing officer's failure to specify how the IEP was inadequate in certain key areas. The IEP proposed for the 1998-99 school year included a behavioral plan and called for an educational technician for one-to-one supervision, who would address the student's behavioral needs and intervene when he behaved inappropriately. **There was little evidence that the student's behavior was uncontrollable in the school environment or that he was ineducable without extensive treatment**. To the contrary, his problems were treatable and did not interfere with his educational development. The district did not violate the IDEA by failing to address the student's out-of-school behavior. The absence of behavior plans in IEPs for the student's second and third-grade years did not constitute grounds for an award of compensatory education, because his in-school behavior never became uncontrollable and the district did not fail to provide him with educational benefit. However, the school district had apparently paid the student's residential school tuition for the prior year and the mother was not required to reimburse the school for complying with the hearing officer's order. The family's subsequent challenge to the magistrate's decision was denied by the district court. *Rome School Comm. v. Mrs. B.*, Civil No. 99-CV-20-B, 2000 WL 762027 (D. Me. 2000).

The school committee then proposed a 1999-2000 IEP calling for the student's placement in a public school with two hours of small-group special education services addressing learning disabilities, and assistance with homework for regular education classes. The rest of the day would be spent in mainstream classes with a behavioral plan calling for self-management, breaks to avoid defiance and disruptiveness, and deceleration targets with rewards for meeting behavior goals. The 1999-2000 IEP also described an alternative placement at a day-treatment school. The parents rejected the 1999-2000 IEP and sought a second administrative hearing. A hearing officer held that the 1999-2000 IEP did not provide the student with a FAPE and approved the student's placement at the Massachusetts residential facility at district expense.

The school committee appealed, and in an opinion issued the same day as the decision regarding the 1998-1999 IEP, the magistrate judge rejected the hearing officer's conclusion that the student required a residential placement. The hearing officer's finding that a residential placement was required was unsupported by the evidence. The magistrate noted that courts have held that residential placements are only warranted when a student's needs are very great, and unpredictable behavior outside of school is not, by itself, sufficient to compel a residential placement. In this case, the student's behavior to not rise to the level necessary to warrant a residential placement, and his out-of-school behavior did not effect his ability to make educational progress under either of the proposed district placements. **Even though the school committee's proposal for the 1999-2000 school year did not maximize the student's potential, it was calculated to provide him with some educational benefit and the behavior plan devised for the student had a 98 percent success rate with other students**. The magistrate recommended that the court reverse the hearing officer's decision, but concluded that the school committee was not entitled to reimbursement from the parent for the student's 1998-1999 residential tuition. Even though the 1998-1999 IEP had been held adequate, the parent had complied with the hearing officer's decision in enrolling the student at the residential facility. *Rome School Comm. v. Mrs. B.*, Civil No. 99-CV-198-B, 2000 WL 761980 (D. Me. 2000).

The parent appealed to the First Circuit, seeking an order preventing the school committee from recovering reimbursement from her for the money it spent on the student's residential placement after the hearing officer's decision. The court stated that even in the IEPs for the 1998-1999 and 1999-2000 school years were deemed adequate, the parent would not be required to reimburse the school committee. School officials are precluded from seeking reimbursement from parents for a school year covered by an agency decision ordering reimbursement. The circuit court also clarified the parties' obligations in a few areas the parties traditionally disputed when developing the student's IEPs, in a n attempt to prevent future disputes. *Rome School Committee v. Mrs. B.*, 247 F.3d 29 (1st Cir. 2001)

◆ A student with a significant sexual disorder that included pedophilia and paraphilia was placed in a segregated program at a regional high school. He improperly touched a classmate and his IEP was amended to require his supervision by an adult at all times. The following year, the student was hospitalized and treated for ongoing pedophilic problems. **Although a treatment plan described him as a sexually deviant youth who required treatment in an intensive residential setting**, the school district indicated that he continued to make educational progress and was improving in appropriate peer relations within his district placement. The student's adoptive parents initiated child protection proceedings due to their inability to supervise him and he was committed to the custody of the state department of social services (DSS). Without notifying the school district, DSS placed the student in a residential school for mentally disabled students with sexually offending behavior. The school district proposed resuming the district placement. A hearing officer determined that the IEP proposed by the school district was inappropriate because it failed to address the student's sexual behavior. The residential school placement was academically appropriate and provided for his maximum possible educational development in the least restrictive environment, as required by Massachusetts law. The school district appealed to a federal district court.

The court held that the student's behavior was intertwined with his educational performance. Evidence indicated that he required the residential placement because his disabilities combined a number of conditions described in state regulations that would each require special education. **Given the student's unique needs, special education for him included counseling and therapy that was available at the residential school, but not in district schools**. The court held that the student's emotional disability entitled him to special education services. The court rejected the district's attempt to separate the student's educational goals from his behavioral controls, and found that the hearing officer had properly relied upon *David D. v. Dartmouth School Comm.*, 775 F.2d 411 (1st Cir.1986). In that case, the U.S. Court of Appeals, First Circuit, held that a student was entitled to a residential placement to receive comprehensive behavior therapy for his sexual misbehavior. The court rejected the district's assertions that the residential placement would require the school to provide the student with medical treatment, and that DSS had violated a state operations protocol in making the unilateral placement. The court affirmed the administrative decision. *Mohawk Trail Regional School Dist. v. Shaun D. by Linda D.*, 35 F.Supp.2d 34 (D.Mass.1999).

◆ A Connecticut student with attention deficit hyperactivity disorder and oppositional defiant disorder often disrupted his classes. When he became increasingly disruptive in school and on his school bus, a school placement team recommended revising his IEP. The student entered a psychiatric treatment program due to his aggressive, suicidal and self-endangering behavior. **Upon his release, the student's behavior again deteriorated, and he was placed in a series of private placements whose educational components were funded by the school district**. By agreement, **the state Department of Children and Families (DCF) funded the residential part** of the placements. After a fire-setting incident, his mother requested a due process hearing. The hearing officer determined that the school district had failed to provide the student with a FAPE. He further held that the student required a residential placement, but rejected the school district's request to join the DCF as a party. The school district appealed to a federal district court, which accepted the hearing officer's determination that the district had denied the student a FAPE by preparing an inadequate IEP and failing to revise it in response to the series of changes in his educational environment.

The court deferred to the hearing officer's findings and rejected the district's arguments that it had provided the student with an adequate IEP and should not be responsible for the student's residential placement. The court rejected evidence that the student's most serious emotional problems had occurred in non-educational settings. Instead, the court applied a deferential standard of review under *Mrs. B. v. Milford Bd. of Educ.*, 103 F.3d 1114 (2d Cir. 1997) and accepted administrative findings that the district had not addressed the student's educational needs. **The court followed a line of federal decisions holding school boards responsible for residential placements where a student has interrelated emotional and educational disabilities.** DCF involvement in the residential placements did not act to reduce the district's burden of providing an adequate IDEA placement, and the court affirmed the administrative order. *Naugatuck Bd. of Educ. v. Mrs. D.*, 10 F.Supp.2d 170 (D.Conn.1998).

In a related proceeding, the court denied summary judgment motions filed by the parties concerning the school district's claim that the state education board and DCF had failed to develop and publish interagency agreements to define the financial responsibility of various state and local agencies as required by the IDEA. *Naugatuck Bd. of Educ. v. Mrs. D.*, 1997 WL 205791 (D.Conn.1997).

◆ A Maryland student with a severe emotional disturbance received good grades in a special education program at a public middle school after attending a private institution for two years. Because he was progressing, his parents considered mainstreaming him in a neighborhood public high school. However, before a scheduled placement meeting, the student attempted suicide and was hospitalized in a psychiatric facility. Upon his release, **his parents placed him at a private residential facility recommended by hospital personnel without any input from the school district. They then demanded tuition reimbursement** from the school district for the costs of the facility, which the district denied. The parents sought an administrative ruling and succeeded in obtaining part of the requested private school funding. The hearing officer awarded funds for the period of time after they had first requested it from the school district. A state level review officer held that the district had no obligation to provide any funding, and the parents appealed to the U.S. District Court for the District of Maryland.

Before the court, the parents argued that they had been deprived of their IDEA procedural rights and that only the private facility was appropriate because of the student's suicide attempt and family problems. The court found no procedural violations by the school district, commenting that the family and their attorney had resisted legitimate school district efforts to meet and confer in order to consider an appropriate placement. The court found that a regional placement facility proposed by the school district was appropriate. **Because a residential placement that is required to remedy emotional problems rather than educational needs is not reimbursable under the IDEA, the district was not required to pay the private school tuition**. The court affirmed the review officer's decision for the school district. *Sanger v. Montgomery County Bd. of Educ.*, 916 F.Supp. 518 (D.Md.1996).

II. CONTAGIOUS DISEASES AND PLACEMENT

Courts have held that students with hepatitis, HIV and AIDS may have disabilities as defined by law and can be admitted to public school programs if their enrollment is not a health threat to the school community. This result follows from the case of School Board of Nassau County v. Arline, *480 U.S. 273, 107 S.Ct. 1123, 94 L.Ed.2d 307 (1987), see Chapter Seven, Section II. In that case, the U.S. Supreme Court ruled that persons with contagious diseases such as tuberculosis may be considered disabled under § 504 of the Rehabilitation Act if they are otherwise qualified to participate in a program and able to perform essential job duties. For more Rehabilitation Act cases, see Chapter Nine.*

◆ A federal district court held **that three brothers who were hemophiliacs and who had tested positive for the HIV virus could not be excluded from public school classes**. The school district contended that although no actual physical harm had been done to their classmates or teachers due to the brothers' class attendance, there was the possibility of future harm. This future harm allegedly included transmission of the HIV virus in the classroom setting and liability of the school district for allowing the brothers to attend classes. The court also cited the Supreme Court's decision in *School Board of Nassau County v. Arline*, where the Supreme Court held that a person with tuberculosis could be considered an individual with a disability under § 504 of the Rehabilitation Act. **Because § 504 prohibits recipients of federal funds from discriminating against the disabled solely because of their disability, the school district could not exclude the brothers from class**. *Ray v. School Dist. of Desoto County*, 666 F.Supp. 1524 (N.D.Fla.1987).

◆ A girl born with respiratory distress received 39 blood transfusions during the first four months of her life and was diagnosed as having AIDS-Related Complex at the age of three. She was classified as trainable mentally handicapped (TMH). At the age of six the girl had a mental age of between one and one-half years in expressive language and three and one-half years in perceptual motor skills. The girl was incontinent and was observed by doctors to drool and suck her thumb continually. In the past, the girl had developed skin lesions. When these occurred, her mother kept her home. When the girl approached school age her mother attempted to enroll her in a Florida public school. The school district operated two schools which each maintained classes for TMH children. However, **the school district excluded the girl from public schools** based upon her incontinence. The school district recommended that the girl be educated in its homebound program. The girl appealed to the Florida State Division of Administrative Hearings. The school district prevailed after an evidentiary hearing. The administrative decision was appealed to a federal district court which held in favor of the school district. *Martinez v. School Bd. of Hillsborough County, Florida*, 675 F.Supp. 1574 (M.D.Fla.1987).

In 1988, the U.S. District Court for the Middle District of Florida held a full trial on the matter of placing the student. **The court allowed the student to join the school's TMH classroom with heavy restrictions**. The court noted that the student was still incontinent and sucked her thumb and fingers continuously.

Because there was a remote theoretical possibility of transmitting AIDS through bodily secretions the court again ruled that the student could not be mainstreamed. The court ordered the school district to construct a separate room within the TMH classroom conforming to the court's order. The school board was also required to provide a full-time aide to remain with the student in her room at all times. Other children in the TMH class who had written parental waivers could be allowed into the separate room during class time. *Martinez v. School Bd. of Hillsboro County, Fla.*, 692 F.Supp. 1293 (M.D.Fla.1988).

The student's mother then appealed to the U.S. Court of Appeals, Eleventh Circuit. The court first determined that the student in this case was entitled to a free appropriate education under the IDEA. She suffered from two disabilities under § 504 as she was both mentally retarded and had AIDS. **The appropriate educational placement was the regular TMH classroom. The district court's finding of a "remote theoretical possibility" of transmission of AIDS was insufficient to exclude her** from the TMH classroom. Because the district court had failed to make findings concerning the overall risk of transmitting AIDS through bodily secretions, it had failed to determine whether the student was "otherwise qualified" to attend the TMH classroom. If the court found on remand that the student was not "otherwise qualified" to attend the TMH classroom, it was bound to consider whether reasonable accommodations would qualify her. The lower court would also be required to hear evidence concerning the stigmatizing effect of segregating the student in a separate room. The appeals court vacated the district court's decision and remanded the case for rehearing.

On remand, the court noted that the American Academy of Pediatrics had eliminated its recommendation that students who could not control their bodily secretions be placed in more restrictive environments. It also noted that the Center for Disease Control had stated that the risk of transmission of HIV and HBV from feces, nasal secretion, saliva, sweat, tears, urine and vomit was extremely low or nonexistent unless visible blood was actually present. The student's behavior had changed since the initial consideration of the case. She sucked her fingers less often and was becoming toilet trained. The court ruled that the student could join the TMH classroom. **The student was otherwise qualified to attend the TMH classroom which was therefore the most appropriate placement under the IDEA.** The court also required the school board to provide an educational program for parents whose children would be in the classroom. *Martinez v. School Bd. of Hillsborough County, Fla.*, 711 F.Supp. 1066 (M.D.Fla.1989). In 1989, Eliana Martinez died at the age of six from complications attributable to AIDS.

◆ A twelve-year-old student contracted the AIDS virus through blood transfusions when he had undergone open-heart surgery as a child. **When the board of education of an Illinois school district learned that the student was infected with the AIDS virus, it excluded him from attending the school's regular education classes and extracurricular activities.** The student filed a complaint in a federal district court, seeking an order to allow him to return to his regular classes as a full-time student. The student's claim was primarily based on § 504 of the Rehabilitation Act. In order for the student to prevail under this section, he had to be an individual with a disability and "otherwise qualified" to attend school.

The court found that the student would likely be considered an individual with a disability. As an AIDS victim, **he was regarded as being impaired and this impairment substantially limited one or more of the student's major life activities.** The court also deemed the student "otherwise qualified" to attend school. Medical authorities found no significant risk of transmission of AIDS in the classroom. The court found that the student had been harmed by loss of self-esteem which could be partially alleviated by returning him to the classroom. Any injury that might occur by issuing the order was insufficient to outweigh the harm to the student. In addition, the public interest would not be disserved by allowing the student to return to school since the threat of the student transmitting the AIDS virus to others was minimal. The court held that the student was entitled to return to school. **The court required carefully-drawn procedures to ensure that any potential risk of harm to the student's classmates and teachers was eliminated**. *Doe v. Dolton Elementary School Dist. No. 148*, 694 F.Supp. 440 (N.D.Ill.1988).

- A California school district learned that an eleven-year-old hemophilic student in the district had been exposed to the AIDS virus. **The district instructed the student not to enroll in school and required him to study at home until the district formulated an AIDS policy**. The student's guardian was unhappy with the home tutor program and repeatedly requested to have the student returned to regular classes. On each occasion the district told her that the student could not attend school until an AIDS policy had been formulated. The guardian filed a complaint in a California trial court, seeking both a preliminary and a permanent order allowing the student to return to school. The guardian also sought attorney's fees. **The school district stated that it was developing an AIDS policy and requested verification from the student's doctor and county health officials that his attendance at school would pose no health risk** to students or staff members. The court issued an injunction ordering the school district to allow the student to attend a regular school within its district, subject to its evaluation of his medical condition every six months. Shortly after the court's order, the district's policy on AIDS and infectious diseases became effective. The matter then proceeded to trial where the court found for the guardian. **An order was granted which required the school district to allow the student to attend a regular school, subject to periodic medical examinations**. The guardian was also awarded attorney's fees. The school district appealed the decision to the California Court of Appeal, Fourth District.

On appeal, the school district argued that the trial court abused its discretion in issuing a permanent order. It insisted that a permanent order was not necessary because the student had been attending school. Alternatively, it contended that even if the order was proper, attorney's fees were not warranted. **The court of appeal ruled that the district had unreasonably delayed the formulation of its AIDS policy** for more than five months. The permanent order was proper even though the school district had decided to allow the student to attend class. The record suggested that the student was allowed to attend solely because it was mandated by the court order. The court also found that attorney's fees were appropriately awarded as the lawsuit was instrumental in motivating the school district to address the issue of AIDS and to effectuate an appropriate policy without impairing the rights of students. *Phipps v. Saddleback Valley Unified School Dist.*, 251 Cal.Rptr. 720 (Cal.Ct.App.4th Dist.1988).

◆ The Appellate Court of Illinois considered the appropriate educational placement of a trainable mentally disabled child with Down's syndrome who was also a carrier of an infectious disease, Hepatitis Type B. **Local school officials contended that because of the risk of the child transmitting the disease to other children, the appropriate placement for her was in a "homebound" setting.** The child maintained that the risk of transmission of the disease was remote and therefore not a sufficient reason to exclude her from classroom participation. A hearing officer, the State Superintendent of Education and a lower court agreed with the child. So did the Appellate Court of Illinois. The question on appeal was whether the child's homebound placement was mandated by the school district's health and safety obligations to its students so that she was being educated in the least restrictive environment as required by Illinois law and the IDEA. The court held it was not. Using the *Rowley* case as its guide, the court first noted that the trial court had given due deference to the state agency's determination of educational policy under the present circumstances. Next, the court noted that there is a strong congressional preference in favor of mainstreaming wherever possible. **A major goal of the educational process is the socialization process that takes place in the regular classroom, with the resulting capacity to interact in a social way with one's peers.** The superintendent of education recognized this and determined that the risk of transmission of the disease did not outweigh the injury to the child if she remained isolated from her peers. After a thorough examination of the testimony of expert witnesses, the court concluded that the trial court's decision was not against the manifest weight of the evidence and thus the child could be integrated into the classroom if appropriate sanitary procedures were followed. *Comm. High School Dist. 155 v. Denz*, 463 N.E.2d 998 (Ill.App.Ct.1984).

III. CHANGES IN PLACEMENT

The IDEA requires school districts to provide parents with prior written notice of any proposed change in the educational placement of a child with a disability. See 20 U.S.C. § 1415(b)(1)(C). This notice requirement also applies when an LEA proposes graduating a student with a disability and awarding the student a regular education diploma. See 34 C.F.R. Section 300.122(a)(3)(iii). A hearing must be granted to parents wishing to contest a change in placement. Under the IDEA "stay put" provision, school officials are prevented from removing a child from a current placement over the parents' objection pending completion of review proceedings.

A. Notice and Hearing

◆ After a student with an emotional disturbance was tardy 20 times during one academic year and was disruptive in class, a family court truancy petition was filed. The family court denied a motion by the student's guardian to dismiss the petition, based on the argument that it called for a change in placement that violated the stay put provision. The court denied the motion and placed the student under county supervision. The New York Supreme Court, Appellate Division, noted that the 1997 IDEA Amendments contain a provision prohibiting an interpretation of the IDEA that would prevent the reporting of crimes committed by students with disabilities or preventing law enforcement officers from exercising their duties. Even though the student had been accused of threatening other students, he was not charged with committing a crime and was not the subject of a juvenile delinquency petition. The truancy proceeding arose under the Family Court Article and the 1997 Amendments had no application in the case. **The court agreed that the filing of the truancy petition triggered the stay put provision and that the county failed to exhaust required IDEA and state special education administrative remedies** prior to filing the petition. Accordingly, the court dismissed the petition.

School officials appealed to the New York Court of Appeals, which observed that the stay put provision requires that parents or guardians of students with disabilities receive written prior notice whenever an education agency proposes to initiate or change the identification, evaluation or educational placement of the student. According to the high court, the key phrase in this dispute was "change in educational placement," which is not defined in the IDEA itself. **The determination of whether a change in placement has occurred must be made on a case-by-case basis in which a number of factors are considered**: whether the student's IEP has been revised, whether the student will be educated with non-disabled students to the same extent as before, whether the student will have the same participation opportunities in nonacademic and extracurricular programs, and whether the new placement option is the same option on the continuum of alternative placements. The court also relied on authoritative guidance from the U.S. Department of Education indicating that a change in placement occurs when the substance of the student's educational program itself has been changed, so that the program has been materially altered. In this case, the school officials were not seeking a change of placement by filing the PINS petition. To the contrary, they sought to enforce his program through probation. His habitual tardiness and aggressive behavior prevented him from fully taking advantage of his individualized education program. Probation primarily sought to improve his attendance record and supervise his activities, not alter his educational services or placement. The student attended the same school, same classes and received the same type and level of services. Since no substantial and material change was effected by the filing of the PINS petition, the high court reversed and remanded the decision of the appellate division. In doing so, **the panel rejected a blanket rule under which the stay put provision barred all PINS proceedings**. *In the Matter of Beau "II,"* 715 N.Y.S.2d 686 (N.Y. 2000).

◆ A Maine student with a learning disability received special education services from his local public school. In his third grade year, his parents requested his removal from the school based on their perception that the school administration, teachers, students, and a bus driver were harassing him. The school agreed to provide tutoring in the superintendent's office for the rest of the school year, but the IEP developed for grade four called for continuing placement at the school.

The parents instead decided to provide a home school curriculum, then sought placement in a neighboring school system 30 miles away. When the school district refused to change the IEP, the parents requested a due process hearing. The district prepared a new IEP calling for special education services and mainstreaming at the local school. **The hearing officer determined that hostility between the family and school staff prevented the implementation of a successful education program at the student's former school**. He ordered the implementation of the student's IEP at a different school but left the actual placement decision to the school administration. The school committee appealed to the U.S. District Court for the District of Maine.

The school committee argued that the hearing officer's decision allowed the parents to prevail in an IDEA dispute based on their hostility to school officials, a result that was contrary to the IDEA's cooperative approach. The court rejected the committee's claim that the IDEA did not allow consideration of parental objections to a proposed IEP. **The hearing officer had properly focused on the student's inability to gain educational benefits from his placement and recognized that his anxiety prevented a successful placement at his former school**. The court affirmed the hearing officer's decision. *Greenbush School Comm. v. Mr. and Mrs. K.*, 949 F.Supp. 934 (D.Me.1996).

◆ A 14-year-old Mississippi eighth grader exhibited symptoms of emotional disturbance and antisocial behavior, causing the district to change his placement from special education classes to the district alternative school. The student's parents consented to the change. He demonstrated hostility to others and damaged school property while fighting with school employees. The district responded by placing the student in a residential care facility. He was returned to the district alternative school when Medicaid funds were exhausted, but resumed his disruptive conduct. **The district then convened an IEP meeting and decided to place him in a self-contained classroom located in a courtroom in the county sheriff's office**. The student's parents refused to consent to the placement and requested a due process hearing under the IDEA. The hearing officer found that the placement would last only 45 days and was appropriate given the student's recent suicide threats. The hearing officer also ordered the district to provide ten hours of instruction per week and to design a behavioral management system and therapy plan. The district was ordered to develop a transition plan to assist the student in returning to the alternative school or a residential placement. When the parties disagreed on implementation of the order, the parents filed a lawsuit against the district in the U.S. District Court for the Northern District of Mississippi, seeking a preliminary order prohibiting the change in placement.

The court found that the school district had not committed any procedural errors under the IDEA and had appropriately notified the parents of the proposed change. **An exception existed to the IDEA stay put provision where a student presents a danger to himself or others and threatens a safe school environment**. The court recounted the district's efforts to place the student in a variety of unsuccessful school environments. It also stated that a 45-day placement in the detention center would allow the school district to provide individualized attention and counseling. The placement was not punitive and would satisfy the IDEA requirement for a meaningful education in view of his violent behavior. The court denied the parents' motion for a preliminary order and adopted the recommended remedies of the hearing officer. *Taylor v. Corinth Pub. School Dist.*, 917 F.Supp. 464 (N.D.Miss.1996).

◆ A Georgia county education board proposed the consolidation and closure of four schools. A taxpayer filed a lawsuit against the board in a Georgia trial court, seeking an order requiring an evidentiary hearing or referendum on the proposals. The trial court permanently enjoined the board of education from consolidating and closing the schools. The decision was based partly upon the court's finding that the board had failed to comply with the IDEA. The court ordered the county board to renovate the schools, utilize school trustees as set forth under Georgia law and comply with state and federal funding statutes. The board appealed to the Supreme Court of Georgia. The supreme court reversed the trial court's holding that the board action had violated the IDEA. Contrary to the trial court's decision, **the transfer of disabled students from one school to another with a comparable program did not constitute a change in placement that would require notification of parents under the IDEA**. *Powell v. Studstill*, 441 S.E.2d 52 (Ga.1994).

B. Stay Put Provision

◆ During the sixth grade, a student with cerebral palsy underwent surgery to implant a pump in his abdomen to deliver medication to his spine. He received home instruction during his recovery and continued to receive it through grade seven due to complications. Meanwhile, the relationship between his parents and school officials deteriorated and both sides requested due process hearings to consider the appropriateness of his program. **The district determined that the student's home was no longer an appropriate learning environment and notified the parents that it would provide him the same services at school**. The parents refused to bring him to school and he received no services until a federal district court issued a preliminary order 10 months later. A due process hearing panel held that the district provided the student with a FAPE and did not violate the stay put provision with its unilateral action. However, the panel ordered the district to provide the student with ESY services and other relief while phasing out his home schooling. The parties appealed unfavorable aspects of the panel's decision to a district court, which held that the decision to change the location of the student's program from home to school violated the stay put provision.

The district appealed to the Eighth Circuit, which noted that the stay put provision requires that a student remain in his or her "then-current educational placement" during the pendency of any IDEA action. The court held that **the stay put provision is to be literally and rigorously enforced in order to strip schools of the unilateral authority they formerly employed to exclude students with disabilities from school**. The district argued that its action did not change the student's placement since it called for the provision of identical services at a different location. The court found that the IDEA does not define the term "then-current." Other courts have held that the transfer of a student to a different school building for fiscal reasons does not constitute a change of placement. On the other hand, an expulsion or other change in the location of a program has usually been deemed a change in placement that violates the stay put provision. The district court had employed a "fact intensive" approach and then made findings on the impact of the change in setting to the student's education. There was no error in this analysis, and the district court findings were not clearly erroneous. The remedy ordered by the district court – to provide the student with ESY services – was also well within its discretion. The Eighth Circuit held that the district court did not error when it concluded no IDEA violation occurred. *Hale v. Poplar Bluff R-I School Dist.*, 280 F.3d 831 (8th Cir. 2002).

◆ During a student with severe dyslexia's third year in public schools, his parents objected to the district's proposed IEP and unilaterally placed him in a private school for students with learning disabilities. The parties were unable to resolve the IEP dispute and the parents requested a due process hearing. The hearing officer agreed with the parents that the district denied the student a FAPE and awarded them reimbursement for two years of tuition. A state review officer denied an appeal by the district and the district paid the parents. However, the parties disputed a subsequent IEP, and the parents again requested an impartial hearing to obtain tuition reimbursement for a third year. The parents invoked the stay put provision, requesting the hearing officer issue an interim ruling requiring the district to fund the private placement during the pendency of the dispute. The hearing officer denied this request, but **a state review officer annulled the decision and ordered the district to reimburse the family for the private placement**. The district sued the parents, state education department, and SRO in federal district court, seeking reversal of the SRO's order.

The court first rejected the school district's claims for monetary damages under 42 U.S.C. § 1983, observing that the 11th Amendment protected the state and SRO from such actions. The Due Process Clause of the 14th Amendment did not protect a state political subdivision such as a school district from action by its own state. The district's opposition to the stay put order was also without merit. **The parties were bound by the most recent final administrative ruling in the case, which had fixed the private school selected by the parents as the student's stay put placement**. The district's incorrect interpretation of the stay put provision rendered it virtually meaningless, so that any district proposing a new IEP could potentially avoid application of the provision. While the district correctly argued that 20 U.S.C. § 1412(c) required a court or hearing officer to first find a current IEP inadequate in order to permit private school tuition reimbursement, the court found that this provision applied only where parents had not yet mounted an administrative challenge under the IDEA. In this case, the stay put provision applied, not Section 1412(c). Because the private facility located by the parents was the student's stay put placement, the court ordered the district to continue funding the placement during the pendency of the dispute. *Board of Education of Pawling Central School District v. Schutz et al.*, 137 F.Supp.2d 83 (N.D.N.Y. 2001).

◆ The parents of a New York student claimed that the IEP devised for the 1998-99 school year was inappropriate and unilaterally placed the student in a private school. At the same time, the parents requested a due process hearing. Before the hearing was held, the parents objected to the proposed 1999-2000 IEP, but did not commence due process proceedings challenging this IEP because of the pending hearing over the 1998-1999 IEP. After a federal district court ordered the state education department to rule on the 1998-1999 IEP, a hearing officer declared this IEP inappropriate and held that the school selected by the parents was an appropriate placement. A state review officer affirmed this decision, ordering the district to reimburse the parents for the private-school tuition costs for part of the 1998-99 school year. Under this proceeding, the private school was deemed the student's stay put placement. The district's IEP proposals for the next two school years were also rejected by the parents, who again challenged each IEP at due process. **A hearing officer held that the private school was no longer the student's stay put placement and that the state review officer's decision on the 1998-99 matter did not create a pendency placement for future school years.** The district refused to pay the student's private school tuition and the student dropped out of school during the 2000-2001 school year. A state review officer reversed the stay put decision and held that the private school remained the student's pendent placement for the duration of the proceedings. The hearing officer then issued a decision determining that the private school was the appropriate placement for the 1999-2000 school year, entitling the family to reimbursement. The hearing officer held that the district's 2000-2001 IEP proposal was inappropriate, but found that the private school was not appropriate either, because the student had regressed while attending the school.

The school district appealed the state review officer's stay put ruling to a district court. The court first held that the family's claims against the state education department were barred by the 11th Amendment. The family failed to state any claims against the state review officer, as there was no error in his decision. **The court stated that the stay put provision works as an absolute rule in favor of the status quo, depriving courts of any discretion about the appropriateness of a student's current placement during the consideration of an IDEA dispute.** The private school was unquestionably the student's placement during the pendency of the dispute, as the state review officer's decision on the 1998-99 school year had approved it and the parties did not subsequently modify it by agreement. Although the case was complicated by the hearing officer's decision that the private school was no longer appropriate for the 2000-2001 school year, that decision was still awaiting a final administrative determination by a state review officer and was not presently before the court. Until then, the student's pendent placement remained the private school, irrespective of any claim by the district that his family would be unable to repay any sums it expended for the school year. *Board of Education of Pine Plains Central School District v. Engwiller*, 170 F.Supp.2d 410 (S.D.N.Y. 2001).

◆ The parents of a Michigan student with disabilities objected to the placement described in his IEP and unilaterally placed him in a private school. Their first attempt to recover tuition reimbursement was rejected by a federal district court due to their failure to exhaust administrative remedies. The parents then commenced an administrative proceeding against the district. A local hearing officer heard six days of testimony, then terminated the proceeding as moot when the parents announced that they intended to place the student in a private school. A state review officer affirmed the decision, and the parents appealed to federal district court.

The court agreed with the parents that the local hearing officer had erroneously failed to consider the substantive question of whether their son had received a FAPE. However, they were not deprived of their due process rights by the abrupt end to the administrative hearing. Although the hearing officer had erroneously dismissed the case as moot, the error was corrected when the state review officer fully reviewed the IEP. The court rejected the parents' argument that the student was entitled to have his IEPs updated during the pendency of the case, which was now in its fifth year of litigation. **The district had prepared a new IEP in 1998 pursuant to the court's order, and the IDEA's stay put provision required the district to maintain that IEP as the student's current educational placement pending the outcome of the proceedings.** In examining the district's proposed IEP, the court agreed with the review officer's conclusion that it was reasonably calculated to enable the student to receive educational benefits under the IDEA. It also satisfied Michigan's higher standard of "maximum potential," which does not require a student to receive the best education possible. Accordingly, the court denied the parents' request for private educational expenses and attorneys' fees. *Kuszewski v. Chippewa Valley Schools*, 131 F.Supp.2d 926 (E.D. Mich. 2001).

◆ A student with autism resided in the Unorganized Territories of Maine, which has no public schools. The local education agency funded his placement in a private school, where he received special education services. In the spring of the year in which the student turned 19, his pupil evaluation team recommended that he graduate with his class. **His parents challenged the recommendation and requested a due process hearing, arguing that he was not ready to graduate.** The hearing officer determined that the agency's decision did not deprive the student of a free appropriate public education. The agency sent the student a diploma and the parent appealed to district court.

The court considered the parents' motion for a preliminary order requiring the agency to maintain the student's placement pending consideration of the merits of the case under the IDEA's stay put provision, 20 U.S.C. § 1415(j). The court agreed with the agency that parents must make the traditional four-part showing required when any party petitions a court for preliminary relief: likelihood of success on the merits of the claim, the potential for irreparable harm if the relief is denied, the balance of hardships between the parties, and the public interest. However, the burden of establishing these four elements rested on the agency, because it was the party seeking to modify the student's existing placement. The court found the hearing officer's decision ambiguous because although it approved the agency's decision to allow graduation, it did not specify the student's current educational placement, referring only to the date of his last IEP. According to the court, in the absence of detailed administrative findings, the student's current educational placement was the one described in his last IEP. The parents had objected to the agency's decision to graduate the student while he was still attending the private school and the court interpreted the hearing officer's ambiguity in their favor. The court further held that **graduation constitutes a**

change in placement for purposes of the stay put provision. Because the agency failed to prove the four required elements for preliminary relief and thus failed to overcome the strong preference for preservation of the educational status quo, the court held that the student should remain in his private school placement under the curriculum established in the previous year's IEP, pending further proceedings. *Bell et al. v. Education in the Unorganized Territories et al.*, 2000 WL 1855096 (D. Me. 2000).

◆ An Illinois student with Rett's syndrome attended regular classes in a public school along with receiving special education services. At the end of her second-grade year, **the school district sought to change her placement to a self-contained classroom. Her parents strongly objected** to the proposal and filed an administrative challenge that did not proceed to a hearing for over two years. The student continued to attend regular classes with her peers through the end of grade five. When the hearing was finally held, the presiding hearing officer held that the placement proposed by the school district satisfied its responsibility to provide the student with a FAPE. The parents petitioned a federal district court for review of the administrative decision. Although the student's disabilities were too severe for her to master the core curriculum, the parents sought to invoke the IDEA's stay-put provision in order to keep her in the same class with her peers as they advanced to junior high school. While their appeal of the substantive parts of the order was pending, the court made a ruling on the stay-put issue.

The court explained that the IDEA provides that children with disabilities must remain in their "then-current" educational placement pending the conclusion of a dispute under the IDEA. The student remains in her stay-put placement during proceedings unless the parties agree otherwise. In this case, the district argued that the student's stay-put placement was the setting it proposed, as affirmed by the hearing officer. The court held that **the advancement of the student's class to junior high school did not mean that there was no longer a current educational placement for her. Instead, to preserve the educational status quo, she should remain with her public school peers in the junior high school setting** pending the outcome of the IDEA proceedings. Although the change to a multi-classroom setting created some complexities, they were insufficient to deny the student a statutory entitlement. *Beth B. v. Van Clay*, 126 F.Supp.2d 532 (N.D. Ill. 2000).

◆ A Minnesota school district and the parents of a student with autism vigorously debated an appropriate placement. The district contended an in-school placement could adequately serve the student's needs, while the parents sought an in-home applied behavioral analysis program. At due process, a level-one hearing officer agreed with the school district's IEP. Both parties appealed. A level-two hearing officer modified the district's IEP in several respects. The parents appealed, and a court affirmed the decision. During the appeal, the district sought to implement the administrative decision by rejecting the parents' requests to pay for the 30 hours of home-based services specified in the student's IEP. After the parties failed to agree on a new IEP, the district threatened to file a truancy report against the student unless the parents moved him into the school-based program approved by the hearing officer. The parents applied to home-school the student and filed a complaint against the district with the state commissioner of the Department of Children, Families and Learning. **The commissioner found the district in violation of the IDEA and ordered it to reimburse the parents for their home-based educational expenses pending appeal.**

The district appealed to a Minnesota court of appeals, where it argued that the stay put provision does not require continuation of a student's program or reimbursement where there is no continuing judicial proceeding in which the need to attend a school-based program is in dispute. It asserted that the pending proceeding pertained only to procedural issues, citing IDEA final regulations that make the stay put provision inapplicable where there is no dispute among parties that is subject to an IDEA proceeding. The court found the district's arguments meritless, finding that the IDEA required it to provide services in conformity with the applicable IEP pending appeal. The policy concerns behind the stay put provision supported this interpretation. The court ruled that the current appeal challenged the student's placement, and that the court's earlier procedural decision had a significant impact on important details of the educational services provided to the student. There were significant matters pending at the time of the appeal regarding his educational program. Accordingly, the application of the stay put provision was proper. The court further held that **the commissioner had the authority to order the district to reimburse the parents for the costs of the home-based program pending appeal because the commissioner had the power to determine whether the district violated the stay put provision**. The court also rejected the district's argument that its obligation to fund the home-based program ceased once the parents elected to home-school their son. The court affirmed the commissioner's decision. *Special School District No. 1 v. E.N.*, 620 N.W.2d 65 (Minn. Ct. App. 2000).

◆ When the parents of a Maine student objected to the proposed public school placement for grade eight, they requested an administrative due process hearing challenging the proposed IEP. Before the hearing was conducted, **the parties reached an agreement under which the student would be placed at a learning center through the end of the school year. The parties further agreed that the IEP team would use the student's progress at the center during the year as a basis for the subsequent school year placement**. The agreement expressed the parties' intent that the student return to public school the next school year and that placement at the center was only temporary. The family agreed to drop their due process hearing request. At the conclusion of the student's eighth grade year, the parents rejected the IEP team's recommendation for returning the student to a public high school for the ninth grade. The parents filed a new due process complaint, contending that the student was entitled to remain at the center at district expense, under the stay put provision. The school district asserted that the parents then agreed at a pre-hearing conference to allow the hearing officer to determine the student's appropriate stay put placement. When the hearing officer held that the public high school was the student's stay put placement, the parents appealed to a federal district court, stating that they had not agreed to be bound by the hearing officer's decision. The court denied their request for a preliminary order requiring the school district to fund the student's continuing placement at the center. The administrative hearing officer then made a final determination ordering a public school placement. Because the hearing officer had issued an order determining the student's appropriate placement, the district court denied the parents' request for temporary relief under the stay put provision, holding that the issue was moot. The court also held that the parents had agreed to submit the stay put placement issue to the hearing officer.

The parents appealed to the First Circuit, which disagreed with the district court's finding that the case was moot, but ultimately agreed with its disposition of the case. The circuit court held that a stay put placement includes both administrative and judicial proceedings. The court explained that the stay put requirement is subject to an exception when the educational agency and parents otherwise agree to another placement. 20 U.S.C. § 1415(j). It upheld the district court's decision that the "otherwise agree" exception applied in this case. **The parents, by submitting the stay put placement issue to the hearing officer, had forfeited any claim that the student was entitled to remain at the center pending administrative or judicial proceedings**. The court rejected the parents' assertion that they had never agreed to be bound by the hearing officer's interim placement decision, but had rather intended that he serve only as an initial adjudicator of the appropriate stay put placement. The agreement of the parties governing the eighth grade placement at the center was clearly a temporary one, and the parties had contemplated the student's return to public school for grade nine. The district court decision was affirmed. *Verhoeven v. Brunswick School Comm.*, 207 F.3d 1 (1st Cir. 1999).

- **The private school placement of a student with a language disability, autism and pervasive developmental disorder was funded by a school district for three years under a settlement agreement** that resolved an earlier due process hearing concerning appropriate placement. The school admission, review and dismissal committee then determined that the student was no longer eligible for services under the IDEA and worked on a transition plan to move him into regular education classes at a district middle school. The parents requested a due process hearing and notified the district by telephone that the student would again attend the private school. The parents failed to notify the district in writing of their intent to reject the public school placement and enroll the student in the private school, as required by Maryland law and the IDEA. An administrative law judge dismissed the case due to the family's failure to provide the district with appropriate notice of the placement, and the parents appealed to the U.S. District Court for the District of Maryland.

The court found that it would be unfair to dismiss the case as a result of the parents' failure to comply with state and federal law requirements, when the district had itself failed to notify the parents of their obligation to comply with the same requirements. The IDEA and corresponding provisions of Maryland law did not bar the claim for reimbursement. The court next considered the parents' assertion that the private school was the student's then current placement for purposes of the IDEA stay put provision. It noted that several years had elapsed between the time of the earlier administrative decision approving of the private school placement. The court therefore rejected the parents' claim that the district was automatically required to fund the student's private school tuition during the pendency of the case. **There was no merit to the claim that the parents were entitled to "perpetual tuition reimbursement" during subsequent litigation concerning school years subsequent to an administrative placement order**. According to the court, a rule permitting automatic tuition reimbursement under the stay put provision would encourage protracted litigation and discourage settlement agreements because schools would risk being bound to pay private school tuition during disputes in later years. The court held that the student's stay put placement was not the private school and the parents were not entitled to reimbursement pending resolution of their claim. The case was remanded for further administrative action. *Mayo v. Baltimore City Pub. Schools*, 40 F.Supp.2d 331 (D.Md.1999).

◆ A student with bipolar disorder and learning disabilities received two hours of occupational therapy weekly. One hour was devoted to hippotherapy, a therapy involving horses. At an IEP meeting, the school district proposed reducing the number of occupational therapy hours per week to one and eliminating hippotherapy. The student's mother agreed to the reduction, but objected to the elimination of hippotherapy. She requested a due process hearing after the district cancelled the student's hippotherapy. A hearing officer held that the school district violated the IDEA's stay put provision by discontinuing hippotherapy during the administrative proceedings and that it violated the IDEA by determining prior to the IEP meeting that occupational therapy would be provided at school and not at an outside facility. He also awarded the student one semester of hippotherapy as compensatory education. **The school district appealed to an administrative appeal officer, who held that the district was entitled to change the location of services**. The district did not violate the stay put provision, and because the proposed IEP offered the student a FAPE, he was not entitled to an award of compensatory education. The family appealed to a federal district court, which granted the school district's summary judgment motion, substantially adopting the appeal officer's factual findings and conclusions of law. The court held that the elimination of hippotherapy was a change in methodology of services, not a change in educational placement that triggered the stay put provision.

On appeal, the Tenth Circuit disagreed with the mother's assertion that the district was required to continue providing two hours of weekly occupational therapy including the hour of hippotherapy until resolution of her appeal. The court observed that the mother had agreed to the reduction in services. It held that **the stay put provision is inapplicable when a parent and school district agree to change the level of services in an educational program**. The district court had properly found that hippotherapy is a treatment modality, and not an educational placement or service delivery provision. According to the court, the intent of the stay put provision is to prevent school districts from unilaterally changing an education program. The student's IEP did not specify service providers or modalities and the elimination of hippotherapy was permissible because the district continued to provide him with occupational therapy addressing the same issues and did not fundamentally change a basic element of his program. There was no merit to the claim that the district had predetermined a reduction in the amount of occupational therapy. The district court had properly found that compensatory education is not a remedy for IDEA procedural violations. Since the proposed IEP was appropriate, the claim for compensatory education was properly dismissed. *Erickson v. Albuquerque Pub. Schools*, 199 F.3d 1116 (10th Cir. 1999).

◆ A student with autism attended a public school self-contained classroom. His IEP team determined that he should be institutionalized or placed in a homebound program after his behavior became severe and self-injurious. However, the student's parents unilaterally placed him in a private Kansas residential facility pending selection of a site by the school board. Because Louisiana law requires that local educational agencies apply to the state for approval of placements outside the agency's territory, **the school board requested the assistance of the state education department for locating an appropriate residential facility. The department declined the request**. The parents requested a due process hearing to obtain funding for the private placement. The school board asked the state to assume the placement costs and participate in the due process hearing. The state education department refused to participate in the due process hearing. The hearing officer held for the school board, finding that the IEP addressed primarily medical concerns and was not required for educational purposes. However, a state level review panel reversed this decision, finding the Kansas residential placement appropriate and assigning liability to the board. It held that the board was not precluded from obtaining reimbursement from the state for its costs.

The parents filed a federal district court action against the state and school board, seeking damages and attorney's fees. The action was stayed pending the board's appeal to federal court concerning liability for the residential placement. The parents moved the court for an order to preserve the Kansas placement. The board argued that the state should fund this placement under the stay put provision of the IDEA. The court agreed, ordering the state education department to pay for the student's placement and related services from the date of the review officer's decision. The state appealed to the Fifth Circuit. The court limited its review to questions of liability for the temporary placement and certain due process issues, refraining from an opinion on the appropriateness of the placement. It observed that **the IDEA does not limit a court's authority to award tuition reimbursement against a state or local educational agency. The district court had not erroneously allocated liability to the state** in this case, since there was no interagency agreement governing the dispute and the IDEA requires that states establish procedures to ensure IDEA compliance. The court noted the primary responsibility for ensuring local compliance with the IDEA rests with the state. The state had received notice and an opportunity to participate in the administrative proceedings, but had declined to do so and had suffered no due process violation. *St. Tammany Parish School Bd. v. State of Louisiana*, 142 F.3d 776 (5th Cir.1998).

◆ A twelve-year-old Florida student with autism attended school in a segregated exceptional education center operated by his public school district. Because of the progress he made there, he was placed in a special education program for students with autism at another district school. He then experienced serious behavioral problems, including 43 instances of aggressive behavior such as hitting, kicking, spitting, pulling hair and throwing objects. He improperly touched a female teacher and hit staff members on at least nine occasions. The district sought to return him to the exceptional education center and applied to a federal district court for an order waiving the requirement that it comply with the stay put provision for 45 days to allow transfer to a more restrictive environment. The court considered the application for temporary relief and noted substantial evidence presented by school board witnesses that the student's behavior was disruptive to the educational process and constituted a danger to himself and others. **Based upon this showing, and the absence of any threat to the student by not enforcing the stay put provision, the court granted the district's motion to prevent enforcement of the stay put provision for 45 days or the completion of administrative due process proceedings.** *School Bd. of Pinellas County, Florida v. J.M.*, 957 F.Supp. 1252 (M.D.Fla.1997).

◆ A New Jersey student with autism attended a public school preschool program for one year. At the beginning of the following school year, his parents unilaterally placed him at a private school and requested a due process hearing at which they sought reimbursement for the private placement. An administrative law judge conducted a hearing, but within two days, the parties reached an agreement under which **the board agreed to pay the student's private school costs for the rest of the school year and the parents agreed that the student should resume a public school program if 14 specific conditions were met.** A few days before the public school program was to resume, the parents complained that the board had failed to fulfill the settlement terms by failing to implement a transition plan for public school reentry. They again filed an administrative complaint in which they argued for the private school placement. They alleged that the private school placement was also the stay put placement pending further consideration. An administrative law judge agreed, and the board appealed to a federal district court.

The court agreed with the parents that the private school program they had selected was the student's stay put placement pending further proceedings. This was because **the board had agreed to a private placement pending the fulfillment of the 14 stipulated conditions. Accordingly, the board could not now challenge the placement because moving the student to a new program at a public school would not maintain the "status quo" of his educational placement.** The court granted summary judgment to the student. *Bayonne Bd. of Educ. v. R.S., by his parents K.S. and S.S.*, 954 F.Supp. 933 (D.N.J.1997).

◆ An Illinois student with autism was unable to care for himself or speak as he approached age 21. Shortly before his birthday, his parents requested a hearing under the IDEA to preserve his placement in a program for autistic students funded by his school district. **The complaint sought compensatory education in the form of continued placement in the program under the IDEA stay put provision,** pending the resolution of administrative proceedings. They claimed that the district had deprived the student of an appropriate placement prior to being placed in the program for autistic students. A hearing officer ordered the district to provide the student with six months of compensatory education, and the district appealed to the U.S. District Court for the Northern District of Illinois. Meanwhile, the court applied the IDEA stay put provision and ordered the school district to pay for the program for autistic students until after the student's twenty-third birthday. The district appealed to the U.S. Court of Appeals, Seventh Circuit. The court stated that while not specified in the IDEA, compensatory education was appropriate in certain cases, even where the student had attained the age of 21. However, **the stay put provision, which preserves a student's placement pending IDEA proceedings, was inapplicable to cases in which a student was beyond the age of statutory entitlement**. Otherwise, parents could file a claim for compensatory education just prior to the student's twenty-first birthday simply to preserve an educational placement. The order requiring the school district to preserve the student's placement was reversed. *Bd. of Educ. of Oak Park and River Forest High School Dist. 200 v. Illinois State Bd. of Educ.*, 79 F.3d 654 (7th Cir.1996).

◆ The parents of a Pennsylvania student with a learning disability rejected the IEP proposed by the student's school district as she prepared to enter ninth grade. **They withdrew her from public school and placed her in a private school** for students with learning disabilities. They then filed an administrative appeal of the school district's proposed placement which resulted in a decision for the district. The parents appealed to a state special education appeals panel, which reversed the decision, holding that the district had proposed an inadequate IEP and that the private school was the student's appropriate educational placement pending further proceedings. The U.S. Court of Appeals, Third Circuit, held that the IDEA stay put provision requires the preservation of the student's current educational placement pending the outcome of an appeal, unless the parents and the state or local education agency agree otherwise. **The appeals panel's decision had the effect of an agreement between the state and the parents to change the placement.** Because the stay put provision was clearly intended to benefit students with disabilities and their parents, it ought to be interpreted to relieve them of the financial burden of an appropriate private school placement during an appeal. The school district was required to pay for the private school placement during the review process and its obligation could not be deferred until the termination of proceedings. The court affirmed the district court order. *Susquenita School Dist. v. Raelee S.*, 96 F.3d 78 (3d Cir.1996).

IV. SUSPENSION AND EXPULSION

The suspension or expulsion of students with disabilities from school may be a change in placement for purposes of the IDEA under the U.S. Supreme Court's decision in Honig v. Doe, *484 U.S. 305, 108 S.Ct. 592, 98 L.Ed.2d 686 (1988). Indefinite suspensions violate the IDEA's stay put provision found at 20 U.S.C. § 1415(e)(3); however, suspensions for up to ten days do not constitute a change in placement. In recent years, courts have considered cases filed by regular education students who claim to have disabilities and seek the protection of the stay put provision to avoid a pending suspension or expulsion. The issue has been addressed in the IDEA Amendments of 1997 which provide that where a school district does not have knowledge that a child is a child with a disability, the child may be subjected to the same disciplinary measures as those applied to nondisabled children. The amendments also provide that a student may be removed from the classroom for up to 55 days if he or she is placed in an appropriate interim alternative educational setting. See 20 U.S.C. § 1415(k). This section is applicable to students who carry weapons to school or school functions, possess weapons at school or school functions, or possess or use illegal drugs (or sell or solicit the sale of a controlled substance) at school or a school function. Also, a hearing officer may order a change in placement where substantial evidence has shown that maintaining the student in his or her current placement is substantially likely to result in injury to the child or others.*

◆ *Honig v. Doe* involved two emotionally disturbed children in California who were given five-day suspensions from school for misbehavior that included destroying school property and assaulting and making sexual comments to other students. Pursuant to state law, **the suspensions were continued indefinitely during the pendency of expulsion proceedings**. The students sued the school district in federal court contesting the extended suspensions on the ground that they violated the IDEA's stay put provision, 20 U.S.C. § 1415(e)(3), which provides that a student must be kept in his or her "then current" educational placement during the pendency of proceedings which contemplate a change in placement. The district court issued an injunction preventing the expulsion of any disabled student for misbehavior resulting from the student's disability, and the school district appealed. The U.S. Court of Appeals, **Ninth Circuit, determined that the indefinite suspensions constituted a prohibited change in placement under the IDEA and that no dangerousness exception existed in the IDEA stay put provision**. It ruled that indefinite suspensions or expulsions of disabled children for misconduct arising out of their disabilities violated the IDEA. The court of appeals also ruled, however, that fixed suspensions of up to 30 school days did not constitute a change in placement. It determined that a state must provide services directly to a disabled child when a local school district fails to do so. The California Superintendent of Public Instruction petitioned the U.S. Supreme Court for review.

The Supreme Court declared that the purpose of the stay put provision was to prevent schools from changing a child's educational placement over his or her parents' objection until all review proceedings were completed. While the IDEA provided for interim placements where parents and school officials were able to agree on one, no emergency exception for dangerous students was included. **The Court concluded that where a disabled student poses an immediate threat to the safety of others, school officials may temporarily suspend him or her for up to ten school days**. The court held that this authority insured that school officials can: 1) protect the safety of others by removing dangerous students, 2) seek a review of the student's placement and try to persuade the student's parents to agree to an interim placement, and 3) seek court rulings to exclude students whose parents adamantly refuse to permit any change in placement. **School officials could seek such a court order without exhausting IDEA administrative remedies "only by showing that maintaining the child in his or her current placement is substantially likely to result in injury either to himself or herself, or to others."** The Court affirmed the court of appeals' decision that indefinite suspensions violated the IDEA's stay put provision. Suspensions up to ten days did not constitute a change in placement. The Court also upheld the court of appeals' decision that states could be required to provide services directly to disabled students where a local school district fails to do so. *Honig v. Doe*, 484 U.S. 305, 108 S.Ct. 592, 98 L.Ed.2d 686 (1988).

A. Generally

◆ **An eighth-grade student with a learning disability brought marijuana to school and was involved in selling it**. After admitting his misconduct, the student was immediately suspended for 10 days. The school board expelled him for the rest of the school year at a disciplinary hearing conducted just before the suspension expired. The day after the hearing, the district special education director attempted to schedule a manifestation review meeting. Although this meeting had to be held within 10 days of the expulsion decision, the district's attempts to schedule the meeting within the 10-day period were unsuccessful and the hearing was held 12 days after the expulsion decision. During the period between the expulsion decision and the manifestation review meeting, the parents requested a due process hearing, and the student received special education tutoring services for two hours per day. **At the manifestation review meeting, it was determined that the student's misconduct was not a manifestation of his learning disability**. The parents attended the meeting, but refused to participate. An IEP for the remainder of the student's expulsion was developed during the meeting that called for two hours of in-home, one-to-one instruction in core subjects and two hours of weekly specialized reading instruction. The parties were unable to agree on who would conduct a functional behavioral assessment. The following day, the parents requested a second due process hearing, challenging the manifestation review meeting. A state hearing officer found that the district did not need to hold the meeting prior to the expulsion decision and that the delay did not deny the student a FAPE. The hearing officer upheld the conclusion that the student's misconduct was not a manifestation of his disability. The new IEP was deemed to provide the student a FAPE, and was calculated to ensure that he progressed in the general curriculum, as required by the IDEA.

On appeal by the parents, a federal district court initially noted that Section 1415(k)(4)(A) requires a manifestation determination within 10 days of a change in placement, regardless of the nature of the disabled student's offense. The court examined the two-day delay that occurred in this case and determined that it did not result in any harm. **The delay had no effect on the parties' participation in the meeting, the result of the meeting, or the student's educational program**. In examining the substantive results of the manifestation meeting, the court rejected the parents' assertion that an undiagnosed impulsivity problem was the cause of the student's misconduct. The court noted that even if the student had an impulsivity problem, the manifestation review committee would have reached the same conclusion. The court examined **the IEP developed at the manifestation review meeting** and concluded that it did not deny the student a FAPE. It **allowed him to participate in and progress in the general curriculum during his expulsion**, as required by 20 U.S.C. § 1415(k)(3)(B).

Although the student was unable to participate in gym, art and computer classes during his expulsion, as he had under his pre-expulsion IEP, this did not violate the IDEA. These classes were not mandatory for graduation, and the student's inability to participate in them did not affect his progress in the general curriculum. In examining the parents' assertion that they did not receive adequate notice of the decision to change the student's placement prior to the board hearing, the court found any violation with respect to notice harmless. The failure to conduct a timely functional behavioral assessment was also characterized as harmless, as it had no bearing on the proceedings and decisions that were made about the student. The court determined the student was not entitled to remain in his pre-expulsion placement for the first 45 days of his expulsion while his parents appealed. The district had the right to suspend the student for 45 days under 20 U.S.C. § 1415(k)(1)(A)(ii), an IDEA provision governing the discipline of students with disabilities who bring drugs to school. The district followed all applicable procedural requirements, and the student's behavior was not a manifestation of his disability. Moreover, the IEP designed for the student during his expulsion was appropriate, and any error that occurred was harmless. For these reasons, the court upheld the hearing officer's decision. The district and parents were ordered to arrange for a functional behavioral assessment, with the stipulation that an outside consultant could be utilized. *Farrin v. Maine School Administrative District No. 59*, 165 F.Supp.2d 37 (D. Me. 2001).

♦ Three months after a new IEP was developed for a student with a history of starting fires and aggressive behavior, he started a fire in the school cafeteria, and school personnel notified the police. A delinquency petition was brought and the student was incarcerated. The parents filed a due process petition against the district, and an expedited hearing was held to consider whether the district's report caused a change in placement under the IDEA. The hearing officer concluded that the district's report to police did not violate the IDEA. He held that he had no authority to grant the parents' request to place their son in another educational setting, inasmuch as the student remained in a juvenile detention center. A state special education review panel did not disturb the hearing officer's decision and the parents appealed to a federal district court, seeking an order requiring the district to prepare an IEP offering their son a FAPE, plus compensatory services, reimbursement for an independent evaluation, and compensatory and punitive damages for IDEA violations under 42 U.S.C. § 1983.

The court noted that the Third Circuit has ordered all Pennsylvania school districts to work with the state education department to ensure that students with disabilities receive appropriate services, under an order resolving a class action suit. The order requires districts to notify the department if no appropriate placement is expected for a student within 30 days. In this case, the district did not notify the department of its failure to obtain a placement for the student for more than three months. The district thus violated the class action order. Since it also failed to provide the student with the services required by his IEP, it was liable to provide them for the two-month period representing the time it was first mandated to report a lack of placement through the date of his offense. **The district did not violate the IDEA by reporting the student to the police. Under 1997 IDEA amendments codified at 20 U.S.C § 1415(k)(9), nothing**

prohibits reporting a crime committed by a student with disabilities to appropriate authorities, and nothing prevents state law enforcement and judicial authorities from exercising their responsibilities. The IDEA requires that agencies reporting crimes committed by students with disabilities ensure that student records are transmitted to authorities for their consideration. The IDEA does not obligate school authorities to conduct a manifestation determination review before notifying authorities that a student with disabilities has committed a crime. The court rejected the district's argument that the claim for failing to provide the student with services required by his IEP was barred due to failure to exhaust administrative remedies. After reviewing the IDEA's legislative history, the court held that Congress intended that claims asserting failure to provide IEP services be exempt from the administrative exhaustion requirement. The court affirmed the special education review panel's decision concerning the district's action in the case. It issued an order that included a provision requiring the district to ensure that the student's name was redacted from court exhibits. *Joseph M. v. Southeast Delco School District*, No. 99-4645, 2001 WL 283154 (E.D. Pa. 2001).

◆ The New York City School Board of Education adopted a policy under which students were required to meet objective criteria for advancing to the next grade. Students not meeting promotional requirements received notices to attend a mandated 100-hour summer program. The system adopted a regulation governing the suspension of students with disabilities that afforded them a hearing when they faced suspension from the summer program. However, the regulation did not provide for a manifestation determination review, as required by the IDEA. **The students alleged that they had been disciplined without required special education procedural protections** and sued the school board in federal district court, seeking a preliminary order enjoining enforcement of the policy for the 2000 summer session.

The court noted that a status report on the summer program characterized it as an integral part of the board's promotional policy, completion of which was the critical factor. Some of the students named in the complaint had already been suspended under the policy and faced the risk of being denied completion of the summer program. **Despite the importance of the summer program, the policy did not provide for alternative instruction of suspended students nor did it attempt to determine whether the conduct giving rise to discipline was related to the student's underlying disability**. The court found that the board's failure to follow statutorily required procedures created a substantial likelihood of harm to the students. An erroneous suspension and exclusion of a student from school would result in his or her inability to be promoted to the next grade. The students demonstrated that they were likely to succeed on the merits of their claim, as the policy appeared to violate both the IDEA and board regulations. Two of the main violations involved parental notification in the case of disciplinary removals and the provision of a manifestation determination review to decide whether the behavior leading to discipline was a manifestation of the student's disability. The board's own regulations required compliance with the suspension procedures of the IDEA, as well as the right to an impartial hearing with the opportunity to confront witnesses and appeal adverse decisions. Certain procedural requirements of the board regulation were more stringent than those of the IDEA itself. The IDEA and its regulations state that the extensive disciplinary protections apply every school day that students are in attendance for instructional purposes. The summer program qualified under the regulatory definition. The court rejected the board's position that the IDEA did not apply to the summer program. For these reasons, the court granted the students' application for a temporary order enjoining the board from implementing the policy governing suspension of students during the 2000 summer session. *LIH ex rel. LH v. New York City Bd. of Educ.*, 103 F.Supp.2d 658 (E.D.N.Y. 2000).

◆ After a 15-year-old special needs student drew a picture of his school surrounded with explosives and the superintendent of schools with a gun to his head in response to a teacher's request that he draw a picture expressing his feelings about being excluded from class. The math teacher turned the drawing over to the school principal, and, two days later, the principal called the student to his office. The student explained that he was only doing an assignment and expressing his feelings. However, **the principal suspended him and later stated that he could return if he was "cleared" by a psychiatrist** and took medication. After the student missed two days of school, his father met with school personnel, who confirmed that the student could remain in school only if he received a psychological evaluation. The student attended classes for another week, but his father advised the principal that he was unable to get the requested evaluation. The principal stated that the student would not be permitted to stay in school. He called an emergency special education team meeting attended by the student and his father. The team determined that the student should be excluded from school for the remaining seven weeks of the school year because he presented a risk to himself and others. The principal notified the parents by letter that the student was excluded from school and that alternative special education services would be provided.

When the student's father inquired about alternative services, the principal responded only that he could arrange for home schooling. The parents obtained counsel and the district offered an alternative school placement. However, the family sued the school district in a federal district court for violations of state and federal law and violations of the U.S. Constitution under 42 U.S.C. § 1983. The action included claims for temporary and permanent injunctive relief and monetary damages. The court held that the student was entitled to IDEA protection since he was a special needs student under Massachusetts law. However, the IDEA and state law require that parties exhaust their available administrative remedies prior to filing a lawsuit. **The family would have to commence an administrative action prior to filing suit, even though it appeared that the district had denied the student his due process rights.** The student was entitled to an expedited hearing before the state bureau of special education appeals. Even students who are not covered under the IDEA must exhaust administrative remedies under the state administrative procedure act. The court denied the family's request for preliminary relief for this reason. *Demers v. Leominster School Department*, 96 F.Supp.2d 55 (D. Mass. 2000).

◆ School security officers found a high school student with a behavioral/emotional disorder in possession of marijuana and he admitted to possessing drugs at an expulsion hearing. **The school determined that the student's drug**

possession was unrelated to his disability, and ordered his expulsion for the rest of the semester. His parents pursued an administrative appeal under the IDEA to contest the school action. They asserted that the offense was related to the student's disabilities and that he was entitled to special education services pending the appeal. A hearing officer ordered the school to allow the student to return to school, pending the outcome of the proceedings, and the student did so after receiving 27 days of alternative, non-special education services during the period of his expulsion. At a later date, the hearing officer held that the student's offense was unrelated to his disabilities, and affirmed the one-semester expulsion. She also held, however, that the school was obligated to provide him with special education services during the expulsion. A level II hearing officer affirmed the decision and ruled that the school would have to provide the student with 27 days of compensatory services for the days it failed to provide them prior to the hearing officer's decision.

The school district appealed to a federal district court, asserting that it should not be required to provide the student with special education services during his expulsion. The parents counterclaimed for an award of attorneys' fees. The court denied the parents' request and awarded summary judgment to the district under *Doe v. Bd. of Educ. of Oak Park*, 115 F.3d 1273 (7th Cir. 1997). By the time the district court issued its opinion, the student was a senior in high school and the expulsion was never imposed. The school provided him with the compensatory services to which he was entitled and he graduated from high school. The parents appealed the district court decision to **the Seventh Circuit**, which **held that it had no jurisdiction to consider the case because of the student's graduation. It ruled that when a case becomes moot while on appeal, the appellate court has no power to hear the merits of the action**, since no action by the court can affect the rights of the parties. The court vacated the district court judgment and remanded the case for dismissal. It also declined to decide whether the parents were entitled to attorneys' fees for the district court action. The parents' claim for attorneys' fees in administrative proceedings was not moot. This claim was independent from the district court action, since it arose from the administrative decision staying the expulsion and imposing a stay-put order. In order to recover attorneys' fees in an IDEA action, parents must demonstrate that they have materially altered the legal relationship of the parties in their favor by bringing the action. The court found that while the parents obtained an emergency stay-put order requiring that the student remain in school until graduation, they were not prevailing parties entitled to attorneys' fees. They did not obtain an enforceable judgment against the school district and obtained only interim relief. The invocation of the IDEA stay-put provision does not entitle parties to an award of attorneys' fees and the court denied the parents' request. *Bd. of Educ. of Oak Park and River Forest High School Dist. 200 v. Nathan R.*, 199 F.3d 377 (7th Cir. 2000).

◆ **A Missouri student with behavior-related disabilities made a number of threats to students and school officials, including a specific threat to blow up the principal's car**. Although the student was characterized as having an explosive temper, he had only instigated one fight. The student's school district filed a lawsuit in the U.S. District Court for the Western District of Missouri, seeking relief from the stay put provision of the IDEA to allow a change in his placement pending an administrative hearing. The court conducted a three-day hearing, after which it determined that the risk of harm presented by the student's continued school attendance was minimal. Despite evidence of threats against other students and faculty members, there was little evidence that the student was more violent than other students his age or that he had the ability to carry out his threats. In denying the school district's motion for relief from the stay put provision, **the court commented that a risk of property damage alone was not enough to authorize injunctive relief. A danger to other students and faculty must not only be very likely, but "substantially" likely if it is to justify exclusion,** and the evidence in this case did not indicate a substantial likelihood of serious personal injury. Even though the risk of causing material physical injury presented by the student may have exceeded that of an average student his age, it would be speculative to anticipate that he would actually cause a serious injury. Because the district could not demonstrate a significant level of danger presented by the student's continued attendance at school, the court denied the requested relief. *Clinton County R-III School Dist. v. C.J.K.*, 896 F.Supp. 948 (W.D.Mo.1995).

B. Interim Placement

- During the seventh grade, a student with attention deficit hyperactivity disorder, pervasive development disorder and a history of aggression and violent outbursts wrote a story for a class about a student who gets revenge on his school, designed a computer game called "101 Ways to Destroy the School" and asked a classmate if he knew anyone who could get guns. After learning of the incident, the school suspended the student pending a manifestation determination committee/multidisciplinary committee (MDC) meeting. At the MDC meeting, various school officials expressed their concern for the possibility of danger to other students if the student continued to attend school. Although the mother presented evidence that the student's psychiatrist concluded that he was not a risk to harm himself or others, **the district concluded that he should not return to school because of his propensity for violence and the danger presented to others.** The team discussed alternative sites but because none were available, the mother suggested an "interim homebound placement." The school district agreed and promised weekly tutoring and social work therapy while searching for an alternative setting for grade eight. The team concluded that the student's conduct was related to his disability. At no time during the meeting was the student's IEP, IEP goals, related services or behavior plan changed. The parents then requested a hearing, which the school and hearing officer considered to be a non-IDEA suspension hearing, but the parents believed was an IDEA proceeding. The parents were never told that the hearing officer was not an authorized IDEA hearing officer. The hearing officer held that the interim placement should remain in effect. The parents subsequently requested an IDEA due process hearing because the district did not provide the specified amount of tutoring and social work therapy. Although the student received no academic, social or psychological assistance, he received good grades. The due process hearing was held, and a hearing officer awarded the parents their costs for counseling services, ruling that the student had been deprived of a FAPE in the LRE.

The school district appealed to a federal district court, which held that the district's numerous procedural errors resulted in the denial of a FAPE. The notice for the MDC hearing did not indicate to the parents that the district was considering a change in placement, stating only that there would be a determination of whether the student's behavior was related to his disability. The district deprived the family of any meaningful opportunity to participate in the MDC. As the IHO found, the district was bound to address the student's behavior after determining that his conduct was related to his disability. Such a finding requires an IEP team to change the IEP, discuss ways to address behavioral problems, or consider what in-school remedies or services could address the behavior. The district instead removed the student from school without considering realistic alternatives. The district apparently intended only to remove him from school under the 45-day period specified under IDEA regulations for weapon and drug violations. It acknowledged the error in making such a removal and was limited to making an interim placement of 10 days or less. **The district violated the IDEA by offering an interim homebound setting without first seeking the expedited due process hearing procedure under 20 U.S.C. § 1415(k) for students posing a threat to themselves or others**. Had it done so, an IHO would have considered the appropriateness of the student's placement and other relevant factors, such as the LRE available for him. The district provided a non-IDEA suspension hearing over which the hearing officer had no true authority. According to the court, the district was more concerned with removing the student from school than complying with the IDEA. The IHO properly found that the defective notices and failure to propose a range of placements forced the family into accepting the homebound placement and denied the student a FAPE. There was no merit to the district's argument that the student was not entitled to relief because he passed his classes. The homebound program was not designed to meet his unique needs and was calculated to remove him from school. The parents were entitled to reimbursement for their counseling expenses and attorneys' fees. *Community Consolidated School District No. 93 v. John F.*, No. 00 CV 1347 (N.D. Ill. 2000).

◆ A student with emotional and learning disabilities and a history of behavioral problems was disciplined numerous times for fighting, disobedience, profanity and other misconduct. He slashed another student in the face with a box cutter while on a school bus, and was placed in juvenile detention and suspended from school. A school staffing committee conducted a manifestation hearing and determined that the bus incident was not a manifestation of his disability, finding that the student had "planned and brought the weapon" on the bus. At the same meeting, **the school principal recommended expulsion for the rest of the school year and the following year, which was permissible discipline in view of the committee's finding that the student's conduct was not a manifestation of his disability**. However, the committee instead placed the student in a temporary homebound program pending a second meeting. At the second meeting, **the committee released the student from the homebound program and placed him in an alternative school**. He was then sentenced to an adolescent residential center under a juvenile court order for aggravated battery with a deadly weapon as a result of the slashing incident. During the intervening summer, the school committee again met and discussed placement. The committee decided to resume the alternative school placement, but scheduled a second meeting at which the student's parent sought to return the student to the high school so that he could play football. The staff responded that the student was expelled and had to remain at the alternative school. The parent then requested a due process hearing. Prior to the hearing, the parties settled some disputed matters, but the parent renewed her request within a few weeks. An administrative law judge held that the alternative school placement provided the student with FAPE and was his stay put placement pending the proceedings.

The parent appealed to the U.S. District Court for the Middle District of Florida, which found that the district provided the student with FAPE. **The alternative school furnished a basic floor of opportunity for the student and was the least restrictive environment in view of his history of aggressive behavior and violence.** While the student's behavior had improved at the alternative school and there was evidence that it had improved further under his juvenile justice program, there was evidence that he would still present a danger to himself or others in a regular school setting. There was no merit to the parent's assertion that the district had committed IDEA procedural violations during the manifestation hearing. The district had not denied the parent the opportunity to participate in relevant meetings and had duly provided adequate notice to the family of relevant meetings and decisions. The district was entitled to summary judgment. The court also dismissed civil rights claims arising under 42 U.S.C. § 1983 against the school principal and special education director in their individual capacities because they had not deprived the student of any federal rights. The student was never expelled and was allowed to attend school throughout the proceedings. There was also no deprivation of rights as a result of the special education director's statements, which were only generalized comments about the unwieldy nature of due process hearings. The administrators were entitled to qualified immunity and the court awarded them summary judgment. *Parent v. Osceola County School Bd.*, 59 F.Supp.2d 1243 (M.D.Fla.1999).

◆ A 15-year-old Arizona student with emotionally disabling conditions brought a knife to school in violation of state law and school district policy. **His immediate short-term suspension was extended to a 175-day expulsion following a meeting of school officials who determined that his misconduct was unrelated to his disabling condition**. The district maintained a written policy that educational services for students with disabilities could be discontinued entirely during a long-term suspension or expulsion for conduct unrelated to the disability. The student claimed that the district violated the IDEA when it failed to consider providing him with alternative educational services. The student's father requested an IEP meeting, which was held, but which resulted in no alternative educational placement. The student was placed in the juvenile court system with no educational services after his conviction on state weapons charges. The student and his father filed a federal district court action against the school district, seeking a declaration that the long-term suspension and expulsion order violated the IDEA. The court considered cross-motions for summary judgment advanced by the parties, and as a preliminary matter rejected the district's argument that it was no longer his home district since the juvenile placement was outside its territory.

The court rejected the district's assertion that it need not provide IDEA procedural protections or educational services for a student with a disability expelled for misconduct unrelated to the disabling condition. **The court held that since the expulsion of a student with disabilities constitutes a change in placement for IDEA purposes, the district had violated the IDEA stay put provision and was presently violating the IDEA by refusing to provide educational services.** Because the district continued to violate the IDEA, the court left open the possibility of an award of compensatory services and ordered the school to ensure that the student received appropriate services within ten days. It ordered the district to refrain from discontinuing educational services for students with disabilities during long-term suspensions or expulsions and granted the student's summary judgment motion. *Magyar v. Tucson Unif. School Dist.*, 958 F.Supp. 1423 (D.Ariz.1997).

◆ A Missouri student with multiple mental disabilities exhibited aggressive behavior towards students and teachers. She was placed in a public school's self-contained classroom for students with mental disabilities and provided with two-on-one staffing at all times. She was also enrolled in several regular classrooms. Despite this placement, her aggressive behavior continued to the point that daily lesson plans were not completed and the parents of other students complained of the negative effect on their children. The student's IEP team reevaluated the placement. The student's art teacher recommended removal from art class because of her consistently disruptive behavior. The parents objected to any change in placement and requested the imposition of the IDEA's stay put provision during the course of administrative proceedings. Shortly thereafter, the student hit another student on the head three times during art class. The school imposed a ten-day suspension, and the parents filed a lawsuit seeking to set it aside in the U.S. District Court for the Eastern District of Missouri. **The school district filed a counterclaim to remove the student from school during the revision of the IEP, based on the student's aggressive behavior and the substantial risk of injury** she presented to herself and others. The court granted the district's motion for an order allowing it to remove the student from school. The parents appealed to the U.S. Court of Appeals, Eighth Circuit.

On appeal, the parents argued that the district court should have inquired into whether the student was truly dangerous, based upon her capacity to inflict injury. The court disagreed, determining that it was only necessary to determine whether a student with a disability posed a substantial risk of injury to herself or others. **There was substantial evidence in the record of a likelihood of injury based on almost daily episodes of aggressive behavior by the student**. Accordingly, removal of the student had been proper and temporary placement at a segregated facility for students with disabilities was appropriate. The interim placement proposed by the school district was appropriate during the administrative review process. The court affirmed the lower court's decision for the school district. *Light v. Parkway C-2 School Dist.*, 41 F.3d 1223 (8th Cir.1994).

◆ A 15-year-old Washington student with Tourette's syndrome and attention deficit hyperactivity disorder became increasingly uncontrollable and frequently disrupted classes with name-calling, profanity, explicit sexual comments, kicking and hitting. The school ultimately expelled him under an emergency order after he assaulted a staff member. **The student's parents agreed with the school's determination that he should be placed in a self-contained program off the school campus** for individualized attention and a structured environment. **The parents soon changed their minds** and requested a due process hearing to contest the interim placement and demand a new IEP. The parties were unable to agree upon a new IEP, and the parents insisted that the student return to regular classes for the rest of the school year. A 10-day due process hearing was held during the summer break, resulting in a determination that the school had complied with the IDEA. The parents appealed to the U.S. District Court for the Western District of Washington, which affirmed the administrative decision. The parents appealed to the U.S. Court of Appeals, Ninth Circuit.

The court rejected the parents' argument that the school district's hiring of an aide to observe the student's behavior triggered IDEA procedural protections. The court also rejected the parents' allegation that the school had violated IDEA procedural requirements by failing to propose a new IEP before putting him in the interim placement. **The court reasoned that because the parents had initially agreed with the interim placement, it could be implemented without a current IEP and could be considered the student's stay put placement for IDEA purposes.** The court also held that the school district had complied with substantive requirements of the IDEA by placing the student in the interim placement that constituted the least restrictive environment in which he could receive educational benefits. The record contained overwhelming evidence that the student's presence in regular classrooms was disruptive and created a danger to other students. The court of appeals affirmed the district court judgment. *Clyde K. v. Puyallup School Dist. No. 3*, 35 F.3d 1396 (9th Cir.1994).

C. Regular Education Students

Section 1415 (k)(8) of the 1997 IDEA Amendments addresses the issue of regular education students seeking IDEA protections in disciplinary cases. A student who has not been determined to be eligible for special education and related services under the IDEA may assert the act's procedural protections if the LEA has knowledge that the student was a child with a disability prior to the misconduct giving rise to discipline. In order to impute such knowledge to an LEA, the parents must have requested an evaluation or have presented written concerns of the student's special education needs, a teacher or other staff member of the LEA must have expressed concern about the student's behavior or performance to an appropriate person, or the student's behavior or performance must demonstrate the need for special education services.

◆ An Alabama student was of normal intelligence but experienced academic and behavioral difficulties at times. His foster parent initially resisted any attempt to place him in special education classes, objecting to a teacher's request for an evaluation. School administrators recommended a voluntary behavior management plan. After a number of disciplinary referrals, the school district transferred him to an alternative school for 45 days as an interim measure to avoid expulsion. The foster parent then asked the district to evaluate the student for special education. Five teachers and the parent completed surveys designed to identify an emotional disturbance. The surveys of the parent and two of the teachers yielded clinically significant results, but those of the other teachers suggested no disturbance. **A hearing officer found** the data supplied by the parent to be incredible, based on bias and possible lack of sincerity, and held that **the student did not qualify for special education as emotionally disturbed**.

The student appealed to a federal district court, where he argued that the survey results should have automatically entitled him to special education. The school district countered that his misconduct was inconsistent with any recognized disorder and that the survey results were unreliable. The court stated that Alabama law defined "emotional disturbance" as "a disability characterized by behavioral or emotional responses so different from appropriate age, cultural, environmental or ethnic norms that the educational performance is adversely affected." In addition, the disturbance must be consistently exhibited in an educational environment for a longer time period, to a marked degree, with an adverse affect on educational performance. The court held that the hearing officer had properly discounted the value of the surveys rating the student's emotional disturbance as clinically significant. Only two of the five teacher surveys indicated emotional disturbance, and the parent's survey was clouded by bias. **The parent had changed his position on special education once it was clear that his son could avoid severe discipline by obtaining classification under a special education category**. Multiple experienced educators testified that the student often acted appropriately. The evidence indicated that the student was not emotionally disturbed under state and federal law and the parent could not force the school district to provide the accommodations he requested. The court awarded summary judgment to the district. *Maricus W. v Lanett City Board of Education*, 142 F.Supp.2d 1327 (M.D. Ala. 2001).

◆ Although a student struggled academically and had repeated fourth grade, he was not identified as a student with disabilities. His parents believed that he had an attention deficit disorder. During his sixth-grade year, the student brought a miniature Swiss army knife to school. He also admitted to possessing a homemade knife. The school held a disciplinary hearing that resulted in a recommendation of expulsion for one year, but suspended most of the punishment. **The school board overruled the recommendation and approved the student's suspension for a full calendar year** under its zero-tolerance policy. The student appealed to a federal district court, claiming that the district should have identified him as having disabilities, and that it violated his procedural rights under the IDEA. He sought preliminary relief from the court preventing the expulsion, asserting that the use of the zero-tolerance policy violated his constitutional rights to due process.

The court rejected the student's claims regarding violation of IDEA procedural protections. The 1997 IDEA amendments require the imposition of the act's stay put provision where a school district intends to discipline a student not currently receiving education or services under the IDEA when the district knows or should know of a student's genuine disability. However, there must also be a showing that the misconduct giving rise to discipline is related to the alleged disability. In this case, **the student failed to show that he was a child with a disability as defined by the IDEA**. He presented only lay witnesses, who could not prove that he had an attention deficit disorder. There was no allegation that these conditions related to the bringing of knives to school. The stay put provision is irrelevant unless the behavior causing the misconduct is related to the student's disability. The court held that the district should formally test the student to determine whether he had a learning disability, if and when he was reinstated to school in light of his history of academic difficulty. It found that the school board did not make an independent evaluation of the case when it considered the recommendation proposed by the hearing officer. Instead, it had deferred to the blanket expulsion policy in a manner that deprived the student of his constitutional due process rights. Where expulsion is threatened, a school board must provide a student with a high degree of due process protection. The court held that the school board clearly had the authority to expel students, but could only do so upon independent consideration of the relevant facts and circumstances of a case. The board was also required to devise individualized punishment by reference to the relevant facts and circumstances. Because the board in this case had "blindly meted out the student's punishment," the court remanded the case to the board for reconsideration. If the board reinstated the student to school, it would be required to administer testing to determine if he was a child with a disability under the IDEA. *Colvin v. Lowndes County School District*, 114 F.Supp.2d 504 (N.D. Miss. 2000).

◆ After a Texas school district disciplined a student for several incidents of misconduct, his parents prepared to transfer him to a private school and commenced an administrative claim against the school district requesting expunction of the discipline from the student's records, reimbursement for evaluation costs and private school tuition reimbursement. **The parents claimed the student was eligible for special education, based on a disability, and that the district had failed to evaluate the student prior to disciplining him**. The hearing officer held for the parents, ruling that the student was entitled to IDEA procedural protections that made his alternative placement inappropriate. The district brought a federal district court counterclaim to challenge the administrative findings when the family asserted claims for monetary damages.

The court held that the district was not obligated to perform a special education evaluation of the student prior to the disciplinary hearing. The student was not enrolled in any special education classes and no party had previously requested an evaluation. **The court recited language from the IDEA providing that students may be subject to the same discipline as applied to students without disabilities in the absence of knowledge that a child is disabled. The district had no knowledge that the student had a disability when it disciplined him**. The court rejected the assertion that assignment to an alternative placement for more than 10 days violated the IDEA. The district did not become aware of any need to evaluate the student for special education services until after his disruptive behavior occurred, and this part of the administrative decision was erroneous. The court issued an order remanding the case to the hearing officer for a determination of whether the district violated the IDEA by failing to evaluate or provide him with special education, but otherwise granted summary judgment to the district and denied summary judgment to the parents. *James C. v. Eanes Indep. School Dist.*, No. A-97-CA-745 JN (W.D.Tex.1999).

◆ A sixth grade student attending regular education classes at a private school in Puerto Rico was indefinitely suspended for serious disciplinary violations. He frequently disrupted classes, used obscenities, fought with other students and walked out of classes. Following the suspension, the student was diagnosed with oppositional defiant disorder, childhood depression and attention deficit hyperactivity disorder. The family filed a federal district court action against the school for violations of the Americans with Disabilities Act (ADA) and the Rehabilitation Act. The school moved to dismiss the case and to compel arbitration based on an arbitration agreement contained in the school's contract with the family. The court denied the motion and granted a preliminary order which required the school to readmit the student. The student's disruptive behavior continued when he returned to school, and school officials refused to reenroll him for the seventh grade. The family brought a contempt motion which the district court denied. However, **the court extended the preliminary injunction to require the school to enroll the student in seventh grade and alter its disciplinary code with respect to the student.**

The school appealed to the U.S. Court of Appeals, First Circuit, where it argued that the district court had improperly suspended the arbitration agreement based upon a perceived conflict between the agreement and rights created by the ADA. The court agreed with the school, observing that enforcement of the arbitration agreement was consistent with the ADA and other civil rights statutes. The court also agreed with the school that the district court had erroneously ordered the student's reinstatement. **The ADA does not require educational institutions to fundamentally alter their programs. In this case, the school was not required to suspend the application of its disciplinary code to accommodate the student**. Since the ADA did not require the school to fundamentally modify its program, and there was significant evidence that the student did not conform his behavior to the code, the district court should have vacated the preliminary injunction. The court remanded the case to the district court. *Bercovitch v. Baldwin School, Inc.*, 133 F.3d 141 (1st Cir.1998).

◆ Maryland school officials questioned a high school student enrolled in a regular education course of study about her possible possession of controlled substances on school grounds. **After signing a written admission that she had brought LSD onto school grounds, she was expelled by the school superintendent**. A school board panel voted to affirm the decision following a hearing and the student appealed to the state board of education. The state board summarily affirmed the local board's decision, and the student appealed to a Maryland circuit court, arguing that the admission had been coerced and that the school district had failed to first assess her special education needs before taking disciplinary action. The court affirmed the expulsion order, and the student appealed to the Court of Special Appeals of Maryland.

The court of special appeals rejected the student's assertion that the district was required to perform a special education evaluation prior to taking disciplinary action against her because it possessed evidence that she had attention deficit hyperactivity disorder. **The procedural safeguards of state special education law applied only to students who were unable to achieve their educational potential in general education programs. A parental request for a special**

education evaluation did not bring regular disciplinary proceedings to a halt. The court also rejected the student's claim that her oral admission had been coerced. She had ratified the admission in writing and again at her hearing where she was represented by an attorney. The court affirmed the expulsion order. *Miller v. Bd. of Educ. of Caroline County*, 114 Md.App. 462, 690 A.2d 557 (Md. Ct. Spec. App. 1997).

◆ An Indiana fourth grader with diabetes attended a public school as a regular education student. Although the district was aware of her diabetic condition, she was not identified as a student with a disability and did not receive special education services. Her blood sugar tested at a low level on a morning that she went on a class field trip. Her teacher suggested that she eat some fruit, and after doing so her blood sugar rose to a level identified by her doctor as unlikely to cause unusual behavior. However, on the return trip to school, **she used a nail file instrument containing a small knife blade to threaten two students** who had been harassing her during the bus ride. The school's principal suspended the student for five days for knowingly possessing or handling a knife during a school activity. A hearing examiner recommended a six-week expulsion for violating the state code, which prohibited any knowing possession or handling of a weapon at school. The hearing officer was not notified of the student's diabetic condition. The student's parents appealed to the school board, and presented evidence that her actions had been caused by her diabetes. **The board upheld the expulsion and found that the evidence did not support the argument that the student's behavior was affected by low blood sugar levels**. The parents filed a lawsuit against the school district in an Indiana superior court, and the district removed the action to a federal district court.

The court agreed with the district that the IDEA and related § 504 claims were barred by the family failing to first request an administrative hearing. There was no merit to the family's assertion that participation in the expulsion hearing satisfied the IDEA's administrative exhaustion requirement. **The court held that the board had not acted arbitrarily or capriciously by expelling the student without finding that her behavior was causally related to her disability**. The district was not obligated to make this finding since she had not been identified as disabled. The expulsion decision had not been based solely upon the student's aggressive behavior; it was also based on a violation of the state code prohibiting possession of a knife at a school activity. The court granted the district's dismissal motion. *Brown v. Metropolitan School Dist. of Lawrence Township*, 945 F.Supp. 1202 (S.D.Ind.1996).

◆ A 15-year-old African-American student was attacked by a group of white students at a Massachusetts high school. When school administrators intervened, the student remained upset and repeatedly assaulted teachers who were trying to restrain him. The school indefinitely suspended the student pending expulsion. **Although the student was not then identified as a student with disabilities, his parents requested an evaluation and asserted that the IDEA stay put provision prohibited suspension or expulsion pending completion of review proceedings**. School district officials evaluated the student and determined that he was entitled to IDEA services and should receive limited home tutoring. The parties disputed his appropriate placement, and the parents filed a lawsuit against the district in the U.S. District Court for the District of Massachusetts, seeking an order that would reinstate the student to school. The court observed that **because the student's academic record included repeating a grade, the district had been on notice prior to the fight that he should have been referred for a special education evaluation**. Because a referral should have been made prior to the incident, the student was entitled to an order under the IDEA stay put provision requiring his return to school. However, the court noted that the parents had unilaterally placed the student in a private parochial school after the disciplinary action and that the order it had prepared was now moot. When the private school placement did not work out, the court denied a motion by the parents to reopen proceedings. The parents would have to refile an IDEA complaint in order to obtain relief. *Richard V. by Marcel V. v. City of Medford*, 924 F.Supp. 320 (D.Mass.1996).

CHAPTER THREE

IDEA Procedural Safeguards

I. DUE PROCESS HEARINGS

The procedural safeguards of the IDEA provide the means for students with disabilities and their parents to enforce their rights under the Act. The safeguards include the right to an "impartial due process hearing" under 20 U.S.C. § 1415(f) when parents or guardians are dissatisfied with any matter relating to the identification, evaluation, or educational placement of the child, or the provision of a free appropriate public education to the child. The state or local educational agency responsible for providing services conducts the hearing with the assistance of an impartial hearing officer. The initial due process hearing may be provided at the state or local educational agency level. If held at the local level, either party may appeal to the state educational agency, which shall conduct an impartial review of such hearing. See 20 U.S.C. § 1415(g). Unless appealed, the initial hearing officer's decision becomes final. Likewise, the state officer's decision becomes final unless a party brings a challenge in state or federal district court. See 20 U.S.C. § 1415(i)(2).

A. Generally

◆ When a school district and the parents of a gifted student were unable to agree on his IEP for the 2000-2001 school year, the parents requested a due process hearing. The hearing officer ordered the parties to develop a new IEP, and required the district to give the student certain credits toward graduation. At the resulting IEP meeting, the district proposed an IEP calling for the student's graduation in 2002, with an agreement that if he completed the 28.5 credits he needed for graduation, he would graduate a semester early. The parents requested a due process hearing, challenging the district's decision that the student would graduate in 2002. A hearing officer upheld the district's IEP and the 2002 graduation date and the parents appealed. A special education due process appeals panel reversed the decision, finding that the IEP contained both substantive and procedural errors. The panel ordered the student classified as a member of the 2000-2001 class, provided he completed the required number of credits. **The school district was ordered to provide certain personnel involved in the student's education with 10 hours of special education in-service education,** and to hire an outside expert to help develop an appropriate IEP.

The district appealed various aspects of the panel's decision to the Pennsylvania Commonwealth Court. Initially, the court determined that although the student had graduated, the dispute was not moot, as it presented the court with an issue "capable of repetition yet evading review,"- the scope of relief a special education appeals panel can award. **Although appeals panels have the authority to order remedies such as compensatory education, the court held the appeals panel was not authorized under Pennsylvania law to order the type of special education in-service it ordered**. No provision of Pennsylvania law indicated that a special education appeals panel preempted the school district's statutory authority over employee professional development, or that the panel could not order this type of remedy. The court found that the consequence of allowing an appeals panel to order this type of relief would interfere with the district's authority under state law to develop of professional education programs employees, drain district resources, and circumvent the provisions of state law allowing for local and community input into the development of a district professional education plan. Since the panel lacked the authority to order district personnel to participate in an in-service session, this part of the panel's decision was reversed. Under applicable Pennsylvania special education regulations, the composition of the IEP team is the school district's responsibility. Because the inclusion of an outside expert was not a statutory requirement for the composition of an IEP team, the panel lacked the authority to order the inclusion of an outside expert on the student's IEP team. In examining the district's contention that the panel overstepped its authority by ordering the district to allow the student to graduate before he earned the statutorily established minimum number of credits toward graduation, the court determined that the student was obligated to earn 28.5 credits, since this was the graduation requirement when he started high school. The panel's order allowing his graduation without the required number of credits may have been an attempt to cure the district's failure to provide an appropriate learning environment, but had no bearing on the fact that the student was required to earn 28.5 credits to graduate. The court reversed the appeals panel's order. *Saucon Valley School District v. Robert O. et al.*, 785 A.2d 1069 (Pa. Commw. Ct. 2001).

◆ According to the divorce decree applicable to the parents of a student with dyslexia, the student's mother had custody of him, along with the ability to make educational decisions. The student's father requested a due process hearing, challenging the tutoring services the student was receiving under his educational plan. An administrative hearing officer dismissed the father's request, and the father appealed to a federal district court. The district court also dismissed the father's suit, finding that **as a non-custodial parent, the father could not bring an IDEA suit challenging his child's educational plan**. Further, the district court found that the provision of the divorce decree that stated the mother had the ability to make educational decisions also precluded the father's suit because he lacked standing.

On appeal, the Seventh Circuit initially determined that the father could not bring a claim on behalf of the student without hiring a lawyer. Because the father filed suit without the assistance of a lawyer, only his individual claims, not those he brought on behalf of the student, were allowed to proceed. Next, the court rejected the school district's assertion that the father's claim should be dismissed for failing to pursue an administrative appeal of the hearing officer's decision, finding that Illinois had eliminated this requirement. In examining the merits of the case, the circuit court concluded that **the divorce decree did not eliminate all of the father's rights regarding the student's education**. Under the terms of the decree, the father was allowed to be informed about and involved in his child's education. The court noted that if the parents disagreed about educational decisions, in most circumstances, the mother's view would prevail under the decree. Since the father was challenging the student's educational plan, and the divorce decree did not appear to bar this type of challenge, the district court erred when it dismissed father's claim for lack of standing without examining the language of the decree. The case was remanded to the district court for examination of the father's claims, a determination of the status of his claims under the divorce decree and resolution of any claims that were not contrary to the mother's exercise of her rights under the decree. *Navin v. Park Ridge School District 64*, 270 F.3d 1147 (7th Cir. 2001).

◆ The mother of a Florida student claimed that the district failed to provide or implement an appropriate IEP for her child, who had mental and physical disabilities. She commenced an administrative action against the school board that was resolved through a settlement agreement prior to a final hearing. The board agreed to place the student in a particular school and provide her with transportation for a four-month period in 1999. It also agreed to pay up to $17,000 for attorneys' fees to the family in return for their waiver of any further claims in a formal administrative proceeding. During the four-month period, the student's mother claimed that the board breached the agreement by failing to provide the student with agreed-upon services. She commenced a new due process action against the board, which was dismissed in view of the settlement agreement. The Florida Second District Court of Appeal affirmed the decision, and **the mother filed a new administrative action against the board, seeking rescission of the settlement agreement and damages** for breaching it.

The hearing officer held that he was without jurisdiction to consider the case, which sought only to enforce, interpret or rescind the prior settlement agreement and did not relate to the student's present educational placement. The board appealed to the district court of appeal, seeking to dismiss the action. **The court held that the hearing officer had correctly found himself without jurisdiction to consider the case**. The agreement pertained to a specific time period for which services had allegedly been withheld from the student. It was not the typical special-education dispute in which a family sought to ensure an appropriate placement. **There was no current claim that the student's IEP was improper or needed to be changed**. Issues such as breach of contract, rescission and attorneys' fees were properly before a state circuit court, and the court affirmed the administrative order. *School Board of Lee County v. M.C.*, 796 So.2d 581 (Fla. Dist. Ct. App., 2d Dist. 2001).

♦ The parents of student with disabilities filed a due process complaint against their school district to determine whether it would continue providing him with reading and comprehension tutoring services in the auditory discrimination in depth/visualize-verbalize method. The parties reached a settlement agreement during the administrative proceedings. The following year, the parents initiated a due process proceeding with the California Special Education Hearing Office, primarily asserting that the district failed to comply with the parties' settlement agreement from the prior administrative action. **The hearing officer held that he lacked jurisdiction to hear any issue related to the previous hearing order,** since due process orders are considered final under the state education code. Compliance with SEHO orders was an issue for the state education department's compliance office, and the hearing officer dismissed the case. The parents then filed a federal district court action against the school district, arguing that the SEHO had jurisdiction to hear compliance issues related to previous due process proceedings.

The district court affirmed the hearing officer's order, and the parents appealed to the U.S. Court of Appeals for the Ninth Circuit. On appeal, the parents asserted that the SEHO had jurisdiction over several of their claims because they related to the settlement agreement. The circuit court disagreed, holding that the SEHO hearing officer lacked jurisdiction to hear issues arising from a final hearing order. The California Education Code states that a special education due process hearing is the final determination in a special education dispute and is binding on all parties. Once a decision is rendered by the SEHO, it becomes final and is not subject to further review on the same issue. In this case, the hearing officer had properly found that the prior order dismissing the case was final. The initial SEHO decision was a final administrative action and **the appropriate recourse for the parents to address alleged noncompliance by the school district was an action before the state education department's compliance office**. *Wyner v. Manhattan Beach Unif. School Dist.*, 223 F.3d 1026 (9th Cir. 2000), *cert. denied*, 122 S.Ct. 1091 (U.S. 2002).

♦ **The Delaware Office of Disciplinary Counsel petitioned the state board on the Unauthorized Practice of Law for a ruling that a New Jersey non-profit advocacy center was engaging in the unauthorized practice of law by attempting to represent students during Delaware special education due process proceedings**. The board agreed with the ODC, and the center appealed to the state supreme court, asserting that the IDEA authorized it to argue on behalf of students with disabilities in state due process hearings, and that Delaware was the only state in the United States that did not permit lay advocates to do so. Its petition was supported by the U.S. Department of Justice, which asserted that the board had erroneously failed to recognize the center's asserted right under the IDEA to represent families of students with disabilities.

The court observed that hearings were conducted by three-person panels that included a lay person with a demonstrated interest in the education of students with disabilities, a certified educator or post-secondary educator of students with disabilities, and an attorney licensed to practice law in Delaware. Hearings were relatively informal, but parties presented evidence through witnesses and cross-examined adverse witnesses. Parties also made closing statements and were sometimes asked to file written submissions. While each of the parties argued that the language of the IDEA clearly supported its position, **the court found that the IDEA was ambiguous, apparently conferring joint authority upon attorneys and non-lawyers to accompany and advise parents at IDEA due process hearings**. The court concluded that the IDEA contains sufficient procedural protections for students with disabilities to guard against the constitutional problems identified by the center and the Department of Justice. The record did not support the assertion that children and parents would be denied "the only assistance available to them" if the center did not argue on their behalf. Legal counsel was available for such students and their families. Delaware had the exclusive authority to regulate the practice of law in the state and to exclude non-attorneys from adversarial hearings such as state due process hearings. The court affirmed the decision of the board, ruling that the IDEA contains no clear language granting the right to lay representation. *In the Matter of Arons*, 756 A.2d 867 (Del. 2000), *cert. denied,* 532 U.S. 1065 (2001).

◆ A Maine school committee and the parents of a student with disabilities went to due process over the parents' decision to unilaterally place the student in a private school. The hearing officer ordered the school committee to reimburse the parents for their tuition costs. Shortly after the hearing concluded, the committee learned the hearing officer had a disabled student who attended private school, and attempted to find out more information about the hearing officer's child and the hearing officer's communications with the parents. Meanwhile, the committee requested a new hearing to consider the family's failure to cooperate with requested evaluations of the student. The same hearing officer was appointed to preside at the hearing, and the committee requested she recuse herself. She declined to recuse herself, and **the school committee appealed her original decision on the grounds that she had a disqualifying personal interest and was biased**. The committee filed a motion asking the court to permit further discovery on the issue.

The court observed that Maine special education regulations permit the challenge of a hearing officer only on the grounds of conflict of interest or bias. The appearance of impartiality alone was insufficient to disqualify a hearing officer. **The fact that the hearing officer had a child with moderate hearing loss in private schools did not indicate any conflict of interest, bias, hostility or prejudgment** against the school committee. The alleged conversations with the parents had been about the hearing officer's son, not the student whose case was being considered. The court disallowed the school committee's request to make further fact finding. The time for development of the record had been during the pre-hearing conference and there was no need to make more intrusive inquiries. The court denied the committee's request for relief and ordered the parties to confer on the status of the case. *Falmouth School Committee v. B.*, 106 F.Supp.2d 69 (D. Me. 2000).

◆ After a school district decided to transfer a deaf student with cochlear implants from his neighborhood school to another school, his parents requested a due process hearing. The first hearing officer recused himself, stating that he was prejudiced in favor of the school board and could not be completely fair in any final decision. Another hearing officer was then appointed to hear the case. She held that although the student was receiving appropriate aids and services in his neighborhood school, the school board had absolute discretion to determine what school he should attend. The parents appealed to a state level appellate panel. Inexplicably, **the hearing officer who had recused himself from hearing the case originally was appointed to the hearing panel.**

The panel affirmed the hearing officer's decision, and the parents appealed to the U.S. District Court for the Middle District of Louisiana, asserting that the recused hearing officer's presence on the review panel denied them the opportunity for a fair hearing. **The court agreed with the parents that the procedural irregularities they identified resulted in the denial of due process at the review panel level**. The student was entitled to another hearing to insure compliance with state special education regulations and constitutional principles of fairness. The court held that the parties should themselves determine whether the new hearing should commence at the hearing officer or administrative review level. This determination would depend on whether the facts in the case had changed from the time of the original hearing. The court's order excluded any hearing officer or panel member who had previously considered the case from serving as a member on a new panel or as a hearing officer. *Veazey v. Ascension Parish School Board*, 109 F.Supp.2d 482 (M.D. La. 2000).

◆ The parents of a student with language, learning and auditory processing disabilities sought public funding of a private school placement and filed an administrative proceeding against the school board and officials. The administrative law judge allowed the school system to call witnesses out of turn and struck the testimony of one of the parents' witnesses because she was unavailable for cross-examination. The ALJ granted the school board and officials' motion to dismiss the case, and the parents appealed to a federal district court. The parents asserted that the ALJ had allowed procedural irregularities and improperly issued a directed verdict in the board's favor, exceeding her authority in issuing this form of decision. The court found nothing in state administrative regulations that restricted an ALJ's broad authority, even though they specifically treated three motions. **The court found that the General Assembly did not intend to limit an ALJ's ability to conduct an efficient hearing by addressing the motions specifically. Although the court expressed curiosity about the ALJ's motivation for issuing a directed verdict instead of a final determination, this was harmless error**. The court also rejected the claim that the school board had denied the student a FAPE by failing to properly implement the IEP. There was evidence that the IEP was being properly implemented at the student's high school and that he was receiving educational benefits. There was also no merit to the claim of the parents that the ALJ had based her findings of educational benefit to the student solely on consideration of his grades and advancement through school. The ALJ had considered more than just the student's grades and advancement when making the determination that he was receiving a FAPE, and the court awarded summary judgment to the school board and officials. *Smith v. Parham*, 72 F.Supp.2d 570 (D. Md. 1999).

◆ Parents obtained a private evaluation of their child's educational needs following her first grade year in public school. The district determined that she had a language disability and devised a public school IEP for her. However, the parents unilaterally enrolled the student in a private school for students with learning disabilities and sought an administrative ruling that the district had failed to provide her with FAPE. An administrative law judge held that the district had not violated the IDEA. The parents appealed to the U.S. District Court for the District of Maryland, challenging not only the placement offered by the school district, but the procedures employed by the ALJ. The student remained in the private school placement selected by her parents, and the district did not devise an IEP for the school year. The parents filed a second administrative hearing request, asserting that the district had again failed to offer the student a FAPE. A different ALJ denied the parents' request for tuition reimbursement and the parents appealed the second action to the federal district court.

The court consolidated the cases, observing that in addition to challenging the placement decisions of the school district, **the parents were seeking to hold state administrative officials liable for failing to provide and train an impartial and competent ALJ**. The court found that while states have the ultimate responsibility to assure that local education agencies provide students with disabilities a FAPE, this did not create a viable cause of action against state officials. The state did not participate in the development of the student's IEP and did not deny her of a FAPE. The parents failed to show that their due process rights had been violated during administrative proceedings in a manner that could create liability for state actors. The state officials were entitled to summary judgment. The parents correctly asserted that the ALJ had improperly delayed the issuance of a decision for 99 days after the hearing, since federal regulations impose a 45-day time frame for administrative decisions. However, there was no showing that the delay had prejudiced them. Any claim based on the alleged incompetence of the ALJ was barred by the Eleventh Amendment to the U.S. Constitution, which precludes federal claims based on alleged state law violations by state officials carrying out official duties. **The court found that the ALJ could not be deemed biased simply because he had a child who benefited from district special education programs. There was no evidence that he had any personal interest in the outcome** of this case, and he had testified under oath about his lack of personal bias in special education cases. The court rejected the parents' assertion that the ALJ had made off-record comments that demonstrated bias. *Jacobsen v. Anne Arundel County Bd. of Educ., et al.*, Civ. No. WMN-97-2016, WMN-99-223 (D.Md.1999).

◆ A hearing officer was placed on the list of independent hearing officers available to preside over special education hearings in Indiana. **Because state and federal law require that hearing officers be independent from public education agencies, he was not a state employee and was not compensated unless he was actually selected to hear a case**. After serving in this capacity for several years, the hearing officer decided a case in favor of the parents of a student with disabilities that resulted in an order requiring the state to reimburse the parents for over $121,000. The decision was reversed by the state board of special education appeals, which expressed concern over the hearing officer's handling of the case. The board's attorney found that the officer had made several inaccurate factual findings and argumentative conclusions of law. The state superintendent of public instruction informed the hearing officer by letter that he would be removed from the list of available hearing officers based on the attorney's findings.

The hearing officer sued the superintendent in a state trial court for constitutional rights violations, asserting the right to a hearing prior to the termination action. The court granted partial summary judgment to the hearing officer and the superintendent appealed to the court of appeals. The court noted that the hearing officer was not a state employee who was entitled to the same constitutional due process protections that government officials enjoy. The Due Process Clause protects deprivations of constitutional liberty and property interests, which are only implicated as the result of some statute, ordinance or contract. The placement of his name on a list of hearing officer candidates did not create a contract and did not guarantee that he would actually be assigned to hear any cases. **Because the placement of the hearing officer's name on a list of candidates did not create any constitutionally protectable property interest, he was not entitled to due process protections such as the hearing he sought**. The trial court had improperly awarded him judgment on this question and the appeals court reversed. *Reed v. Schultz*, 715 N.E.2d 896 (Ind.Ct.App.1999).

◆ A student was diagnosed with attention deficit disorder with hyperactivity and his parent brought an action against the River Falls School District asserting the student's entitlement to special education services. The parties reached a settlement that the parent later repudiated. The settlement was voided in administrative proceedings in which a hearing officer ruled that the case was moot. While that action was pending, the school district claimed that the student was not entitled to special education services under the IDEA. The parent initiated a new action against the district to challenge the district's findings, but the family moved out of the school district before the matter was heard. The state educational agency held that the case was moot in view of the family's move, and the parent appealed to a federal district court. **The court dismissed the case, ruling that the family resided in another school district and that further litigation over the River Falls evaluation of the student's needs would not benefit any party**. *School Dist. of River Falls v. Iversen*, 210 F.3d 376 (7th Cir. 2000).

◆ For most of his academic career, a student attended schools that were part of a special services district (SSD). He then moved to another school district and requested a due process hearing to challenge the services he had received while attending school in the Minneapolis system. **The hearing officer dismissed the case, finding that he was without jurisdiction to hear a case involving a student who no longer attended school in the district**. The student appealed to a review officer, who affirmed the decision, and then appealed to the state court of appeals, which dismissed the case for untimely service. The family initiated a federal district court action against the SSD and several state officials, alleging violations of the IDEA, the Americans with Disabilities Act (ADA), § 504 of the Rehabilitation Act, 42 U.S.C. § 1983, and state law. The court dismissed the IDEA claims for failure to bring suit within the statute of limitations, which the court determined was 30 days from the date of the hearing review officer's decision. The court also entered summary judgment against the student on his § 1983 claims, and concluded that the student had no right to file a due process action against the SSD, because he was not a resident of the district.

The student appealed to the Eighth Circuit, which agreed with the school district and officials that the student had no right to obtain a hearing against the SSD because he did not reside in the district. It also rejected the student's claim that his procedural rights under the IDEA had been violated for lack of notice. The record established that the student's mother had received a parents' rights brochure, informing her that a hearing must be conducted by the district directly responsible for a student's education. Receipt of the brochure established the required notice, according to the court. **The student attempted to revive his claims by notifying the court**, without supplementing the record, **that he had moved back to the SSD. Even if true**, said the court, **that fact would only be relevant to new claims based on current conditions**, not on claims for which he had exhausted his administrative remedies. The court affirmed the judgment for the school district and officials. *Smith by Townsend v. Special School Dist. No. 1 (Minneapolis)*, 184 F.3d 764 (8th Cir.1999).

◆ A West Virginia student with a genetic disorder described as Fragile X syndrome attended a public school special education program until he entered high school, when his school board agreed to pay for a residential placement. His mother requested an independent evaluation to determine an appropriate placement. The parents retained an advocate who proposed that the evaluation be performed by a multidisciplinary team made up of evaluators from outside the state of West Virginia at a cost of $4,480. A school board administrator consented to an evaluation, but rejected the request to use the proposed evaluators, stating that most independent special education evaluations cost $800 or less. The parents requested a due process hearing at which an independent hearing officer held that the school board was not required to pay for an independent educational evaluation under the IDEA. However, **the hearing officer held that the administrator's statement created a contract** under which the board should be required to pay $1,350 for occupational therapy and speech evaluation costs.

The school board failed to appeal the administrative decision, and the parents filed an action in a state circuit court, seeking a declaration that the reimbursement obligation arose under the IDEA, and not under a contract created by the administrator's statement. The court dismissed the action, and the parents appealed to the Supreme Court of Appeals of West Virginia, which held that **the hearing officer's decision was final since the board had failed to appeal the circuit court order**. The lawsuit was not a dismissal of the hearing officer's decision and the board was required to fulfill its obligation under the contract analysis employed by the hearing officer. The court affirmed and remanded the case. *P.T.P., IV by P.T.P., III v. Bd. of Educ. of County of Jefferson*, 488 S.E.2d 61 (W.Va.1997).

◆ A New Jersey student with autistic-like neurological impairments received special education services for three years in a neighboring school district because his own district of residence did not have the necessary facilities. The student's residence district paid tuition to the neighboring district for its services. After three years, the neighboring district claimed that the student was capable of attending regular education classes with resource room support. It conducted an evaluation and determined that the student should be returned to his district of residence. The student's family filed an emergency appeal with the state office of administrative law. **The hearing officer granted the neighboring district's motion for dismissal from the case**, finding that it was a provider of services that was not legally bound to provide special education services under New Jersey law. The student's family appealed to the U.S. District Court for the District of New Jersey. The court rejected the neighboring district's argument that it was a mere provider of services. **The district should not be dismissed from the lawsuit because the student would not be able to gain complete relief against the residence district alone.** The student was familiar with students and staff in the neighboring district and required its services to advance educationally. The administrative agency was bound to consider all claims brought by the student in the same litigation because they arose from the same set of circumstances, and the administrative hearing officer had improperly granted the neighboring district's motion for dismissal. *D.K. v. Roseland Bd. of Educ.*, 903 F.Supp. 797 (D.N.J.1995).

B. Evidence

◆ The parents of a private school student with learning disabilities, language impairments and attention-deficit hyperactivity disorder rejected an IEP proposed by the school system. They enrolled the student in a private school for learning and language disabled students, and then commenced an administrative proceeding for reimbursement of their private school tuition costs. **An ALJ determined that the parents should bear the burden of demonstrating that the IEP prepared for the student was inappropriate**. After assigning the burden of proof, he found that the school system had offered the student a FAPE and denied the claim for tuition reimbursement. The parents appealed to a federal district court, which concluded that the burden of proof in IEP challenges should be placed on the school district, since it is the party with better access to relevant educational records and information. The district court reversed and remanded the case, while school officials appealed to the Fourth Circuit. The ALJ held that the proposed IEP would not have provided the student with a FAPE. In doing so, he imposed the burden of proof on the school district, as the district court ordered.

The Fourth Circuit took note of the intervening administrative decision and declined to consider the case in view of it, stating that **the question of which party has the burden of proof in an action challenging an initial IEP should be considered in the context of a mature case and controversy**, not in a piecemeal manner. It was unclear at this stage of the case what the allocation of the burden of proof would do to the student's claim and it was possible that the parties would appeal the current administrative decision. The panel vacated the district court decision and remanded the case with directions to consolidate the burden of proof questions with consideration of the merits of the student's claims. *Schaffer et al. v. Vance et al.*, 243 F.3d 540 (4th Cir. 2001).

◆ A student was 21 years old and had cerebral palsy, mental retardation, a degree of cortical blindness and the expressive language level of a 2-year old. Her communication skills were rudimentary and her vocabulary was limited to about 10 words. The student's parents expressed dissatisfaction with her IEPs by filing complaints against their school district with the U.S. Department of Education's Office for Civil Rights (OCR) and the Florida Education Department. The state education department ordered the district to provide the student with transition planning. The parties settled the OCR complaint through an agreement to transfer the student to a high school for which the parents expressed a placement preference. After the student was transferred to the new high school, the parents filed a due process complaint against the school district that raised numerous issues about the IEP and its implementation. Although they did not specifically challenge the qualifications of their daughter's teachers, **an administrative law judge ordered the district to provide her with a qualified speech and language pathologist or therapist**. He found that **the school's speech and language teacher was unqualified**, since she was out of the field areas for which she was certified and had only received six hours of field course work in speech pathology. The administrative order noted three deficiencies in the student's IEP, but otherwise held for the school board, finding that it had neither violated the IDEA's free appropriate public education requirement nor inadequately implemented her IEP.

The school board appealed to a Florida district court of appeal, which found that the ALJ had applied proper IDEA legal standards when considering the IEP. However, he exceeded his authority by ordering the district to attempt to ensure the attendance of an outside agency at future transition service meetings. IDEA regulations at 34 CFR Part 300.344 permit local education agencies to take other steps to obtain the participation of other agencies, but such attendance is not compelled. **The ALJ also abused his discretion by determining that the student's speech therapist was not qualified simply because she was teaching outside her field of certification.** There was no evidence to support this finding. Since the issue had not been raised prior to the hearing, the board had no opportunity to present evidence concerning her credentials. There was evidence indicating that the student had significantly improved her communication skills through augmentative communication and that she had increased her verbal skills. The court reversed the parts of the administrative decision which ordered the district to replace the student's speech and language therapist and required it to take specific action to ensure the attendance of outside agencies at future meetings. The administrative decision was otherwise affirmed. *School Bd. of Lee County v. S.W.*, 789 So.2d 1162 (Fla.Dist.Ct.App.2d Dist. 2001).

◆ The parents of an eight-year-old student with autism rejected a proposed IEP and unilaterally enrolled her in a private school. They requested reimbursement for their tuition costs and sought a due process hearing. After considering extensive documentary evidence and testimony by witnesses at a two-day hearing, an administrative law judge held that the IEP prepared by the school district did not comply with the IDEA and awarded the parents the requested reimbursement. **The school district appealed to a federal district court, and moved for a hearing to present additional evidence beyond that considered at the administrative hearing.** The court required a proffer of evidence by the district and it responded with a list of 19 witnesses and three categories of documentary evidence. The court excluded most of the evidence offered by the school district, finding it was cumulative and/or irrelevant and affirmed the administrative decision for the parents.

The school district appealed to the U.S. Court of Appeals for the 11th Circuit, which observed that the IDEA's provision for judicial review has been described as puzzling and somewhat confusing, creating issues of the appropriate amount of deference due administrative decisions. Under established law, administrative decisions in IDEA cases are entitled to due weight and courts cannot substitute their own judgment for that of state education officials. In *Town of Burlington v. Dept. of Education*, 471 U.S. 359 (1985), the U.S. Supreme Court affirmed a First Circuit decision construing the IDEA's "additional evidence" clause as not authorizing trial witnesses to repeat or embellish their administrative testimony. **Trial courts in IDEA actions must make an independent ruling based on a preponderance of the evidence, supplementing the administrative record for reasons such as gaps in the administrative transcript, unavailable witnesses, improper exclusion of evidence by the hearing officer and relevant events occurring after the administrative hearing.** The court held that the determination of what additional evidence should be allowed was within the discretion of the trial court. Administrative hearing witnesses were presumed to be foreclosed from testifying at trial. Motions should be made to consider the appropriateness of allowing witnesses to testify at the trial court level, with concern for possible unfairness by one party reserving its best evidence for trial and undercutting the statutory role of the administrative tribunal. Courts should consider the reasons why a witness did not testify at the administrative level and assert broad discretion in deciding whether to receive any supplemental evidence in the form of deposition transcripts or affidavits in lieu of personal appearances. Expressing its approval of the evidentiary rulings by the district court in this case, the 11th Circuit affirmed its decision in all respects. *Walker County School Dist. v. Bennett*, 203 F.3d 1293 (11th Cir. 2000).

◆ After enrolling their son in a private school for students with disabilities, parents sought reimbursement for the cost. The parents asserted that the school system failed to provide the student with a FAPE. The student had learning disabilities, language impairments and was diagnosed as having attention deficit hyperactivity disorder. He attended a private school from kindergarten through grade seven, with limited success. The student's parents then requested public school services. The school system determined that the student was eligible for services and proposed a public middle school placement. The parents rejected the proposed IEP and requested a due process hearing. An administrative law judge presided over three days of hearings and determined that the school system had offered the student a FAPE. The ALJ denied the parents' claims for tuition reimbursement. In doing so, **the ALJ found that the parents should bear the burden of demonstrating that the IEP prepared for the student was**

inappropriate, since the IDEA contemplates deference to the decisions of school officials.

The parents appealed to a federal district court where they challenged the decision, including the ALJ's assignment of the burden of proof. In many kinds of cases, courts assign the burden of proof to the party seeking to change the status quo, which in IDEA cases is the party challenging the IEP. However, as discussed by the New Jersey Supreme Court, the burden of proof should be on the party with better access to relevant information. *Lascari v. Bd. of Educ of Ramapo Indian Hills Regional High School Dist.*, 116 N.J. 30, 560 A.2d 1180 (1989). In IDEA cases, this is normally the school board, which has ready access to IEP team records and evaluations and has the expertise needed to formulate an IEP. By contrast, parents lack the necessary expertise to formulate an appropriate education for a child. **The court noted that if parents had the burden of persuasion at the administrative level, the school district would never have to show any evidence in justification of an IEP. Allocation of the burden of persuasion to school officials did not have the effect of improperly deferring to their judgment in cases involving the appropriateness of an initial IEP.** Since the administrative law judge in this case had failed to properly allocate the burden of proof, the court remanded the case. *Brian S. v. Vance*, 86 F. Supp.2d 538 (D. Md. 2000).

◆ A nine-year-old Pennsylvania student was identified as having attention deficit disorder with hyperactivity (ADHD). The student's school district conducted a multidisciplinary evaluation and determined that she was not entitled to special education services. The multidisciplinary team found that although the student exhibited ADHD symptoms, she had strong verbal skills and achievement levels and abilities that were at or above average. It determined that she could be educated in regular classrooms. A school IEP team agreed with the multidisciplinary team evaluation. The student's parents requested a hearing, which resulted in reversal of the proposed placement decision. A state appeals panel reversed, and the U.S. District Court for the Eastern District of Pennsylvania affirmed. In doing so, **the court disallowed the family's attempt to supplement the administrative record** and held that it was confined to a review of the administrative record. It also held that the IDEA preempted other claims by the student, including those filed under § 504 of the Rehabilitation Act, the Americans with Disabilities Act and Pennsylvania school law. The family appealed to the U.S. Court of Appeals, Third Circuit.

The court of appeals noted that **language in the IDEA required a district court to hear additional evidence at the request of a party**. Although a district court should exclude cumulative evidence and testimony offered only to bolster the record, it was required to consider evidence acquired after the administrative hearing that pertained to the reasonableness of a school district's initial placement decision or denial of special education services. The district court erroneously held that the IDEA preempted other state and federal claims. The IDEA expressly allowed students to advance multiple claims under state and federal law after exhausting their administrative remedies. The court vacated and remanded the district court's decision. *Susan N. v. Wilson School Dist.*, 70 F.3d 751 (3d Cir.1995).

II. EXHAUSTION OF ADMINISTRATIVE REMEDIES

The exhaustion of remedies doctrine, as articulated by the U.S. Supreme Court in Myers v. Bethlehem Shipbuilding Corp., *303 U.S. 41, 58 S.Ct. 459, 82 L.Ed. 638 (1938), provides that "no one is entitled to judicial relief for a supposed or threatened injury until the prescribed administrative remedy has been exhausted." The U.S. Supreme Court in* McKart v. U.S., *395 U.S. 185, 89 S.Ct. 1657, 23 L.Ed.2d 194 (1968), explained that the doctrine allows for the development of an accurate factual record, thereby allowing more informed judicial review, encouraging "expeditious decision making," and taking advantage of agency expertise.*

A. Operation of the Exhaustion Doctrine

Parents or guardians of a child with a disability generally have the duty to exhaust all administrative channels before resorting to a state or federal court. Where a student adds other claims to an IDEA lawsuit, the exhaustion requirement remains in effect and subjects all claims to dismissal upon failure to exhaust agency remedies.

◆ Although a Massachusetts student with ADHD received a high school diploma, her family sued the school committee and several of its employees in a federal district court. The complaint sought monetary damages under 42 U.S.C. § 1983, based on alleged violations of her right to receive a FAPE under the IDEA. The student also included claims for damages resulting from violations of other federal laws including Section 504 of the Rehabilitation Act, the Violence Against Women Act, Title IX of the Education Amendments of 1972 and the Federal Educational Rights and Privacy Act. **The court observed that students with disabilities may seek relief under other laws in an IDEA action or in a case seeking relief that is available under the IDEA, but that the IDEA requires exhaustion of administrative procedures "to the same extent as would be required had the action been brought under" the IDEA.** The court rejected the student's assertion that because she was seeking compensatory and punitive damages under Section 1983, and this relief was unavailable under the IDEA, she was excused from the administrative exhaustion requirement, finding that adopting this reasoning would lead to abuse. Administrative exhaustion was required even where a party was seeking relief under Section 1983, since the underlying basis for the claim was rooted in alleged IDEA violations. The court dismissed the student's Section 504 discrimination claim for failure to exhaust administrative remedies since, like the Section 1983 claim, it was based on alleged IDEA violations. The U.S. Supreme Court has declared the Violence Against Women Act unconstitutional, requiring the court to dismiss the student's claim brought under that statute. There was insufficient evidence of retaliation or harassment based on sex to permit the student's claim under Title IX to proceed, since she only claimed that a school employee peeked at her while she was using the bathroom. In same-sex harassment cases, the complaining party must prove that the complained-of conduct is discriminatory on the basis of sex. There was no merit to the student's claims under the Federal Educational Rights and Privacy

Act, 42 U.S.C. 2000d or the Revenue Sharing Act of 1972, and the school committee was entitled to judgment on those claims. *Frazier v. Fairhaven School Committee*, 122 F.Supp.2d 104 (D. Mass. 2000).

On appeal, the First Circuit affirmed the district court decision. *Frazier v. Fairhaven School Committee*, 276 F.3d 52 (1st Cir. 2002).

◆ The New York City Board of Education classified a student as hearing impaired and developed an IEP calling for a public school kindergarten placement. His mother disagreed with the proposal and filed an impartial hearing request. After a hearing, a hearing officer issued an interim order requiring the board to place the student in a different public school and to provide him with a paraprofessional trained in American Sign Language. When the hearing reconvened some weeks later, the student had yet to enroll in the placement specified in the interim order. The board stated that the IEP it had proposed could not be implemented due to insufficient enrollment. The hearing officer recommended that she retain jurisdiction over the case while the school's committee on special education devised a new IEP. **The mother withdrew from the administrative hearing process**, and the hearing officer dismissed the case. The board recommended that the student attend school at the location specified in the interim order until a new IEP could be developed.

The mother then sued school officials in a federal district court, asserting that they violated the Americans with Disabilities Act by denying equal educational opportunities to her son on the basis of his disability. The court considered a dismissal motion by the officials based on their argument that the mother's withdrawal from the administrative action deprived the court of jurisdiction under the IDEA's administrative exhaustion requirement. The court held that claims under the ADA and Section 504 of the Rehabilitation Act are subject to the IDEA's exhaustion requirement if the relief sought is clearly available under the IDEA. The relief sought by the mother in this case was the registration of her son in a general education program in public school. The remedy for her action was available under the IDEA, since she was challenging the adequacy of the IEP and seeking to modify it. This remedy was best left to education experts. Although an exception to the exhaustion requirement exists where the pursuit of administrative remedies would be futile, the mother had failed to make any such showing. The interim order called for registering the student at the school in which the mother sought to place him. Instead of continuing with the hearing process, she withdrew from it and precluded the hearing officer from creating a final remedy. Had the administrative proceedings continued, the hearing officer would still have had the authority to order appropriate relief. **The mother's action resulted in failure to comply with the IDEA exhaustion requirement**. The court granted the motion to dismiss the action, but granted leave to the mother to amend her complaint within 30 days to allege facts demonstrating how exhaustion of administrative remedies would be futile. *Kielbus v. Wertheimer*, No. CIV.01-CV-1130-FB, 2002 WL 24446 (E.D.N.Y. 2002).

◆ A Kansas student was hospitalized for seven days at the beginning of seventh grade and diagnosed with diabetes mellitus. As a result, she missed a large portion of the first quarter of the school year. The school nurse prepared an individual health care plan for her. The student's parents requested a Section 504 accommodation plan. The student's 504 team devised a plan that addressed accommodations for the student's absences, make-up tests, blood sugar testing and alternative assignments in band, physical education, art and English. The parents removed the student from school and sought to educate her at home after a grade dispute. The parents then requested a due process hearing, seeking reimbursement for the student to attend school in another district. The hearing officer denied reimbursement, but held that the district failed to properly implement Section 504 regarding the student. The parties developed a 504 accommodation plan and the hearing officer incorporated it into the decision, ordering the district to select a Section 504 coordinator and review the student's grades under the revised accommodation plan. The parents appealed the decision to the district's board of education. **The board denied the appeal** and adopted the majority of the hearing officer's decision. **The parents did not pursue their administrative remedies by appealing to the state education department**.

After 19 months, the parents sued the district and several employees in a federal district court, claiming "educational discrimination" under the IDEA and the ADA. The court considered a summary judgment motion by the district and officials and rejected the parents' attempt to include claims under Section 504 of the Rehabilitation Act, the Family Education Rights and Privacy Act, and 42 U.S.C. § 1983 as an untimely attempt to assert new issues in response to summary judgment. The court recited IDEA language requiring parents who file suit under other laws to exhaust IDEA remedies to the same extent as if the suit had been filed under the IDEA, if the suit could also have been filed under the IDEA. The parents did not pursue IDEA administrative remedies by appealing the board's decision with the Kansas Department of Education. They claimed that exhaustion of administrative remedies was unnecessary in this case, because they sought monetary damages that could not be obtained through the administrative process. The court noted that while the parents sought monetary damages, they also brought claims for injunctive, non-monetary relief against the district based on the theory that the student was denied a FAPE. **A party seeking monetary damages must exhaust available administrative remedies, if educational issues remain unresolved. Since the complaint regarded failure to accommodate the student and was literally related to the student's identification, evaluation or educational placement, its subject matter was presumptively redressable through IDEA administrative procedures**. Therefore, the court dismissed the case for lack of jurisdiction. *Eads v. Unif. School Dist. No. 289, Franklin County, Kansas*, No. 00-4010-SAC, 2002 WL 225919 (D.Kan. 2002).

◆ A student with mild mental retardation attended a public high school. His IEP stated that he was to receive reading and mathematics instruction toward a special education diploma, and work with school custodial staff for one or two hours daily. After a dispute over how much time the student was spending working with the school's custodial staff, his mother withdrew him from school and contacted the school board to authorize a home based program. The school multidisciplinary team scheduled a meeting to discuss the student's program. A member of the team later testified that the notice for the meeting included a brochure describing the rights of students with disabilities and their parents, including appeal rights. The student and mother attended the meeting, where a team member verbally informed them of their procedural rights, including the right to an administrative hearing. The team advised the mother that a home teacher would not be provided. **The mother refused to approve an IEP and kept her son out of school for the rest of the year. She then commenced a federal district court action against the school district**. The court found that the mother failed to exhaust administrative remedies with the state education department before bringing suit and dismissed the case. She appealed to the Sixth Circuit, arguing that the district's failure to provide her with the required IDEA notices excused the exhaustion requirement.

The circuit court rejected the mother's assertion. Initially, the court recited the general rule that parties bringing IDEA complaints must exhaust available administrative remedies before resorting to litigation. Exhaustion enables the development of a record by the appropriate agency, which may resolve the problem through agency expertise and discretion. It also permits the agency to correct mistakes and promote various goals, including judicial economy. **A party seeking to avoid administrative exhaustion bears the burden of showing that use of administrative procedures is futile or inadequate to address the relief being sought.** The mother's primary evidence of an IDEA violation was her attendance at a school board meeting where she complained about violations of her son's IEP. Although she asserted that the board did not provide her with appropriate IDEA notices at the meeting, the court held that it was under no obligation to do so. The mother did not assert that Tennessee's administrative procedures were inadequate or futile, and she did not claim that a state administrative proceeding could not resolve the disputed issues. The IDEA requires notice to parents of their procedural safeguards in the specific circumstances described in 20 U.S.C. § 1415(d)(1), which does not include school board meetings. Since the IDEA does not require parental notification of rights at a school board meeting, the mother was incorrect in asserting that she was not provided with proper notice of her due process rights. The court affirmed the judgment for the school district. *Donoho v. Smith County Board of Education*, 21 Fed.Appx. 293 (6th Cir. 2001).

◆ A New York student with hearing impairments whose primary language was American Sign Language was excluded from her district's limited English proficient (LEP) program and not provided with bilingual education services. Her parents asserted that the board provided her with unqualified and improperly trained ASL instructors and that the board removed her from a gifted and talented program because her primary language was ASL. They also claimed that the board excluded the student from a public school for deaf and hearing-impaired students. The parents requested an impartial hearing to challenge the student's IEP and participated in a series of hearings. However, **the family withdrew from the administrative hearing process** during the final stages of negotiations with the school board **and commenced a federal district court action** against it, asserting violations of Section 504 of the Rehabilitation Act and the ADA. They asserted that the board discriminated against their daughter by excluding her from the LEP program and denying her equal access to educational opportunities, including the general education curriculum, solely because of her disability.

The board moved to dismiss the action, arguing that the family's claims arose under the IDEA and that it was required to exhaust administrative remedies. The court referred the case to a magistrate judge, who observed that while the family had filed claims under Section 504 and the Americans with Disabilities Act, the conduct giving rise to them was covered by the IDEA. The IDEA exhaustion requirement applies to Section 504 and ADA claims that seek remedies that may also be available under the IDEA. The family was challenging the adequacy of the student's educational program and the goal of the suit was to expand the student's program to include general education classes with ASL instruction. There was no merit to the family's argument that her status as a gifted student was a legally significant distinction. The claims were not removed from the scope of the IDEA for this reason. The family's withdrawal from the IDEA administrative procedure deprived the hearing officer of reaching a final determination, so that the state and local educational agencies had no opportunity to address their concerns. It also resulted in the lack of an administrative record for the court to review. **The IDEA clearly states that Section 504 and ADA claimants must first seek administrative redress before commencing any action in court**. The magistrate found that the board had made several attempts to provide the student with resources to function and learn in a general education class and offered her bilingual education services during a prior school year. It had placed her in a gifted and talented student program and provided her with a full-time ASL interpreter. The family resisted the board's educational recommendations and none of the exceptions to the exhaustion requirement applied. The magistrate judge recommended dismissal of the case, noting that the relief sought by the family was available under the IDEA, Section 504 or the ADA. *Kielbus v. New York City Board of Education*, 140 F.Supp.2d 284 (E.D.N.Y. 2001).

◆ The IEP team of a student with an ankle impairment met to consider moving her to another school where she could receive special education services. The student's mother rejected placing her daughter at another school and the district sought an administrative due process hearing. Three months later, the parties agreed that the student should be bused to the other school for a two-week trial period. The parties reached an agreement through mediation, and the district withdrew its request for a hearing. During **the next school year, the student's mother filed a federal district court action against school officials**, seeking an independent evaluation, an award of compensatory damages and related services. She also sought an injunction preventing the district from transferring the student. The district moved to dismiss the case, arguing that the family failed to exhaust available administrative remedies under the IDEA.

The court stated that the IDEA's extensive system of procedural safeguards provides parents with the opportunity to fully participate in all decisions concerning the education of their children and to obtain administrative and judicial review of decisions with which they disagree. In general, parents must first exhaust state administrative remedies before filing a court action in a case involving IDEA subject matter. **The student's mother never filed a formal complaint or requested a hearing and therefore, she was required to exhaust IDEA administrative remedies before filing suit**. Although limited exceptions to the exhaustion rule exist where filing an administrative complaint would be futile or inadequate, there were no such circumstances in this case. The court rejected the mother's assertion that the district was on notice of her disagreement with the student's IEP and should have commenced administrative due process proceedings. The court found that school districts have no IDEA obligation to initiate due process proceedings prior to the implementation of an IEP. The family's ADA claim sought relief that was also available under the IDEA and had to be dismissed because of the IDEA's exhaustion requirement. *Deveaux v. Vallas*, No. 01 C 1422, 2001 WL 699891 (N.D. Ill. 2001).

◆ **A high school student who claimed that her school violated the Montana Human Rights Act by failing to provide an accessible building was not required to exhaust administrative remedies under the IDEA because her complaint did not raise issues of inadequate educational services and was properly before the state human-rights commission**, according to the Montana Supreme Court. The student was paralyzed below her mid-back with camptomelic syndrome and used a wheelchair. She claimed that her school presented numerous physical barriers for her, and provided insufficient accommodations. The student filed an administrative complaint against the school district with the state human-rights commission, alleging discrimination in violation of the Montana Human Rights Act. A hearing examiner held that the district's failure to adequately monitor and address the student's physical access problems was discriminatory. The district appealed to a state district court, which reversed the decision and held that the human-rights commission exceeded its authority by ordering the district to proactively monitor accommodations. On appeal, the state supreme court held that there was no compelling reason to preclude the student's Montana Human Rights Act claim in favor of IDEA exhaustion, since the MHRA provided an administrative remedy through the human-rights commission. There was no legal basis for holding that the IDEA should limit applicable state human-rights laws pertaining to discrimination. Because the hearing examiner's decision was supported by substantial evidence, the state supreme court held that the affirmative relief awarded by the human-rights commission was within its statutory authority. The court held that the commission had broad discretion to remedy discrimination, and it reversed the judgment and reinstated the administrative decision. *Great Falls Public Schools v. Johnson*, 26 P.3d 734 (Mont. 2001).

◆ Hawaii's highest court determined that **state family courts have no jurisdiction to order the state department of health to pay for certain special education services in the absence of a proceeding under the IDEA.** Families of students must first exhaust administrative procedures to establish who is obligated to pay these costs. The decision was the result of two consolidated cases involving who was responsible for paying the costs of private special education services obtained for two special education students with multiple disabilities who were under the supervision of the state department of human services. *In the Interest of Doe*, No. 23149, 2001 WL 988839 (Haw. 2001).

◆ The mother of an elementary school student filed three complaints with the Rhode Island Education Department under the federal complaint resolution procedure challenging various aspects of the student's educational program. The third complaint also claimed the child's school district retaliated against the mother. In resolving the first two complaints, the education department concluded the district was fully compliant with all applicable state and federal requirements. The third complaint resulted in an order directing the district to take certain actions. The mother also requested mediation over the student's IEP and classification. **The mother** then **filed a federal district court action against the district that included a retaliation claim based on her attempts to enforce the student's rights under the IDEA and Section 504** of the Rehabilitation Act. The district court awarded summary judgment to the school district and the mother appealed to the First Circuit.

The circuit court rejected the district's argument that the mother had no standing to assert retaliation claims under the IDEA and Section 504. It found that Rehabilitation Act remedies broadly extend to any person aggrieved under the act or by the failure of any recipient of federal funding to take action. Courts have construed this language to permit standing to the fullest extent possible and it applied to any individual who had been intimidated, threatened, coerced or discriminated against for the purpose of protecting rights. The circuit court held that the mother had standing to pursue her IDEA-based retaliation claim against the school district. Although the IDEA lacked the enforcement language found in the Rehabilitation Act, the structure of the IDEA "reveals the central role played by parents in assuring that their disabled child receives a 'free appropriate public education.'" The parent had standing to advance retaliation claims under the Rehabilitation Act and the IDEA. However, the parent had failed to exhaust her administrative remedies as required by the IDEA prior to filing the federal district court action. **The three CRP complaints filed with the state education department and the mediation action were not due process hearings as contemplated by the IDEA and could not be considered attempts to exhaust IDEA administrative procedures**. The parent had failed to assert that resort to a due process hearing was futile or that any of the exceptions to the exhaustion requirement applied. The court affirmed the summary judgment order for the school district. *Weber v. Cranston School Committee,* 212 F.3d 41 (1st Cir. 2000).

◆ In examining a claim brought by the parent of a student with mental retardation covering a five year time period, a hearing officer held that the student's IEPs for the two most recent years were inappropriate and awarded her two years of compensatory education. The mother failed to appeal the hearing officer's denial of any relief for three earlier years in which she alleged that the district failed to provide appropriate services. However, the school district appealed the award of compensatory education to a state special education appeals panel. The special education appeals panel reduced the award of compensatory education to one year. The mother then commenced a federal district court action against the district.

Because the mother had failed to appeal the adverse part of the hearing officer's decision, the claims for the first three years of educational deprivation were unexhausted, and therefore, the court granted the district's motion for to dismiss this portion of the suit for failure to exhaust administrative remedies. The district conceded liability for the most recent year of claimed educational deprivation, but asserted that the claim for the one remaining year was barred because of the family's failure to commence an action within one year. It claimed that compensatory education claims, like claims for tuition reimbursement, should be dismissed where a party failed to pursue them with reasonable diligence. The court disagreed, noting that failure to object to a student's placement should not deprive the student of the right to an appropriate education. The U.S. Court of Appeals for the Third Circuit, whose jurisdiction includes the states of Pennsylvania, Delaware and New Jersey, has treated claims for compensatory education differently than those for tuition reimbursement. The failure to commence a claim for compensatory education was not a bar to the family's claim for the remaining one year of deprivation of educational services, and the court refused to dismiss it. *Kristi H. v. Tri-Valley School Dist.*, 107 F.Supp.2d 628 (M.D. Pa. 2000).

◆ Because a school district's actions made a parent's request for a due process hearing over her child's placement moot, a hearing was never held. When a second dispute arose between the parties, the parent requested a pre-hearing conference with the school district. When the parties were unable to reach an agreement, she filed a complaint against the district with the Pennsylvania Right to Education Office. A hearing officer held that the district must reimburse the parent for certain transportation expenses. While the administrative action was still pending, **the parent filed a federal district court action against the school district on issues that were not addressed in her current administrative complaint or mooted in the first action**. She asserted violations of the IDEA, Section 504 of the Rehabilitation Act, the Americans with Disabilities Act, and 42 U.S.C. § 1983 on behalf of herself and her son.

The school district moved to dismiss the action on grounds that the parent had failed to exhaust her administrative remedies under the IDEA. The court found that while she had initiated two administrative proceedings against the district, none of the issues raised in the complaint had been fully adjudicated at the administrative level. There was also no reason to allow an exception to the general rule that a party seeking relief under the IDEA must first exhaust all available state administrative remedies. The first administrative compliant had become moot by the private school placement. The parent was not a prevailing party in the second action for reimbursement of her transportation expenses and could not continue the action in district court since she was not an aggrieved party in an IDEA action. **The court also found that the non-IDEA issues could not be resolved in a federal district court since the statute requires that administrative remedies be exhausted in those actions to the same extent as an IDEA action, where relief is also available under the IDEA**. The district's motion to dismiss was granted. *Mapp v. William Penn School District et al.*, No. Civ.A. 99-4440, 2000 WL 1358484 (E.D. Pa. 2000).

◆ A California student with autism who filed a lawsuit seeking monetary damages and compensatory education because of his school district's failure to comply with an administrative decision was also barred from bringing a federal district court action under Section 1983 against his school district because he failed to first exhaust his administrative remedies. Much of the relief he sought was available through an administrative appeal, and **he was** also **required to exhaust administrative remedies in order to pursue his claims for monetary damages arising under 42 U.S.C. § 1983**. The court stated that a contrary ruling would mean that a party could improperly circumvent the administrative exhaustion requirement simply by including a claim for monetary damages in an IDEA case. The court dismissed the action in its entirety. *Porter v. Board of Trustees of Manhattan Beach Unified School District*, 123 F.Supp.2d 1187 (C.D. Cal. 2000).

◆ The IEP of a seven-year-old student with ADHD, depressive disorder with obsessive compulsive features, coordination delays and mental retardation included a behavior plan that established procedures for his challenging classroom behavior. The plan designated "cool down areas," or in cases of severe escalation, a "private quiet room," where he could go until he became calm. **The student destroyed the existing time out room during a violent episode, and the school built an enclosure within the classroom that was six feet by six feet by eight feet, open at the top with a large window in the door. The door could not be locked, but could be held in a closed position** by a staff member. On one occasion, the student experienced a number of oppositional, defiant, and violent incidents. A teacher's assistant decided to place him in the enclosure. Once inside the enclosure, the student removed his clothes and urinated on the walls and floor. He later wrapped his shoelaces around his neck, prompting the assistant to remove all clothing from the room to prevent injury. The student defecated in the room and was covered with feces and urine when his father arrived. He reported the incident to law officers, and school officials agreed in writing to discontinue using the enclosure for disciplining the student.

The father commenced a federal district court action against the school district, teacher, teacher's assistant, principal and others for constitutional rights violations, negligence, assault and battery and other state law claims. He sought special damages in the form of medical expenses, compensatory damages, punitive damages and attorney's fees. The district and employees moved to dismiss the case for failure to exhaust available administrative remedies under the IDEA, arguing that the complaint was based on its alleged failure to properly administer discipline under his IEP. The court agreed with the district that the complaint alleged that the school employees used the enclosure in a manner that grossly and wantonly violated the IEP. **According to the court, the complaint arose under the IDEA, even though the family asserted that only monetary damages were being sought and that this relief was unavailable under the IDEA**. The court held that the form of relief available to a party may not necessarily be the particular relief it requests, but is instead dictated by governing law. The informal meeting of the parties did not constitute exhaustion of IDEA remedies. There was also no merit to the family's argument that the presence of constitutional claims excused the exhaustion of administrative remedies. The court relied on a line of cases involving non-disabled students in which corporal punishment and the removal of dangerous students from school was permitted. In this case, the behavior plan contained disciplinary guidelines concerning the use of time out areas, and the IEP process provided the family with the opportunity for a hearing where one was requested. Although the family characterized the use of the enclosure as "medieval-like punishment," the Eighth Amendment was inapplicable in school cases, and the district and employees were entitled to summary judgment. *Sabin v. Greenville Pub. Schools*, 1999 U.S. Dist. LEXIS 19469 (W.D.Mich.1999).

◆ Two 14-year-old Alabama students with mental retardation began cursing each other and misbehaving in their classroom. They did not obey their teacher's instructions to stop. A school administrator helped to evacuate other students when they became violent and dangerous. Police escorted the students away as they threatened each other. **The school board imposed three-day suspensions on both students and moved a state court for an order allowing it to suspend or remove the students for longer terms**. The court issued a temporary order that included the parties' agreement to remove the students from the school system. However, the students later removed the case to a federal district court, claiming that the board had failed to exhaust its administrative remedies in violation of the IDEA. The court considered the board's motion to declare the case moot.

The students argued that the board was obligated by the 1997 IDEA Amendments to request an expedited hearing before bringing a court action, since the amendments provide for such a hearing where injury to a student or others is likely. The board asserted that the exhaustion of remedies question was moot since the students were presently enrolled in homebound programs by an agreement of the parties that changed their placements. The court held that the issue was not moot since the students might return to public school settings at some time. However, **the expedited hearing procedure contained in the 1997 Amendments was optional and the board was not required to seek an expedited hearing when trying to remove dangerous students from classrooms**. The court commented that expedited hearings might be inadequate in some cases. School officials still needed the immediate authority to prevent a dangerous student's return from a suspension. The 10-day period called for in the proposed IDEA regulations would be inadequate in these cases. Despite the existence of the new expedited hearing procedure, school boards retain their authority under *Honig v. Doe*, 484 U.S. 305, 108 S.Ct. 592, 98 L.Ed.2d 686 (1988) to seek a temporary order from a court. Because exhaustion was not required by the 1997 Amendments, the court held that the preliminary order remained in effect. *Gadsden City Bd. of Educ. v. B.P.*, 3 F.Supp.2d 1299 (N.D.Ala.1998).

◆ The parents of a Michigan student with cerebral palsy claimed that an aide assigned to care for their son intentionally humiliated and tormented him. They complained to school employees but they asserted that no action was taken. After rejecting the outcome of an IEP meeting and requesting a due process hearing, the parents removed the student from the school system. **At the hearing, they asserted that the administrative proceeding was moot, and the case was dismissed**. The parents then brought a federal district court action against the school board and employees including the aide, asserting constitutional rights violations under 42 U.S.C. § 1983 and related state law claims. The school board and employees argued that the case should be dismissed because the family had failed to exhaust its administrative remedies as required by the IDEA. The court agreed, rejecting the argument that the complaint did not concern IDEA subject matter. **The court noted the IDEA's exhaustion requirement applied to all IDEA-subject matter claims, even where the claim alleges a constitutional violation**. There were many references to IDEA requirements in the parents' own pleadings, including the fundamental claim that the student had been deprived of a free appropriate public education. The parents could not avoid IDEA procedural requirements by labeling their IDEA claims as due process violations. The court granted judgment to the school board and employees. *Franklin v. Frid*, 7 F.Supp.2d 920 (W.D.Mich.1998).

◆ A Texas student with disabilities arrived late to class one day and was refused admittance. The teacher alleged that the student then made an improper comment and the teacher poked him in the chest with his index finger, even though he was aware that the student had no right pectoral muscle. **The student filed a personal injury lawsuit against the teacher and school district in a Texas trial court, which granted summary judgment to the district and teacher**. The student appealed to the Court of Appeals of Texas, where he argued that the trial court had improperly held that the teacher was entitled to immunity. The court stated that while the Texas Tort Claims Act provides for teacher immunity for any act by a teacher within the scope of employment, an exception exists for the use of excessive force in the discipline of a student or negligence resulting in bodily injury to a student. Because the teacher had failed to state in his responsive papers that he was not imposing discipline on the student at the time of the incident, he was not entitled to summary judgment. However, the Texas education code requires that all complaining parties bringing disputes arising under the school laws of Texas first exhaust their administrative remedies. The court determined that this provision applied even to a grievance against a school district employee. **Because the student had failed to exhaust his administrative remedies prior to filing the lawsuit, the court dismissed the case**, requiring the student to first exhaust his administrative remedies. *Grimes v. Stringer*, 957 S.W.2d 865 (Tex.App.–Tyler 1997).

◆ Although Arizona law requires the provision of necessary special education services to students incarcerated in county jails, **the state department of education failed to provide any special education services to 22 inmates with disabilities under the age of 22 in a county jail who were waiting to be tried as adults.** One of the inmates filed a federal district court action against the department and certain education and correctional officers on behalf of all incarcerated Arizona students with disabilities, asserting that they had been denied a free appropriate public education in violation of the IDEA, Rehabilitation Act and the Fourteenth Amendment. The department asserted that it had been unaware of the juveniles in the adult jail and that it began performing identification and evaluation services and providing special education services as soon as it became aware of them. The department and state officials moved to dismiss the case based on the students' failure to exhaust their administrative remedies prior to filing suit. The inmates appealed to the U.S. Court of Appeals, Ninth Circuit.

The court recited the general rule that the IDEA requires the exhaustion of administrative remedies prior to the commencement of a lawsuit. However, exhaustion is excused where resort to the administrative process would be futile or would offer inadequate relief. The inmates argued that their complaint described systemic or structural violations which could not be remedied in an administrative proceeding. The court disagreed, finding that the complaint involved the treatment of juveniles at one jail and not all incarcerated Arizona juveniles. **Because the claimed violations did not threaten the IDEA's goals**

on a system-wide basis, and the complaint could have been adequately addressed in an administrative proceeding, exhaustion of administrative remedies was not excused. The district court had properly dismissed the IDEA, Rehabilitation Act and constitutional claims since the IDEA makes related claims subject to its administrative exhaustion requirement. *Doe by Brockhuis v. Arizona Dept. of Educ.*, 111 F.3d 678 (9th Cir.1997).

◆ A Illinois school district principal and a local police officer investigated a fire in an elementary school locker. They found a propane torch in a locker near the site of the fire and questioned a learning disabled student about it. Although another student admitted starting the fire with matches, the principal continued to question the learning disabled student and obtained a signed confession that the student had brought the torch to school and given it to the student who had admitted starting the fire. **The school district suspended the learning disabled student from school and recommended expulsion through the following school year. It also redesignated him as nonlearning disabled** and held a disciplinary hearing at which he was expelled. The student filed a state court action against the school district for constitutional rights violations, resulting in an order to limit the expulsion to the current school year. The student then filed a federal court action against the school district, school board president, principal and police officer seeking monetary, declaratory and injunctive relief for constitutional rights violations including unlawful search, seizure and interrogation.

The school officials filed a dismissal motion, asserting that the student's claims arose under the IDEA and were barred due to his failure to first exhaust his administrative remedies. The court agreed in part, finding that **the questions of reclassification as a nonlearning disabled student, expulsion and inadequate notice were IDEA claims. Since the student was not excused from the administrative process, those claims were dismissed**. However, the assertion that the principal had repeatedly interrogated the learning disabled student even after another student admitted starting the fire made out a sufficient claim for unreasonable seizure and interrogation that precluded pretrial dismissal. The court denied the dismissal motion for this claim. *Bills by Bills v. Homer Consol. School Dist. No. 33-C*, 959 F.Supp. 507 (N.D.Ill.1997).

◆ A Nebraska student with disabilities including cerebral palsy and seizure disorder was entitled to receive special education and related services from his school district. The district contracted for necessary services with an educational service unit and regional office of human development, which in turn utilized a private hospital to provide related services. **The student's program of related services included physical therapy, but the hospital failed to provide therapy for a period of eight months, causing severe contractures and dislocated hips**. The student and his parents filed a lawsuit against the school district, educational service unit, human development office and hospital for violations of the IDEA, state special education act, failure to monitor the physical services and failure to notify the parents of the discontinuance of physical therapy. A Nebraska trial court held that special education students had no cause of action for medical malpractice or other negligence against a school district and that the student had failed to exhaust his administrative remedies. It further observed that the IDEA and state education act provided exclusive remedies to the student and parents in this case. The Supreme Court of Nebraska agreed to review the case.

The court affirmed the district court's decision concerning exhaustion of administrative remedies, determining that even in a case in which the relief sought was prohibited by the IDEA, the exhaustion requirement must be met. The court determined that the claims against the school district, educational service unit and human development office arose under the IDEA and the state education act, and were outside the district court's jurisdiction because of the exhaustion requirement. However, the negligence claims against the hospital for abandonment of treatment and malpractice were not barred by the IDEA or state special education act. Although the family had failed to state a claim against the school district, the district court decision was reversed for consideration of the claim against the hospital with leave to amend the petition in accordance with the supreme court's decision. *Crider v. Bayard City Schools*, 250 Neb. 775, 553 N.W.2d 147 (1996).

B. Exceptions to the Exhaustion Doctrine

There are several instances where the exhaustion doctrine will not apply or exhaustion will be excused. The exhaustion doctrine does not apply when it would be futile or cause irreparable harm. Delay by an agency in making a decision or the fact that the agency may not be empowered to grant relief may excuse the exhaustion requirement. The unavailability of a state or local remedy or a predetermined result by an agency may also excuse the requirement.

◆ A Kansas student suffered from several disabling conditions including Asperger's Syndrome, a high-functioning form of autism. Her parents claimed that her school district failed to provide her with a FAPE and sued the district and officials in a federal district court. The district and officials moved to dismiss the case for failure to exhaust administrative remedies, as required by the IDEA. **The parents** admitted that they had not availed themselves of Kansas' state administrative review process, but **claimed that they were excused from the requirement because the state's administrative process was "not adequate."**

The court observed that the U.S. Court of Appeals for the 10th Circuit, which has authority over federal courts in Kansas, Oklahoma, New Mexico, Colorado, Wyoming and Utah, has held that **administrative remedies may be found inadequate or futile where a complaining party alleges "structural" or "systematic" failures requiring system-wide reforms**. The parents in this case alleged only that the student's IEP was improperly formulated and implemented. This did not call into question the structural or due process concerns of the state and therefore did not excuse the exhaustion requirement. The parents asserted that they should also be excused from filing a due process hearing request because some of the relief they sought for their daughter could not be obtained under the IDEA. However, the 10th Circuit has held that complaining parties in special education disputes cannot avoid exhaustion based solely on the character of relief they are seeking. Instead, the court was required to look at whether the alleged injuries could be redressed to any degree by IDEA administrative procedures and remedies. The family's allegations had to do with the student's educational program and were squarely within the scope of the IDEA. The court found no reason to excuse the administrative exhaustion requirement and dismissed the case. *Marlana G. v. Unified School District No. 497, Douglas County, Kansas*, 167 F.Supp.2d 1303 (D. Kan. 2001).

◆ A school board decided to remove a child with disabilities from school unless a parent remained with him during the school day. **The parents** asserted that the board's action deprived the student of access to a FAPE, and they **petitioned a federal district court for an order enforcing the stay put provision**. In addition to an order requiring the student's immediate reinstatement to school, the parents sought monetary damages and an order requiring the board to provide the student with appropriate education services under his IEP.

The board moved the court for dismissal based on the parents' failure to first commence an administrative action under the IDEA. The parents argued that this would be too time-consuming and was excused under the "futility exception" to the administrative exhaustion requirement. The court noted that the U.S. Court of Appeals for the Fifth Circuit, whose jurisdiction includes Texas, Mississippi and Louisiana, has held that **the general rule of administrative exhaustion in IDEA cases applies in any action under 20 U.S.C. § 1415(b)(1)(E), which guarantees parents an opportunity to present complaints concerning identification, evaluation, placement or the provision of a free appropriate public education** to a student with disabilities. The parents' complaint fell within this section, and thus administrative exhaustion was required. The court also recited language from a recent Fifth Circuit decision emphasizing that a party's non-IDEA claims are also subject to administrative exhaustion. There was no merit to the parents' argument that exhaustion was futile in this case because of the unavailability of monetary relief for IDEA violations. The court granted the board's motion to dismiss the case. *Comeaux v. Tangipahoa Parish School Board*, No. CIV. A. 00-2836, 2001 WL 175230 (E.D. La. 2001).

◆ In response to a high school student's worsening asthma, his IEP was amended. When the student's symptoms persisted, the district placed him in a different high school on a temporary basis and sought a psychological assessment. The student's family objected to the psychological testing and pursued an administrative hearing. After the district amended the student's IEP again, the parents withdrew their request for a hearing. The student experienced academic difficulties at the new school and the district proposed that he return to the school from which he had transferred. The parents objected and initiated new due process proceedings on grounds that the district had failed to comply with the amended IEP. The district countered by offering a placement at the new school with no psychological testing. However, the family moved to a new school district and the student began attending a school there. The parties stipulated for withdrawal from the due process proceedings. Within two months, **the parents sued the student's former school district in a federal district court for IDEA violations**. The court awarded summary judgment to the district based on the parents' failure to exhaust their administrative remedies.

The parents appealed to the U.S. Court of Appeals for the First Circuit, asserting that the district discriminated against their son by requiring that he undergo psychological testing as a condition of school attendance. The circuit court held that the complaint related unmistakably to the evaluation and placement of the student in school and his entitlement to a FAPE. Thus, it was subject to the IDEA's administrative exhaustion requirement. The circuit court rejected each of the parents' arguments that they should be excused from administrative exhaustion. They had mischaracterized the nature of their agreement with the school district for the temporary placement, and the school did not violate any agreement by requiring reevaluation of the student. The IDEA requires reevaluation of students with disabilities if conditions require reevaluation or if a parent or teacher makes such a request. **The parents' decision to abandon the administrative process did not permit them to claim that the process was futile**. They failed to show that the student would have suffered severe harm by awaiting further administrative proceedings and returning to his former school. The court affirmed the judgment for the school district. *Rose v. Yeaw*, 214 F.3d 206 (1st Cir. 2000).

◆ **Two unrelated families** with autistic children **brought a civil rights action against their school district** in a federal district court **for violations of Section 504 of the Rehabilitation Act, the ADA and state common-law claims for personal injury**. The claims arose from the families' assertion that the district regularly allowed other individuals to enter into, observe and/or participate in regular education programs, but that their requests for limited access into the classroom to allow observation were denied. They sought monetary relief, an order requiring district administrators and teachers to attend and pay for training in civil rights and disability discrimination, and a declaration that district policies violated Section 504 and the ADA.

The district moved to dismiss the action, asserting that while the parents had couched the complaint in terms of disability discrimination, it actually was an IDEA action that required the families to exhaust available administrative remedies prior to filing a federal district court action. The parents argued that they were exempt from the IDEA administrative exhaustion requirement because they were seeking relief that was not available under the act, including monetary relief. According to the parents, there was no current controversy about the availability of appropriate educational services, since two of the students now attended private schools and the two others were receiving a FAPE in the district. The district argued that a party may not avoid the administrative exhaustion requirement by adding a claim for monetary relief to a civil complaint otherwise claiming relief available under the IDEA. It noted that the non-monetary forms of relief sought by the families could be ordered by a state hearing officer. The court observed that the parents were satisfied with the present educational placements of their children. Although the case was "a close call," **the court held that the issues raised and the relief sought did not require exhaustion of administrative remedies under the IDEA**. The court expressed doubt that the state claims for common-law negligence could survive a motion for summary judgment, but refused to strike them at this stage of the litigation. It denied the district's motions. *Glass v. Hillsboro School District 1J*, No. 00-1058-JO, 2000 WL 1877647 (D. Or. 2000).

◆ A Tennessee student attended a public special education program at the Knoxville Adaptive Education Center until graduating with a special education diploma. His mother alleged that the school system and its employees locked him in a time-out enclosure on various occasions during a four-year period. She asserted that the system used the enclosure for disciplinary reasons, and that it was a dark, vault-like box about four feet by six feet, with a concrete floor and no heat, furniture or ventilation. The parent claimed that the student was repeatedly locked in the enclosure, and was often left there unsupervised. The parent filed an administrative complaint against the school system and officials with the Tennessee Department of Education. The system denied the allegations and the parent requested an IDEA due process hearing, asserting that her son had been improperly disciplined. The hearing was repeatedly scheduled, delayed and rescheduled over the next three years. Before an administrative hearing was ever held, **the parent sued the system and its officials in federal district court for civil rights violations under 42 U.S.C. § 1983, adding state law claims for intentional infliction of emotional distress and false imprisonment**. The complaint asserted no IDEA violations, but the system moved to dismiss it on grounds of the parent's failure to exhaust her IDEA administrative remedies. The school system argued that the claims involved IDEA subject matter, since they revolved around allegations of improper disciplinary measures under the student's IEP.

The court agreed with the school system and granted its summary judgment motion. The parent appealed to the U.S. Court of Appeals for the Sixth Circuit, which recited the general rule that parties must exhaust their administrative remedies before filing an IDEA action in court. The parent argued that her claim concerned abusive behavior by school employees that violated the U.S. Constitution and did not arise under the IDEA. Without determining whether the parent's claim arose under the IDEA, the court held that it would be futile for her to seek administrative relief in this case. It disagreed with her argument that she was excused from the administrative exhaustion requirement by virtue of her damage claim alone. Courts have rejected this argument because a party could defeat the exhaustion requirement simply by seeking monetary damages in a claim otherwise arising under the IDEA. The court observed that the administrative exhaustion requirement is also excused if the process would be futile or inadequate to protect a party's rights, and where a party does not receive notice of IDEA procedural protections. **The student had graduated and non-monetary relief could not redress his claimed injuries. Under the unique circumstances of this case, proceeding through the state's administrative process would be futile**. The court reversed and remanded the district court decision. *Covington v. Knox County School System*, 205 F.3d 912 (6th Cir. 2000).

- **A complaint was filed in federal district court alleging a student with Tourette's syndrome and other disabilities was physically and psychologically abused by his teacher and an instructional assistant**. He claimed that the two punished him by force-feeding him oatmeal mixed with his vomit while his hands were held behind his back, despite knowing that he had an allergy to oatmeal. The student also claimed that staff members strangled him, leaving red marks on his neck, and that he was forcibly restrained, left to stand outside or in the corner for long time periods, and deprived of food as punishment for making involuntary body movements or tics. The student claimed that the teacher and assistant repeatedly tackled him and restrained him. The student's mother alleged that the principal was aware of the treatment and threatened that her son would be taken away from her if she tried to remove him from the school.

The family sued the school district, teacher, and principal in a federal district court, asserting that they subjected the student to physical and emotional abuse in violation of § 504 of the Rehabilitation Act, the Americans with Disabilities Act, 42 U.S.C. § 1983, and state law tort law. The court dismissed the action for lack of subject matter jurisdiction, because there had been no prior administrative hearing and the family had failed to exhaust their administrative remedies under the IDEA. The family appealed to the Ninth Circuit, which observed that the complaint sought only monetary damages. It found no congressional intent in the language of the IDEA that granted courts the power to provide monetary damages. **Because the parties had resolved all educational issues through the IEP process, and the family was seeking relief that was not available under the IDEA, administrative exhaustion was not required**. The court observed that any available remedies under the IDEA were not well suited to addressing past physical injuries, which are typically remedied by an award of monetary damages. Since the family was not required to exhaust administrative remedies prior to filing the federal district court action, the court reversed and remanded the case. *Witte v. Clark County School Dist.*, 197 F.3d 1271 (9th Cir. 1999).

◆ A Massachusetts sixth grade student attended regular education classes with the exception of language arts and homeroom. His mother asked his school special education team to determine whether he had a learning disability. The team determined that while the student had no learning disability, he should be placed in a small, structured classroom. The following year, the student attended a private school since the only special education accommodation offered by the district was a teacher advocate. **The school district prepared a new IEP for the student in the event that he returned from the private school**. The student eventually withdrew from the private school for academic reasons and was later expelled from another private school for bringing a gun to school. The mother then asked the school district's special education department for an evaluation and alternative placement. The school superintendent responded that the district was not required to provide educational services to a student expelled from another school for gun possession, but offered to provide him ten hours of tutoring per week.

Although the parties later agreed that the district would pay for a private school placement, the mother filed a federal district court action against school officials for educational malpractice, wrongful exclusion from public school in violation of the IDEA and monetary damages. **The court agreed with the mother that she was excused from exhausting her administrative remedies under the IDEA, since there was evidence that the IEP was fraudulent or based on a misrepresentation and had been prepared only in case the student returned to public schools**. The court dismissed the educational malpractice claim since this cause of action is not recognized under Massachusetts law. However, the court refused to dismiss the claim for monetary damages against school officials pending further proceedings. *Doe v. Town of Framingham*, 965 F.Supp. 226 (D.Mass.1997).

III. LIMITATION OF ACTIONS

The IDEA does not specify a time limitation in which parties may bring suit in state or federal court after exhausting administrative remedies or in which they may appeal adverse administrative decisions. Federal courts are required to apply the most analogous state statute of limitations from the district in which they are located, consistent with underlying IDEA policies. State laws govern administrative procedures and often specify a relatively brief limitation on appeals. Parties also often make claims for attorneys' fees, requiring courts to determine if the claim constitutes an independent claim or a claim subject to the limitations period.

A. Administrative Appeals

◆ The parents of a student with disabilities sought tuition reimbursement from their school district, claiming that it denied him of a FAPE. The district asserted that the parents' administrative claim was barred by an Oregon law that required the commencement of any action based on liability created by a statute within two years. **The hearing officer agreed with the parents that a state law allowing two years for personal injury claims against a government entity was the proper limitation period**, and that this period applied to the initiation of their request for a due process hearing. A federal district court reversed the decision, and the parents appealed to the Ninth Circuit.

The circuit court noted that because the IDEA lacks its own limitations period, courts are required to apply the most analogous local limitations period that does not undermine IDEA policies. It employed the same analysis for determining the correct limitations period for commencing an administrative hearing as used by courts to determine when to limit civil actions under the IDEA. The parents' claim could reasonably be characterized as one arising from liability created by a statute, as the district court had done. However, the Ninth Circuit noted that the school district was a "public body" as defined by the Oregon Tort Claims Act. The IDEA was the source of the district's alleged duty, and the student's claim was within the statutory definition of "tort." Because the two-year limitation period employed by the hearing officer applied specifically to breaches of duty by public bodies, and a two-year limitations period was consistent with underlying IDEA policies, the court reversed the district court's judgment and reinstated the hearing officer's decision. **The two-year statute of limitations best served IDEA policies because it was short enough to allow expeditious claims resolution, but long enough for parents to protect their children's rights**. *S.V. v. Sherwood School Dist.*, 254 F.3d 877 (9th Cir. 2001).

◆ The families of two students with autism moved to North Carolina from other states and brought separate actions against their school districts after their requests for funding of Lovaas programs were denied. In the first case, the student's progress in the Lovaas program resulted in a medical determination that he was no longer disabled, yet the district refused to reimburse the family for his past participation in Lovaas therapy. The parties exchanged letters discussing resolution of the reimbursement claim. **The family filed an due process**

petition, which an ALJ rejected as untimely filed under the state's 60-day limitation law. The parents appealed to a federal district court, which affirmed the ALJ's decision. The second family moved to North Carolina to take advantage of a TEACCH program for their child, but soon removed her from the program in favor of Lovaas therapy. Their school district proposed a full-day TEACCH program for successive school years. The district did not explain that it was making a final decision or refer to the 60-day state law limitations period in its interactions with the parents. The second family's administrative appeal also resulted in a decision for the school district, and the federal district court affirmed the decision.

On appeal, the Fourth Circuit consolidated the cases. It stated that Congress did not provide a statute of limitations in the IDEA, leaving the courts to consider the most analogous limitations period from local law. The North Carolina statute was unique in that it specifically referred to special education cases. For this reason, the court was not required to determine the most appropriate local limitations period in the jurisdiction. However, federal courts must additionally consider whether a limitations period borrowed from state law is consistent with federal policies. The circuit court found that **while local limitations periods are most frequently raised as a defense to a late-filed federal court action arising from a final administrative decision, the same policy concerns applied to the commencement of an administrative appeal arising from a final school decision**. While the court had previously held that a very short limitations period, such as 30 days, was disfavored under the IDEA, the North Carolina limitations period was entitled to special deference. The 60-day period was twice as long as the one previously held insufficient and took account of all relevant federal policies under the IDEA. The state statute explicitly required school authorities to clearly and fully notify parents in writing of the 60-day limitations period. In both cases, the school districts failed to provide the notice required by the statute. There was nothing in the district correspondence that signaled the end of negotiations and the onset of the statutory limitations period. Because neither district provided with the required notice, the limitations periods could not be applied, and the administrative dismissals of both cases were incorrect. *CM et al. v. Board of Education of Henderson County et al.*, 241 F.3d 374 (4th Cir. 2001).

On remand, the district court found that the issue was whether the district had to provide due process notice to the family under the circumstances. The family had moved to North Carolina to take advantage of TEACCH methodology, but unilaterally removed the child from a TEACCH program after only three months, without giving notice or making a complaint about the student's program. Even after the parents asked for contribution toward Lovaas therapy, they still raised no complaint or objection to the IEP. The court agreed with the ALJ that a school system could not provide due process rights notification to a family that was "not aggrieved" by school action. The limitations period commenced "when notice is given of the agency decision to all persons aggrieved who are known to the agency." Because the parents unilaterally removed the child from district schools when there was no special education dispute, the due process notice requirement of state law had never been triggered. The court held that **in the absence of a complaint by the parents, the county could not be**

faulted for failing to provide a due process notice to the family. The parents were unable to show that due process notices were necessary for the 1993-94 and 1994-95 school years, and they received a parents' handbook explaining their parental rights during the 1995-96 school year. They were not entitled to reimbursement for any of those years, since there was no showing that the IEP proposed by the district for those years was inadequate. The court held that the district's IEPs satisfied North Carolina's heighten special education standards, and noted that the student made more progress under the TEACH program than she did under the Lovaas program. *CM v. Bd. of Public Educ. of Henderson County*, No. CIV 1:98CV66, 2002 WL 172434 (W.D.N.C. 2002).

◆ At due process, an ALJ ordered a school board to develop an IEP for a student with disabilities, but ruled that her parents were not entitled to reimbursement for the cost of IEEs or private school tuition. A state review officer reversed the decision in part by ordering the board to reimburse the parents for the cost of the IEEs. The order provided that any party aggrieved by the decision was entitled to institute an IDEA action in state or federal court within 30 days of the receipt of the decision. The parents filed a federal district court action against the board at the end of the 30-day period, seeking reimbursement for private school tuition costs. Instead of filing an action within the 30-day timeframe, the board responded to the parents' complaint with an answer and appeal from the administrative decision. **The parents moved to dismiss the action as untimely, asserting that the board had failed to comply with the 30 days allotted for appealing the administrative decision**. The district court disagreed. The court then considered the merits of the claim and counterclaim and held that the board was required to develop an IEP for the student. However, it denied the parents' request for private school tuition reimbursement and the amounts claimed for IEEs.

The parents appealed to the Fourth Circuit, arguing that an action filed in a federal court under the IDEA is an appeal from an administrative decision that requires the other party to also file an appeal in the prescribed time period. The board argued that an IDEA lawsuit is an original civil action for which a counterclaim is permitted beyond that time period. The court reviewed the language of the IDEA and noted that it specifically referred to a civil action, not an appeal. In reviewing the legislative history of the law, it was clear that Congress was aware of the distinction and deliberately chose to characterize an IDEA lawsuit as a civil action. The fact that courts were permitted to supplement the administrative record in an IDEA lawsuit was further evidence that IDEA cases were original civil actions. Although reviewing courts were required to give deference to administrative findings, this did not mean that IDEA cases more closely resembled "appeals." The deferential standard of review was a judge-made rule that only recognized the expertise of administrative agencies in handling educational questions. This was not enough to convert IDEA actions into appeals in view of explicit statutory language declaring them to be original civil actions. Under principles of federalism, it would be improper for federal courts to review final state agency decisions if they were considered appeals. **The district court properly ruled that the board's response was an answer and compulsory counterclaim that was not time-barred**; therefore, the circuit court affirmed the decision for the school board. *Kirkpatrick v. Lenoir County Board of Education*, 216 F.3d (4th Cir. 2000).

◆ An Ohio student with a severe form of dyslexia attended public schools through the start of his fourth grade year. His parents grew dissatisfied with his lack of progress in basic language skills and his regression in reading, writing and arithmetic. During a fourth-grade IEP meeting, the school district indicated that the student's existing IEP would not be modified and the parents unilaterally withdrew him from the school system. They placed him in a private special education school where he experienced success for three years. He later attended two other special education schools. **More than six years after withdrawing the student from the public school system, and after having expended over $150,000 on private schools, the parents requested a due process hearing** to obtain tuition reimbursement from the school district. An administrative hearing officer determined that the parents had failed to timely initiate due process procedures and dismissed the action. On appeal, a district court found that the parents had been advised of their rights under the IDEA but had failed to do so for seven years and had deprived the district of an opportunity to remedy the student's educational program.

The parents appealed to the Sixth Circuit. While the parents did not request a due process hearing for almost seven years after the start of the present dispute with the school district, they had maintained interaction with the district at various times through the years. The parents had attempted to negotiate the return of their son to public school two years before their formal hearing request, but had been rebuffed by school officials. Although the district never refused to enroll the student or offer him a post-enrollment IEP, district employees had discouraged the parents from re-enrolling the student. The special education director had incorrectly advised them that the student had to be re-enrolled before the district had any obligation to prepare him a new IEP. The obligation to prepare an IEP derives from a student's residence in a school district, not from enrollment in school. The district was excused from taking no action for the first five years in which the student attended private schools, as there was evidence that the parents knew of their due process rights but sat on them during that time period. However, **it was not excused from claims arising during the next two years, since there was evidence that it had refused to prepare a pre-enrollment IEP**. This constituted a violation of the IDEA. The parents' request for a due process hearing preserved this claim, and it was not barred under either the two or four-year statutory limitation periods of Ohio law. Their claim could still be considered by the district court. The Sixth Circuit further held that the parents had an obligation under the IDEA to challenge their son's IEP through administrative channels. Under the circumstances, **the claims for the five school years preceding the district's rejection of their attempt to re-enroll the student in public school were barred**, and the court reversed that part of the judgment. *James v. Upper Arlington City School Dist.*, 228 F.3d 764 (6th Cir. 2000).

◆ Although they signed two separate initial IEPs for their child, a student with autism, parents made several requests during the school year to implement the services included in the IEPs and increase the amount of services the child received. The district rejected their requests and the parents removed him from school and placed him in private tutoring programs. Over a year later, the parents learned about IDEA administrative hearing procedures and within two months, they filed a request for a due process hearing. One of the forms of relief sought by the parents was money damages. A local hearing officer found that the district had a pattern and practice of failing to follow IDEA procedures. The LHO ordered the district to reimburse the parents nearly $118,000 in educational expenses incurred from 1993 through 1998. **A state hearing officer deleted the claims for educational expenses incurred prior to the commencement of the administrative action under a Virginia two-year state statute of limitations.**

The parents appealed to a federal district court, which held that the LHO failed to apply the statute at all and the SHO applied it improperly by barring all claims arising before the due process request. The appropriate date to consider was July 1995, when there was evidence that the parents first received notice of their right to commence administrative proceedings. The IDEA mandates that parents be informed of their due process hearing rights on three separate occasions, including each notification of an IEP meeting. The court found that the rights guaranteed by the IDEA were nothing more than an empty promise if parents remained unaware of their due process rights. **The failure to comply with IDEA notice provisions constituted a violation and the court upheld the LHO's factual findings imposing liability on the school district for keeping the parents in the dark about their due process rights** over a two-year period. The court found that the damages available in IDEA cases were "limited to the amount of money expended for educational purposes, irrespective of the number of violations committed by the state." Because the school district committed at least one violation by failing to inform the parents of their procedural rights, they were entitled to full relief from July 1995, the approximate date they first learned of their right to request a due process hearing. *Jaynes v. Newport News School Board*, No. 4:99cv146 (E.D. Va. 2000).

◆ At due process, a hearing officer determined a student with multiple disabilities had been improperly declassified as eligible for special education by his school district. When the student's parent and the district were unable to subsequently agree on an IEP, the district requested another due process hearing, seeking a determination that the recommended day treatment program placement was appropriate. The mother sought tuition reimbursement for the costs of a home-based program offered by a private school that she had enrolled the student in. Unhappy with the hearing officer's determination that the district had developed appropriate IEPs for the student, the home-program was not adequate and the denial of her request for reimbursement, the mother appealed. A state level review officer held that the two most recent IEPs were inappropriate, but affirmed the decision not to award reimbursement.

The mother then commenced a federal district court action against the school district on behalf of the student, asserting violations of the IDEA, Section 504 of the Rehabilitation Act, the Family Education Rights and Privacy Act (FERPA) and educational malpractice under state law. She also sought to recover an award of damages under 42 U.S.C. § 1983 for IDEA and Section 504 violations. The court considered the district's motion for summary judgment and held that some of the student's claims were time-barred. In examining which statute of limitations applied, **the court determined that New York's four-month limit on appeals from Article 78 proceedings applied to bar the claims arising from the first administrative proceeding. However, the claims arising from the second administrative proceedings had been timely filed and were not barred**. The court determined the student was not entitled to compensatory or punitive damages under the IDEA. Courts have not held that the IDEA is a means of obtaining personal injury type damages, since the statutory scheme favors the restoration of educational rights. However, the court refused to prevent the student's claims for damages under Sections 504 and 1983, finding he had presented sufficient evidence that several of the IEPs prepared by the district were inappropriate and failed to provide him with special education services. He was entitled to the opportunity to show that the school acted with deliberate indifference to his rights. Courts have construed Section 504 as allowing punitive damages, and if the student proved his case, he would be entitled to recover punitive damages from the individually named school officials, who were not entitled to immunity. The court dismissed the student's FERPA and state law claims, finding no justification for allowing them to proceed. *Butler v. South Glen Falls Central School Dist.*, 106 F.Supp.2d 414 (N.D.N.Y. 2000).

◆ A West Virginia student was diagnosed with a specific learning disability, received consistently poor grades, exhibited socially delinquent behavior and was frequently absent from school. However, **the school district placement advisory committee recommended that she continue in her regular education classes, and her mother consented**. Nearly seven years later, the mother took the student for evaluation and testing. She was diagnosed as having attention deficit hyperactivity disorder and a severe learning disability. After conducting its own assessment, the school's IEP committee found the student ineligible for special education services and the mother requested a due process hearing. The hearing officer found that the school district had failed to complete a timely multidisciplinary hearing evaluation. However, she found no violation on the issue of the eligibility assessment. The IEP committee reconvened and determined that the student was eligible for special education services, rendering the hearing decision moot. The parent requested another hearing challenging the initial special education assessment, the failure to refer the student for special education services, and the most recent eligibility determination.

The hearing officer held the current IEP appropriate and the mother appealed to a federal district court, seeking eight years of compensatory education based on the school district's initial failure to provide services. The district claimed that the action should be barred under West Virginia's two-year statute of limitations for personal injury actions. **The court agreed that two years was the appropriate limitations period to apply to an initial request for special education services. The two-year limitation protected student rights and promoted the IDEA's preference for expediency**. Because the student's mother had failed to appeal from the initial eligibility assessment, she was barred from challenging the decision. The court granted summary judgment to the school board. *Leake by Shreve v. Berkeley County Bd. of Educ.*, 965 F.Supp. 838 (N.D.W.Va.1997).

◆ A Rhode Island student with mental disabilities was entitled to receive 230 days of special education services under state special education regulations. However, the state school department failed to provide her with 50 days of summer educational services in three consecutive years, and the department admitted that she was entitled to a total of 150 additional days of special education services. The department refused to provide services when it learned that the student had moved to Pennsylvania. The family filed an administrative complaint against the department and an impartial hearing officer upheld its decision. **The family appealed to a review officer who determined that the student was entitled to compensatory education services even though she now lived in Pennsylvania**. The review officer's decision was forwarded to a state agency as allowed by state law, and was not received by the school department until almost two weeks later. The department appealed to the U.S. District Court for the District of Rhode Island within 30 days of its receipt of the decision, but 41 days after the issuance of the decision.

The court held that **the department's appeal was barred by a 30-day state limitation statute under which the time limit runs from the date of issuance of a decision by the state education commissioner or board of regents for elementary and secondary education**. The department appealed to the U.S. Court of Appeals for the First Circuit, where it argued that the state Administrative Procedure Act (APA) was the local limitation statute that was most analogous to the IDEA. The court held that while the IDEA has no limitation period, it incorporates the most analogous limitation period from the state in which the case is filed. The APA was most analogous to the IDEA and because its 30-day time limit did not begin to run until the receipt of an administrative decision, the appeal had been timely. The court reversed and remanded the case. *Providence School Dept. v. Ana C.*, 108 F.3d 1 (1st Cir.1997).

◆ The U.S. District Court for the Western District of Pennsylvania applied a two-year limitations period from state law in the cases of two special education students asserting IDEA, Rehabilitation Act and Americans with Disabilities Act violations. Without consolidating the cases, the court heard them simultaneously and considered arguments by the parents that the statute of limitations should not begin to run since they alleged that the school districts were engaged in continuing practices that violated their statutory and constitutional rights. **The court agreed that the continuing violation doctrine applied in this case because the complaints alleged discriminatory practices that continued to within two years of the filing of the actions.** Accordingly, the claims were not time-barred and the court denied motions by the school districts to dismiss them. *Jeffery and Mary Y. v. St. Marys Area School Dist.*, 967 F.Supp. 852 (W.D.Pa.1997).

◆ A New York student with learning disabilities attended regular education classes with resource room support. Her parents disagreed with the IEP proposed by her school district and placed her in a private school for students with learning disabilities. The school was not approved by the state of New York. **Although her parents had complained earlier about the board's handling of the student's education program, they did not file a formal complaint until her third year at the private school.** At a hearing, they requested tuition reimbursement.

The hearing officer granted tuition reimbursement for the third year, finding that the IEP was inappropriate and that the private school program was appropriate. However, reimbursement for the first two years of tuition was inappropriate since the parents had failed to file a timely complaint. The parties appealed and a review officer reversed the order for tuition reimbursement for the third year. The parents appealed to the U.S. District Court for the Southern District of New York. The board filed a dismissal motion.

The court found that **even if the parents had correctly followed IDEA administrative procedures, an untimely claim could be allowed only if there was good cause for delay and the delay did not prejudice the board**. The parents argued that the board had not properly informed them of their IDEA rights and that the school principal had misled them. The court held that the parents had been adequately informed of their rights through other sources. It also found that the board had been prejudiced by having to defend an IEP developed three years earlier. However, there was evidence that the board had failed to develop an appropriate IEP. Because factual issues remained concerning placement, the court granted the dismissal motion with regard to the first two years but denied the motion to dismiss the reimbursement claim for the third year. *Phillips v. Bd. of Educ. of Hendrick Hudson School Dist.*, 949 F.Supp. 1108 (S.D.N.Y.1997).

◆ A Montana student had speech impairments and was eligible for special education services from his school district. The district assumed partial financial responsibility for a series of hearing evaluations over the next few years. Later, the parents sought reimbursement from the school district for hearing aids and evaluations, which the school district denied. The parents filed a request for administrative review, resulting in a decision which required the school district to reimburse them for approximately $4,000 for related services. **The school district appealed** to the U.S. District Court for the District of Montana **but did not file the complaint until over one month after being served with the administrative decision**. The family filed a motion to dismiss the complaint as barred by the 30-day statute of limitations from the Montana Administrative Procedure Act. The court denied the motion and entered summary judgment for the school district, reversing the hearing officer's substantive rulings. The family appealed to the U.S. Court of Appeals for the Ninth Circuit.

The school district argued that a 60-day limitation period for review of decisions by the state superintendent of public instruction should apply to IDEA cases. Alternatively, Montana's two-year limitation period for statutory liability could preserve the appeal. The court stated that the IDEA was designed to assure the speedy resolution of disputes involving students with disabilities. **It agreed with decisions by the First, Seventh, and District of Columbia Circuits that IDEA appeals were more similar to administrative than statutory appeals. Because the 30-day limitation period was the most analogous to the IDEA, the court applied it** to this case. It reversed and remanded the district court decision. *Livingston School Dist. Numbers 4 and 1 v. Keenan*, 82 F.3d 912 (9th Cir.1996).

B. Attorneys' Fees

- Parents contended that their school district unilaterally changed the placement of their three children without prior notice or consultation. They commenced an administrative due process hearing in which a hearing officer ultimately agreed with them and held that the district violated the IDEA. A state appeals board affirmed the decision and the district did not appeal further. **More than nine months later, the parents filed separate suits in a federal district court seeking attorneys' fees**. The court consolidated the cases, and held that the parents were prevailing parties in an IDEA action and thus entitled to an award of fees. It also adopted their argument that Kentucky's five-year limitation on actions for liability created by a statute should apply to their claim, and awarded them over $37,000. The district appealed to the Sixth Circuit, asserting that the state's 30-day limitation on appeals from administrative proceedings barred the claims.

The Sixth Circuit noted that U.S. circuit courts have been divided on the issue, with some accepting the notion that a claim for fees was a separate action from IDEA due process procedures. The 11th Circuit, which includes Florida, Georgia and Alabama, has accepted this view. The Seventh Circuit, comprised of Indiana, Illinois and Wisconsin has found that claims for attorneys' fees are a part of the due process procedure. The court agreed with this view, finding that **claims for attorneys' fees were another phase of the administrative proceeding. Because it was unlikely that the claims were independent from the administrative action, the 30-day limitation period applied**. The case was reversed and remanded. *King v. Floyd County Board of Education*, 228 F.3d 622 (6th Cir. 2000).

- A parent challenged the educational program provided for her son at an administrative hearing. The hearing officer determined that the school board failed to provide the student with a FAPE under the IDEA. Forty days later, the parent filed a federal district court action against the board for recovery of her legal fees. The board moved for summary judgment, asserting that an Alabama law requiring appeal from an administrative hearing within 30 days was the most analogous state limitation period for IDEA actions. The parent asserted that a two-year limitations period on actions for injury to the person or rights of another was more appropriate. The court stated that the IDEA permits the award of attorneys' fees to the parents of a student with disabilities who prevail in an IDEA proceeding. The IDEA does not contain a limitations period for attorneys' fees actions, and courts must look to the local limitations statute most analogous to the case that is consistent with federal policies. An award of attorneys' fees is not analogous to an administrative appeal. Instead, actions for attorneys' fees are founded on statutory liability. **Alabama had no limitations period governing actions founded on statutory liability, and its two-year limit on actions arising from injury to the person or rights of another, was most analogous to the claim for attorneys' fees**. Because the action for attorneys' fees was filed within two years, it was not time barred, and the court denied the board's motion for summary judgment. *Dickerson ex rel. Ingram v. Brodgen*, 80 F.Supp.2d 1319 (S.D. Ala. 1999).

◆ The parents of a student with autism withdrew him from the Puerto Rico public school system and placed him in a Boston private school. The Puerto Rico Department of Education failed to timely respond to their requests for a hearing and a federal district court held that the department's denial of any hearing was sufficient to demonstrate an IDEA violation. The court held that the parents were entitled to partial tuition reimbursement and their attorney's fees. The district court then considered the parents' claim for over $108,000 in attorney's fees. It commented that **the IDEA contains a statutory method for computing appropriate fee awards, based on the amount normally paid for legal services in the community**. It determined a reasonable rate for the parents' local counsel, and held that they were also entitled to an enhanced award for an attorney they had hired for the litigation who had a specialized IDEA practice outside Puerto Rico. However, it rejected their claim that the Washington, D.C. market rate should be applied, even though the education department had hired a D.C. attorney for the case. **The court reduced the award for certain items that were not justified, such as filing motion papers**, before awarding the family its attorney's fees and costs plus the student's educational expenses. The total attorney's fees award was just under $80,000. *Gonzalez v. Puerto Rico Dept. of Educ.*, 1 F.Supp.2d 111 (D.PR. 1998).

◆ A New Jersey student needed care for his basic needs due to cerebral palsy. His school district classified him as multiply disabled and placed him in a regional day school clinic where he had occupational, physical and speech therapy and a full-time aide. However, his mother demanded full inclusion within his neighborhood school district, which the district rejected. She requested mediation, at which she continued to demand an inclusive program at the neighborhood school with a full-time aide, in-home tutoring and other support. The parties reached a settlement at which the district agreed to the neighborhood placement, and agreed to conduct another IEP conference. However, the mother later rejected the neighborhood school placement since it was in a self-contained classroom with no mainstreaming opportunities. The mother filed a petition for emergency relief to enforce the mediation agreement and allow the student to attend a resource room, pending placement in a more inclusive setting. The parties reached a partial agreement, but the school was unable to fully accommodate the student's personal needs and the mother came to school to care for him in the absence of a full-time aide. She later commenced an administrative due process hearing that resulted in another settlement by which the district modified the IEP and placed the student in four regular classes at the neighborhood school.

Two years later, the parent petitioned the court for her attorney's fees from the mediation and administrative proceedings. She also sought reimbursement for her own services at the school and for interest accrued on her credit cards to pay expenses related to the dispute. The court considered the parties' cross-motions for summary judgment. It stated that the IDEA lacks a limitation period, and that courts must apply the most appropriate local limitations period consistent with IDEA purposes. **Application of a short limitations period for attorney's fees claims, as sought by the district, would be inconsistent with the IDEA, but these claims must be brought within a reasonable time**. Courts are to use equitable principles as guidance in each case. Because the mother in this case had changed attorneys during the dispute, the two-year delay was not unreasonable and the action was not barred. However, she was not entitled to summary judgment regarding her status as a prevailing party under the IDEA, since there were factual disputes concerning whether the school district had changed the IEP as a result of the threatened due process hearing. The court also denied the parent's claim for her personal care of the student at school and her credit card interest. It ordered a hearing to resolve the remaining factual disputes. *B.K. v. Toms River Bd. of Educ.*, 998 F.Supp. 462 (D.N.J.1998).

◆ The parents of an Indiana student with disabilities requested a due process hearing concerning the student's placement. A hearing officer determined that the student's present placement was deficient and mandated certain changes to his IEP. The administrative order notified each party that appeal of the decision should take place within 30 calendar days of receipt of the decision. Neither party appealed, but because the local educational agency failed to immediately implement the decision, the family filed a complaint with the state education department. All of the issues were resolved in the student's favor within six months. **The educational agency rejected the family's claim for attorney's fees, and the family commenced a lawsuit for fees in a state circuit court**. The educational agency removed the case to a federal district court and moved for summary judgment on the ground that the 30-day appeal period had expired.

The court observed that the IDEA gives courts the discretion to award reasonable attorney's fees to parents who are prevailing parties in IDEA proceedings. The IDEA contains no statute of limitations and courts are to borrow an applicable limitations period from the state in which they are located. **The court held that Indiana's 30-day statute of limitations for appeals of agency decisions was the most appropriate state limitations period**. There was no merit to the family's assertion that the educational agency's failure to implement the administrative order extended the limitations period. Since the petition for fees was not filed until over seven months after the issuance of the administrative decision, the court granted the educational agency's summary judgment motion. *Wagner v. Logansport Community School Corp.*, 990 F.Supp. 1099 (N.D.Ind.1997).

◆ Seven students with disabilities and their families prevailed in separate administrative proceedings brought under the IDEA against an Iowa school district. **They individually sought reimbursement for their attorneys' fees for successfully prosecuting their cases at the administrative level**. When the school district failed to pay any of the attorneys' fees claims, the families filed lawsuits against the district in the U.S. District Court for the Northern District of Iowa, which consolidated the cases and considered the district's motion for summary judgment on the basis of the passage of a 30-day limitation period taken from Iowa administrative law. The court observed that the IDEA lacks a statute of limitations, leaving courts to apply the most analogous state statute. The borrowed state statute of limitations must not conflict with important policy considerations of federal law. The district maintained that the 30-day administrative review statute was most analogous to IDEA requirements because of the public policy favoring prompt disposition of IDEA cases. The court found that this time restriction was far too short to allow for effective settlement negotiations.

Instead, **the court agreed with the students and parents that either a two or five-year statute of limitations from Iowa personal injury law was the most analogous to the IDEA**. Under either statute, the claims for attorneys' fees were not barred. The court denied the district's summary judgment motion. *Curtis K. by Delores K. v. Sioux City Community School Dist.*, 895 F.Supp. 1197 (N.D.Iowa 1995).

IV. OTHER IDEA PROCEDURES

◆ A California elementary school district with a long history of non-compliance with the IDEA was the subject to an extensive corrective action plan designed to bring the district in compliance. The plan was adopted as the result of a class action lawsuit brought on behalf of students with disabilities who attend or will attend district schools. Through implementation of the plan, the district was to come into compliance with the IDEA, and the plan included specific actions for the district to take, described the expected results, contained a timeline for completing the goals, identified the responsible individual for each objective and established measures for determining compliance. A federal district court approved the plan in January 2000, and a court-appointed monitor began overseeing the district. **The plaintiff class requested that the court sanction the school district, arguing the district was not complying with the plan or attempting to follow the plan**. At a hearing in April 2001, the court gave the district three additional months to show its commitment to complying with the plan and ordered the California Department of Education to furnish additional assistance to the district.

After the district's IDEA compliance did not improve dramatically within the three-month period, the court ordered it to demonstrate at a hearing why the court should not hold the district in contempt. Before a civil contempt finding can be made, a court must determine that a specific and definite order of the court has been violated. Once this determination is made, the court then looks to whether every reasonable effort has been made to comply. If this standard is met, civil contempt has not occurred.

In applying the first part of the contempt test, the court rejected the district's argument that the order requiring implementation of the corrective action plan was too vague to be enforced through a contempt motion. It found the plan very clear, establishing specific actions, setting deadlines and designating the responsible person for each action. The court stated there was no dispute over the district's failure to comply with the court's order regarding the plan. Turning to the second part of the test, whether the district used all reasonable steps within its power to comply with the plan, the court found that the evidence overwhelmingly supported the conclusion that the district failed to meet this standard. **There was little evidence that district personnel were committed to implementing the plan, and there appeared to be an entrenched resistance to the plan among district employees, including the superintendent**. According to the court, once the plaintiff class filed the motion for contempt, the district began to take steps to better implement the plan, but these steps were still not enough to prevent the district from being held in contempt. The court held the district in contempt, but gave it seven months to demonstrate its commitment to compliance with the plan, refusing to adopt the plaintiffs' suggested remedy of turning over control of the district to the state superintendent of education for appointment of a receiver. Within the seven-month period, the district was required to take certain steps in order to comply with specific portions of the plan. The court issued a very detailed order explaining what was expected of the district and set up a monthly monitoring procedure, while retaining authority to impose additional remedies if necessary. *Emma C. et al. v. Eastin et al.*, No. C96-4179 T E H, 2001 WL 1180363 (N.D. Cal. 2001).

◆ A New York City school district student with a learning disability in reading received resource room instruction from grades five through seven. When the student was 15 years old, his mother filed an administrative action against the school board, challenging the lack of individual instruction. A hearing officer ordered the city to provide him with instruction in a more-restrictive modified instruction services class setting with a student-teacher ratio of 3-to-1. A 12-year-old New York City student with a learning disability also received resource room instruction for years in groups of about eight students without any individual assistance. The 12-year-old's mother commenced an administrative action against the city board of education, challenging the student/teacher ratio in the student's resource room. The proceeding led to the development of a new IEP for the student, calling for instruction in a group of no more than three students. A state review officer reversed the decision, holding that the student was entitled to intensive, specialized direct instruction in a special education class. **The students later filed a federal district court action against the city school board, seeking to represent a class of New York students with learning disabilities who were denied necessary individual instruction** because of placement in resource rooms with inappropriately high student-teacher ratios.

The court found that **neither of the students could adequately represent the class because during the course of the action, they had obtained relief addressing their educational needs that separated their interests from other students in the proposed class**. The 12-year-old student no longer attended resource rooms, and thus could not fairly or effectively represent a class seeking relief from deficient instruction in resource rooms. The school board further argued that the case should be dismissed because of failure to exhaust administrative remedies. The 15-year-old student admitted that the hearing officer's order modifying his IEP fully addressed his educational needs and the court found that this mooted the dismissal motion. The same was true of the 12-year-old's case, even though he had exhausted his administrative remedies, since he obtained all the relief he sought. The court held that because the intervening decisions by the administrative officers had substantially altered the status of the case, the action should be dismissed without prejudice to allow the amendment of the complaint to reflect these changed circumstances. *Adrian R. v. New York City Board of Education*, No. 99CIV9064(WK), 2001 WL 77066 (S.D.N.Y. 2001).

◆ The parents of a student with clinical depression and tremors refused to consent to an IDEA evaluation. School officials became concerned about the student's poor grades and isolation from other students, and made numerous attempts to evaluate him for special education services. After three years, the parents allowed the district to classify the student as disabled under Section 504 of the Rehabilitation Act and provide him with an alternative learning plan. The student tried out for the high school basketball team, but was cut. School officials sought an evaluation and suggested that the parents consider home schooling. **The parents requested an IDEA due process hearing, asserting that the district failed to follow proper evaluation procedures, threatened them by proposing home schooling and discriminated against their son** by cutting him from the basketball team. A hearing officer held for the school district, and the Indiana Board of Special Education Appeals affirmed the decision.

The parents appealed to a federal district court, asserting claims under the IDEA, Section 504 and 42 U.S.C. § 1983 for deprivation of a free appropriate public education and discrimination on the basis of disability. Soon after filing the lawsuit, the family moved out of the school district. When school officials discovered this, they expelled the student, as allowed by Indiana law. The court awarded summary judgment to the district, and the parents appealed to **the Seventh Circuit, which dismissed the case as moot. The case involved a dispute over the placement of a 20-year-old who had not attended district schools for three years.** The district had agreed to end its attempts to evaluate the student during administrative proceedings, and continued litigation could provide no meaningful relief to the parties. The parents' claim for attorneys' fees failed because they had won only small, tactical victories at the administrative level, losing on the major issues in litigation. *Doe v. Eagle-Union Community School Corp.*, 2 Fed.Appx. 567 (7th Cir. 2001).

◆ A federal district court awarded expert-witness fees incurred during IDEA administrative proceedings to the parents of a Massachusetts student with disabilities. A magistrate judge noted that no U.S. circuit court has yet ruled on whether expert-witness fees are recoverable as part of an attorneys' fee award under the IDEA. The act itself does not mention experts' fees, but a U.S. House of Representatives conference report from the 1986 Handicapped Children's Protection Act stated that House conferees intended that the term "attorneys fees as a part of the costs" include expert-witness fees and the reasonable cost of any test or evaluation necessary to prepare for an action or proceeding under the act. This provision is now a part of the IDEA, at 20 U.S.C. § 1415(i)(3)(B). **The magistrate rejected the district's argument that expert-witness fees could not be awarded in the absence of direct statutory authority. The magistrate held that the award of expert-witness fees was consistent with IDEA purposes** as well as the explicit language of the House committee report, and recommended that the court approve an award of $3,250 for the costs of presenting expert testimony. The district court adopted the magistrate's recommendation in its entirety. *Pazik et al. v. Gateway Regional School District*, 130 F.Supp.2d 217 (D. Mass. 2001).

◆ **The parents of a group of children with autism and pervasive developmental disorder advanced an action on behalf of the children, asserting that county, state and city officials deprived the children of due process rights**

to individualized treatment plans in violation of the IDEA and Section 504 of the Rehabilitation Act of 1973. They also asserted claims under the New York Public Health Law and federal civil rights claims arising under 42 U.S.C. § 1983. The parents asserted that county officials attempted to prevent, discourage and limit the use of applied behavior analysis (ABA) therapy and that the state deliberately failed to enforce special education laws in violation of their obligation to do so. The families sought a declaratory judgment, compensatory and punitive damages, remedial treatment, costs and attorneys' fees. The county brought a cross-claim against the state.

The court denied a motion by the county for a declaration that the state was the party ultimately responsible for provision of early intervention services as required by the IDEA. The state was already a party to the action because of the claim brought against state education officials, and the county's payment for services would have to be resolved at trial. The county was not entitled to an award of attorneys' fees arising from a motion by one of the students who sought to be dismissed from the action. The court had permitted this student to withdraw from the suit. The state argued that it was entitled to have the county's action against it severed from the case advanced by the students, claiming that the issue of the ultimate financial responsibility for serving the students was a separate matter. The court disagreed, finding that severance would require presentation of some evidence twice. The compliant by the families asserted that the state knew about the failure by county and city employees to provide ABA therapy but failed to take remedial action. **While the county's action against the state centered on the question of financial responsibility for the provision of early intervention services, the court held that the general overlap of witnesses and evidence made severance inappropriate**. The families moved the court to exclude from evidence three spreadsheets offered by the county and state containing information compiled from case files. They asserted that the spreadsheets were inadmissible for a variety of reasons, including inaccuracy. The court rejected their claim that presentation of the spreadsheets at a trial would confuse the jury and carry an improper "aura of respectability" as county records, or that they were incomplete and confusing. This was so even though only portions of the spreadsheets would be offered and critical evidence tending to show an illegal policy custom or practice of limiting the use of ABA therapy to 10 hours per week might be excluded. **The court refused to narrow the issues to those identified by the county as related to the formulation of individual family service plans**, since the existence of an illegal policy might go beyond the formulation of the plans. It also permitted the families to introduce videotapes of their children and tapes of other students intended to instruct and familiarize the jury on use of ABA therapy. The court made a number of other pretrial rulings and indicated that no trial would be held until at least September of 2000. *B.D. v. DeBuono*, 2000 U.S. Dist. Lexis 2186 (S.D.N.Y. 2000).

◆ Despite a history of deficient performance by a District of Columbia institution for detained and committed students, the appointment of a receiver by a trial court was inappropriate in view of the creation by Congress of a new District financial authority and the appointment of a new superintendent. **The District of Columbia Court of Appeals held that the appointment of a**

receiver was a drastic remedy that should be employed only as a last resort. The dispute arose from a class action brought against the District of Columbia, which alleged the defendants failed to provide students confined to juvenile facilities with appropriate care, rehabilitation and treatment. A consent decree was entered into by the parties, and a special master was eventually appointed to help the defendants comply with the consent decree and related orders. The students later requested the appointment of a receiver to oversee the institution's education system. *District of Columbia v. Jerry M.*, 1999 WL 796847 (D.C. 1999).

◆ A student had chronic encephalopathy and a developmental delay. She experienced seizures, behavioral problems, and had difficulty functioning in school. Her school opposed certain accommodations sought by her mother. The mother refused to attend meetings or supply requested medical records, and eventually filed a due process challenge to the school's proposed IEP. After the mother failed to comply with three orders by the administrative hearing officer, the school petitioned a state superior court to enforce the orders. **The school also sought appointment of a guardian for the student for the limited purpose of participating in her educational placement decisions.** The court ordered the mother to sign a medical records release, but she initially failed to comply with the order. After the court found her in contempt, she signed the release. Although the court absolved the mother of contempt, it ordered the appointment of a limited educational guardian to act on the student's behalf.

The mother appealed to the Court of Appeals of Indiana, which stated that **while the trial court had properly applied a standard incorporating the best interest of the student, it failed to find that the appointment of a guardian was necessary for her care or supervision.** Although the school argued that the mother refused to attend case meetings and "consistently obstructed" efforts by the school to finalize an IEP, her only obstructive actions were failing to provide the requested medical records and refusing to sign the IEP. The school district was nonetheless able to draft an IEP. There was no evidence that the mother prevented the school from providing the student with a FAPE or that an educational guardian was necessary to prepare an appropriate IEP. The mother was not legally obligated to attend case conference meetings, and her failure to attend them did not prevent the school from adopting and implementing an IEP. Lack of parental consent neither prevents a school from providing, nor relieves a school of its duty to provide a FAPE to students with disabilities. When parents refuse to approve an IEP, schools may seek review by an independent hearing officer. The court reversed and remanded the trial court order appointing a limited guardian for the student. *E.N. v. Rising Sun-Ohio County Comm. School Corp.*, 720 N.E.2d 447 (Ind.Ct.App. 1999).

◆ The parent of a New York student with disabilities brought a federal district court action on behalf of her son against his school district, alleging violations of the IDEA and 42 U.S.C. § 1983. The parent's attorney informed the court during the course of a hearing that the parties had reached a tentative settlement pending approval by the school district's insurance carrier. The judge agreed to discontinue the action so that the school district could obtain the necessary approval and stated that the parties were entitled to reopen the matter if the settlement fell through within 45 days. He also said that the case could be reopened by means of a letter to the court rather than a formal motion. Within three weeks of the hearing, **the parent wrote the court a letter stating that she was firing her attorney and wished to reopen the matter**. She also sought a conference with the school district as soon as possible. However, the court held that the district had ratified the settlement, and that the case was now closed.

Eleven months later, the parent appealed to the U.S. Court of Appeals, Second Circuit, which noted that the 45-day period specified by the court applied to both parties and that the court had indicated that the parties could reopen the case if the settlement fell through. **Since the mother had followed the court's suggested procedure for abandoning the settlement by mailing a letter to the court within 45 days, it should have granted her motion to reopen the case.** The eleven-month delay in bringing an appeal was not grounds for barring the challenge since there was no evidence of undue delay or prejudice to the school district. The court reversed and remanded the case. *Cappillino v. Hyde Park Central School Dist.*, 135 F.3d 264 (2d Cir.1998).

◆ The parents of a Missouri student with a disability requested a due process hearing to contest the services provided to their son. The parties and their attorneys met and agreed to postpone the proceedings to discuss a formal resolution. **A settlement was reached, but the parents never signed the written version**. Some months later, the school district commenced a state court action against the parents, seeking to enforce the agreement. A federal district court rejected the parents' attempt to remove the action, and a state trial court ordered the agreement enforced. The parents appealed to the Missouri Court of Appeals, Southern District.

The court reviewed statements made by the school district's attorney at the hearing and found reference only to an agreement by the parties to a recess in the hearing. The hearing panel had taken no action that could form a record for the trial court to review. State law permitted appeals only where administrative remedies had been exhausted, and **judicial review could only occur where there was a full, written opinion including findings of fact and conclusions of law. Accordingly, the trial court lacked the power to enforce the agreement and its order was void.** The court vacated the trial court decision and denied the school district's request for attorney's fees. *Neosho R-V School Dist. v. McGee*, 979 S.W.2d 537 (Mo.Ct.App.S.D.1998).

◆ A North Carolina student with Attention Deficit Hyperactivity Disorder obtained an administrative order holding that his school board's IEP was inappropriate and that his parents' decision to place him in a Wisconsin public school (where he lived with his grandparents) was appropriate. A state review officer affirmed the administrative order for the reimbursement of certain costs associated with evaluations, private tutoring, travel and related expenses. However, she reversed the part of the order allowing the parents to recover claims for lost wages and other incidental expenses and for two independent evaluations. The review officer also found that the IEP devised for the student for a subsequent school year was appropriate, and she denied recovery for any expenses during that year. **The parents filed a federal district court action seeking attorneys'**

fees and expert witness fees incurred in the IDEA action. The court considered several motions including the school board's motion for dismissal and agreed with the board that the IDEA does not provide for expert witness fees. **The court noted that the IDEA makes no provision for expert witness fees. The parents were thus entitled only to the $40 fee allowed under federal law**. There was no merit to the claim that 42 U.S.C. § 1988, a federal civil rights statute permitting the recovery of attorney's fees, provided an alternative means of recovering expert witness fees. The court also made a favorable ruling for the board based on its desire to keep certain requested attorney fee information from the parents' attorney. *Eirschele by Eirschele v. Craven County Bd. of Educ.*, 7 F.Supp.2d 655 (E.D.N.C.1998).

◆ The parents of an autistic Florida student disagreed with the IEP proposed by their school district. They urged the school board to furnish the student with a residential placement in a private Massachusetts facility. When the school board denied the requested placement, the parents requested a due process hearing at which the student's father represented the family. The hearing officer agreed that the IEP was insufficient, but denied the request for a residential placement. The parents appealed to a federal district court on several grounds, including claims that the student was entitled to an order for extended eligibility, an award of monetary damages and the residential placement. The family contracted with an attorney who represented them through the first day of trial, but then discharged him. The student's father then moved the district court to allow the attorney's withdrawal and to grant permission to proceed on behalf of his son. The court denied the motion, and the father appealed to the U.S. Court of Appeals, Eleventh Circuit. The court found that **while the IDEA allows parents to bring lawsuits on behalf of their children, it does not authorize them to act as their children's counsel. This is true even though parents have a right to represent their children in due process hearings**. There was no authority in the federal rules of civil procedure or other federal law allowing parties to be represented by non-attorney parents. The court affirmed the district court order denying the father's motion. *Devine v. Indian River County School Bd.*, 121 F.3d 576 (11th Cir.1997).

CHAPTER FOUR

Private School Tuition

I. TUITION REIMBURSEMENT

In Burlington School Committee v. Department of Education of Massachusetts, *below, the U.S. Supreme Court ruled that parents who unilaterally place children in private schools may nevertheless receive tuition reimbursement from the school district if the IEP proposed by the school is later found to be inappropriate. If the proposed IEP is found to be appropriate, however, the parents will not be entitled to reimbursement for the tuition and related expenses incurred in unilaterally changing their child's placement.*

A. Unilateral Placement by Parents

◆ In the *Burlington* case, the father of a learning disabled third grader became dissatisfied with his son's lack of progress in the public school system. A new IEP was developed for the child that called for his placement in a different public school. **The father**, however, followed the advice of specialists and **unilaterally withdrew his son from the public school system, placing him instead at a state-approved private facility**. He then sought reimbursement for tuition and transportation expenses from the public school, contending that the IEP, which proposed a public school placement, was educationally inappropriate. The state Board of Special Education Appeals (BSEA) ruled that the proposed IEP was inappropriate and that the father was justified in placing his son at the private school. The BSEA ordered the school committee to reimburse the father for tuition and transportation expenses, and the school committee appealed to federal court. A Massachusetts federal district court held that the parents had violated the IDEA by enrolling their child in the private school without the agreement of public school officials. Thus, they were not entitled to reimbursement. The U.S. Court of Appeals for the First Circuit reversed the district court's ruling, and the school committee appealed to the U.S. Supreme Court.

In upholding the court of appeals, **the Court ruled that parents who place a disabled child in a private educational facility are entitled to reimbursement for the child's tuition and living expenses if a court later determines that the school district proposed an inappropriate IEP**. Conversely, reimbursement could not be ordered if the school district's proposed IEP was appropriate. The Court observed that to bar reimbursement claims under all circumstances would violate the IDEA, which requires appropriate interim placement for children with disabilities. In addition, under the school committee's reading of the IDEA's stay put provision, parents would be forced to leave children in what might later be determined to be an inappropriate educational placement, or would obtain the appropriate placement only by sacrificing any claim for reimbursement. This result was not intended by Congress. However, **parents who unilaterally change the placement of a child during the pendency of IDEA proceedings do so at their own financial risk**. If the courts ultimately determine that a child's proposed IEP is appropriate, the parents are barred from obtaining reimbursement for an unauthorized private school placement. *Burlington School Comm. v. Dept. of Educ. of Massachusetts*, 471 U.S. 359, 105 S.Ct. 1996, 85 L.Ed.2d 385 (1985).

◆ An Illinois student exhibited behavior problems by second grade but was not identified as disabled or eligible for special education services until the end of her eighth-grade year, when a private evaluator concluded that she had emotional disabilities. Her elementary school district scheduled an IEP meeting, at which the district offered two summer placement options and a primarily mainstream placement for grade nine. She agreed to attend high school summer classes. The student failed several eighth grade classes but was "placed" in ninth grade. The student's mother was not allowed to participate in the decision to exclude the student from elementary school graduation. When the student withdrew from summer classes after only two days, her mother contacted the district to request immediate services. The mother's request for a residential placement at district expense was unsuccessful. **Two weeks prior to the next IEP team meeting, the student's mother enrolled her in a residential facility in Maine that utilized controversial methods**. The team revised the student's IEP by proposing placement in a self-contained program with two periods of regular education, counseling and community-based services. The student's mother did not attend the meeting and initiated separate administrative proceedings against the elementary and high school districts, seeking reimbursement. The hearing officer in the elementary district case upheld the student's proposed ninth-grade placement. However, a review officer reversed part of the decision, finding that the district failed to timely identify the student as eligible for special education and excluded her mother from the decision to place her in grade nine. She ordered the elementary district to provide compensatory education, but denied the request for tuition reimbursement. The hearing officer in the high school district case held that the district was not responsible for the student's education until after she actually started high school and that the proposed IEP was appropriate. A review officer upheld the decision and the mother appealed both cases to a federal district court.

The court stated that because the student no longer attended school in either district, all placement issues were moot. Only the question of reimbursement remained. The high school district appropriately intervened by helping develop the IEP and placing the student in an adequate program in a highly structured environment. The student's mother had signed the IEP and it was in accord with the recommendations of the student's therapist and psychologist. The IEP team considered extended-year services for the student and found that they were not required. The administrator's inappropriate comments about residential placement undermined the purposes of the IDEA and understandably prompted the student's mother to seek a private placement. However, she should have waited for the scheduled meeting before making her unilateral placement decision, since she knew the IEP team would be discussing the case. Moreover, **the private school was inappropriate, as it employed a confrontational method that was contrary to the recommendations of the student's own experts**. The placement segregated the student with disabled students, in violation of the IDEA's least restrictive environment requirement. The districts' technical violations of the IDEA did not compromise the provision of FAPE. The IDEA was not implicated in the decisions to place the student in ninth grade and exclude her from graduation. While the elementary district had not acted with any urgency to evaluate her despite her deteriorating performance, the IEP was approved within IDEA deadlines. The student's eighth-grade school year had ended by that date, and she would not have received IEP services until the following year. Any delays were minimal and did not violate the IDEA. **Because the districts had offered the student an appropriate placement and the placement selected by her mother was inappropriate, the court denied the request for tuition reimbursement**. *Board of Education of Arlington Heights School District No. 25 v. Illinois State Board of Education*, No. 98 C 5370, 2001 WL 585149, 2001 WL 969043 (N.D.Ill. 2001).

◆ During the 1996-1997 school year, a student with disabilities received resource room services and therapy while classified as learning disabled. His parents placed him in a private school during the course of the school year. The following year, the district declassified the student as learning disabled and classified him as speech impaired. As a result, the board reduced his speech and language therapy. The parents placed the student in another private school for the 1997-98 school year. The student's committee on special education failed to include a general education teacher on his IEP team, as required by the IDEA. It also failed to determine whether additional evaluations should be conducted prior to his declassification and did not consider whether he required declassification support. After reviewing evidence that the student was progressing well at his private school, the board declassified him from special education entirely and recommended his placement in a general education program with no special services. The parents requested a due process hearing, seeking continuation of the private school placement. A hearing officer held that **the IEP proposed by the school board for 1998-99 was void because of procedural errors. However, the parents were not entitled to tuition reimbursement, because the record did not indicate that the student had a disability**. A state review officer agreed that the proposed IEP was procedurally flawed. The review officer declared the IEP invalid and determined that the student was speech impaired at the beginning of the 1998-99 school year. Despite this finding, there was no objective basis for placing him at the private school, and the parents were not entitled to tuition reimbursement.

The parents appealed to a federal district court, which considered the parties' cross-motions for summary judgment. It recited the general rule that parents of a student with disabilities are entitled to private school tuition reimbursement if the student's IEP is inadequate and the private educational services obtained by the parents are appropriate. Reimbursement is appropriate only if the parents show that the private placement they select is proper under the IDEA. The U.S. Supreme Court has held that reimbursement is possible for a unilateral parental placement even if the private school is not approved by the state education agency. In this case, the IEP prepared by the school committee was procedurally flawed and the student should not have been declassified. However, **the evidence indicated that the student had no special education needs warranting placement in the private school his parents selected**. Test results indicated that he was in the average to superior range in cognitive ability and academic achievement, and was no longer in need of speech and language services. The record did not indicate that he even received special education services at the private school. While he would benefit from the school's advantageous student-teacher ratio, this would be true for any student. The IDEA does not require the best education possible, and the court granted the board's motion for summary judgment. *J.B. v. Board of Education of City School District of the City of New York*, No. 00 CIV. 7099 (SAS), 2001 WL 546963 (S.D.N.Y. 2001).

◆ A student of average intelligence was diagnosed with ADHD and dyslexia during his kindergarten year. His IEP team devised a first-grade IEP that called for 30 minutes of speech and language therapy, 45 minutes of academic special education services three times weekly, consultation services twice a month and two daily administrations of Ritalin. His parents obtained an independent evaluation, which, according to them, recommended a substantially separate language-based classroom with regular speech and language therapy. They enrolled the student in a private school prior to a scheduled IEP team meeting and notified the district after the student's enrollment. The team held the meeting and considered the private evaluation, preparing an IEP for the student's second-grade year that greatly expanded the level of special education services provided to him. **The parents rejected the proposed IEP and commenced an administrative action against the school district in which they sought approval of the private-school placement and tuition reimbursement**. A hearing officer ruled that the IEP was designed to assure the student's maximum possible educational development in the LRE. Since this satisfied Massachusetts IEP requirements, the hearing officer denied the parents' request for tuition reimbursement, also holding that the private school they selected was inappropriate.

The parents appealed to a federal district court, arguing that the hearing officer made a number of errors and should have considered a subsequent third diagnosis. A magistrate judge held that the hearing officer had correctly applied Massachusetts law by considering whether the IEP could be implemented to assure that the student would receive the maximum possible educational development in the least restrictive environment. There was no error in the failure to consider the student's third diagnosis. The focus of the hearing officer was properly on the IEP as originally proposed. She had relied on the reports and testimony of appropriate experts who had evaluated the student. **There was evidence that the parents intended to enroll their son in the private school before the IEP was ever formulated**, despite the school's lack of a language-based program, as recommended by the private evaluation. In contrast, the public school's proposed classroom teacher testified that she could provide these services in her classroom. The IEP included most of the services, goals and objectives recommended by the experts who prepared the private evaluation. The hearing officer had committed no error in finding that the program provided for an FAPE in the LRE. The parents were not entitled to tuition reimbursement, and the district was entitled to summary judgment. *Douglas W. by Douglas v. Greenfield Public Schools*, 164 F.Supp.2d 157 (D. Mass. 2001).

◆ Despite his history of severe emotional and behavioral problems, a Minnesota elementary school student made reasonable academic progress in public schools. He was enrolled in a special program for elementary needs for the third grade. During that year, his IEP team held numerous planning and team meetings to discuss his placement. The IEP called for reduced homework assignments, separate classroom space, behavior reinforcement and time-out periods. The student's mother was a team member, but her ideas often conflicted with those of the team. Less than halfway through the year, the mother unilaterally removed the student from school, but later agreed to his placement in the same special program at another school. After a serious behavioral incident at the second school, the student's mother again removed him from school. At her suggestion, the school began to provide him with homebound academic instruction. Within weeks, **the mother unilaterally enrolled him in a private school offering one-on-one instruction for at-risk students**. He was isolated from other students there, but continued to exhibit significant behavioral problems. The mother initiated a due process hearing request, seeking recovery of the private school tuition expenses. A hearing officer found that the district provided the student with a FAPE during grades one and two, but failed to design an appropriate IEP for third grade. A hearing review officer reversed the decision, holding that the district developed and implemented an appropriate third-grade IEP, and that the mother's unilateral action denied the district an opportunity to assess and refine the IEP. She appealed to a federal district court, which held that the district provided the student a FAPE during third grade.

The court held that the district kept the student's behavioral challenges in mind and tailored the IEP to his needs. It provided the mother with opportunities to participate in the development of his IEPs, even though the team did not always endorse her ideas. The IEP team made continual efforts to refine the student's program during his third-grade year. He was in the average range in his academic subjects, demonstrating educational progress. The IDEA does not compel schools to maximize student potential and achieve outstanding results. So long as a student benefits from instruction, a district may determine the appropriate methodology. **Because the student's IEP was reasonably calculated to enable him to receive educational benefits, the court** affirmed the review officer's decision, and **refused to award the mother reimbursement for the costs of the private school**. While the mother was not entitled to tuition reimbursement, the district was bound to pay her a sum under a settlement agreement reached by the parties after the student's third-grade year. *Nygren v. Minneapolis Public Schools*, No. CIV.01-1305 ADM/AJB, 2001 WL 1690048 (D. Minn. 2001).

◆ A New York school district prepared an IEP for a student with a learning disability that called for resource room services, but did not specify how often the student would receive these services. The district subsequently began providing him with resource room support for one period each day. The district's special education director agreed with the father that the student's IEP goals did not address his learning needs. The district then proposed increasing the student's resource room usage to two periods per day. The student's father unilaterally removed him from the public school system and placed him in a private school for students with learning disabilities. At due process, a hearing officer held in the school district's favor, but a state review officer held that the IEP offered by the district was inappropriate. According to the SRO, the IEP failed to adequately describe the student's educational needs and to construct goals and objectives specifically addressing those needs. However, the SRO held that **the private school placement selected by the father was also inappropriate and that reimbursement was improper**. The father appealed to a federal district court, which agreed with the SRO that the IEP was inappropriate. However, the district was required to fund the private school placement because it was suited to the student's "love of hands-on activities," provided for remedial academic classes twice a week and employed phonics instruction that improved his grade level.

The school district appealed to the Second Circuit, which recited the general rule that in tuition reimbursement cases, an award is permitted only where the IEP is inadequate to afford the student a FAPE, and the private placement obtained by the parents is appropriate. The court found that the IEP suggested for the student did not reference his problems in word analysis, decoding skills and spelling. The district conceded that the IEP was materially incomplete in identifying the student's learning deficits, and was ineffective in setting baselines and measuring progress. For this reason, it could not rely on the fact that the student was advancing in school as evidence that he was still making progress. The district failed to show that the IEP was reasonably calculated to provide the student with educational benefits and this part of the district court decision was upheld. However, **the district court failed to appropriately defer to the SRO's finding that the private school selected by the father was improper**. The district court failed to explain why the SRO's finding was discredited and improperly relied on evidence that the student was happier at the private school. It substituted its judgment for that of the SRO; therefore, **the portion of the decision awarding tuition reimbursement to the father was reversed**. *M.S. v. Board of Education of City School District of City of Yonkers,* 231 F.3d 96 (2d Cir. 2000).

◆ A Connecticut school district and the parents of a seventh grader with ADHD, depression, a learning disability in written expression, and difficulties processing verbal information agreed that a placement outside the district was necessary. Until an appropriate placement was located, the parents consented to home schooling. The parents then sought the student's placement in a private summer program. When the district refused, they unilaterally placed the student in the private summer program and, after he completed it, sought his placement at the private school for grade eight. The district agreed that the school was appropriate but made the student's placement there contingent on entering into a contract with the school to ensure that it followed the student's IEP. The school and district were unable to reach an agreement and the parents filed a due process complaint, seeking reimbursement for tuition, along with reimbursement for private psychological services they had obtained. **The hearing officer held that the private school placement was appropriate and that the parents were entitled to tuition and tutoring reimbursement** for the student's eighth-grade year. However, the placement was inappropriate for grade nine because of the private school's refusal to sign the contract with the school district and the parents' failure to provide necessary information. The administrative decision also denied the parents' request for reimbursement of psychological services. The parents appealed to a federal district court, which held that they were entitled to reimbursement for the costs of the ninth-grade private school placement and the psychological counseling services. The district court also awarded the parents attorneys' fees.

The district appealed to the Second Circuit, which held that **the district court had failed to properly apply the correct analysis** for evaluating tuition reimbursement cases. In these cases, **courts must first determine whether the school district's proposed placement was adequate under the IDEA. The district court in this case had only considered whether the school district had a valid reason for rejecting the private placement, and did not evaluate the adequacy of the IEP team's proposals**. The court had then concluded that the lack of a contract between the district and the private school did not bar reimbursement. The Second Circuit held that this reasoning was flawed, since it ignored the analysis approved by the U.S. Supreme Court in *School Comm. of Burlington v. Department of Education of Massachusetts*, above. The Second Circuit vacated the portion of the judgment awarding reimbursement to the parents for grade nine and remanded the issue to the district court. The panel also reversed the award of reimbursement for psychological services. Under the IDEA, no-cost psychological counseling is required only if the services are required to assist the student to benefit from special education. Courts have uniformly barred psychological counseling reimbursement where parents unilaterally arrange for the services without first notifying their school boards of dissatisfaction with an IEP. The parents brought the issue to the district's attention about eight months after the services were obtained, making it impossible for the district to determine whether the expenditures were necessary. The appeals court reversed the portion of the judgment awarding reimbursement for these costs. *M.C. v. Voluntown Board of Education*, 226 F.3d 60 (2d Cir. 2000).

◆ A Maine student attended public schools during grades five, six and seven and had a learning disability. She attended a combination of regular and special education classes. Although her IEP goals were not consistently met, her teachers believed that she was making meaningful academic progress, had appropriate peer interactions and was "bright, creative, artistic, sensitive, kind, caring, humorous, bubbly and flamboyant." However, the student's parents believed that she suffered from depression arising from her learning disability and contended that she had become suicidal. They asserted that the student's placement team failed to recognize her depression and social isolation, resulting in inadequate IEPs that failed to address her emotional and social problems. **Prior to the student's entry into eighth grade, the parents removed her from public schools and placed her in a private residential school for students with learning disabilities.** The school district nonetheless prepared an IEP for the student and commenced an administrative proceeding to validate its proposal for the year. The hearing officer approved the IEPs created by the district for each of the student's years of public school attendance and the proposed eighth grade IEP.

The parents appealed the hearing officer's decision to a federal district court, asserting that the hearing officer was biased against the student and that the IEPs failed to address the student's social and emotional disabilities. They sought tuition reimbursement for the private facility and an award of compensatory enhanced services. **The court found no merit to the parents' assertion that the hearing officer had improperly disregarded evidence that the IEPs failed to address the student's emotional and social problems.** There was contrary evidence that the parents had exaggerated these problems, as her teachers had testified that she was generally happy in school. The hearing officer had been faced with contradictory testimony and had not discounted the parents' testimony. Rather, she placed greater weight on the testimony of the student's teachers. The hearing officer's factual findings were entitled to deference, since she was in a better position to assess the credibility of the witnesses. There was ample evidence in the record to support her findings and the court affirmed them. The court found the parents' assertion that the hearing officer showed "hostility" toward them to be both unsupported and irresponsible, since she was simply required to choose between two possible but contrary factual representations. The court affirmed the administrative decision for the school district. *B.A. v. Cape Elizabeth School Committee*, No. 99-164-P-C, 2000 U.S. Dist. Lexis 7498 (D. Me. 2000).

◆ Because a student had a history of emotional and behavioral problems, school officials recommended placing him in a behavior disorder resource program. The student's mother disagreed with the proposal and unilaterally enrolled the student in a private parochial school that had no formal special education behavior disorder program. The school informed the mother at the end of the school year that the student would not be readmitted, and she re-enrolled him in district schools. However, **she placed him in a private residential school in Maine for the following year without consulting with the district, and sought reimbursement**. The district declined the request and the mother commenced administrative proceedings, seeking tuition reimbursement. The district obtained an order dismissing the request. Rather than appealing the decision to a second-level hearing officer as required by state law, the mother commenced a new action against the district for tuition reimbursement, which was denied by another administrative hearing officer. A second-level hearing officer affirmed on the merits, declining to rule on the school district's argument that the second action was barred by claim preclusion. The mother appealed to a federal district court, which agreed with the school district that the first administrative decision on the merits of the claim precluded her from advancing the virtually identical claim in the second action. However, the court also ruled on the merits of the case, finding that the claim for tuition reimbursement was properly dismissed.

On appeal, the U.S. Court of Appeals for the Seventh Circuit held that the district court had appropriately considered the merits of the case, despite the school district's assertion that the second action was barred by the first. Even though typically deemed "orders for summary judgment," district court decisions in actions filed under the IDEA are evaluated under a preponderance-of-the-evidence standard. Courts considering IDEA administrative appeals must give due weight to administrative proceedings and refrain from substituting their judgment for that of administrative hearing officers. The mother was required to show only that the administrative findings were clearly erroneous. **The IDEA provides for a cooperative placement procedure** in which school officials, parents and others who are knowledgeable about the student meet and confer about the student's educational needs. School authorities are obligated to reimburse parents for private school tuition expenses only if a court ultimately determines that the private placement, and not the proposed IEP, is appropriate. Without some minimal cooperation from parents, schools cannot evaluate students with disabilities as contemplated by the IDEA. **The circuit court held that parents who fail to cooperate with a school district's attempts to evaluate children with disabilities and make unilateral private placements forfeit their claims for tuition reimbursement.** Courts will look harshly upon any party's failure to reasonably cooperate under the IDEA. The district court correctly found that the mother did not cooperate with school officials by placing the student in an out-of-state residential school and declining to allow district officials to evaluate him in the state of Illinois. The circuit court affirmed the district court's grant of summary judgment in favor of the school district. *Patricia P. v. Bd. of Educ. of Oak Park and River Forest High School Dist. No. 200*, 203 F.3d 462 (7th Cir. 2000).

◆ A Maryland student with multiple disabilities was musically talented and exceeded academic expectations. After attending public school pre-kindergarten and kindergarten programs, her parents sought placement in a private special education school. An administrative law judge ordered the school district to pay for the private placement for two years. The student progressed academically at the school, but, after the two years were up, the district proposed an IEP placing the student in a public school learning center. The parents wanted to maintain the private school placement. **At due process, the parents argued that the public school program offered by the school district was inappropriate for a variety of reasons.** The ALJ agreed, and issued an order requiring the school district to fund the private school placement because it had failed to provide the student with a FAPE. He held that the public school placement was inappropriate because of the student's emotional fragility and that the public school could not meet the student's IEP goals.

The school board appealed to a federal district court, arguing that the administrative order was contrary to the testimony of its employees. The court disagreed, noting that a private educational consultant and tutor hired by the student's parents testified that the public school did not provide a differentiated level of instruction, which the student required. The ALJ was in the best position to determine the credibility of the witnesses. The school board argued that the private school placement would not provide the student with a placement in the least restrictive learning environment as required by the IDEA and the IDEA regulations at 34 CFR Part 300.500, which require mainstreaming of students with disabilities to the maximum extent appropriate. The court again disagreed with the board, noting that the finding that the school district failed to provide the student with a FAPE made the mainstreaming issue inconsequential. Although the IDEA requires mainstreaming to the maximum extent appropriate, it does not require mainstreaming when it results in no educational benefit to the student or is otherwise inappropriate. The tutor's testimony indicated that **the student required stability in her learning environment, was frightened by unfamiliar situations and was confused by a large school setting. These factors would make it difficult for her to benefit from the proposed public school placement**. Because there was no error in the administrative decision, the court affirmed it and awarded summary judgment to the student. *Bd. of Educ. of Montgomery County v. Hunter*, 84 F.Supp.2d 702 (D. Md. 2000).

◆ The parents of an Indiana student with dyslexia objected to the school district's proposed IEP near the end of his seventh grade year. During the summer, they placed the student in the Landmark School in Massachusetts and sought an administrative ruling on the adequacy of the proposed IEP. An administrative hearing officer held that the district was required to provide the student with weekly sessions for remedial reading and accommodation strategies and provide compensatory education during the next two summers to make up for failing to provide this assistance prior to the hearing. However, **the decision rejected further summer education and affirmed the proposed placement in a mainstream public school setting**. The parents removed the student from public school and placed him full time at the Landmark School. A federal district court substantially affirmed the administrative decision and the parents appealed to the Seventh Circuit.

The circuit court explained that the district court had appropriately deferred to the administrative proceedings in reaching its decision. It disagreed with the parents that the Landmark School placement constituted the student's stay put placement. Although the administrative decision held that the student required summer instruction to address flaws in his IEP, the court stated that parents take the financial risk of placing a student in a private school pending IDEA proceedings and must show more than that a proposed IEP is deficient to obtain private school tuition reimbursement. In addition to showing that the school district's proposal is inadequate, parents must show that placement in a private school is proper under the IDEA. The district court had found that **private school tuition reimbursement was inappropriate because the extra summer sessions and the continuation of the mainstream public school program would be preferable to the segregated Landmark School placement**. Even though the public school had fallen behind in providing extra services to the student, this did not require a private school placement. The court also refused to award the parents their requested attorneys' fees, finding that they did not prevail in the case despite receiving $1,000 as compensation for private tutoring. This amount was insignificant in comparison with the relief they were seeking. The court affirmed the district court decision. *Linda W. v. Indiana Dept. of Educ.*, 200 F.3d 504 (7th Cir. 1999).

◆ Two gifted brothers with learning disabilities attended district schools for several years. Their parents became dissatisfied with both programs and obtained independent evaluations. The parties failed to reach any agreement on IEPs and the parents enrolled the students in a private school for students with learning disabilities. The school district sent the parents IDEA notices concerning due process hearings, but they did not request a hearing for either student for over one year. Even after the family initiated administrative proceedings against the district, the hearings did not take place for several months. As a result over two years elapsed from the time the students were placed in the private schools until the hearing officer rendered a decision. The hearing officer found that the IEPs proposed by the district were appropriate and denied the family's request for reimbursement. **A special education review panel reversed the decision, finding that the district was liable for tuition reimbursement for proposing inadequate IEPs, but reducing the amount of liability because of unreasonable demands by the parents.** A federal district court affirmed the review panel's decision and the parties appealed to the Third Circuit.

The school district argued that the private school selected by the parents was inappropriate because it was not approved by the state of Pennsylvania. The court disagreed, observing that the U.S. Supreme Court's decision in *Florence County School Dist. Four v. Carter*, 510 U.S. 7 (1993) disposed of the notion that a non-approved school is always an inappropriate placement. The court held that the private school placement was appropriate, affirming the district court's finding that it was not overly restrictive. However, **the Third Circuit reversed the district court's reduction in tuition reimbursement based on the parents' conduct**, which the lower court had characterized as "uncooperative and unreasonable." **The Third Circuit held that such a reduction in appropriate benefits would be contrary to the core IDEA policy of encouraging parental participation in special education decisions.** The circuit court approved of the reimbursement of private school tuition for both students as of the time the family requested the administrative hearings. The family was also entitled to reimbursement for the cost of independent evaluations for both students. The court affirmed the district court judgment, except for the limitation on tuition reimbursement for parental behavior. *Warren G.; Grant G. by Tom G. v. Cumberland County School Dist.*, 190 F.3d 80 (3d Cir.1999).

◆ A Missouri student who had attended his neighborhood elementary school began seventh grade at a middle school. He came home after the first day of school with stomachaches, vomiting, crying and other physical symptoms that he continued to experience throughout the school year. A psychiatrist determined that he had general and separation anxiety but had no impediment to attending school. The student completed seventh grade, receiving mostly As and Bs and showing marked improvement in managing his anxiety. However, **he began to cry when he returned home from his first day in eighth grade, and his parents enrolled him in a private school without consulting the school district**. Over a year later, the parents requested reimbursement for the private school placement, which the school district denied. They commenced a federal district court action against the district for reimbursement of their costs. The court granted summary judgment to the district, finding that the student was not disabled within the meaning of the IDEA because his anxiety did not cause his academic performance to fall below his age level. The parents appealed to the U.S. Court of Appeals, Eighth Circuit.

The court observed that the parents had unilaterally transferred the student to the private school without informing the school district. The IDEA contains specific requirements for school administrators, parents and students regarding the formulation of IEPs. **The district had received no opportunity to provide an appropriate public education for the student through possible accommodations**. Because the district had been excluded from the parents' decision making process, reimbursement was inappropriate. The court affirmed the district court judgment without reaching the issue of whether the student was disabled within the meaning of the IDEA. *Schoenfeld v. Parkway School Dist.*, 138 F.3d 379 (8th Cir.1998).

◆ A Kentucky student with Pervasive Development Disorder was enrolled in his school district's infant-toddler intervention program. He attended a preschool program in the county school system. His parents obtained an evaluation from a Boston private school and later sought to place him there. They asked school officials to delay formulation of the student's IEP because he had been accepted for a summer program at the Boston school and they wished to incorporate his expected progress there into the IEP. **Before the IEP was developed, the parents decided to place the student at the Boston school for the regular school year**. The school district offered placement in a general ungraded primary school, and the parents sought an administrative ruling on their entitlement to funding for the Boston placement. A hearing officer held that the school district did not offer an appropriate placement, but a state appeal board reversed the decision. The parents appealed to a federal district court and initiated a second administrative proceeding, seeking an order that the student should remain in the Boston school and seeking tuition reimbursement from the school district for both school years. The hearing officer held that the school district had formulated an appropriate IEP, and the parents filed a second district court action.

The court consolidated the cases and stated that **the parents had failed to give the school district an opportunity to develop an appropriate IEP for the first school year. The parents were not entitled to any of their expenses for either school year**. The parents appealed to the U.S. Court of Appeals, Sixth Circuit, which held that the IDEA Amendments of 1997 did not affect its decision, since they have no retroactive application and the school years in issue were prior to 1997. The district had proposed an appropriate, comprehensive IEP. There was evidence that the Boston school was unable to match the school district's ability to offer the student daily one-on-one speech and language therapy, occupational and physical therapy, computers and appropriate peers. The parents were not entitled to dictate educational methodology to the school district or obtain a specific program for the student. Because the district had proposed an appropriate placement, the court affirmed the judgment. *Tucker by Tucker v. Calloway County Bd. of Educ.*, 136 F.3d 495 (6th Cir.1998).

◆ A New Jersey student had attention deficit hyperactivity disorder, and while he was not classified as a student with disabilities under the IDEA, he was eligible for special services under § 504 of the Rehabilitation Act. **The parents claimed that the school board did not timely inform them that he qualified for § 504 services,** and later requested a hearing with the state education department **to obtain reimbursement** for the unilateral private placement they arranged. An administrative law judge held that the board had failed to develop and implement an appropriate § 504 accommodation plan and that the private school placement was appropriate. Finding the board's § 504 plan "seriously deficient," the administrative judge ordered it to reimburse the parents for their private school costs. The board appealed to a federal district court and the parents counter-claimed, alleging that the board had failed to inform them of their § 504 rights and was in contempt of the administrative order. The board moved to stay the administrative order while its tuition reimbursement appeal was pending.

The court found that **under § 504 regulations at 34 CFR Part 104.33(c)(1), school boards are obligated to provide educational services to qualified students or to place them in an appropriate program not operated by the board.** The school board had failed to provide the student with a free appropriate public education as required by § 504. Private school tuition was an appropriate remedy in this case, and the parents were entitled to the temporary relief they had requested, based on the likelihood that they would prevail on the merits of the case. The court rejected the board's arguments that budgetary constraints precluded a temporary order pending further consideration of the case. It was not entitled to a stay of the administrative order and was required to reimburse the parents for over $12,000 in tuition and transportation costs. The expenditure did not present irreparable harm to the board, whose budget for the year exceeded $10 million, while a contrary order might present great harm to the family. *Borough of Palmyra, Bd. of Educ. v. F.C.*, 2 F.Supp.2d 637 (D.N.J.1998).

◆ An 18-year-old multiply disabled New Jersey student attended a public school program for two years. The student's parents unilaterally placed him at a private school in Maryland. The parents requested a due process hearing, seeking reimbursement for the private school costs. The parties agreed to **a settlement under which the school board paid a portion of the private school costs for the school year, and also agreed that the board would contribute the same amount for the next year's private school tuition plus 90 percent of the increase for the following school year for specified services.** Under the stipulation, the board was relieved of responsibility for other costs. The following year, the private school determined that the student required the services of a one-on-one aide, which resulted in his tuition almost doubling, to over $62,000. The school board refused to pay for the aide based on the stipulation from the prior year. An administrative law judge dismissed a complaint filed by the parents, ruling that the prior stipulation was legally enforceable. The administrative law judge also dismissed a second claim by the parents. The parents appealed to the U.S. District Court for the District of New Jersey, which upheld the agreement. The district court stated that the school board was not allowed to contract out of responsibilities imposed upon it by the IDEA. **The court found that the student must have an opportunity to show a change of circumstances that would make the settlement unenforceable** under the IDEA. The court remanded the case to the administrative law judge for a determination of whether the student had received the opportunity at the prior hearing to raise the issue of educational necessity. If there had been a change in circumstances such that continued enforcement of the stipulation would violate the student's educational rights, the agreement would be void.

On remand, **the ALJ concluded that the student's circumstances had not changed, therefore, the agreement was binding**, and the school district did not have to fund the personal aides. The parents appealed to the district court, which reversed, finding the student's circumstances had changed, and that the disputed personal aides were necessary for him to receive a FAPE. Accordingly, the district court voided the agreement and ordered the district to pay for the personal aides. The district appealed to the U.S. Court of Appeals, Third Circuit, which reversed, agreeing with the ALJ's determination that the student's circumstances had not changed. The circuit court stated that the only change was in the cost of the student's private school program. **Parents cannot void settlement agreements just because the cost of a private placement increases**, and public policy supported upholding the agreement. Since the agreement was valid, the district was not obligated to fund the personal aides. *D.R. by M.R. and B.R. v. East Brunswick Bd. of Educ.*, 109 F.3d 896 (3d Cir. 1997).

B. Placement in Unapproved Schools

The U.S. Supreme Court's decision in Florence County School Dist. Four v. Carter, *below, held that parents who placed their child in an unapproved private facility were entitled to tuition reimbursement despite the lack of state approval of the facility. The Court's analysis focused on the appropriateness of the placement selected by the parents and the inability of the local school district to provide an appropriate alternative. While state approval remains a factor in selecting an appropriate placement, the lack of state approval by itself no longer determines the appropriateness of the placement.*

◆ The parents of a South Carolina ninth-grader with a learning disability disagreed with the IEP proposed by their public school district. The IEP called for mainstreaming in most subjects, with individual instruction three periods per week, and specific goals of increasing the student's reading and mathematics levels by four months for the entire school year. The student's parents requested an IDEA due process hearing under 20 U.S.C. § 1415(b)(2). Meanwhile, they unilaterally removed the student from public school and placed her in a private school that specialized in teaching students with disabilities. The hearing officer held that the IEP was adequate. After the student raised her reading comprehension three full grades in one year at the private school, the parents sued the school district for tuition reimbursement in the U.S. District Court for the District of South Carolina. **The court found that the educational program and achievement goals of the proposed IEP were "wholly inadequate" under the IDEA. Even though the private school did not comply with all IDEA procedures**—by employing noncertified staff members, for example—**it provided the student with an excellent education that complied with IDEA substantive requirements.** The court held that the parents were entitled to tuition reimbursement, a result that was upheld by the U.S. Court of Appeals, Fourth Circuit. The school district appealed to the U.S. Supreme Court.

The Court expanded upon its decision in *Burlington School Comm. v. Dept. of Educ. of Massachusetts*, subsection A, above, where it held that parents had the right to unilaterally change their children's placement at their own financial risk. To recover private school tuition costs, parents must show that the placement proposed by the school district violates the IDEA, and that the private school placement is appropriate under the act. Here, **the failure by the school district to provide an appropriate placement entitled the parents to an award of tuition reimbursement, even though the private school was not approved by the state, because the education provided to the student at the private school had been determined by the district court to be appropriate.** The Court further noted that federal courts have broad discretion in granting relief under the IDEA, and may reduce tuition reimbursement awards found to be unreasonable. The lower court decisions in favor of the parents were upheld. *Florence County School Dist. Four v. Carter*, 510 U.S. 7, 114 S.Ct. 361, 126 L.Ed.2d 284 (1993).

◆ A New York two-year old with developmental delay and autism was eligible for early intervention services. The New York City Early Intervention Program devised an individualized family service plan for him that included treatment at a development center, social work and speech therapy. The parents requested the inclusion of applied behavioral analysis (ABA) therapy, but the city did not provide it for students under three. **The parents arranged for in-home ABA therapy under the direction of a social worker, and withdrew the student from the city program. The social worker trained the parents and six college students to provide ABA therapy**. The parents then requested an administrative hearing to obtain reimbursement for the in-home therapy. An administrative law judge agreed that the city program was inappropriate and ordered the city to reimburse the parents for in-house therapy. The city and state department of developmental health appealed to a New York trial court.

The parents removed the action to a federal district court, which dismissed the case. The city and department appealed to the U.S. Court of Appeals, Second Circuit. The court determined that Part H of the IDEA requires states to provide appropriate early intervention services to all infants and toddlers with disabilities and their families. The U.S. Supreme Court has held that parents can obtain reimbursement for privately obtained special education services, even where the services do not completely satisfy a state education agency's standards or regulations. The right of parents to unilaterally withdraw a student from a state-approved program must be preserved where the local education agency's program is inappropriate. In this case, **the order for reimbursement for ABA therapy was affirmed because the city's placement decision was inappropriate, there was a demonstrated lack of ABA therapists in the area, and evidence indicated that the students were qualified to provide the services.** *Still v. DeBuono*, 101 F.3d 888 (2d Cir.1996).

◆ The parents of an emotionally disturbed student requested their school district evaluate the student for special education placement. **They requested approval for a private school placement at a school that offered small classes and employed unlicensed professionals to work with students with disabilities.** The student had attended classes at the private school since the previous fall. The school district convened an IEP meeting; however, it excluded the parents in the development of the IEP in violation of the IDEA (see 20 U.S.C. § 1415(b)). The placement team's confidential report was not signed by all multidisciplinary team members, nor was it created with the input of the student's current teachers, which also violated the IDEA's requirements. The parents rejected the proposed placement and the school district expressly disapproved of the private school placement. The parents requested a due process hearing at which the hearing officer concurred with the parents that the placement outlined in the IEP was deficient. He ordered a new IEP, but the school district proposed another placement without developing a new IEP. The result was a second due process hearing after which the hearing officer again found that the school district had not made an appropriate placement because of the lack of parental participation in the IEP.

The hearing officer ruled that the private school placement selected by the parents was inappropriate because the institution failed to provide special education and related services according to the standards set by the appropriate educational agency. The school district was not required to provide tuition reimbursement for the parents' unilateral private school placement. The parents did not contact the school district concerning further placement issues as instructed by the hearing officer; instead, they filed a lawsuit for reimbursement of the private school tuition in the U.S. District Court for the District of Columbia. The court ruled that there could be no tuition reimbursement in this case. This would be contrary to the IDEA's requirement for an appropriate education, defined in 20 U.S.C. § 1401(a)(18) as "special education and related services that ... meet the standards of the State Educational Agency." Even though the school district had repeatedly failed to include the parents in the IEP process, they were not entitled to private school tuition reimbursement, and the decision of the hearing officer was affirmed. *Fagan v. Dist. of Columbia,* 817 F.Supp. 161 (D.D.C.1993).

- A 20-year-old New Jersey student was entitled to receive special educational services under the IDEA because of autism and severe behavioral problems. The state Division of Developmental Disabilities (DDD) placed her in a Delaware school that was not an approved special education facility. The student's mother sought a transfer to a residential facility located in the family's home town. When the DDD refused to transfer the student, her mother filed a due process hearing under 20 U.S.C. § 1415(e)(2). **An administrative law judge granted the mother's summary judgment motion, ordering the DDD to place the student at the residential facility in the family's home town**. The DDD failed to transfer the student, and the mother filed a petition for enforcement of the administrative order in the U.S. District Court for the District of New Jersey. The DDD responded with a complaint for review of the administrative decision, and the district court consolidated the matters. Before the district court, the DDD changed its position, arguing that the Delaware school retained a "conditional approval" for special education. The student's mother argued that the programs were comparable and that the IDEA's requirement of placement in the least restrictive environment included placing the student as close as possible to the family's home. The district court agreed, citing 34 C.F.R. § 300.552(a)(3), a regulation which requires school districts to take into account the location of the placement, "particularly in a residential program." **Because the educational program available to the student in her home town was comparable to the Delaware placement, it was the appropriate placement**. The court affirmed the administrative law judge's decision for the student and awarded attorneys' fees and costs. *Remis v. New Jersey Dept. of Human Serv.*, 815 F.Supp. 141 (D.N.J.1993).

C. Notice

The IDEA contains provisions requiring notice when parents decide to unilaterally enroll their child in a private school. These provisions are listed at 20 U.S.C 1412(a)(10)(C)(iii), which states when reimbursement for the costs of a unilateral private school placement can be limited, and 20 U.S.C. 1415. Before reimbursement can be limited under 20 U.S.C. 1412(a)(10)(C)(iii), the school district must have previously provided the parents with all applicable IDEA notices and in most cases, the parents are required to notify the district, in writing, of their objections to the district's program and their intent to enroll the child in a private program before actually doing so. Some states have comparable statutory provisions, as illustrated by the following cases.

- A student with disabilities attended public schools under IEPs for three years. The parents agreed to an IEP proposed by the system during March of one school year, without mentioning that they had submitted an application for the child's admission to a private school. After the student was accepted in June of the same year, the family's attorney sent a letter to the public school principal, stating that the parents intended to place their son at the private school. He enclosed new assessments and requested that the school system consider the private school as the student's appropriate placement. The parties met to discuss the new evaluations, but the system maintained its recommendation for placement in a public school. The student attended the private school for the remainder of the year, and the parents commenced an administrative proceeding for tuition reimbursement. **The district moved to dismiss the action, arguing that the IDEA required the parents to provide prior notice of the rejection of an IEP as a prerequisite to any reimbursement claim**. An ALJ granted the motion, even though it was untimely filed, ruling that the parents did not comply with Section 8-413(i)(1), a provision of Maryland special education law that parallels 20 U.S.C. § 1412(a)(10)(C). Both provisions, among other things, preclude private school tuition reimbursement for a unilateral parental placement unless the parents timely notify a school IEP team of a placement rejection and state the reasons for the rejection.

The parents sued the school system and officials in a federal district court, which awarded summary judgment to the district and officials. On appeal to the Fourth Circuit, the court determined the ALJ did not abuse her discretion in considering the system's late dismissal motion. There was no evidence of prejudice and the parents did not argue that they had insufficient time to prepare a response. Although the parents now asserted they had expressed reservations about signing the IEP, they did not inform school officials they were rejecting it. **The letter from the parents' attorney did not serve as a proper rejection,**

as it did not explain that they no longer considered the IEP legally adequate. The parents thus waived the issue of whether they failed to provide timely notice of their son's enrollment in the private school. The circuit court rejected the parents' argument that the school system was required to show it was prejudiced by their failure to provide the rejection notice required by state and federal laws. **Section 8-413(i)(1) clearly explained the consequences of failing to provide timely notice of a student's private school enrollment**, and the claim for tuition reimbursement was properly denied. The system had provided the parents with notice of their procedural rights at the March IEP meeting. They were not entitled to receive any additional notifications, and were not excused from providing appropriate notice of their decision. The court affirmed the summary judgment order for the school district. *Pollowitz v. Weast et al.*, No. CA-99-3118-S (4th Cir. 2001).

◆ Because a student with disabilities did not perform well in a district middle school, his parents removed him from the school in favor of a private placement. He was eventually transferred to a private residential placement in Connecticut. The parents requested reimbursement l and a reevaluation. Before an IEP was approved, the parents requested a hearing on their tuition reimbursement claim on grounds that the district failed to provide a residential placement for the student. The district later approved an IEP calling for a 45-day diagnostic placement, but the plan was not approved until after the hearing date. The board moved to dismiss the administrative proceeding on grounds that the family failed to provide it with a notice required by Maryland special education law. It cited a statute which provides, in part, that **parents who enrolled their children in nonpublic schools are not entitled to tuition reimbursement if they did "not provide to the county board prior written notice rejecting the program proposed by the county board, including the reason for the rejection, and stating an intention to enroll the student in a nonpublic school."** An administrative law judge granted the board's motion and the parents appealed to a federal district court. The court granted summary judgment to the board on grounds that the parents failed to comply with state special education law.

On appeal, the parents argued that the state law did not apply in their case, because the board had not proposed an IEP at the time they enrolled the student in the residential school. The court agreed with the parents, noting that **because there was no IEP for them to reject, the notice contemplated by the state law was impossible**. To preclude the parents from seeking reimbursement because they failed to give the notice specified in the statute would create an absurd result. The court construed the law as applying only when an IEP has actually been proposed by a school district prior to the time a student is enrolled in a nonpublic school. The court explained that this interpretation would not allow parents to bypass required steps for seeking a FAPE for their children within the public school context. This was because any entitlement to reimbursement could only result from a decision by an administrative hearing officer or court that a school district did not make a FAPE possible before the parents enrolled a student in a nonpublic school. Districts would still receive the opportunity to timely fashion appropriate educational programs for students with disabilities. The Fourth Circuit reversed the district court judgment and remanded the case for further proceedings. *Sandler et al. v. Hickey et al.*, 5 Fed.Appx. 233 (4th Cir. 2001).

II. RELIGIOUS SCHOOLS

Public aid to students who attend private religious schools implicates the Establishment Clause of the First Amendment. Public school funding for students with disabilities for private religious school education and related services has been held constitutionally permissible, as the benefit to the private school is only attenuated. In contrast, a direct payment of government funds to a private religious school would violate the U.S. Constitution.

◆ An Arizona student attended a school for the deaf from grades one through five and then transferred to a public school for grades six through eight. During his public school attendance, the school district furnished the student with a sign language interpreter. The student's parents enrolled him in a parochial high school for ninth grade, and requested the school district to continue providing a sign language interpreter. The school district refused, and the student's parents sued it in the U.S. District Court for the District of Arizona. **The court granted the school district's summary judgment motion, finding that "the interpreter would act as a conduit for the religious inculcation" of the student**, promoting his religious development at government expense. On appeal, in the U.S. Court of Appeals for the Ninth Circuit affirmed the district court decision, determining that the furnishing of a sign language interpreter to a parochial school student had the primary effect of advancing religion, in violation of the Establishment Clause of the U.S. Constitution. The court of appeals stated that the placement of a public school employee in a parochial school would create the appearance that the government was a joint sponsor of the private school's activities. The U.S. Supreme Court granted the parents' petition for a writ of *certiorari*. On appeal, the school district cited 34 CFR § 76.532(a)(1), an IDEA regulation, as authority for the prohibition against using federal funds for private school sign language interpreters.

The Court stated that **the Establishment Clause did not completely prohibit religious institutions from participating in publicly sponsored benefits.** If this were the case, religious groups would not even enjoy police and fire protection or have use of public roads and sidewalks. Government programs which neutrally provide benefits to broad classes of citizens are not subject to Establishment Clause prohibition simply because some religiously affiliated institutions receive "an attenuated financial benefit." **Providing a sign language interpreter under the IDEA was part of a general program for distribution of benefits in a neutral manner to qualified students. The provision of the interpreter provided only an indirect economic benefit to the parochial school and was a neutral service** that was part of a general program that was not "skewed" toward religion. A sign language interpreter, unlike an instructor or counselor, was ethically bound to transmit everything said in exactly the same way as it was intended. Because the Establishment Clause did not prevent the school district from providing the student with a sign language interpreter under the IDEA, the Court reversed the court of appeals' decision. *Zobrest v. Catalina Foothills School Dist.*, 509 U.S. 1, 113 S.Ct. 2462, 125 L.Ed.2d 1 (1993).

◆ The New York City Board of Education attempted to implement Title I programs at parochial schools by allowing public employees to instruct students on private school grounds during school hours. In 1985, the U.S. Supreme Court agreed with a group of taxpayers that this violated the Establishment Clause in *Aguilar v. Felton,* 473 U.S. 402, 105 S.Ct. 3232, 87 L.Ed.2d 290 (1985). On remand, **a federal district court ordered the city board to refrain from using Title I funds for any plan or program under which public school teachers and counselors furnished services on sectarian school grounds**. In response to *Aguilar,* local education boards modified Title I programs by moving classes to remote sites, including mobile instructional units parked near sectarian schools. A new group of parents and parochial school students filed motions seeking relief from the permanent order.

The district court denied the motions, and the U.S. Court of Appeals, Second Circuit, affirmed the decision. On further appeal, the U.S. Supreme Court agreed with the city board and students that recent Supreme Court decisions required a new ruling on the question of government aid to religious schools. For example, the provision of a sign language interpreter by a school district at a private school was upheld in *Zobrest v. Catalina Foothills School Dist.,*509 U.S. 1, 113 S.Ct. 2462, 125 L.Ed.2d 1 (1993), above. The Court held that it would no longer presume that the presence of a public school teacher on parochial school grounds creates a symbolic union between church and state. The provision of Title I services at parochial schools resembled the provision of a sign language interpreter under the IDEA. **New York City's Title I program was constitutionally permissible because it did not result in government indoctrination, define funding recipients by reference to religion or create excessive entanglement between education officials and religious schools**. The Court reversed the lower court judgments. In the process, the Court substantially overruled *Aguilar v. Felton* and its companion case, *School Dist. of Grand Rapids v. Ball,* 473 U.S. 373, 105 S.Ct. 3216, 87 L.Ed.2d 267 (1985). *Agostini v. Felton,* 521 U.S. 203, 117 S.Ct. 1997, 138 L.Ed.2d 391 (1997).

◆ A student attended regular classes in public schools through fifth grade. A psychologist reported that her anxiety and depression inhibited her intellectual potential, and she was classified as an exceptional student. The school district developed an IEP for her sixth grade year including mainstream classes with learning disabled resource room support. The student's academic performance declined through the seventh grade and she was assessed by a school psychiatrist as having signs of ADHD, which was confirmed during her eighth grade year. During eighth grade, the student's academic and behavior problems became severe. The student's parent objected to the inclusion of emotional support in the proposed ninth grade IEP, emphasizing her belief in the student's need for a college preparatory program without emphasis on emotional problems. **The parent placed the student in a private Quaker school that was not state approved**. The student excelled at the private school, but the school district's proposed IEP for the following year called for a different placement. The student's mother rejected the IEP and requested an administrative hearing to challenge the district's placement decisions for both years. The hearing officer determined that the district had prepared an appropriate IEP for the ninth grade but not for the tenth grade. She determined that because the placement selected by the parent was for a private, sectarian institution, the state could not be compelled to fund the placement. She also ordered the school district to prepare an adequate IEP for the tenth grade. A special education appeals panel affirmed the hearing officer's decision, but the district failed to propose an alternate placement until April of the student's tenth grade year. The parent appealed to the U.S. District Court for the Eastern District of Pennsylvania.

The court affirmed the administrative decisions concerning the claim for ninth grade tuition at the private sectarian school. There was evidence that the district IEP had been reasonably calculated to enable the student to receive educational benefits. The court rejected evidence of the student's later educational achievement at the private school, noting that the proper consideration in determining the appropriateness of an IEP was whether it was reasonably calculated to afford educational benefits at the time it was developed. There was evidence that the student required emotional support. The court then observed that the district had failed to act on the administrative orders to devise an appropriate placement for the tenth grade. The student was therefore entitled to private school tuition reimbursement for tenth grade. **There was no merit to the school district's argument that payment of private school tuition to a sectarian school violated the Establishment Clause**. The U.S. Supreme Court has ruled that private school tuition reimbursement under the IDEA primarily benefits students, not private schools. The court substantially affirmed the administrative decisions, but required the school district to pay the private school tuition for tenth grade. *Christen G. v. Lower Merion School Dist.*, 919 F.Supp. 793 (E.D.Pa.1996).

- A blind person sought vocational rehabilitative services from the state of Washington's Commission for the Blind pursuant to a state law which provided that visually disabled persons were eligible for educational assistance to enable them to "overcome vocational handicaps and to obtain the maximum degree of self-support and self-care." However, because the plaintiff was a private school student intending to pursue a career of service in the church, the Commission for the Blind denied his request for assistance. The Washington Supreme Court upheld this decision on the ground that the First Amendment prohibited state funding of a student's education at a religious college. The U.S. Supreme Court reversed, finding that the operation of Washington's program was such that the commission paid money directly to the student, who would then attend the school of his or her choice. **The fact that the student in this case chose to attend a religious college did not constitute state support of religion because the individual, not the state, made the decision to support religious education**. The First Amendment was therefore not offended. The case was remanded to the Washington Supreme Court. *Witters v. Washington Dept. of Servs. for the Blind*, 474 U.S. 481, 106 S.Ct. 748, 88 L.Ed.2d 846 (1986).

On remand, the Washington Supreme Court reconsidered the matter under the Washington Constitution, which provides a more strict prohibition on the expenditure of public funds for religious instruction than the U.S. Constitution. **The disbursement of vocational assistance funds for the student's religious education violated the state constitution because it would result in the**

expenditure of public money for religious instruction. The court rejected the student's argument that the restriction on public expenditures would violate his right to free exercise of religion. The court determined that the commission's action was constitutional under the Free Exercise Clause because there was no infringement of the student's constitutional rights. Finally, denial of the funds to the student did not violate the Fourteenth Amendment's Equal Protection Clause because the commission had a policy of denying any student's religious vocational funding. The classification was directly related to the state's interest in ensuring the separation between church and state as required by both state and federal constitutions. The court reaffirmed its previous order disallowing financial assistance. *Witters v. State Comm'n for the Blind*, 771 P.2d 1119 (Wash.1989).

CHAPTER FIVE

Related Services

I. RELATED SERVICES UNDER THE IDEA

The IDEA requires states to provide a free appropriate education to each child with a disability. Related services are part of the state's obligation to provide a free appropriate education. Related services are defined by the IDEA, at 20 U.S.C. § 1401(22), to include transportation, speech pathology, psychological services, physical and occupational therapy, recreation and medical services that are necessary for the student to receive an educational benefit. Other services, such as sign language interpreters, rehabilitation services, family counseling, transition services and extracurricular activities may also be required for children with disabilities.

A. Voluntarily Enrolled Private School Students

- When the parents of New York student with mental retardation requested that the student receive special education services at a parochial school, the district refused, stating that the provision of services by public employees on parochial school grounds violated the Establishment Clause. The parents obtained administrative review of the action, but the school district prevailed. The parents appealed to a federal district court, and obtained a favorable order. The school district appealed to the U.S. Court of Appeals for the Second Circuit, which held that **individualized special education services must be made available to private school students on the same basis as public school students**. The provision of these services did not violate the Establishment Clause. However, the U.S. Supreme Court vacated and remanded the case in view of the 1997 Amendments to the IDEA.

On remand, the Second Circuit held that the amendments do not require a district to provide on-site special education services to voluntarily-placed private school students. A school district need only allocate a proportionate share of IDEA funds to such students. This share is typically only a fraction of a school district's cost of educating students with disabilities. **While the district had the discretion to provide such services on-site at private schools, it was not bound to do so by the IDEA**, and the court reversed the district court judgment. The case was sent back to the district court for further analysis of the issues.

In examining whether New York education law compelled the provision of the requested services on-site at the parochial school, the district court analyzed the language of two sections of New York education law and concluded **the school district could, but was not required to, provide the services on-site**. Further, the court determined that the school district's refusal to provide the services on-site at the parochial school did not violate the Free Exercise Clause. The school district's refusal to provide the disputed service on-site at the parochial school did not impinge on the exercise of the parents' right to practice their religion, as the student had no right to on-site services at the parochial school. *Russman by Russman v. Board of Education of the Enlarged City School District of the City of Watervilet,* 92 F.Supp.2d 95 (N.D.N.Y. 2000).

During the pendency of the student's appeal to the Second Circuit, she received an "IEP diploma" and withdrew from school. As a result, the Second Circuit determined the case was moot, as the student's education was no longer in dispute, and her academic career had most likely ended. *Russman v. Board of Education of Enlarged City School District of Watervliet,* 260 F.3d 114 (2d Cir. 2001).

◆ A Pennsylvania county intermediate unit provided speech and language services to a parochial school student during his kindergarten year. It then notified the family that it intended to discontinue services to Diocesan schools. A district multidisciplinary team devised an IEP calling for biweekly speech/language therapy sessions, on the condition that the student be exclusively enrolled in district schools. The parents rejected the IEP and requested a due process hearing. A hearing officer held that the district was not obligated to provide the student with services while he was enrolled in a private school. A state appeals panel affirmed the decision.

The parents appealed to the Pennsylvania Commonwealth Court, which agreed with the parents that a state law, 24 Pa. Stat. § 5-502, prevented the district from denying their child services by reason of his attendance at a parochial school. The IDEA did not relieve school districts of their obligation to provide services to students with disabilities, only from requiring them to provide services at nonpublic schools. The parents made no claim of an entitlement to services at their son's school. The court agreed with them that **state and federal special education law did not permit school districts to dictate the conditions imposed on private school students in order to receive services.** The district did not assert that it had no room for the student or that his attendance in district programs would cause significant expenditures. It also failed to assert that it expended a proportionate share of federal funds in other ways that benefited private school students. State law did not prevent dual enrollment of a student in a private school and a district gifted program such that the student had to forego the right to receive special education. State guidelines recommended dual enrollment as a "genuine opportunity for equitable participation." The 1997 IDEA

Amendments did not change decades of educational jurisprudence, but instead clarified certain points related to unilaterally enrolled private school students. Services offered to private school students had to reflect a genuine opportunity to participate in programs, the court found, reversing the administrative decisions. *Veschi v. Northwestern Lehigh School District*, 772 A.2d 469 (Pa.Commw.Ct. 2001).

◆ A Pennsylvania student with Down syndrome began attending a parochial school early intervention program until the first grade, when he transferred to a public school under the terms of his IEP. The student did not like the public school, partially because his peers did not accept him, and because he did not like being separated from his siblings. After three weeks, his parents withdrew him from the public school and placed him at the parochial school. **The parents sought** funding for the placement and **the provision of auxiliary services at the parochial school** from their school district and the local intermediate unit. The claim for reimbursement was settled, but the dispute over auxiliary services proceeded to federal court.

In considering the parents' motion for an order that would require the IU to provide auxiliary services to the student at the parochial school, the court noted that the IU received state education funds to "furnish on an equal basis auxiliary services to all pupils in the Commonwealth in both public and nonprofit nonpublic schools." According to the court, the IU was required to provide auxiliary services to the student at the parochial school, even though the parents conceded that the services offered at the public school were appropriate under the IDEA. **State law plainly indicated that auxiliary special education services should be provided to students with disabilities on an equal basis, which the court found to mean a proportional allocation of a fixed allotment to all qualified students.** Private school students had no individual entitlement to services, but the student was entitled to receive auxiliary services at the parochial school. State law required the IU to provide for the proper education and training of the student, who did not attend public school and was "not otherwise provided for." The parochial school was the only appropriate placement for the student under the circumstances, and he could only achieve meaningful progress with special education services. The court held that the student was entitled to speech and occupational therapy, a classroom aide and an itinerant teacher. *John T. et al. v. Delaware County Intermediate Unit*, 2000 U.S. Dist. Lexis 6169 (E.D. Pa. 2000).

◆ A student with spinal meningitis required constant medical care and supervision. He lived with his parents and received special educational services at home from the school district in which they resided. **The parents moved the student to a licensed nursing facility that was located within the school district for non-educational reasons.** The district discontinued the student's educational services and the parents filed an administrative complaint. A hearing officer held that the parents were not entitled to relief because they had unilaterally placed the student at the nursing facility. The parents appealed to a state trial court, and the school district removed the case to federal district court. The district court held that state law and the IDEA required the school district to provide services at the nursing facility.

The district appealed to the U.S. Court of Appeals for the Eighth Circuit, which noted that the school district remained willing to provide the student with a FAPE at school facilities or at his home. The parents had chosen the nursing facility for non-educational reasons and had acted without the consent or approval of the student's IEP team. The parents' arguments were foreclosed by the 1997 amendments to the IDEA, which clarified that **local education agencies are not required to pay for the cost of a private school education if they have offered a FAPE to the student and the parents nonetheless make a voluntary private school placement**. Further, under Eight Circuit precedent, parents who unilaterally place a student with disabilities in a private school or facility have no individual right under the IDEA to special education and related services, and no right to a federal court order mandating that those services be provided at a particular location. The court considered the parents' state law claim, which arose from a section of the Nebraska Special Education Act that requires school districts to provide visiting teachers for homebound students with disabilities. The section did not mandate the provision of on-site teaching services to homebound students; it only listed on-site teaching services as one of the authorized methods by which a school district may provide a FAPE to a student with disabilities. According to regulations published by the Nebraska Department of Education, school districts were not required to pay for the costs of educating a student with a disability at a non-public school or facility if the school district made a FAPE available at the student's home and the parents made a unilateral choice to place the student in the private facility. Since the district offered the student a FAPE, the district complied with the IDEA and with Nebraska special education laws and regulations. The district court judgment was reversed. *Jasa v. Millard Public School Dist. No. 17*, 206 F.3d 813 (8th Cir. 2000).

◆ **The parents of a student with disabilities unilaterally enrolled him in a private religious school and sued the school district and area education association when their request for an on-site assistant was denied**. The district offered to provide the services in a public school setting but refused to provide an assistant on-site at the religious school. A federal district court held that the denial of services violated Iowa law but did not rule on a related IDEA claim. The court nonetheless awarded attorney's fees to the parents based on its finding that they were prevailing parties within the meaning of the IDEA.

The district and education agency appealed to the Eighth Circuit, which rejected their arguments that state law vested educational agencies with absolute discretion when determining where to provide special education services for private school students. **The applicable state law mandated the provision of services to students attending private schools, since it required that school districts make public school services available to private school students in the same manner and to the same extent as provided to public school students**. The court held that the school district violated state law when it refused to provide an assistant to the student. The court also observed that the district's actions before 1997 violated the IDEA, stating that the school board had not considered how best to serve the student in its placement decision. However, its actions after 1997 did not violate the amended IDEA. The 1997 Amendments are not retroactive, and as the law no longer confers an individual right to IDEA services, parents do not have a right to federal court orders mandating that services be provided at a particular location. The court remanded the issue of relief for pre-1997 IDEA violations to the district court. *John T. v. Marion Indep. School Dist.*, 173 F.3d 684 (8th Cir.1999).

◆ An Oregon student, who was blind and had cerebral palsy, initially attended public schools. There, he received physical therapy and services from a vision specialist, along with special equipment. His parents transferred him to a sectarian school for religious reasons. **The district** continued to provide him with braillers, computers, and other special equipment after the transfer, but **declined to provide a vision specialist. Instead, it provided the service at a nearby fire hall**, with transportation. The family sued the school district and state superintendent of public instruction in a federal district court for an order requiring the district to furnish the services at the sectarian school. The court determined that the IDEA did not require the district to provide the services at the sectarian school. However, a state regulation requiring the provision of services for private school students in religiously neutral settings violated the Free Exercise, Establishment, and Equal Protection Clauses of the U.S. Constitution. The district and superintendent appealed.

The Ninth Circuit held that the 1997 IDEA amendments do not require the provision of services on-site at a private school and affirmed that part of the judgment. It rejected the family's assertion that the state regulation violated the Free Exercise Clause. **The regulation did not force the family to choose between enrolling the student in a sectarian school and forgoing services, nor did it burden their free exercise of religion**. Moreover, the regulation did not discriminate against religious school students or suppress religion or religious conduct. The circuit court rejected the district court's holding that the regulation violated the Establishment Clause, because it did not result in entanglement between the state and religion. Under *Zobrest v. Catalina Foothills School Dist.*, 509 U.S. 1 (1993), and *Agostini v. Felton*, 117 S.Ct. 1997 (1997), the presence of public school employees on private school grounds is not longer presumed to violate the U.S. Constitution, and the superintendent would not be required to perform a case-by-case analysis of whether particular school settings were religious, as the district court had found. The Ninth Circuit also rejected the district court's finding that the regulation violated the Equal Protection Clause, finding the district court applied the wrong standard of review. The district court had subjected the regulation to the strict scrutiny analysis, which was not warranted in this case, as students with disabilities are not regarded as a class of persons for which the strict scrutiny analysis is required. The court held that the regulation did not violate the family's constitutional rights, and reversed the judgment. *KDM v. Reedsport School Dist.*, 196 F.3d 1046 (9th Cir. 1999).

◆ A Louisiana student with hearing impairments attended a public school under an IEP that included sign language interpretation services. His parents then enrolled him at a parochial school and requested on-site sign language interpretation services from the school board. The board refused to provide the services and the parents requested an administrative hearing. The hearing officer upheld the board's decision and the parents appealed to a federal district court, claiming

IDEA violations. **The court** granted summary judgment to the parents and **ordered the board to provide a sign language interpreter at the parochial school,** even though the parties had previously agreed that the student's public school IEP was appropriate. The U.S. Court of Appeals for the Fifth Circuit, issued a decision that was favorable to the student in some respects, but remanded the case for further consideration.

The court of appeals then granted petitions for rehearing filed by the parties. It also solicited an opinion from the U.S. Department of Education, which stated that the IDEA does not require school districts to expend non-IDEA funds for students voluntarily enrolled in private schools. **A local education agency's obligation is to make a FAPE available to all disabled students and provide a proportionate share of IDEA funds to students enrolled in private schools**. The court accepted this opinion, and added that the IDEA Amendments Act of 1997 specifies that an education agency need only provide students enrolled in private schools with a proportionate share of IDEA funds. Because the district had offered the student an appropriate public school IEP, it was not required to provide him with an on-site interpreter. The circuit court reversed the district court judgment. *Cefalu v. East Baton Rouge Parish School Bd.*, 117 F.3d 231 (5th Cir.1997).

◆ A multiply-disabled Indiana student attended public school with assistance for positioning, self-help skills, motor movements, mobility and expression. She attended a kindergarten class with related services including speech and occupational therapy, transportation and a full-time instructional assistant. Her parents chose to enroll her in a private school and requested the assistance of an on-site instructional assistant. When the school denied the request, the parents sought a hearing. The hearing officer held that the school was not obligated to provide the student with an instructional assistant at the private school. The parents then appealed to a federal district court, asserting IDEA violations. The court held that IDEA regulations required the school district to provide related services to private school students that were comparable to those received by public school students. The school district appealed to the U.S. Court of Appeals for the Seventh Circuit. The court of appeals held that public schools need not provide voluntarily-placed private school students with related services that are comparable to those received by public school students. School districts maintain the discretion to decide what benefits will be provided to private school students and need only provide voluntarily-placed private school students with a genuine opportunity for equitable participation. The court reversed the district court judgment, but the U.S. Supreme Court vacated and remanded the case for reconsideration in view of the IDEA Amendments of 1997. The court then found that **the 1997 amendments relieve a local education agency from the obligation to pay for a private school student's special education and related services if the agency has made a FAPE available and the parents voluntarily place the child in the private school**. Because the school district had afforded the student a genuine opportunity to receive a free appropriate public education, the court again reversed the district court judgment. *K.R. by M.R. v. Anderson Community School Corp.*, 125 F.3d 1017 (7th Cir.1997).

◆ A profoundly deaf twelve-year-old Kansas student attended a public school for four years before his parents voluntarily placed him in a private nonsectarian school. They asked the school district to provide the student with interpretive services on site at the private school. The district denied the request and its decision was upheld in administrative proceedings. The parents appealed to a federal district court, which held that the district had to pay for the requested services. The school district appealed to the U.S. Court of Appeals for the Tenth Circuit, which reversed the district court decision, ruling **that the district had to pay an amount up to, but not more than, the average cost to the district of providing the same services to public school students**.

The U.S. Supreme Court agreed to review the case and remanded it for reconsideration in view of the IDEA Amendments of 1997. On remand, **the court of appeals held that the amendments did not apply retroactively and that its prior decision remained in effect for all activity in the case up until June 4, 1997, the effective date of the amendments**. After that date, the amended act applied, and the district court would have to reconsider the student's entitlement to funding. The court found that **under the amendments, a local education agency is not required to pay for an interpreter for a voluntarily-placed private school student if the agency offers the student a FAPE**. The local education agency is obligated only to allow private school students to participate in special education and related services and to provide them with a proportionate amount of IDEA funds. The state would not be required to spend any of its own funds for on-site private school interpretive services, and the student was not entitled to any additional rights under Kansas law. The court reversed and remanded the case. *Fowler v. Unif. School Dist. No. 259, Sedgwick County, Kansas*, 128 F.3d 1431 (10th Cir.1997).

◆ Two Minnesota students with disabilities attended private religious schools. Education officials determined that both students could benefit from paraprofessional services. **Both school districts denied requests by the students to furnish on-site paraprofessional services at the sectarian schools**. The families then became financially unable to continue paying private school tuition. A group representing parents of Minnesota students with disabilities joined the two families in filing a federal district court action against the two school districts, the state education commissioner and other education officials, claiming that state regulations and policies implementing the IDEA were unconstitutional and that state and local officials had violated the IDEA by denying their requests. **The district court grated summary judgment against the parents on their IDEA claim, finding the IDEA grants broad discretion to local boards in determining what services to provide to special education students who voluntarily attend private schools**. The statute and regulations do not require local education agencies to provide on-site paraprofessional services to private school students. After the one district decided to provide services, the parents of the other student appealed, challenging the grant of summary judgment against them on the IDEA, free exercise, free speech and equal protection claims.

The U.S. Court of Appeals, Eighth Circuit, reversed the district court's decision with respect to the equal protection and IDEA claims. The district's policy of denying on-site special education services to students with disabilities who attended sectarian schools while providing services to students who were home schooled or attended nonsectarian schools appeared to be unconstitutional. According to the court, the evidence suggested impermissible religious discrimination by the district. Turning to the parents' IDEA claims, the court stated that under IDEA 1997, the student was not entitled to on-site services at a sectarian school. However, the court determined that **the denial of on-site services before the effective date of IDEA 1997 was improper**. Under the old version of the IDEA, the student was entitled to special education services that were "comparable in quality, scope, and opportunity for participation" to the services furnished to public school students. The appropriate remedy for this violation was left for the district court to determine on remand. *Peter v. Wedl,* 155 F.3d 992 (8th Cir. 1998).

B. Home Schooled Students

◆ The parents of a home schooled student who needed speech therapy requested speech therapy from the district, and indicated their willingness to bring the student to a public school for therapy. The district rejected the request, stating that the student was being educated at home and did not attend a public or nonpublic school. The state department of education denied mediation and due process hearing requests by the parents, and they commenced a state court action against the district in which the state department of education intervened. A trial court found that the student was entitled to a *pro rata* allocation of federal funds available for New Jersey nonpublic school students. It also held that the department had improperly engaged in rulemaking in violation of the state administrative procedure act when it created its regulatory definition of "nonpublic school." Moreover, the department and district violated the student's equal protection right to receive special education under the New Jersey Constitution. The court ordered the department and district to reimburse the family for weekly speech therapy sessions.

On appeal, the New Jersey Superior Court, Appellate Division, noted that the IDEA allows school districts to treat nonpublic-school students and home-schooled students differently. IDEA regulations state that local districts must provide services to students in "private schools" under a funding formula that compares the number of private school students with the total number of students with disabilities in the district. Because the student in this case was not attending a "nonpublic school," he was not included in this calculation. Under the IDEA, state law determines whether a home-schooled student is enrolled in a "private school." New Jersey did not include home schooling within the definition of "nonpublic school" and there was no indication that the Legislature intended to provide services to students elsewhere than at a school. The appeals court rejected the parents' argument that the term "nonpublic school" encompassed home education. It observed that **the amended IDEA creates no individual entitlement to funds and allows the states to differentiate among students who attend nonpublic schools and those who are educated at home.** State law, the IDEA and an OSEP opinion letter provided a clear statutory basis for the exclusion of home schooling from the definition of "nonpublic school" in department regulations. Although it was permissible for New Jersey school districts to differentiate between nonpublic-school students and those who received home education, the district in this case violated the student's equal protection rights by refusing entirely to provide him with services, even after his parents agreed to follow a recommended treatment plan that was to take place at a public school in the district. **Because the district did not provide the student with services it provided for other students who needed speech therapy services, and they would be delivered at the same cost to the district, the district violated the student's equal protection rights.** The appeals court affirmed the trial court's decision regarding the alleged equal protection violation, and rejected the district's assertion that the department was responsible for paying for the disputed services. *Forstrom v. Byrne et al.*, 775 A.2d 65 (N.J. Super. Ct. App. Div. 2001).

C. Sign Language Interpreters

◆ An Arizona school district furnished a sign language interpreter to a student with hearing impairments who attended public schools. When the student's parents enrolled him in a parochial school, they requested the school district continue providing the interpreter. The district refused to provide this service on Establishment Clause grounds and the parents filed a lawsuit against the district in a federal district court. Appeal reached the U.S. Supreme Court, which held that **the provision of a sign language interpreter was a religiously-neutral distribution of IDEA benefits that provided only an indirect financial benefit to the parochial school.** It reversed the lower court decisions and held that the Establishment Clause of the First Amendment to the U.S. Constitution did not prohibit the school district from sending the sign language interpreter to the parochial school for the student's benefit. *Zobrest v. Catalina Foothills School Dist.,* 509 U.S. 1, 113 S.Ct. 2462, 125 L.Ed.2d 1 (1993). For a full summary of this case, see Chapter Four, Section II.

◆ Three Nebraska students with hearing impairments required the use of sign-language interpreters in their classrooms. Their school district provided a modified SEE-II system that was based on the use of SEE-II principles 85 percent of the time, with the remaining time spent using modifications that helped beginning students learn sign language more easily. However, **the students used strict SEE-II signing systems at home, and their parents made numerous requests to use strict SEE-II systems at school.** After the district refused to comply with their requests, the parents filed an administrative complaint, alleging that the modified signing system did not provide their children with an adequate individualized special education program. The hearing officer held for the school district but imposed on it the requirement to develop IEPs for each student that called for interpreters during both academic and nonacademic activities. The parents appealed to the U.S. District Court for the District of Nebraska, which affirmed the administrative decision. The parents then appealed to the Eighth Circuit.

On appeal, the parents renewed their argument that the IDEA and Americans with Disabilities Act (ADA) required the district to provide their children with the signing system of their choice, rather than the one selected by the school district. They argued that the use of the modified SEE-II system amounted to a failure to develop an appropriate IEP. They also claimed that the district violated the ADA by depriving them of access to educational programs and discriminating against them. The court of appeals disagreed, finding no error in the district court's decision. **There was no requirement under the IDEA for a school district to maximize the educational potential of each student. Parents and students were not entitled to compel a school district to provide a specific signing system of choice as a related service.** Although ADA regulations required a public entity to provide an auxiliary aid or service of choice to an individual with disabilities, the public entity was allowed to demonstrate that another effective means of communication existed. The school district had complied with the ADA by providing the modified SEE-II system as an effective means of communication. The circuit court affirmed the district court's decision. *Petersen v. Hastings Pub. Schools*, 31 F.3d 705 (8th Cir.1994).

D. Transition Services

Transition services must be included in each IEP as a part of the duty to provide a FAPE. Under IDEA 1997 and the corresponding regulations, transition services must be considered by the IEP team starting at age 14, or earlier, if deemed appropriate by the student's IEP team. Transition services help students prepare for post-school life by teaching them employment and independent living skills. Further, transition services can be a related service if required to assist a student with a disability in benefiting from special education.

◆ The parents of a 20-year-old student with disabilities requested a due process hearing to resolve a dispute with the school district over the district's diagnosis of the student. The hearing resulted in an administrative order requiring the school district to conduct an evaluation and devise a new IEP. The parents disputed the resulting IEP and arranged for independent evaluations. The parents did not participate in further IEP and multidisciplinary team meetings and requested a second hearing. A hearing officer held for the school district and the parents appealed. A state appeals panel affirmed the hearing officer's decision that the appropriate classification of the student was physically disabled and mentally retarded, and denied the parents' request for reimbursement of the costs of the independent evaluations. **The appeals panel held that the IEPs for the student's three most recent school years were inadequate in the areas of transition planning** and assistive technology. As relief, the student was awarded over 600 hours of compensatory education.

The district appealed to a federal district court, which noted that in two-tiered administrative systems, courts should generally accord due weight to the appeals panel's findings, rather than those of the hearing officer, except for determining witness credibility. In examining the transition services issue, the court stated that the IDEA requires a statement of transition services for students no later than age 16. In this case, **the transitional evaluation prepared by the school multidisciplinary team was inadequate because the team did not include personnel who had evaluated the student's transition needs. The district also failed to include aspects of transition planning in the student's IEP.** The court adopted the panel's decision, finding that the IEP was not sufficiently tailored to meet the student's needs. The district had also improperly delayed providing assistive technology to the student. After identifying the student's needs in this area, no equipment was provided for over one year, and the student received inadequate training once the equipment was provided. Applying the Third Circuit's standard for awarding compensatory education, the court found that the district knew or should have known the student's IEP lacked appropriate transitional planning and assistive technology provisions. Accordingly, compensatory education was appropriate. The court modified the appeals panel decision by slightly decreasing the amount of compensatory education awarded, but otherwise upheld the appeals panel's decision. *East Penn School Dist. v. Scott B.*, 1999 WL 178363 (E.D.Pa.1999).

♦ A 17-year-old South Dakota student with cerebral palsy was classified as orthopedically impaired. She obtained good grades and participated in extracurricular activities. Her special education program provided adaptive physical education, physical therapy and transportation. After she completed her physical education requirements in ninth grade, the district advised her parents that she was no longer eligible for special education services. The parents requested a due process hearing, claiming that the district had failed to provide transition services, as required. The hearing officer determined that even if the student was not eligible for special education, the need for transition services alone justified providing them. **The hearing officer determined that the district must provide training in independent living skills and self-advocacy as necessary transition services** and furnish a transition plan in coordination with other agencies. A federal district court concluded the student had severe orthopedic impairments and was in need of special education and related services under the IDEA. The district was obligated to provide transition services and the court ordered it to convene an IEP meeting. The court denied the student's request for compensatory education.

The school district appealed to the U.S. Court of Appeals for the Eighth Circuit, where it argued that the student should not be deemed disabled since she was an excellent student who was not adversely affected by her disabilities. The court disagreed, stating that if it were not for the specialized accommodations, instruction and services provided by the school district, the student's grades would be adversely affected. The district had failed to incorporate the services it was providing the student into its written IEP and her need for the services had not ended. **The student would be entitled to receive transition services from the school district until the age of 21 or her graduation date**. The court affirmed the district court judgment. *Yankton School Dist. v. Schramm*, 93 F.3d 1369 (8th Cir.1996).

E. Occupational Therapy and Rehabilitation Services

♦ A 14-year-old Massachusetts student with ataxia telangiectasia received physical, occupational and speech therapy services at a private, nonsectarian school under a public school IEP. The student's disorder eventually required the assistance of a full-time instructional aide. **His parents and their local school district agreed that he needed an aide, but disputed the financial**

responsibility for providing this assistance at the private school. The parents rejected a proposed IEP calling for the provision of an aide at a public school and began paying for a special education aide on-site at the private school. They sought an administrative order requiring the school district to fund the service, but an administrative hearing officer determined that the district had fulfilled its obligation to provide the student with a genuine opportunity for equitable participation in special education services by offering to provide the aide at a public school site. The hearing officer expressly held that the district was not obligated to fund an aide at the private school because the IEP provided for a FAPE. The parents appealed to the U.S. District Court for the District of Massachusetts, which granted the school district's motion for summary judgment.

The student then graduated from the private school and began attending a public high school. The parents appealed to the U.S. Court of Appeals for the First Circuit. **The court of appeals held that the student's graduation deprived it of jurisdiction over the case, since no controversy remained between the parties** and there was no evidence that he would reenroll at the private school or transfer to a private high school. Because the parents had failed to bring a claim for damages at the district court level, the court of appeals was without jurisdiction to determine their entitlement to reimbursement. Since the controversy was moot, the court vacated the judgment and remanded the case for dismissal. *Thomas R.W., by Pamela R. v. Massachusetts Dept. of Educ.*, 130 F.3d 477 (1st Cir.1997).

- A preschooler with ataxic cerebral palsy received occupational, physical and speech therapy services from a Texas school district's early childhood program. The district prepared an IEP for the student calling for 30 minutes of occupational therapy per week. The family moved to Mississippi and their new school district adopted the Texas district's IEP, providing him with occupational and physical therapy for the rest of the school year and summer. As the district prepared a revised IEP for the upcoming school year, the parents decided to enroll the student in a private religious school. **The district discontinued occupational therapy services and quit developing an IEP**. The parents requested a due process hearing, seeking continuation of related services under IDEA regulations. The hearing officer ordered the district to provide occupational therapy and the district appealed to the U.S. District Court for the Southern District of Mississippi, which considered the parties' cross-motions for summary judgment.

The court found that there was no merit to the district's argument that it had satisfied IDEA obligations by simply offering related services to the student should the family decide to return him to public schools. **The district was required to make meaningful efforts to provide educational benefits to the student and could not condition the provision of services on whether the family decided to enroll the student in public schools**. The court affirmed this aspect of the hearing officer's decision but held that he should not have ordered the district to provide the student with an occupational therapist. Because the IEP prepared by the Texas school district was still in place, the student was entitled to receive the 30 minutes of occupational therapy it specified. *Natchez-Adams School Dist. v. Searing*, 918 F.Supp. 1028 (S.D.Miss.1996).

◆ The parents of two children with disabilities who received physical therapy as related services were covered by health insurance policies issued by the same insurer. The students attended two intermediate educational units formed as part of the Pennsylvania public school system. Physical therapy was provided by licensed physical therapists either employed by or affiliated with the units. **Both sets of parents and the two intermediate educational units sought coverage from the insurer, which was denied**. The insurer's basic coverage provided that the policy would pay for "physical therapy prescribed by the attending provider as to type and duration when performed by a duly qualified physical therapist." The parents and educational units filed a class action suit in a federal district court. The insurer moved to dismiss their case, contending that the policy covered only "medically necessary hospitalization and medical benefits," and that the physical therapy which had been provided to the children would never have been prescribed by doctors without the IDEA. The district court granted the motion for dismissal, and the parents and educational units appealed to the U.S. Court of Appeals for the Third Circuit.

The court of appeals refused to accept the insurer's position that the IDEA does not authorize the shifting of costs to private insurers when intermediate educational units have a statutory duty to provide an appropriate public education for children with disabilities at public expense. **Under some circumstances, the insurer would be obliged to pay for physical therapy services furnished under a disabled student's IEP. However, the court noted that the students in this case were entitled to physical therapy services under the IDEA** and that the parents were not legally obligated to pay for those services. Since the insurer had contractually excluded coverage for services that were provided for free under the IDEA, the court refused to hold it liable for the costs of the physical therapy. The court thus affirmed the district court's decision and dismissed the case. *Chester County Intermediate Unit v. Pennsylvania Blue Shield*, 896 F.2d 808 (3d Cir.1990).

F. Other Services

◆ A Utah student received special education services from kindergarten through grade three in California schools. The parent claimed that the Utah school district violated the IDEA's child find obligation by failing to evaluate the student during his sixth grade year and filed an administrative proceeding against the district. A hearing officer held that the district denied the student a FAPE through grade nine and ordered it to provide him with tutoring through grade 10 and the intervening summer vacation.

The parent appealed to a federal district court, asserting that the award was inadequate and alleging that the student's IEP for grade 10 was inadequate. The court granted the district's dismissal motions regarding the parents' claims for monetary damages under 42 U.S.C. § 1983, and considered a separate motion for partial summary judgment on IDEA claims arising from the hearing officer's decision. The court held that factual issues existed for most of the issues, including the sufficiency of the remedy for alleged IDEA violations. It declined to resolve whether the ninth and tenth grade IEPs were sufficient without further consideration. The court was unable to resolve questions concerning the district's failure to provide transition services, related services such as counseling, speech therapy and a laptop computer. However, the district was entitled to summary judgment on the parent's claim of entitlement to ESY services for her son. **State rules required the provision of ESY services to a student who required them to remain at his current least restrictive environment and/or for whom attainment of the expected level of self-sufficiency was otherwise unlikely**. There was no evidence in this case that the student needed ESY services to remain in public school or would not be self-sufficient by the time he graduated. *Wiesenberg v. Bd. of Educ. of Salt Lake City School Dist.*, 181 F.Supp.2d 1307 (D.Utah 2002).

◆ A Connecticut school district and the parents of a seventh grader with ADHD, depression, a learning disability in written expression and difficulties processing verbal information agreed that a placement outside the district was necessary. Until an appropriate placement was located, the parents consented to home schooling. The parents then sought the student's placement in a private summer program. When the district refused their request, they unilaterally placed the student in the private summer program and, after he completed it, sought his placement at the private school for grade eight. The district agreed that the school was appropriate but made the student's placement there contingent on entering into a contract with the school to ensure that it followed the student's IEP and remained accountable for him. The school and district were unable to reach an agreement and the parents filed a due process complaint, seeking reimbursement for the costs of the school, along with reimbursement for private psychological services. The hearing officer held that the private school placement was appropriate and that the parents were entitled to reimbursement for the student's eighth-grade year. However, the placement was inappropriate for grade nine. **The administrative decision** also **denied the parents' request for reimbursement of the cost of psychological services because the student's IEP for grade seven called only for school counseling**. The parents appealed to a federal district court, which held that they were entitled to reimbursement for the costs of the ninth-grade private school placement and the psychological counseling services. The district court also awarded the parents attorneys' fees.

The district appealed to the Second Circuit, which held that the district court had failed to properly apply the correct analysis for evaluating tuition reimbursement cases. In these cases, courts must first determine whether the school district's proposed placement was adequate under the IDEA. The district court in this case had only considered whether the school district had a valid reason for rejecting the private placement, and did not evaluate the adequacy of the IEP team's proposals. The court had then concluded that the lack of a contract between the district and the private school did not bar reimbursement under the IDEA. The Second Circuit vacated the portion of the judgment awarding reimbursement for grade nine costs and remanded the issue to the district court for determination of the adequacy of the proposed IEP. The panel also reversed the award of reimbursement for psychological services. Under the IDEA, no-cost psychological counseling is required only if the services are required to assist the student to benefit from special education. **Courts have uniformly barred psychological counseling reimbursement where parents unilaterally**

arrange for the services without first notifying their school boards of dissatisfaction with an IEP. The parents brought the issue to the district's attention about eight months after the services were obtained, making it impossible for the district to determine whether the expenditures were necessary. The court reversed the judgment awarding reimbursement for these costs. *M.C. v. Voluntown Board of Education*, 226 F.3d 60 (2d Cir. 2000).

◆ As a result of an accident, a student became quadriplegic. He required continuous nursing care and monitoring of his ventilator, wheelchair alignment, catheterization and tracheostomy, as well as feeding and medication. A no-fault insurance carrier paid all of the student's nursing expenses from the time of the accident, including in-school nursing services and services while the student was transported to and from school. **The school district refused to reimburse the insurer for the in-school and in-transit nursing services when the insurer sought reimbursement**. A Michigan trial court agreed with the insurer and the school district appealed to the state court of appeals, arguing that the trial court had been without jurisdiction to consider the case because no IDEA administrative proceeding had been requested.

A court of appeals held that the case arose under the state no-fault insurance act and that the trial court had jurisdiction. The parties did not dispute that the benefits available under the IDEA served the same purpose as the no-fault benefits paid by the insurer for services provided to the student during school hours. The state no-fault act provided that where government benefits are available and an injured person does not exercise reasonable efforts to obtain them, an insurer is entitled to set off such benefits. The court rejected the school district's assertion that an IDEA proceeding was required to show that the nursing services were required and that the insurer had no standing to bring such a proceeding. The insurer had not brought the action to ensure that the services were included in the student's IEP. The school district had already stipulated to the provision of such services for the student, and it was within the trial court's power to apply this fact to the dispute between insurer and school district. **Because the school district was obligated to provide nursing services to the student during school hours and during school transportation, and these were "related services" within the meaning of the IDEA, the trial court had correctly found that they were "required to be provided" by the school district**. The insurer was entitled to subtract the costs of care during school and school transportation from the no-fault benefits otherwise payable to the student. *Farmers Ins. Exchange v. South Lyon Comm. Schools*, 602 N.W.2d 588 (Mich.Ct.App.1999).

◆ A Rhode Island school committee employed a registered nurse to provide tracheostomy monitoring services for a student with disabilities. She assisted the student at home, rode with her on the school bus and remained with her throughout the day, including her return trip home. The services were provided under the student's IEP but included no instruction and the nurse provided no other services to the school committee. **The Rhode Island Department of Elementary and Secondary Education issued an advisory opinion to the committee that employment of the nurse in this capacity violated a state law** which required the employment of only certified nurse-teachers for school health programs. A hearing officer affirmed the department's decision, but the state board of education regents reversed the hearing officer's decision. A teachers' union representing employees of the school district intervened in the matter and appealed to the Supreme Court of Rhode Island.

On appeal, the school committee argued that the provision of related services to a single student with disabilities did not constitute a school health program under state law. Therefore, it did not need to provide a certified nurse-teacher in this case. The court stated that one-on-one nursing services were essential for the student to attend school. **The nurse's services could not be construed as being part of a school health program as defined in state law, and the court affirmed the judgment** of the regents **permitting the registered nurse to provide related services.** *Rhode Island Dept. of Elementary and Secondary Educ. v. Warwick School Comm.*, 696 A.2d 281 (R.I.1997).

- A New Jersey student with cerebral palsy and other disabling conditions required personal assistance for many daily tasks. He also needed close monitoring in classrooms. His parents disputed a public day school placement made by the school district and sought placement for him in a residential program. They filed a petition for a due process hearing with the state education department in which they sought an out-of-state residential placement. **The school board then agreed to fund part of the residential placement and 90 percent of any cost increase for the following school year. The agreement specifically excluded the board's obligation to pay for related services.** The following school year, the student's private school tuition almost doubled because the residential school stated that it could only maintain the placement with the services of two classroom aides.

The board refused to pay for the increased cost of tuition, asserting that the increase reflected the added cost of the personal aides and was a related service that was excluded under the settlement agreement. An administrative law judge agreed with the board, but a federal district court reversed and remanded the decision for a determination of whether the student's personal circumstances had changed since the agreement. The administrative law judge again ruled for the board, and the district court reversed the decision. The board appealed to the U.S. Court of Appeals for the Third Circuit, which rejected the parents' claim that the student's circumstances had changed in a manner that required voiding the settlement. **The only changed circumstance from the time of the settlement was the school's staffing decision. The settlement remained enforceable and thus the school board was not liable for the costs associated with hiring the two aides.** *D.R. by M.R. and B.R. v. East Brunswick Bd. of Educ.*, 109 F.3d 896 (3d Cir.1997).

- An Illinois student with speech impairments attended regular education classes. After the first diagnosis of impairment, the student's parents contacted their school board and requested speech therapy. A school speech therapist conducted an evaluation and determined that the student did not require speech therapy services. **The parents discontinued their efforts to obtain services from the school district and obtained private speech therapy services.** The following year, the parents renewed their request for speech therapy and requested a multi-disciplinary conference and testing. The district again denied the request for services and the parents appealed the decision. A hearing officer agreed with the school district, but a level two hearing officer reversed the decision and held for the parents. **The district appealed to the U.S. District Court for the Northern District of Illinois, which awarded the parents reimbursement for their out-of-pocket expenses for speech therapy services**, but only from the date they had first filed for administrative review through the date of the court order. The parents requested the court to amend its order to award retroactive reimbursement from the date that they had originally requested speech therapy services. The court observed that the parents had failed to diligently pursue this claim. Therefore, they were properly limited to a recovery that did not take their expenses during this time into account. The court amended the judgment to include reimbursement for expenses from the time of the district's final eligibility determination until the court's prior order. *Mary P. v. Illinois State Bd. of Educ.*, 934 F.Supp. 989 (N.D.Ill.1996).

II. MEDICAL SERVICES

The IDEA specifically excludes medical services from its definition of related services, unless provided for diagnostic or evaluative purposes. In determining whether a service is an excluded medical service, courts tend to focus on who has to provide the service and the nature of the service to determine whether it is part of the school district's obligation under the IDEA.

◆ In 1984, the U.S. Supreme Court ruled that clean intermittent catheterization (CIC) is a related service not subject to the "medical service" exclusion of the IDEA. **The parents of an eight-year-old girl born with spina bifida brought suit against a local Texas school district after the district refused to provide catheterization for the child while she attended school**. The parents pursued administrative and judicial avenues to force the district to train staff to perform the simple procedure. After a U.S. district court held against the parents, they appealed to the U.S. Court of Appeals, Fifth Circuit, which reversed the district court ruling. The school district then appealed to the U.S. Supreme Court.

The Supreme Court affirmed that portion of the court of appeals decision that held CIC is a "supportive service," not a "medical service," within the meaning of the IDEA. The Court was not persuaded by the school district's argument that catheterization is a medical service because it is provided in accordance with a physician's prescription and under a physician's supervision, even though it may be administered by a nurse or trained layperson. The Court listed four criteria to determine a school's obligation to provide services that relate to both the health and education of a child. First, to be entitled to related services, a child must be disabled so as to require special education. Second, **only those services necessary to aid a child with disabilities to benefit from special education must be provided**, regardless of how easily a school nurse or layperson could furnish them. Third, **IDEA regulations state that school nursing services must be performed by a nurse or other qualified person, not by a physician**. Fourth, the child's parents in this case were seeking only the services of a qualified person at the school; they were not asking the school to provide equipment. The Court reversed those portions of the court of appeals ruling which held the school district liable under the Rehabilitation Act and which held that the parents were entitled to attorney's fees. *Irving Indep. School Dist. v. Tatro*, 468 U.S. 883, 104 S.Ct. 3371, 82 L.Ed.2d 664 (1984).

◆ In 1999, the Supreme Court decided another case involving the extent of a school district's obligation to provide medical services, adopting a bright-line, physician/non-physician test to determine whether a requested service is a related service or a medical service. An Iowa student suffered a spinal cord injury that left him quadriplegic and ventilator dependent. For several years, his family provided him with personal attendant services at school. **When the student entered grade five, his mother asserted that the district should provide him with continuous one-on-one nursing services**. The district refused, and the family requested due process. An ALJ determined that the school district was required to reimburse the family for nursing costs in the current school year and provide the services in the future. The school district appealed to a federal district court, which granted summary judgment to the family, and the district appealed. The U.S. Court of Appeals, Eighth Circuit, found that the services provided for the student were related services as defined by the IDEA that were necessary to enable him to benefit from special education. The court rejected the school district's argument that the services were medical services that were excluded under the IDEA and state special education law. **Because the district's nurse could provide the required services, they were not excluded from IDEA coverage as medical services** and the district court's summary judgment order was affirmed.

On appeal to the U.S. Supreme Court, a majority of the court affirmed the Eight Circuit's opinion, agreeing that the requested services were not medical services. The Court based its decision on the IDEA definition of related services, the *Tatro* decision, and the purpose of the IDEA to make special education available to all disabled students. **Adopting a bright-line, physician/non-physician standard, the court held that since the disputed services could be performed by someone other than a physician, the district was obligated to provide them**. The district's assertion that a multi-factor standard that includes cost as a consideration was appropriate was rejected. *Cedar Rapids Community School Dist. v. Garret F.*, 526 U.S. 66, 119 S.Ct. 992, 143 L.Ed.2d 154 (1999).

◆ A student had over 150 absences and numerous behavioral referrals during her sophomore year of high school. The student had a problematic relationship with her mother and exhibited signs of drug use. A school support team began an initial evaluation for special education and a social worker urged the student's parents to have her tested for drug use late in her junior year. Two days later, the mother confronted the student about drug use and the student responded by threatening to kill her mother. The student was hospitalized and tested positive for marijuana. She underwent a special education evaluation that resulted in her classification as emotionally impaired. **She spent time in a juvenile detention center but eventually completed a residential program at another hospital** during the summer. She received tutoring and graduated the following spring. Her parents filed an administrative action against state education officials seeking reimbursement for the hospitalization costs, characterizing them as IDEA related services. A hearing officer concluded that the costs were reimbursable and awarded the parents $7,713.

The Hawaii education department appealed to a federal district court, which stated that under the IDEA, medical services are subject to parental reimbursement as "related services" if they are for diagnostic and evaluation purposes. The IDEA's affirmative duty to identify, locate and evaluate children with disabilities in the state applied to all students suspected of being disabled, even those who advanced from grade to grade. The IDEA states that a state or local education agency is deemed to have knowledge that a child has a disability if behavior or performance demonstrates the need for special education and related services. The hearing officer found reason to suspect that the student was disabled and that she might need special education services to address her emotional impairment as early as the beginning of her junior year. She was absent from school 79 times and had many behavior referrals the previous year. The court rejected the state's argument that the student's graduation under the IEP it eventually developed satisfied its obligation to provide a FAPE. The student's receipt of some educational benefit was not determinative in this case, because instruction was not provided under an appropriate IEP, despite numerous warning signs, before the end of her junior year. The state violated the IDEA's child-find provisions by failing to evaluate her earlier. **The services provided at the hospital were diagnostic and for evaluation. While they had been precipitated by a crisis, the student's disability might never have been addressed and she might not have ever received IDEA services if not for her hospitalization**. The student's parents were entitled to reimbursement for her hospitalization costs. *Department of Education, State of Hawaii v. Cari Rae S.*, 158 F.Supp.2d 1190 (D. Haw. 2001).

• After an Indiana student was released from a medical center, her parents contacted local school officials, seeking a residential placement. The local coordinating committee forwarded an application for residential placement to the state education department. The parties met at an IEP conference and agreed on the need for a residential placement. While the student awaited the outcome of the administrative process, she was placed in a psychiatric hospital for over sixth months, incurring significant costs for psychiatric counseling, medication and therapy. Shortly after the student was hospitalized, her parents filed a state court petition to have her involuntarily committed. The court accepted the petition and held that the student was mentally ill, schizoaffective, paranoid, suicidal, and required long-term education in a locked, residential, protective placement. She remained in the hospital for an additional five months, since the least restrictive appropriate facility had no available space. The hospital notified the court that she was no longer a threat to herself or others and recommended termination of her civil commitment. In a separate action, a class of Indiana students with disabilities and their parents sued the Indiana Department of Education, alleging that the department's long delays in residential placement matters violated the procedural protections of the IDEA. The parties settled that lawsuit under an order that provided a procedure for recovery of certain educational and related services costs from the state where there was a delay between the date of the IEP and the date of the placement. The state agreed to place eligible students in residential facilities within 30 days of the development of their IEPs, "except where special circumstances require otherwise." **The student and her parents joined the action and sought reimbursement for the services she received while hospitalized.** The state board of special education appeals reversed an administrative decision in their favor, ruling that the hospitalization was not "education or related services" that required reimbursement under the settlement order.

A federal district court affirmed the appeals board order and the student and parents appealed to the Seventh Circuit, arguing that the hospitalization costs were reimbursable under the settlement agreement. The court held that the hospitalization charges incurred by the student resulted from "special circumstances" as described in the settlement order, therefore, the delay in placing her in a residential facility, as called for in her IEP, did not violate the terms of the settlement agreement. Her IEP was designed for homebound services and contemplated a residential placement for her educational needs, not a placement based on medical treatment. The student's unstable condition made hospitalization necessary, and resulted in her inability to be placed at a residential facility. Medical services are not reimbursable under the IDEA unless they are for diagnostic or evaluative purposes, which was not the case here. **The hospital placement was for medical reasons related to the student's psychiatric crisis, therefore, reimbursement was not warranted.** The student's IEP team had unanimously concluded that she did not require hospitalization, and her parents had failed to challenge the adequacy of the IEP. The hospital was not equipped to serve as an educational provider. The court affirmed the district court decision. *Butler v. Evans*, 225 F.3d 887 (7th Cir. 2000).

◆ The mother of a Rhode Island student who was profoundly retarded, paraplegic and required a ventilator challenged the student's IEP. The city school department prevailed in administrative proceedings, and the mother appealed. However, she voluntarily dismissed the action. At the time of the voluntary dismissal, an IEP team meeting was already one month overdue under a state special education law. A state education department compliance officer requested an IEP review meeting. Although a meeting was held, it was not attended by any representative from the city school department. The state education department then initiated compliance proceedings against the city school department for failure to conduct an annual IEP review. Following a hearing, the education department authorized the compliance officer to take necessary action to develop a revised IEP for the student. At a final hearing in the compliance action, the officer testified that nursing services were appropriate for the student in order to provide her with a safe environment in which to receive a FAPE. **The city later refused to pay for a full-time nurse to assist the student, and the commissioner deducted almost $55,000 from the city's operation aid to pay for nursing services** rendered to the student.

The city appealed the deduction to the state Board of Regents for Elementary and Secondary Education. The board denied the appeal, and the Rhode Island Supreme Court denied the city's subsequent petition. The case then came before the Rhode Island Superior Court, which found that the state's general laws authorized the commissioner to deduct funds from a city's operation aid for a violation or neglect of law, or for a municipality's violation or neglect of rules and regulations. State special education law required an annual meeting to review a student's IEP. In this case, the city had violated the law by failing to timely arrange for an IEP meeting, despite requests from the student's mother and the compliance officer. Withholding of funds by the commissioner had therefore been appropriate. The court then considered whether the provision of full-time nursing services while the student was weaned from her ventilator constituted "related services" under the IDEA. According to the court, "related services" included supportive services that may be required to assist a student with disabilities to benefit from special education. In this case, the record indicated that **full-time nursing services were necessary for the student to maintain her health and safety while she received public education**. She was a technology-dependant child who was in need of respiratory suctioning, special feeding, catheterization and a ventilator. The disputed services could be provided by a nurse and were thus not subject to the IDEA's medical services exclusion. *City of Warwick v. Rhode Island Dept. of Educ.*, No. PC 98-3189, 2000 WL 1879897 (R.I. Super. Ct. 2000).

◆ An Illinois preschool student had developmental disabilities as the result of a rare neurological-muscular disease. He used a wheelchair and had a tracheostomy tube to keep his airway clear. His parents filed an administrative complaint against the district when it refused to place him in a public early childhood center for students with disabilities that was operated by another school district. A hearing officer determined that the student was entitled to the placement and a review officer upheld the decision. **The school district** appealed to an Illinois circuit court and **refused to provide a nurse to perform tracheostomy suctioning while he rode the school bus**. The student's mother performed the suctioning and **the parents initiated a separate action in a federal district court to require the district to provide a licensed nurse during bus rides**.

The court considered the family's application for a temporary order requiring tracheostomy suctioning for bus rides pending further consideration of the case. The court observed that federal regulations published under the IDEA exclude medical services from the IDEA's definition of related services. Excluded medical services are defined in the regulations as those that are provided by a physician. In this case, **the services did not require a physician and could be performed by any individual with minimal training**. The U.S. Supreme Court has ruled that services that can be provided in the school setting by a nurse or qualified layperson are not subject to the medical services exclusion. Because it appeared that the student in this case required only a nurse, he was entitled to a preliminary order requiring the district to furnish tracheostomy suctioning during his bus rides. *Skelly v. Brookfield LaGrange Park School Dist. 95*, 968 F.Supp. 385 (N.D.Ill.1997).

◆ An eight-year-old Ohio student with spina bifida required regular suctioning of her tracheostomy tube. Despite her impairment, she was bright and highly motivated. The special education services provided by her public school district were limited to one hour of home instruction per day. She received no physical or speech therapy. The student's mother requested additional home instruction or an in-school placement. **The school board denied an in-school placement, stating that the student's disability required the services of a full-time licensed practical nurse and that this would not be covered by the IDEA as a medical service.** A hearing officer determined that the student's IEP should be modified to include placement at a school for disabled students with the services of an attendant at regular intervals. A state level review officer reversed the hearing officer's decision and held that the student was receiving a free appropriate public education under her present IEP. The Hamilton County Court of Common Pleas held that the district's failure to place the student in a school with necessary related services violated the IDEA and the Rehabilitation Act. The court noted that the student had improved her ability to communicate since the filing of the administrative action and could be accommodated in a manner not unduly burdensome to the school district.

The school board appealed to the Court of Appeals of Ohio, First District, which rejected the board's argument that the trial court had erroneously substituted its judgment for that of the review officer. The IDEA expressly permits reviewing courts to consider evidence in addition to that produced at administrative hearings. **The evidence in this case overwhelmingly demonstrated that the single hour of home instruction provided by the school district each day was inadequate for the student to receive educational benefits.** The student's progress to date was mainly attributable to her mother's efforts, and the trial court had refrained from ruling on the provision of a full-time nurse. The court affirmed the trial court's judgment, modifying its findings on the cost of a full-time aide. However, it reversed the permanent order in favor of the student as violative of the IDEA requirement for annual review of each IEP. *Tanya by Mrs. X v. Cincinnati Bd. of Educ.*, 100 Ohio App.3d 52, 651 N.E.2d 1373 (1995).

III. TRANSPORTATION

The IDEA expressly requires school districts to furnish students with disabilities necessary transportation as a related service. School districts must also furnish transportation to disabled students attending private schools if necessary for the student to receive a FAPE.

- A school district placed a student with autistic-like behaviors in a private school for students with autism during the regular school day. The district provided him with transportation from the private school to the family home each day. The parents petitioned the school district's committee for special education to add a private after-school program to the student's IEP, pay for the after-school program, and provide transportation to and from the program twice a week. The district declined the request, and the family initiated due process proceedings. **A hearing officer upheld** the decision not to add the program to the student's IEP and **the refusal to provide transportation**. A state level review officer annulled the portion of the hearing officer's decision denying transportation, but affirmed the decision that the program need not be added to the student's IEP. Both parties appealed unfavorable aspects of the review officer's decision to a New York trial court, which confirmed the review officer's decision. The parties appealed to the New York Supreme Court, Appellate Division.

The court determined that the issue in this case was whether the private after-school program was a mandated "related service" under the IDEA, and therefore, a service for which the district was required to furnish transportation. The court observed that the review officer had correctly held that the district was not required to fund the after-school program in order to provide the student a FAPE, since his private school placement met his educational needs. Since the student's IEP was appropriate, the district was not required to modify it by adding the after-school program. **The obligation created by state and federal special education regulations to provide equal opportunities for students to participate in non-academic and extracurricular activities did not extend to the provision of equivalent or alternative transportation** simply because a district's after-school program was unsuitable for students with disabilities. There was no evidence in this case that the district had excluded the student from its existing extracurricular programs. To the contrary, it had offered to modify its existing program to accommodate him. The district did not deprive the student of any opportunities that he would have received had he attended a district school. Access to the after-school program was not required by the IDEA or state law, and it was error for the appellate court to require the district to pay for transportation home from the alternate after-school program chosen by the parents. The court modified the portion of the trial court judgment requiring the district to provide the student with transportation home from the after-school program. *Roslyn Union Free School Dist. v. Univ. of State of New York, State Educ. Dept.*, 711 N.Y.S.2d 582 (N.Y. App. Div. 2000).

◆ An Iowa student with severe disabilities, including cerebral palsy and spastic quadriplegia, participated in the special education program of her regularly assigned, neighborhood school. She was transported there with a lift bus that traveled a special route for her. **Her parents sought to transfer her to a different school under the intra-district transfer program, and asked for special transportation despite the program requirement that they furnish their own transportation**. The district approved the transfer but denied the transportation request. An administrative law judge held that the parents had established no need for special transportation beyond parental preference for placement at a specific school. A federal district court reversed the administrative decision, ruling that the district had impermissibly limited the student's opportunity to participate in the transfer program.

The district appealed to the Eighth Circuit, which observed that in § 504 cases, complaining students must demonstrate that there has been discrimination on the basis of disability. A defendant school district is entitled to show that the requested accommodation is unduly burdensome. This may be demonstrated by proof of undue financial and administrative burdens to the district, or by showing that the requested accommodations require the fundamental alteration of a school program. The court found that the student was not denied the benefit of participating in the intra-district transfer program, since she was allowed to participate in it on the same terms as other applicants. There was no evidence of discrimination in the administration of the transfer program, and the student was not denied access to it on the basis of her disability. Instead, her parents did not wish to comply with "the main condition of the program applicable to all students who wish[ed] to participate - parental transportation." **Requiring the district to spend additional funds on transportation to the transfer program would fundamentally alter this requirement, creating an undue burden on the school district**. The court reversed and remanded the district court decision. *Timothy H. and Brenda H. v. Cedar Rapids Comm. School Dist.*, 178 F.3d 968 (8th Cir.1999).

◆ A parochial academy attended by a student with speech impairments was located three blocks from a public school which offered a speech therapy program. **The school board agreed to provide the student with speech therapy at the public school under an IEP, but declined to furnish transportation** or to send a speech therapist to the private school. The student's mother filed an administrative appeal, and a hearing officer upheld the board's decision. The mother appealed to the U.S. District Court for the Southern District of Alabama, which found that the student was not entitled to receive transportation or speech therapy services at the parochial school. The mother appealed to the U.S. Court of Appeals for the Eleventh Circuit.

The court stated that public schools need only provide those services necessary to help a student with disabilities benefit from special education. **In determining whether a student with disabilities needs transportation as a related service, the court must consider the student's age, the distance which the student must travel, the nature of the area over which the student must travel, the availability of private assistance, and the availability of public transit and crossing guards**. In this case, the student was only six years old, but was only required to travel a short distance. His mother failed to show that she was unavailable to provide private transportation and there was no evidence that the school was in a high crime or high traffic area. Because the student was unable to establish that he could not reach the public school without the board's assistance, the district court had properly determined the board need not provide transportation. There was no evidence that the offering of a speech therapy class at the public school denied the student appropriate access to a free appropriate public education, and the court affirmed the judgment for the school board. *Donald B., by and through Christine B. v. Bd. of School Commissioners of Mobile County, Alabama*, 117 F.3d 1371 (11th Cir.1997).

◆ A Pennsylvania student with disabilities attended a public school where he was enrolled in a hearing impaired support resource room program. The student's parents were divorced and had a joint physical custody arrangement by which his residence alternated between parents each week. **The mother resided within the school district, but the father lived outside the district, and school officials refused to provide transportation to and from his residence**. The father requested a due process hearing at which a hearing officer determined that the district had no obligation to provide transportation while the student stayed with his father. A special education appeals panel reversed the hearing officer's decision and ordered the district to reimburse the father for his transportation costs. The district appealed to the Commonwealth Court of Pennsylvania.

The court observed that transportation is a related service under the IDEA that must be provided where it is an integral part of the student's IEP and is required to assist the student in benefiting from a special education program. Although the U.S. Court of Appeals for the Fifth Circuit has approved of supplemental transportation outside a school district where required to prevent significant regression of a student's educational progress, **the requested transportation in this case did not address the student's special education needs. Transportation to the father's residence served only to accommodate the custody arrangement of the parents**. While separated parents face greater difficulties and expenses in meeting their parental obligations, the IDEA and state education code require additional transportation only for a student's educational needs. The court reversed the appeals panel's decision. *North Allegheny School Dist. v. Gregory P.*, 687 A.2d 37 (Pa.Commw.Ct.1996).

◆ A hearing-impaired Philadelphia student received a scholarship for bi-weekly hearing treatment at a therapy clinic. **His mother requested that the school district provide her son with transportation to the clinic**. When the district refused, the mother requested a due process hearing. The hearing officer determined that the district was not obligated to provide transportation to the clinic. The mother appealed to the Pennsylvania Secretary of Education. The secretary determined that the district had to provide transportation because the combination of the student's regular education and the additional therapy constituted "sufficient services reasonably calculated to give real educational benefit." The district appealed this decision to the Pennsylvania Commonwealth Court. On appeal, the district argued that it was already providing the student with an appropriate education. In upholding the secretary's decision, **the court determined that the combined therapies constituted services calculated to afford the student real educational benefit**. Since the additional therapy program was approved by the Department of Education, the school district was obligated to provide free transportation. The court noted that although the student was progressing satisfactorily, evidence showed that students with the same problem require additional assistance later on in their education and that providing additional therapy now would allow the student to become more independent. Thus, the district was required to provide transportation to the clinic. *School Dist. of Philadelphia v. Dept. of Educ.*, 547 A.2d 520 (Pa.Commw.Ct.1988).

◆ Because the mother of a hearing impaired student disagreed with the school IEP committee's proposed placement, she requested local and state level administrative hearings. Both hearing officers upheld the committee's report. They found that it would best develop the student's potential in the least restrictive environment. The mother instead placed the student in a special education school in Washington, D.C. because she believed that both the IDEA and the Michigan Mandatory Special Education Act (MMSEA) required placement there. The school was part of a federally funded program which did not require tuition or residence charges. **The student's mother then sought reimbursement from her local school district in the amount of $2,500 per year for transportation**

expenses to and from Washington. The district refused and she sued various state and local school officials in a federal district court.

The court upheld the hearing officer's decision. It agreed with the school officials that the mother's argument turned upon a discussion of the merits of mainstreaming versus placement in a segregated setting. The court refused to substitute its judgment for that of the committee on decisions of this nature. Although the state of Michigan had not defined "maximum potential," there were geographical and physical limits to its commitment to educate students with disabilities to their maximum potential. Michigan law indicated that "maximum potential" meant neither "utopian" nor the best education possible. **Because the mother had not met her burden of proving that the IEP failed to meet IDEA requirements, including the MMSEA's "maximum potential" requirement, she was not entitled to transportation costs**. *Barwacz v. Michigan Dept. of Educ.*, 681 F.Supp. 427 (W.D.Mich.1988).

CHAPTER SIX

School Liability

I. GOVERNMENTAL IMMUNITY

The doctrine of governmental immunity, based on the Eleventh Amendment to the U.S. Constitution, prohibits lawsuits against the government and its officials. However, the doctrine has been limited in several aspects by legislative action or judicial decisions.

A. Federal Suits

Generally, the Eleventh Amendment bars a private citizen from seeking in federal court an award of money damages against a state or state officials in their official capacities. However, local political subdivisions do not constitute "states" and they are thus subject to suit. Additionally, the Eleventh Amendment does not bar prospective relief that allows federal courts to issue injunctions ordering states and state officials to conform their future conduct to the dictates of federal law. Immunity also does not attach to suits brought by the federal government against a state, or lawsuits brought in state court.

◆ In 1974, a Pennsylvania state school and hospital resident brought a class action suit against the school and its officials as well as various state and local mental health administrators. The resident claimed that conditions at the institution violated § 504 of the Rehabilitation Act, the Developmentally Disabled Assistance and Bill of Rights Act, 42 U.S.C. §§ 6001-6081 (DDABRA), Pennsylvania mental health legislation, and the Eighth and Fourteenth Amendments to the U.S. Constitution. A federal district court held that the state legislation provided a right to adequate habilitation, but did not determine whether the student and class had habilitation rights in the least restrictive environment. On appeal, the U.S. Court of Appeals, Third Circuit, affirmed the district court decision and ruled that the class had habilitation rights in the least restrictive environment based on its interpretation of the DDABRA. The U.S. Supreme Court reversed, holding that the DDABRA created no substantive rights. It remanded the case to the court of appeals. *Pennhurst State School and Hospital v. Halderman*, 451 U.S. 1, 101 S.Ct. 1531, 67 L.Ed.2d 694 (1981).

On remand, the court of appeals affirmed its previous decision in full. The U.S. Supreme Court again granted certiorari, and again reversed and remanded the case. **It held that the Eleventh Amendment to the U.S. Constitution prohibited federal courts from ordering state officials to conform their conduct to their own state laws.** On remand, the court of appeals would be permitted to consider a judgment based on the federal legislation. *Pennhurst State School and Hospital v. Halderman,* 465 U.S. 89, 104 S.Ct. 900, 79 L.Ed.2d 67 (1984).

When Pennhurst was closed in 1987, litigation continued with county and commonwealth defendants arguing that there should be no continuing obligation to abide by the final settlement agreement. In 1993, the county and commonwealth defendants filed a motion in the district court, seeking to be dismissed from the matter under the Eleventh Amendment to the U.S. Constitution, which has been construed by the U.S. Supreme Court as barring an award of compensatory relief against a state or its officials. The district court found no merit to the county and commonwealth defendants' argument that the 1985 final settlement constituted compensatory relief. **The commonwealth's obligation to correct constitutional violations was not relieved by the release of Pennhurst residents, who were entitled to benefit from the 1985 agreement. The court decree was not a remedy for past constitutional violations, and was prospective in nature. Accordingly, the Eleventh Amendment did not bar the claims.** *Halderman v. Pennhurst State School and Hospital*, 834 F.Supp. 757 (E.D.Pa.1993).

The district court subsequently reviewed the commonwealth's and county's record of compliance with district court orders and noted the substantial accomplishments and progress achieved by certain class members. While the commonwealth and county had previously been found in violation of almost every substantive requirement of the 1985 court decree, the closure of the institution had resulted in the relocation of almost all class members into smaller, community living arrangements. The parties had cooperated in developing heathcare, quality assurance, and access to community employment plans to provide class members with minimally adequate habilitation services. All active class members had current individual habilitation plans and 35 had obtained employment in positions paying at least the minimum wage. However, the court retained the case for several months to conduct a comprehensive review of individual class members to determine whether they were actually receiving mandated services under its prior decree. The special master who had been appointed in 1994 was directed to conduct a comprehensive review of a sample of class members prior to the conclusion of court supervision. *Halderman v. Pennhurst State School and Hospital*, 995 F.Supp. 534 (E.D.Pa.1998).

After completion of the review ordered by the district court, the court concluded the city and state were substantially complying with the 1985 consent decree, and purged the 1994 contempt order. The special master was directed to close his office approximately two months after the date the court's decision was issued. The court further stated that it would terminate any active supervision over the Philadelphia members of the Penhurst class. *Halderman v. Pennhurst State School and Hospital,* 9 F.Supp.2d 544 (E.D.Pa. 1998).

◆ A student with disabilities had a history of severe behavior problems, which included accosting other students, screaming obscenities, cutting her tongue with scissors, and hitting. Upon the student's return to school after being hospitalized, her behavior problems escalated, to the point that she spat at a counselor and head-butted him. **School staff members began to wrap her in a sheet or blanket to ensure her safety, and when she escaped the wrap, they began to secure it with safety pins or duct tape**. On one occasion, school staff wrapped the student in a blanket and secured it to a cot with tape. The student's mother removed her from school for about three months because of this treatment, but later returned her to school. The school discontinued the practice of wrapping or taping the student, but her mother commenced a state court action against the district and school officials, which was removed to federal court.

The mother asserted that the school's restraint methods violated the student's constitutional rights, the Texas Education Code and other state law obligations. In considering the district's motion for summary judgment, the court noted that school personnel had testified that the wrapping incidents were not designed to punish the student but were intended to protect her and those around her. The school officials were entitled to qualified immunity. **There was no legal authority for the mother's claim that her daughter had a constitutional right to be free from restraint**. The boundaries of the asserted right to bodily integrity were simply not sufficiently well-established to create liability in a civil rights violation case. The court held that an emotionally disturbed student does not have a due process right to be free from restraints used to control outbursts for preventing harm to the student or others. Given the severity of the student's condition, the reaction of school officials was not unexpected. Their actions were taken to deal with out-of-control behavior, not as punishment. The officials had relied on the professional judgment of a therapist who testified that the wrapping technique was preferable to allowing the student to injure herself. The court found no deliberate indifference or conscious-shocking behavior by school officials, and they were entitled to immunity. The court was unable to find a violation of the state education code, which prohibits excessive force when disciplining a child. The court rejected the other claims presented by the mother, finding these claims legally insufficient. The case was dismissed in its entirety. *Doe v. S & S Consol. Indep. School Dist.*, 149 F.Supp.2d 274 (E.D. Tex. 2001).

◆ A 16-year-old New Mexico special education student had psychological and emotional problems and received instruction under an IEP. The student twice mentioned suicide to a school aide. The school's principal reprimanded and suspended the student for threatening physical harm to a teacher. She then instructed the teacher to drive the student home, without first contacting the parents. She did, however, call the police with instructions to detain the student if he returned to school. The school's disciplinary policy called for the temporary suspension of a special education student on the same basis as regular students, but provided that students should remain at school if their parents were not home. The teacher also failed to contact the parents and dropped the student off at home, where he committed suicide with a rifle.

The parents sued the district, its board and certain employees in a federal district court under 42 U.S.C. § 1983, alleging constitutional and IDEA violations. The court dismissed the IDEA claims and the constitutional claims based on failure to properly train school employees. However, it refused to award judgment to the employees on the family's due process claims. This was based on evidence that **some of the employees were aware that the student was at risk for suicide. The reasonableness of taking a potentially suicidal student home without notifying his parents was a question that should be considered by a jury**. The parties appealed unfavorable aspects of the district court decision to the U.S. Court of Appeals, Tenth Circuit, which affirmed the summary judgment order on the IDEA claims. It recited the general rule that government officials enjoy qualified immunity from liability under § 1983. There can be liability under § 1983 only where government officials violate clearly established rights of which a reasonable person would know. There is no requirement that officials provide private parties with protective services, or otherwise protect them from harm, except in the rare circumstances where there is a special relationship between the party and the government entity. This relationship not been found in an educational setting. The student was not restrained by the teacher at the time of his suicide, and any custodial relationship with her ended when he was dropped off at home. The district court had erroneously denied immunity to the school employees on that ground. However, **it was possible that by suspending the student and taking him home without notice to his parents, the actions of the principal and teacher had placed him in danger, or increased the risk of harm**. There was evidence that the principal and teacher had knowledge of the student's suicidal threats, and that he had access to firearms at home. Summary judgment was thus properly denied to the teacher and principal. *Armijo v. Wagon Mound Public Schools*, 159 F.3d 1253 (10th Cir.1998).

◆ A visually impaired and developmentally disabled Illinois student attended the Illinois School for the Visually Impaired for ten years. During that time, he was allegedly subjected to sexual assaults by other students. **His guardian filed a lawsuit against the school superintendent** in the U.S. District Court for the Central District of Illinois, **claiming that the superintendent had personal knowledge of some of the assaults**. The court considered the superintendent's motion to dismiss the case on the basis of qualified immunity. It observed that government entities and their employees have no affirmative constitutional duty to protect individuals from third party violence. The Due Process Clause has not been construed as conferring a right to governmental protection and no court has held that a full-time residential student at a special state-run school has a constitutional right to a safe environment. The student did not have a special relationship with the school that was sufficient to create an exception to this rule. His parents retained legal custody of him and he was not committed or otherwise incarcerated. The superintendent was protected from liability under the Eleventh Amendment and was entitled to judgment.

On appeal, the U.S. Court of Appeals, Seventh Circuit, upheld the district court decision, agreeing with the district court's conclusion that the state did not have an obligation to protect the student from his classmate. Neither of the two exceptions to the general rule that a state has no obligation to protect from third party violence applied in this case. Further, **the superintendent was entitled to qualified immunity because the student had no constitutional right to be protected from the classmate**, therefore, the superintendent's actions could not have violated a "clearly established" constitutional right. *Stevens v. Umsted,* 131 F.3d 697 (7th Cir. 1997).

B. IDEA

Congress may remove a state's Eleventh Amendment protection by specifically abrogating it for particular and specified purposes. In the 1990 amendments to the IDEA, Congress authorized lawsuits against the states for violations of the IDEA.

◆ In 1989, the U.S. Supreme Court in *Dellmuth v. Muth*, 491 U.S. 223, 109 S.Ct. 2397, 105 L.Ed.2d 181 (1989), ruled that while local school districts could be sued under the IDEA, states were immune from IDEA liability under the Eleventh Amendment. In response, Congress passed the Education of the Handicapped Act Amendments of 1990—known as the Individuals with Disabilities Education Act (IDEA), and included a new section, 20 U.S.C. § 1403, which specifically abrogates a state's Eleventh Amendment immunity to suit in federal court for violations of the IDEA. This section allows suits against a state for both legal and equitable remedies in federal court for violations that occur in whole or in part after October 30, 1990.

◆ Part H of the IDEA provides federal funds to the states for the development and implementation of early intervention services for infants and toddlers from birth through age two. States receiving federal funds under Part H are required to establish a comprehensive early intervention system to assist disabled students from birth through age two and mandates that a state have in effect a statewide intervention system when it applies for its fifth year of funding. Although the state of Illinois began participating in the Part H program in 1987 and received federal funding for its statewide early intervention system, it did not have a statewide service system fully implemented by its fifth year of participation. An audit of the state's implementation progress revealed that many services were not available in all parts of the state and that many eligible children were not being served and instead remained on waiting lists. **A class action suit was filed in federal court against state officials on behalf of eligible Illinois children who were not receiving early intervention services** under Part H. The court denied motions to dismiss the complaint.

The state officials appealed to the U.S. Court of Appeals, Seventh Circuit, arguing that the action was barred by Eleventh Amendment immunity and that Part H was too vague to impose binding obligations upon the state. **The court held that the Eleventh Amendment does not bar a suit against state officials for relief from ongoing violations of federal law. Part H of the IDEA imposes significant and specific duties on individual state executive officers and may be enforced under 42 U.S.C. § 1983**. Part H contains 14 minimum system components conferring specific rights upon eligible children to be identified and referred for special education services. Because Illinois was required to have an early intervention system in place under Part H and the IDEA identified the specific services and beneficiaries of those services, the district court had properly granted summary judgment to the students. The court of appeals affirmed the judgment. *Marie O. v. Edgar*, 131 F.3d 610 (7th Cir.1997).
[Editor's Note: Under IDEA 1997, Part H has been changed to Part C.]

◆ An Illinois student with severe psychiatric and behavioral disabilities was placed by his parents in a 24-hour residential care facility even though the state Department of Mental Health and Development Disabilities (DMHDD) refused to provide them with an individual care grant. The parents appealed to an administrative hearing officer who denied their claim. Their school district convened a multidisciplinary conference and determined that the student was not eligible for special education services. The parents again requested a hearing, at which they agreed with the school district that the DMHDD should be joined in the proceedings. **The hearing officer denied the motion and ordered the school district to fund the entire cost of the residential placement**. The school district complied, but the following year the parents rejected the district's proposed IEP and requested another hearing. The school district filed a motion to join DMHDD and the Illinois State Board of Education (ISBE) as parties to the suit. The hearing officer denied the motion. The district was ordered to continue funding the residential placement and a review officer affirmed the decision. The district then filed a federal district court action against the ISBE and DMHDD, seeking to shift the financial burden of the placement to the state agencies.

The court held that the school district lacked standing to proceed with the complaint except as it pertained to the placement decision. The court then vacated its order and invited the parties to submit additional evidence. The court again held for the state board, DHS and state officials, **finding that the school district was not authorized to seek DHS funding on behalf of the student and that it had**

no jurisdiction to consider the DHS decision. The DHS was not required to share residential placement costs. The claims for tuition reimbursement were moot since the state education board had reimbursed the school district for some costs and was in the process of paying others. The district was unable to show that the lack of an interagency agreement reduced available IDEA funding. The court granted summary judgment to the state education board, DHS and state officials. *Bd. of Educ. of Community High School Dist. 218 v. Illinois State Bd. of Educ.*, 979 F.Supp. 1203 (N.D.Ill.1997).

C. State Statutory Immunity

Congress has enacted the Federal Tort Claims Act that allows individuals to sue the federal government in limited circumstances. Many states have enacted similar legislation wherein they effectively consent to be sued in certain instances.

◆ A student was placed at a private school for students with emotional problems. Due to continuing knee problems, the student presented her gym teacher with a note from her doctor stating that she should not participate in any sport requiring lateral movement. During one class, the student sat at a desk performing academic P.E. instead of playing dodgeball. **A teacher observed her talking to a classmate and told her that if she did not join the game, she would receive a failing grade for physical education and not be able to graduate**. The student had already received a D+ in gym class, so she joined the game. While attempting to dodge a thrown ball during the game, she injured herself. The student and her mother sued the school in an Illinois trial court, alleging willful and wanton misconduct. The court awarded summary judgment to the school under the state Tort Immunity Act, finding that it was entitled to immunity for negligence and for willful and wanton misconduct.

The student appealed to the Illinois Appellate Court, First District, which observed that the state's supreme court distinguished between public and private schools in the context of the immunity act in *Cooney v. Society of Mt. Carmel*, 75 Ill.2d 430 (1979). The school argued that the Legislature amended the immunity act after *Cooney* by including not-for-profit corporations organized for the purpose of conducting public business within the definition of "local public entity." Under this definition, the school qualified for the immunity act's protection. The appellate court disagreed, finding no indication that the Legislature sought to overrule the outcome in *Cooney*. The Illinois Supreme Court had reiterated its determination that the immunity act did not apply to private schools in *Henrich v. Libertyville High School*, 186 Ill.2d 381 (1998), a case that contrasted the immunity act from 105 Ill. Comp. Stat. 5/24-24. In *Henrich*, the court reaffirmed its decision that **the tort immunity act does not apply to private schools**. Moreover, there is a distinction between the public interest and public business, as defined in the immunity act. The court reversed the trial court's order for summary judgment based on the immunity act. Because the student had presented evidence that the teacher had exhibited reckless disregard for her safety when he ordered her into the game, the case could not be dismissed without further consideration by the trial court. The teacher's statements created a factual dispute that made the case inappropriate for summary judgment. The court reversed and remanded the case to the trial court for further consideration. *Brugger v. Joseph Academy Inc.*, 760 N.E.2d 135 (Ill. App. Ct., 1st Dist. 2001).

◆ The mother of a student with disabilities brought a stroller to school for transporting the student from class to her resource room. However, the district allegedly used the stroller for physically restraining the student during time-outs, during which she was placed in a closet for 15 to 20 minute time periods. On one such occasion, the student fell out of the stroller and fractured her skull, resulting in complications, including an increase in seizure activity. In a federal district court decision, the district court held that the school district was not entitled to pretrial dismissal of the student's claim for compensatory damages under the IDEA. **The student** then **filed a state trial court action against the school district and its board. The court held that the district was entitled to immunity, and the student appealed** to the state court of appeals. A state appeals court affirmed, and the student appealed to the Colorado Supreme Court, arguing that the trial court had improperly failed to apply an exception to government immunity for the creation or maintenance of a dangerous condition in a public building.

The supreme court observed that the state governmental immunity act (CGIA) provides for the waiver of sovereign immunity by a public entity in an action for injuries resulting from a dangerous condition of any public building. The condition must be associated with the construction and maintenance of a building, not solely its design, and must constitute an unreasonable risk to public health and safety. There must be a sufficient connection between the government negligence and the construction or maintenance of a facility. In a previous decision, the court had found that the CGIA refers to injuries arising from the state of a building itself, not the activities conducted within the building. Maintenance of a building encompassed the ongoing repair and upkeep of a facility as well as alterations. In this case, the student alleged that her serious injuries directly resulted from the conversion and use of the storage closet to a seclusion room for disabled students, creating an unreasonable risk to the public. However, the substance of her claim was that school officials failed to keep her within their view in order to prevent her from falling out of her stroller. While she alleged an act of negligence, she did not demonstrate a connection between the use of the building and a construction or maintenance activity. **Her claim that the district should have upgraded the closet for use as a "time-out room" was inadequate to waive immunity under the CGIA.** *Padilla v. School District No. 1, City and County of Denver, Colorado, et al.*, 25 P.3d 1176 (Colo. 2001).

◆ A school administrator who served as a special education diagnostician with responsibility for disciplining special education students investigated allegations that a 17-year-old student with disabilities was sexually assaulted on a school elevator three times by a male special education student. She determined that the first incident was consensual, even though the student stated that it was not. Accordingly, **she decided to discipline both students with reprimands**, with the agreement of the school's principal. After the student told one of her teachers that the incident was not consensual, the teacher prepared a memorandum to the administrators explaining this sentiment. The administrators implemented new policies designed to prevent a recurrence. The male student assaulted the student again on the elevator on two occasions, despite the immediate implementation of the policies. He was removed from the classroom and placed into in-school suspension. The victimized student's family commenced a state court lawsuit against four district administrators for failure to perform their duties and for negligently disciplining her. The trial court ruled that the administrators were not entitled to immunity under the Texas Education Code, and they appealed.

The state court of appeals explained that **professional employees of school districts are entitled to immunity from personal liability for any act within the scope of their employment involving the exercise of judgment or discretion, except for the use of excessive force in the disciplining of students or negligence resulting in bodily injury to a student**. Whether an employee is entitled to immunity depends on the ability of the employee to exercise discretion when performing an act. The administrators had created new policies in response to the first assault, but did not enforce them. The elevator door was not locked and the second assault occurred during class time, when the students were both tardy. The policies left the administrators with no judgment or discretion, and the evidence indicated that they did not carry out their ministerial duties. They were not entitled to summary judgment on their claims to immunity under the state education code, and the court affirmed the judgment. *Myers v. Doe*, 52 S.W.3d 391 (Tex. App.–Fort Worth 2001).

◆ The mother of a student with disabilities commenced a state court action for damages based on allegations that a classmate sexually molested her daughter twice, and that school employees were aware of the risk that the classmate presented for this kind of conduct. The court awarded summary judgment to the school district on grounds that the actions at the time of the alleged assaults were discretionary. Accordingly, **the district was entitled to immunity** under Wisconsin Statute § 893.80(4).

The family appealed to the court of appeals, which observed that the case required drawing the distinction between ministerial and discretionary duties of public employees, a distinction that was long recognized in Wisconsin law. The family asserted that school employees had failed to act when faced with a known danger presented by the assaultive classmate. The court observed that the "known danger" theory is limited in application and applies only when the nature of the danger is compelling, known to the public officer and is of such force that the officer has no discretion not to act. In this case, **the classmate had presented some possibility of danger to others, but nothing indicated that the threat was compelling or certain to cause injury if school employees took no corrective action**. This was not a case in which danger was certain to occur. The court of appeals therefore affirmed the trial court judgment dismissing the complaint. *Keiko B. v. Madison Metropolitan School Dist.*, 2000 Wis. App. Lexis 895 (Wis.Ct.App. 2000).

◆ **A Pennsylvania student with a severe emotional disturbance became extremely agitated and started screaming** after being physically threatened by another student. **After running to the principal's office, she was restrained by three district employees** and was eventually handcuffed by police officers.

The officers placed her legs in restraints and she was taken by ambulance to a medical center. The student eventually transferred to a private facility approved by the state education department. Her family initiated a federal district court action against state and local education officials, asserting a variety of state and federal claims. Local education officials moved for dismissal of certain claims, and the court issued two opinions dismissing some of the claims, but retaining others for further proceedings.

In the first opinion, the court found that the student's family was seeking monetary damages that could not be obtained through IDEA due process proceedings. Therefore, the family was not required to exhaust administrative remedies. The court refused to dismiss the student's allegations regarding her IEP and placement and the district's control proceedures at the pre-trial stage, finding these claims should survive for further consideration. The family's claims under the Americans with Disabilities Act also survived pre-trial dismissal, since the student successfully asserted that she was excluded from services as the result of her disability. According to the court, the student failed to allege sufficient facts to show that local school officials violated her constitutional rights. In an action against a political subdivision, such as a school district, a complaining party must show that an official policy or custom inflicts injury to the party's federally protected rights in order to prevail in a civil rights violations claim brought under 42 U.S.C. § 1983. The family had claimed only that the student's rights under the IDEA, ADA and § 504 had been violated, and there was no basis for the constitutional rights violation claim. Accordingly, the Section 1983 action was properly dismissed. The court also dismissed the state law claims against the local officials for false imprisonment under the Pennsylvania Political Subdivision Tort Claims Act. *O.F. by N.S. v. Chester Upland School District,* 2000 WL 424276 (E.D. Pa. 2000).

In a second opinion issued a few weeks later, the court considered the dismissal motions filed by state education officials, including the state education department and its secretary. The court held that **states, state agencies and state officials acting in their official capacities are not subject to liability for civil rights violations under 42 U.S.C. Section 1983**. The courts have not deemed these officials and government entities to be "persons" within the meaning of the act. The state education department and secretary of education were not persons and were entitled to dismissal of the claims against them. The false imprisonment claim against the state officials failed because they, like the local education officials, were entitled to immunity under state law when acting within the scope of their duties. *O.F. by N.S. v. Chester Upland School District*, No. CIV. A. 00-779, 2000 WL 572708 (E.D. Pa. 2000).

◆ A student with developmental disabilities and Down's syndrome rode a bus to a training center for students with developmental disabilities. A private transportation service, which operated the bus under a contract with the board, employed an attendant to accompany student riders. The student was allegedly raped by a male student during the ride home. Her parent sued the board and transportation company in a state trial court for negligence and intentional misconduct, asserting that the board and company had a duty to prevent or intervene in the assault. The complaint asserted that the school board knew that male passengers on the bus were likely to assault female riders, and that the board knew of a propensity by male passengers to commit sexual assault. **The trial court dismissed the case, holding that a section of the state Tort Immunity Act barred claims of negligence and intentional misconduct for governmental failure to prevent crimes by third parties**. The court also held that even though the state school code imposed an affirmative duty on the board to maintain discipline among students, it also immunized the board from claims based on ordinary negligence in the exercise of school discipline. The parent appealed to the Illinois Appellate Court, First District.

The appeals court agreed with the parent that the school board had an affirmative duty under the school code to maintain discipline among students. However, this duty did not encompass execution and enforcement of the law under a section of the Tort Immunity Act allowing for public employee liability in cases of willful and wanton misconduct. While state law created a duty of disciplinary enforcement in educators, the law was not enforced or executed as contemplated by the public employee liability section. The court rejected the parent's argument that the Police and Correctional Activities section of the Tort Immunity Act did not apply to school districts performing duties described by the act. A part of the act specifically included school boards as local public entities. **This part of the act did not include an exception to immunity for willful and wanton misconduct, and there was a clear legislative intent that this section should provide unqualified immunity to all local public entities for both negligent and intentional misconduct**. The parent's claim was thus barred under the section. The court observed that the Illinois Supreme Court has construed the Tort Immunity Act according to its plain language. In the absence of express exceptions to immunity, it could only be concluded that the legislature intended to provide unqualified immunity to local public entities for both negligent and intentional misconduct under the Police and Correctional Activities section of the Tort Immunity Act. While state law requires educators to maintain school discipline, teachers and other school employees stand in the same relationship to students as do parents and cannot be subject to liability arising from the exercise of authority over a child. Parents are entitled to immunity for negligent conduct inherent to the parent-child relationship, and educators are entitled to immunity for negligence in the imposition of school discipline. The fact that the assault took place on a school bus did not defeat immunity, and the appellate court affirmed the judgment for the school board. *A.R. v. Chicago Bd. of Educ.*, 724 N.E.2d 6 (Ill. App. Ct. 1999).

◆ A Texas student with disabilities arrived late to class one day and was refused admittance. The teacher alleged that the student then made an improper comment and the teacher poked him in the chest with his index finger, even though he was aware that the student had no right pectoral muscle. The student filed a personal injury lawsuit against the teacher and school district in a Texas trial court, which granted summary judgment to the district and teacher. The student appealed to the Court of Appeals of Texas, where he argued that the trial court had improperly held that the teacher was entitled to immunity. **The court stated that while the Texas Tort Claims Act provides for teacher immunity for any act by a teacher within the scope of employment, an exception exists for the use of**

excessive force in the discipline of a student or negligence resulting in bodily injury to a student. Because the teacher had failed to state in his responsive papers that he was not imposing discipline on the student at the time of the incident, he was not entitled to summary judgment. However, the Texas education code requires that all complaining parties bringing disputes arising under the school laws of Texas first exhaust their administrative remedies. The court determined that this provision applied even to a grievance against a school district employee. Because the student had failed to exhaust his administrative remedies prior to filing the lawsuit, the court dismissed the case, requiring the student to first exhaust his administrative remedies. *Grimes v. Stringer*, 957 S.W.2d 865 (Tex.App.–Tyler 1997).

◆ An Illinois high school senior wrote suicide notes and told other students that he was going to kill himself. The students reported his intentions to a school counselor. When the student took a drug overdose at school, the counselor notified his mother that she should take him to the hospital. Nothing was said about the suicide threats. Later that day, the student killed himself by jumping from a highway overpass. The student's estate sued the school board in a state court for negligently failing to inform the student's mother of the suicide threats and failure to implement a suicide prevention program. The court dismissed the lawsuit, and the estate appealed to the Appellate Court of Illinois, Third District. **The appellate court observed that the student had left the control of school administrators at the time of the suicide**, removing any possibility of a claim for negligence based on breach of a special duty to protect him. There was no state requirement to develop a suicide intervention program and **the board and its employees were entitled to immunity despite the failure to inform the mother of the suicide threats**. The court affirmed the dismissal of the case. *Grant v. Bd. of Trustees of Valley View School Dist. No. 365-U*, 676 N.E.2d 705 (Ill.App.Ct.3d Dist.1997).

II. LIABILITY FOR NEGLIGENCE

In the absence of immunity, courts have held schools and their agents liable for personal injuries which resulted from the negligent failure to provide a reasonably safe environment, failure to warn of known hazards or to remove known dangers where possible, failure to properly instruct participants in an activity, or failure to provide adequate supervision.

A. Negligent Supervision

1. Student Injuries

◆ **A special education student alleged his bus driver made inappropriate sexual comments** to him, and offered to arrange a sexual experience between the student and a woman. The student's mother relayed the information to a school counselor, and a state agency social worker reported the incident to the district transportation director. The director questioned the driver about the incident and advised an assistant superintendent about her investigation. The transportation director placed a video/audio camera in the driver's bus, but did not reassign the driver or report the incident to the district's complaint manager. After several uneventful weeks, the camera was removed from the bus. Shortly thereafter, the student claimed that the driver placed his hand inside the student's pants. The student's mother reported the harassment to school employees, but they again failed to notify the district complaint manager. For a two-week period, the student was taken to school by taxi and attended some classes at another high school. The student sued the school district in a federal district court for discrimination and retaliation on the basis of sex in violation of Title IX of the Education Amendments of 1972 and for intentional infliction of emotional distress.

The district moved the court for summary judgment, arguing that the claims were barred for failure to exhaust administrative remedies under the IDEA. The court concluded the district was not entitled to summary judgment on the basis of administrative exhaustion. The court further held that the student raised sufficient facts to avoid dismissal of his claims for Title IX violations and intentional infliction of emotional distress. A Title IX claim for damages exists where an official with authority to address alleged discrimination and institute corrective action is deliberately indifferent to harassment of which he or she has actual knowledge. The harassment must be so severe, pervasive and objectively offensive that it deprives the victim of access to educational opportunities or benefits. In this case, the district did not interview the student and took no other corrective action besides placing the camera in the bus for several weeks. The student presented evidence that this measure was incomplete and that school officials failed to ask him about the allegations because they assumed he was lying. The court held that **an incomplete investigation and failing to make proper inquiries could constitute a clearly unreasonable response to allegations of harassment**. The student raised factual issues about the severity of the harassment by claiming that sexual talk and gestures continued while he was on the driver's bus, and that he was forced to stop taking the bus altogether for two weeks. There was sufficient evidence to avoid pretrial judgment on the Title IX claim as well as the claim for intentional infliction of emotional distress, and the court denied the district's summary judgment motion. *Landon v. Oswego Unit School District No. 308*, No. 00 C 1803, 2001 WL 649560 (N.D. Ill. 2001).

◆ **A special education student and her brother attended an elementary school where they claimed they were victimized by continuous harassment from other students**. Their mother alleged that she witnessed students assaulting and harassing her mentally disabled daughter and that when she directed her son to help, he too was assaulted. The school's principal suggested that the mother pick her children up at another location and the plan worked for the rest of the school year. The disabled sibling was bruised on the playground during a recess period when another student bumped into her. Her brother stated that on a later date, some other students spit on him and punched him while he stood near a drinking fountain. The mother commenced a federal district court action against the school district, principal, an assistant principal and the school superintendent for civil rights violations arising from these incidents, asserting that the defendants failed to protect her children from abusive students.

The court considered a summary judgment motion filed by the district and officials, and observed that the mother did not submit any evidence that the students required medical attention as a result of the incidents and did not include doctor or therapist reports concerning problems or treatment received by the students. There was insufficient evidence of harm to establish that a due process violation occurred and was caused by the district or district officials. **There was also no showing that the incidents from which the injuries arose were foreseeable to district employees. The playground incident was apparently accidental** and there was no showing of a dangerous condition at the playground after school. The spitting incident was unforeseeable to district employees and not the result of the district's action or inaction. The perpetrators in this incident were not the same as those who caused the playground injuries and the cases were not similar enough to support the family's argument that the district should be held responsible under the theory of a "state created danger." The court held that the incidents could not have been foreseen and noted that the principal's suggestion had remedied the situation. There was no showing of willful disregard by the district in failing to transfer the mentally disabled student to another school. The court awarded summary judgment to the district and officials. *Nordo v. School District of Philadelphia*, 172 F.Supp.2d 600 (E.D. Pa. 2001).

◆ A New York court refused to award damages to a 15-year-old special education student injured while playing basketball at school. No amount of supervision, however intense, would have prevented the accident and there was no practical way to ensure against similar accidents. The student was 15 years old with mild cerebral palsy and an intellectual functioning range near the seven-year-old level. He collided with another student while playing basketball and fell to the floor. The student sued his board of cooperative educational services for personal injuries in a state trial court on the theory of inadequate supervision. The court held in his favor and the BOCES appealed to the New York Supreme Court, Appellate Division. The appellate court rejected the student's assertion that he required constant and intensive supervision. There was contrary evidence that his doctor had cleared him for all gym activities and that his mother allowed him to "go as far as he felt he could go" while outside school. **The BOCES and its agents were not negligent, because supervision could not have prevented the injury**. Since there was no way to ensure against such injuries short of barring all physical activities, the court reversed the decision and dismissed the complaint. *Ancewicz v. Western Suffolk BOCES*, 730 N.Y.S.2d 113 (N.Y. App. Div., 2d Dep't 2001).

◆ **A mobility service employee sexually molested two students while he was supposed to be providing them with mobility training** under a contract between the district and service. One of the students was legally blind, while the other was blind and had mental retardation. The families of the students filed lawsuits against the school board for negligence when they learned of the molestation, asserting failure to properly supervise, negligent hiring and screening of employees, negligently allowing the employee to leave school with the students, failing to protect them from wrongful and criminal acts and provide them with a safe environment, failing to identify risks of harm posed by the employee, and failing to investigate a prior reported molestation. Moreover, the families alleged wanton and reckless disregard for the students' rights by allowing them to be molested while in the district's care and custody. The board and mobility service filed cross-claims against each other and moved the court for summary judgment, seeking interpretation of indemnity language in the contract. The court held that the service did not need to indemnify the board, and the board appealed to the Louisiana Fourth Circuit Court of Appeal.

The board argued that it was entitled to indemnification, since all of the acts causing injury to the students arose from the employee, who was employed by the service. The fact that the students had alleged negligence by the board should not affect the service's obligation to provide indemnity under the contract, according to the board. The court found that the contract provided for indemnity between the parties "regardless of whether or not it is caused in part by a party indemnified." This language, plus a reference to "all claims" in the contract mandated indemnification. **The contractual language required the service to indemnify the board for the students' claims, and this interpretation did not violate a public policy disfavoring the indemnification of a party that is solely responsible for the causation of damages through negligence**. The board was not solely responsible for the damage in this case and its negligence could be described as secondary to that of the service, since the latter employed the offending party. The court reversed the trial court judgment and remanded the case. *Berry v. Orleans Parish School Board*, 802 So.2d 861 (La. Ct. App. 5th Cir. 2001).

◆ After being reprimanded for misconduct by a teacher, an eighth grader attempted suicide in a locker room. **The student's parents sued the town, the school board and school officials in federal district court, alleging that the defendants had failed to respond appropriately to an alleged epidemic of suicide attempts** at the middle school the student attended. The complaint further alleged the school failed to provide appropriate counseling and monitoring programs. The district court dismissed the lawsuit.

The parents appealed to the First Circuit, asserting constitutional and state law claims. The court refused to find a constitutional due process violation based upon alleged school inaction toward a student, since there is no general duty for schools to protect students. It held that "school children are not captives of the school authorities and the basic responsibility for their care remains with the parents." Even if school employees had been negligent, there would be no due process violation. **There was no merit to the claim that the teacher's reprimand was malicious or created a risk that the student would attempt suicide**. The court distinguished the case from *Armijo v. Wagon Mound Public Schools*, 159 F.3d 1253 (10th Cir. 1998), which involved a special education student who committed suicide at home after school employees sent him home with the knowledge that he would be alone and had access to a gun. *Armijo* involved facts that were more aggravated than in this case, and the court emphasized that the Due Process Clause is no substitute for state legal or administrative remedies. The court affirmed the district court judgment. *Hasenfus v. LaJeunesse*, 175 F.3d 68 (1st Cir.1999).

◆ On three occasions, nurses employed by a health services provider under contract with the county in which two private schools were located noted possible spine curvature in a student. However, school employees did not review the student's health records. The student's family physician also failed to detect the spinal problems over an 11-year period. The physician then detected a slight spinal curvature and referred the student to a specialist for surgery and braces. **The student filed a state court action against the schools and the health services provider for personal injuries**, asserting that the private schools negligently failed to furnish his parents with written notification of an abnormal curvature of his spine and advise them of the necessity of treatment. The court granted summary judgment to the schools, finding no evidence that they knew of the abnormal spine condition and ruling that the schools had no legal duty to supervise nurses employed by a health services provider under contract to perform professional services.

The student appealed to the Supreme Court of Nebraska, where he argued that a state law requiring school districts to screen students for sight, hearing and dental problems and to report defective conditions to parents created a similar duty which required the schools to report his spinal condition. The student asserted that the schools had a duty to report his medical condition to his parents, noting that the state published a school guide for maintaining health service programs which discussed scoliosis screening by school nurses and recommended advising parents to consult a physician upon recognizing signs of scoliosis. The court held that this was not a requirement of law. **The guide created no duty requiring school districts to screen students for abnormal spinal conditions. There was also no potential liability for the schools under general liability theories based on allowing a negligent condition to occur on school premises**. The court held that the schools had no duty to supervise or monitor the nurses, or to take any affirmative steps to ensure that they were performing their professional duties. The schools had no actual knowledge of the nurses' findings and the trial court had correctly granted summary judgment to the schools. *Koltes v. Visiting Nurses Assn., et al.*, 591 N.W.2d 578 (Neb.1999).

◆ A student with mental retardation and seizures went on playground equipment described as "the high tower," which she had been forbidden from using by her special education teacher. The teacher was absent on the day in question. **The student slid down a pole and fell, suffering a fractured tibia**. At the time of the accident, two teachers were on the playground supervising special education students. Another adult supervisor was assigned to watch 100 regular education students. The student's parents sued the school district for failing to properly supervise the student. A jury determined that the substitute teacher had not acted negligently and held for the district. The court denied the parents' motion for a new trial.

The parents appealed to the Montana Supreme Court, which observed that a verdict cannot be reversed where it is supported by substantial credible evidence. In this case, the substitute teacher had been the only eyewitness to the incident, and she had testified that she was watching five low-functioning disabled students who all required special attention. **The court agreed with the parents that the substitute teacher had a duty to closely supervise the student. However, the fact that the substitute had failed to see her climbing the high tower did not require a finding that she had breached this duty**. The question of negligence had been properly submitted to the jury. There was no merit to the parents' claim that the substitute's testimony was not credible. The court found that the substitute's statements were substantially similar, and that the jury was aware of any potential inconsistency in her testimony. The jury had received proper instructions from the trial court and was entitled to evaluate the substitute's credibility. The court found substantial credible evidence in support of the verdict and affirmed the trial court's order denying the motion for a new trial. *Morgan v. Great Falls School Dist. No. 1*, 995 P.2d 422 (Mont. 2000).

- A student with spina bifida and hydrocephalus was unable to walk due to paralysis of his legs. The student's school district provided transportation in a specially equipped bus with a wheelchair. A district bus aide typically secured the student in the wheelchair with a lap restraint, but the wheelchair did not have a means of securing his upper body. **The bus driver backed the bus into a car after picking up the student for school** one day, and the student's mother asked the student if he had been injured. The student did not respond and the mother permitted him to go to school. A police investigator relied on the driver's assurance that no one had been injured. However, **the student returned home from school that day with a bruised forehead. He also complained of head and back pain**, and the family took him to an emergency room for treatment. The student then began a two-month chiropractic treatment program costing more than $1,000. The family sued the school board for the costs of the chiropractic treatment and emergency services. The court found the board liable for the injuries and added a general damage award of $6,000 to the cost of services incurred by the family.

The school board appealed to the Court of Appeal of Louisiana, Second Circuit, which found ample evidence that the student's injuries had been caused by the accident. An injury is presumed to have resulted from an accident if the injured party did not exhibit symptoms before the accident and is later observed to have them. The student had no bruise on his forehead before the accident and did not report head or back problems. The trial court was entitled to discredit testimony by the aide that she had been observing the student the entire time and could not see that he had been hurt. The trial court was also permitted to reject the school board's evidence that chiropractic treatment of the student was unnecessary and inappropriate. There was no evidence of bad faith by the family and there had been testimony that the treatment reduced the student's pain and decreased muscle spasms. The court held that the $6,000 general damage award was not unreasonable. General damage awards are intended to compensate personal injury claimants for mental or physical pain, suffering, inconvenience, and other losses that cannot be measured in exact monetary terms. **There was sufficient evidence that the student had suffered physical pain as the result of the accident, and continued to experience pain.** The court affirmed the judgment. *Marshall v. Caddo Parish School Bd.*, 743 So.2d 943 (La. Ct. App. 1999).

- An elementary school student had congenital myopathy, resulting in weakening of his muscles. The school prepared an IEP for him that called for the assistance of an aide during gym class and recess. **The student and his family claimed that the district and a teacher were negligent for allowing him to**

trip over a door during a fire drill, in view of the precautions stated in his IEP. The parents brought a personal injury suit against the district. A Minnesota district court held for the district and teacher. On appeal, **the court of appeals agreed with the family that the case could not be dismissed prior to a trial, given the school district's knowledge of the student's condition and his IEP recommendations**. This was because there were factual issues concerning the reasonableness of the teacher's conduct when the student was injured. The district court had erroneously awarded summary judgment to the school district and had also improperly granted immunity to the teacher, since her duties were outlined in the IEP and were only ministerial in nature. Official immunity is appropriate in negligence cases only where employees are engaged in discretionary duties. The court reversed and remanded the case to the district court, and allowed the family to amend the complaint to include claims of assault and battery. However, it upheld the district court's decision to preclude the addition of constitutional claims arising under 42 U.S.C. § 1983. This was because a single incident does not establish an official policy or custom sufficient to allow § 1983 liability. *Moses v. Minneapolis Pub. Schools*, 1998 WL 846546 (Minn.Ct.App.1998).

2. Student on Student Injuries

◆ A Georgia student complained to her teacher of sexual harassment by a male student. The teacher did not immediately notify the principal of the harassment. Although the harassing student was eventually charged with sexual battery, school officials took no action against him. The student sued the school board in a federal district court under Title IX of the Education Amendments of 1972, which prohibit sex discrimination by education programs receiving federal assistance. The court dismissed the case and the student appealed to the U.S. Court of Appeals for the Eleventh Circuit. The court reversed the judgment but granted the board's petition for rehearing. On rehearing, **the court observed that under the student's argument, a school board must immediately isolate an alleged harasser to avoid a Title IX lawsuit**. Because Congress did not discuss student-on-student harassment when considering the Title IX amendments, there was no merit to this argument and the court affirmed the dismissal of the case.

The U.S. Supreme Court accepted the student's petition for certiorari. The Supreme Court reversed, holding that **school districts may be liable for deliberate indifference to known acts of peer sexual harassment under Title IX, in cases where the response of school administrators is clearly unreasonable under the circumstances**. A recipient of federal funds may be liable for student-on-student sexual harassment where the funding recipient is deliberately indifferent to known student sexual harassment and the harasser is under the recipient's disciplinary authority. In order to create Title IX liability, **the harassment must be so severe, pervasive and objectively offensive that it deprives the victim of access to the funding recipient's educational opportunities or benefits**. The Court stated that the harassment alleged by the student was sufficiently severe to avoid pretrial dismissal, thus reversing and remanding the case. *Davis v. Monroe County Bd. of Educ.*, 526 U.S. 629, 119 S.Ct. 1661, 143 L.Ed.2d 839 (1999).

◆ Two 12-year-old students with mental retardation were placed in the same class. One of the student's parents claimed that the classmate had disciplinary problems, repeatedly bullied their son, and frequently stole his lunch money. Their teacher observed both of them leaving the rest room one day and noticed that the classmate had an erection and that the student looked surprised. **The student complained that the classmate sexually assaulted him**, but the classmate denied it. According to the teacher, the student then changed his story, saying there was no sexual contact. The teacher took both students to the assistant principal's office. There was conflicting evidence about whether sexual contact had occurred, and the school did not notify the student's parents about the incident. The student told his sister about it three days later, and the parents notified the state child-protection agency and school principal. The principal began an administrative investigation in which he interviewed the students, spoke with the child-protection agency and the police. He also met with the student and his parents and with teachers and administrators, ultimately deciding to transfer the classmate to another school.

The student's parents sued the district in a federal district court on behalf of their son, asserting sexual harassment claims under Title IX and various state law negligence claims. The court recited the test for Title IX liability in student-on-student harassment cases as described by the U.S. Supreme Court in *Davis v. Monroe County Board of Education*, 526 U.S. 629 (1999), above, which requires the victim to show that the sexual harassment was so severe, pervasive and objectively offensive that it deprived him or her of educational benefits. It must be proven that school officials had actual knowledge of the harassment and were deliberately indifferent to it. Although it is possible for a single incident of harassment to be so severe, pervasive and objectively offensive that it deprives the victim of educational benefits, the Supreme Court has held that the behavior must have the systematic effect of denying the victim equal access to a program or activity. **Although there was evidence of prior bullying by the classmate in this case, there were no other incidents of gender-related harassment that could give rise to Title IX liability**. Contrary to the parents' argument, school officials were not deliberately indifferent to the suspected sexual assault. The principal's investigation of the incident was reasonable and would have prevented further harassment. The court awarded summary judgment to the district and officials on the Title IX claim. It held that the district and officials were entitled to state law immunity from the negligence claims, but dismissed the claims so that the parents had the opportunity to bring them in a state court action. *Wilson v. Beaumont Independent School District*, 144 F.Supp.2d 690 (E.D. Tex. 2001).

◆ A Colorado student had developmental and physical disabilities including spastic cerebral palsy and hearing impairments. Her mother stated that she advised school officials that the student had been sexually assaulted at another school. However, the student came into contact with another student with disabilities who had exhibited disciplinary and behavioral problems, including sexually inappropriate conduct. **The mother asserted that the other student began making inappropriate, sexual contact with her daughter and twice sexually assaulted her. She claimed that teachers and the school principal did nothing to stop the assaults and took deliberate steps to conceal them**. The student became suicidal and was placed in a psychiatric hospital. School employees continued to deny the sexual assaults, and the student returned to school. The mother then claimed that the student was ridiculed by other students who knew of the attacks. Although the school conducted a meeting among staff and parents to discuss the situation, the mother asserted that the principal still failed to investigate the matter and suspended only her daughter after suggesting that the contact might have been consensual.

The mother filed a federal district court action against the school district, school board and school employees, asserting violations of Title IX of the Education Amendments of 1972 and the Constitution. The court dismissed the case and the mother appealed to the Tenth Circuit, which abated the proceedings pending the U.S. Supreme Court's decision in *Davis v. Monroe County Bd. of Educ.*, 119 S.Ct. 1661 (1999), above. The Tenth Circuit then considered the case under the analysis adopted by the *Davis* Court. **The court stated that the employees' knowledge of assaults towards the student, if true, could be charged to the school district and that the alleged deliberate indifference of school officials to the abuse reports was sufficient to create Title IX liability**. The principal had the authority to suspend the other student yet allegedly failed to take corrective action. The student had been hospitalized and rendered unable to participate in the school's educational programs. She thus met each of the factors of the *Davis* test, requiring reversal of the Title IX judgment. The circuit court determined the district court had properly rejected the family's equal protection complaint against the school district, since such a cause of action depended upon the existence of an official policy or custom of deliberate indifference to sexual harassment by the school district. There was no such allegation in the complaint and the court reversed the judgment. The principal and teachers were not entitled to immunity in their individual capacities for equal protection violations. The case was reversed and remanded to the district court for further proceedings. *Murrell v. School Dist. No. 1, Denver, Colorado*, 186 F.3d 1238 (10th Cir.1999).

◆ **A student with mental retardation and a history of sexual abuse told her mother that a male educable mentally impaired student raped her in a back room at school** after the teacher had allowed him to accompany her to her locker at lunchtime. She also stated that the male EMI student and two others had fondled her on a school bus and in the back of their class when the teacher was in the hallway, and that they had threatened her with violence if she told anyone. The student's mother reported the rape to school, law enforcement, and child protection officials. Staff commenced an investigation and devised a plan for the protection and increased supervision for the student. The rape suspect claimed that the contact with the student was consensual, but after police charged him, the school expelled him for the rest of the year. The police did not prosecute the two other male students and the school did not discipline them. The school implemented several remedial steps, including the installation of windows on doors in the school, placement of an aide in the student's classroom and bus, and implementation of a hall pass rule. The student's mother kept her at home until the expulsion of the male EMI student. The family commenced a federal district court civil rights action against the school district, the school board, and a number of employees for violations of the U.S. Constitution and Title IX of the Education Amendments of 1972. The court awarded summary judgment to the school defendants and the family appealed to the Sixth Circuit.

The circuit court held that the superintendent of schools was entitled to absolute immunity under state law as the district's highest executive. It further noted that Michigan law provides for governmental immunity for other government officers and employees in the absence of gross negligence, which was defined as conduct so reckless as to demonstrate a substantial lack of concern for injury. The Sixth Circuit rejected the family's assertion that the conduct of the district and its employees was grossly negligent. The district's alleged improper supervision of students and failure to have a policy in effect to protect at-risk students was shielded by governmental immunity since it did not demonstrate recklessness or a substantial lack of concern for injury. The court summarily rejected the assertion that there was a violation of the student's equal protection rights, since there was no evidence that she was treated differently than male students. Although a constitutional violation exists where a school official physically harms a student, liability for harm caused by a third party, such as another student, requires the existence of a special relationship between the school and the victim. The court rejected the family's theory that compulsory attendance laws create such a special relationship and held that there was no constitutional rights violation by the school district or its employees. Because there was no underlying constitutional rights violation, the family's claim under 42 U.S.C. § 1983 also failed. **The Sixth Circuit noted that under *Davis v. Monroe County Bd. of Educ.*, 119 S.Ct. 1661 (1999), the student could not prevail because the school officials had no actual knowledge of any harassment until after the fact. As soon as they learned of it, they took immediate steps to remedy the situation**, including expulsion of the rape suspect. Because of this prompt and thorough response, the Title IX claim failed and the court affirmed the judgment. *Soper v. Hoben*, 195 F.3d 845 (6th Cir. 1999), *cert. denied*, 530 U.S. 1262, 120 S.Ct. 2719, 147 L.Ed.2d 984 (2000).

- After a special education student was murdered by a classmate, her family filed a state court action against the school district, asserting negligent failure to properly supervise students. According to the complaint, the perpetrator had previously told a teacher at the school that he intended to "stick his girlfriend with a needle and try killing her." The family produced additional evidence that the perpetrator had threatened his girlfriend, was dangerous, and required mental health counseling and monitoring. However, there was no proof that this information was passed on to school personnel, and the court awarded summary judgment to the school district.

On appeal, the New York Supreme Court, Appellate Division, held that while school districts in the state are required to adequately supervise their students, school liability is limited to foreseeable injuries that are proximately related to the absence of adequate supervision. **In order to establish whether school supervision has been adequate, it must be shown that school authorities have specific knowledge or notice of dangerous conduct that causes injury. When the injury is caused by a third party, the action must have been reasonably anticipated**. In most cases, actual or constructive notice to school personnel is required in order to impose liability on a school entity. In this case, there was no competent evidence that the school was in breach of its duty to adequately supervise the students. The court held that the school had no additional duty to provide security based on the theory that the wooded area presented an inherent danger to students. It also rejected the argument that the school owed the student a heightened duty of care because she was a special education student. *Marshall v. Cortland Enlarged City School Dist.*, 697 N.Y.S.2d 395 (N.Y. App. Div. 3d 1999).

◆ A student with an IQ of 38 was enrolled in the district's trainable mentally handicapped (TMH) program. She was raped by another TMH student outside a school district building while two other students stood watch. She was reported to be hysterical immediately after the incident and became anxious and insecure about going to school. The district did not remove either the student or the perpetrator from the TMH classroom and they remained in the same class as of the time of trial. A jury awarded the student $1 million in damages in her negligence lawsuit against the district, which the court later reduced to $250,000. The school district appealed to the state court of appeals, which found that the question of liability hinged on whether the district had been grossly negligent within the meaning of the state Tort Claims Act. It found evidence from which **a jury could reasonably make a finding of gross negligence because the employee who was supposed to be supervising the students at the time of the incident left them unattended** while she used the restroom, **despite her knowledge of sexual contact between two students** in the same class within the previous two weeks. There was also evidence that TMH students required constant supervision to ensure their safety, and evidence that the student was hysterical after the rape. She had become withdrawn and disinterested in school as a result of the incident. This justified a large award of damages, and the court denied the school district's motion for a new trial. It affirmed the trial court orders. *Duncan v. Hampton County School Dist. #2*, 517 S.E.2d 449 (S.C.Ct.App.1999).

◆ A ninth grade New York student was injured in a drawing class when another student shot a pencil at him with a ruler, striking him in the eye. The student's family sued the school district and the other student in a state court for personal injury, claiming that the district failed to maintain a safe environment and did not provide adequate supervision and discipline in the classroom. Evidence was offered showing that disruptive and unruly behavior was common in the drawing class. The court denied a summary judgment motion by the board and district, and they appealed to the New York Supreme Court, Appellate Division. **The court found that the board and district were on notice of a pattern of undisciplined, disruptive and unruly behavior in the drawing class.** The trial court appropriately denied the summary judgment motion. *Maynard v. Bd. of Educ. of Massena Central School Dist.*, 663 N.Y.S.2d 717 (N.Y. App. Div. 1997).

3. Injuries to Others

◆ A student was identified as multiply disabled, with an IQ below 30 and severe developmental delays. He did not speak, read or write and had trouble following directions. He frequently attacked teachers and other students, causing over 1,300 documented injuries to school staff. One staff member who complained about frequent injuries was told that injuries were to be expected and that she might look for another job. The student required restraint between 10 and 48 times daily, often by two adults. On one occasion, a staff member injured her shoulder, back and neck while attempting to move the student to another room. A second aide injured her neck, back and shoulders while escorting the student to a picture taking session, and she requested reassignment. **The injured aides sued the district in a state trial court**. The court granted summary judgment to the district, which held that the suit was barred by the state industrial insurance act.

The employees appealed to the court of appeals, which observed that an exception to the industrial insurance regime exists where an employer deliberately injures an employee. Washington courts have previously held that a deliberate injury may be found where an employer has actual knowledge that an injury is certain to occur, yet willfully disregards this knowledge. In this case, **there was evidence that the district had knowledge of the student's dangerous propensities, and even tolerated injuries to staff persons**. There was also evidence that the district had either improperly trained staff or failed to address the student's programming to provide for classroom safety. Because a reasonable jury could conclude that the district had willfully disregarded the risk of injury to employees, the trial court had improperly awarded summary judgment to the district. *Stenger v. Stanwood School Dist.*, 977 P.2d 660 (Wash.Ct.App.1999).

One of the aids also sued the state of Washington, claiming the state was liable for her injuries as a result of the failure of the state Department of Social and Health Services to place the student in a more restrictive environment. The aide's complaint also included claims alleging assault and battery, negligence and civil rights violations under 42 U.S.C. § 1983. DSHS obtained summary judgment at the superior-court level, and the aide appealed to a state appellate court, arguing that DSHS failed to disclose the student's violent behavior during dependency proceedings, willfully disregarded staff safety at district schools, failed to place him in a properly restrictive environment and negligently supervised him.
The court discussed the claim based on failure to exercise proper supervision over the student in the context of the public duty doctrine. Under that doctrine, a governmental agency may be liable to an individual or the public based on negligent conduct if the individual can show the existence of "a special relationship." **The court agreed with the DSHS that because it lacked the authority to change the student's placement under state and federal law, it could not be held liable for failing to place him in a more-restrictive setting**. There was no special relationship between the student and DSHS sufficient to trigger any duty under the public duty doctrine. The record indicated that the school district had met with the student's aunt to devise his IEP without any input from DSHS. The agency was not a "public agency" as defined by federal special education regulations. The superior court had properly awarded summary judgment to DSHS on the aide's negligence claims. *Stenger v. State of Washington*, 104 Wash.App. 393, 16 P.3d 655 (2001).

◆ A psychologist diagnosed a Wisconsin grade school student as having Attention Deficit Hyperactivity Disorder (ADHD). After the student repeatedly kicked, bit, spit, and yelled at other students and teachers, his psychologist prescribed Dexedrine, a medicine designed to reduce impulsive and aggressive behavior in children. **The parents kept him on the medication for one term but then discontinued it due to side effects without consulting the psychologist, teachers, or any member of the special education staff**. The student again became disruptive. On one occasion, he pulled a teacher's hair, causing her to fall down a flight of stairs and suffer a herniated disc. There was some dispute as to whether the student's action was intentional. The teacher sued the parents and their homeowner's insurer in a Wisconsin trial court, alleging that the parents were negligent in failing to inform anyone at the school that they had removed the student from medication. The trial court held for the teacher, but the Wisconsin Court of Appeals reversed, ruling that the jury had improperly based its decision upon speculation. The teacher appealed to the Supreme Court of Wisconsin.

The supreme court held that **the parents' negligent conduct was a substantial cause of the teacher's injury. They had inadequately researched both the consequences of discontinuing Dexedrine and alternative forms of treatment. They had also neglected to inform the school that the medication had been discontinued**, precluding development of a plan to manage the student's behavior. The court rejected the insurer's public policy arguments, ruling that the injury was not too remote from the negligence, that liability would not impose unreasonable burdens on similarly situated parents, and that the decision would not "open the floodgate of litigation." The parents were negligent in failing to control the student, and their negligence was a substantial factor in causing the teacher's injuries. No public policy considerations precluded a finding of liability, and the supreme court reinstated the trial court's decision. *Nieuwendorp v. American Family Ins. Co.*, 529 N.W.2d 594 (Wis.1995).

◆ A Louisiana special education teacher's aide assisted profoundly mentally disabled students at a school for the trainable mentally retarded. Although the teacher's aide had 18 years of experience in a conventional classroom setting and could not swim, her school decided to assign her to the adapted aquatics program. She injured her back when she lunged to grab a disabled student who was struggling in the water. The teacher's aide filed a personal injury lawsuit against the state of Louisiana through the state Department of Education, alleging that the state owed her a duty of care under the IDEA and Louisiana special education statutes. A Louisiana trial court awarded judgment to the state and the aide appealed to the Court of Appeal of Louisiana, Third Circuit. The court of appeal stated that **the IDEA and Louisiana special education statutes did not confer a legal cause of action upon a teacher to recover for personal injuries. These statutes imposed duties upon the state to serve students with disabilities and the duty did not extend to teachers or aides**. The teacher's aide was protected by the state workers' compensation system and she had in fact applied for and received workers' compensation benefits from the school board. Because the state had no duty to protect the aide from personal injury, the court of appeal reversed the trial court's judgment. *Durham v. State of Louisiana through the Dept. of Educ.*, 638 So.2d 1129 (La. Ct. App. 1994).

◆ The mother of a Florida student was severely injured when she was struck in the mouth by a 16-year-old junior high school student as she walked down a school corridor. The student had a long history of disciplinary problems. **The injured parent sued the school board, claiming that it had breached a duty to protect her from a known or foreseeable threat of violence by the student**. A Florida trial court granted the board's summary judgment motion, stating that there was no evidence of prior violence by the student toward nonstudents and nonteachers that would place the school board on actual notice of an attack. The court then granted the injured parent's motion for a rehearing, but entered another order granting the board's summary judgment motion. The parent appealed to the District Court of Appeal of Florida, Second District.

The court of appeal reviewed Florida legal authority that established school boards are required to appropriately supervise students. School boards had a further duty to protect students from assaults by other students. Florida statutes require school boards to protect teachers and other school personnel from assaults by students. Accordingly, **the school board owed visitors to school premises a duty to keep reasonably safe conditions, including a duty to protect parents and other visitors from reasonably foreseeable student attacks**. Since the parent had been on school grounds to obtain books and assignments for her son, and the evidence indicated that the student was "extremely volatile and was becoming more difficult, unruly, and violent as time went on," the record did not support the trial court's grant of summary judgment for the school board. The court of appeal reversed and remanded. *Garufi v. School Bd. of Hillsborough County*, 613 So.2d 1341 (Fla. Dist. Ct. App. 1993).

B. Negligent Placement

◆ A Massachusetts student who attended a middle-school program for students with special needs was brutally beaten by a classmate. The classmate had recently transferred from another school, where he had allegedly threatened another student with a weapon. **When the classmate arrived at the school, he was placed in a restrictive program for students with serious behavioral disorders**. The program, which required "100 percent supervision" at all times, did not expressly apply to after-school activities. On the day of the beating, the classmate and another student were supposed to board a school bus, however, they left the supervision of school employees and caught up with the disabled student in a field behind the school. The classmate attacked the student and kicked him repeatedly in the forehead. The student suffered a permanent closed-head injury and suffered chronic headaches as a result of the incident. Although the classmate was found delinquent in the state juvenile justice system, he returned to the school and was never disciplined. The student's parents sued the school committee, special-education director, school psychologist, principal, classmate and classmate's parents. The school committee and officials moved for summary judgment on the parents' claims of negligence and constitutional rights violations.

The court observed that state actors such as school officials have no general constitutional duty to protect individuals from harmful conduct by third parties, such as classmates. Compulsory school attendance laws did not create a "special relationship" between the officials and the student that entitled him to heightened protection. At most, the officials demonstrated poor judgment by accepting the classmate into the restrictive program and failing to supervise him after school. This conduct did not rise to the level of a constitutional rights violation. The Massachusetts Torts Claims Act provided immunity for any claims based on the exercise or performance, or the failure to exercise or perform, a discretionary function by a public employer or employee within the scope of office or employment. **The placement of the student in a program involved a high degree of discretion and judgment by a special education team**. The state's highest court held in a 1977 case that a school's adoption of a plan to integrate disabled students into public schools was an activity protected by immunity. The failure of school officials to prevent one student from injuring another was also protected under the state tort claims act. The court held that the state tort claims act could not be construed to hold municipalities and public schools liable for the release of students after the regular school day. The officials were entitled to summary judgment. *Willhauck v. Town of Mansfield*, 164 F.Supp.2d 127 (D. Mass. 2001).

◆ A Virginia high school student was identified as having a learning disability when he was 18 years old. His parents claimed that the school district's failure to identify his disability while he was in the fourth grade violated a number of his rights under state and federal law. They initiated administrative proceedings against the school district and resolved all placement issues that had been in dispute. However, the hearing officer denied their request for compensatory and punitive damages. The parents appealed to a federal district court, seeking damages under the IDEA, § 504 of the Rehabilitation Act, Virginia law and the U.S. Constitution for failing to identify the student's disability. **The court rejected the IDEA claim, observing that the act does not create a private cause of action for educational malpractice.** Monetary relief under the IDEA has been limited by many courts to the reimbursement of costs. The § 504 claim failed to state a valid cause of action because any damage recovery under § 504 required a showing of intentional discrimination or bad faith, which the student had failed to allege. His state law educational malpractice claim also failed, because Virginia's supreme court has refused to recognize this cause of action, as have all other U.S. jurisdictions except Montana. The court granted the school board's dismissal motion.

The parents appealed to the Fourth Circuit, which agreed with the district court that **the IDEA claim was indistinguishable from one for educational malpractice. The award of compensatory or punitive damages in an IDEA case was inconsistent with the IDEA's statutory scheme, and would transform the IDEA into a personal injury statute**. Although other courts have allowed monetary damage awards in claims filed under § 504 of the Rehabilitation Act, such claims require proof of bad faith or gross misjudgment. In this case, the parents had alleged no facts indicating that the school district had discriminated against the student or had acted with bad faith or gross misjudgment. The district court had properly dismissed the Rehabilitation Act and 42 U.S.C. § 1983 claims, and the court of appeals affirmed the judgment. *Sellers v. School Bd. of City of Manassas, Virginia*, 141 F.3d 524 (4th Cir.1998).

◆ A New York student encountered great difficulty in his classes but consistently scored well on standardized citywide tests. The tests indicated that he was an above average student, which resulted in his being placed in regular classes. He did not receive any special education services. The student finally received a learning disabled classification when he entered high school, and he was then placed in appropriate classes. **He claimed that the school district's earlier failure to evaluate and properly place him constituted educational malpractice.** He also claimed that his elementary school principal had altered his citywide test answer sheets, which had the effect of denying him access to special education programs and services. He filed a lawsuit in a New York trial court, claiming educational malpractice. The court stated that the cause of action for educational malpractice did not exist in New York, but refused to dismiss the lawsuit at the pretrial stage. The district and principal appealed to the New York Supreme Court, Appellate Division, Second Department. The appellate division court stated that New York did not recognize a legal cause of action for educational malpractice. Those portions of the complaint were dismissed. However, **the student's allegations of fraud and other intentional wrongdoing could be viable if properly pleaded and proven at trial.** In such cases, only actual financial losses could be the basis for a damage award. The student's present complaint had failed to allege any damages, and the court dismissed it, allowing him an opportunity to refile claims for fraud and intentional tort. It would also be possible for the student to raise the question of the city board of education's knowledge of the principal's alleged wrongdoing based on the dramatic improvement in the ranking of his school as the result of citywide test results. *Helbig v. City of New York*, 622 N.Y.S.2d 316 (N.Y. App. Div. 2d Dept.1995).

III. LIABILITY FOR INTENTIONAL CONDUCT

Parties injured as the result of intentional conduct by school employees or third parties, including students, have sought to hold school districts and their officials liable for constitutional rights violations. Courts have rejected claims for school district liability based on intentional conduct except where a special relationship exists between the victim and district and where proof of an official policy of deliberate indifference to the victim's clearly established constitutional rights exists. State compulsory attendance laws have been held not to create the required special relationship; instead, the victim must be completely dependent upon and in the custody of the agency for liability to attach, such as in cases of involuntary commitment or incarceration.

A. School Employees

◆ At the start of her eighth-grade year, a special education student transferred schools. She claimed that she was targeted by several male classmates for harassment and that school officials were unresponsive to her complaints. The school suspended the student seven times that year and reported numerous incidents of disruptive behavior and unexcused absences. She then jabbed a male classmate with a pen after he made sexual remarks and threatened to poke her breast. While she was detained in the office, **the assistant principal called her mother to offer her a choice of punishments: suspension or three swats with a paddle** under the school's corporal-punishment policy. The mother agreed to the paddling, which resulted in bruises requiring medical attention. The mother notified the county child-protection agency of the paddling and it determined that "there had been abuse by inappropriate discipline." The family sued the district, principal, assistant principal and other school officials in a federal district court for constitutional rights violations and for violating Title IX of the Education Amendments of 1972.

The court considered noted that the complaining party in an action for constitutional rights violations against a school district or its employees must show the existence of a policy or custom that is causally connected to an injury. There must be an official act taken with the requisite degree of culpability, and a causal link between the action and a deprivation of federal rights. **The court found no evidence that the corporal punishment policy, as written, led to a constitutional injury**. The policy did not prescribe the amount of force to be used in relation to a student's offense, and the student offered no evidence of other incidents of excessive corporal punishment. There was no showing of unlawful discrimination against a disadvantaged group, and no evidence of purposeful discrimination to counter the district's evidence that the disparate punishments given to the students corresponded to each student's disciplinary history. The student had a record of disruptive behavior and was found to be the perpetrator. Her mother had selected corporal punishment and it was imposed in her presence. The officials had a reasonable belief that they were complying with the student's due process rights, as they followed district policy when administering discipline. The student was not entitled to more elaborate procedures than a regular-education student would receive, since laws protecting special-education students provide heightened due process procedures for expulsion or suspension, not for ordinary discipline related to unacceptable classroom behavior. There was no merit to the student's Title IX claim, as she failed to show that the more severe discipline imposed on her was based on her gender rather than her record of misconduct. The district and officials were awarded summary judgment on all of the student's claims. *B.A.L. v. Apple*, No. 00-0068-C-B/G, 2001 WL 1135024 (S.D. Ind. 2001).

♦ A special education student claimed that a substitute teacher locked the classroom door, confining her with disruptive classmates. She alleged that the substitute responded to the disruption by saying "I don't care what you do as long as you do not bother me." According to the student's account, two classmates attempted to rape another student in the back of the classroom. After the other student broke free and returned to her seat, **the student claimed that the two classmates assaulted and raped her behind a portable blackboard in the back of the class**. She sued the school district, superintendent, school principal and substitute for civil rights violations under 42 U.S.C. § 1983 in federal district court.

The substitute moved the court for summary judgment. The court first rejected the assertion that the district had a duty to protect the student from the actions of the third party students based on the existence of a special relationship between the student and the district. Even though she had limited mental abilities, there was no custodial relationship between her and the district that gave rise to liability under this theory. The court also rejected the student's claim that the district had a policy or custom of allowing classroom rapes because the substitute was not a policymaking employee of the district. However, the court accepted the student's argument that **there was potential liability on the theory that the substitute had placed her in danger by locking the door and telling the class that she would not enforce classroom discipline as long as she was not bothered**. Since the substitute was alleged to have isolated the student by locking the classroom and telling students that she would not control their behavior, the student met each part of the test for state created danger. The court accordingly denied the substitute's motion for summary judgment. *Maxwell v. School Dist. of Philadelphia*, 53 F.Supp.2d 787 (E.D.Pa.1999).

◆ A Kentucky school district maintained a policy allowing corporal punishment unless parents notified school officials otherwise. The parents of an eighth grade student advised his school's assistant principal that corporal punishment should not be used on him. However, the parents allegedly told a teacher that he had permission to paddle the student. The teacher paddled the student after he became involved in a fight with another student. The family sued the school board and employees in a federal district court for constitutional violations. The court denied summary judgment motions by the school officials, and they appealed to the U.S. Court of Appeals, Sixth Circuit. The court found that **the teacher and assistant principal had a good faith belief that the parents had withdrawn their instructions not to paddle the student. The paddling was not so severe or disproportionate to the violation to be considered an abuse of official power**. The constitutionality of corporal punishment was sufficiently unclear to prove a constitutional violation, and the district court had erroneously denied qualified immunity to the employees. *Saylor v. Bd. of Educ. of Harlan County, Kentucky*, 118 F.3d 507 (6th Cir.1997).

◆ Two school administrators wrote a favorable employment reference for an employee without revealing his history of sexual misconduct with students. A California middle school hired the employee and he later sexually assaulted a student, who filed a lawsuit against him in a California superior court. She also sued the former employer and administrators for fraudulent employment references. The court dismissed the claims against the school district and administrators, but the Court of Appeal of California reversed the decision concerning negligent misrepresentation and fraud. The district and administrators appealed to the Supreme Court of California, which held that it was reasonably foreseeable that the positive references could have led to the hiring district's reliance and created the opportunity for the sexual assault. **Employers who write recommendation letters have a duty to prospective employers and third parties not to misrepresent the qualifications and character of a former employee where misrepresentation would present a foreseeable risk of physical injury.** The supreme court reinstated the negligent misrepresentation and fraud claims. *Randi W. v. Muroc Joint Unif. School Dist.*, 60 Cal.Rptr.2d 263, 929 P.2d 582 (1997).

◆ An Alabama student with spina bifida underwent bladder surgery and had to be catheterized while at school each day. **The school system hired a special aide to provide care for the student, but she allegedly failed to catheterize the student on one occasion**. She also allegedly allowed the wheelchair which the student was using to roll down a flight of stairs. The student and her parents sued school district officials including the school principal, school nurse, special education services supervisor and the aide in an Alabama trial court, which dismissed all the claims except those advanced against the aide. The student and her parents appealed to the Supreme Court of Alabama. The supreme court considered whether the action was one against the state, in which case the officials would have absolute immunity, or whether it was best characterized as a claim against the individual officials, in which case the officials could be entitled to qualified immunity under the defense of performing discretionary duties. The court determined that the action was not against the state and held that the employees were not entitled to absolute immunity. However, **the actions of hiring and retaining the aide were properly characterized as discretionary. Therefore, the principal, nurse, and supervisor were entitled to qualified immunity**. The trial court had properly dismissed the lawsuit against those officials. *Nance by and through Nance v. Matthews*, 622 So.2d 297 (Ala.1993).

B. Sexual Abuse Reporting

◆ A teacher's aide noticed abnormalities in the genital area of a nine-year-old student with severe disabilities when changing her diaper and alerted the classroom teacher. The teacher notified the school principal, who contacted a state trooper. Although the trooper suspected child abuse, she could not verify her suspicions without physical evidence and asked school employees to inform her immediately if they discovered further symptoms. Several weeks later, the principal reported additional symptoms. **The trooper instructed the principal to take the student to a doctor's office immediately, stating that she had legal authority to do so. However, the trooper did not obtain a warrant or other court order allowing an examination**. A child protection worker signed a consent form purporting to authorize the examination that falsely indicated he was the student's legal guardian. The principal and aide transported the student to a doctor's office where a doctor performed oral, vaginal and rectal swabs. They returned the student to school, and soon learned the laboratory results did not indicate sexual abuse. The trooper did not inform the school employees or child protection worker that the test results were negative and none of those involved contacted the student's parents. However, the trooper met with the student's parents and accused the father of molesting his daughter. No evidence of abuse was discovered and no criminal abuse charges were ever filed against the parents.

The student's conservator sued the aide, principal, trooper and child protection worker in a Michigan court alleging false imprisonment, battery and constitutional rights violations. The court awarded summary disposition to the government employees, finding they were entitled to immunity from liability under the state Child Protection Law since they were engaged in a good-faith investigation of child abuse. The conservator appealed to the Michigan Court of

Appeals, which agreed with the trial court that there could be no personal monetary liability by government employees for constitutional rights violations arising from an unlawful search and seizure. **The trial court had properly dismissed the remaining claims against the aide and principal under the Child Protection Law, which immunizes persons who act in good faith in reporting abuse, or otherwise cooperating or assisting in an investigation.** This statutory immunity extended not only to the making of a report, but to a party's cooperation with an investigation. The aide's observations indicated unusual conditions in the student's genital area, creating reasonable cause to believe that she was a victim of child abuse. Even though no charges were ever filed against the parents, the principal had acted in good faith when she took the student to the doctor's office. The trooper and child protection worker were not entitled to immunity under the Child Protection Law because they had violated some of its provisions. The law generally requires a court order to perform a medical evaluation of a child suspected to be the victim of child abuse. The trooper and worker made no effort to obtain a court order and there was no evidence of serious danger to the student's health. Because the two were not acting pursuant to the Child Protection Law at the time they arranged the doctor's examination, the court reversed the portion of the trial court order awarding them summary judgment. On remand, the trial court was to reconsider this issue, as well as the conservator's claims for battery and false imprisonment. *Lavey v. Mills*, 639 N.W.2d 261 (Mich. Ct. App. 2001).

- **Three special education students were sexually abused by a teacher. Allegedly, they informed their homeroom teacher about the abuse, but she did not report it for several weeks.** According to the students, the teacher's abuse did not stop until it was reported to the state Department of Social Services by a doctor. The DSS took immediate action to separate the students from the teacher after receiving the report. The homeroom teacher eventually reported the allegations to a city civil rights officer. She asserted that she was unaware that Massachusetts law and Boston Public Schools policy required immediate reporting of such incidents to the DSS. The civil rights officer also failed to contact DSS, as did a school special education supervisor and school principal who learned of the suspected abuse. The students sued the city and a number of school employees in a federal district court, alleging civil rights violations under Title IX, 42 U.S.C. § 1983 and state law. The city moved for summary judgment, asserting a number of defenses.

The court stated that in order to establish municipal liability under Section 1983 or Title IX, the complaining party must identify a municipal custom or policy that causes a deprivation of federal rights. Even where a municipal policy is constitutionally valid on its face, the municipality may still be held liable under Section 1983 if it is implemented with deliberate indifference. In this case, **the city had a written policy requiring teachers to immediately report sexual abuse charges to the DSS**. Moreover, the state had enacted legislation mandating immediate reporting to the DSS. The court agreed with the students that **there was evidence that could support a finding that the city failed to train employees under this policy and to ensure employees were aware of their reporting requirements** under state law. Four school employees who were bound by law to report the allegations had failed to do so, therefore, the court denied the city's motion for summary judgment on the Section 1983 and Title IX claims. It found that a jury could conclude that the city was a moving force behind any violation occurring after the report to the homeroom teacher. The court rejected the city's argument that it was not on "actual notice" of the abuse, concluding that there was evidence the school principal had knowledge of the allegations before the doctor made his report. The court further determined that all four school employees who were notified of the teacher's abuse had the power to stop it. The city was awarded summary judgment on the students' claims for punitive damages, since they are unavailable in Title IX cases. The city was also entitled to summary judgment on the students' state law claims, according to the court. Only the Title IX and Section 1983 claims against the city would proceed to trial. *Booker v. City of Boston et al.*, Nos. CIV.A.97-CV-12534MEL, CIV.A.97-CV-12675MEL and CIV.A.97-CV-12691MEL, 2000 WL 1868180 (D. Mass. 2000).

◆ A family enrolled their 4-year-old child with disabilities in a school for speech therapy. Although a teacher had received only one training session in the use of facilitated communication, she decided to use FC with the student without the parents' consent. The teacher placed the student on her lap and, despite the student's inability to read or write, she produced messages indicating her father had sexually abused her. A state agency then initiated parental rights termination proceedings. The father was denied contact with the student for three years, and the mother was only allowed supervised visits, even though there was no medical evidence of abuse. The teacher continued using FC with the student, even after being told not to do so. The state agency dismissed the parental termination action, but the father claimed that he had lost his job as a result of the investigation. **The parents asserted that the charges destroyed their marriage and deprived them of three years of contact with their child**, in violation of their constitutional rights, the IDEA and various state and federal laws. The parents sued the teacher, school district and others in federal court. When the court denied the teacher's motion for summary judgment in part, she appealed to the U.S. Court of Appeals for the Fifth Circuit.

The court stated that in cases alleging constitutional rights violations by public officials, the complaint must involve a clearly established right of which a reasonable official would have knowledge. The right to family integrity was clearly protected by the Constitution, and the district court had correctly determined that a teacher's fabrication of sexual abuse by a parent was shocking to the conscience. The use of a highly controversial FC device with a four-year-old who could not read or write was a clear abuse of governmental power. **The right to family integrity was well established at the time of the alleged violation, and the teacher was deemed to know that she could not manufacture false evidence of sexual abuse**. Accordingly, **the teacher was not entitled to immunity** from the claims alleging denial of the right to family integrity. The district court was deemed to have improperly denied the teacher summary judgment on the IDEA claim, since the use of FC did not give rise to a cause of action regarding some aspect of the student's education. The circuit court determined that the district court was correct in denying the teacher summary judgment on the state law claims. The case was remanded for further proceedings. *Morris v. Dearbourne*, 181 F.3d 657 (5th Cir. 1999).

The district court then considered a motion for summary judgment and dismissal by the Texas Department of Protective and Regulatory Services and the employees named in the suit, noting that facilitated communication is highly controversial. Caseworkers overlooked evidence that the child could not type any words confirming abuse unless the teacher held her wrists. The court stated that child protection workers had covered up certain information during the course of the investigation that was favorable to the parents. The investigation was deficient and resulted in the separation of the child from her father for three years, and limited contact with her mother. **The court held that the county employees were not entitled to immunity because the law required them to investigate child abuse allegations, allowing no discretion to omit information from their investigations**. They depended on unreliable information and omitted pertinent information in official reports. The officials violated the family's clearly established constitutional right to family integrity and privacy. No sensible person would defend the belief that holding an illiterate child's wrists would make her capable of generating the disputed reports, and the county employees' actions shocked the conscience. The court denied the TDPRS motions, holding that its employees conducted a sham investigation, withheld evidence, violated state law and TDPRS policies and procedures, and misrepresented facts to a state court. *Morris v. Dearborne*, 69 F.Supp.2d 868 (E.D. Tex. 1999).

◆ A teacher and a speech therapist employed by a New York school district utilized facilitated communication to communicate with a student with disabilities. **Based on the student's responses to them as solicited through facilitated communication, they began to suspect that she was a possible victim of child abuse**. The teacher and speech therapist reported their suspicions to the school principal, who determined that reasonable cause existed to make a report to the New York State Child Abuse Central Registry, and **the student was temporarily removed from the custody of her parents**. The family then filed a federal district court action against state and county education, social services and sheriff's department employees, alleging that the action violated an asserted constitutional right to remain together as a family. The court dismissed the social services and sheriff's department employees from the lawsuit, and considered a motion for summary judgment by the school district employees.

The court considered specific allegations by the family that facilitated communication is an experimental and unreliable method which had yielded false information and that its use had violated their constitutional rights. The court found no evidence that the teacher, speech therapist and principal had reason to believe that facilitated communication would yield false results. They were therefore entitled to summary judgment. **The school district and superintendent were also entitled to judgment since there was no evidence that the district had failed to train personnel in proper child abuse reporting procedures or that there had been previous problems with facilitated communication** which could have put them on notice of the need to further train district personnel. Because the district and superintendent maintained no unconstitutional policy or practice that deprived the family of their rights, the district and officials were entitled to summary judgment. *Zappala v. Albicelli*, 980 F.Supp. 635 (N.D.N.Y.1997).

◆ A Pennsylvania student was diagnosed with severe autism and mental retardation. He relied on nonverbal communication, and his IEP recommended using facilitated communication. The decision to use facilitated communication was approved by the student's parents. One of the student's teachers believed that the student told him through facilitated communication that his father was abusing him. **The teacher reported this to the school social worker and another teacher, but no report was made to the child protection agency until the following year** when the teacher learned that other incidents of sexual abuse had been reported through facilitated communication. The county social service agency advised school personnel that facilitated communication reports had to meet several criteria including a description of the alleged abuse with specific details. The report should also be consistently conveyed through more than one facilitator. When the student came to school one day in an agitated state, the teachers believed that the distress was from sexual abuse perpetrated by the student's father, and a report was made to the social service agency. **The student was taken into protective custody, but released after a medical examination revealed no signs of abuse**. The student remained in protective custody until a hearing over two months later, when he was released to the parents. They then filed a lawsuit against the school district, county social service agency, teachers, social workers and other individuals in the U.S. District Court for the Eastern District of Pennsylvania claiming constitutional violations under 42 U.S.C. § 1983. Their claims included invasion of personal privacy rights, violation of due process and unreasonable search and seizure in violation of the Fourth Amendment.

The school, county and employees filed summary judgment motions. The court stated that the complaining party in a § 1983 suit must establish the violation of a clearly established constitutional right in order to demonstrate liability against a government entity or employee. **The court rejected the parents' assertion that the use of facilitated communication violated their clearly established rights simply because it was under criticism within the scientific community. It was well-established that teachers and childcare workers were entitled to qualified immunity in the performance of their discretionary duties**, and there was no constitutional violation of any well-established rights. Objectively reasonable facts supported the taking of the student into protective custody and the teachers might have risked criminal penalties if they had failed to take action. The court granted summary judgment to the school, county and employees. *Callahan v. Lancaster-Lebanon Intermediate Unit 13*, 880 F.Supp. 319 (E.D.Pa.1994).

C. Third Parties

◆ The parents of a student with a cortical visual impairment commenced a federal district court action against their school district, **alleging the district committed civil rights violations when it placed the student in a fourth grade class with another student who had tormented and abused her during the previous school year**. According to the complaint, the district was aware of the abuse, but instead of rectifying the situation, increased the risk. The complaint stated that the district's actions violated the student's civil rights under the IDEA, the ADA, Section 504 of the Rehabilitation Act and 42 U.S.C. § 1983. The court dismissed the IDEA, ADA and Section 504 claims for failure to exhaust administrative remedies and awarded summary judgment to the district on the merits of the Section 1983 claim. The family appealed the district court's ruling on the Section 1983 claim to the Second Circuit.

The circuit court stated that the complaining party in an action under 42 U.S.C. § 1983 must allege that the conduct giving rise to a civil rights violation is attributable at least in part to "a person acting under color of state law," and that the conduct deprived the party of a right, privilege or immunity secured by the Constitution or laws of the United States. In this case, the student alleged that school employees had increased the likelihood that the classmate would abuse her. The court noted that the U.S. Supreme Court held in a Section 1983 case that the Due Process Clause of the 14th Amendment to the U.S. Constitution "does not require the government to prevent private citizens from harming each other." While states are prohibited from harming individual rights without due process of law, there is no affirmative obligation on the states to protect individuals from acts of private violence. The Second Circuit stated that **Section 1983 claims are not barred if state officials in some way assist in creating a danger or increasing the risk of harm** to the complaining party. In this case, however, **the student's parents had failed to allege that the school district was warned of the classmate's alleged abusive conduct toward the student during grade three**. The mother's sworn statement failed to affirmatively state that the district was notified of any abuse. It indicated only that she had requested that the students be separated, and that the request had been refused. This was insufficient for a reasonable jury to conclude that the classmate had abused the student and the district court had properly awarded summary judgment to the school district. *Robertson v. Arlington Central School Dist.*, 229 F.3d 1136 (2d Cir. 2000).

- **A Florida high school student was shot and killed by non-student assailants while he awaited a ride in his school parking lot**. The student had attended a school-sponsored function and had been denied a request to telephone his father from the school administrative office. The student's estate filed a lawsuit in a federal district court against the school board and school officials claiming that its policies deprived the student of certain constitutional rights. The court granted the board's dismissal motion, and the estate appealed to the U.S. Court of Appeals, Eleventh Circuit. The court held that **a government entity has no duty to protect individuals from the criminal acts of third parties**. The court therefore rejected the estate's assertion that the school had violated a constitutional duty owed to the student. The court also rejected the estate's claim that the board was under a duty to protect the student from a danger which the district had created. There were other places to wait for rides, including inside the building. The court affirmed the dismissal of the case. *Mitchell v. Duval County School Bd.*, 107 F.3d 837 (11th Cir.1997).

- An eight-year old Georgia student with hearing impairments attended a state-operated residential school, spending weekends at home. **The student claimed**

that he was sexually assaulted on a number of occasions by a 13-year-old student who also attended the school. When the student's mother learned about the assaults, she withdrew the student from the school and filed a lawsuit in the U.S. District Court for the Northern District of Georgia against the school's education director and education supervisor, alleging violations of the student's constitutional rights. The court entered summary judgment for the school officials, and the student's mother appealed to the U.S. Court of Appeals for the Eleventh Circuit. The court of appeals discussed the difficult legal standard that applied to persons seeking to hold government officials liable for the intentional acts of third parties. In such cases, **the victim must establish that she or he enjoyed a special relationship with the state entity, and that state officials violated a clearly established constitutional right** of the victim. Although many attempts have been made to find government officials responsible for acts of third party violence, the only "special relationships" that have been recognized by the courts are those existing between the state and incarcerated prisoners, committed mental patients and involuntarily placed foster children. In this case, the court reasoned that the student, while dependent to an extent on school officials during the school week, still depended on his parents for his basic needs. The state also exercised considerable control over the student because of his age and disability. However, the court was not persuaded by the argument that he had been committed to the care of the state. **The school officials were entitled to qualified immunity because it could not be shown that the student had a clearly established right to be protected from third party intentional conduct.** The court of appeals affirmed the district court's award of summary judgment for the school officials. *Spivey v. Elliott*, 29 F.3d 1522 (11th Cir.1994).

The court of appeals reviewed its prior opinion and found that it was only necessary to determine whether there was a clearly established constitutional right implicated in the complaint, not whether a violation itself had been alleged in the complaint. The court stated that it was sufficient that no violation of a clearly-established constitutional right had been alleged against the school officials. Accordingly, the court withdrew all of its prior opinion relating to whether the complaint had alleged the violation of a constitutional right in order to take away any precedential value of that issue. **The court reaffirmed its prior decision that there was no clearly-established constitutional duty to protect the student at the time of the sexual assault.** The school officials were entitled to qualified immunity. *Spivey v. Elliott*, 41 F.3d 1497 (11th Cir.1995).

IV. AWARDS AND DAMAGES

A. Attorneys' Fees

In Smith v. Robinson, *468 U.S. 992, 104 S.Ct. 3457, 82 L.Ed.2d 746 (1984), the U.S. Supreme Court held that attorneys' fees were not recoverable for special education claims made under the IDEA. Congress responded by enacting the Handicapped Children's Protection Act (HCPA) (20 U.S.C. § 1415(i)(3)), a 1986 amendment to the IDEA, which allows recovery of attorneys' fees where a student or guardian prevails in "any action or proceeding." The HCPA overruled* Smith *and provided for retroactive recovery of attorneys' fees to the date of* Smith.

1. Administrative Proceedings

◆ After an evaluation, a school planning and placement team (PPT) found inconsistencies in a regular education student's grades and signs that he had ADHD, but did not find him in need of special education services or accommodations. The next year, the student allegedly vandalized a bus and the school notified his parents of an expulsion hearing. The parents contested the hearing through an attorney and sought a due process hearing and an independent evaluation. The school board cancelled the hearing and scheduled PPT meetings. A hearing officer postponed a hearing until after an evaluation. The PPT determined that the student had a disability and that his actions on the school bus manifested his disability. The school terminated expulsion proceedings and the PPT drafted an IEP that provided all the relief the parents sought. The parties agreed to adopt the PPT decision as an official hearing decision. Before the hearing, the school board backed down from the agreement due to fears that it would create liability for attorney's fees. The hearing officer declined to adopt the PPT decision as an official order, but allowed it to be read into the hearing record "as an agreement between the parties only." The hearing officer issued a final decision dismissing the hearing as moot. **The parents sought attorneys' fees from the board, asserting that they were prevailing parties** under the IDEA and § 504 of the Rehabilitation Act. A federal district court awarded them $14,140 in attorney's fees and costs, not including attorney time spent preparing for and attending PPT meetings.

The board appealed to the Second Circuit, and the parents cross-appealed for fees related to the PPT meetings. The court stated that the IDEA authorizes attorney's fees for parents who are prevailing parties in a lawsuit or administrative proceeding. The U.S. Supreme Court clarified the term prevailing party in *Buckhannon Board and Care Home, Inc. v. West Virginia Dept. of Health and Human Resources*, 121 S.Ct. 1835 (2001). The *Buckhannon* Court held that **prevailing party status results only from a judgment on the merits of a case or settlement agreement that is expressly enforced by a court through a consent decree. Without an enforceable court order, there is no basis for an attorney's fee award.** The Supreme Court rejected the less exacting "catalyst test" as a basis for attorneys' fees. The Second Circuit explained that while the *Buckhannon* decision involved the ADA and Fair Housing Amendments Act, it was applicable in IDEA cases. The IDEA's legislative history indicated that "prevailing party" was to be construed in the same way it was in other federal "fee-shifting" laws. Congress deliberately chose not to allow attorney's fees for PPT meetings. PPT meetings are mechanisms for compromise and cooperation, not adversarial confrontation. The parents were not entitled to an award of fees under the IDEA or § 504, and the Second Circuit affirmed the judgment. *J.C., By His Parents and Next Friend, Mr. and Mrs. C. v. Regional School Dist. 10, Bd. of Educ.*, Nos. 00-9408(LEAD), 00-9484(XAP), 2002 WL 89061 (2d Cir. 2002).

◆ As a New Jersey student with mental retardation and other congenital conditions prepared to enter high school, his parents rejected the proposed classroom, seeking to enroll him instead in a self-contained special education class at a different school. The district believed that the class it selected was appropriate and denied the parents' intra-district transfer request. The parents responded by initiating a due process hearing. **When the district agreed to transfer the student, the parents withdrew their administrative complaint**. The district refused to pay the parents' request for attorneys' fees incurred in litigating the administrative complaint, and they commenced a federal district court action for their fees and costs.

The court considered the district's motion for summary judgment and noted that the IDEA provides for attorneys' fee awards for parents who are prevailing parties in disputes over identification, evaluation and placement. In this case, the only relief sought by the parents was the placement of their son in a particular classroom in a district school. The district contended that the transfer was not a change in educational placement under the IDEA, even though the parents obtained the transfer only after commencing due process proceedings. It argued that the student's IEP remained the same in either school, as did the teaching methods. The court found that the student's program of instruction remained virtually identical in either school. **Transfer to another school was not a change in placement under the IDEA that gave rise to an award of attorneys' fees**. Since there was no change in placement, the court held that the student was not entitled to an award of attorneys' fees, and awarded summary judgment to the district. *J.S. by D.S. and H.S. v. Lenape Regional High School Dist. Bd. of Educ.*, 102 F.Supp.2d 540 (D.N.J. 2000).

◆ The parent of a special education student and a school board disagreed about whether the parents were entitled to reimbursement for the costs of a private school placement. An administrative hearing officer denied the parents' claim for reimbursement, and the decision was upheld by a Maryland circuit court. Meanwhile, the school's admission, review and dismissal committee determined that the student should be reevaluated before his IEP for the upcoming school year was developed. The parent declined to provide independent evaluation reports to the board, resulting in the district's request for a due process hearing seeking to compel the parent to allow the board to conduct an evaluation of the student. An administrative law judge agreed with the parent that a board evaluation was not required, and the board appealed to federal court. The court granted the parent's motion to dismiss the case. The board moved to alter or amend the decision. Because the student had stopped attending the private school and the parent stated she was not seeking tuition reimbursement for the disputed school year, the court issued the order requested by the board. After the district court denied the parent's motion for attorneys' fees, she appealed to the U.S. Court of Appeals for the Fourth Circuit. The circuit court recited the general rule that in order to recover attorneys' fees in an IDEA action, a party must be a prevailing party. **The parent had voluntarily disavowed her claim for tuition reimbursement, therefore, the district court properly denied her request for attorneys' fees**. *Board of Educ. of Harford County v. Thomas,* 205 F.3d 1332 (4th Cir. 2000).

◆ After issuing an opinion in a case involving a placement dispute, a federal district court considered the parents' claim for more than $30,000 in attorney's fees. The district resisted the claim on the grounds that it was not filed on a timely basis. Observing that the IDEA lacks a statute of limitations, the court applied a Maryland law requiring administrative appeals within 180 days. It rejected the parents' claim that the three-year general statute of limitations from Maryland law should apply. According to the court, the passage of time makes it difficult to analyze the merits of the claim underlying a request for attorneys' fees. **While a limitations period that was too short would frustrate IDEA purposes, the 180-day limitations period was reasonable.** Since all of the events upon which the parents had based their claim had occurred more than 180 days prior to the filing of the petition for fees, the court held that it was barred. The court nonetheless proceeded to the merits of the underlying dispute, observing the possibility of an appeal. It held that the parents were not entitled to recover attorney's fees for any claims for which they were not prevailing parties in administrative proceedings. This included the two years following the settlement agreement pertaining to the first year of private school tuition. Regarding the first year of contested tuition liability, the court held that, even if the claim was not barred by the statue of limitations, the parents had not prevailed on their claim for compensatory speech services. The family did not establish an appropriate number of hours expended by their attorneys. There was no merit to the family's claims for transportation expenses and reimbursement for expert witness fees. The IDEA does not provide for reimbursement of such costs. *Mayo v. Booker,* 56 F.Supp.2d 597 (D. Md. 1999).

◆ A student was diagnosed as having dyslexia and dysgraphia and was eligible for special education services. However, the school district failed to provide any transition planning and the family filed an administrative complaint. The state found the district had failed to live up to its obligations under the IDEA and directed it to develop a transition plan. The district failed to do so and did not devise a plan even after a subsequent administrative compliant was filed. It then developed an IEP for the student for the following school year without the participation of his parents. The parents requested another due process hearing, which prompted the district to propose an individualized transition plan, although it was developed in the parents' absence. **The district then offered an IEP that was essentially the same as one they had rejected previously, but agreed on the eve of the hearing that another one should be used**. The parents filed a federal district court action seeking attorneys' fees and costs.

The school district argued that the parents were not prevailing parties in an IDEA action. The court held that a party prevails in an IDEA action if it receives relief that materially alters the legal relationship of the parties. Administrative proceedings, as well as litigation, may be deemed to bring such relief even in the absence of an order or decree, if the pressure of the lawsuit was a material contributing factor in obtaining relief. In this case, the parents reasonably believed that the school district was not complying with its statutory obligation to provide transition planning for the student. **The state twice found the district in noncompliance with the IDEA, and the parents obtained a binding agreement during administrative proceedings that materially altered the**

parties' legal relationship to their benefit. Their success was significant and was causally related to the initiation of administrative proceedings. The court approved an award in excess of $13,000 for the parents. *T.F. and F.F. on Behalf of T.F. v. North Penn School Dist.*, 1999 U.S. Dist. LEXIS 12618 (E.D.Pa.1999).

◆ A Minnesota student with epileptic seizure disorder attended public school under an emotional/behavioral disordered classification. The student's mother sought his classification as "other health impaired" in order to obtain speech and language therapy for him. The district proposed a revised IEP that continued to be based upon the emotional/behavioral disordered classification, and the mother made numerous requests that the student spend more of his school day in regular education. She removed him from public school, placed him in a private school, and requested a due process hearing, objecting to the revised IEP calling for continued public school education. A state hearing officer determined that the school district had properly classified the student as emotional/behavioral disordered and appropriately placed him under an IEP designed to provide him with educational benefits. However, the hearing officer ordered the school district to provide the student with ten meetings in a facilitated friendship group. A state review officer upheld the district's classification decision and determined that the district had provided the student with a FAPE. However, it ordered the district to amend the IEP to reflect the mother's choice of schools, at her expense if a private school was chosen, and to add "other health impaired" as a secondary handicapping condition.

The mother initiated a federal district court action against the school district, seeking $158,000 in attorneys' fees as a prevailing party under the IDEA. The court held that the mother had not prevailed on the actual merits of her claim or received the relief that she sought, but was nonetheless a prevailing party who was entitled to attorney's fees because the administrative proceedings had resulted in a material alteration of the legal relationship of the parties. It awarded the mother over $63,000, and the school district appealed to the U.S. Court of Appeals for the Eighth Circuit. The court held that **the district court had improperly awarded the mother attorneys' fees since she had not obtained actual relief on the merits of her claim. A material alteration in the legal relationship of the parties is relevant in a determination of the amount of attorney's fees awarded, but fees are unavailable to a party who does not prevail.** The court reversed and remanded the district court judgment, observing that the award would have been excessive even if the mother had been the prevailing party. *Warner v. Indep. School Dist. No. 625*, 134 F.3d 1333 (8th Cir.1998).

◆ An Indiana preschool student had developmental delays attributable to his premature birth. His parents contacted their local education agency (LEA), which developed an IEP calling for two days of special education preschool with evaluation for occupational, physical and speech therapy. **Although the parents accepted the IEP, they also placed the student in a private regular education preschool for two days per week at their own expense.** The parents later asked the LEA to provide transportation and private school tuition. The LEA responded that the local Head Start program handled other students in special preschool programs and that regular education was unnecessary for the student. The parents requested an administrative hearing at which the hearing officer determined that a dual placement in part-time special education preschool and regular education preschool was appropriate. He also held that the Head Start preschool was appropriate and that the LEA was required to fund this component. The parents claimed that they were prevailing parties in the administrative action, and requested attorneys' fees. When the LEA declined the request, the parents filed a lawsuit against it in an Indiana superior court, which granted summary judgment to the parents.

The LEA appealed to the Court of Appeals of Indiana, which first rejected its statute of limitations defense, ruling that it had waived the defense by failing to appropriately raise it before the trial court. It also rejected the LEA's claim that the parents were not prevailing parties in the administrative action. Although the LEA claimed that the Head Start program was its recommended placement during the administrative process, the court noted that the LEA had never offered to pay for it. **The parents prevailed because the hearing officer determined that regular education was appropriate and that the LEA was obligated to fund it**. The court affirmed the order for summary judgment in favor of the parents. *Madison Area Educational Special Services Unit v. Daniels*, 678 N.E.2d 427 (Ind.Ct.App.1997).

◆ The District of Columbia Public Schools (DCPS) notified the parents of certain students enrolled at a private school in the District of its intention to change each student's placement. The parents requested an administrative hearing to oppose the changes, and a hearing officer ordered DCPS to restore funding for each of the students at the private school. The superintendent of DCPS schools appealed the administrative decision to a federal district court in an action that was dismissed almost five years later as moot. The effect of the dismissal was to deny the relief sought by DCPS and to preserve the administrative decision. The parents then sought an award of attorneys' fees and costs in excess of $90,000. DCPS claimed that the parents could not be considered prevailing parties in an IDEA action because the dismissal was based on mootness and because the parents were the defending parties in the federal court action. The court rejected both arguments, observing that **the parents were entitled to prevailing party status because they had preserved a favorable status quo under which they obtained funding for the private school placements. It was irrelevant that their position in federal court was defensive**, and the court approved an award of $82,663. *Smith v. Roher*, 954 F.Supp. 359 (D.D.C.1997).

◆ The U.S. District Court for the Northern District of Illinois denied a request for attorney's fees by a regular education student who had received special education services from another school district prior to transferring to his present district. The student's school expelled him for one year for drug possession at a time when he was only two classes short of his graduation requirement. The family retained an attorney who demanded transition services and an evaluation within one week, and requested an administrative hearing when the district failed to comply. The hearing officer rejected the family's assertion that the school district had improperly terminated special education services, failed to provide transition services or a vocational plan and was obligated to develop an IEP. The hearing officer upheld the expulsion but ordered the school district to set up a meeting with a state rehabilitation agency and to allow the student to graduate by a specific date. The family petitioned the court for attorney's fees claiming prevailing party status. The court rejected the request, noting that a party must obtain an enforceable judgment to prevail in an IDEA action. **The student could not be deemed a prevailing party because he was entitled to graduate regardless of the outcome of the hearing, and the hearing officer had found for the school district on all significant claims.** Further, the district had voluntarily evaluated the student for learning disability eligibility. Prevailing party status may not be awarded on the basis of voluntary action. Because the benefits received by the family were incidental and insignificant to the relief sought, the court denied the claim for fees. *Petrovich v. Consol. High School Dist. No. 230, Palos Hills, Illinois,* 959 F.Supp. 884 (N.D.Ill.1997).

◆ A student with autism received special education services in an intensive residential program at a private school. His program was pursuant to an IEP developed by a New Jersey public school district. His parents moved to Massachusetts and enrolled him in public schools there. His new school's IEP team was unable to develop an appropriate IEP because evaluations from the private school were incomplete. The district placed the student in a public school program for students with special needs. The student's behavior deteriorated at school and home and after several violent outbursts, he was hospitalized, then placed in a highly structured behavioral program. The parents requested payment for short-term placement in a residential school and after the district refused to pay for the placement, they requested a special education hearing. The district agreed to pay for eight weeks in the residential program and consented to an independent evaluation. The district then prepared an IEP incorporating the parties' agreement. A second hearing was held concerning other disagreements and the district agreed to an extension of the private school placement. The parents then sought an award of attorneys' fees, asserting that they were prevailing parties under the IDEA. **The court held that the student and his parents had achieved the relief they sought by filing the special education hearing request.** They had obtained substantial relief and were prevailing parties under the IDEA. The court therefore approved an award of attorneys' fees in excess of $60,000. *Arunim D. by Ashim D. v. Foxborough Pub. Schools*, 970 F.Supp. 51 (D.Mass.1997).

2. Court Proceedings

◆ The parents of a student with cerebral palsy unilaterally enrolled him in a private religious school and asked their school district to provide an on-site assistant. The district denied the request. The parents then initiated a state administrative proceeding, which resulted in a decision for the district. The parents commenced a federal district court action against the district and state education department. **The court held that the denial of services violated Iowa special education law and awarded attorneys' fees to the parents as prevailing parties.** It awarded fees against the department for its advocacy in support of the administrative decision.

The district and department appealed to the Eighth Circuit, which explained that attorneys' fees are available to parents who prevail in an IDEA action and succeed in modifying the non-prevailing party's behavior. The district court had correctly found that the parents prevailed. The IDEA places primary responsibility on state education agencies to ensure local compliance with the act. The district court had properly found that the parents were prevailing parties against the department. However, the district court should not have imposed liability against the department for the parents' attorneys' fees incurred during the administrative proceedings, because the department did not participate in those proceedings. The IDEA does not make state educational agencies liable for the transgressions of all local agencies. **It was appropriate to apportion part of the fees against the department for its opposition to the federal district court decision in the parents' favor**, and the court reversed and remanded this part of the case. *John and Leigh T., as Individuals and as Guardians and Next Friends of Robert T. v. Iowa Department of Education*, 258 F.3d 860 (8th Cir. 2001).

- The parents of a child with Down's syndrome and their local intermediate unit disputed what auxiliary services the student would receive while attending a parochial school. When the dispute was initially heard in federal court, the court held that the intermediate unit was required to provide auxiliary services to the student at the parochial school, and agreed to join the state department of education as a part to the dispute. Due process proceedings were initiated when the parents objected to a new IEP. A hearing officer ruled for the parents, but a review panel reversed. Both parties appealed to the district court, which issued an order finding the intermediate unit in contempt for failing to provide services at the parochial school during the previous school year, and vacating its prior order due to changed circumstances- specifically the child's enrollment in public school. While the district's appeal of the contempt order was pending before the Third Circuit, **the family moved the court to voluntarily dismiss the case and sought an award of attorneys' fees in excess of $136,000.**

The court stated that federal rules permit a party to voluntarily dismiss a case if there is no prejudice to the adverse party. The intermediate unit claimed that it would be unable to proceed with its claim for funding from the education department if the case was dismissed, and sought to recover $60,000 in costs paid on behalf of the student, plus over $120,000 in its attorneys' fees. The court observed that the intermediate unit had only a contingent claim for contribution against the education department that could be adjudicated in a direct action against the department. The intermediate unit would suffer harm if it were exposed to another lawsuit by the parents, and the court held that the case should be dismissed without allowing the parents any opportunity to relitigate the case. The court allowed voluntary dismissal of the action, and held that the parents' motion to reverse the appeals panel decision was moot. In moving for dismissal, the parents withdrew any claim they had for reimbursement of $26,000 for the expenses of an aide, in view of their other successes. **The parents' claim for over $136,000 in attorneys' fees was also subject to dismissal, since they had not prevailed on the merits of their case by securing a judicially sanctioned change in the legal relationship of the parties**. In the event that they successfully defended the contempt issue currently pending before the Third

Circuit, they would be allowed to submit a motion for fees on that issue alone. The intermediate unit was forbidden from recovering any of its attorneys' fees, as the IDEA allows recovery for prevailing parents, not school districts. The intermediate unit had created much of the delay and expense in the action. The court rejected the intermediate unit's motion to recover $60,000 in expenses paid to implement the court's preliminary order, as there was no legal or equitable justification for reimbursement of costs already paid. *John T. v. Delaware County Intermediate Unit*, No. CIV. A. 98-5781, 2001 WL 1391500 (E.D. Pa 2001).

◆ A student had academic difficulties in eighth grade and his parents requested a special education evaluation. After he was referred to a planning and placement team for evaluation, the school suspended him pending an expulsion hearing. The district refused to complete the special education evaluation prior to the expulsion hearing and expelled the student, despite his assertion that he was entitled to return to school under the IDEA's stay put provision. The parents requested a due process hearing and a hearing officer determined that his stay put placement was suspension, rather than his regular education placement. The parents complained that his hearing was not concluded within 45 days as required by state law and IDEA regulations. **They sought relief against the state education department and board for maintaining a policy or custom of failing to hold special education hearings within 45 days and for determining that suspension was their son's correct stay put placement**. The hearing officer reversed his previous decision and ruled that the district had failed to perform a timely evaluation of the student and that he was entitled to return to school.

The parties entered into settlement negotiations, and a federal district court ultimately held that the state education department and board were responsible for procedural compliance with the IDEA, including the student's right to remain in a previous placement, not suspension, pending IDEA proceedings. While the case was proceeding, the state education department conducted a thorough review of special education in Connecticut and sought comments from special education attorneys and hearing officers throughout the state. The student's attorney made written responses to regulations proposed by the department concerning timely procedures and the stay put placement of disciplined students. The student then asserted that he was entitled to an award of attorneys' fees for bringing his due process complaint, since the state adopted regulations that raised the same issues under consideration in his case. The court considered his petition for an award of fees, noting that in order to obtain such relief, a party must prove that it has prevailed on a significant claim in litigation that effects a material alteration in the parties' legal relationship or is a catalyst for obtaining relief. The court found evidence that the state had finalized the new regulations in response to the student's lawsuit. Although the department was considering special education reform some time before the action was commenced, **the court found a causal connection between the filing of the action and the adoption of the new regulations. Because the lawsuit was a catalyst for change to the state regulations, the student was entitled to prevailing party status**. However, he had not obtained a sufficient degree of success to justify an award of the entire amount he claimed, and the court reduced it by half. *E.S. v. Ashford Board of Education et al.*, 134 F.Supp.2d 462 (D. Conn. 2001).

◆ The parents of a 29-year-old Michigan resident with severe mental disabilities obtained an order from a federal court that the student had been denied services to which he was entitled for five years. The parents then filed a motion seeking attorneys' fees. The local education agency filed a responsive motion, which the parents claimed was untimely. In examining the parents' claim, the court noted that the IDEA permits an award of reasonable attorneys' fees to prevailing parties in IDEA actions or proceedings. A prevailing party, according to the U.S. Supreme Court, is one who succeeds on any significant issue in litigation that achieves some of the benefit sought in bringing suit. The parents were entitled to attorneys' fees, as they were the prevailing party on the IDEA and Rehabilitation Act claims. The only issue before the court was whether the amount claimed was reasonable. **The court considered the applicable factors to consider when evaluating the reasonableness of a claim for attorneys' fees and determined that the amount requested was reasonable**. Special education law is highly specialized and requires an attorney familiar with the legal issues involving individuals with disabilities, along with the educational and psychological issues encountered by the disabled. The issues in the case were complex, and the prospects for success were deemed uncertain. The amount claimed by the parents was deemed reasonable and fair under the circumstances. The parents were awarded over $53,000 in fees and costs. *Wayne County Regional Educ. Service Agency v. Pappas,* No. 99-40011 (E.D. Mich. 2000).

◆ A private school placed a student on indefinite suspension for repeated disciplinary violations. His family sued the school in a federal district court, alleging violations of the ADA, § 504 of the Rehabilitation Act, and Puerto Rico law. The court issued a preliminary injunction in favor of the student, requiring that he remain in school, then issued an order requiring the school to allow him to reenroll there the following year. The school appealed to the First Circuit, which vacated the injunction and remanded the case to the district court, holding that the lower court had failed to enforce an arbitration agreement between the parties. On remand, the district court dismissed the case. **Claiming that it was entitled to prevailing party status under federal law, the school sought attorneys' fees from the family**. The district court denied the school's motion, holding that it could only be entitled to an award of attorneys' fees against the family if the lawsuit was totally frivolous and unfounded. The court declined to make such a finding.

The school appealed to the First Circuit, arguing that the text of both statutes mandated an award of fees to the school as a prevailing party. The court rejected the school's argument, noting that an award of fees under the ADA is discretionary with the court. **The First Circuit held that a school or other entity defending a federal discrimination lawsuit stands in a different posture than the complaining party in such a lawsuit**. This was because a student or other complaining party prevailing in a disability discrimination lawsuit is awarded fees because the effect of the lawsuit is to vindicate an important congressional policy against a violator of federal law. Those considerations did not exist with respect to a prevailing defendant, and a decision to award fees to a defendant should be rare. In this case, the lawsuit was not frivolous and raised questions of first impression before the court. Accordingly, no award of fees to the school against the family was warranted, and the court affirmed the district court judgment. *Bercovitch v. Baldwin School, Inc.*, 191 F.3d 8 (1st Cir.1999).

◆ A Florida school board sought to temporarily block the entry of a student into district schools, pending an agreement between the parties. A state trial court held that the student did not present a danger to himself or others, and denied the school's motion. However, **it refused to award attorneys' fees to the family, finding that only federal courts have this power.** The family appealed to the District Court of Appeal of Florida, Fifth Circuit, which found no language in the IDEA indicating a Congressional intent to limit the powers of state courts. On the contrary, the statute granted concurrent jurisdiction to state and federal courts. Language relied upon by the school board referred only to the minimal jurisdictional requirements of federal courts and did not deprive the state courts of jurisdiction over attorneys' fee disputes. The court agreed with a New Jersey appellate court decision, *J.H.R. v. East Brunswick Bd. of Educ.*, 705 A.2d 766 (N.J.Super.App.Div.1998), in which the court found that **state and federal courts have concurrent jurisdiction to award attorneys' fees to parties prevailing in IDEA actions**. It reversed and remanded the trial court's decision for an assessment of fees. *W.R., by Doe v. School Bd. of Osceola County*, 726 So.2d 801 (Fla.Dist.Ct.App.5th Dist.1999).

◆ A Minnesota student with severe dyslexia attended public schools under a series of IEPs that called for regular education classes in most of her subjects. A neuropsychological test concluded that the student had severe learning problems and a specialist recommended a private school placement, but the school district refused to pay for private school services. The parents later disagreed with a proposed IEP and placed the student in the private school. The family requested a due process hearing, at which **a hearing officer found that the IEP was appropriate and denied reimbursement for the private school. However, the district was ordered to reimburse the parents for certain extended year services and evaluation costs.** A hearing review officer reversed the decision, and the district appealed to the U.S. District Court for the District of Minnesota.

The court rejected the hearing review officer's findings that the IEP had been inappropriate and that the family had been denied their due process rights under the IDEA. The court reinstated the original decision for the school district. The district court later considered the family's application for attorney's fees since the hearing officer had allowed them to recover the cost of extended year services, the cost of a private evaluation and counseling. Generally, a prevailing party in an IDEA action is entitled to recover reasonable attorneys' fees and costs, even where the party prevails on only part of the relief requested. **The court rejected the family's application for over $40,000 in attorneys' fees and adjusted the claim to reflect the minimal success obtained**. The court approved an award of 20 percent of the claimed fees and expert witness costs. *Indep. School Dist. No. 283, St. Louis Park, Minnesota v. S.D., by and through J.D. and N.D.*, 948 F.Supp. 892 (D.Minn.1996).

3. Settlement

◆ The parents of an Illinois student with a mild learning disability sought a due process hearing when the student was midway through the fifth grade, asserting that he should receive an extended-year placement in a private facility. Prior to the hearing, the school district's attorney sent the parents' attorney a settlement offer addressing the issues raised in the due process request. The letter included continued provision of district summer programming with remedial programs in three subjects at no cost. The parents rejected the offer and the case proceeded to a hearing. The hearing officer denied their request for extended-year services at the facility they selected, and found that the district's summer program was calculated to provide the student with educational benefits and offered the student a less restrictive environment than the private program. The hearing officer found that the district could include a few modifications in the student's IEP and denied the parents' request for social work services during the summer.

The student attended only five days of the summer program. His parents then sought reimbursement for legal fees incurred in the administrative proceeding, asserting that they were prevailing parties under the IDEA. A federal district court held that in order to obtain attorneys' fees in an IDEA proceeding, parents must prevail by succeeding on any significant issue in litigation that achieves some of the benefit sought by bringing the action. The relief obtained must significantly alter the legal relationship of the parties. **The parents did not meet the prevailing-party standard because they did not obtain the primary relief they sought** — to place the student at the private facility with the provision of social work services during summer months. The hearing officer awarded them the exact relief the district offered prior to the hearing, which was the continuation of district summer programming. The commencement of an IDEA action did not alter the relationship of the parties. Because the parents did not receive any benefit on the issues of extended year or social work services, they were not prevailing parties and were not entitled to an award of attorneys' fees. The court noted that a further reason to deny relief to the parents existed in **IDEA language** that **bars awards of attorneys' fees when a written settlement is tendered by a district more than 10 days prior to an administrative hearing and the eventual relief is no more favorable than the settlement offer**. The district's attorney had sent a written offer within the specified time period and the relief awarded was no more favorable than that of the offer of settlement. *Joshua H. v. Lansing Public Schools*, 161 F.Supp.2d 888 (N.D. Ill. 2001).

◆ A Pennsylvania school district identified a student as being in need of special education services, and engaged in a series of IEP meetings. When the parties could not agree on an IEP, the district requested a due process hearing. The parents' attorney requested a settlement conference, expressing the desire to avoid a hearing, but also requested a due process hearing. The parties and their attorneys attended a settlement conference at which the district made a number of concessions that led to an acceptable IEP. **The district withdrew its due process request, and the parents sought their attorneys' fees related to the settlement conference.** The school district refused the request, and the parents commenced a federal district court action to recover their attorneys' fees. The court found that the conference was not truly a "settlement conference," but was an IEP team meeting. The district's request for a due process hearing had initiated an "administrative proceeding" under the IDEA for which attorneys' fees were available. Because the parents obtained what they sought in the proceeding, they were entitled to their attorneys' fees.

The district appealed to the Third Circuit, which found that the 1997 IDEA amendments authorize attorneys' fees for work performed at an IEP team meeting convened as the result of an administrative proceeding. Whether fees should be awarded in such cases was a question of causation. The court held that an administrative proceeding can be causally connected to the prevailing party's relief if the pressure of the proceeding is a materially contributing factor in its success. It rejected the district's argument that fees were unavailable unless a due process hearing was actually held. In this case, there were a series of unsuccessful IEP meetings, writings and telephone calls that became counterproductive and eventually came to impasse. The final meeting was unlike all others in significant ways. The parties' attorneys attended it, and each of them sought a hearing, indicating that the IEP process had broken down. The district court did not commit error by finding that the meeting led to an acceptable IEP and would not have occurred without the intervention of attorneys. The court affirmed the decision that the parents were entitled to attorneys' fees. *Daniel S. v. Scranton School District,* 230 F.3d 90 (3d Cir. 2000).

◆ A school district and the parents of a special education student agreed to revise the student's program at various meetings, and eventually prepared an IEP calling for learning support services and weekly counseling. The student experienced behavioral difficulties during the school year and the parties initially agreed to increase his learning support services to three times per week. However, the parents demanded a hearing to determine an appropriate educational placement. The hearing was postponed as the parties discussed possible solutions, including a behavior modification plan. **The parents accepted behavior plans prepared by the district, and the parties agreed on a placement. They also agreed to explore alternative placements** for the student outside the school district, and ultimately agreed to place the student in a non-approved private school. The agreement was reached four days before a scheduled due process hearing.

The parents then sought an award of attorneys' fees from the school district, asserting that they had obtained the placement they sought as the result of representation by their counsel, rather than the normal special education evaluative process. The court found that a prevailing party in an IDEA action is entitled to attorneys' fees if the relief requested is actually achieved and there is a causal connection between the litigation and the relief obtained. In this case, the parents admitted that they did not have to engage in the IDEA due process appeal process in order to obtain the private school placement for their child. There was a genuine issue of material fact concerning the causal connection between the litigation and the relief obtained. **Because it was possible that the parents would have achieved the alternative educational placement as a normal part of the reevaluation and IEP process, the court denied their motion for summary judgment.** *Christopher P. v. Upper Merion Area School Dist.*, 2000 U.S. Dist. LEXIS 323 (E.D. Pa. 2000).

◆ A New Jersey student classified as neurologically impaired attended self-contained public school special education classes through grade four. After attending a private school for two years, he returned to public school self-contained programs. One of the student's treating psychologists and his physician recommended a residential placement, but the school district instead prepared an IEP calling for an in-district placement with resource center support in English, math, history and science. The parents retained an attorney, requested a due process hearing and continued seeking a residential placement. However, they refused to attend intake meetings scheduled by the district at two institutions and failed to provide the school district's attorney with requested copies of materials relating to schools they had screened. **On the scheduled day of the due process hearing, the parties reached a partial settlement**. An expert retained by the school district diagnosed the student as having Asperger's Disorder and stated that he presented a danger to himself and others due to his aggressive and destructive behavior. The parties then agreed to place him in a residential program.

The parents filed a federal district court action for their attorney's fees as prevailing parties in the administrative proceeding. The court considered cross motions for summary judgment by the parties, and rejected the school district's assertion that the residential placement was the result of a convergence of expert opinions. **The parents had obtained the result they sought in the administrative action, and the proceeding had been the catalyst for change**. Prior to the request for a hearing, the school district had repeatedly denied requests for a residential placement, and the change in position was attributable to the threat of litigation. Although the parents were prevailing parties under the IDEA and thus entitled to an award of fees, they had failed to adequately support their claim, leaving the court to speculate about the appropriate amount of an award. There was evidence that the award should be reduced because the parents had failed to cooperate with the district on certain occasions. The request for attorney's fees was denied without prejudice to allow the filing of a properly supported fee application. *S.D. v. Manville Bd. of Educ.*, 989 F.Supp. 649 (D.N.J.1998).

◆ A 14-year-old Alabama student was diagnosed with attention deficit hyperactivity disorder and emotional problems including depression. After physically attacking his adoptive mother, the student was placed in an adolescent adjustment center under the custody of the Alabama State Department of Human Resources and subsequently placed in a sequence of temporary foster homes. The adoptive mother was unable to secure special education services for the student from her district of residence. **After the mother obtained a private evaluation and threatened the district with a due process appeal, the district agreed to provide the student with IDEA services**. However, the district's change of position occurred while the student was temporarily in the custody of another party. The matter was settled and the student's mother petitioned a federal district court for an award of attorney's fees.

The court first stated that the IDEA permits an award of attorney's fees to a prevailing party in an action or proceeding under the act. The correct manner for determining prevailing party status in the Eleventh Circuit remains the catalyst test, under which a party may be entitled to fees if the lawsuit prompts some remedial action by the school district. In this case, the district had changed its position within a few months of the threatened litigation after two years of inaction. This was compelling evidence that the lawsuit was the catalyst for the requested relief. **The court rejected the district's claim that the adoptive mother had no standing and was required to exhaust her administrative remedies because she had not had custody of the student at the time of the parties' settlement.** Other courts have recognized that non-custodial parents may have a legal interest in IDEA actions. The mother was not required to renew the administrative appeal process because of her temporary lack of custody. *W.T. by Tatum v. Andalusia City Schools*, 977 F.Supp. 1437 (M.D.Ala.1997).

4. Other Proceedings

- Special education advocates who challenged New Jersey's amended special education regulations were entitled to a partial award of their attorneys' fees, a state appeals court ruled. Because the advocates succeeded in convincing the court that eight of the 60 regulations violated the IDEA, they were entitled to prevailing party status under the IDEA. In response to the advocates' challenge to the state's special education regulations, a federal court concluded that most of the regulations conformed with federal mandates and were not arbitrary, capricious or unreasonable. However, the court identified eight major problem areas requiring new or amended regulations in order to conform with federal IDEA requirements. In examining the advocates' motion for an award of $340,000 in attorneys' fees related to their regulatory challenge, the court noted there was no other case law on the issue of whether the IDEA applied to regulatory challenges as well as actions by parents seeking specific relief under the act. It determined that a successful regulatory challenge could form the basis for an award of attorneys' fees, since the IDEA was designed to protect children with disabilities. State education officials were correct in asserting that there could be no award for the 15 amendments that had been adopted without any court judgment or consent order. The state officials acknowledged that **the advocates had prevailed in eight specific regulatory areas, and the court awarded fees to the advocates as prevailing parties with respect to these eight areas**. The court found that the advocates succeeded in at least one significant issue in litigation that achieved some of the benefit they sought in bringing suit. The court awarded the advocates $45,000 for their attorneys' fees. The advocates were also entitled to an award covering their expenses. *Baer v. Klagholz*, 786 A.2d 907 (N.J. Super. Ct. App. Div. 2001).

- The parents of two students with learning disabilities requested a due process hearing to obtain specialized instruction for their son. On the morning of the hearing, the district made a settlement offer and the parties negotiated an agreement on educational programs for the son and his older sister, who had a specific learning disability. The settlement agreement was transcribed and entered into the hearing record as two separate agreed orders. In subsequent IEP meetings, the parties decided that both children would be placed at a private school for students with learning disabilities. The **parents sought reimbursement from the district for their attorneys' fees, costs and expert fees associated with obtaining an appropriate placement for their son**. The district declined to respond, and the parents filed a federal district court action seeking recovery of these costs.

The court considered the district's motion for summary judgment and stated the general rule that attorneys' fees are available as costs to the parents of children with disabilities who are prevailing parties in actions under the IDEA. Under a recent U.S. Supreme Court decision, prevailing party status is only possible upon achieving an alteration in the legal relationship of the parties through a judgment or a consent decree. The court found that the agreed orders entered by the hearing officer changed the legal relationship of the parties and qualified the parents as prevailing parties. However, **the 1997 IDEA amendments limited the recovery of attorneys' fees by precluding awards related to IEP team meetings, unless the meetings were convened as the result of an administrative proceeding or judicial action**. In this case, the IEP team meetings were by official or formal consent and were unrelated to any administrative proceeding or judicial action. The parents were barred from recovering any attorneys' fees for the meetings. Although the IDEA does not specifically refer to reimbursement for the cost of experts, the court found evidence that Congress intended to include them as part of the costs payable under the act. The court concluded that many cases have held that properly documented and reasonable expert fees are payable, and ruled that the parents were entitled to recover their expert fees under the IDEA. *Brandon K. v. New Lenox School District*, No. 01 C 4625, 2001 WL 1491499 (N.D. Ill. 2001).

◆ **A mediation agreement between an Illinois family and a school district did not confer prevailing party status on the family under the IDEA**. The hearing officer made no findings or rulings, so the mediation agreement was a private settlement, not an enforceable consent decree. The agreement was read into the record before a hearing officer. The hearing officer did not make any findings of fact or deliver a ruling. The mother filed a federal district court action against the district, seeking attorneys' fees and costs. The court observed that the IDEA authorized attorneys' fee awards for parents who are prevailing parties in an IDEA action and that the U.S. Supreme Court has held that prevailing party status is achieved only through a favorable judgment on the merits of a case or through a settlement agreement that is enforced by a consent decree. A prevailing party is one who has been awarded some relief by a judicial body. See *Buckhannon Board and Care Home, Inc. v. West Virginia Dept. of Health and Human Resources*, 121 S.Ct. 1835 (2001). The district court found that a consent decree is a contract between parties that is entered into the record with the court's approval and sanction. The hearing officer had not approved or sanctioned the agreement in this case. **The settlement agreement resembled a private settlement, not a consent decree, and did not confer prevailing party status on the mother**. Although the *Buckhannon* case involved the ADA and Fair Housing Amendments Act, nothing suggested that the Supreme Court's holding did not apply to IDEA cases. The court denied the mother's motion for reconsideration and awarded summary judgment to the school district. *Luis R. v. Joliet Township High School Dist.*, No. 01 C 4798, 2002 WL 54544 (N.D.Ill 2002).

◆ Prior to a student's junior year in high school, his parents and school district unsuccessfully sought to create an IEP for him. The student had been diagnosed with attention deficit disorder and a history of not attending classes. The parents requested a due process hearing, believing the student should receive an independent educational evaluation, a transition planning consultant, and modification of his IEP to build on his strengths and provide more positive behavioral reinforcement. The district agreed to mediate the dispute and to pay for a second IEE and the transition consultant. The parties reached a settlement agreement incorporating the suggestions from the IEE into the student's IEP. The district reduced the number of credits he needed to graduate and provided a detailed list of classroom modifications, including a short school day and off-site tutoring. The plan proved to be ineffective, as the student continued cutting classes and did not graduate. **The student's parents commenced a federal district court action against the district to recover their legal fees associated with the mediation proceedings**. The court refused their request, and they appealed to the Seventh Circuit.

The circuit court observed that parents seeking to recover attorneys' fees in an IDEA action must show that their claims were the cause for achieving redress, and that the school district did not act wholly gratuitously. The parents were not entitled to a second IEE under the IDEA because they did not significantly disagree with the first one. They also failed to identify any areas of disagreement with the school district's diagnosis or methodology. The parents had sought action to prevent the student's frequent absences and the removal of sanctions for this conduct. The district responded to the parents' requests by removing all punitive measures from the student's IEP and adding positive behavior reinforcements. The IEE did not identify the incentive structure from his IEP as deficient. **Because the parents were challenging the methodology employed by the district and sought a successful transition from school to work, their claim to attorneys' fees could not rest only on the district's agreement to pay for a second evaluation**. The granting of interim relief such as ordering the second IEE did not make the parents prevailing parties under the IDEA. The court affirmed the judgment for the school district. *Edie F. v. River Falls School District*, 243 F.3d 329 (7th Cir. 2001).

◆ A 16-year-old student with learning disabilities and emotional problems was placed in a residential treatment facility as an exceptional student. He claimed that the facility, school district and county mental health and retardation department sought his discharge from the facility based on the belief that he was abusing inhalants. His parent requested an expedited special education due process hearing through the Pennsylvania education department. The facility, district and department agreed to rescind the attempt to discharge him at the hearing, and the student and parent petitioned a federal district court for an award of attorneys' fees. The school district asserted a cross-claim against the mental health department for indemnification or contribution for its share of the attorneys' fees, and the department moved to dismiss the cross-claim. The district asserted that if it was found liable for any attorneys' fees, the department should be required to pay all or part of the award because the attempt to discharge the student arose from the department. The department countered that the district's cross-claim for indemnity and contribution was insufficiently specific because it did not allege that the department was the party responsible for the residential placement and related issues. The court found that the district had sufficiently pleaded a cross-claim against the department for contribution and indemnity. **When multiple parties have failed to comply with the IDEA, a court may apportion an award of attorneys' fees to the prevailing party according to its relative fault**. The district had sufficiently alleged that the department was responsible for the student's residential placement and had attempted to discharge him. The claims were specific enough to avoid dismissal, and the court issued an order in the district's favor. *Jeremy M. ex rel. L.M. v. Central Bucks County School District et al.*, No. Civ. A. 99-4954, 2001 WL 177185 (E.D. Pa. 2001).

- The parents of a student with autism made informal complaints to the Oregon education department about their son's education program, then filed a formal complaint under the state complaint resolution procedure, alleging IDEA violations. The department conducted an investigation of the school district, identified IDEA violations and ordered the district to hold an IEP meeting. The district held several meetings to devise a new IEP, some of which were attended by the parents' attorney. The parties agreed on a revised IEP for the student, and **the parents filed a federal district court action against the district for reimbursement of attorneys' fees incurred for their attorney's attendance at the department-ordered IEP meetings**. The court granted the request, and the school district appealed.

The Ninth Circuit initially noted that there are two ways for parents of students with disabilities to bring IDEA challenges, through the impartial due process hearing method or by filing a complaint under a state CRP. 34 C.F.R. Part 300.660-662 requires state education agencies, as part of their state CRPs, to conduct independent, on-site investigations and allow complaining parents an opportunity to provide information about a suspected IDEA violation. Within 60 days, the state agency must issue a written decision with factual findings and conclusions. The state CRP must include procedures for the effective implementation of a final decision. The circuit court rejected the school district's argument that an IEP meeting ordered by a state agency to resolve a CRP complaint was not an action or proceeding brought under the IDEA for which attorneys' fees might be awarded. Nothing in the text of the IDEA required this result. The IDEA permits a district court to award fees in "any action or proceeding brought under this section." The CRP and due process hearings were alternative methods for addressing IDEA complaints. The school district's assertion that no award of attorneys' fees should be allowed under a CRP action was in conflict with the federal policy of encouraging less costly and litigious resolution of special education disputes. The court determined that **if a CRP addresses a dispute that is subject to resolution in a due process hearing, the CRP is a proceeding brought under the IDEA for which attorneys' fees are permissible**. The court held inapplicable the general IDEA prohibition on attorneys' fee awards that are related to any IEP-team meeting, because the IDEA specifically allows such awards if the IEP meeting is convened as the result of an administrative proceeding or judicial action. In this case, the IEP-team meeting had arisen from an order pursuant to the CRP. This was an IDEA proceeding for which an award of attorneys' fees was available to a prevailing party. Because the parents had obtained affirmative relief under the department's order, they were prevailing parties who could recover attorneys' fees for their lawyer's attendance at the department-ordered IEP meetings. *Lucht v. Molalla River School Dist.*, 225 F.3d 1023 (9th Cir. 2000).

◆ Shortly after a student with ADHD was referred to a school district committee on special education, he was suspended indefinitely from school for behavior reasons. The student's parents asserted that the behavior difficulties he experienced were the result of disabilities that the district had failed to address. They retained an attorney who threatened to file due process proceedings unless the district immediately convened a CSE meeting to classify the student as other health impaired or emotionally disturbed, and to provide him with an appropriate educational program. The school district declined to take the reclassification action and the attorney sent the district a letter proposing a settlement that called for reclassification of the student with a functional behavioral assessment, an individualized behavior intervention plan, and counseling. **The district agreed to reclassify the student as other health impaired and place him in a special program outside the district.**

After the parties agreed to this resolution, the student's attorney sought $2,000 in attorney's fees for his activities in bringing about the settlement. The district refused the request and the family petitioned a federal district court for its attorney's fees. The district moved to dismiss the action, arguing that 1997 amendments to the IDEA specifically prohibit attorneys' fee awards relating to any IEP team meeting that does not arise as the result of administrative proceedings or litigation. Without determining whether the parents were prevailing parties in this action, the court found that the 1997 IDEA Amendments do not alter the law regarding attorney's fee awards in cases where an IEP meeting is held in direct response to an attorney's request for a due process hearing. The amendment was only intended to discourage attorney participation in routine IEP meetings. **Attorney's fees remain available in cases where an impartial hearing has been requested, but the district has changed its course under the threat of impending litigation or a due process hearing.** The district in this case had agreed to hold a CSE meeting in response to the parents' attorney's demands, and had reclassified the student and placed him in a new program as requested by the attorney. Accordingly, the court denied the district's motion on the question arising under the 1997 IDEA Amendments. *F.R. v. Bd. of Educ., Plainedge Public Schools*, 67 F.Supp.2d 142 (E.D.N.Y. 1999).

B. Compensatory Education

Compensatory education involves the belated provision of necessary educational services by a school district to a student with a disability. Courts may award compensatory education to students with disabilities who have been deprived of their right to a free appropriate public education pursuant to 20 U.S.C. § 1415(i)(2)(B)(iii), which recognizes the power of a court to grant such relief as it deems appropriate in IDEA cases. In recent years, courts have shown an increased willingness to award compensatory education beyond the age of 21.

1. Generally

◆ A federal district court approved a settlement between the Arizona Department of Education and a class representing students with special needs who sued the department for failing to ensure local compliance with the IDEA. Under the settlement, **students claiming injury due to local noncompliance with special education laws may apply for compensatory education services if they lodged a complaint with the education department** between June 4, 1997, and the date of the court's final order, and if they remain dissatisfied with the local response to the resolution ordered by the department. A five-member committee will review requests for compensation and other remedial action. The settlement calls for the appointment of a monitor to regulate policies and procedures specified in the order to prevent the reoccurrence of noncompliance and eliminate past effects of any violation. The lawsuit was the result of a complaint by the parent of a Paradise Valley School District student who claimed that the district did not comply with the findings of a state education department compliance officer. *Dunajski v. Keegan*, No. CIV. 99-0353 PCT RCB (D. Ariz. 2001).

◆ In examining a claim brought by the parent of a student with mental retardation covering a five year time period, **a hearing officer held that the student's IEPs for the two most recent years were inappropriate and awarded her two years of compensatory education**. The mother failed to appeal the hearing officer's denial of any relief for three earlier years in which she alleged that the district failed to provide appropriate services. However, the school district appealed the award of compensatory education to a state special education appeals panel. The special education appeals panel reduced the award of compensatory education to one year. The mother then commenced a federal district court action against the district.

Because the mother had failed to appeal the adverse part of the hearing officer's decision, the claims for the first three years of educational deprivation were unexhausted, and therefore, the court granted the district's motion for to dismiss this portion of the suit for failure to exhaust administrative remedies. The district conceded liability for the most recent year of claimed educational deprivation, but asserted that the claim for the one remaining year was barred because of the family's failure to commence an action within one year. The court disagreed, noting that failure to object to a student's placement should not deprive the student of the right to an appropriate education. The U.S. Court of Appeals for the Third Circuit, whose jurisdiction includes the states of Pennsylvania, Delaware and New Jersey, has treated claims for compensatory education differently than those for tuition reimbursement. **The failure to commence a claim for compensatory education was not a bar to the family's claim for the remaining one year of deprivation of educational services**, and the court refused to dismiss it. *Kristi H. v. Tri-Valley School Dist.*, 107 F.Supp.2d 628 (M.D. Pa. 2000).

◆ A Pennsylvania special education due process review panel ordered a school district to provide compensatory education to a student with disabilities. The district appealed to a federal district court, and the parents asserted counterclaims against the district, including claims for monetary damages under the IDEA, Section 504 of the Rehabilitation Act, the ADA and 42 U.S.C. 1983. **The parents also sought to recover damages against parties such as the state education secretary, education department and 10 individuals** alleged to have been involved in the evaluation and provision of compensatory education to the student. These individuals included the district superintendent, the principal, director of special education, school board president, school psychologist, three teachers and two outside consultants who were hired to assess the student's need for compensatory education.

The court agreed with the education department and its secretary that the 11th Amendment to the U.S. Constitution **prohibits a federal court from exercising jurisdiction in cases brought against a state.** As in most cases, the state agencies and officials were entitled to immunity in federal court actions. Therefore, the court refused to join these individuals to the action. The court refused to dismiss the claim for money damages brought against the outside evaluators, rejecting their assertion that the IDEA does not contemplate individual liability. The court found instead that Congress had expressly allowed for individual claims under the IDEA in response to a 1984 U.S. Supreme Court decision. The evaluators were necessary parties to the Sec. 1983 action, therefore, the court denied their motion to dismiss. *Salisbury Township Sch. Dist. v. Jared M.*, 1999 U.S. Dist. LEXIS 11687 (E.D. Pa. 1999).

◆ A Maryland student with pervasive developmental disorder, mental retardation and a substance abuse problem received special education services from his public school district. His mother agreed to a recommendation by the school to place him in a Pennsylvania residential training and counseling school. The student attended different programs within the school at various times. Included was a career training and therapeutic services program through which he obtained off-campus employment. The student's substance abuse problem worsened, and his mother believed that the school's program emphasized employment over classwork. She sought a community-based program located within his home community. The student then attained the age of 21 and met his high school graduation requirements. The school district filed a federal district court motion seeking to relieve itself of further educational obligations. The court granted the motion, and the mother initiated a separate administrative proceeding in which she sought compensatory services. **A hearing officer agreed with the mother and ordered the district to provide the student with one and one half years of compensatory services.** A review board reversed, and the mother appealed to the U.S. District Court for the District of Maryland.

The mother asserted that the school district had violated the IDEA and should have taken a more active role in providing her with assistance in the student's placement. She also asserted that the use of different programs at various times within the residential school constituted changes in placement under the IDEA. The court rejected the mother's arguments, finding that school officials had complied with the IDEA. The movement within programs at the private school did not constitute fundamental program or IEP changes. **School officials had made strong efforts to comply with the mother's wishes and there was evidence that she had created delays and failed to participate in the process**

by walking out of an IEP meeting. The court affirmed the review board's decision. *McGraw v. Bd. of Educ. of Montgomery County*, 952 F.Supp. 248 (D.Md.1997).

◆ A 19-year-old Connecticut student had a learning disability and emotional and social maladjustment. He was entitled to receive special education services under the IDEA and state law. He was arrested on a felony charge and held by the state department of corrections (DOC) for eight months. **A special school district within the DOC failed to offer the student special education services during this period, but his local education board resumed a special education program for him upon his release from prison.** The student was soon arrested on new felony charges and remained in custody for at least six more months. Although the local education board developed an IEP to be used upon his release from custody, the student's mother requested a due process hearing. The special school district then began an education program for the student while he remained in custody. The special district failed to convene a planning and placement team meeting and did not develop a new IEP for him. The student was finally placed on probation and entered a private residential treatment and education program. An administrative hearing officer found the special school district liable for over ten months of educational services during the student's period of incarceration and ordered it to provide compensatory education at the private residential program after the student reached the age of 21.

The special school district appealed to the Superior Court of Connecticut, where the court upheld the hearing officer's decision on liability since the special school district had clearly violated state and federal special education laws by depriving the student of an appropriate placement. State law charged the district with providing special education services for all incarcerated students, not simply those that had been sentenced. However, **the hearing officer had abused her discretion by approving the placement in the private facility commencing after the student reached age 21. This prospective placement, issued two years in advance of the time when services were to be provided, did not comply with the law**, and it would be necessary to convene a planning and placement team meeting to evaluate the student's needs when he turned 21. The court ordered the education department to issue a new decision requiring the special district to provide compensatory special education services to the student and to reconvene a placement meeting at the appropriate time. *State of Connecticut-Unif. School Dist. No. 1 v. State Dept. of Educ.*, 45 Conn.Sup. 57, 699 A.2d 1077 (1997).

2. Beyond Age 21

◆ The parents of a student with Down's syndrome rejected the proposed district IEP and placement for the student's final year of eligibility and requested an administrative hearing. The hearing officer rejected the parents' claim that the district committed procedural violations, but held that the IEP was deficient in several areas. The parents sought reversal in federal court, and the district filed a counterclaim. The court consolidated the actions, and the parties filed a sequence of motions that continued past the end of the school year covered by the disputed IEP. The district court referred the case to a federal magistrate judge to consider the district's argument that the case was now moot, in view of the student's graduation. The parents claimed that the case was not moot, even though the student had graduated and reached his 20th birthday, because they were seeking compensatory education.

The magistrate observed **an eligible student may seek compensatory education even after becoming too old to qualify for services, if it is claimed that the district denied the student an appropriate education in the past**. The court noted that in *Thomas R.W. v. Massachusetts Department of Education*, 130 F.3d 477 (1st Cir. 1997), the First Circuit held that in order to avoid dismissal for mootness, a claim for compensatory education must be "evident from the record" or included as an alternative pleading by a party, if no live controversy among the parties remains that can be remedied by injunctive relief. The parents had raised the issue of compensatory education by claiming it as a remedy in a reply memorandum filed with the court. Accordingly, the court found the claim "evident from the record." A claim for compensatory education could only arise after a student became ineligible for services. **However, the student had received the very relief that his parents sought when they initiated the action by virtue of the administrative stay put order**. The parents had sought to overcome the district's proposal to place their son in a vocational training program for the entire day, and they obtained this through the stay put order's continuation of the 1999-2000 IEP. The case was moot because there was no longer any live controversy between the parties. Federal courts have no jurisdiction where, as in this case, a party no longer has a stake in the outcome of the litigation. Because the family received all the relief it had sought, the magistrate judge recommended dismissal of the consolidated actions as moot. *Maine School Administrative District No. 35 v. Mr. and Mrs. R.*, 176 F.Supp.2d 15 (D. Me. 2001).

- The mother of a student with disabilities petitioned the West Virginia Supreme Court of Appeals for an order compelling the school district to provide her child with certain special education services she claimed he was entitled to but had not received. After numerous court proceedings, a special master issued a report in favor of the mother, finding that the district did not perform its obligations from 1993 to 1995. Moreover, **the district's performance of make-up services did not compensate the student for depriving him of them at the time they were actually required, justifying an award of compensatory education**. The district challenged the action in a federal district court, which first referred the case to mediation, then dismissed it because the district failed to exhaust its administrative remedies.

When mediation attempts failed, the mother moved the state court of appeals for relief based on allegations of "a 14-year history of inadequate, bad-faith malfeasance" by the district and sought a private placement for the student at the district's expense. She also sought a court-appointed monitor and reimbursement for the costs of all of the services she had previously arranged for the student. The court stated that it intended a prompt hearing to determine whether the services provided to the child were adequate. The record supported the special master's finding that the district did not comply with its legal duty to provide the student with special education from 1993 to 1995, and that the corrective measures it took did not fully address the lack of services during the relevant time period. The record also supported her finding that a new IEP and medical evaluation were currently necessary. The court granted the mother's request for relief, ordering the parties to promptly create a new IEP. The mother was ordered to permit a full physical and psychological examination of her son. Any conflict was to be addressed in an appropriate trial court or administrative proceeding, not by further proceedings. **The district was responsible for providing special education services for two additional years beyond the student's statutory entitlement to compensate him for past service deficiencies**. The mother was a prevailing party in the action and thus entitled to her attorneys' fees. *State of West Virginia ex rel. Justice v. Board of Education of County of Monongalia*, 539 S.E.2d 777 (W.Va. 2000).

- A 15-year-old New York student suffered severe brain injuries in an automobile accident. After remaining in a coma for six months, he was transferred from a hospital to a rehabilitation facility in Pennsylvania. His parents requested a special education evaluation by their school district. The district's committee on special education recommended a daily special services program that it attempted to implement by contract with a Pennsylvania school district. **The student returned to a hospital in New York where only part of the IEP was implemented, with some services withheld**. The parents requested a due process hearing to address the failure to provide services, which the district had discontinued on the basis of the lack of medical information. The hearing officer ordered the school committee to prepare a new IEP for the upcoming school year but did not address the lack of services for the current school year. A state level review officer held that the school district had failed to provide the services described in the IEP, but denied the parents' request for compensatory special education and related services.

The parents appealed to the U.S. District Court for the Northern District of New York, which found the IEP appropriate and affirmed the administrative decisions. In a later opinion, the court held that **compensatory education is a permissible form of relief for a student over 21 years of age where there has been a gross violation of the IDEA. However, the parents had failed to show that the student's condition regressed** because of the failure to provide a free appropriate education. The court agreed with the administrative decisions that compensatory education and related services would not be appropriate to remedy the lack of services during the year after the injury. On appeal to the U.S. Court of Appeals for the Second Circuit, the circuit court issued a brief memorandum affirming the district court decision in all respects, for substantially the same reasons. **The circuit court noted that an award of compensatory special education and related services beyond a student's 21st birthday was inappropriate**, and that the IDEA does not provide for monetary damage awards. *Wenger v. Canastota Central School Dist.*, 208 F.3d 204 (2d Cir. 2000).

- A Michigan student with severe mental disabilities began receiving special education services in 1974 and was identified as severely multiply handicapped. His placement committee recommended a minimum 230 days of annual instruction.

However, from 1974 to 1979, the local education agency (LEA) provided only 180 days of annual instruction. It provided special education services to the student until he turned 27. Several years later, the parent requested a due process hearing, seeking compensatory services as relief. **A hearing officer granted the LEA's dismissal motion and denied the request for compensatory education. A review officer reversed this decision, finding that the student had been denied services to which he was entitled**. The LEA appealed to a federal district court, and the family counterclaimed for monetary damages under the IDEA, § 504 of the Rehabilitation Act and 42 U.S.C. § 1983.

The court dismissed related state law claims without prejudice and retained the IDEA and § 1983 claims. A resulting state court action in Wayne County led to conflicting stay put orders from each court during the pendency of the proceedings. **The federal court affirmed the review officer's decision that the student had been deprived of services to which he was entitled from 1974 through 1979**. It upheld the compensatory education award. Applying Michigan law, the federal court found that individuals with mental disabilities are entitled to relief from application of a statute of limitations during a period of disability, even when their rights are capably handled by an attorney or guardian. The action was not barred by Michigan's statute of limitations or by laches, an equitable remedy applied by courts when a party has failed to timely file an action, and the delay results in prejudice to the adverse party. The court affirmed the review officer's decision, but rejected each of the counterclaims. The court applied the decision of the U.S. Court of Appeals, Sixth Circuit, in *Crocker v. Tennessee Secondary School Athletic Assn.*, 980 F.2d 382 (6th Cir.1992), which interprets the IDEA as not permitting monetary damages. The LEA was entitled to dismissal of the § 504 claim for punitive damages, and the court also declined to award monetary damages under § 1983. *Wayne County Regional Educ. Service Agency v. Pappas*, 56 F.Supp.2d 807 (E.D.Mich.1999).

◆ An autistic student attended a Texas public school district. His parents disputed an IEP proposed by the district when he was 19 years old. The following spring, they also disagreed with the district's admission, review and dismissal (ARD) committee's recommendation and requested a due process hearing before the Texas Education Agency, claiming that the district had failed to provide the student a free appropriate public education. They sought compensatory special education. **The hearing officer determined that the student was no longer entitled to special education services because he had reached the age of 22 prior to the hearing date**. The parents filed a lawsuit against the school district in the U.S. District Court for the Southern District of Texas, which determined that compensatory education was an appropriate equitable remedy that was not barred when a student passed the age of statutory entitlement. The court remanded the case to the education agency, which referred the matter to a hearing officer who determined that the district's proposed IEP was appropriate. This decision was affirmed by the district court, and the parents appealed to the U.S. Court of Appeals, Fifth Circuit.

On appeal, the parents argued that the school district had violated IDEA procedural requirements by failing to notify them about 15 informal staff meetings at which the student's progress was evaluated. The parents argued that many of the short-term objectives of their son's IEPs were discontinued or modified, depriving them of any input as mandated by the IDEA. They also claimed that some special education services were terminated without notice. **The court found no evidence in the record that the parents had been deprived of input into IEPs or ARD meetings or had not received an opportunity to participate**. Evidence indicated that the parents had actively participated in the development of their son's special education programs and that they were not entitled to notice of the informal meetings. The court affirmed the judgment for the school district. *Buser by Buser v. Corpus Christi Indep. School Dist.*, 51 F.3d 490 (5th Cir.1995).

C. Monetary Damages

Courts seem unable to agree on whether money damages are available under the IDEA. Although the IDEA allows courts to award any appropriate relief, some courts have taken the position that the only form of money damages available is for reimbursement of the costs incurred in providing a necessary placement or services. Other courts have stated that compensatory monetary damages may be available under the IDEA. Given the lack of decisions awarding money damages for IDEA violations, it remains to be seen which view will prevail.

◆ A Missouri student with behavior problems commenced a federal district court action against his school district after a security guard sprayed him with mace for behavior that could have been attributed to his mental illness. He alleged that the action caused an unlawful change in placement in violation of the IDEA's stay put provision, and that it violated his right to procedural due process. The student also sought monetary damages under 42 U.S.C. § 1983 for pain and emotional distress against the guard, the school district and its insurer. The court dismissed the claims, and the student appealed to the U.S. Court of Appeals, Eighth Circuit. The court agreed with the school district that the student failed to allege that he had undergone any change of placement in violation of the IDEA stay put provision. It also held that **the IDEA does not allow the recovery of monetary damages in an action under 42 U.S.C. § 1983.** The student's procedural due process claim failed because he did not allege that the school district maintained a policy or custom of requiring the use of mace to discipline students, or that any school official made an executive decision to have him maced. The court affirmed the district court judgment for the district. *Wolverton v. Doniphan R-1 School Dist.*, 16 Fed.Appx. 523 (8th Cir. 2001).

◆ The parent of a student with disabilities claimed a school administrator changed the placement of her son to another school based solely on a telephone call without first performing an assessment, as required by the IDEA. She brought an administrative complaint against four local education agencies and several administrators. A hearing officer found that the agencies failed to provide the student with a FAPE and should be required to reimburse the parent for a private residential school placement. The agencies and officials appealed to a federal district court, and **the parent counterclaimed against the agencies and officials for monetary damages**.

The court affirmed the administrative findings on all grounds except one, that an assessment was timely completed. The court affirmed the monetary award and the administrative ruling that the agencies and officials violated rights secured by the IDEA. The administrator moved the court for relief from any liability for monetary damages under Section 1983, arguing that there can be no monetary liability under the IDEA and that she was entitled to immunity. The court held that **the IDEA does not foreclose remedies, including monetary damages under Section 1983**. Congress expressly authorized Section 1983 claims to vindicate IDEA rights when it amended the IDEA in 1986. Although the family was entitled to bring a Section 1983 action against the districts and officials for monetary damages for IDEA violations, the court found that **California school districts are arms of the state and thus protected from liability by 11th Amendment immunity**. To the extent that the 11th Amendment barred a suit against any California school district, it also barred them against school officials who were sued in their official capacities. The administrator and her employing school district were entitled to 11th Amendment immunity from any official capacity claims. The court rejected an alternative argument by the administrator that she was entitled to official immunity for any claims brought against her in her individual capacity, finding the administrator was charged with knowledge of IDEA requirements that prevent a student change of placement at the request of the student's parent without first performing an assessment. While a government official is entitled to qualified immunity for objectively reasonable conduct, it was implausible that an official with the administrator's level of responsibility would not know that it was unlawful to change a special education student's placement on the basis of a phone call from the parents. Since her decision involved disregard for IDEA procedures and the act's requirement to provide an education reasonably calculated to provide some educational benefit, the court denied her motion for qualified immunity. *Goleta Union Elementary School District v. Ordway*, 166 F.Supp.2d 1287 (C.D. Cal. 2001).

- After an incident in which the teacher of a nonverbal student with Down's syndrome allegedly spat water in the student's face, his parents learned that she had restrained the student by strapping him to a chair with a belt on some occasions without their consent. The new teacher assigned to the student after this incident physically restrained him at least once. Shortly thereafter, the parents rejected a proposed behavior management plan for the student that allowed physical restraint. They filed separate requests for administrative hearings challenging both the district's provision of a FAPE and proposed summer program. After the resolution of the administrative proceedings, the parents brought federal district court actions to recover their attorneys' fees. The district agreed to pay them $15,500 in settlement of both actions. **The parents** then **filed a federal district court action against the school board and school officials for federal civil rights violations and against the special education teachers for state law assault and intentional infliction of emotional distress**. The parents included a claim for monetary damages under 42 U.S.C. § 1983.

The board and officials moved for summary judgment, arguing that there can be no Section 1983 claim based on a violation of the IDEA. The court disagreed, noting that 1986 amendments to the IDEA's predecessor legislation made Section 1983 available as a remedy to vindicate IDEA violations. The court also denied the board's motion for judgment on the parents' substantive due process claim arising from the spitting and physical restraint incidents. There was insufficient information in the record for the court to determine whether the use of physical restraint had been necessary for the safety of the student or others. The board was entitled to summary judgment on the procedural due process violations claim, as there was no evidence that state due process procedures were insufficient to address the parents' claims. The court held that **the school board, as a municipal entity, could not be held liable for any Section 1983 violations, since it was not alleged that the harm suffered by the student was the result of an official board policy or custom of physically restraining disabled students**. The teachers were not final policymakers whose conduct could be attributed to the board for Section 1983 purposes. There was insufficient evidence to create supervisory liability for the Section 1983 claims against the superintendent, the director of pupil services and another administrator, as it was not shown that they had actual knowledge of the restraint or spitting incidents and there was no evidence they were personally involved in developing the student's behavioral management plan or his IEPs. However, the district supervisor of special education was not entitled to summary judgment on the parents' Section 1983 claims for supervisory liability. There was evidence that she was familiar with the student's IEP and behavioral management plan. She was in a position to know that the methods used by the teachers were not included in the student's IEPs and were not agreed to by the parents. The court held that the superintendent, the director of pupil services and the supervisor of special education were not entitled to qualified immunity. The teachers were entitled to immunity concerning the state law claims for assault and intentional infliction of emotional distress, as they acted pursuant to the delegated state responsibility of providing special education. *M.H. v. Bristol Board of Education*, 169 F.Supp.2d 21 (D. Conn. 2001).

- The mother of a student with medical and developmental disabilities and a history of behavior problems brought a stroller to school for transporting the student from class to the resource room. However, **the district allegedly used the stroller for physically restraining the student during time outs, in which she was placed in a closet for 15 to 20 minute time periods. On one such occasion, the student fell out of the stroller and fractured her skull**, resulting in complications, including an increase in seizure activity. The parents never requested a due process hearing. The family moved out of the district and sued the district and five employees in federal district court, seeking to hold the school district and the employees individually liable for compensatory damages under the IDEA through 42 U.S.C. § 1983. In addressing the district's motion to dismiss the complaint, the court noted that while three federal circuits (the Sixth, Fourth and Eighth) have held that general damages are unavailable in IDEA cases, it would not follow these decisions. **The court instead followed other federal district courts and the Third Circuit, which have held that the IDEA does not specifically forbid an award of compensatory damages.** It applied a general rule announced by the U.S. Supreme Court in a Rehabilitation Act case allowing federal courts to award any appropriate relief, absent an explicit contrary directive from Congress. The court further held that the school employee defendants could be held individually liable for any damage award.

On appeal to the 10th Circuit, the court noted that some federal courts have agreed with the district court's conclusion that monetary damage awards are permitted under Section 1983 for IDEA violations, and that these damage awards may be enforced against individual school officials. However, the district court's analysis presupposed that Section 1983 could be used to enforce IDEA rights. Although a majority of the courts that have considered the issue have held that Section 1983 actions may be based on IDEA violations, the U.S. Supreme Court has held that the IDEA creates a comprehensive enforcement scheme that preempts other "overlapping but independent statutory or constitutional claims," *Smith v. Robinson*, 468 U.S. 992 (1984). Congress amended the IDEA in 1986 to address *Smith*'s prohibition on the joinder of Rehabilitation Act and other claims to IDEA cases. **The court stated that the legislative changes did not preempt *Smith*'s ruling that the IDEA provided a comprehensive remedial framework that foreclosed Section 1983 as a remedy for IDEA violations, therefore, it reversed the district court's denial of the defendants' motion to dismiss the IDEA-based Section 1983 claims** against the school district, board and the remaining school officials. The court did not directly rule on whether the IDEA imposes individual liability or permits damage awards. The court affirmed the denial of the board and district's motion to dismiss the case for failure to exhaust administrative remedies and reversed the denial of the motion to dismiss the Section 1983 action. *Padilla v. School District No. 1, City and County of Denver, Colorado*, 233 F.3d 1268 (10th Cir. 2000).

◆ A California student with autism who filed a lawsuit seeking monetary damages and compensatory education because of his school district's failure to comply with an administrative decision was barred from bringing a federal district court action under Section 1983 against his school district because he failed to first exhaust his administrative remedies. Much of the relief he sought was available through an administrative appeal, and **he was** also **required to exhaust administrative remedies in order to pursue his claims for monetary damages arising under 42 U.S.C. § 1983**. The court stated that a contrary ruling would mean that a party could improperly circumvent the administrative exhaustion requirement simply by including a claim for monetary damages in an IDEA case. The court dismissed the action in its entirety. *Porter v. Board of Trustees of Manhattan Beach Unified School District*, 123 F.Supp.2d 1187 (C.D. Cal. 2000).

◆ Although the IEP of a student with an emotional disturbance called for his placement in a residential school at district expense, his school board never located an appropriate school for him. Instead, the board placed the student in a modified instructional services program located within a public school until a private placement was found. When the student was suspended during his first week in the MIS program, an interim placement calling for home instruction, speech/language therapy and counseling was developed. The parents initialed a due process hearing when the interim services were not provided. A hearing officer directed the board to provide the specified interim services while it located an appropriate private placement. When the board failed to implement the hearing officer's order, **the parents commenced a federal district court action**

against the board seeking monetary damages under Section 1983 due to the failure to comply with the IDEA.

The board moved to dismiss the case, asserting that the parents had failed to exhaust their administrative remedies by filing the action prior to appealing the administrative decision. The court rejected the board's argument, finding such an appeal is required only where a party is aggrieved by the findings and decision of an administrative hearing officer. Since the parents had prevailed at the hearing and were not entitled to appeal, the exhaustion of administrative remedies was unnecessary. The court further rejected the board's argument that the claim for monetary damages under 42 U.S.C. § 1983 based on IDEA violations should be dismissed. While courts have disagreed on whether damages may be available for alleged IDEA violations, **the court found that Congress had clearly authorized monetary damages when it amended the IDEA in 1986** to add 20 U.S.C. § 1415(f) (now 20 U.S.C. § 1415[1]) to clarify that the IDEA does not "restrict or limit the rights, procedures, and remedies available under the Constitution, the Americans With Disabilities Act of 1990, Title V of the Rehabilitation Act of 1973, or other Federal laws protecting the rights of children with disabilities." The parents had sufficiently alleged the presence of deliberate indifference by school authorities to meet the pleading standard for federal court actions arising under Section 1983 and had also pleaded the requisite bad faith or gross misjudgment necessary to avoid pre-trial dismissal of their claims arising under the Americans with Disabilities Act and the Rehabilitation Act. They successfully asserted that the board acted intentionally, recklessly and willfully to deny the student of his right to a FAPE. Therefore, the court dismissed the school board's motion to dismiss the entire case. *R.B. v. Board of Education of City of New York*, 99 F.Supp.2d 411 (S.D.N.Y. 2000).

◆ Despite a special education student's behavior and attendance problems, this district changed his classification and determined that he should no longer receive special education services. More than two years later, the student was diagnosed as having attention deficit hyperactivity disorder. The following year, the student was classified as having multiple disabilities. His mother challenged the district recommended day treatment program, also rejecting a home school program. The mother initiated due process proceedings and obtained an administrative order in the student's favor. The hearing officer determined the student had been improperly declassified, was never offered counseling and his most recent IEP was inadequate. Neither party appealed. The CSE met to develop another IEP, which the mother rejected. Instead, she enrolled the student in a home-based program offered through a private school. The school district contested the unilateral placement. **A hearing officer held that although the school district had devised IEPs that were appropriate for the student, the private program was inappropriate**, and therefore, the mother was not entitled to tuition reimbursement. The order directed the school district to implement the most recent IEP and provide home tutoring for 18 months or until the student received his GED. The mother appealed to a state level review officer, who held that the two most recent IEPs were inappropriate, but affirmed the decision not to award tuition reimbursement.

The mother then commenced a federal district court action against the school district on behalf of the student, asserting violations of the IDEA, Section 504 of the Rehabilitation Act, the Family Education Rights and Privacy Act (FERPA) and educational malpractice under state law. She also sought to recover an award of damages under 42 U.S.C. § 1983 for IDEA and Section 504 violations. The court considered the district's motion for summary judgment and held that some of the student's claims were time-barred. In examining which statute of limitations applied, the court determined that New York's four-month limit on appeals from Article 78 proceedings applied to bar the claims arising from the first administrative proceeding. However, the claims arising from the second administrative proceedings had been timely filed and were not barred. **The court determined the student was not entitled to compensatory or punitive damages under the IDEA**. Courts have not held that the IDEA is a means of obtaining personal injury type damages, since the statutory scheme favors the restoration of educational rights. **However, the court refused to bar the student's claims for damages under Sections 504 and 1983**, finding he had presented sufficient evidence that several of the IEPs prepared by the district were inappropriate and failed to provide him with special education services. He was entitled to the opportunity to show that the school acted with deliberate indifference to his rights. Courts have construed Section 504 as allowing punitive damages, and if the student proved his case, he would be entitled to recover punitive damages from the individually named school officials, who were not entitled to immunity. The court dismissed the student's FERPA and state law claims, finding no justification for allowing them to proceed. *Butler v. South Glen Falls Central School Dist.*, 106 F.Supp.2d 414 (N.D.N.Y. 2000).

◆ An administrative review officer held that a student's IEP for the 1992-93 school year was adequate and denied his claim for compensatory education. The school district allowed the student to graduate. The student then sued the district and certain officials in federal district court, alleging IDEA procedural due process claims for allowing him to graduate. **In addition to the wrongful graduation claim, the former student sought monetary damages for IDEA violation under 42 U.S.C. § 1983**. The court considered a motion by the district and officials to dismiss the claims for monetary damages and observed that four federal circuit courts have held that monetary damages are unavailable under the IDEA.

The court observed that the U.S. Court of Appeals for the Third Circuit has interpreted the IDEA as allowing compensatory damage claims, and found the Third Circuit's reasoning persuasive. **According to the court, the 1986 amendments to the IDEA do not limit a student's right to seek monetary damages. The court found this particularly true in this case, since the former student had graduated some time ago and claimed to be struggling from the effects of the earlier deprivation of services**. The court held that "it is entirely possible that his earning capacity since graduation was diminished, and that such diminution may only be remediable via damages...." Finding that nothing in the IDEA limited a claim for damages under 42 U.S.C. § 1983, the court denied the school district's summary judgment motion. *Cappillino v. Hyde Park Central School Dist.*, 40 F.Supp.2d 513 (S.D.N.Y. 1999).

◆ A student was diagnosed with autism at birth and received services from an early childhood learning center until the age of three, when his school district assumed responsibility for providing educational services. The district and family disagreed about the student's program, and disputed whether the program should be integrated or nonintegrated. He was first placed in an integrated public school program, which the family attacked because of the school's inadequately trained staff. After the student was reevaluated, the program was modified to include increased staff training. The parents alleged that the training never took place, and they requested a hearing before the state board of special education appeals, seeking a new placement. The hearing officer issued a preliminary order that called for some improvements in the placement but declined the parents' request for an off-site program. They petitioned a federal district court for reversal of the administrative decision, and requesting placement in the early learning center. The court denied their request for an immediate, off-site placement. The court made extensive efforts to assist the parties in reaching a mediated solution and a neutral expert retained by the court for this purpose recommended placement in a district school with some changes in the existing program. The district implemented these changes, but the student eventually transferred to a school in another district. **The family then sought compensatory and punitive damages from the district for IDEA violations under 42 U.S.C. § 1983.**

The court noted that § 1983 does not create substantive rights, but instead provides a vehicle for persons to obtain monetary damages for violations of rights created by the Constitution and other federal laws. The IDEA was amended in 1986 with an explicit provision allowing plaintiffs in IDEA actions to seek remedies available under the Constitution and other federal laws, but federal courts have disagreed on the availability of damages under § 1983 for IDEA violations. The court held that § 1983 liability has been found in cases of alleged misconduct of constitutional proportions, but not for mere statutory violations. **The intent of Congress in amending the IDEA could not be seen as allowing a § 1983 claim whenever a school district and family disagreed about an educational placement.** Among the reasons given by the court for declining to recognize an independent cause of action for IDEA violations under § 1983 was that such actions are reserved for the vindication of civil rights. Moreover, the IDEA is a funding statute, establishing a federal-state contract relationship that a state may theoretically reject by declining to accept federal funds. In reaching its decision, the court relied extensively on the opinion of the U.S. Court of Appeals for the Fourth Circuit in *Sellers v. School Bd. of City of Manassas*, 141 F.3d 524 (4th Cir.1998). In that case, the court found a student's claim for damages indistinguishable from an impermissible claim for educational malpractice. The family in the present case had failed to argue that the alleged civil rights violations by the school district were the product of a custom or practice. Having failed to meet this threshold for § 1983, the court dismissed the claim. However, the parents were entitled to an award of attorney's fees. The court reduced the amount of fees claimed by the family, but required the school district to pay in excess of $26,000 in fees within 45 days. *Andrew S. v. School Comm. of Town of Greenfield*, 59 F.Supp.2d 237 (D.Mass.1999).

◆ **A district disciplinary review board recommended placing a regular education student in an alternative education program for parts of two semesters after he became involved in a number of disciplinary incidents**, including abusive confrontations with teachers. The superintendent and school board upheld the alternative placement. The student's parents removed him from school and commenced an IDEA action against the board. A special education hearing officer held that the district had violated the IDEA by failing to provide the student with a FAPE. The hearing officer issued an order recommending the removal of the alternative placement from the student's record, reimbursement to the parents for certain evaluation costs, and reimbursement for private school costs and expenses. The school district appealed adverse aspects of the administrative decision to a federal district court, and the family commenced an action for monetary damages against the school district for IDEA violations via 42 U.S.C. § 1983.

The court separated the family's claim for damages from the appeal of the administrative decision, and considered the district's motion for summary judgment, which incorporated an argument that § 1983 damages are never available for IDEA–based claims, even where constitutional violations are also asserted. The court rejected this argument, but agreed with the school district that a § 1983 claim based exclusively on IDEA violations has no legal merit. This is because the IDEA has a comprehensive remedial scheme. Because the parents prevailed at the hearing level and had obtained partial relief, they had no standing to bring a direct IDEA claim, and had improperly inserted the § 1983 claim based on IDEA violations in its place. Allowing a § 1983 claim would contravene the Congressional intent to limit judicial review of special education cases involving school districts. Section 1983 is reserved for cases involving state violations of federal rights, and the alleged denial of a free appropriate public education does not amount to a violation of due process or equal protection rights. Moreover, a local government entity such as a school district may be held liable for monetary damages under § 1983 only where it has an official policy or custom that deprives a person of federally protected rights. Allegations of isolated injuries do not rise to this level. In this case, the family failed to allege that the district had a policy or custom of discrimination or deliberate indifference to individual rights. **Because there was no showing that the district maintained unconstitutional practices or policies, and the § 1983 claim based exclusively on IDEA violations was meritless, the court awarded summary judgment to the school district**. The court determined the Section 504 claim was unsupported by the evidence. *James C. v. Eanes Indep. School Dist.*, No. A-97-CA-745 JN (W.D.Tex.1999).

◆ **The parents of a student with autism claimed that school employees had frequently strapped the student to a chair with a vest-like device, resulting in bruises and psychological trauma**. They asserted that on one occasion he became hysterical and passed out when resisting the restraint. The family filed an administrative action against the school board, asserting that it had violated the IDEA by failing to provide the student with a free appropriate public education. The parties reached a settlement concerning the implementation of goals and objectives for his program, the location of his placement, and his classification.

The proceeding was dismissed pursuant to the settlement, and the parents commenced a state court action against the board for monetary damages and injunctive relief arising from use of the restraining device.

The court granted summary judgment to the school board, ruling that the settlement agreement and the IDEA precluded the action, and that the parents had failed to exhaust administrative remedies prior to filing suit. They appealed to the Supreme Court of Appeals of West Virginia, which found that **the settlement agreement did not mention the use of the restraint, was limited to IDEA issues and did not bar the action for damages**. The family had already exhausted all available IDEA remedies by pursuing the action before the state board. Further administrative consideration would have been futile in view of the fact that the settlement and the damage claim neither referred to nor related to the IDEA claim. The court reversed and remanded the case to the circuit court for trial. At trial in 1999, a jury awarded the parents $339,000 in damages. The district has indicated it will appeal. *Ronnie Lee S. v. Mingo County Bd. of Educ.*, 500 S.E.2d 292 (W.Va.1997).

A jury later returned a verdict in favor of the family for $250,000, finding district employees violated the state human rights law and were liable for negligent supervision, intentional infliction of emotional distress and loss of consortium by the student's father. The award included lost wages claimed by the student's mother and $100,000 in punitive damages.

◆ A student diagnosed as mildly mentally retarded alleged that the District of Columbia Public Schools (DCPS) failed to provide him with an appropriate special education in violation of the IDEA. He claimed that he was misdiagnosed and that the DCPS's failure to provide timely due process hearings violated not only the IDEA but § 504 of the Rehabilitation Act and 42 U.S.C. § 1983. He claimed that he was entitled to damages for the IDEA violations under § 1983, which provides an enforcement mechanism for violations of federal and state laws by government agencies and employees. The parties brought summary judgment motions before the U.S. District Court for the District of Columbia. The court rejected the DCPS's argument that no § 1983 action was available for an alleged denial of rights under the IDEA. The student had alleged sufficient facts to support the claim such that DCPS was not entitled to judgment prior to a trial. However, the student's allegations did not establish that DCPS had a custom or practice of IDEA violations that would entitle him to summary judgment. Accordingly, the court would consider these matters further, prior to any dismissal action. **Although the IDEA has not been construed to allow an award of damages, the student could be entitled to damages under § 504 if violations could be proven in later stages of the litigation. However, punitive damages were unavailable** as a matter of law. *Walker v. Dist. of Columbia*, 969 F.Supp. 794 (D.D.C.1997).

CHAPTER SEVEN

Employment

I. DISCIPLINE AND DISCHARGE

Each state code establishes permissible grounds for disciplinary action against a teacher, typically reserving discretion to the school district for necessary action. Two of the most frequently stated grounds for employee discipline are misconduct and incompetence. Courts which review employee suspension and discharge actions must analyze each case under applicable state laws, collective bargaining agreements and school board policies and procedures. Constitutional issues usually arise where a school board is charged with violating fundamental employee rights such as free speech.

A. Misconduct

♦ After a Washington state school district's special education program reported a high error rate, the state education compliance monitoring agency scheduled a verification review. On the night before the review, the special education director obtained a faxed list of 41 files that the agency intended to audit. He reviewed the files with an administrative intern and made significant alterations to a number of them. **The director and intern forged and back-dated some documents, making changes in an effort to make their program appear to comply with state and federal special education laws.** Although the director denied any misconduct, many of the changes were obvious, and the district terminated him. He sought administrative review before a hearing officer, who concluded that documents had been back-dated under his participation, direction or approval and that there was probable cause to terminate his employment. The director appealed to a state superior court, which affirmed the hearing officer's decision.

On appeal, the Washington Court of Appeals observed that the director had attempted to create records, not merely correct dates. One of the glaring examples of the alterations reflected a classroom observation that allegedly took place on a Sunday. Another indicated a date that never existed — Feb. 29, 1995. The court determined that the director's conduct established sufficient cause for employment termination under state law. Sufficient cause existed to terminate a certificated employee where there was an irremediable deficiency that materially and substantially affected performance, or conduct that lacked any positive educational aspect or legitimate professional purpose. There was no need to consider remediability in this case, as this was a concern only when a discharge followed deficient performance. **The director's conduct lacked any positive educational aspect or legitimate professional purpose, was unprofessional and was dishonest.** Since unprofessional conduct was grounds for revocation of a teaching certificate and discharge, the court affirmed the judgment. *Weems v. North Franklin School District*, 37 P.3d 354 (Wash. Ct. App., 3d Div. 2002).

◆ Several teacher aides worked for a board of cooperative educational services. A BOCES representative instructed them that they should report any concerns about classroom matters to the supervisor of special education or school principal. Within one month, **the aides became aware of bizarre and inappropriate sexual conduct by a teacher toward a student.** They did not report the misconduct for over one month, and then brought it to the attention of a union representative, not a BOCES supervisor. The union representative informed the BOCES of the report and the BOCES discharged the aides for insubordination.

The aides filed improper-practice charges against the BOCES with the New York Public Employment Relations Board, asserting that the BOCES violated the state Civil Service Law by discharging them for reporting a teacher's suspected misconduct to their union representative, instead of a BOCES supervisor. An administrative law judge found that the BOCES committed an improper practice because the report by the aides was protected conduct. The Public Employment Relations Board reversed and dismissed the charges and the aides appealed to the New York Supreme Court, Appellate Division. The court held that the PERB and administrative law judge had correctly found that the aides were engaged in protected activity when they consulted with their union representative. However, **their discharges had not been improperly motivated, since there were legitimate educational and business reasons for the actions.** The evidence indicated that BOCES had discharged the aides for failing to follow a supervisor's directive and jeopardizing the safety of a child under their supervision, not for engaging in protected conduct. The court confirmed the PERB decision. *Hoey et al. v. New York State Public Employment Relations Board*, 725 N.Y.S.2d 449 (N.Y. App. Div. 2001).

◆ Three teacher aides were non-certified, untenured employees who worked under annual contracts. They refused to attend a required training session on clean intermittent urinary catheterization. A board policy permitted teacher aides to avoid performing catheterization procedures if a supervising nurse or aide was uncomfortable in doing so. The aides attended individual conferences to discuss their refusal to attend the training session, and a new session was arranged. They were advised that **failure to attend the rescheduled training session would be considered insubordination and would result in a recommendation that they be discharged**. The aides again refused to attend the training session, and the district superintendent recommended discharge. The school board voted to terminate the aides' employment contracts on grounds of insubordination. The aides convinced a county circuit court that the board had arbitrarily terminated their contracts. The court awarded the aides pay and benefits for the remainder of their contract terms, and the board appealed. A state appeals court affirmed the trial court's decision concerning the arbitrariness of the termination action, but held that the aides had a reasonable expectation of continued employment with the district that extended beyond their contract terms. It held that they might be entitled to wages and benefits beyond the expiration of their contracts and remanded the case.

The Tennessee Supreme Court considered the board's argument that the correct measure of damages for noncertified, untenured teacher aides was limited to the contract term and that the aides were not entitled to additional compensation and benefits beyond their contract terms. **The court held that awarding damages for a period beyond the term stated in a contract such as the type at issue in this case would put the aides in a better position than they would have enjoyed if they had fully performed their contracts**. They had no reasonable expectation of continued employment beyond their contract terms and were ineligible for protection under the state Teacher Tenure Act. The aides had no additional rights under a county employment manual, county charter or a state civil service law requiring government employers to provide pretermination due process. They never alleged that they were denied notice and an opportunity to respond to the charges against them prior to the termination action. The aides were entitled only to payment for the remainder of their contract terms, and the high court reinstated the circuit court judgment. *Cantrell et al. v. Knox County Board of Education*, 53 S.W.3d 659 (Tenn. 2001).

◆ A high school student complained to her mother after viewing *1900*, an R-rated film with violence and sexual content, in class. The school board proposed dismissing the teacher who showed the film for insubordination and neglect of duty. A hearing officer recommended that the district retain the teacher because the board's controversial learning resources policy did not give sufficient guidance for determining whether the film was controversial. Under the policy, **teachers were required to provide written notice to principals before using controversial learning resources, not less than 20 days in advance of the planned presentation.** The board rejected the hearing officer's recommendation and discharged the teacher. On appeal, the Court of Appeals of Colorado held that the discharge violated the teacher's First Amendment rights. The board appealed to the Supreme Court of Colorado.

The supreme court upheld the teacher's discharge, finding he had violated the controversial learning resource policy by showing the film without prior approval. The court followed a line of federal circuit court decisions holding that **schools, not teachers, have the right to determine the curriculum**. School officials must demonstrate that the curriculum is reasonably related to legitimate educational concerns in order to avoid First Amendment problems. Because the policy reasonably addressed the use of controversial materials, **the teacher had no First Amendment right to use unapproved controversial materials without following district procedure.** The policy was not unconstitutionally vague since the teacher did not have to guess that *1900* was controversial, given its graphic sexual content and violence. The court reversed the judgment. *Bd. of Educ. of Jefferson County v. Wilder*, 960 P.2d 695 (Colo.1998).

◆ A Missouri high school teacher with over 20 years of experience taught an English class that included a drama segment. **She allowed students to write, perform, and videotape plays that contained extensive profanity**. She neither encouraged nor discouraged the use of profanity by students and was aware that the school student discipline code prohibited student profanity. Based on the videotapes, the district superintendent charged the teacher with willful or persistent violation of board regulations and recommended employment termination. **The school board held a hearing and voted to terminate the teacher's employment** for wilful or persistent violations of school policy. The teacher filed a lawsuit against the school district in the U.S. District Court for the Eastern District of Missouri, which considered cross-motions for summary judgment by the parties.

The court considered evidence that the board had established a clear policy of prohibiting student profanity and observed that Missouri law allows school districts to fire tenured teachers on the basis of wilful and persistent violation of school board regulations. In determining whether a teacher's conduct is wilful or persistent, a school board must prove not only intentional conduct but also an intent to violate or disobey a particular regulation. Because the teacher had presented evidence that there was an unwritten exception to the profanity prohibition and that many other teachers and administrators allowed class-related profanity, a fact question existed that prohibited summary judgment prior to trial. The court reversed the school board's order and ordered the district to reinstate the teacher.

On appeal to the Eighth Circuit, the court overturned the judgment, finding that the teacher had received sufficient notice of board policies. **The disciplinary code prohibited student profanity with no exception for creative speech by students.** The district court had erroneously found no legitimate academic interest in prohibiting student profanity, and the judgment on the First Amendment claim was reversed. Although there had been references to race by the superintendent and board members during consideration of the teacher's contract, the court held that the decision was not racially motivated. *Lacks v. Ferguson Reorganized School Dist. R-2*, 147 F.3d 718 (8th Cir.1998).

B. Incompetence

◆ A Texas school district employed a special education teacher for several years under a continuing contract until notifying her of its intention to terminate the contract based on myriad deficiencies noted in her observation reports, appraisals and evaluations. **The stated deficiencies included: failure to fulfill her duties and responsibilities; incompetency and insufficiency in performing classroom duties; inability to maintain classroom discipline**; failure to comply with reasonable district requirements for professional improvement and growth; and failure to attain stated goals in consecutive school years. Following a hearing, the district accepted the hearing examiner's findings of good cause to terminate the teacher's contract. The state commissioner of education adopted the hearing examiner's findings and a Texas district court affirmed.

The teacher appealed to a state court of appeals, which held that a school district may reject hearing examiner findings only if they are unsupported by substantial evidence. Courts are similarly bound to the standard of substantial evidence when reviewing state education commissioner decisions. In this case, **the evidence supported the hearing examiner's finding that the teacher had failed to fulfill her job duties and responsibilities, particularly with regard to adequate classroom management and discipline**. The appeals court agreed with the commissioner that the teacher's performance was so deficient that the district was not required to offer her the opportunity for remediation. The teacher's failures included improperly assigning special education students low grades for defiant behavior, failing to maintain classroom order and failing to conduct required academic achievement tests and reading style inventories for each student. She also failed to teach in accordance with student IEPS. Because there was substantial evidence supporting the termination decision, the appeals court affirmed the trial court decision. *Ramirez v. Edgewood Independent School District*, No. 04-00-00137-CV, 2001 WL 22043 (Tex. App.–San Antonio 2001) (unpublished).

◆ A South Dakota school district contracted for 15 years with a community health nurse to provide sex education for elementary students. The board never prescreened the program. After a video presentation by the nurse, a teacher with 29 years of experience in the district solicited questions from a group of boys, as had been the practice for 15 years. **The teacher responded to a question about homosexual practices in explicit language, prompting complaints** from parents. The school board notified the teacher of a hearing to consider his discharge. At the hearing, only two parents testified that they were bothered by his statements, and the principal testified that there was no evidence that students had been harmed or that there had been an increase in discipline problems. However, the school superintendent testified that the teacher's ability to perform his duties had been affected and the board voted to discharge him.

A South Dakota circuit court upheld the discharge, and the teacher appealed to the Supreme Court of South Dakota. The court noted that incompetence has been described as arising from a course of conduct, series of incidents or habitual failure to perform work with the degree of skill usually displayed by persons regularly employed in such work. **Although a single incident may be sufficient**

to support a finding of incompetency, the teacher's conduct here did not rise to that level since there was no showing that his teaching ability had been impaired or that students were detrimentally affected. The school administration had abdicated its control over the sex education program and no school officials ever took steps to place limits upon it. The teacher had participated in the questioning for the past 15 years without incident. Accordingly, the one ill-advised answer did not support the finding of incompetence. The court reversed and remanded the case for reinstatement of the teacher. *Collins v. Faith School Dist. No. 46-2*, 1998 SD 17, 574 N.W.2d 889 (S.D.1998).

◆ The Supreme Court of Montana affirmed a state district court decision in favor of a school board which discharged a high school science teacher for incompetence, unfitness and violation of its policies. The teacher was accused of joking about menstrual periods, making obscene gestures at students and making inappropriate jokes and comments. Although the county superintendent was presented with evidence of at least seven such incidents, she determined that the board had failed to establish the teacher's incompetence or unfitness to teach. The state superintendent of public instruction reversed the county superintendent's order, and a state district court affirmed the decision. On appeal, **the supreme court observed that each of the incidents constituted inappropriate conduct by the teacher and indicated his unfitness to continue teaching.** Because the county superintendent had improperly applied the law in this case, the court affirmed the discharge action. *Baldridge v. Bd. of Trustees, Rosebud County School Dist. No. 19, Colstrip, Montana*, 951 P.2d 1343 (Mont.1997).

◆ A Louisiana school board demoted a tenured special education teacher for failing to control his behavior disordered and emotionally disturbed students. The teacher challenged the demotion, and at a school board hearing he unsuccessfully sought to present evidence indicating that misbehavior from behavior disordered and emotionally disturbed special education students was to be expected. The board upheld charges for wilful neglect of duty, but dropped charges based on incompetence. A Louisiana trial court ordered the board to reinstate the teacher with his full salary and the board appealed to the Court of Appeal of Louisiana, Fourth Circuit. The court held that under Louisiana law, **wilful neglect of duty is a permissible statutory ground for demoting a teacher but it must be supported by evidence that the teacher has deliberately violated a direct order or an identifiable school policy**. There was no evidence in this case that the teacher had violated any direct order or identifiable school policy. Because no testimony indicated wilful misconduct and the incompetence charges had been dropped, the trial court order was affirmed. *Coleman v. Orleans Parish School Bd.*, 688 So.2d 1312 (La.App.4 Cir.1997).

◆ A five-year-old Louisiana kindergarten student with a behavior disorder exhibited several incidents of disruptive conduct within a one-week period. The student's classroom teacher brought him to the principal's office on a day when he was experiencing severe behavior problems. **The principal bound the student to a desk with rope and duct tape** and placed him in the doorway of her office, where he remained for approximately two hours. The school board voted to demote the principal for incompetence, and she appealed to a Louisiana district court, which affirmed the board's action. The principal then appealed to the Court of Appeal of Louisiana, First Circuit.

The principal advanced several arguments supporting her position that the vote to demote her was improper. She claimed that one board member was biased against her due to political differences with her husband. She also alleged that the trial court had made evidentiary errors concerning her right to cross examine witnesses and obtain the student's medical records. The court found no merit to these arguments, finding that the overwhelming majority of the board had found in favor of demotion and that the single vote of the board member was not evidence of bias. **The principal had been afforded the due process to which she was entitled and had not been deprived of her due process rights by the presentation of tape recorded statements by adverse witnesses** at her hearing. There was no merit to her argument that she should be entitled to receive the student's medical records, as they were irrelevant to the issue of her actions. Because there was substantial evidence that the principal was incompetent, the court affirmed the decision to demote her. *Sylvester v. Cancienne*, 664 So.2d 1259 (La.App.1st Cir.1995).

C. Speech Rights and Retaliation

1. Speech Rights

◆ A district employee was promoted to the position of assistant superintendent for curriculum and program accountability in 1997. By the fall of 1998, she was reassigned to an administrative assistant position. **She asserted that she was improperly reassigned for reporting misconduct by district employees associated with the Texas Assessment of Academic Skills**. The administrator claimed that teachers "paced" students on the untimed TAAS. She alleged that the district exempted a disproportionate number of recent immigrants, special education students and "second-year sophomores" from taking the TAAS and that some teachers had advance knowledge of a TAAS writing-test prompt. The administrator filed a federal district court action against the district, board and superintendent, asserting federal civil rights violations and a claim against the district under the Texas Whistleblower Act. The court awarded summary judgment to the district, board and superintendent, and the administrator moved for reconsideration.

The court stated that in order to hold a school district liable for civil rights violations for inaction under 42 U.S.C. § 1983, a complaining party must show a policy of inaction when a decision-maker is deliberately indifferent to the risk of clear constitutional violations. **The administrator could produce no evidence of deliberate indifference by the district in her reassignment**. There could be no district liability through the superintendent because the board did not delegate final decision-making authority to him. The superintendent was entitled to qualified immunity because the administrator's allegations of testing improprieties were not protected forms of speech, since they did not involve a public interest nor did they involve a public controversy. An employee may invoke the Texas Whistleblower Act only where there is a good faith report based on a subjective and objectively reasonable belief that the reported conduct violates the law. It was not clear that the practice of pacing, by itself, violated Texas law. She had no firsthand knowledge that pacing actually took place, and her report was therefore not in good faith. The administrator also did not make a good faith report of improper coding of special education students by the district. Although the court found that the administrator made a good faith report of the disclosure of a TAAS writing prompt, it rejected the possibility that there was evidence that her report was the reason for her reassignment. **There was evidence that the superintendent reassigned her for failing to follow his orders**. Finding no evidence to support the teacher's claims, the court denied her reconsideration motion. *Rodriguez v. Board of Trustees of Laredo Indep. Sch. Dist.*, 143 F.Supp.2d 727 (S.D. Tex. 2001).

◆ A group of Arkansas special education teachers worked at a middle school that was the site of increasing tension over the needs of special education students. The teachers were openly critical of the principal. The principal allegedly instructed the teachers not to discuss incidents involving special education students. However, one of the teachers was quoted in a local newspaper, and another teacher told her she should leave the school. The other teachers engaged in an ongoing conflict with the fifth-grade teachers concerning special education, and the superintendent recruited a consultant to mediate the dispute. The consultant's efforts were unsuccessful and the staff became deeply divided. **The teachers claimed in a lawsuit that the principal** lowered their performance evaluations, **stifled their personal speech rights** and violated their right to equal protection. A federal district court summarily denied the principal's motion for immunity from suit and he appealed to the Eighth Circuit.

The circuit court held that the teachers offered no evidence that they were treated differently than other teachers and thus failed to make the threshold showing for a claim based on equal protection. In examining the First Amendment claims, the circuit court explained that a balancing-of-interests test applied, under which the teachers' interest in public speech was outweighed by the school's interest in promoting efficient public service. Although the teachers' speech about special education students involved a matter of public concern, there was undisputed evidence that it resulted in disharmony and created factions that negatively affected the efficient administration of the school. **Where a teacher's speech causes upheaval, it does not outweigh the interest of efficient school administration even if it touches on a matter of public concern**. Under these circumstances, the principal's motion for summary judgment based on qualified immunity should have been granted. The district court decision was reversed and remanded. *Fales v. Garst*, 235 F.3d 1122 (8th Cir. 2000).

◆ A teacher with over 12 years of experience teaching socially and emotionally disturbed high school students underwent "a dramatic conversion to Christianity." After being admonished against discussing religious topics in his classes, he did not abide by a cease and desist memorandum. The order instructed him not to incorporate noncurricular religious references into his classes. The special education director suspended the teacher indefinitely for violating the directive, which was later adjusted to a six-month suspension. The teacher then signed an affirmation indicating that he would adhere to the directive, but wrote a letter to the director requesting clarification. The director reassigned the teacher to a comprehensive development skills class attended by students with autism and other disabilities who had little or no communication skills. After a student's parent sent a tape of religious songs to calm his son at school, the teacher sent him a thank you note containing religious references. The teacher's supervisor advised him that the letter violated the directive, but took no disciplinary action. **The teacher responded by filing a federal district court action against the board of cooperative educational services** (BOCES), asserting violations of his speech rights and **claiming that the directive was unconstitutionally vague.** The court granted summary judgment to the BOCES and the teacher appealed to the Second Circuit.

The court found that schools have the ability to restrain teacher speech rights in view of legitimate government interests, such as avoiding litigation over possible Establishment Clause violations. In this case, the teacher's letter introduced religious content into a curricular matter. The agency could not risk giving the impression that it endorsed religion, and the directive did not infringe on the teacher's speech rights. **There was no merit to the teacher's claim that the directive was unconstitutionally vague since its basic meaning gave him fair notice of what he was not supposed to do.** The agency was not required to explain the term "instructional program" or describe every possible example of prohibited speech. The court affirmed the judgment for the board. *Marchi v. Bd. of Cooperative Educ. Services of Albany*, 173 F.3d 469 (2d Cir.1999).

◆ An untenured kindergarten teacher worked at an Illinois early childhood education center serving students with learning disabilities and behavior problems. Because of student disciplinary problems, she requested assistance more frequently than other teachers at the school and asked that certain students be removed from her classroom. **She took a medical leave when the school principal denied her request to remove a student from her class and wrote a lengthy memorandum protesting the center's management approach**, asserting that its lack of disciplinary procedures had led to the deterioration of her health. The principal did not respond to the memorandum but circulated a copy of it to the school superintendent and assigned the teacher a poor performance evaluation. The school board did not renew her employment contract for the following year.

The teacher demanded arbitration, and an arbitrator who sustained the board's action heard the case. The teacher then filed a federal district court action against the board for violation of her speech rights. The court granted summary judgment to the school board, and the teacher appealed to the U.S. Court of Appeals, Seventh Circuit, where she asserted that she had been fired for engaging in constitutionally protected speech. The court stated that **while a public school teacher's speech can be protected where it addresses both public and private matters, the decision to deliver a message in private supports an inference that it is only a private employment matter, not a matter of public concern**. The school board was entitled to insist that its staff carry out the school's educational philosophy and the court affirmed the district court judgment. *Wales v. Bd. of Educ. of Community Unit School Dist. 300*, 120 F.3d 82 (7th Cir.1997).

◆ A Massachusetts special needs teacher supervised a small therapy session attended by seventh grade male students. **During a discussion of words with multiple meanings, one student interrupted the discussion with an obscenity**. The teacher allowed the discussion to continue as the word had multiple meanings. The last ten minutes of the class were devoted to a discussion of similar words and their literal definitions. At the end of class, the teacher admonished students not to use these words and to consult an adult or dictionary if they had further questions. When a parent complained about the discussion, the school superintendent suspended the teacher for two days and refused to recommend her for reappointment. The teacher was not reappointed and did not gain tenure. She filed a lawsuit against the school committee in a Massachusetts trial court, asserting a constitutional right to academic freedom. The court granted summary judgment to the school committee and the teacher appealed to the Supreme Judicial Court of Massachusetts.

The court stated that a teacher may not be punished for exercising speech rights protected by the First Amendment and that constitutionally protected conduct must not be a motivating factor in an unfavorable employment decision. The teacher had demonstrated that she was not rehired because of the classroom discussion. **The district's resource room discipline guidelines required her to respond to difficult situations in creative ways** without sending students to the principal's office for discipline. **The evidence indicated that she had responded to the situation appropriately**. The court ruled that the teacher was entitled to be reinstated for one year of untenured service and her economic damages. The court reversed and remanded the trial court decision. *Hosford v. School Comm. of Sandwich*, 421 Mass. 708, 659 N.E.2d 1178 (1996).

◆ A Wyoming school board published **an employee conduct policy making it unethical for any staff member to criticize another staff member before third parties**. Criticisms were allowed when directed to designated school officials or the person being criticized. Continued disregard for the policy would result in disciplinary action. A special education teacher was disciplined for violating the criticism policy and she filed a lawsuit against the school district and officials in the U.S. District Court for the District of Wyoming, claiming violations of her First Amendment right to free speech. The court considered her motion for an injunction prohibiting the district from enforcing the policy. **The court found that the policy's blanket restriction on criticism had a deterrent effect on speech and failed to specify adequate guidelines**. The word "criticism" was ambiguous, having six definitions in Webster's dictionary. **The policy was void as unconstitutionally vague as well as overbroad** for restricting protected speech. The policy violated constitutional requirements for content-neutrality and was written more broadly than necessary. The teacher was entitled to an order prohibiting enforcement of the policy. *Westbrook v. Teton County School Dist. No. 1*, 918 F.Supp. 1475 (D.Wyo.1996).

2. Retaliation

◆ **Three Chicago public school teachers filed a federal district court action against the principal of their school and the city education board alleging**

retaliation and civil rights violations under 42 U.S.C. § 1983. The first teacher complained that the school failed to sufficiently comply with special education students' IEPs. The teacher met with district special education administrators, who found no evidence to support her allegations. The principal disciplined the teacher for bringing IEP documents to a meeting after she removed them from files without permission, in violation of Illinois law. The alleged retaliation was lowered evaluations and a classroom reassignment. The second teacher also criticized the principal for improper implementation of special education programs, and was then cited for chronic tardiness and conduct unbecoming a teacher. Her evaluations were poor and the principal recommended her termination. The school board instead issued her a warning. The principal assigned her an unsatisfactory performance evaluation for each year thereafter, and each year, she challenged the evaluation. A third teacher attended a school board meeting in support of the first teacher and complained to the principal about various issues. He was reprimanded for tardiness and received a one-day suspension. A federal district court conducted a trial and a jury returned a verdict for the principal and board.

The teachers appealed to the Seventh Circuit, which stated that a party seeking an award of damages in a Section 1983 case based on First Amendment violations must show that his or her conduct is entitled to constitutional protection and that this conduct was the motivating factor in the adverse employment action. **The court found ample evidence that the principal's actions had nothing to do with free speech, and would have occurred even in the absence of the complaints**. The principal had continued to rate the first teacher "superior," even after she complained. He only lowered her evaluation for the year in which she violated state law. She was one of several teachers who were moved to different classrooms due to vacancies. The principal and board acted with restraint when disciplining the second teacher, in view of her frequent tardiness and insubordination. Prior decisions of the court had held that employee insubordination toward supervisors and coworkers may justify adverse employment action, even when it coincides with otherwise protected activity. There was nothing in the record to show that the second teacher was disciplined for anything more than insubordinate conduct. The evidence also indicated that the third teacher had been disciplined in response to his severe tardiness and other substantive violations, and these reasons were not a pretext for retaliation. Because the evidence supported the jury findings, the circuit court affirmed the district court decision. *Love v. City of Chicago Board of Education*, 241 F.3d 564 (7th Cir. 2001).

◆ **A federal jury awarded an adapted physical education teacher $1 million against her school district after she complained** that it intentionally deprived students of adequate scheduling, equipment, and facilities and did not properly teach or supervise the students. She asserted that school officials retaliated against her by not renewing her contract after she complained about the treatment of special education students, including her allegations that the district discriminated against them and did not provide them with a free appropriate public education. The jury found that a pair of school administrators should each pay the teacher $50,000. *Settlegoode v. Portland Public Schools*, No. CV-00-313-ST, *verdict rendered* (D. Or. Nov. 16, 2001).

◆ During her fourth year of employment by a New York school district, a teacher was called to testify before an impartial hearing officer in IDEA proceedings. She gave testimony that supported the position advocated by a student's parent. The parent prevailed in the IDEA proceeding. Almost five years later, the district superintendent of instruction notified the teacher by letter that she would be terminated. The letter stated that the teacher had refused to turn in a grade for a student, failed to respond to repeated requests for work samples by the same student, failed to schedule an appointment with the superintendent, and cited her "record of instruction." The school district discharged the teacher several months later.

Over two years after receiving her discharge notice, and over seven years after she testified in the IDEA hearing, the teacher sued the school district in a federal district court for retaliatory discharge. **She asserted that the district discharged her because of her testimony at the hearing**, in violation of her speech rights under the First Amendment and her due process and equal protection rights under the 14th Amendment. She also advanced state law claims for defamation, intentional infliction of emotional distress, breach of contract and wrongful discharge. The court conducted a hearing on the district's motion to dismiss the teacher's amended complaint and determined that she had failed to state a claim for deprivation of her constitutional rights. It also dismissed her state law claims in conformity with federal rules. The teacher appealed to the Second Circuit, which affirmed the judgment for the same reasons given by the district court. **She failed to make out a claim for retaliation under the First Amendment or demonstrate that the district deprived her of any due process rights under the 14th Amendment**. Her claims regarding a hostile work environment were time-barred, according to the court. *Reynolds v. Bd. of Educ. of Wappingers Central School Dist.*, 208 F.3d 203 (2d Cir. 2000).

◆ An Oklahoma school administrator had been suspended and reprimanded for insubordination and not getting along with a co-worker during his service as an elementary school principal. After the suspension, he filed an EEOC claim, which he later voluntarily withdrew. He became active in unionizing district administrative employees, and was eventually reassigned to serve as an assistant high school principal. He filed a second claim with the EEOC, alleging that the reassignment was discriminatory and that a reprimand issued to him was retaliatory. A federal district court granted summary judgment to the school district and superintendent in that action. The administrator continued having difficulties and received poor performance evaluations. The principal's refusal to change an evaluation of the administrator led to a third EEOC claim. The board then voted to discharge the administrator. **The administrator filed an action in federal district court alleging his termination was retaliatory**. When the district court granted summary judgment in the board's favor, the administrator appealed to the U.S. Court of Appeals for the Tenth Circuit.

The circuit court rejected the administrator's arguments that he had been discharged for his union activities and EEOC complaints, finding no evidence that the decision to terminate his employment was based on his union activities or previous EEOC charges. Further, **there was no evidence the legitimate, nondiscriminatory reasons offered by the board for the administrator's**

discharge were a pretext for retaliation. The administrator had a history of not getting along with co-workers, and the individual who recommended his termination was also a union official. The district court decision was upheld. *Grady v. Shawnee Pub. School Dist. I-93,* 166 F.3d 347 (10th Cir.1998).

- An untenured Massachusetts teacher received a superlative evaluation during her first year. Three months later, officials attempted to serve a subpoena on her on school grounds to secure her testimony in felony child abuse charges against her live in fiancée. She then learned that she would not be rehired. She sued the town and school officials in a federal district court for violation of her constitutional right to intimate association. The town and officials moved to dismiss the action on the basis of qualified immunity. The court stated that because the rights implicated in the complaint were not clearly established, the claims against the officials in their individual capacities were properly dismissed. However, **the town might be held liable for constitutional violations if the teacher could show that town officials had made a deliberate choice not to rehire her because of her intimate association**. Because privacy rights, including the right to raise a family, cohabitate or marry, are fundamental rights implicating personal liberty, the court refused to dismiss the action against the town. *LaSota v. Town of Topsfield*, 979 F.Supp. 45 (D.Mass.1997).

- A Dallas high school math teacher alleged that his principal told him to give a student-athlete a passing grade even though the student was failing the class. After the teacher refused to change the grade, the principal allowed the student to transfer to another class. The Texas Education Agency (TEA) investigated the school, and disqualified it from the state football playoffs. The school district then transferred the teacher to a middle school, placed him on probation, froze his salary and assigned him an unsatisfactory performance rating. An administrative panel upheld the school board's decision, but the TEA reversed it. Although prevailing in the TEA action, the teacher resigned from teaching and filed a Texas district court action against the district and certain officials, including the principal. The court granted judgment to the district and officials, and the teacher appealed to the Court of Appeals of Texas, Dallas. **The court held that the teacher had no constitutional right to refuse to assign a grade to a student. This was not an example of academic freedom protected by the First Amendment**, and the court affirmed the trial court judgment. *Bates v. Dallas Indep. School Dist.*, 952 S.W.2d 543 (Tex.App.–Dallas 1997).

- An untenured special education teacher performed well during her first year of employment at a Maine middle school. However, during her second year, her class size increased from six to 18 and she had to deal with more difficult students, including some who were considered violent. **The teacher expressed her disapproval of the district's special education director at a school board meeting** which she attended at the invitation of a school board member. Within several days, the special education director presented the teacher with an unfavorable employment evaluation. The teacher complained to her union representative, who filed a grievance on her behalf. The teacher's contract was not renewed, and she filed a lawsuit against the school board in the U.S. District

Court for the District of Maine, which dismissed her claims for constitutional violations under 42 U.S.C. § 1983, the Maine Whistleblowers' Protection Act and other state laws. The teacher then appealed to the U.S. Court of Appeals for the First Circuit.

On appeal, the teacher renewed her argument that the district was prohibited from firing her based on her constitutional right to express disagreement with the special education director's policies. She claimed that her protected speech was the motivating factor in her employment nonrenewal. The court of appeals observed **a public employer that dismisses an employee based on a number of factors, including an unconstitutional one, may still escape liability by showing that the same decision would have been made in the absence of the protected conduct**. The court of appeals agreed with the district court that the teacher's contract would not have been renewed because of her inability to develop a working relationship with the special education director and other employees. The court affirmed the judgment for the school board. *Wytrwal v. Saco School Bd.*, 70 F.3d 165 (1st Cir.1995).

II. EMPLOYMENT DISCRIMINATION

State and federal anti-discrimination laws prohibit specific forms of employment discrimination. Title VII of the Civil Rights Act of 1964 is the primary federal law prohibiting discrimination on grounds including race, sex, national origin and religion. State civil rights acts are based upon Title VII, often directly incorporating its language and standards. Discrimination on the basis of disability may violate § 504 of the Rehabilitation Act, the Americans with Disabilities Act (ADA) and/or analogous state laws. Many other state and federal acts prohibit employment discrimination on the basis of other grounds, such as age.

A. Disability

The following employment discrimination cases arise under § 504, the ADA and related state laws. For § 504 and ADA cases involving students, please see Chapter Nine.

• **States are entitled to 11th Amendment immunity from employee's ADA suits seeking monetary damages**, according to a recent U.S. Supreme Court decision. **In the Supreme Court's view, Congress exceeded its authority by authorizing monetary damage awards against the states in Americans with Disabilities Act cases**. The court held that Congress did not show a history and pattern of irrational employment discrimination by the states against individuals with disabilities when it enacted the ADA. In determining whether two Alabama state employees were subjected to disability discrimination, the Supreme Court analyzed the enforcement provisions of Section 5 of the 14th Amendment, which grants Congress the power to enforce the substantive guarantees of the 14th Amendment. The Supreme Court has held previously that legislation enacted under Section 5 must demonstrate "congruence and proportionality between the injury to be prevented or remedied and the means adopted to that end." In this case, there was no such congruence and proportionality. Although Congress had identified negative attitudes and biases against individuals with disabilities as reasons for enacting the ADA, it did not identify a pattern of irrational discrimination by the states against them. The information relied on by Congress in finding that "historically, society has tended to isolate and segregate individuals with disabilities" included a handful of examples dealing with discrimination by states. The Supreme Court held that this limited evidence fell far short of showing a pattern of unconstitutional discrimination under Section 5 of the 14th Amendment. Since there was no pattern of unconstitutional behavior by the states, the ADA failed the "congruence and proportionality" test for 11th Amendment analysis. *Board of Trustees of University of Alabama v. Garrett*, 531 U.S. 356, 121 S.Ct. 955, 148 L.Ed.2d 866 (2001).

- In a 2002 case, **the U.S. Supreme Court restricted the number of individuals covered by the ADA, finding the statute only applies to persons with impairments that prevent or severely restrict them from activities that are of central importance to daily life**. When considered in light of the *Sutton* and *Murphy* decisions, below, it appears the Court has adopted a fairly narrow interpretation of the definition of disability under the ADA. The plaintiff in the case was restricted from performing certain aspects of her manufacturing position due to carpal tunnel syndrome. When the employer allegedly refused to accommodate the employee, she filed a federal ADA lawsuit. The district court awarded summary judgment to the employer, finding the employee was not disabled at the time she sought the accommodation. The Sixth Circuit reversed, finding the employee was disabled. The Supreme Court agreed to review the case to consider the proper standard for determining when an ADA claimant is substantially limited in the major life activity of performing manual tasks. The court held that the standard was met only where a person has "an impairment that prevents or severely restricts [her] from doing activities that are of central importance to most people's daily lives. The impairment's impact must also be permanent or long-term." The Supreme Court concluded the Sixth Circuit had erroneously concluded that the employee was disabled by finding that she was prevented from performing a class of manual tasks associated with some assembly line jobs, without examining other relevant evidence. That evidence included consideration for whether she could perform tasks of "central importance to most people's daily lives," such as those involved in personal hygiene. In the Court's view, the ADA's definition of disability covers individuals with disabling impairments regardless of a connection to the workplace. The court reversed and remanded the case to the Sixth Circuit for reconsideration. *Toyota Motor Manufacturing, Kentucky, Inc. v. Williams*, 534 U.S. 184, 122 S.Ct. 681, 151 L.Ed.2d 615 (2002).

- In two ADA disability discrimination cases, the U.S. Supreme Court decided that the question of whether an impairment rises to the level of "substantially limiting" should be made with reference to the mitigating measures employed. This contradicts established EEOC guidelines. In the first case, **twin sisters with uncorrected vision of 20/200 or worse but corrected vision of 20/20 or better**

were denied jobs as global airline pilots with an airline because their uncorrected vision did not meet the airline's minimum uncorrected vision standard. The sisters filed an ADA claim against the airline, which was dismissed by a federal district court. On appeal, the U.S. Court of Appeals for the Tenth Circuit affirmed.

The Supreme Court agreed with the lower court decisions, finding the sisters had not demonstrated they were disabled as defined by the ADA. **The Court concluded that mitigating measures had to be taken into account when evaluating whether an individual was disabled**, and that, because glasses or contacts corrected the sisters' vision to 20/20 or better, they were not substantially limited in a major life activity. The sisters were also not regarded as having a disability because there was no evidence that the airline perceived them to be substantially limited in a major life activity. *Sutton v. United Air Lines, Inc.*, 527 U.S. 471, 119 S.Ct. 2139, 144 L.Ed.2d 450 (1999).

In the second case, the Supreme Court held that a mechanic with high blood pressure who was fired from his job was not disabled under the ADA. **Because the mechanic was able to control his high blood pressure with medication, he was not substantially limited in a major life activity**. He was also not regarded as disabled. At most, the employer regarded the mechanic as being unable to perform the single, particular job of mechanic because it believed his high blood pressure exceeded the U.S. Department of Transportation's requirements for drivers of commercial motor vehicles. *Murphy v. United Parcel Service, Inc.*, 527 U.S. 516, 119 S.Ct. 2133, 144 L.Ed.2d 484 (1999).

- The U.S. Supreme Court ruled that an individual with tuberculosis may be considered an individual with a disability under § 504 of the Rehabilitation Act. Federal regulations published under § 504 define an individual with a disability as "any person who (i) has a physical or mental impairment which substantially limits one or more of such person's major life activities, (ii) has a record of such impairment or (iii) is regarded as having such an impairment." It defines "physical impairment" as a disorder affecting, among other things, the respiratory system and defines "major life activities" as "functions such as caring for one's self ... and working."

The case involved a Florida elementary school teacher who was discharged because of the continued recurrence of tuberculosis. The teacher sued the school board under § 504 but a U.S. district court dismissed her claims. However, the U.S. Court of Appeals, Eleventh Circuit, reversed the district court's decision and held that persons with contagious diseases fall within § 504's coverage. The school board appealed to the U.S. Supreme Court.

The Supreme Court ruled that the teacher was a person with a disability under § 504 because her tuberculosis affected the respiratory system and affected her ability to work. The school board contended that in defining an individual with a disability under § 504, the contagious effects of a disease can be distinguished from the disease's physical effects. However, the Court reasoned that the teacher's contagion and her physical impairment both resulted from tuberculosis. It would be unfair to allow an employer to distinguish between a disease's potential effect on others and its effect on the afflicted employee in order to justify discriminatory treatment. Allowing discrimination based on the contagious effects of a physical impairment would be inconsistent with the underlying purpose of § 504. **Contagion cannot remove a person from § 504 coverage**. The Supreme Court remanded the case to the district court to determine whether the teacher was "otherwise qualified" for her job and whether the school board could reasonably accommodate her as an employee. *School Bd. of Nassau County v. Arline*, 480 U.S. 273, 107 S.Ct. 1123, 94 L.Ed.2d 307 (1987).

On remand, the U.S. District Court for the Middle District of Florida held that the teacher was "otherwise qualified" to teach. The teacher posed no threat of spreading tuberculosis to her students. When she was on medication, medical tests indicated a limited number of negative cultures. Her family members tested negative and she had limited contact with students. The court ordered reinstatement or front pay in the amount of $768,724 for earnings until retirement. *Arline v. School Bd. of Nassau County*, 692 F.Supp. 1286 (M.D.Fla.1988).

◆ **A wheelchair-bound teacher with disabilities asserted in a state lawsuit that her employing district and superintendent made inadequate accommodations to enable her to continue working, and that the offered accommodations caused physical injuries and emotional distress**. The teacher also alleged the superintendent had made derogatory comments about her disability. As relief, the teacher requested compensatory and punitive damages. The district and superintendent moved to dismiss the action, asserting immunity from suit under Article 5, Section 20 of the Arkansas Constitution. The court denied the motion, ruling that school districts are not entitled to immunity under that provision of the state constitution.

The district and superintendent appealed to the Arkansas Supreme Court, which stated that when a complaint alleges an action against the state, a trial court has no jurisdiction. Even where the state is not a named party, the payment of monetary damages from the state treasury would violate constitutional principles of sovereign immunity. The court noted in previous cases that school districts are political subdivisions of the state that are not state agencies. Their functions were public in nature, and they were created for public convenience and necessity. The definition of political subdivision embraced school districts, since they operated schools in their territory, purchased and held title to real property and supervised maintenance. Unlike school districts, state agencies such as the department of education enjoyed immunity. **School districts themselves were considered creatures of the state that could not avail themselves of constitutional immunity safeguards**. State law granted immunity to political subdivisions that was not as comprehensive as that provided to state agencies under the Arkansas Constitution. This protection limited immunity to the extent political subdivisions were covered by liability insurance, prohibiting recovery for any excess over that amount. The trial court properly denied the motion to dismiss the case brought by the district and superintendent under the state constitution, and the state supreme court affirmed the trial court's decision. *Dermott Special School District v. Johnson*, 32 S.W.3d 477 (Ark. 2000).

◆ A school bus driver was employed by an Ohio school district for seven years, and then transferred to a custodial position. After **the employee was observed**

drinking beer at an elementary school while on duty, the school board recommended discharging him for drinking alcohol at work, violating workplace policy, and leaving his post. The employee was allowed to keep his job under a "last chance agreement." **The school district later rejected the employee for a part-time bus driver/garage worker position**, even though he was the most senior applicant. He filed a grievance and won the position after a binding arbitration hearing. The arbitrator found that the board did not demonstrate that the employee posed a safety threat. The board appealed to an Ohio trial court, which reversed and vacated the arbitration award. The Ohio Court of Appeals reversed and reinstated the arbitrator's award. The employee received the position, but with no back pay or other benefits.

The employee sued the board in a federal district court, asserting violations of federal and state disability discrimination laws. The district court awarded summary judgment to the board because it found that the employee had no disability, whether perceived or real. On appeal, the Sixth Circuit noted that the employee's request to be awarded the jobs was now moot. The only issue was whether he should receive compensatory and punitive damages, including back pay due to discrimination. The court found that in order prevail under the ADA, the employee was required to show that he had a disability; that he was otherwise qualified to perform the essential functions of the job; that he suffered an adverse employment action; and that he was replaced by a nondisabled person. The Sixth Circuit held that there was a distinction between taking an adverse job action for unacceptable misconduct and taking action solely because of a disability, even if the misconduct was caused by the disability. **An employer may hold an alcoholic employee to the same performance and behavior standards to which it holds other employees**. The court ruled that the ADA did not require the district to put a person guilty of drinking on the job in a bus driver position. **The ADA** did not protect the employee from his own bad judgment, and **did not compell the board to hire him as a bus driver**. There was a serious risk that the employee might drink on the job, run the risk of an accident, and potentially subject the district to liability. The court affirmed the district court judgment. *Martin v. Barnesville Exempted Village School District Board of Education*, 209 F.3d 931 (6th Cir. 2000).

◆ A visually impaired Illinois social worker applied for work at an alternative high school for students with behavior disorders. The school served students described as the toughest two percent of the student population, including those with conduct and emotional disorders who sometimes required physical restraint. **School officials determined that the applicant should have a two-day trial observation period prior** to making an employment decision. When the evaluators noticed that she failed to detect cues from students, which indicated the possibility of imminent violent behavior, the school decided not to hire her. The applicant filed a complaint against school officials with the state human rights commission, asserting discrimination on the basis of her visual disabilities. The commission found that the applicant had failed to demonstrate her ability to interpret inappropriate gestures and cues by the students and that she had never before worked with behavior disordered students. It also found that her visual impairment interfered with her ability to recognize impending aggressive situations, and that the employment decision was unrelated to her disability.

The applicant appealed to the Appellate Court of Illinois, Second District, which found that she was inexperienced with the behavior disordered population and that **her application had been denied on the basis of legitimate safety concerns. She failed to show her ability to perform the job and failed to demonstrate that she had not been hired for reasons related to her disability**. The court rejected the applicant's argument that the school had failed to offer her reasonable accommodations. An employer's duty to provide reasonable accommodations does not attach until an employee asserts the ability to perform essential job functions if afforded a reasonable accommodation. Since the applicant had presented no evidence that she had even asked for a reasonable accommodation, the court affirmed the commission's decision dismissing the complaint. *Truger v. Dept. of Human Rights*, 688 N.E.2d 1209 (Ill.App.Ct.2d Dist.1997).

◆ An Illinois elementary school custodian complained that certain staff members were trying to get rid of him. He exhibited behavior which caused the school's principal to fear for her personal safety. The principal called a meeting with the employee, a union representative and the school district's personnel director to discuss the custodian's threat against the principal to booby trap an office. The custodian brought a Bible to the meeting, interrupting the meeting with references to it. After the meeting, **the district placed the custodian on a paid leave of absence pending a psychiatric examination**. A psychiatrist diagnosed the custodian with paranoid psychotic symptoms which could predispose an individual to violent behavior. The district later allowed the custodian to return to work but placed a warning letter in his personnel file stating that insubordination, baseless accusations and threats would not be tolerated.

The custodian filed a grievance to protest the psychiatric examination and disciplinary letter. An arbitrator held that the examination was appropriate but that the letter was improper. The school district removed the letter from the custodian's file, but he filed a federal district court action against the district, asserting ADA and Title VII claims. The district moved for summary judgment. The court noted that the action was moot as to the disciplinary letter, since it had already been removed from the custodian's file. It also rejected his argument that the psychiatric examination requirement violated the ADA. **The district had shown that the examination was job-related and consistent with business necessity since there was concern for the safety of others. The ADA prohibits only medical examinations that are not job-related** and does not prohibit an employer from inquiring into an employee's ability to perform job-related functions. The Title VII claim was also baseless, since the district had never raised any issue of religious expression. The court granted the district's summary judgment motion. *Miller v. Champaign Community Unit School Dist., No. 4*, 983 F.Supp. 1201 (C.D.Ill.1997).

◆ A Colorado school psychologist was injured in a fall. Her contract was not renewed by her employer the following year. However, she was rehired as an assessment psychologist with the primary job duty of testing students. This position differed from her previous position, and she sought reinstatement as a school psychologist. **The district refused to reassign her, but offered to accommodate her work restrictions by modifying her schedule**. It scheduled a meeting to discuss further accommodations, but the psychologist refused to attend and resigned. She filed a lawsuit against the district in the U.S. District Court for the District of Colorado, alleging violations of the ADA, the Colorado workers' compensation act and Title VII of the Civil Rights Act of 1964. The court considered the district's motion for summary judgment.

The court observed that **the ADA does not require employers to provide the best accommodations possible for a disabled employee or to provide exactly the accommodations sought**. It simply prohibits discrimination on the basis of a disability. The psychologist had rejected a number of accommodations to her work schedule and continued to demand reinstatement to school psychologist, a position that was now unavailable. Because the job title she held at the time of her resignation was assessment psychologist, this was the relevant position for ADA purposes, and **the employer's attempts to accommodate her** in it **had been reasonable**. Accordingly, the district was entitled to summary judgment on the ADA claim. The district was entitled to immunity on the psychologist's retaliatory discharge claim brought under the state workers' compensation act. There was no merit to the Title VII complaint as the employee had failed to show any evidence of a connection between her reassignment and her engagement in protected activities. The court granted summary judgment to the school district. *Dyer v. Jefferson County School Dist. R-1*, 905 F.Supp. 864 (D.Colo.1995).

◆ A New York school librarian sustained serious neurological injuries in an automobile accident. She was unable to completely recover, but obtained a job several years later as a library teacher at two elementary schools. **As her probationary employment term reached a conclusion, two evaluators determined that she had difficulty controlling her library skills class and that she had improperly remained seated during class.** When she was denied tenure for these reasons, she filed suit against the school district in the U.S. District Court for the Southern District of New York, claiming that the district had violated § 504 of the Rehabilitation Act. The court granted summary judgment to the school district, and the librarian appealed to the U.S. Court of Appeals for the Second Circuit.

The court analyzed the appropriate legal framework for § 504 employment cases. A complaining party with the ability to perform the essential functions of a job with or without a reasonable accommodation is an otherwise qualified person under the Act. If an employer is aware of the party's disability, it has an affirmative obligation to make reasonable accommodations available unless they present an undue hardship to the employer, such as an excessively burdensome cost. The complaining party must demonstrate that a reasonable accommodation exists that makes employment feasible. The employer must then rebut this evidence by showing that the proposed accommodation causes undue hardship. In this case, **the librarian had presented evidence that an aide could help her control unruly students. Rehabilitation Act regulations specifically mention that aides may be used as reasonable accommodations** for employees with disabilities. The school district had failed to present any evidence concerning its budget, the cost of providing an aide or any other relevant factors indicating whether the proposed accommodation was reasonable or presented an undue hardship. Accordingly, the district court had inappropriately granted summary judgment to the school district, and the court of appeals vacated and remanded its decision. *Borkowski v. Valley Central School Dist.*, 63 F.3d 131 (2d Cir.1995).

◆ The Omaha School District employed two diabetic school van drivers. The state Department of Motor Vehicles and state Department of Education modified the licensing procedures, requiring school van drivers to undergo examinations and be certified by doctors to work under federal Department of Transportation regulations. The Department of Motor Vehicles then refused to issue licenses to either of the drivers. **The school district demoted the drivers to van aide positions, at lower pay rates**. The drivers sued the school district, Department of Motor Vehicles and Department of Education in the U.S. District Court for the District of Nebraska, claiming violations of § 504 of the Rehabilitation Act. The court granted motions to dismiss the lawsuit, and the drivers appealed to the U.S. Court of Appeals for the Eighth Circuit. The court of appeals held that the drivers had shown that their disabilities could be reasonably accommodated and that they were at low risk for hypoglycemic episodes. Because they had demonstrated a material fact issue under the Rehabilitation Act, summary judgment was inappropriate.

On remand, **the district court determined that the drivers were Type II insulin-using diabetics who had an appreciable risk of developing hypoglycemic symptoms without warning. Because this constituted a danger** to students and others using public roads, **there was no reasonable accommodation that could be offered** by the school district. Accordingly, the Rehabilitation Act afforded no protection to the drivers. The drivers appealed again to the U.S. Court of Appeals for the Eighth Circuit, which found that the district court's factual findings were not clearly erroneous. Because hypoglycemia created an increased risk of sudden and unexpected vision loss and loss of consciousness, the district court's decision that the van drivers presented a danger to themselves and others was supported by the evidence. The circuit court affirmed the district court's judgment. *Wood v. Omaha School Dist.*, 25 F.3d 667 (8th Cir.1994).

B. Title VII and Related State Laws

1. Sex Discrimination

◆ A school district employee met with two male co-workers to review psychological evaluation reports from job applicants. She alleged that during one meeting, her supervisor read from a report that one applicant had commented to a co-worker, "I hear making love to you is like making love to the Grand Canyon," and that the supervisor then said, "I don't know what that means." According to the complaining employee, the other employee responded, "Well, I'll tell you later," and then both male employees chuckled. **The employee asserted that when she complained that this incident constituted sexual harassment, she was transferred to another position in retaliation**. The transfer took place 20 months after the alleged harassment. The employee filed a federal district court action against the school district. The court awarded summary judgment to the district. The Ninth Circuit reversed, observing that the employee had a reasonable belief that the harassing incident violated Title VII and that the EEOC had issued the employee a right-to-sue letter within three months of the job transfer, making summary judgment improper.

The U.S. Supreme Court accepted the district's petition for review concerning the question of the employee's reasonable belief that a Title VII violation had occurred. It held that no reasonable person could have believed that the single incident giving rise to the lawsuit violated Title VII. Sexual harassment is actionable only if it is so severe or pervasive as to alter the conditions of the victim's employment and create an abusive working environment. According to the Supreme Court, **simple teasing, offhand comments and isolated incidents that are not extremely serious will not amount to discriminatory changes in the terms and conditions of employment**. In this case, the employee's job required that she review the offensive statement. She conceded that it did not upset her to read the written remark in the applicant's file. Significantly, the supervisor's comment and the male employee's response was at worst "an isolated incident" that could not remotely be considered serious under recent Supreme Court precedents. The high court found "no causality at all" between the job transfer proposed by the school district and the employee's complaint. It noted that there must be a very close proximity in time between an employer's knowledge of an employee's protected conduct and an adverse employment action if this is the employee's only evidence of retaliation. The court reversed the Ninth Circuit's judgment, in effect reinstating the district court's summary judgment order for the school district. *Clark County School District v. Breeden*, 532 U.S. 268, 121 S.Ct. 1508, 149 L.Ed.2d 509 (2001).

◆ A 55-year-old New York state special education school employee claimed that her supervisor made sexual remarks and derogatory comments about her age. She was fired by the school and filed a lawsuit against the supervisor and school in the U.S. District Court for the Southern District of New York, claiming violations of Title VII of the Civil Rights Act of 1964 and the Age Discrimination in Employment Act. She also alleged violations of New York law, asserting that her supervisor had sexually harassed her and discriminated against her. The court considered the supervisor's dismissal motions. It observed that the statutory language of Title VII and the ADEA provided that a supervisor could not be sued in an individual capacity under those federal acts. This was because only entities with 15 or more employees are subject to Title VII and ADEA liability. However, New York's highest court has determined that a supervisor discriminating on the basis of age or sex may be held subject to liability under the state Human Rights Law. This depends upon the supervisor's ownership interest in the employing entity or the ability to hire or fire the complaining party. **Because the employee alleged that the supervisor had participated in the creation of a hostile work environment by his remarks, the state human rights claims could not be dismissed prior to a trial**. *Storr v. Anderson School*, 919 F.Supp. 144 (S.D.N.Y.1996).

◆ A mentally disabled custodian with a mild personality disorder and epilepsy worked for a Pennsylvania school district for eight years without difficulty. He was then subjected to physical and sexual harassment by two male coworkers and endured severe harassment for several months. He finally complained to his supervisor and quit the next day. The custodian filed a sexual harassment complaint with state and federal human rights agencies, and then filed a Title VII complaint against the district in a federal district court. **The court held that a same-sex harassment claim was possible under Title VII, but required a showing that the harassment was based on the victim's sex**. The harassment in this case had resulted from the custodian's vulnerability, not his sex, and there was no evidence any of the parties were homosexual. The custodian had failed to complain to a supervisor until the day before he quit. Because an employer cannot be liable for harassment of which it has no knowledge, the district was entitled to summary judgment. *Ward v. Ridley School Dist.*, 940 F.Supp. 810 (E.D.Pa.1996).

2. Race Discrimination and Affirmative Action

◆ State law prohibited the California Commission for Teacher Preparation and Licensing from issuing credentials, permits or certificates to applicants who were unable to demonstrate reading, writing and mathematics skills in English. CTPL used a basic skills proficiency test, the California Basic Education Skills Test to make this assessment. **Groups representing minority educators asserted that they historically failed the test at a higher rate than Caucasians, and that the test had a disproportionately adverse impact on minorities** that violated Titles VI and VII. A federal district court awarded summary judgment to the state. The educators appealed to a three-judge panel of the Ninth Circuit, which held that Title VI was inapplicable to the state commission's administration of the test, since it received no federal funds. The Title VII claim had also been properly dismissed, according to the panel, since the test was a properly validated licensing exam that was exempt from liability. The panel withdrew its decision when a majority of the judges of the Ninth Circuit voted to rehear the case *en banc*.

The full Ninth Circuit observed that Title VII may apply to an entity that is not the complaining party's "direct employer" if it interferes with the party's employment opportunities with another employer. The level of control exerted over local school districts by the state of California was particularly strong and extended to day-to-day local operations. Districts were considered state agencies in other legal contexts, so that the state was in a practical position to "interfere with" local employment decisions. This brought the state within the reach of Title VII, as determined by the district court. Because a decision on the Title VI question was unnecessary to resolve the case, the court did not determine whether it applied in this case. Under a test first described by the U.S. Supreme Court in *Albemarle Paper Co. v. Moody*, 422 U.S. 405 (1975), discriminatory employment tests are held unlawful unless they are proven to be predictive or significantly correlated with important elements of work behavior that comprise or are relevant to the job for which applicants are being tested. The complaining parties successfully showed that the CBEST requirement had a disparate impact upon minority applicants. However, the circuit court concluded that the district court correctly held that **the test was properly validated in that it had a manifest relationship to school employment. It adequately identified specific job duties to which the CBEST could be correlated and established a minimum level of competence in three areas of basic education skills**. Validation studies adequately considered the specific positions for which the test was required and the skills measured by it were important elements of work behavior for employment in public schools. The state did not set passing scores at an impermissible level. For these reasons, the circuit court concluded the CBEST requirement did not violate Title VII. *Association of Mexican-American Educators v. State of California*, 231 F.3d 572 (9th Cir. 2000).

◆ The University of Nevada used an unwritten affirmative action policy to achieve balance in the faculty's racial composition. A white female instructor was hired at a substantially lower wage than that paid to an African-American male hired for a similar job. She sued the state university system in a Nevada district court for violation of the Equal Pay Act and Title VII. The court conducted a trial and denied the system's post-trial motion to set aside a $40,000 jury award. The university system appealed to the Supreme Court of Nevada, which observed the tension between affirmative action goals and Title VII's prohibition on employment discrimination. **The affirmative action plan did not violate Title VII because it included nonracial criteria such as educational background, publishing history, and work experience.** The plan did not violate the Equal Pay Act because there was a legitimate business reason for the wage disparity between the two employees. The court reversed the district court judgment. *Univ. and Community College System of Nevada v. Farmer*, 930 P.2d 730 (Nev.1997).

III. LABOR RELATIONS

Collective bargaining agreements between local education agencies and their employees are contracts that are subject to interpretation under a state education code as well as a state labor code. Since collective bargaining agreements typically refer employment disputes to an arbitrator, the jurisdiction of the courts to consider disputes arising under collective bargaining agreements is usually limited to the consideration of major issues, most frequently those arising under the category of unfair labor practices.

A. State Law Conflicts

◆ Ohio public university regents can set standards for faculty instructional workloads in order to emphasize undergraduate instruction, according to a U.S. Supreme Court decision. **The law required state universities to adopt faculty workload policies and made them an inappropriate subject for collective bargaining.** Any university policy prevailed over the contrary provisions of collective bargaining agreements. One university adopted a workload policy pursuant to the law and notified the collective bargaining agent of its professors that it would not bargain over the policy.

The professors' union filed a state court action, seeking an order that the law violated public employee equal protection rights. The Supreme Court of Ohio struck down the law and the U.S. Supreme Court accepted the university's appeal. It held that Ohio could reasonably conclude that the policy would be undercut if it were subjected to collective bargaining. **The state legislature could**

properly conclude that collective bargaining would interfere with the legitimate goal of achieving uniformity in faculty workloads, and the Court reversed and remanded the case. *Central State University v. American Assn. of Univ. Professors, Central State Univ. Chapter*, 526 U.S. 124, 143 L.Ed.2d 227, 119 S.Ct. 1162 (1999).

On remand, the Supreme Court of Ohio concluded that the statute did not violate either the Equal Protection Clause of the Ohio constitution, or the provision of the state constitution authorizing the legislature to pass laws regarding certain employment matters. *American Assn. of Univ. Professors, Central State Univ. Chapter v. Central State University,* 87 Ohio St. 3d 55, 717 N.E.2d 286 (Ohio 1999).

♦ **A school nurse filed a grievance against the school committee after a principal ordered her to administer medication to a special education student**. Her collective bargaining association argued that any increase in her workload was not covered by the collective bargaining agreement and that the nonemergency medication of special education students attending the collaborative program located at the school was not permitted. According to the association, the matter had to be negotiated by the parties and the collaborative program was not a party to the agreement. An arbitrator held that a school administrator could not order the nurse to dispense medication to a student who was not a member of the regular student body. A Rhode Island superior court confirmed the arbitrator's decision, and the school committee appealed.

The Rhode Island Supreme Court observed that an arbitrator exceeds his or her powers by resolving a non-arbitrable dispute or by making an award that does not draw its essence from the agreement, is not based on a plausible interpretation of the contract, manifestly disregards a contractual provision or reaches an irrational result. The school district had a non-delegable managerial duty to provide health services to students attending the collaborative education program. The arbitrator was powerless to address the issue because a ruling against the district would cause a violation of state law. The district was bound by state law to operate a school health program and to provide special education programs. These duties were non-delegable and could not be bargained away in a CBA. State law and regulations stated that special education students in the collaborative program were within the public school system and entitled to receive health services. There was no collective bargaining provision limiting the provision of services to students within the exclusive control of the school district. **The principal acted according to law when he ordered the nurse to provide medication to the student.** The arbitration award contradicted a collective bargaining agreement provision stating that the parties maintained the common goal of providing public education to all children. The court vacated and remanded the award. *Woonsocket Teachers' Guild, Local 951, AFT v. Woonsocket School Comm.*, 770 A.2d 834 (R.I. 2001).

♦ A school district subcontracted its printing services to a Board of Cooperative Education Services (BOCES) district with the consent of its only printing employee, who continued performing his duties in the same shop. **The employee association filed an improper practice charge with the state Public Employment**

Relations Board (PERB), **claiming the printing services could not be subcontracted out without first submitting the matter to collective bargaining**. An administrative law judge held that the district's actions constituted an improper practice and that printing services were not covered by New York Education Law § 1950(4)(d) nor exempt from the law's mandatory collective bargaining requirement. On appeal, the PERB reversed and dismissed the improper practice charge. A New York trial court affirmed, but an appellate division court reversed.

The court of appeals first determined that printing was a service falling within the scope of § 1950(4)(d). That section of the law gave BOCES districts the authority to provide certain services to other districts on a cooperative basis. Because printing was not within the statutory list of prohibited services, and was the type of service that promoted the policy behind the BOCES statute, the court said it was a service that the education commissioner could approve on a cooperative basis through BOCES districts. The court then analyzed whether the statute permitted school districts to subcontract printing services without first submitting the issue to collective bargaining. While the BOCES statute did not refer to collective bargaining, it was apparent from the statute's strict timetable that schools needed to plan for the provision of services no later than Feb. 1 for programs beginning in September. Section 1950(4)(d) did not include job protection provisions for public employees whose jobs were transferred to BOCES districts under shared services contracts. **The broad state law recognition that BOCES program takeovers were to be considered transfers implied that an action taken pursuant to § 1950(4)(d) was not subject to collective bargaining**. Accordingly, the court held that the school district's decision to subcontract its printing services to the BOCES district was not subject to mandatory collective bargaining. *In the Matter of Vestal Employees Assn., NEA/NY v. Public Employment Relations Bd. of State of New York*, 94 N.Y.2d 409 (N.Y. 2000).

- An Ohio school board employed a tutor to instruct students with learning disabilities. It paid her at a specified hourly rate for five hours per day. The following school year, her workload was reduced to two hours per day, and she refused to accept additional work instructing homebound students. The board gave the tutor an unsatisfactory performance evaluation and advised her that she would not be reemployed the following year. The tutor filed a lawsuit against the school board in an Ohio trial court, claiming the right to compensation at the rate specified by state law, and seeking an order that the reduction in hours was an illegal wage decrease. The court granted summary judgment to the school board, and the tutor appealed to the Supreme Court of Ohio. The court stated that under Ohio law, **the terms of a collective bargaining agreement supersede the general provisions of state law. Because the tutor was bound by the terms of a collective bargaining agreement, she was not entitled to the higher statutory rate**. She was not salaried, and the reduction in hours did not violate state law. *State ex rel. Burch v. Sheffield-Sheffield Lake City Sch. Dist. Bd. of Educ.*, 661 N.E.2d 1086 (Ohio 1996).

- A Pennsylvania school district and the education association representing its teachers were unable to reach a new agreement upon the expiration of their collective bargaining agreement. After six months, the association called a two-day strike that ended with an agreement to extend the terms of the expired agreement. As the school year reached its end, the association called a second strike because of continuing unsuccessful negotiations. **The strike jeopardized the district's ability to provide 180 days of instruction per year as required by the state public school code**. The state secretary of education filed a complaint against the association in a Pennsylvania county court for a preliminary order to compel a return to work because the district had provided only 163 days of instruction for the year. The court granted the request and ordered the association and school board to engage in court-monitored bargaining. The district and board appealed to the Commonwealth Court of Pennsylvania, which ruled that the trial court had no authority to order the parties to bargain. The secretary appealed to the Supreme Court of Pennsylvania. On appeal, the board and district argued that the state Public Employee Relations Act did not grant state courts the authority to order negotiations between parties to collective bargaining agreements. **The court ruled that the Public Employee Relations Act must be read in conjunction with the state public school code, which empowers the secretary of education to compel a return to work in order to provide at least 180 days of instruction annually**. Because the trial court had correctly construed the statutes together in ordering the parties to resume bargaining, its order was affirmed. *Carroll v. Ringgold Educ. Assn.*, 680 A.2d 1137 (Pa.1996).

B. Unfair Labor Practices

◆ A school district declared an impasse after bargaining with the district's education association. Pursuant to the rules of impasse, **the district** implemented its "last best offer," which **called for replacing the reduction in force and recall policy from the previously negotiated agreement in favor of a non-negotiated board policy**. The education association filed an unfair labor practices complaint against the district with the South Dakota Department of Labor, which held that the unilateral modification of the policy was an unfair labor practice. A state circuit court affirmed the decision, and the district appealed to the South Dakota Supreme Court.

The court explained that under state law, a negotiable item for public employees is one that must relate to rates of pay, wages, hours of employment and other conditions of employment. A subject is negotiable only if it "intimately and directly affects the work and welfare of public employees," and is a matter on which negotiated agreement would not significantly interfere with the exercise of the employer's inherent management prerogatives. On the other hand, an item is not negotiable if it has been preempted by a statute or regulation. In this case, the reduction in force and recall policy intimately and directly affected the work and welfare of teachers working under the collective bargaining agreement. There was no state law or regulation preempting the policy and there was no statutory basis for preempting the policy from negotiation. Finally, the court found that negotiation of the policy did not significantly interfere with the exercise of the district's inherent management prerogatives. In reaching this conclusion, **the court distinguished between a public employer's substantive decision to transfer or assign employees, which came within the employer's managerial discretion, and procedural processes to be followed after making a**

decision, which were mandatory subjects of negotiation. Because the policy in this case involved only procedures, the court affirmed the judgment in favor of the association. *Webster Education Association v. Webster School District*, 631 N.W.2d 202 (S.D. 2001).

◆ The University of Alaska adopted a non-smoking policy applicable to all university facilities and motor vehicles. Prior to the adoption of the policy, a union representing certain university employees requested bargaining. One union member continued to smoke in a vehicle assigned to him and was censured. He circulated a petition asking the union to negotiate the policy. The university refused to bargain, but the parties reached a collective bargaining agreement without any reference to the non-smoking policy. The union filed an unfair labor practice complaint against the university, asserting that the policy was a mandatory subject of bargaining. The Supreme Court of Alaska observed that **because the collective bargaining agreement contained no reference to the non-smoking policy, the union had contractually waived its right to bargain the issue by agreeing to the contract**. The union could also be deemed to have waived its right to bargain under the management rights section of the agreement. *Univ. of Alaska v. Univ. of Alaska Classified Employees Assn.*, 952 P.2d 1182 (Alaska 1998).

◆ A Wisconsin school district established a pilot program to increase the promotion rate among ninth graders in its schools. Each teacher in the program was directed to call the parents of participating students. However, the teachers' association advised the school that the calling would create a burden upon teachers that could not be unilaterally imposed. It filed a prohibited practice complaint with the state employment relations commission, asserting that the district had a duty to bargain over the subject. The commission dismissed the complaint, finding that the calling had no impact on teacher wages, hours or employment conditions. A Wisconsin trial court affirmed the decision, and the teachers' association appealed to the Court of Appeals of Wisconsin. The court agreed with the commission that **telephoning parents is fairly within the scope of a teacher's regular job duties. It required only five to six hours during the first two weeks of school and did not adversely affect teacher wages, hours or working conditions**. The telephone contact was expected of teachers and did not represent a new duty for them. The court affirmed the judgment in favor of the school district. *Madison Teachers, Inc. v. Wisconsin Employment Relations Commission*, 580 N.W.2d 375 (Wis.Ct.App.1998).

◆ A New Jersey school board adopted a 186-day school calendar providing for three additional makeup days for school closings due to weather emergencies. Because of severe weather, schools in the district were closed for 12 days during the school year and the school superintendent proposed eliminating several school holidays including the spring break, with additional make-up days to be added to the end of the school year. Although he notified parents and employees of the proposed changes, he presented the changes to the school board without consulting the employees' labor organization. **After the board unilaterally adopted a revised calendar, the employees' association filed an unfair labor**

practices complaint against the board, alleging that the changes affected terms and conditions of employment that could not be unilaterally changed by the board. A hearing officer dismissed the complaint and the state public employment relations commission declined to review it.

The association appealed to the Superior Court of New Jersey, Appellate Division. The court noted that the establishment of a school calendar is a traditional management decision that is not a term or condition of employment. However, even non-negotiable management decisions may have an effect on terms and conditions of employment that are negotiable. **The court stated that a case-by-case analysis must be applied to non-negotiable management decisions to determine whether negotiating their impact upon employees would significantly or substantially encroach upon a management prerogative.** Because the hearing officer had not conducted such an analysis in this case, the court reversed and remanded the case to the employment relations commission. *Piscataway Township Educ. Ass'n v. Piscataway Township Bd. of Educ.*, 307 N.J.Super. 263, 704 A.2d 981 (N.J.Super.Ct.App.Div.1998).

◆ The collective bargaining agreement between a New Hampshire education board and the union representing its custodians expired. The agreement generally provided for full-time employment for represented employees at a stated wage. During negotiations for a new contract, the board announced a reorganization under which full-time custodians would be laid off and replaced by part-time employees working for $2 per hour less with no benefits. **The union filed an unfair labor practice charge against the board, asserting that the layoff and hiring of part-time employees was a unilateral change in the conditions of employment** in violation of the collective bargaining agreement. The state Public Employee Labor Relations Board (PELRB) ordered the board to pay part-time custodians at the contractual hourly rate with prorated benefits. The board appealed to the Supreme Court of New Hampshire, which found that **the reorganization was a mandatory subject of collective bargaining**. The reorganization was not reserved to the board's exclusive managerial authority, affected terms and conditions of employment and did not involve governmental functions. The court affirmed the PELRB's order. *Appeal of City Nashua Bd. of Educ.*, 695 A.2d 647 (N.H.1997).

◆ An Illinois cooperative special education district provided special education services for 37 member school districts. The special district independently hired its own teachers under a collective bargaining agreement that was separate from those between its member districts and their employees. **The collective bargaining agreement between the special district and its employees provided that if a member district took back any special education programs from the special district, the member district had to notify the special district of new positions** created by the action so that the special district could advertise the job openings to tenured special district employees. One member district took back certain special education programs that had been previously delegated to the special district but failed to advise the special district of three teaching vacancies created by the action. The union representing employees in the special district filed a grievance pursuant to their collective bargaining agreement and submitted the matter for arbitration. The Illinois Educational Labor Relations Board rejected the special district union's unfair labor practice charge, and the union appealed to the Appellate Court of Illinois, First District. The court affirmed the board's order, finding that **the special district had no authority to bind member districts to the collective bargaining agreement between the special district and its employees.** It agreed with the member district that such an interpretation would violate the member district's collective bargaining agreement with its own employees, noting that no special district teacher had lost employment due to the take back action. *SEDOL Teachers Union v. IELRB,* 668 N.E.2d 1117 (Ill.App.Ct.1st Dist.1996).

IV. TENURE AND DUE PROCESS

State tenure laws protect qualified school employees by establishing minimum procedural protections for adverse employment actions proposed by an education agency. These protections, in conjunction with existing contract rights and constitutional rights to notice and an opportunity to be heard, are referred to as due process rights.

A. Tenure and Due Process Rights

◆ A Pennsylvania state university police officer was charged with felony counts related to marijuana possession. State police notified the university about the charges, and **the university immediately suspended the officer without pay** pursuant to a state executive order requiring such action where a state employee is formally charged with a felony. University officials demoted the officer but did not inform him that they had obtained his confession from police records. He filed a federal district court action against university officials contesting his suspension without pay. The court granted summary judgment to the officials, but the U.S. Court of Appeals for the Third Circuit reversed and remanded the case. The U.S. Supreme Court agreed to hear the case, and **held that the university did not have to suspend the officer with pay pending a hearing**. The criminal complaint established an independent basis for believing that he had committed a felony, and the suspension did not violate his due process rights. The Court reversed and remanded the case. *Gilbert v. Homar*, 520 U.S. 924, 117 S.Ct. 1807, 138 L.Ed.2d 120 (1997).

◆ A principal's first-year evaluation expressed concerns and she received a preliminary notice of contract nonrenewal the next year. At the hearing she requested, the board renewed her contract. At the start of the principal's third year, a district administrator developed a formal assistance plan for her. During the same school year, a group of five or six students violently and aggressively assaulted a student. When the principal called law enforcement and suspended the students, parents of the disciplined students began to actively denounce her. The district administrator initially voiced support for the principal, and he recommended renewal of her contract. When a complaining parent reported that the closed board vote renewing the principal's contract violated the state open-meetings law, the board rescinded its action and held a second meeting. By the time the board met again, it was bound by state law to renew the contract. However, all district employees were notified that the board had revised the principal's title and job description. Subsequently, **the principal resigned, stating that the removal of her main job duties amounted to constructive discharge**.

She sued the school district, school board, and district administrator in federal district court, asserting violation of an asserted constitutional property right in continued employment duties, constructive discharge, and violation of her liberty interest in her reputation. The court awarded summary judgment to the board and administrator, and the principal appealed to the Seventh Circuit, which noted that a constitutional property right in employment arises from state laws and contractual relationships, not the Constitution. Wisconsin law provided that a principal must perform administrative and leadership responsibilities and receive preliminary notices of non-renewal. The law and the principal's contract did not encompass any right to perform particular job duties. The district did not transfer the principal and she retained her title and salary. **Her expectation of retaining certain job duties did not create a protectable property interest**. According to the court, the principal had no constitutionally protected claims against the board, district or administrator. Her constructive-discharge claim failed because she had abruptly resigned and had declined the opportunity to participate in the creation of her new job duties. There was no violation of her liberty interest in reputation because **a charge of mismanagement or incompetence does not rise to a constitutionally protected level**. The court affirmed the district court's judgment. *Ulichny v. Merton Community School Dist.*, 249 F.3d 686 (7th Cir. 2001).

◆ A long-term probationary teacher was identified as being present while a cheat sheet was prepared to improve student performance on citywide reading and math tests. The school district reassigned her to nonteaching duties in another school. The teacher denied the allegations against her at a disciplinary hearing, but the district held that she had violated school policies. The district placed a strong letter of reprimand in her employment file and instructed her principal to assign her an unsatisfactory performance evaluation. The teacher filed a notice of claim against the city, special commissioner and two investigators for defamation and violation of her civil rights. The commissioner issued a supplemental report accusing her of helping students cheat during testing, pressuring other teachers to do the same, and assaulting another teacher. The district provided the teacher a second hearing at which the district affirmed its earlier findings and **the superintendent of schools denied her certification of probation, disqualifying her from district employment**.

The teacher sued the district, superintendent, school board and board chancellor in a federal district court for violating her due process rights and terminating her employment in retaliation for filing a notice of claim. The board moved to dismiss the complaint, asserting that she was a probationary employee with no constitutionally protected due process rights. The court held that a civil rights plaintiff attempting to show a due process violation must identify a protected interest and a deprivation of that interest without the provision of the constitutional minimum procedures. **When state law defines an employment position as probationary, the employee lacks a legal claim of entitlement and has no property interest in continued employment**. Unlike permanent employees, probationary employees have no property rights in their position and may be lawfully discharged without a hearing. This was true even though the teacher had worked for the district for ten years. Although the district's accusations impugned the teacher's honesty, touching on her constitutional liberty interest in reputation, she had an adequate state remedy to redress these allegations. Because state law provided for a hearing and redress that was adequate to meet due process requirements, there was no federal constitutional violation. The court dismissed the teacher's constitutional claims, but allowed her 30 days to come forward with sufficient facts to avoid dismissal of her retaliation claim. *Rivera v. Community School Dist. Nine*, 145 F.Supp.2d 302 (S.D.N.Y. 2001).

◆ Two Kentucky special education teachers were assigned to a school that had some of the lowest scores in the state on student tests, tense relations among faculty and the administration, and significant problems with student discipline. Six staff members, including **the special education teachers**, who had opposed a recommended school improvement plan, **received notices on the last day of school that they would be transferred for "good cause and extenuating circumstances"** pursuant to the collective bargaining agreement. Neither teacher received an opportunity for a hearing, and they sued the superintendent in a federal district court, asserting that they had been transferred based on the exercise of their speech rights. Days before school resumed, the court held that the superintendent had not violated the First Amendment rights of the teachers when deciding to transfer them, but had deprived them of their due process rights. The morning before school resumed, the superintendent provided the teachers with written notices of the transfers, listing the reasons for them, and scheduling hearings for a few hours later that same day. The transfers were upheld and the teachers appealed.

The Sixth Circuit observed that the teachers had clearly spoken on matters of public concern. According to the court, due process is a flexible principal in which its requirements depend on the facts of each case and its essential requirements are notice and an opportunity to respond. The district court had correctly ruled that **the teachers received all the process to which they were due**. Although they received little time to prepare for their hearings, their attorneys had advised the district court that they were prepared to be heard. There was an urgency for immediate hearings, since school was to start the following day, and the teachers could still file grievances against the board under the collective bargaining agreement. The court affirmed the judgment. *Leary v. Daeschner*, 228 F.3d 729 (6th Cir. 2000).

◆ A New York special education teacher was assigned to teach, for one year, a regular education class in which six learning disabled students were mainstreamed. The following year, the same class was assigned to a regular education teacher who had a probationary appointment in the elementary tenure area. Two years later, **the school district abolished four elementary education positions and**

determined that the special education teacher had more seniority in the elementary tenure area than did the regular education teacher. It did not renew the regular education teacher's position and she filed a state court action against the school board. The court held that the special education teacher had more seniority in the elementary tenure area than the regular education teacher. She was thus entitled to seniority credit for the year she had served as a regular education teacher, even though the district had not expressly notified her that this assignment was outside her initial special education tenure area appointment as required by New York education regulations.

The trial court dismissed the case and the New York Supreme Court, Appellate Division, affirmed the judgment. The regular education teacher appealed to the Court of Appeals of New York, which stated that **the regulation protected teacher tenure and should not be applied to prevent the special education teacher from receiving seniority credit to which she was entitled**. Although the regular education teacher's argument was technically correct, a teacher assigned out of a tenure area could waive entitlement to the statutory notice and consent if enforcement of these requirements would work to the teacher's detriment. The special education teacher was entitled to receive her elementary tenure area credit even though some of her students had learning disabilities, and the court affirmed the lower court judgment for the school board. *Kaufman v. Fallsburg Central School Dist. Bd. of Educ.*, 91 N.Y.2d 57, 666 N.Y.S.2d 1000, 689 N.E.2d 894 (1997).

◆ New York Education Law requires teachers to serve a three-year probationary period to obtain tenure. The law allows regular substitutes to earn credit toward tenure, but does not define "regular substitute." A teacher served as a substitute for two terms. Although she later received a probationary special education teaching position, her employer decided not to renew her position just prior to the expiration of the three-year probationary term. The substitute filed an action in a New York trial court to annul the agency's decision. The court granted her petition and reinstated her, but the New York Supreme Court, Appellate Division, reversed the trial court decision. The teacher appealed to the Court of Appeals of New York, which held that **a substitute teacher is entitled to earn credit for continuously performing the duties of a regular substitute for at least one term. This is without regard to whether the employer designates the substitute as a regular or per diem substitute**. The court reinstated the trial court judgment. *Speichler v. Bd. of Cooperative Educ. Services*, 90 N.Y.2d 110, 659 N.Y.S.2d 199, 681 N.E.2d 366 (1997).

B. Seniority and Reductions in Force

◆ A South Dakota school district and its teachers association negotiated a collective bargaining agreement that set out mandatory procedures for reductions in force. If normal attrition did not succeed in reducing the workforce, teachers with less than full certification would be released first, followed by those without continuing contract status, then those with continuing contract status, according to "length of service." **The board voted for a workforce reduction because of budgetary constraints, and notified a teacher and a teacher/coach that they**

were subject to release. The teacher/coach had three years of continuous service to the district, but the other teacher had more than five years of overall service. She had worked as a substitute, taught summer school and worked as a full-time contract teacher. The board determined that because the teacher/coach would reach continuing contract status first, he had seniority over the teacher. The teacher appealed to the school board, which upheld the decision to release her. The state labor department held that the collective bargaining agreement was binding on the district. The reduction-in-force policy measured seniority by "length of service," not "continuous service." Because the teacher's overall service was greater, the board should have retained her.

A state trial court affirmed the department's decision, and the district appealed to the South Dakota Supreme Court. The court rejected the district's argument that a state law governing teacher termination allowed the non-renewal of an untenured teacher's contract. The teacher's case was governed by the collective bargaining agreement, not the contract renewal statute. By acting under the agreement, the district had to abide by its terms and could not add words that the parties left out of it.

The agreement enumerated the specific protocol for implementing a reduction in force, using a principle of seniority measured by length of service within the school system. The board was not permitted to insert or delete contract language to make it mean more than its plain words. The contract included no language such as "continuous" or "uninterrupted" to define length of service. Since the teacher should have been retained under the plain language of the agreement, the court affirmed the department's decision to reinstate her. *Gettysburg School District 53-1 v. Larson*, 631 N.W.2d 196 (S.D. 2001).

◆ In order to fund an alternative learning center, **a Kentucky school board reduced extended employment days for 46 of its 600 certified employees** based on a "budget allocation." Several of the teachers sued the school board in a Kentucky circuit court for violations of state law. The court held that the reduction in extended employment days had been accomplished according to a uniform plan in compliance with state law, and that there had been no violation of the state open meetings law. The teachers appealed to the state court of appeals, which stated that Ky. Rev. Stat. § 161.760 provided that teacher salaries shall not be lowered unless the reduction is part of a uniform plan affecting all teachers in the entire district, and there is a reduction in responsibilities. The reduction in extended employment days was a reduction of responsibilities under the law. The court noted that the board's records indicated that the plan included only 46 of 600 certified employees and that specific teachers were targeted for reductions. **While a school board was permitted to adjust its budget to meet district needs, the legislature had provided that there be uniformity when making such adjustments so that no teacher or class of teachers was "sacrificed."** All teachers were to be encompassed in such a plan, even though not all were affected by the implementation of the plan in order to prevent arbitrary salary reductions of a targeted class. Because the circuit court did not reach the issue of whether the teachers had received a reduction in responsibility or proper notice as required by the law, the court remanded the case for further proceedings. *Pigue v. Christian County Board of Education*, 65 S.W.3d 540 (Ky. Ct. App. 2001).

- New Jersey law provides for jointure commissions, through which two or more local boards may jointly provide educational services to students with disabilities upon approval by state education officials. After the board eliminated a tenured teacher/guidance counselor's position, it contracted with a jointure commission board of education to obtain guidance services. Some of the services were provided to students with no disabilities. **The teacher filed a complaint with the state education commissioner, asserting that the district violated her tenure and seniority rights by eliminating her position** and contracting with the jointure commission to replace her services. An administrative judge held that the employment action was permissible, but that the contract requiring the provision of guidance services to students without disabilities was unlawful. The state education board agreed, finding that the legislature intended to provide for the education and training of students with disabilities when it created the jointure commission law.

The New Jersey Superior Court, Appellate Division, held that the state board's interpretation of the law was correct; the legislature clearly stated that the purpose of jointure commissions was to provide educational and training services to students with disabilities. There was no merit to the school district's argument that the jointure commission law had a secondary purpose of providing local boards with flexibility in order to promote efficient financial operations. This was evident when the jointure commission law was compared with other legislation providing for pooled services and facilities or programs that made no distinction between students with disabilities and regular education students. The powers described in the jointure commission law were narrowly defined and applied only to special needs students. The court affirmed the decision of the state education board. *Colantoni v. Board of Education of Township of Long Hill*, 748 A.2d 630 (N.J. Super. Ct. App. Div. 2000).

- An Oklahoma school superintendent advised his school board that the district should eliminate four teaching positions in order to reduce the annual budget. The board eliminated a driver education position occupied by a tenured teacher with 19 years of experience. The district retained some nontenured, probationary teachers who instructed classes in academic areas in which the tenured teacher was also certified to teach. He filed a lawsuit against the school district in an Oklahoma district court, claiming breach of employment contract. The court granted summary judgment to the school district, and the Court of Appeals of Oklahoma affirmed. The teacher appealed to the Supreme Court of Oklahoma. The court stated that school boards were allowed to exercise discretion when making necessary reductions in force but were required to conform their actions to the state tenure act. **Although boards were allowed to make necessary economic adjustments, they were required to retain tenured teachers before rehiring nontenured or probationary teachers pursuant to any reduction in force.** Because the tenured teacher presented evidence that he was certified to teach in other areas and also showed that the school district could have accommodated him through minimal efforts, the summary judgment order had been improper and the case was reversed and remanded. *Barton v. Indep. School Dist. No. I-99, Custer County*, 914 P.2d 1041 (Okla.1996).

◆ A West Virginia special education school devoted itself primarily to mentally retarded students. Federal law required the school district that operated the school to provide certain seriously disabled students with education and related services beyond the normal 180-day school year to prevent educational regressions during summer vacation. The school could not charge tuition or fees for this summer session. The school's principal posted the job vacancies for the special education summer program, and then conducted interviews with the applicants. **The principal's decision on whom to hire focused on the applicants' relationship with the students, giving preference to those who had existing relationships** with the students. An applicant who was not hired brought a grievance, claiming that his seniority required the principal to hire him. A hearing examiner ordered the board of education to pay the teacher back wages and benefits. A West Virginia trial court reversed, holding the examiner's decision to be contrary to the law. The teacher appealed to the Supreme Court of Appeals of West Virginia.

On appeal, the teacher argued that West Virginia law on summer schools mandated that the more experienced teacher be hired. The supreme court disagreed. **The court stated that the special education summer session was not a traditional summer school and was not governed by the normal hiring mandates** of West Virginia law. IDEA hiring requirements for special education summer programs are governed by West Virginia law. Under that law, vacant teaching positions are filled according to the applicants' qualifications. Seniority is only considered for otherwise equal applicants. **The principal had made a diligent, professional, and reasonable attempt to hire the best-qualified teachers**. Therefore, there was no basis for an award of backpay or benefits. *Bd. of Educ. v. Enoch*, 414 S.E.2d 630 (W.Va.1992).

C. Certification Issues

◆ A group of Chicago public school students commenced a lawsuit in federal district court against the city board of education and the Illinois State Board of Education, alleging systemic failure to comply with the IDEA's LRE requirement. In a 1998 decision, the district court held that Chicago's reliance on placing students based on their identified disability, which segregated them in classrooms according to categories of disability, resulted from the district's continuing use of pre-1990 special education regulations issued by the ISBE. It held that the ISBE failed in its responsibility to ensure local compliance with the IDEA. The court found it permissible to hold the ISBE responsible for the Chicago district's systemic failures, since it had accepted IDEA funds and was the party responsible for ensuring local compliance. It ordered the ISBE to submit a comprehensive compliance plan for several areas, including the practices of segregating students by category of disability, and the use of teacher certification standards that relied on labels associated with such categories. **The court specifically ordered the ISBE to ensure that teacher certification in Illinois complied with, rather than contradicted, the IDEA's LRE requirement**.

Subsequently, the court issued an order reflecting the ISBE's efforts to bring itself into compliance with the 1998 order. A court-appointed monitor recommended accepting the ISBE's new certification framework, and directives were issued requiring two administrative rules concerning state certification standards.

The monitor recommended the elimination of language from an ISBE rule that prohibited special education certificate holders from serving only in classrooms composed of students with the particular disability for which the holder's certificate was endorsed. The students objected to a final ISBE teacher certification proposal on grounds that it could be implemented in a manner replicating the existing categorical certification system. The court approved of the rule recommended by the monitor, and ordered its implementation. It reserved a specific ruling on the ISBE's draft rules for the implementation of standards for certification in special education, in view of ongoing settlement efforts by the parties. The court also approved an agreed-upon order between the parties requiring the ISBE to issue public notification of its proposed rules for the transition to the new certification structure and standards for certification in special education. The transition rules would describe procedures for teachers to acquire and maintain special education certification designations reflected in the new standards. The ISBE was to hold public meetings for consideration of the proposed rules and submit a final certification proposal for transition rules following the end of the public comment period. *Corey H. et al. v. Board of Education of City of Chicago*, No. 92 C 3409 (N.D. Ill. 2001).

◆ The Ohio administrative code was amended to require teachers to complete certain coursework before receiving "Early Education of Handicapped" certification. **The code contained a grandfather clause allowing the certification of degreed individuals already employed to teach handicapped infants, toddlers or young children** by a chartered school or school district as of the effective date of the amendment. One teacher who was employed by an Ohio school district to teach handicapped children in grades one through three sought to obtain her early education certification under the grandfather clause, asserting that young children as defined by the code could include students in first through third grade. The state board of education denied her application because she was not a teacher of handicapped infants, toddlers or young children as of the date of the amendment.

An Ohio county court denied her petition for review, and she appealed to the Court of Appeals of Ohio, where she renewed her argument that the term "young children" could encompass first through third graders and that the cognitive ages and abilities of her students were comparable to those of younger children. **The court found that the department's definition of the term "young children" reasonably applied only to prekindergarten special-needs children.** This interpretation was consistent with separate certification requirements for teachers maintained by the state in other grade classifications. The court rejected the teacher's claim that a student's cognitive or mental age should be considered. The court affirmed the decision for the state board. *State ex rel. DeMuth v. State Bd. of Educ.*, 113 Ohio App.3d 430, 680 N.E.2d 1314 (Ohio Ct. App. 10th Dist. 1996).

CHAPTER EIGHT

School District Operations

I. BUDGET AND FINANCE

Local educational agencies that receive federal funding are required to comply with federal law requirements. The oversight role of the federal government often includes the threat of withholding funds for local noncompliance with federal requirements. Since local educational agencies depend upon a combination of state, federal and local tax revenues, reviewing courts have been presented with challenges involving funding at all levels of government.

A. State and Local Educational Funding

◆ After publication of *Bd. of Educ. v. Wieder*, 72 N.Y.2d 174, 531 N.Y.S.2d 889, 527 N.E.2d 767 (1988), in which the New York Court of Appeals held that school districts had to make special education services available to all students residing within district boundaries even if they were attending private schools, **the New York legislature enacted a statute which created a new school district whose boundaries were coterminous with a Hasidic community** (whose residents demanded education of their children in accordance with their tradition of segregating the sexes in school). New York taxpayers and an association representing New York school districts filed a lawsuit seeking a declaration that the statute was unconstitutional. The board of education of the Hasidic village and the education board of the larger school district in which the Hasidic community was located intervened as defendants. The parties brought summary judgment motions for declaratory relief concerning the constitutionality of the statute. The trial court held that the statute violated the New York and federal constitutions, and the New York Supreme Court, Appellate Division, affirmed. The education boards appealed to the Court of Appeals of New York, which held that **the statute had the primary effect of establishing a symbolic union of church and state that could be perceived as an endorsement of religion**. Because the legislation conveyed a message of governmental endorsement of religion, it violated the Establishment Clause of the U.S. Constitution. The court of appeals affirmed the lower court decisions, as modified. *Grumet v. Bd. of Educ. of Kiryas Joel Village School Dist.*, 81 N.Y.2d 518, 601 N.Y.S.2d 61, 618 N.E.2d 94 (1993).

The U.S. Supreme Court agreed to review the matter and held that a state may not delegate authority to a group chosen by religion. **Although the statute did not expressly identify the Hasidic community as a recipient of governmental authority, it had clearly been passed to benefit them. The result was a purposeful and forbidden fusion of governmental and religious functions.** The creation of a school district for the religious community violated the Establishment Clause. The legislation extended a special franchise to the Hasidic community that violated the constitutional requirement of religious neutrality by the government. The statute crossed "the line from permissible accommodation to impermissible establishment," and the Supreme Court affirmed the judgment of the court of appeals. *Bd. of Educ. of Kiryas Joel Village School Dist. v. Grumet*, 512 U.S. 687, 114 S.Ct. 2481, 129 L.Ed.2d 546 (1994).

The New York legislature promptly repealed the statute and abolished the Kiryas Joel Village School District, passing two statutes that provided a mechanism for the organization of new school districts. **They authorized school districts consisting of the entire territory of a municipality coterminous with preexisting school districts when the educational interests of the community required such action, and where certain student enrollment and property tax requirements were satisfied**. The taxpayers filed a motion for a temporary restraining order or preliminary injunction in a New York trial court, seeking a declaration that the new statutes were unconstitutional. The court determined that the 1994 statutory amendments were non-specific, religiously neutral, general statutes that were justified by reasonable educational concerns. Although Kiryas Joel Village was currently the only district taking advantage of the statutes, other municipalities might also seek to use them. Any harm alleged by the taxpayers was outweighed by the risk of harm to students attending the village school, which limited its services to disabled students, and the court denied the taxpayers' motion for a temporary order.

The parties then filed cross-motions for summary judgment. **The court held that the 1994 amendments had an identifiable secular purpose**: to create new school districts where municipalities met religiously-neutral objectives and standards. **The amendments were neutral in language and were not motivated by a religious purpose**. The amendments did not create a new Kiryas Joel Village school district, but merely gave municipalities the opportunity to create school districts where they met certain minimum requirements. The school board's exclusively Hasidic composition did not result in excessive entanglement and the individual board members could not be denied their political rights. The court dismissed the taxpayers' complaint.

The taxpayers appealed to the New York Supreme Court, Appellate Division, where they argued that the new legislative criteria for authorizing school districts created the same result as under the prior unconstitutional law. The court agreed, and observed that one of the criteria was apparently meaningless and had been included only to limit the applicability of the statute and afford special treatment to village residents. **The legislation had no educational purpose, was not generally applicable and had been enacted as a subterfuge to avoid the prior U.S. Supreme Court decision**. The trial court decision was reversed and remanded, and the court declared the legislation unconstitutional under the Establishment Clause. The Court of Appeals of New York agreed to review the case, and found that **despite the apparently neutral criteria in the amendments, the Hasidic village was the only municipality that could ever avail itself of the statutory mechanism**, and the legislation impermissibly favored that group. The law could be perceived as being for the sole benefit of the sect, and the court affirmed the judgment for the taxpayers. *Grumet v. Cuomo*, 90 N.Y.2d 57, 659 N.Y.S.2d 173, 681 N.E.2d 340 (1997).

In 1997, the legislature passed similar legislation to that passed in 1994, but broadened its applicability to municipalities that were as yet unformed. A school district for Kiryas Joel was reconstituted under the new act, and a new challenge was mounted in the state court system. A state appellate division court held that the 1997 law impermissibly extended a preference to the village based on the religious beliefs of its residents and thus had the unconstitutional effect of endorsing religion.

The court of appeals reviewed the case and found that while the 1997 law was facially neutral with respect to religion, its actual effect benefited only the Kiryas Joel district, and its potential benefit extended to only one other district in the state. Since other religious groups would be unable to benefit from the law in the manner enjoyed by the Satmar sect in Kiryas Joel, the law was not neutral in effect. The 1997 law had the same unconstitutional effect as the 1994 law, and violated the Establishment Clause by preferring one religion to others. **The law required the delegation of governmental power to a religious group without assuring that other groups would receive such a benefit and was an impermissible religious accommodation**. It had no secular purpose since it did not extend benefits to a broad spectrum of groups and had the primary effect of advancing religion. The court of appeals noted that the U.S. Supreme Court has now held that the provision of on-site services at religious schools does not create an impermissible union of church and state, and affirmed the judgment of the appellate division. *Grumet v. Pataki*, 93 N.Y.2d 677, 720 N.E.2d 66 (N.Y.1999).

◆ In separate proceedings, two school districts challenged orders requiring them to support the educational costs of students with disabilities who did not attend public schools. In the first case, an ALJ held that the school district was required to reimburse the family of an 18-year-old student with disabilities for private school tuition. A federal magistrate judge held that the district had made so many procedural and substantive errors in preparing the student's IEP that tuition reimbursement was proper. **The judge ordered the state to pay for the costs of the student's private education and half of the parents' legal costs**, on the theory that it was the guarantor of local compliance with the IDEA. In the second case, a hearing officer held that parents were entitled to their costs for supplying an intensive home-based program for their five-year-old child, who had autism. On appeal to a federal district court, **a magistrate judge rejected the hearing officer's order that the state should contribute to the costs of the home-based program**. The court accepted the magistrate judge's finding that the state was not required to contribute to the cost of the home-based program.

The Seventh Circuit consolidated the state's appeal in the first case with the appeal of the school district in the second case. The state argued that it was protected from any liability by the 11th Amendment and that the school boards lacked the power to sue the state. The circuit court disagreed, noting that Congress had successfully abrogated 11th Amendment immunity when it amended the IDEA. States receiving IDEA funds accept federal money under the condition that they subject themselves to the jurisdiction of the courts. The court agreed with the state that **the IDEA does not permit the courts to reallocate reimbursement awards among state and local educational authorities.** Under 20 U.S.C. § 1411(f), states were required to distribute at least 75 percent of the total grants received under the IDEA to the states, keeping the remainder for their direct educational services, administration, technical assistance, training hearings and subgrants. School districts were not entitled to receive anything more than their annual statutory allocation. The allocation was based on a formula stated in the IDEA that was intended to supplement funding for students with disabilities at a level that was 30 percent above the average cost per student for primary education in the U.S. Neither school district alleged that it had received less than its statutory allotment of IDEA funds from the state. **By attempting to force the state of Illinois to pay more than the statutory share described in the IDEA, the school districts were impermissibly trying to gain additional funds**. The court ruled in favor of the state in both cases. *Board of Education of Oak Park and River Forest High School District No. 200 v. Kelly E.; T.H., L.H. and S.H. v. Board of Education of Palatine Comm. Consolidated School District No. 15*, 207 F.3d 931 (7th Cir. 2000).

◆ The New Jersey Supreme Court issued its sixth opinion in a case involving educational quality, finance and reform in the state's poorest urban school districts. It characterized the state education department's failure to implement its 1998 decision as the result of misunderstandings, but refused to find that it acted in bad faith. **The court issued guidance to the parties for implementation of education reforms in the districts, and found that the state's use of community care providers staffed by uncertified teachers violated its order to establish quality preschool programs**. The legislature had recognized the need for early childhood education for three- and four-year-olds in the state's poorest school districts, and every year of delay threatened another generation of children. The state education commissioner was required to ensure that programs were adequately funded and to assist the schools in meeting transportation, service, support and resource needs. The state was required to clarify the regulations and eliminate the disparity among preschool programs and was ordered to comply with the 1:15 teacher-to-student ratio established by the trial court, which was supported by educational research. New regulations and substantive standards developed by the education department were to establish a baseline for upgrading daycare centers into well-run preschools. The court disagreed with the districts that judicial oversight was required to ensure state compliance with the quality preschool network established by state law. *Abbott by Abbott v. Burke*, 748 A.2d 82 (N.J. 2000).

- The Michigan Constitution was amended in 1978 to include a complex system of revenue and tax limits on state and local government. As a result, the state can only change state revenues in an amount based on the change in personal income in the state and is prohibited from requiring any new or expanded activity by local governments without full state financing. The state is also prohibited from reducing the proportion of state assistance to local government units. Local government units cannot levy any new taxes or increase existing taxes above authorized rates without the approval of local voters. **A group of resident taxpayers filed a lawsuit against state education and finance officials, asserting that the state had violated the constitutional amendments by failing to maintain the state-financed portion of the necessary costs of required activities.** A second group of taxpayers and Michigan school districts filed another action seeking a money judgment for the school districts on the basis of the state's failure to maintain funding required by the amendments.

The Court of Appeals of Michigan consolidated the cases and issued a judgment favorable to the taxpayers and districts. The state then appealed to the Supreme Court of Michigan, where it argued that it was not required to comply with the constitutional mandate concerning special education, special education transportation, and state-matched school lunch payments, since these programs were federal rather than state mandates. **The supreme court observed that the programs identified by the state were also covered by comparable state legislation and were therefore not excluded federal mandates.** The court substantially affirmed the judgment of the court of appeals, but modified the remedy so that **the state would be liable for monetary damages to be distributed to the plaintiff school districts, taxpayers within the prevailing districts, or used for other public purposes.** *Durant v. State of Michigan*, 566 N.W.2d 272 (Mich.1997).

On remand, the court of appeals held that the 1997 and 1998 legislation complied with the Headlee Amendment, a 1963 Michigan constitutional amendment that imposes tax and revenue limitations on state and local governments. The amendment limits the changes in total state revenues to an amount based on changes in personal income. It prohibits local government units from levying new taxes or increasing existing taxes above authorized rates without electoral approval, and also prevents the state from requiring new or expanded activities by local government units without full state financing. Moreover, the Headlee Amendment prevents the state from reducing the proportion of state spending by shifting the tax burden to local units. The state is obligated to finance the necessary costs of special education, transportation, and school lunch programs at fixed percentages.

The court of appeals further determined that the 1997 and 1998 legislation was constitutional. However, the per student funding guaranteed to local and intermediate school districts to reimburse them for the costs of school operations was solely intended to reimburse local districts for general school operating expenses. **The acts violated the constitutional guarantee of a specific base level of unrestricted, mandated per student aid, to the extent that they restricted the use of a portion of per student funding attributed to special education students solely to the satisfaction of state funding obligations for mandated programs, services, and transportation**. The taxpayers were entitled to summary disposition of their claim for violation of the Michigan Constitution in this regard. The state conceded that it violated the constitution by underfunding school lunch programs. However, the court held that local districts had failed to use certain state funds provided under the state school aid act in an amount necessary to operate school lunch programs, and the state was entitled to summary disposition on that claim. The state was entitled to summary disposition on the claim that it improperly allocated revenues. Because of the separation of powers, the court denied the taxpayers' claims for injunctive relief, monetary damages, and other relief. *Durant v. State of Michigan,* 238 Mich. App. 185, 605 N.W.2d 66 (Mich.Ct.App. 1999).

◆ The Wisconsin legislature enacted the Milwaukee Parental Choice Program in 1989 to allow moderate to low-income resident students to attend any nonsectarian private school located in the city at public expense. **The program was amended** in 1995 **to greatly increase the number of participating students and allow their attendance at sectarian schools**. Groups of taxpayers, teachers, parents and civic organizations challenged the program's constitutionality in two state court actions brought against the state superintendent of public instruction and other officials. The cases were consolidated by a Wisconsin trial court, which found that the amended program violated the Wisconsin Constitution. The state appealed to the Court of Appeals of Wisconsin, which held that the program violated the religious establishment provisions of the state constitution.

The Supreme Court of Wisconsin granted the state's petition for review, and considered the case under both the Wisconsin and U.S. Constitutions. It held that **the program had a secular purpose of providing low-income students with opportunities to receive an education outside the Milwaukee public school system in a manner that did not have a primary effect of advancing religion, was religiously neutral and did not lead to religious indoctrination**. Religious school attendance came only as the result of individual private choices by parents. Because state administration of the program required no oversight beyond existing efforts to monitor the quality of education provided at private schools, the program did not excessively entangle the state with religion. The court upheld the program under the Establishment Clause and on three additional state constitutional grounds. The court rejected arguments that the program violated student equal protection rights and found it constitutional in its entirety. *Jackson v. Benson*, 578 N.W.2d 602 (Wis.1998).

◆ The Massachusetts legislature required municipalities to obtain voter approval for any appropriation of money, unless the general court provided for the assumption of the cost by the state as an unfunded local mandate. Municipalities could submit notices to the state requesting a determination that certain costs were unfunded local mandates for which they were entitled to reimbursement by the state. **The city of Worcester requested the state auditor's office to determine whether some of its special education costs were unfunded local mandates**. The auditor's office held that some, but not all, of the expenditures were unfunded local mandates and determined that there was a deficiency of over $985,000. The city then filed a complaint in a Massachusetts trial court, requesting a declaration that all of the expenditures examined by the auditor's office were unfunded local mandates. The court reserved and reported the case to the state appeals court, which transferred the matter to the Supreme Judicial Court of Massachusetts.

The supreme judicial court held that **none of the special education expenditures under review were unfunded local mandates. The city was not entitled to any part of the reimbursement that the auditor's office had ordered**. One of the mandates at issue was a 1986 amendment to a state law definition of "substantial disability for children." The court held that the definition in the amendment was merely a verification of an existing law, and did not impose a new direct service or cost on the city, as the city had argued. Thus, the amendment was not an unfunded local mandate. The city had been obligated prior to the effective date of the legislation to provide special education to children residing within its area. Its obligation was unchanged by the amendment. It did not matter that the city had believed it was not required to provide special education services to some of its children prior to the amendment's passage. The court remanded the case to the trial court for judgment dismissing the governor from the case and declaring that none of the special education expenditures under consideration were unfunded local mandates. *City of Worcester v. Governor*, 416 Mass. 751, 625 N.E.2d 1337 (Mass.1994).

B. Federal Funding Issues

◆ A group of Louisiana citizens sued the Jefferson Parish School Board in 1985 for violating the First Amendment, alleging that the board improperly provided Chapter Two funds to parochial schools for the purpose of acquiring library materials and media equipment. **The group asserted that expenditures for books, computers, software and other audiovisual equipment violated the Establishment Clause**, since 41 of 46 participating private schools were religiously affiliated. The district court agreed, granting summary judgment to the group since the funding failed the religious advancement test from *Lemon v. Kurtzman*, 403 U.S. 602 (1971), and that the loan of materials to sectarian schools constituted impermissible direct government aid to the schools. Two years later, the district court reversed itself in post-judgment activity, citing an intervening U.S. Supreme Court decision in which the court held that a state could provide a sign-language interpreter on-site at a parochial school. The citizens appealed to the U.S. Court of Appeals for the Fifth Circuit, which held that the Chapter Two grants were unconstitutional. The U.S. Supreme Court agreed to review the decision.

The Supreme Court found no basis for ruling that the school board's use of Chapter Two funds had the effect of advancing religion in violation of the Establishment Clause. The use of the funds by private schools did not result in government indoctrination of religion because eligibility was determined on a neutral basis and through private choices made by parents. Chapter Two had no impermissible content and did not define its recipients by reference to religion. Chapter Two funding in the school district did not create an improper incentive for parents to select religious schools for their children. A broad array of schools was eligible for assistance without regard to religious affiliation. **The program was neutral with regard to religion, and private decision-making controlled the allocation of funds to private schools.** Students who attended schools receiving Chapter Two funds were the ultimate beneficiaries of the assistance, even though the schools used them to purchase computers, software, books and other equipment. The court upheld the board's use of Chapter Two funding and held that the parish did not need to exclude religious schools from the program. *Mitchell v. Helms*, 530 U.S. 793, 120 S.Ct. 2530, 147 L.Ed.2d 660 (2000).

◆ Title I of the Elementary and Secondary Education Act of 1965 provides federal funding through states to local educational agencies to provide remedial education, guidance and job counseling to at-risk students and students residing in low-income areas. Title I requires that funding be made available for all eligible students, including those attending private schools. Local agencies retain control over Title I funds and materials. **The New York City Board of Education attempted to implement Title I programs at parochial schools by allowing public employees to instruct students on private school grounds during school hours**. The U.S. Supreme Court agreed with a group of taxpayers that this violated the Establishment Clause in *Aguilar v. Felton*, 473 U.S. 402 (1985). On remand, **a federal district court ordered the city board to refrain from using Title I funds for any plan or program under which public school teachers and counselors furnished services on sectarian school grounds**. In response to *Aguilar*, local education boards modified Title I programs by moving classes to remote sites including mobile instructional units parked near sectarian schools. However, a new group of parents and parochial school students filed motions seeking relief from the permanent order.

The district court denied the motions, and the U.S. Court of Appeals, Second Circuit, affirmed the decision. On further appeal, the U.S. Supreme Court agreed with the city board and students that recent Supreme Court decisions required a new ruling on the question of government aid to religious schools. For example, the provision of a sign language interpreter by a school district at a private school was upheld in *Zobrest v. Catalina Foothills School Dist.*, 509 U.S. 1 (1993). The Court held that **it would no longer presume that the presence of a public school teacher on parochial school grounds creates a symbolic union between church and state**. The provision of Title I services at parochial schools resembled the provision of a sign language interpreter under the IDEA. **New York City's Title I program was constitutionally permissible because it did not result in government indoctrination, define funding recipients by reference to religion or create excessive entanglement** between education officials and religious schools. The Court reversed the lower court judgments. *Agostini v. Felton*, 521 U.S. 203, 138 L.Ed.2d 391, 117 S.Ct. 1997 (1997).

◆ The Stewart B. McKinney Homeless Assistance Act authorizes grants by the Secretary of the U.S. Department of Education to states for educating homeless children. **The District of Columbia applied for and received funds under the act, and a group of homeless parents sued the district in federal court for failing to place students** within 72 hours. The district's mayor and city council took action to withdraw from the McKinney Act program in the face of a budget crisis. The district moved to vacate an injunction issued prior to the withdrawal and the parents objected, claiming that the district was still required to provide services under the act. **The court determined that the mayor and city council had enacted appropriate emergency legislation to overcome extreme financial difficulties and that the McKinney Act did not apply to entities that no longer participated in its programs**. Nothing in the act created any entitlement to emergency services for homeless persons and the court dissolved the injunction. *Lampkin v. Dist. of Columbia*, 886 F.Supp. 56 (D.D.C.1995).

C. Residency Disputes

◆ A New Jersey student was classified as neurologically impaired by the Somerville school system, where her parents lived before they divorced. Their divorce decree provided for joint legal and shared physical custody of the student. The mother moved into the Manville school district, while the father continued to reside in Somerville. The IEP prepared by the Somerville district placed the student in a school located in a third district, where she remained for several years under an unwritten agreement between the Somerville and Manville school boards to split the cost of educating the student. The Manville district hired a new director of special services, who determined that it should not continue paying tuition to the third district because the student was not a Manville resident. The Somerville district then commenced a New Jersey state court action against Manville for a declaration that the student was jointly domiciled in both districts and that the oral agreement to share tuition expenses at the third district remained enforceable. The Manville district counter-claimed for the amount it had already contributed on behalf of the student. The court held that the student was domiciled in Somerville for the purposes of obtaining educational funding and that Somerville should bear the costs of educating her in the future. Manville was liable only for the balance of the student's current tuition under the oral agreement of the parties. On appeal, the New Jersey Superior Court, Appellate Division, concluded that special education statutes should be construed to ensure that a disabled student's education is not interrupted by disputes between school districts over financial responsibility. **The court found that a child may be domiciled in both parental households if the evidence indicates actual residence with both parents.** Fairness dictated that both Manville and Somerville equally share the student's special education costs. The court reversed the lower court judgment.

The Manville school district appealed to the New Jersey Supreme Court, where the parties raised collateral issues including the receipt of state funding, the authority to modify the student's IEP and the possibility that new state special education regulations might address issues raised on appeal. The court noted that **the parties had voluntarily agreed to share the costs of educating the student and had agreed to share state and federal categorical aid on an alternating annual basis**. The district paying tuition for a given year would count the student for the purposes of receiving state and federal assistance. The parties had also agreed to share the responsibility of providing transportation. The state supreme court affirmed the appellate court's decision, finding its opinion to be thoughtful and comprehensive. It stated that it did not anticipate any significant problems in resolving cost allocation questions when the case returned to the trial court level. The state supreme court recited a portion of the appellate division opinion verbatim with regard to the parties' continuing obligation to cooperate in developing and reviewing the student's IEP, with appropriate concern for consistency and continuity. As the appellate division court had acknowledged, new regulations by the department of education might supersede the court's opinion, but they had not yet been officially published. *Somerville Board of Education v. Manville Board of Education*, 768 A.2d 778 (N.J. 2001).

◆ **A three month old who was severely injured in an accident was placed in a home for children located in Pittsfield, New Hampshire** in 1989. Her parents divorced and the father received sole legal and physical custody. Neither parent had any substantial or meaningful contact with the child. The state education department appointed a surrogate parent to act on her behalf concerning her right to a FAPE. **The father moved to Ohio in 1995 from Manchester, N.H., and the Manchester school district sought to discharge the child from the children's home**. The surrogate parent objected and filed a request for due process. A hearing officer agreed with the surrogate parent that the child should remain in the children's home and the district appealed to a federal district court. The state enacted new legislation redefining residency for public school purposes and the case was remanded to the state education department for further consideration. The hearing officer held that the district remained financially responsible for the placement and the district again appealed to the federal district court, which considered the parties' cross-motions for summary judgment.

The court examined the state's public school statutory scheme and determined that the legal residence of a student is generally that of his or her parents. However, when parents divorce and the parent with sole physical custody moves outside the state, the student has no New Hampshire residence. **Nothing in state law limited the right of any child "placed" in a home for children to attend public school in the district in which the home is located.** Even though the child did not have a right to attend a New Hampshire public school based on legal residence, she might have a right to be placed in the home for children. Since the family last resided in the Manchester school district, Manchester would be obligated to pay for her education in the home for children if the court determined she had been "placed" there within the meaning of state law. Because the parties had not fully developed the issue of whether the student was "placed" in the home for children as defined by state law, the court denied the cross-motions for summary judgment and invited the parties to present arguments on questions of state law that would determine the case's outcome. Another issue for the parties to address was the possibility that the Manchester district might remain financially responsible for the placement because it did not raise the issue in 1992 and was now barred from contesting it. *City of Manchester School District v. Crisman*, No. Civ. 97-632-M, 2001 DNH 61, 2001 WL 311202 (D.N.H. 2001) (unpublished).

◆ The parents of a Kansas student divorced when he was two. The student lived with his mother until age 10, then resided with his father, and eventually moved in with an adult sister. He was identified as eligible for special education when he was seven, and attended a number of schools, some with IDEA financing and some financed by his mother. The mother moved from a residence within the Wichita Unified School District to a home that was located in the Andover Unified School District in March 1995. Eight months later, the student pleaded guilty in a state district court to criminal charges. The court ordered the student to serve 24 months of probation and complete a program at a private, residential facility. The mother then attempted to obtain a placement for her son in the specified facility in order to avoid his potential incarceration. At the same time, she sought public financing from the Wichita school district for the residential placement. She made the actual placement before an IEP was prepared. The Wichita system refused to fund the placement sought by the mother. At a due process hearing against the Wichita school system, the hearing officer refused to join the Andover district as a party to the action. **The hearing officer found that the student was not a resident of the Wichita district** as of the time of his conviction, and therefore the Wichita district did not have to fund the placement. The administrative decision was affirmed by a due process reviewing officer, and later by a federal district court. The student's mother appealed to the Tenth Circuit.

The circuit court rejected the mother's assertion that the Andover school district was a necessary party to the action. By her own admission, the student had lived within the Wichita school district boundaries all his life. The mother's residency was not relevant, as the student did not live with her and his residency controlled the case. Andover was not a necessary party simply because the Wichita district had asserted that Andover was responsible for his education. The court held that **Wichita was not liable for any residential placement costs. Neither parent resided in Wichita** and the student's adult sister was not a "person acting as a parent" within the meaning of state law. The circuit court affirmed the district court's residency determination and adopted its view that the mother's unilateral placement of her son in the Tennessee facility was "manipulative, was not undertaken for education purposes, and essentially obstructed the IDEA process." The mother had attempted to gain funding for a placement that she had already decided on, and her IDEA, Rehabilitation Act and other federal claims failed. The court affirmed the judgment for the school districts and officials. *Joshua W. and Anita O. v. Unified School District 259 Board of Education, Wichita Public Schools*, 211 F.3d 1278 (10th Cir. 2000) (unpublished).

◆ A special education student, his mother and his brother lived in a rented townhouse located in the Cumberland Valley School District during the week and spent some weekends and holidays with the father, who lived in a house owned by the family. The house was located in a different school district. After the student was hospitalized twice, a private placement was recommended. Cumberland Valley school officials refused to fund a private placement, stating that the family had never established residency in the district. The parents unilaterally enrolled the student in a private school for students with learning disabilities. **An administrative board determined the townhouse was a temporary residence, and concluded**

that the family resided in the district within which the home was located. A Pennsylvania trial court concluded that the student's residence was the place of his physical presence. Accordingly, the student resided in the Cumberland Valley school district. Due process proceedings resulted in a determination that the Cumberland Valley school district was responsible for providing the student with a FAPE, and was obligated to pay the costs of the private school.

Cumberland Valley officials appealed the residency issue to the Pennsylvania Supreme Court, which concluded that under the state public school code, a student is a resident of the district in which his parent or guardian resides. The board had erroneously interpreted resides to mean the custodial parent's primary residence and domicle. Under the board's interpretation, primary residence and domicle were largely equivalent, which would result in children being able to claim residency in the district of their choice, regardless of where the parents paid property taxes. **The state supreme court agreed with the lower courts that a person resides in the place they are physically present.** This definition of resides was appropriate for use when interpreting the school code. As a general rule, the court noted that a minor has the same residence as the parent with whom he lives. The supreme court found nothing in the public school code that indicated that the terms resident or resides had any special meaning beyond the classical definitions of those terms. The court affirmed the judgment in favor of the family. *In re Residence Hearing Before the Board of School Directors, Cumberland Valley School Dist.,* 744 A.2d 1272 (Pa. 2000).

- The parents of a New York student with Down's syndrome placed him in a group residence home for permanent care. They retained financial responsibility for him and participated in his special education meetings. The student remained in the residence home when the parents moved to Massachusetts, but the school district from which they had moved discontinued funding his educational program under a New York education law requiring a school district to fund a student's education only when the student resides within the district. **The state commissioner of education interpreted the law as creating a presumption that children reside with their parents, even where they are not physically present in the parents' home.** The parents sued the state education commissioner in a federal district court, arguing that this interpretation violated the Constitution and IDEA. The court held that the commissioner's interpretation did not violate the Equal Protection Clause of the Constitution because it furthered the legitimate educational interest of preserving special education services for legitimate state residents and reserving local control over education. However, the court held that the law as applied in this case violated the Due Process Clause. The commissioner appealed to the U.S. Court of Appeals, Second Circuit, which ruled for him on both constitutional issues.

The parents then filed a district court motion seeking an order that the school district could not seek tuition reimbursement from them for the student's residence home costs. The district and commissioner cross-moved for summary judgment. The district argued that the motion regarding tuition reimbursement should be denied because it was filed eleven years after the institution of the lawsuit. The court found that the key to the parents' motion was their claim that the state of Massachusetts was now liable for the student's tuition. However, **the**

Massachusetts school district into which the parents had moved had never been afforded the opportunity to evaluate or place the student. Consequently, Massachusetts had no financial responsibility for the student's continued placement in New York. The motion regarding tuition reimbursement was denied, and the school district and commissioner were entitled to summary judgment. *Catlin v. Sobol*, 988 F.Supp. 85 (N.D.N.Y.1997).

◆ The parents of an Illinois student with disabilities voluntarily transferred custody of their son to licensed foster parents. The parents retained legal guardianship of their son while the foster parents became his primary care givers. Three years later, **the foster parents moved to a different county and enrolled the student in special education classes in the county school district**. When the school district in which the foster parents lived learned that they were not the student's legal guardians, it sought reimbursement for special education costs from the natural parents and their district of residence. When the district and parents refused the request, the foster parents' residence district filed a lawsuit against the parents' residence district in an Illinois trial court, seeking reimbursement. The court granted summary judgment to the foster parents' district, and the natural parents' district appealed to the Appellate Court of Illinois. The court held that **Illinois law defines the school district of residence as the district in which the parent or guardian of a student resides when the parent has legal guardianship of the student and resides within the state of Illinois**. Because this was the situation presented in this case, the court affirmed the judgment for the foster parents' district. *Bd. of Educ. of Community Unit School Dist. No. 428 v. Bd. of Educ. of High School Dist. No. 214*, 680 N.E.2d 450 (Ill.App.Ct.2d Dist.1997).

◆ A 16-year-old Florida student with special needs lived with his mother until she became unable to care for him. The student then went to live with his grandmother in North Carolina and applied to the local school board for enrollment as a student with special needs. **School administrators denied the application, stating that he was neither a resident nor a domiciliary of the district**. The student appealed to the state office of administrative hearings, which found that he was a resident of the county and that his grandmother acted as his guardian. The student was entitled to a free appropriate education. This decision was affirmed in later administrative proceedings and by a North Carolina superior court. The school board appealed to the Court of Appeals of North Carolina.

The court considered the difference between residence and domicile, observing that they are distinct in that a student may reside in one district and be domiciled in another. Because an unemancipated minor may not establish a domicile that is separate from his parents or guardian, the student remained domiciled in Florida. However, his actual place of residence was with his grandmother in North Carolina. Although North Carolina law generally provides for the education of students domiciled in a school administrative unit, the statute pertaining to students with special needs specifies that each local education agency provide free appropriate special education services to all students with special needs residing in the district. **The specific requirements of state special education law superseded the more general provisions of state education**

law, and imposed an obligation on the district to provide a free appropriate education for each student with disabilities residing in the district. Compliance with the statute was necessary for the state to receive federal funds under the IDEA and the trial court decision was affirmed. *Craven County Bd. of Educ. v. Willoughby*, 466 S.E.2d 334 (N.C.Ct.App.1996).

◆ The parents of an Indiana student with dyslexia obtained a divorce and took up residences in different cities. Although the student spent most of his time with his mother, he spent substantial time with his father under a divorce decree that provided for joint custody. **The parents sought special education services for their son from the father's local education agency**, which denied that it was obligated to provide any services because the student spent most of his time at his mother's house. The parents brought an administrative appeal before a special education appeals board which held for the school district. The parents filed a lawsuit in the U.S. District Court for the Northern District of Indiana against the state Department of Education and the local school authority, asserting violations of the IDEA. The court considered motions for summary judgment by the state department and the local board. The court rejected their arguments that the father's residence district was not required to provide services. **Under Indiana law, a student's residence may be deemed to be both the mother's and father's when the parents are divorced and joint custody has been granted**. The IDEA looked to state law to resolve questions of residency for determining which school district was obligated to provide services. The court denied the motions for summary judgment. *Linda W. v. Indiana Dept. of Educ.*, 927 F.Supp. 303 (N.D.Ind.1996).

◆ A 13-year-old U.S. citizen resided with his parents in Mexico until he was sent to live with his aunt in Illinois. The aunt's school district of residence refused to recognize foreign documents granting custody to the aunt and denied the student's application for tuition-free enrollment. The aunt obtained a temporary restraining order from an Illinois circuit court allowing enrollment of the student. The court then made the order permanent and the district appealed to the Appellate Court of Illinois, First District, which observed that **a child is presumed to reside in the school district where his parents reside. This presumption may be rebutted by circumstances** including the permanency of the student's residence, the extent to which the parents exercise control over the student and the presence of noneducational reasons for living apart from the parents. Because there was sufficient evidence that the student was not applying for residence in the district solely for educational purposes, the court affirmed the circuit court decision. *Joel R. v. Bd. of Educ. of Mannheim School Dist. 83, Cook County, Illinois*, 686 N.E.2d 650 (Ill.App.Ct.1st Dist.1997).

◆ Oklahoma law allows student transfers upon the approval of education boards in the residence and receiving districts. Graduating seniors in counties having a population in excess of a specified number who are previously enrolled in a school district are exempt from the requirement of approval by the residence district. A student who attended a public school as a transfer student for 11 years reapplied for attendance in the school district for his senior year. However, the district denied his application for transfer, and the student's parents appealed to a county court. The court found that Oklahoma law required the receiving school district to approve the transfer. The district appealed to the Supreme Court of Oklahoma, which held that **where a previously-transferred student seeks a transfer and the requirements of law are otherwise met, the receiving district has no discretion to disapprove the request**. Because the district was within a county in excess of the specified population level and had previously allowed the student to transfer into the district, it had no discretion to disapprove the current request. *Hill v. Bd. of Educ., Dist. I–009, Jones, Oklahoma*, 944 P.2d 930 (Okla.1997).

II. STUDENT RECORDS AND PRIVACY

The federal Family Educational Rights and Privacy Act (FERPA) prohibits the unauthorized release by an educational agency of personally identifiable student information without prior parental consent. State laws also impose obligations upon local educational agencies to protect student privacy. These laws occasionally come into conflict with public information disclosure acts.

◆ An Oklahoma parent asserted that her school district's allowance of peer grading was embarrassing to her children, one of whom received special education services. Peer grading policies allow students to grade each other's assignments and call out the results in class. The parent sued the school district and school administrators in a federal district court for violations of FERPA, the IDEA and the federal Constitution through 42 U.S.C. § 1983. The court held that the policy did not violate any constitutional privacy rights and did not involve "education records" under FERPA. It then denied the parent's motion for reconsideration, ruling that because there had been no distinct claim under the IDEA, she could not use the Act as the basis of a constitutional claim. The parent appealed to the Tenth Circuit, which rejected her constitutional claim, ruling that school work did not rise to the level of constitutionally-protected information. It further held that **neither FERPA nor the IDEA created constitutional privacy rights. However, the circuit court held that FERPA could establish the basis for a suit for damages under 42 U.S.C. § 1983**. According to the court, FERPA is intended to protect student and parent privacy rights and creates a binding obligation on schools not to disclose personally identifying student information without permission. The district court decision was reversed with respect to the FERPA claim.

The U.S. Supreme Court accepted the district's petition to review the question of whether the peer grading policy violated FERPA. The Court observed that FERPA defines an education record as one that is "maintained by an educational agency or institution," or by a person acting for an agency or institution. According to the Court, student papers are not maintained under FERPA when students correct them or call out grades in class. The word maintain suggested that FERPA records were kept in files or cabinets in a "records room at the school or on a permanent secure database." The momentary handling of assignments by students did not conform to this definition. FERPA's language implies that education records are "institutional records..., not individual assignments handled by many students graders in their separate classrooms." According to the Court, the circuit court's decision would drastically alter the balance of authority among state and federal governments. The circuit court committed error by deciding that a student acted for an educational institution under FERPA when assisting with grading, according to the Supreme Court. **The Court noted the educational benefits of peer grading, such as teaching the same material a different way, demonstrating how to assist and respect classmates and reinforcement of concepts, and held that FERPA should not be construed to prohibit these techniques**. Congress would not burden teachers in this manner, nor would it extend any obligation to maintain records to students. Because Congress did not intend to intervene in drastic fashion with traditional state functions by exercising minute control over specific teaching methods, the Court reversed and remanded the case. *Owasso Indep. School Dist. No. I-011 v. Falvo*, 534 U.S. 426, 122 S.Ct. 934, 151 L.Ed.2d 896 (2002).

◆ A Massachusetts school district acted reasonably by submitting a student's schoolwork to local law enforcement officers for comparison to racist graffiti found on school grounds. **The Massachusetts Supreme Judicial Court held that the use of student papers as handwriting samples did not violate state regulations or student privacy expectations**. A school vice principal provided the police with written samples of the student's schoolwork to help determine whether it matched racist and obscene writing found at the school and in the student's classroom. A handwriting expert determined that the student had likely written the graffiti. The commonwealth of Massachusetts commenced proceedings against the student for malicious destruction of property and violation of civil rights. A trial court held that the handwriting samples had been obtained in violation of a state law requiring student or parental consent prior to the release of a "student record." On appeal, the Supreme Judicial Court rejected the student's argument that his handwriting samples were protected "student records" within the meaning of state law. **The handwriting samples provided to the police were not student records and were not protected by state confidentiality requirements**. The information was turned over to a governmental agency, not a private third party, and although the provision of samples to the police was a "search" for purposes of the Fourth Amendment, the action was reasonable in view of the reduced privacy expectation of students in school cases. The school had a clear obligation to use the student's papers only for educational purposes, but it also had an obligation to prevent racial harassment of a teacher and further property damage. The court vacated the trial court judgment and remanded the case. *Commonwealth of Massachusetts v. Buccella*, 434 Mass. 473, 751 N.E. 2d 373 (Mass. 2001).

◆ **A Utah school district disciplined and eventually suspended an elementary school student from school for verbal and physical abuse of other students. The school district notified the parents of several victims and witnesses.** In its reports to the parents, the district stated that each child had been questioned about the incident, that each had reported abuse of some kind by the student, and that the student had been advised "that if he had been abusive, he must stop such behavior immediately." In addition, the student was warned that there would be consequences for abusive behavior. The district did not disclose to parents whether the student was ultimately held at fault or punished. The district eventually suspended the student for 10 days, and his parents sued the district, principal and other school officials in a federal district court, asserting civil rights violations under the state and federal constitutions, Section 504 of the Rehabilitation Act, FERPA and state law.

The 10th Circuit held that **the parents' privacy claims failed because the disclosure of information about their son to the parents of student victims and witnesses did not constitute prohibited disclosures of an "educational record" under FERPA**, 20 U.S.C. § 1232g. The court held that the district memorandums did not violate FERPA because "the contemporaneous disclosure to the parents of a victimized child of the results of any investigation and resulting disciplinary actions taken against an alleged child perpetrator does not constitute a release of an 'education record' within the meaning of 20 U.S.C. § 1232g." If this were not the case, educators would lack the ability to assure parents of affected students that they were taking adequate steps to protect harassment victims. The court stated that **the targeted, discrete disclosure of information to the parents of victims was permissible under FERPA**. It was unnecessary to directly address the issue of whether the contemporaneous disclosure of information to the parents of witnesses, as opposed to victims, was permitted under FERPA. The memorandums in this case did not disclose anything that qualified as an educational record under FERPA. The circuit court agreed with the district court's disposition of the parents' other claims. The district court judgment was affirmed in its entirely. *Jensen et al. v. Reeves et al.*, 3 Fed.Appx. 905 (10th Cir. 2001).

◆ A six-month-old child with numerous health problems, including cerebral palsy, and was placed in foster care. **Three school district employees** worked at the foster home. They became concerned about the home's environment and **wrote a letter supporting the guardian *ad litem's*** advocacy for the child in an ongoing custody dispute. A copy of the letter was faxed to the county child protection agency, but it declined to investigate the home. **After the foster parents learned of the letter, they demanded the school district rescind it.** The district refused and the foster parents appealed to the state commissioner of administration. An ALJ recommended that the letter be rescinded and destroyed, and the commissioner issued an order adopting the recommendation.

The school district appealed to the Minnesota Court of Appeals. The court stated that if a letter is classified as a confidential mandated report of child neglect or abuse under Minn. Stat. § 626.556(7), the commissioner of administration has no jurisdiction to hear the dispute. Under Section 626.556(7), a confidential mandated report was "any report received by the local welfare agency, police department, or county sheriff pursuant to this section." However, if it was not a confidential mandated report, it was public or private government data, which the parents had the right to challenge under another chapter of state law. In that case, the commissioner acquired jurisdiction to order the correction of factual errors and conclusions. The court held that the letter was written to the guardian *ad litem* of the child in connection with a custody dispute, not to a local welfare or law enforcement agency, and it did not indicate that it was a "report." The employees were child-care professionals who were presumed to know their obligation to report abuse and neglect to a welfare or law enforcement agency, not a guardian *ad litem*. **Because the letter was not a mandated report of abuse or neglect, it was government data coming under the commissioner's jurisdiction**. The allegations contained in the letter were based on the observations of the district employees, and its accuracy or completeness was not communicated to the agency. The court affirmed the order requiring the district to rescind and destroy the letter. *In re Determination of the Responsible Authority for the South Washington County School District 833*, 620 N.W.2d 45 (Minn. Ct. App. 2000).

- A student with disabilities had boasted to classmates that he would have sex with a school paraprofessional and her daughter. The paraprofessional supervised the in-school suspension (ISS) and behavior rooms where the student was often sent for discipline. The school's assistant principal suspended the student for 10 days after observing an incident in the school cafeteria in which the student claimed that he had had sex with a classmate. School employees then learned that he had been charged with raping the paraprofessional's daughter. **The assistant principal scheduled a meeting with the student's parents and invited the paraprofessional** so that she could explain that ISS was no longer possible as a disciplinary measure. The meeting was acrimonious and included the paraprofessional's accusation of the rape of her daughter by the student. The parents demanded homebound instruction, which the school agreed to provide. However, the parents left the meeting without receiving written notice of the suspension, as required by Minnesota law. The principal later mailed the notice. The student remained in homebound instruction after the end of his suspension, and he graduated from a different school system the following year. He sued the assistant principal, the paraprofessional, his former school district and its superintendent in a federal district court, claiming many state and federal law violations.

The court dismissed the student's state law claim for revealing educational data to the paraprofessional, finding little reason to show that the school's behavior room supervisor was not entitled to receive a behavior-related record. While there had been a technical violation of the state pupil fair dismissal act, the suspension notice had been mailed on the same day as the meeting and there were no grounds for awarding damages. The court rejected the claim that the student had actually been expelled, observing that he had received homebound education according to the parents' wishes. It also dismissed the student's claim that the district had violated its student manual and that the manual created a contract that could be legally enforced. While the student had been excluded from the suspension conference, he had received an opportunity to present his side of the story as required by *Goss v. Lopez*, 419 U.S. 565 (1975). Despite the technical violation of his procedural right to personally present his story, he had not been prejudiced in any way. The assistant principal suspended the student for conduct that she had personally observed, and it was unnecessary for her to evaluate the credibility of any third-party accuser. The court found that even if the student had denied the conduct, he would have still been suspended. Finally, the court found no basis for any damage claim as the result of FERPA violations. **While the court recognized the possibility of a cause of action under 42 U.S.C. § 1983 for FERPA violations, the student failed to show that the school district maintained a policy or practice of violating FERPA by improperly releasing student data without written parental consent**. A one-time violation was insufficient to show the existence of a policy or practice. The court granted the school district and employees' motion for summary judgment. *Achman v. Chisago Lakes Indep. School Dist. No. 2144*, 45 F.Supp.2d 664 (D.Minn.1999).

◆ A Louisiana physics teacher became suspicious that a student's classroom grade was changed on his cumulative report. This was reported to a school board member, who sent the records to the state department of education for investigation. The student filed a lawsuit against the school board in a Louisiana district court, asserting violation of her privacy rights. The court held for the board, and the student appealed to the Court of Appeal of Louisiana, Third Circuit. The court found no invasion of privacy and held that teachers had a legitimate interest in reviewing student records, even those of former students. **The board member was entitled to receive the records as a person charged with public education oversight and he did not violate state law or the student's privacy rights by forwarding the records to the state education department**. Louisiana school boards routinely sent student records to the department to verify graduation eligibility. The court affirmed the trial court judgment. *Young v. St. Landry Parish School Bd.*, 673 So.2d 1272 (La.Ct.App.3d Cir.1996).

◆ A South Dakota school district that adjoined the Iowa border contained no municipalities, and students who resided in the district attended school in an Iowa district. One student from the South Dakota district received special education services at the Iowa district until he was placed in a residential school in Connecticut. The district paid for tuition, room and board for the student as well as for periodic visits by his parents. The cost of the Connecticut placement rose dramatically one year and property taxes in the district were raised significantly to cover the increase. Although the Family Educational Rights and Privacy Act (FERPA), requires local school districts to protect student privacy by preventing the unauthorized release of personally identifiable information, a South Dakota statute requires the publication of school board meeting minutes within 20 days, with a detailed statement of all expenditures and the names of persons to whom payment is made. After obtaining a legal opinion concerning the conflict between the statutes, **the school board decided that it was obligated to disclose the cost of the student's out-of-state special education placement in district notices and a local newspaper**. A newspaper report documented the cost of special education for the student, concluded that the local tax increase was caused by the increase in cost of the placement, and identified the student by name with a picture. The district held a public hearing on the issue of the tax increase, but took no action to reduce taxes. The parents of the student then received harassing phone calls urging them to move out of the district. The parents filed a lawsuit against some outspoken local taxpayers whom they alleged had made inflammatory statements, and sued the school district, board members, and a newspaper reporter for violations of FERPA and other federal and state laws. The defendants filed dismissal and summary judgment motions which were considered by the U.S. District Court for the District of South Dakota.

The court observed that the school district had sought a legal opinion concerning its conflicting obligations under state and federal law. The board members were entitled to qualified immunity, as the release of personally identifiable information to third parties without parental consent was not a matter of school board policy but was mandated by state law. **The school board's decision to publish meeting minutes was an attempt to accommodate conflicting statutory requirements and did not open board members to liability for FERPA violations**, requiring dismissal of that claim. The court also rejected the parents' argument for a finding of civil conspiracy under federal law and dismissed several other state law claims against the reporter, the board and its individual members. The court granted partial summary judgment to the outspoken taxpayers but was unwilling to dismiss all claims against them. *Maynard v. Greater Hoyt School Dist. No. 61-4*, 876 F.Supp. 1104 (D.S.D.1995).

III. GIFTED STUDENT PROGRAMS

The IDEA does not create rights or entitlements for gifted and exceptional students. State laws may establish gifted student programs and requirements, but they do not confer a property interest in gifted student program participation.

◆ Before a gifted student with emotional and behavior problems entered grade 10, his parents expressed their concerns to the district that the school district was not meeting the student's intellectual and emotional needs. A private psychologist chosen by the parents recommended that the district classify the student as having an emotional and behavioral disability, provide him with individual and family counseling and place him in an academically challenging program with his intellectual peers. **A school evaluation and planning team determined that the student had an emotional-behavioral disability under Vermont special education Rule 2362.1(h), but concluded that his disability did not "adversely affect" his educational performance,** as required by the rule. The EPT referred the request to a Section 504 team, which determined that the student was a qualified individual with a disability who was eligible for accommodations, and offered him a support program. The parents unilaterally enrolled the student in an out-of-state higher education boarding school for academically gifted students, and requested funding from the district. The Section 504 team identified three possible placements for the student, along with specifically rejecting the placement selected by the parents. A hearing officer held that the student was ineligible for special education services under the IDEA because he was performing at or above age and grade norms in each of eight basic skill areas. The hearing officer also determined that the school district had provided the student with a FAPE under Section 504, and was not obligated to place him among his intellectual peers.

The parents appealed to a federal district court, which upheld the administrative decision, and then appealed further to the Second Circuit. Observing that the IDEA does not prescribe substantive educational standards, the court scrutinized Vermont special education regulations establishing eligibility criteria for special education consistent with the IDEA. The relevant state regulation deemed eligible for special education those students meeting one or more of the listed categories of disability who exhibited "adverse effect of the disability on educational performance" and who were "in need of special education." The regulation defined "adverse effect of the disability" in part as "functioning significantly below expected age or grade norms," as documented and supported by two or more measures of school performance. The court agreed with the district's argument that **the student did not meet the regulatory definition of "adverse effect"** as set forth in Rule 2362(1). **He consistently performed above the mean in basic skills and did not meet the regulatory definition of below expected age or grade norms in at least two measured areas.** Accordingly, the district had correctly found that the student's educational performance was not adversely affected by his disability and that he was ineligible for special education services under the IDEA. The court also rejected the student's Section 504 claim for asserted denial of FAPE, since the IEP proposal was a reasonable accommodation of his disability. The school had offered him individual counseling and the refusal to fund his college level program did not amount to discrimination. The student was essentially claiming that the proposed accommodation was not an optimal placement, and there was no requirement under Section 504 to provide students with "potential-maximizing education." The court rejected additional arguments by the student based on violation of IDEA procedures and affirmed the judgment for the school district. *J.D. v. Pawlet School Dist.*, 224 F.3d 60 (2d Cir. 2000).

◆ A student placed in the top five percent nationally in three academic subjects while in kindergarten, and his parents requested that he be placed in accelerated and enriched programs. However, the district provided no specialized program for the student until the fifth grade, when it prepared an IEP for a gifted program. The parents later asserted that the district had not offered the student an appropriate curriculum and requested a due process hearing. An administrative hearing officer determined that the district had violated the student's rights in several ways. **The hearing officer ordered the district to provide the student with an individualized program of instruction beyond the district's general enrichment program.** The order required the district to provide the student with 1954 hours of compensatory education to be used within six years of his graduation from high school. The order further required a reevaluation of the student and called upon the district to reevaluate its in-service training for teachers and to restructure its gifted student program.

A state appeals panel affirmed the order and the district appealed to the commonwealth court, which observed that state law requires each school district to identify and evaluate gifted students, and to prepare IEPs for them. While compensatory education is an appropriate remedy for a district's failure to provide an adequate program, it is limited to educational services that are within the district's curriculum. **The administrative remedy in this case was inappropriate because it called for the district to provide college-level instruction that went beyond its own curriculum.** Because the appeals panel had exceeded its authority in creating this award, the court reversed its decision. *Brownsville Area School Dist. v. Student X*, 729 A.2d 198 (Pa.Commw.Ct.1999).

◆ A Connecticut special education statute defined "gifted children" as being "exceptional children" who did not progress effectively without special education. Although this definition coincided with the state law definition of children with disabilities, the statute did not mandate special education for gifted students, as it did for students with disabilities. **The parents of a Connecticut student identified as gifted demanded that his school board provide him with special education individually designed to meet his needs**. The board refused to provide an individualized education program for the student and the parents filed a lawsuit in a Connecticut trial court for a declaration that he was entitled to special education. The court granted summary judgment motions by the state and local education boards and the state commissioner of education, finding that gifted children did not have a right to special education under the state statute or constitution. The Supreme Court of Connecticut transferred an appeal by the student and parents from the state appellate court.

The supreme court observed that although the legislature had categorized gifted children within the definition of exceptional children, **the statute did not create a right to special education for gifted children. Special education was mandatory only for students with disabilities**. Because students with disabilities had different needs than gifted children, there was a rational basis for the legislature to treat the two groups differently, and there was no violation of the state constitution on equal protection grounds. The court affirmed the trial court's order for summary judgment. *Broadley v. Bd. of Educ. of the City of Meriden*, 229 Conn. 1, 639 A.2d 502 (1994).

IV. STATE REGULATORY AUTHORITY

Cases in this section involve state law conflicts arising from the exercise of school district authority and the operation of state compulsory attendance and delinquency laws. Because school districts are government entities that have only the powers granted to them by state law, a reviewing court may set aside a local decision as an abuse of authority. Courts have approved innovative educational approaches including charter schools and community service obligations when challenged on constitutional grounds.

A. School District Authority

◆ **An Indiana school board entered into an agreement with a non-public high school to operate an alternate education program**. Under the agreement, the board agreed to pay the high school $2,334 per semester for each student enrolled in the program, based upon a statutory formula that included state and local funds. **A group of taxpayers**, some of whom had children attending public schools in the district, **commenced a state superior court action** against the state department of education, state board of education, local educational agency and the high school, **challenging the agreement**. The taxpayers sought recovery of the monies paid under the agreement, asserting that the Indiana Constitution prohibited the arrangement. They also asserted violations of state law. The court granted motions to dismiss the case filed by the school board and other school entities and the parents appealed to the Court of Appeals of Indiana.

The court held that in order to attain standing to bring a lawsuit, a party must demonstrate a personal stake in the outcome of the case, and show immediate danger of suffering a direct injury as a result of the conduct at issue. The parents claimed that they would suffer direct injury due to the agreement, since public money used to fund the high school would result in less money for other programs attended by their children. The court disagreed, finding no threat of a direct injury to them as a result of the school board's action. The argument that less funding would be available for other programs was speculative. **Taxpayers typically have only a general interest in the spending of public funds that is common to all members of the public, and the taxpayers in this case had no personal stake in the expenditure of funds**. Since the taxpayers had no standing, the court affirmed the dismissal of the case. *Fort Wayne Educ. Assn. v. Indiana Dept. of Educ.*, 692 N.E.2d 902 (Ind.Ct.App.1998).

- A North Carolina school board adopted a student accountability policy to provide that students in grades three through eight who failed a state-developed standardized test would be retained in their grade instead of promoted. The policy contained a waiver for students who achieved passing grades during the school year and received teacher and principal approval. A group of North Carolina public school students and their parents filed a federal district court action against school officials, challenging the constitutionality of the policy. **The court held that the students failed to present the court with a valid constitutional claim, since a student who is not promoted would be given a remedial year to catch up on skills in which future performance could be enhanced**. Public policy discourages a federal court from substituting its judgment for that of publicly-elected school board members. The policy employed rational means to further a legitimate academic purpose. The court denied the motion for a preliminary order. *Erik V. by Catherine V. v. Causby*, 977 F.Supp. 384 (E.D.N.C.1997).

- A Phoenix middle school academy established a mandatory dress code. The school district justified the dress code as promoting an effective learning climate, increasing campus safety, fostering school unity and pride, eliminating label competition and minimizing clothing expenses. The school notified students that failure to comply with the code would result in transfer to another school. A number of students failed to comply with the code and some parents and students staged a protest on the academy's campus. The school district and a group representing the dissenting students and parents filed separate actions in an Arizona trial court, seeking declaratory and injunctive relief. The court consolidated the cases and held that the code did not violate the First Amendment. The students and parents appealed to the Court of Appeals of Arizona, which affirmed the judgment, ruling that **the dress code was not intended to restrict speech, was content-neutral and furthered the reasonable policies and goals of the academy**. *Phoenix Elementary School Dist. No. 1 v. Green*, 943 P.2d 836 (Ariz.Ct.App.Div.2 1997).

- A New York school district instituted a mandatory community service program. **Each high school student was required to complete 40 hours of community service** and participate in related classroom discussions. A student who objected to the program filed a lawsuit against the district in a federal court, claiming that it violated his constitutional rights. His parents asserted a constitutional right to direct the upbringing and education of their son. The court held that the program violated no constitutional rights, and the family appealed to the U.S. Court of Appeals, Second Circuit. The court agreed with the district court that the program did not implicate the Thirteenth Amendment, because the work was neither severe nor exploitative. It had an educational purpose and did not resemble slavery. **Although the parents had a liberty interest in raising their son, the court did not extend constitutional protection to their purely secular claim.** The program was reasonably related to the state's legitimate function of educating students and the court affirmed the district court judgment. *Immediato v. Rye Neck School Dist.*, 73 F.3d 454 (2d Cir.1996).

◆ Ohio law allows school districts to charge students for the use of certain instructional materials, with an exception for necessary textbooks. A school district that assessed a fee withheld the grades and credits of a high school student because his parents failed to pay the fee. The family filed a petition for an extraordinary order from the Supreme Court of Ohio, seeking the release of grades and credits. The family argued that the school board had a legal duty to issue the grades and credits since the fees were properly characterized as administrative costs and not classroom materials. The court disagreed, stating that there was evidence that proceeds from the instructional fee were used for classroom supplies and instructional materials. **Because the fees were used in compliance with the statute, the family was not entitled to an order compelling the district to issue the grades and credits.** *State ex rel. Massie v. Bd. of Educ. of Gahanna—Jefferson Pub. Schools*, 669 N.E.2d 839 (Ohio 1996).

B. Compulsory Attendance and Delinquency

State compulsory attendance and delinquency laws impose obligations on students that conflict when a juvenile court order requires incarceration of the student. Many states have acted to create alternative placements for students who would otherwise be suspended or expelled for violation of state laws. For a full discussion on the rights of students with disabilities in suspension and expulsion cases, please see Chapter Two, Section Four.

◆ The Pennsylvania Department of Public Welfare contracted with a private children and youth agency to operate a day treatment program located within the Bethlehem Area School District. The program served students attending school in the Bethlehem district and nonresident students who had been ordered into treatment by the county juvenile court. **The facility had an educational component for which the agency sought reimbursement from the Bethlehem school district.** When the district refused, the agency filed a state court petition seeking an order requiring the district to either pay for the educational services provided by the facility to nonresident students or provide the services to students regardless of their residency. The court granted the requested order, and the school district appealed to the Commonwealth Court of Pennsylvania.

On appeal, the school district argued that state law imposed no duty upon it to pay for the education of nonresident students, but created an option to provide or purchase services for its own students while the home districts of nonresident students were required to pay for the education of those students. The court disagreed, finding that **the school district had an obligation to provide for the educational component of all students attending the day treatment program.** The option it had under state law was to either provide the services or to pay another district to provide them. Because the provision of education to all students assigned to a day treatment program is the responsibility of the school district in which the program is located, the court affirmed the judgment. *Community Service Foundation, Inc. v. Bethlehem Area School Dist.*, 706 A.2d 882 (Pa.Commw.Ct.1998).

◆ A twelve-year-old Georgia student stabbed another student with a knife at school. School administrators permanently expelled her from all district schools, and this decision was affirmed by the state board of education. The student appealed to a state superior court, which affirmed the expulsion, then appealed to the Court of Appeals of Georgia. She claimed that the Georgia Constitution prohibited permanent expulsion, that the action violated the state compulsory attendance law and that it was an abuse of school board discretion. The court disagreed, holding that the state constitutional requirement to provide a free public education was limited by the need for student discipline. Local school boards were entitled to take appropriate disciplinary action and courts were not allowed to interfere with their decisions unless they were contrary to law or a gross abuse of discretion. **Permanent expulsion did not violate the state compulsory school attendance act in view of the local board's authority to impose discipline.** The court affirmed the expulsion order. *D.B. v. Clarke County Bd. of Educ.*, 220 Ga.App.330, 469 S.E.2d 438 (1996).

V. INCARCERATED STUDENTS

Section 1412(a)(1)(B)(ii) of the IDEA provides that a FAPE need not be provided to children with disabilities "aged 18 through 21 to the extent that State law does not require that special education and related services under this part be provided to children with disabilities who, in the educational placement prior to their incarceration in an adult correctional facility" were not identified as a child with a disability or did not have an IEP. Section 1412(a)(11)(C) allows states discretion as to whether they will provide services to students with disabilities who are convicted as adults under state law and subsequently incarcerated in adult prisons. As a result of these provisions, cases have arisen over exactly what obligations states have to incarcerated students with disabilities, primarily under state law.

◆ A 21-year-old Connecticut student had an IQ of 61 and was classified as educable mentally retarded. He attended a self-contained, bilingual special education program at a public high school until being arrested and hospitalized. A hospital placement team found him eligible for special education and determined that he required further assessment. The team prepared an IEP and placed him in an ungraded self-contained classroom in the hospital with related services. After his discharge, he returned to public school until being arrested again. He was then incarcerated in a correctional center that did not attempt to obtain his educational records despite knowing that he had a history of receiving special education. Within a few weeks of his release, he was again incarcerated on new charges and a social worker referred him to the Connecticut Office of Protection and Advocacy for Persons with Disabilities. The office assisted the student in obtaining services from the state department of children and families. Following his placement in punitive segregation, the student appeared for a competency determination and remained hospitalized. **A child-student team at the hospital certified the school district's determination of eligibility and implemented his IEP**. However, the hospital released the student and returned him to the custody of the correctional center, where he was admitted to the mental health unit. An evaluation determined that he was mentally retarded and needed a supervised, but not institutional, setting. The department of children and family services determined that the student's English coursework had deteriorated and a consultant informed the center that the student was a special education student with an IEP. The student submitted a form indicating his interest in receiving special education services. The advocacy and protection office contacted a social service agency that submitted a proposal for services on the student's behalf. The center began providing services to the student in a segregated housing unit and an IEP team meeting was convened. The student then inflicted wounds on himself and was placed in a restrictive housing unit due to chronic disciplinary problems.

Following a stalemate concerning the student's transition plan, the office of protection and advocacy requested a due process hearing on his behalf. A hearing officer awarded him one year of compensatory education, and a Connecticut trial court affirmed the decision. The special school district appealed to the state court of appeals. The court stated that the district knew that the student was entitled to special education services when the center received a call from the consultant. It was the district's responsibility to comply with the IDEA, not the student's. Any delay could not be attributed to the office of protection and advocacy for educational entitlements. **The district was charged with the responsibility of identifying students with special educational needs. The district was required to follow IDEA procedural requirements** and it was charged with the knowledge that he had an IEP from the time of the consultant's call. The district had no IEP for the student and was required to implement a program for him. Because the district failed to provide him with a free appropriate public education, he was entitled to compensatory education, even though he was over the age of 21. *Unified School District No. 1 v. Connecticut Department of Education*, 64 Conn. App. 273 (Conn. App. Ct. 2001).

- Pennsylvania law provided **that persons under the age of 21 who are confined to adult county correctional facilities and otherwise eligible for educational services are entitled to services only to the extent as expelled students**. This level of services translated into about five hours of services per week, in contrast to the 27.5-hour per week program of educational services enjoyed by regular students. The law differentiated between juveniles who were convicted as adults based on their place of incarceration, since those placed in state facilities received full education programs. Generally, juveniles who were sentenced to two years or less were confined in county facilities, while those sentenced to terms of five years or more were confined in state facilities.

Sentences of between two and five years could be served at either type of facility at the sentencing judge's discretion. Students over the age of 17 in county facilities received no educational services at all, since state law did not provide for any services to expelled students. A group representing juveniles incarcerated in adult county facilities sued the state of Pennsylvania and numerous state officials in a federal district court, asserting violation of their constitutional right to equal protection under the laws. The parties agreed that all students who were confined as pre-trial detainees should receive full educational programs. Students with disabilities who required special education services were also entitled to receive full educational programs. The court then held that the remaining students were not entitled to a preliminary order mandating full educational services.

On appeal, the Third Circuit observed that education is not a fundamental right. Accordingly, equal-protection claims based on deprivation of educational services do not warrant a heightened degree of constitutional scrutiny. The court held that **the state was required only to show that the disproportionate allocation of state educational resources had some rational relationship to a legitimate end. It then found that the state had met this showing** by providing four justifications for the distinction between county and state adult corrections facilities. County correctional institutions, unlike state facilities, had space limitations. State facilities also had higher youth populations, reducing the cost of providing education there. Pennsylvania argued convincingly that the discontinuation of full educational services at state institutions would result in significant new security concerns. There was also a greater need for educational services at state facilities where longer terms were served since by contrast, county jails served a more transient student population. The legislature was entitled to allocate state resources on these grounds, and its judgment was not subject to judicial second-guessing. The Third Circuit affirmed the district court decision denying relief to the students. *Brian B. et al. v. Commonwealth of Pennsylvania Department of Education*, 230 F.3d 582 (3d Cir. 2000), *cert. denied,* 532 U.S. 972 (2001).

- The Washington legislature enacted a law in 1998 providing for the education of juveniles incarcerated in adult prisons. After two school districts began providing services at correctional facilities under the new law, **a group of inmates brought a class-action lawsuit** in the state court system against Washington state, the school districts, and a number of state officials, **alleging that the various entities failed to provide special education services in violation of state and federal law**. They also asserted violations of the U.S. and Washington constitutions. The court granted summary judgment to the inmates on their state-law claims and invalidated the 1998 legislation as unconstitutional because it failed to provide special educational opportunities. The court dismissed all of the federal claims, and the parties appealed unfavorable aspects of the decision to the Washington Supreme Court.

The state supreme court observed that the 1998 legislation, not the state's basic and special education acts, determined the outcome of the state-law claims. The legislature had specifically acted to exempt incarcerated juveniles from the state compulsory school attendance law. The state special education law did not specifically address the education of juveniles incarcerated in adult facilities. It ensured educational opportunities "for all children with disabilities who are not institutionalized." Inmates were outside the state's school system and were exempt from the provisions of the state special education act. The court rejected the inmates' argument that the state constitution required basic and special education for all inmates in adult prisons up to the age of 22. The provision of education to inmates up to the age of 18 satisfied the U.S. Constitution. The 1998 legislation did not violate the Washington Constitution, since the court found that the state had no obligation to provide an identical education to all children within the state, regardless of their circumstances. The court rejected the inmates' assertion that the state had a duty under the IDEA to provide special education to students with disabilities under the age of 22. **IDEA language specifically exempts the states from their duty to provide special education services "where its application would be inconsistent with state law or practice" for students age 18 through 21. It also exempted those students who were not identified as disabled or did not have IEPs prior to incarceration**. The state was not required to provide special education services to students over the age of 18 if it did not also provide education services to students without disabilities in this age group. Since the 1998 law clearly stated that inmates were entitled to education until the age of 18, the trial court had properly dismissed the inmates' IDEA claim. Because the IDEA claim was without merit, a related claim brought by the inmates under Section 504 of the Rehabilitation Act had also been properly dismissed. The school districts were not required by state law or the Washington Constitution to provide educational services to juvenile inmates, and the trial court had properly dismissed the claims against them. *Tunstall v. Bergeson*, 5 P.3d 691 (Wash. 2000), *cert. denied,* 532 U.S. 920 (2001).

◆ The Maryland Court of Special Appeals held that **a juvenile court judge could not order a county education board to provide educational services to a delinquent student who was ordered to attend a children's institute. The board was not a party to the delinquency proceeding and the court lacked the power to order it to provide the student with services**. The student was adjudicated delinquent at the age of 13. A juvenile court judge entered an order placing him in a regional institute for children and adolescents. As part of the order, the judge held that the student's school board was required to provide him with educational services at the institute. The board appealed to the state court of special appeals, where it argued that the juvenile court had no authority to enter the order and that the order violated the constitutional separation of powers. The court of special appeals reviewed the state Juvenile Causes Act and noted that its purpose was to provide for the care, protection and development of juveniles and to provide them with treatment, training and rehabilitation. The act's relevant provisions did not authorize a juvenile court to order a school system to provide educational services to juveniles. While a court could commit a delinquent child to the custody of the state Department of Juvenile Services for appropriate placement, the separation of powers doctrine prohibited the judge's order in this case. The court vacated the judgment and remanded the case to the juvenile court. *In re Nicholas B.*, 768 A.2d 735 (Md. Ct. Spec. App. 2001).

- A 16-year-old Florida student with disabilities was eligible for special education services and his school district developed an IEP for him. One month later, he was sentenced to a two-year prison term and transferred to the custody of the Florida Department of Corrections, which failed to provide him with any educational services. The student requested a due process hearing, resulting in an adverse order by the state Division of Administrative Hearings. The correctional institution in which the student was incarcerated developed a transition plan for the student without notifying him, his parents or their attorney. **The family then petitioned a federal district court for a preliminary order declaring the denial of an administrative hearing to be improper, requesting reinstatement of the IEP pending a due process hearing, and declaring that the state could not change the transition plan without prior notice to the parents.**

The corrections department asserted that under existing Florida law, inmates under 22 years of age could lawfully be denied a special education due process hearing. The court noted that **the corrections department was required by the IDEA to provide prior written notice to parents regarding any change in the placement of a student or the provision of a free appropriate public education.** The corrections department argued that the Individuals with Disabilities Education Act Amendments of 1997 called for the transfer of the due process notification rights of an inmate convicted as an adult from the parents to the inmate, relieving the department of its duty to provide notice to the parents. The court disagreed, stating that although the rights accorded to parents under the IDEA transfer to students upon reaching the age of majority, these rights do not transfer where a minor student is convicted as an adult. However, since the family failed to show the propriety of the IEP after his incarceration at the correctional facility, the court denied the request to reinstate the IEP. **The department was enjoined from altering or changing the IEP or transition plan and the student was entitled to a due process hearing**. *Paul Y. by Kathy Y. v. Singletary*, 979 F.Supp. 1422 (S.D.Fla.1997).

- **A 1985 amendment to a New Hampshire statute required school districts to perform evaluations, develop individualized education plans and hold staffings for incarcerated special education students between the ages of 18 and 21** in their jurisdictions. It also made school districts that sent students to residential schools in other districts liable for all special education costs associated with these placements. Prior to the amendment, liability for the cost of a court-ordered juvenile placement in a residential school was placed on the town in which the student lived. A New Hampshire school district filed a lawsuit against the state in the state court system, claiming that the amendment created an unfunded mandate in violation of the state constitution. The district argued that the amendment unfairly required school districts to provide services for incarcerated special education students between the ages of 18 and 21. The court upheld the amendment, and the district appealed to the Supreme Court of New Hampshire.

The court held that the 1985 amendment did not create an unconstitutional unfunded mandate because it represented no new, expanded, or modified program for school districts that might require additional local expenditures. Although recognizing the burden of the responsibility for districts to enter state prisons to perform evaluations, conduct IEPs and hold annual staffings, school districts bore the responsibility for the education of each child residing in their jurisdiction. **The school district was responsible for developing plans for each of its resident incarcerated students between the ages of 18 and 21**, and the court affirmed the judgment for the state. *Nashua School Dist. v. State of New Hampshire*, 667 A.2d 1036 (N.H.1995).

CHAPTER NINE

Discrimination

I. FEDERAL ANTIDISCRIMINATION LAWS

The Rehabilitation Act of 1973 and the Americans with Disabilities Act of 1990 prohibit discrimination against individuals with disabilities. They state that no individual with a disability is to be excluded from employment, programs, or services if the individual is otherwise qualified to participate in the program or to receive benefits to which he or she is entitled. Under the statutes, it is discriminatory for a school or educational facility to impose eligibility criteria that screen out disabled individuals. It is also discriminatory for the facilities to fail to reasonably accommodate disabled individuals. This chapter deals primarily with disabled students. However, there is a substantial body of disability employment cases in Chapter Seven, Section II, subsection A. For cases involving the placement of students with disabilities, see Chapter Two.

A. Generally

◆ The U.S. Supreme Court concluded that **no private cause of action exists to enforce federal regulations published under Title VI of the Civil Rights Act** of 1964. It dismissed a class action suit advanced by non-English speakers who claimed that Alabama's exclusive reliance on English for state driver's license examinations had a discriminatory effect based on national origin. Title VI is one of the principal federal laws preventing discrimination on the basis of race, color, or national origin. It prohibits federal funding recipients, including states and educational institutions, from discriminating in any covered program or activity and is commonly cited in education cases alleging discrimination on those grounds. Title IX of the Education Amendments of 1972 was patterned after Title VI. Alabama amended its Constitution in 1990 to declare English its official language. The state began administering driver's license examinations only in English, and a federal district court agreed with a class of individuals that the state's actions violated a Title VI regulation. The district court decision was affirmed on appeal. The Supreme Court agreed to review the case and noted that **Title VI prohibits only intentional discrimination and cannot be used to enforce a disparate impact action**. Thus, there could be no private right of action to enforce Title VI disparate impact regulations. Federal private causes of action can originate only from Congress. In the absence of congressional action, courts cannot create new ones, and the judgment was reversed. *Alexander et al. v. Sandoval*, 532 U.S. 275, 121 S.Ct. 1511, 149 L.Ed.2d 517 (2001).

◆ The parents of two unrelated students with autism alleged that their local school district denied their requests for limited classroom access to allow observation of their children by independent autism experts. The parents sued the district in a federal district court for discrimination under Section 504 of the Rehabilitation Act and the ADA, and for personal injury under state law. They sought monetary relief, an order requiring district administrators and teachers to attend civil rights and disability discrimination classes and a declaration that district policies violated Section 504 and the ADA. **The parents added claims on their own behalf for "associational discrimination," asserting that they had suffered separate, direct injuries as a result of the discriminatory exclusion of their experts**. The district initially moved to dismiss the action, asserting that the case was actually an IDEA action involving the students' entitlement to a FAPE and therefore the parents were required to exhaust IDEA administrative remedies.

The court denied the motion, and the district filed a subsequent motion to dismiss the parents' individual claims for "associational discrimination" for failure to state a claim and lack of jurisdiction. The district argued that the parents failed to show they had suffered direct injuries separate from any injuries to their children. The court stated, in order to have legal standing in this case, the parents had to show that they themselves had suffered specific, direct and separate injuries traceable to the district's actions. **There was no evidence the district had singled out the parents and treated them differently than the parents of nondisabled students**. They only sought to have their experts admitted to observe their children's classrooms. In order to prevail on this claim, the court found that the parents would have to show that they, and not their children, had a right to district services, and that they were discriminated against solely because of their association with disabled persons. The court held that the parents had not alleged any separate and distinct denial of services to them. Their attempts to gain classroom access for their experts related solely to their children's educational needs and did not amount to an attempt to exercise personal rights for their own benefit. The parents did not allege that the district provided the parents of nondisabled children with unrestricted classroom access. The court held that the parents had no valid claims for associational discrimination, and it granted the district's dismissal motion. *Glass et al. v. Hillsboro School District 1J*, 142 F.Supp.2d 1286 (D. Or. 2001).

◆ A federal district court dismissed an Illinois family's claims against a school district and a principal under Title III of the ADA because of untimely filed papers and because Title III applied only to private entities operating places of public accommodations. **Public entities are covered under Title II of the ADA, which does not provide for personal liability**. The parents claimed in a lawsuit that the principal and school district discriminated against the student. The principal moved to dismiss the case, asserting that she could not be held liable for a Title III violation and that the family had filed untimely motion papers. The court agreed, refusing to review the family's papers. Even if it had considered them, the Title III claim was untenable because the action was governed by Title II of the act. There was no merit to the family's assertion that the school district was an "operator of a public accommodation" as defined by Title III. The school district and high school were "quintessential public entities" under Title II, and that part of the act was the student's exclusive means of enforcing her ADA rights. **Because Title II does not provide for personal liability, the principal was entitled to dismissal of the claims against her**. *Block ex rel. Block v. Rockford Public School District No. 205*, No. 01 C 50133, 2001 WL 1195757 (N.D. Ill. 2001).

◆ A Louisiana student with cerebral palsy, scoliosis and learning disabilities used a wheelchair and required the assistance of an aide for toileting. **His parents alleged the school district denied him a FAPE under the IDEA and other state and federal laws because of accessibility concerns and lack of transition services**. They requested a due process hearing to contest the lack of accessible facilities at the student's school. The hearing was continued to allow time for the parties to revise the student's IEP. The hearing officer inspected the high school to view its accessibility. After the hearing resumed, the student's attorneys presented several documents, then walked out. The hearing continued in their absence and the hearing officer determined that the school board had provided the student with a FAPE in the least restrictive environment. A state-level review panel upheld the decision and the parents appealed to a federal district court. The court affirmed the panel's decision that the district did not violate the IDEA. The student's program was appropriately individualized and addressed his special needs in the least restrictive environment.

The school district then moved for dismissal of the family's remaining claims under the ADA, Section 504 of the Rehabilitation Act, 42 U.S.C. § 1983 and provisions of the Louisiana Civil Code. The district argued that the non-IDEA claims had already been adjudicated by prior decisions of the court, a review panel and an administrative hearing officer. This was because the claims were redundant and subsumed in the IDEA decisions. The court noted that the IDEA permits students to include other claims in an IDEA action, so long as they exhaust available administrative remedies when doing so. Where a Section 504 or ADA claim had a factual basis that was indistinct from an IDEA claim, it was appropriate to dismiss it as redundant. In this case, the hearing officer, review panel and court had previously held that the school facilities were not improper, deficient or defective. **The factual basis for the Section 504 and ADA claims was identical to the IDEA claim and had been resolved in the district's favor.** The claim for civil rights violations under Section 1983 was untenable because there was no finding of intentional discrimination and no statutory violation. The student's state-law claims also arose from the same facts that had been considered and resolved in prior activity and were precluded because they were "part and parcel of the IDEA cause of action." The court granted the district's motion to dismiss the non-IDEA claims and dismissed motions by the state education board and department of education as moot. *Pace v. Bogalusa City School Board*, No. Civ. A. 99-806, 2001 WL 969103 (E.D. La. 2001).

◆ A Kentucky ninth grader with hemophilia and hepatitis B joined the junior varsity basketball team. Upon learning of the student's medical condition, **the high school's principal instructed the coach to put the student on "hold" pending further investigation into whether it was medically appropriate for him to play**. After school officials spoke to the student's mother and obtained information from his physician, the principal directed the coach to allow the student to play. Before this decision was communicated to the family, the student decided that he no longer wanted to play. The family commenced a federal district court action against the school district, board and school officials, asserting violations of Section 504 of the Rehabilitation Act and the Americans with Disabilities Act. The district court entered judgment for the school district and officials, and the family appealed to the U.S. Court of Appeals for the Sixth Circuit.

The circuit court noted that under either Section 504 or the ADA, a person with disabilities may be excluded from a program if participation presents a direct threat to the health and safety of others.
In this case, the student was placed on hold while **the school district was legitimately attempting to determine whether his participation on the junior varsity basketball team presented a serious health risk to others**. Congress created a narrow exception to the broad prohibition against discrimination mandated by the ADA in cases where an individual with disabilities presents a direct threat to the health and safety of others. School officials had never actually removed the student from the team and had reasonably placed him on hold status while awaiting medical advice. The school's action was appropriate in view of the potential liability faced by the school if another student became infected as a result of the student's participation. It appeared that the student had chosen not to participate on the team of his own volition and there was no violation of his rights under either Section 504 or the ADA. The school district had not violated the student's rights in any manner, and the circuit court affirmed the judgment in its favor. *Doe v. Woodford County Board of Education,* 213 F.3d 921 (6th Cir. 2000).

◆ **A student with a form of dwarfism and another student with disabilities were left with an adult in a otherwise evacuated middle school for approximately 70 minutes during a bomb threat**. The student filed a disability discrimination complaint against the school board with the U.S. Department of Education's Office for Civil Rights, which resulted in an agreement calling for the board to adopt a new emergency preparedness plan. The parents dropped the case and the board adopted a policy regarding the evacuation of students with disabilities during emergencies. Within two months, an unscheduled fire alarm went off and the student was left alone for approximately two minutes. The student's math teacher stayed with her during the incident, while non-disabled students were evacuated. The family sued the school board in a federal district court, claiming that its actions during both evacuations violated Section 504 and the ADA. The court denied the board's motion to dismiss, but later awarded it summary judgment on the basis of the OCR settlement and lack of bad faith or gross misjudgment by the board. The court denied the family's motion to reconsider the summary judgment order and they appealed to the Fourth Circuit.

The Fourth Circuit held that the motion for reconsideration was properly denied. However, the OCR settlement was not a waiver of the student's federal civil rights under Section 504 or the ADA. The right to file actions under these laws was a statutory right created by Congress that could not be barred without a knowing waiver. Since the settlement did not contain a waiver or release of rights under federal discrimination laws, the claims could not be dismissed on that basis. The district court had also considered the summary judgment motion under an erroneous standard, requiring proof of either bad faith or gross misjudgment. This standard was applicable in the context of the development of an IEP, but had no relevance in a case involving the emergency evacuation of a disabled student from a school building. The relevant consideration was whether the board denied the student access to safe evacuation procedures afforded to others. The student was not excluded from these procedures during the fire drill incident because the board had by then devised an emergency preparedness plan to safely evacuate students with disabilities during emergencies. The board was not liable for its conduct and summary judgment had been correct. However, **the student had been excluded from safe evacuation procedures during the bomb threat incident**, as the board had no reasonable plan to evacuate students with disabilities at that time. Because the board discriminated against the student on the basis of her disabilities during the bomb threat, the district court order for summary judgment regarding this aspect of the student's claims was improper. **The appropriate remedy for the violation was an order requiring the board to develop and implement a reasonable plan of evacuation for students with disabilities**. Since it had already done this in response to the OCR proceeding, the student was not entitled to further relief. *Shirey v. City of Alexandria School Board*, 229 F.3d 1143 (4th Cir. 2000).

◆ A Louisiana student underwent a private evaluation after her mother noticed she was having reading and writing difficulties. The evaluating physician identified the student as having dyslexia and the mother sought to have her evaluated by the school system in accordance with state regulations implementing the state Dyslexia Law. The school formed a Section 504 committee that followed the five-step state regulatory plan for students with dyslexia, ultimately concluding that the student was already receiving an appropriate reading program and accommodations. The committee ruled that she should not be evaluated for special education services. After obtaining another private evaluation, the motion filed a due process complaint against the district, resulting in a decision that the district was in compliance with the law and provided the student with a FAPE.

A state review panel affirmed the decision and the mother appealed to the Louisiana Court of Appeal, claiming the district violated the state Dyslexia Law, the IDEA and Section 504. The court found that **while there is significant overlap between Section 504 and the IDEA, students who are covered only by Section 504 are not entitled to IDEA rights and protections**. A student with dyslexia whose disabilities qualify for services under Section 504 might not qualify under the IDEA. In this case, the school district had fully complied with the dyslexia law and its implementing regulations to determine whether the student had a disabling condition. The evidence indicated that the district provided her appropriate accommodations and remediation under Section 504, including extra time, repeated directions and leniency for misspellings. The district's methodology was reasonably calculated to enable the student to receive educational benefits and her performance supported this finding. Not every student with dyslexia was entitled to special education under the IDEA, and the district had properly refused to evaluate her. *Grant v. St. James Parish School Board et al.*, No. 99-3757, Section N, 2000 U.S. Dist. LEXIS 16544 (E.D. La. 2000).

◆ An Iowa student with severe disabilities, including cerebral palsy and spastic quadriplegia, participated in the special education program of her regularly assigned, neighborhood school. She was transported there with a lift bus that traveled a special route for her. **Her parents sought to transfer her to a different school** under an intra-district transfer program, **and asked for special transportation, despite the program requirement that they furnish their own transportation**. The district approved the transfer but denied the transportation request. An administrative law judge held that the parents had established no need for special transportation beyond parental preference for a specific placement. A federal district court reversed the administrative decision, ruling that the district had impermissibly limited the student's opportunity to participate in the transfer program.

The district appealed to the Eighth Circuit, which observed that in § 504 cases, complaining students must demonstrate that there has been discrimination on the basis of disability. A defendant school district is entitled to show that the requested accommodation is unduly burdensome. This may be demonstrated by proof of undue financial and administrative burdens to the district, or by showing that the requested accommodations require fundamental alteration of a school program. The court found that the student was not denied the benefit of participating in the intra-district transfer program, since she was allowed to participate in it on the same terms as other applicants. There was no evidence of discrimination in the conduct of the transfer program, and the student was not denied access to it on the basis of her disability. Instead, her parents did not wish to comply with "the main condition of the program applicable to all students who wish[ed] to participate - parental transportation." **Requiring the district to spend additional funds on transportation for the transfer program would fundamentally alter this requirement, creating an undue burden on the school district**. The court reversed and remanded the district court decision. *Timothy H. and Brenda H. v. Cedar Rapids Comm. School Dist.*, 178 F.3d 968 (8th Cir.1999).

◆ A student was accepted into her school's show choir. The student suffered recurrent sinus infections that caused frequent absences. The choir director advised the student's father that continuing absences caused potential problems for her participation. The student was picked for a minor role in the spring play. She soon attempted suicide, allegedly in the belief that the director had intended that she fail her audition. She was diagnosed as having severe depression and placed on a treatment plan. After the student returned to school, the director announced to the entire class that the student would not be permitted to participate in the spring play, which was then less than two weeks away. The student's mother intervened, arguing that the student knew the routines and that her mental health and recovery required that she be allowed to continue participating. The school principal advised the director that she must either enforce a previously unenforced written absence policy, or allow all students to perform. **The director announced that she would enforce the attendance policy, which had the effect of precluding the student and three others from some of the routines in the spring play**. The family sued the director, principal, school board, and others in a state court for Americans with Disabilities Act violations and intentional infliction of emotional distress. A federal district court held that the student had not been discriminated against on the basis of depression, and that she was excluded from full participation in the spring play for reasons other than her disability, a valid and uniformly enforced attendance policy.

The family appealed to the Fourth Circuit, which held that the district court decision was based on a misunderstanding of the complaint. The complaint alleged that the exclusion of the student had occurred after the director was informed of the student's depression, and that the instructor had made the decision to exclude her based on the alleged disability. The complaint also stated that that the attendance policy was not uniformly enforced. These allegations were adequate to support federal disability discrimination claims. Alternatively, the complaint alleged that the policy was used as a pretext for unlawful discrimination. **The discriminatory application of a neutral rule, if proven, would be grounds for an ADA violation**. On remand, the district court was to evaluate the complaint under the same analysis as employment discrimination claims arising under Title VII of the Civil Rights Act of 1964. Because Congress expressly stated that Title VII remedies apply to ADA actions, the court agreed with the school employees that the ADA does not authorize any remedies against individuals. Only employers are liable for damages in Title VII actions, and the district court had properly dismissed the claims against the director and principal in their individual capacities. However, the district court had improperly dismissed the state law claims for intentional infliction of emotional distress, and that claim was reinstated. The court remanded the case for further proceedings. *Baird v. Rose*, 192 F.3d 462 (4th Cir. 1999).

◆ Despite having been diagnosed with Attention Deficit Hyperactivity Disorder, a student was ineligible for special education and related services under the IDEA. The student received excellent grades. His parents challenged the eligibility determination in a due process hearing that resulted in dismissal of the IDEA claims. The district then agreed to develop a § 504 plan for the student calling for peer and teacher monitoring, positive reinforcement, extra time to complete assignments and regular evaluations to assess progress. **The parents rejected the plan and sought to enroll the student into a reading program utilizing a phonetic approach**. The parents pursued their objections in administrative proceedings, and ultimately appealed to a federal district court.

The court considered motions for summary judgment by the parties, and observed that § 504 of the Rehabilitation Act prohibits disability-based discrimination by recipients of federal funding. In order to prevail in a § 504 case, a student must show not only that a school district has failed to provide a free appropriate public education, but that the district has acted intentionally. In this case, the evidence indicated that the district had provided the student with a FAPE. Although he tested below average in some categories, he received all A and B grades. Because the student's academic achievements indicated that he was receiving a FAPE, he was not entitled to relief under § 504. **The court found that the suit was an attempt by the parents to maximize their child's potential, which is not required by § 504**. Accordingly, the school district was entitled to summary judgment. *Benik v. Lisle Comm. Unit School Dist. #202*, 1999 U.S. Dist. LEXIS 8007 (N.D. Ill. 1999).

- An Illinois school's athletic code of conduct called for partial loss of athletic eligibility following an alcohol-related violation and loss of eligibility for a full year after a second incident. The school revoked a student's athletic eligibility after he was involved in an alcohol-related auto accident, his second violation of the policy in a one-month period. **The student was later diagnosed as an alcoholic and requested reinstatement to sports eligibility**. The school superintendent and board denied his request, and his mother sued under the Americans with Disabilities Act and Section 504 of the Rehabilitation Act.

The school board moved for judgment on the pleadings, noting that not even the student himself was aware of his alcoholism at the time of the incidents and that, therefore, discrimination could not have played a role in the decision to revoke his athletic eligibility. The court agreed, noting that in order to prevail on his federal disability discrimination claims, the student was required to show unlawful discrimination. **Even if school officials had been aware of the student's condition at the time of revocation, they would not have violated the law because the Rehabilitation Act expressly permits schools to punish students for using alcohol, and students with disabilities are subject to punishment to the same extent as others**. See 29 U.S.C. § 705(20)(C)(iv). The court also rejected the student's claim that school officials refused to grant reasonable accommodation to his disability. It held that the accommodation he requested was not a reasonable one, because it was at odds with the purposes behind the no-alcohol rule, which was intended to establish ideals of good sportsmanship and respect for rules and authority. The court awarded judgment to the board and officials. *Stearns v. Bd. of Educ. for Warren Township High School Dist. No. 121*, 1999 U.S. Dist. LEXIS 17981 (N.D. Ill. 1999).

- The treating physician of a Missouri student with attention deficit hyperactivity disorder issued her a prescription for Ritalin that was in excess of the daily recommendation listed in the *Physicians' Desk Reference*. Her parents asked the student's school nurse to administer part of the dosage during the school day. **The nurse refused to administer the dose because the district maintained a written policy against the administration of drugs in excess of the recommended dosage** as listed in the *Desk Reference*. Although the school board offered the student several alternatives, including alteration of her class schedule or administration by a family member, the family filed a federal district court action against the school board, claiming discrimination in violation of § 504 of the Rehabilitation Act and the Americans with Disabilities Act (ADA). The court granted summary judgment to the school district, and the family appealed to the U.S. Court of Appeals for the Eighth Circuit.

The court commented that to succeed on either claim, the family had to show that the school district had refused to administer medication to the student because of her disability. **The drug administration policy had an objective standard, was neutral, and applied to all students regardless of disability**. There were alternative means for the student to receive her medication, which the parents had rejected. The district did not knowingly administer prescription drugs to any student in excess of the recommended dosage and nothing suggested that the policy or its application had the purpose or effect of discriminating against students with disabilities. There was no merit to the family's claim that the district had failed to reasonably accommodate the student by rejecting their request for waiver of the policy. The waiver request was unreasonable because it would impose an undue hardship on the district to verify the risk of harm for an excess dosage in each individual case. The court affirmed the judgment for the school board. *DeBord v. Bd. of Educ. of Ferguson-Florissant School Dist.*, 126 F.3d 1102 (8th Cir.1997).

◆ In a similar case involving another Missouri student, a school nurse refused to administer medication exceeding the maximum daily dosage recommended in the *Physicians' Desk Reference* despite two medical opinions obtained by the student's parents. The parents changed their work schedule and child care arrangements to give the student his required dosage, then filed a lawsuit against the school district for violations of the Americans with Disabilities Act (ADA), § 504 of the Rehabilitation Act and 42 U.S.C. § 1983. **The U.S. District Court for the Eastern District of Missouri issued a temporary restraining order requiring school employees to continue administering the medication**. The court then held a hearing and dissolved the restraining order, and the parents appealed to the U.S. Court of Appeals for the Eighth Circuit. The court held that the family had failed to present evidence that the district violated any federal civil rights law by refusing to administer medication. **There was no evidence that the school's decision had been based on the student's disability rather than school policies and concerns about liability and student health**. The family's claims that their lives had been disrupted did not demonstrate irreparable harm that would require a temporary order pending a trial on the matter. The court affirmed the district court decision.

The district court later granted summary judgment to the school district on the merits, and the student appealed again to the Eighth Circuit, which found no evidence that he had been treated differently from other students because of his disability. The district's policy was nondiscriminatory and aimed at protecting student health. The district had offered the family alternatives which reasonably accommodated the student's disability. **The family had offered no evidence that the district failed to evenhandedly implement or enforce the policy on the basis of the student's disability and the accommodations proposed by the family presented an undue burden** to the district. The court affirmed the judgment. *Davis v. Francis Howell School Dist.*, 138 F.3d 754 (8th Cir.1998).

◆ A Texas student suffered a traumatic brain injury and as a result had frontal lobe syndrome. His parents resisted efforts by their school district to evaluate him for special education programs and he achieved reasonable progress in regular education classes. This included passing the Texas Assessment of Academic

Skills test and receiving passing grades. The school district created a written accommodation plan for the student under § 504 of the Rehabilitation Act. **His parents claimed that school employees stigmatized the student as being "special" and discriminated against him in reaction to their complaints.** They requested a hearing after which a hearing officer held that the school district had exercised good faith in implementing the § 504 program and provided reasonable accommodations for the student. The parents appealed to a Texas district court, and the school district removed the case to a federal district court.

The court observed that § 504 regulations compel federal funding recipients such as school districts to provide disabled students a free appropriate public education and to refrain from discrimination. In order to bring a successful § 504 complaint, a student must demonstrate failure by the funding recipient to provide a free appropriate education and bad faith or gross misjudgment. As long as educators have exercised professional judgment that does not grossly depart from accepted standards, there can be no § 504 liability. **The student had failed to show any § 504 violation and the discrimination claims were mainly based on the perception of retaliation by school employees due to the parents' behavior.** Also, a single remark by one teacher implying that the student was brain damaged failed to rise to the level necessary for a showing of discrimination. Because of the absence of gross misjudgment or bad faith, the court dismissed the § 504 claim. It also dismissed claimed violations of the Due Process and Equal Protection Clauses and the First Amendment. *K.U. by Michael U. v. Alvin Indep. School Dist.*, 991 F.Supp. 599 (S.D.Tex.1998).

- The Oakland Unified School District (OUSD) and a group representing resident students with disabilities entered into a consent decree settling an action brought by the students to enforce OUSD's compliance with the Americans with Disabilities Act and the Rehabilitation Act. Under the consent decree, **OUSD agreed to undertake a programatic self-evaluation and to survey its existing facilities and programs** to identify architectural and physical barriers to students with mobility impairments. OUSD also agreed to identify and remediate safety hazards and to reimburse the class of disabled students for some of the costs of monitoring the consent decree. The students filed a motion in the U.S. District Court for the Northern District of California, asserting that OUSD was not in compliance with the consent decree, and the court considered their motion to compel compliance.

The court found evidence that OUSD had failed to conduct a programatic self-evaluation or a survey of existing facilities as specified in the consent decree. Both OUSD and the class representing the students had failed to identify all of the possible hazards covered under the consent decree. The court ordered the parties to identify these hazards and report to the court at a later date. **The court ordered OUSD to comply with the decree by performing the programatic self-evaluation and survey of existing facilities as soon as possible and to reimburse the students for their monitoring costs.** The court granted the students' motion and approved an award of attorney's fees. *Putnam v. Oakland Unif. School Dist.*, 980 F.Supp. 1094 (N.D.Cal.1997).

B. Reasonable Accommodation

Under the ADA and the Rehabilitation Act, educational facilities, as well as many other entities, are required to make reasonable accommodations for disabled individuals. For places of public accommodation, such as schools, this entails the reasonable modification of policies, practices or procedures when such modifications are necessary for disabled individuals to participate in the schools' programs or to benefit from their services. However, modifications which would fundamentally alter the schools' programs or services or which would result in an undue burden or hardship are not required.

◆ A 12-year-old student with AIDS sought admission to group karate classes at a private karate school, and his parents signed an application for admission asserting that he was in good health and suffered from no illness or condition that would pose a threat to other students. The school taught exclusively traditional Japanese, combat-oriented martial arts. Students learned techniques that involved substantial body contact, and often received minor, bloody injuries from sparring. After the student's first class, the owner was informed that the student had AIDS. **The owner banned the student from further group classes** based on the belief that the student posed a direct threat to the health and safety of other class members. **Instead, the owner offered to give the student private lessons**. This offer was rejected and the family filed a federal district court lawsuit against the school under Title III of the ADA. The court held that the student's condition threatened the health of others and refused to order the school to admit him.

On appeal to the Fourth Circuit, the court agreed that the school did not violate Title III of the ADA. **The offer of private lessons was a reasonable accommodation, and placement in the group classes posed too great a risk to the safety of other students**. The suddenness of injuries, the tendency of some wounds to splatter blood, the continuous movement and contact of karate, and the inability to immediately detect injuries undermined the effectiveness of precautions like eye coverings and gloves. Also, the school was not required to fundamentally alter the nature of its karate program. The court affirmed the district court judgment for the school. *Montalvo v. Radcliffe*, 167 F.3d 873 (4th Cir.1999).

◆ A New York man was diagnosed as suffering from anxiety disorder, social phobia, and panic attacks. Despite his disability, he obtained a degree in anthropology through a state college's distance learning program. In 1996, he applied for admission into the Masters of Arts and Liberal Studies program at the college and was accepted. He advised the college that he would not be able to attend the required residency program due to his disability, and asked whether he could attend the program via satellite uplink. **The college offered to accommodate his disability by having him attend the program under certain modified circumstances**. However, the student rejected the accommodation based on his belief that it was neither reasonable nor feasible. He brought suit against the state and a university official in the U.S. District Court for the Western District of New York, alleging violations of the ADA and the New York Human Rights Law. The student moved for a preliminary injunction.

The court found that the student met the essential eligibility requirements to participate in the masters program. In order to receive an injunction, he had to show that a monetary award would not adequately compensate him for his injuries. The court found that the student sufficiently demonstrated that he would not be able to participate in that or any other masters program at the college. However, educational institutions are not required to lower or effect substantial modifications of standards to accommodate a handicapped person. The only remaining issue therefore was whether his requested accommodation was reasonable or would constitute a fundamental or substantial modification of the program. The court noted that **the administrators at the college made efforts to accommodate his disability, and it was the severe nature of his handicap rather than the college's failure to offer reasonable accommodation that limited the student's ability to achieve his educational objectives**. The court therefore found that allowing the student to participate in the residency program via satellite uplink would be a substantial modification of the educational program, and as such, his requested accommodation was unreasonable. The court rejected the student's motion for a preliminary injunction. *Maczaczyj v. State of New York*, 956 F.Supp. 403 (W.D.N.Y.1997).

◆ A Nevada elementary school music instructor volunteered as a helping dog trainer. The volunteer work required her to acclimate a helping dog to its future master's home and public environment. This included having the dog lie down or sleep next to her for extended time periods. **The instructor asked her employer for permission to bring a golden retriever she was training to class each day to lie down or sleep under her desk**. The school district denied the request, stating that this would create a distraction and that students might be afraid of or allergic to the dog. The teacher filed a complaint against the school district in a state trial court under a Nevada law making it an unlawful practice for a place of public accommodation to refuse admittance to a person with a helping dog or service animal. The court granted the instructor's request for a temporary order allowing her to bring the dog to class pending further consideration, subject to any serious difficulties or dangers created by the presence of the dog at school. The district appealed to the Supreme Court of Nevada.

The supreme court observed that **the district had refused to negotiate a reasonable compromise with the music instructor, despite the mandatory language of the statute requiring a place of public accommodation to allow a training dog**. The district court had correctly granted the instructor's request for an injunction, as there was a high probability that she would succeed on the merits of her claim since the school was a place of public accommodation and she was a trainer of helping dogs. If a legitimate health concern could be proven, the employer would be entitled to place reasonable restrictions on her right to train the helping dog as necessary to prevent health problems. The court affirmed the trial court order. *Clark County School Dist. v. Buchanan*, 924 P.2d 716 (Nev.1996).

II. STUDENTS WITH DISABILITIES IN SCHOOL ATHLETICS

Students with disabilities may not be excluded from any athletic activity conducted by a school receiving federal financial assistance as long as the student is "otherwise qualified" to participate in spite of his or her disability. However, problems can occur where students with disabilities have been held back one or more years. In such cases, students are sometimes prohibited from participating in interscholastic athletics.

- An Ohio student with cerebral palsy and hearing impairments functioned in the average range and had average scores on intelligence tests. He was a 17-year-old ninth-grader when a teacher suggested he try out for the school cross-country and track teams. After the student did so, he demonstrated notable improvement in his academics and sense of personal well being. At the end of the cross country season, the student's coach and the school athletic director advised his family that Ohio High School Athletic Association regulations would make his continued participation on varsity teams impossible. An OHSAA rule declared ineligible all students who reached the age of 19 before Aug. 1 in order to prevent any team or participant from having an unfair advantage and to ensure safety. **The student's parents insisted on including cross-country team participation as part of his IEP**. School IEP team participants refused to consider team membership as an IEP goal, since the student's participation would result in sanctions against the team. The parents refused to sign a proposed IEP and requested a due process hearing. Three expert witnesses testified at the hearing that participation in track and cross-country as a team member was a necessary component of the student's IEP.

A hearing officer held that the IEP proposed by the district was not reasonably calculated to enable the student to receive educational benefit and denied him a FAPE. The hearing officer held interscholastic sports participation was a necessary component of the student's IEP. His IEP team was ordered to develop an appropriate IEP that would address his communication skills, social and psychological needs, and promote his self-esteem and motor skills by placing him on the track and cross-country teams. A state review officer upheld the administrative decision, and the school district and OHSAA appealed to a federal district court. The court recited overwhelming evidence in the student's favor concerning his improved attitude, self-esteem and performance on school work since joining the teams. He felt proud of being a team member and of finishing races, even though he typically came in last. **The student was entitled to a preliminary order allowing him to compete in interscholastic sports, since he would be irreparably harmed otherwise**. Two state administrative tribunals had found that he should be placed on the team, despite his age. The court held that OHSAA should not be permitted to override state administrative hearing officers in a due process review involving a student's entitlement to special education services. The student was entitled to preliminary relief, since OHSAA and the school district would not suffer any harm if he were allowed to compete, and this would not fundamentally alter Ohio's student athletic rules. *Kling v. Mentor Public School District*, 136 F.Supp.2d 744 (N.D. Ohio 2001).

◆ The IEP for a student with learning disabilities who was classified as educable mentally retarded called for his participation in extracurricular activities as part of his need for socialization and education. The student did not reach high school until he was 16 years old and attended as a non-graded student. Under the IDEA, the student was entitled to attend high school at least until he turned age 21. **The student turned 19 years old prior to the start of his fourth year of high school, 28 days before the date when a Pennsylvania Interscholastic Athletic Association** (PIAA) **by-law operated to exclude him** from further interscholastic sports eligibility. The PIAA rejected his request for a waiver, and he commenced a federal district court action against it under the ADA, § 504 and the IDEA.

The court denied his motion for a temporary order that would have allowed him to compete in football, wrestling and track. In examining the merits of the student's claims, the court found that the student had not exhausted available administrative remedies under the IDEA, and that the PIAA was not a recipient of federal funding, as required to create § 504 liability. Since these factors were fatal to the claims, the court disposed of both of them in the PIAA's favor. After examining the student's ADA claim, the court found that "a rule is essential to a program unless it can be shown that the waiver of it would not fundamentally alter the nature of the program. This determination must be made on an individual basis." The student was seeking modification of a program covered by the ADA and the court considered the student's ADA claim under the analysis established in *PGA Tour, Inc. v. Martin*, 121 S.Ct. 1879 (2001). In *Martin*, the U.S. Supreme Court held that the ADA requires an individualized inquiry to determine whether a requested modification is reasonable and necessary for the disabled individual, and whether the modification would fundamentally alter the nature of the competition. **The court found that the student's participation in football and track would not fundamentally alter the nature of interscholastic competition, as he lacked a competitive advantage.** He was entitled to a permanent order prohibiting the PIAA from enforcing its age by-law unless it did so under a waiver rule providing for an individual evaluation. This would not unreasonably burden the PIAA, especially if it only considered waivers for students having IEPs that required interscholastic sports participation. Evidence indicated that only a few requests of this kind were ever made. The court's order did not extend to the student's request to participate on the wrestling team, as there was evidence the student excelled in wrestling and might have a competitive advantage if allowed to participate. *Cruz v. Pennsylvania Interscholastic Athletic Assn.*, 157 F.Supp.2d 485 (E.D. Pa. 2001).

◆ The Indiana High School Athletic Association maintains an "eight semester rule" that limits a student's eligibility to compete in interscholastic sports to the first eight semesters following the commencement of the student's ninth grade year. One student experienced learning difficulties early in his educational career and was held back for a year. He entered ninth grade and later dropped out of public school. He was persuaded to return to a private school by one of the school's teacher/coaches. The student was tested and determined to have a learning disability. Under the IHSAA rule, the student was ineligible to play interscholastic basketball because he had already participated in varsity sports for eight semesters. **The school requested a waiver of the rule on behalf of the student, asking that the association not count the semesters he was not enrolled in school** for purposes of eligibility. Under other rules of the association, exemptions from the "eight semester rule" could be requested, and had been granted, to injured students who were forced to withdraw from school because of injury. The association nonetheless denied the student's application for an exemption from the rule. The student sued the IHSAA under the Americans with Disabilities Act, asserting that the denial of eligibility failed to reasonably accommodate his learning disability. The court granted a preliminary injunction against enforcement of the rule, concluding that the student would suffer irreparable harm for which he had no adequate remedy at law if he was denied the opportunity to play. The court also concluded that the student had demonstrated a substantial likelihood of success on the merits of the case. It held that the waiver would be a reasonable modification because it would not conflict with the purposes of the rule, and the potential harm to the association would be insignificant.

The Seventh Circuit agreed to hear the case, even though the student had graduated, because the school was also a party and had a continuing interest in the case. It concluded that the student did not have to prove intentional discrimination to prevail in the matter. Instead, it was possible to demonstrate disability-based discrimination by the IHSAA by showing a failure to make a reasonable accommodation. **The court rejected the IHSAA's argument that the student had not been excluded from playing because of his disability, but because of the passage of time.** It affirmed the district court's conclusion that in the absence of the student's disability, the passage of time would not have made him ineligible. The record demonstrated that basketball was an important part of the student's life, helping him to perform academically and to gain self-confidence. These benefits outweighed the corresponding financial and administrative interests asserted by the association. The court affirmed the district court judgment. *Washington v. Indiana High School Athletic Association, Inc.,* 181 F.3d 840 (7th Cir.1999).

◆ An Oregon high school student was diagnosed with Attention Deficit Disorder (ADD) in the sixth grade, but was not held back a grade until after his sophomore year. At the end of his junior year, he had participated in six semesters of high school athletics, but had attended eight semesters of school (he did not play interscholastic sports his freshman year). Under the state school athletic association's rules, students who had attended high school for more than eight semesters were ineligible to play. The school's special education team developed an IEP for the student and **he petitioned the state activities association for a waiver from the eight-semester rule**. Unlike the other eligibility rules set forth by the association, the eight-semester rule did not allow any exceptions for learning disabled students. Accordingly, the association told him he was ineligible to compete in school sports during his senior year. The student sued.

The U.S. District Court for the District of Oregon held that the association was in violation of Title II of the ADA. **The association failed to explain the "essential" requirement that there be no exceptions to the eight-semester rule for learning disabled students while allowing such exceptions to the**

academic-grade and age rules. Further, even if the eight-semester rule was an essential rule of eligibility, a waiver of the rule was a reasonable accommodation of the student's learning disability. The court ordered the association to allow the student to compete during his senior year, and further ordered the association to rewrite its eligibility rules to provide exceptions for learning disabled students. *Bingham v. Oregon School Activities Ass'n*, 37 F.Supp.2d 1189 (D.Or. 1999).

In reviewing the proposed new eligibility rule, the court stated it would afford deference to the association's findings in waiver requests "in direct proportion to the thoroughness of those findings." The court stated that a major purpose of the ADA is to provide reasonable accommodations to individuals who qualify for them. Such accommodations represent a balance between the student's individual circumstances and the need of institutions such as the association to be free from inordinate expense and overly complicated procedures. The court found that it would reduce the burden on the association by giving deference to its findings in future waiver requests if they were thorough. **Eligibility would involve consideration of whether the student was a qualified individual with a disability, and whether participation in sports would result in undue risk to other participants or an undue competitive advantage**. The standard for determining whether a student was qualified was based on the IDEA definition of eligibility for special education services. The court would consider claims of undue risk or unfair competitive advantage on the basis of additional evidence submitted by affidavit. *Bingham v. Oregon School Activities Assn.*, 60 F.Supp.2d 1062 (D.Or.1999).

◆ A Montana student with attention deficit disorder repeated kindergarten and third grade due to learning difficulties. **Because he turned 19 prior to his senior year of high school, his principal petitioned the state athletic association for a waiver of its age rule disqualifying from athletic participation students who turn 19 prior to August 31 of a school year**. Based on this rule, the association denied the request to allow the student to participate in wrestling and football during his senior year. The student appealed the decision under a bylaw of the association allowing appeals by special education students. Although the student was disabled within the meaning of § 504, he did not receive special education services under the IDEA and consequently had no formal IEP. The association denied the student's appeal, and he petitioned a Montana district court for a preliminary order allowing him to compete in wrestling. The court granted the order on the basis of its belief that he was entitled to prevail on his § 504 argument. The athletic association appealed to the Supreme Court of Montana. **The court determined that because the student was not receiving special education services pursuant to a formal IEP, he had no federally protected right to participation in interscholastic sports**. The district court had wrongly issued the preliminary order under the belief that a § 504 claim would be successful despite the lack of an IEP. The supreme court reversed the district court decision and dissolved the injunction. *M.H., Jr. v. Montana High School Assn.*, 929 P.2d 239 (Mont.1996).

◆ A special education student claimed in a lawsuit that several National Collegiate Athletic Association Division I schools recruited him to play football until the NCAA ruled that some of his high school special education courses did not satisfy its core course requirement. As a result, the student was ineligible for participation in Division I athletics during his freshman year. The student filed a federal district court action claiming the NCAA core course requirement violated the Rehabilitation Act and the ADA. Named as defendants were the NCAA, three universities, and the ACT/Clearinghouse, which administers college entrance examinations. **The court denied the NCAA's summary judgment motion, finding evidence that its blanket exclusion of all courses taught "below the high school's regular instructional level (e.g., remedial, special education or compensatory)" from consideration as core courses was not facially neutral** and was premised on a specified level of academic achievement that persons with disabilities were less capable of meeting. The student was entitled to a trial at which the NCAA's liability for money damages would be considered along with the question of his athletic eligibility. After the NCAA changed its rules to allow partial or non-qualifying students to regain all four years of athletic eligibility in certain circumstances, the court amended its order to dismiss the claims seeking relief under the ADA and Rehabilitation Act. It denied motions by the universities that the student should not be allowed to proceed with the case because he lacked the skills necessary to play Division I football.

The student enrolled as an ordinary student without an athletic scholarship at Temple University, one of the three universities named in the complaint, and he added claims against the NCAA and universities under the New Jersey Law Against Discrimination. The court held that **the student was entitled to proceed with his Rehabilitation Act claims only to the extent that he sought monetary damages for intentional discrimination**, dismissing the remaining ADA claims for injunctive relief. Temple sought to bring other universities that had recruited the student into the lawsuit, including Memphis, seeking an order that would require them to contribute to any damage award. The court held that neither statute expressly created a right to contribution in a private right of action for damages, but found that it was an appropriate complement to other remedies they contained. The court stated that sovereign immunity protects the states against federal court lawsuits seeking damages when they do not consent to be sued by private individuals. State-created entities stand in the place of the states and must be provided with this immunity. As an arm of the state of Tennessee, Memphis was entitled to immunity because any judgment would come from Tennessee. However, Congress validly abrogated Tennessee's immunity under Title II of the ADA because it was "appropriate legislation" under the 14th Amendment. Tennessee's acceptance of Rehabilitation Act funds resulted in a knowing waiver of immunity under that act. The court denied Memphis' motion under these federal laws, but granted its motion to bar contribution claims under the New Jersey Law Against Discrimination. *Bowers v. NCAA et al.*, 171 F.Supp.2d 389 (D.N.J. 2001).

III. CIVIL RIGHTS REMEDIES

A 1986 amendment to the IDEA known as the Handicapped Children's Protection Act expressly allows disabled students to cumulate all available remedies under federal law. One of the most commonly used federal civil rights statutes is 42 U.S.C. § 1983, a post-Civil War statute that protects individuals from violations of their constitutional rights by state actors.

◆ The parents of a student with autism claimed that the Hawaii Department of Education failed to implement a home autism program and did not communicate with them concerning the implementation of weekly services required by their daughter's IEP. They alleged that despite repeated complaints, the DOE failed to communicate with them, provided improperly trained staff and materials, and failed to provide any support until they filed an administrative complaint. A hearing officer held that the DOE failed to provide the student a FAPE and ordered it to pay the parents $13,772 as reimbursement for their home programming expenses. The administrative order also required reimbursement for future expenses for an undetermined time. The DOE reimbursed the parents for their out-of-pocket expenses and did not appeal the administrative decision. **The parents then sued the DOE and state education officials in federal district court under 42 U.S.C. § 1983, the Americans with Disabilities Act and Section 504 of the Rehabilitation Act, seeking monetary damages** for lost wages, emotional distress and other injuries.

Both parties moved the court for summary judgment and the DOE sought dismissal, asserting 11th Amendment immunity against the claims for monetary damages and failure to allege federal law claims. The court observed that two recent Ninth Circuit decisions have held that Congress effectively abrogated 11th Amendment immunity under Section 504 and the ADA. Both Section 504 and the ADA clearly stated the intention that states have no immunity to suits filed under these laws, and both acts were valid exercises of congressional power. Moreover, states that have accepted federal funds under Section 504 are deemed to have waived sovereign immunity. The court rejected the DOE's claim that the suit was barred by a consent decree in a 1993 class action suit. The court agreed with the DOE that **the Section 1983 claim against state officials was barred by sovereign immunity**. However, there was no reason to bar claims for punitive damages under Section 504. The parents had standing to advance Section 504 and ADA claims on their own behalf in order to vindicate the rights of their daughter. **The parents presented sufficient evidence of discrimination to avoid dismissal of the Section 504 and ADA claims**. There was evidence the DOE knew that the student was entitled to a FAPE but ignored its responsibility to provide necessary services, requiring the parents to drain their own resources. There was a question of whether DOE officials acted with deliberate indifference to the student, requiring further consideration by the court or a jury. The court denied summary judgment to both parties on the deliberate-indifference issue. In further proceedings, the DOE would be bound by the administrative finding that it had failed to provide the student with a FAPE, since it did not appeal that decision. *Patricia N. v. Lemahieu,* 141 F.Supp.2d 1243 (D. Haw. 2001).

◆ A 10-year-old student with mild to moderate mental retardation used the toilet in the boys' lavatory. Sometime later, the teacher observed him with some classmates going into the same lavatory and laughing. A classmate told her that the toilet was stopped up. The teacher asked the student if he had put paper into the toilet, and he responded that he had. **Believing that the student had intentionally clogged the toilet, the teacher ordered him to go into the lavatory with a trash can and pick the paper out of the toilet**. The student cleared the paper from the toilet with his bare hands, washed his hands and returned to class. The teacher had him return to the lavatory to wash his hands again and stated that he was apparently not upset. However, the student was taunted on the bus ride home from school and his parents complained about the incident. The principal and district superintendent met with the parents the following day and rejected their request for the teacher's dismissal or resignation. Instead, the teacher apologized and the superintendent issued her a formal, written reprimand. The parents removed the student and their other son from school and began home education programs for them. They commenced a federal district court action against the teacher and district alleging constitutional rights violations. The court awarded summary judgment to the teacher and district, and the parents appealed to the 10th Circuit.

The court stated that in school discipline cases, a substantive due process violation occurs only where there is force that causes severe injury that is so disproportionate to the circumstances and inspired by malice or sadism, rather than mere carelessness, as to be a brutal or inhumane abuse of official power that is "literally shocking to the conscience." The court compared the teacher's conduct in this case with two cases in which constitutional violations were found. One case involved a student who was so severely beaten with a paddle that she suffered a two-inch cut and permanent scarring. *Garcia by Garcia v. Miera*, 817 F.2d 650 (10th Cir. 1987). The other involved a mentally disabled student who was left alone in a lavatory for hours and told to clean up feces. *Gerkes v. Deathe*, 832 F. Supp. 1450 (W.D. Okla. 1993). **The court held that the teacher's conduct in this case may have been negligent, but fell far short of the deliberate, malicious, conscience-shocking conduct** seen in the *Garcia* and *Gerkes* cases. **At most, she exhibited poor judgment and carelessness** by failing to further investigate the incident and not providing the student with gloves or tools. The teacher was entitled to qualified immunity because she did not violate any clearly established law of which a reasonable teacher should have known, reasonably believing that she was ordering the student to remove clean paper from the toilet. The district court had properly awarded summary judgment to the teacher and did not commit error by awarding judgment to the school district. There was no evidence that the district had an official policy or custom that violated student rights and the teacher was reprimanded. *Harris v. Robinson*, 273 F.3d 927 (10th Cir. 2001).

◆ After a middle school student with mental retardation, attention-deficit hyperactivity disorder and Cohen syndrome was told she and other special education students "did not belong" at a school dance, the assistant principal telephoned the student's mother and told her she did not belong at the dance because she was a sixth grader. The mother explained that the student was in fact a seventh grader, but **the assistant principal stated that she could not remain at the dance**. The student's parents sued the school district and officials, including the assistant principal, in a federal district court, which referred the matter to a magistrate for a recommendation. The complaint alleged violations of Section 504 and the ADA. The student added state law claims asserting that she was made to feel different, subjected to ridicule and suffered severe emotional distress when she was excluded from the dance. She also claimed that her rights were violated during a choral concert.

A magistrate judge recommended dismissal of the Section 504 and ADA claims against the officials, noting that the majority of courts addressing the issue have held that neither act permits claims to be brought against officials in their individual capacities. They were also entitled to dismissal of the claims based on the Maine Human Rights Act. **Because Section 504 and the ADA contain their own comprehensive remedial schemes, the court found that the student was not entitled to advance a claim for damages under 42 U.S.C. § 1983 based on alleged Section 504 and ADA violations**. The officials were entitled to dismissal of the Section 1983 claim based on IDEA violations. Even though the student stated sufficient facts on which to base a claim for violation of her equal protection rights, she had failed to oppose the officials' motion for qualified immunity on this claim. Accordingly, the magistrate dismissed those claims. The magistrate refused to dismiss the remaining state law claims and the claims brought against the school administrators in their official capacities because they had not yet sought dismissal of those claims. If the magistrate's recommendation was accepted, the federal claims would still remain to be resolved. The interests of judicial economy, convenience and fairness would be best served by retaining any remaining state law claims instead of remanding them to state court. *Smith et al. v. Maine School Administrative District No. 6 et al.*, No. 00-284-P-C, 2001 WL 68305 (D. Me. 2001).

◆ A student was identified as having medical and developmental disabilities and attended a public school on a half-day basis. Her IEP team identified her needs for augmentative/alternative communications systems, auditory and speech training, a behavior management plan and behavior consultations. The student's behavior problems increased when she was transferred on two occasions to other schools. After the second transfer, her new school held several meetings to address behavior modification techniques and devised a new IEP calling for a behavior management plan. The student's mother brought a stroller to school for transporting the student from class to the resource room. However, **the district allegedly used the stroller for physically restraining the student during time outs, in which she was placed in a closet for 15 to 20 minute time periods**. On one such occasion, the student fell out of the stroller and fractured her skull, resulting in complications including an increase in her seizure activity. The parents never requested a due process hearing. The family moved out of the district and sued the district and five employees in federal district court, seeking to hold the school district and the employees individually liable for compensatory damages under the IDEA through 42 U.S.C. § 1983.

In addressing the district's motion to dismiss the complaint, the court noted that while three federal circuits (the Sixth, Fourth and Eighth) have held that general damages are unavailable in IDEA cases, it would not follow these decisions. **The court** instead **followed other federal district courts and the Third Circuit, which have held that the IDEA does not specifically forbid an award of compensatory damages.** It applied a general rule announced by the U.S. Supreme Court in a Rehabilitation Act case allowing federal courts to award any appropriate relief, absent an explicit contrary directive from Congress. The court further held that school employee defendants could be held individually liable for any damage award.

On appeal to the 10th Circuit, the court noted that some federal courts have agreed with the district court's conclusion that monetary damage awards are permitted under Section 1983 for IDEA violations, and that these damage awards may be enforced against individual school officials. However, the district court's analysis presupposed that Section 1983 could be used to enforce IDEA rights. Although a majority of the courts that have considered the issue have held that Section 1983 actions may be based on IDEA violations, the U.S. Supreme Court has held that the IDEA creates a comprehensive enforcement scheme that preempts other "overlapping but independent statutory or constitutional claims," *Smith v. Robinson*, 468 U.S. 992 (1984). Congress amended the IDEA in 1986 to address *Smith*'s prohibition on the joinder of Rehabilitation Act and other claims to IDEA cases. **The court stated that the legislative changes did not preempt *Smith*'s ruling that the IDEA provided a comprehensive remedial framework that foreclosed Section 1983 as a remedy for IDEA violations**, therefore, it reversed the district court's denial of the defendants' motion to dismiss the IDEA-based Section 1983 claims against the school district, board and the remaining school officials. The court did not directly rule on whether the IDEA imposes individual liability or permits damage awards. It agreed with the board and district that the student's ADA claim was subject to dismissal for failure to exhaust her administrative remedies. The IDEA required the student to exhaust administrative remedies prior to commencing an ADA suit since she was seeking relief that was also available under the IDEA. Even if damages were available under the IDEA, they would be awarded in a civil action, not as the result of an administrative hearing. The court affirmed the denial of the board and district's motion to dismiss the case for failure to exhaust administrative remedies and reversed the denial of the motion to dismiss the Section 1983 action. *Padilla v. School District No. 1, City and County of Denver, Colorado*, 233 F.3d 1268 (10th Cir. 2000).

- Although the IEP of a student with an emotional disturbance called for his placement in a residential school at district expense, his school board never located an appropriate school for him. Instead, the board placed the student in a modified instructional services program located within a public school until a private placement was found. When the student was suspended during his first week in the MIS program, an interim placement calling for home instruction, speech/language therapy and counseling was developed. The parents initialed a due process hearing when the interim services were not provided. A hearing officer directed the board to provide the specified interim services while it located an appropriate private placement. **When the board failed to implement the hearing officer's order, the parents commenced a federal district court action against the board** seeking monetary damages under Section 1983 due to the failure to comply with the IDEA, along with alleging claims under the ADA and the Rehabilitation Act.

The board moved to dismiss the case, asserting that the parents had failed to exhaust their administrative remedies by filing the action prior to appealing the administrative decision. The court rejected the board's argument, finding such an appeal is required only where a party is aggrieved by the findings and decision of an administrative hearing officer. Since the parents had prevailed at the hearing and were not entitled to appeal, the exhaustion of administrative remedies was unnecessary. The court further rejected the board's argument that the claim for monetary damages under 42 U.S.C. § 1983 based on IDEA violations should be dismissed. While courts have disagreed on whether damages may be available for alleged IDEA violations, the court found that Congress had clearly authorized monetary damages when it amended the IDEA in 1986 to add 20 U.S.C. § 1415(f) (now 20 U.S.C. § 1415[1]) to clarify that the IDEA does not "restrict or limit the rights, procedures, and remedies available under the Constitution, the Americans With Disabilities Act of 1990, Title V of the Rehabilitation Act of 1973, or other Federal laws protecting the rights of children with disabilities." **The parents had sufficiently alleged the presence of deliberate indifference by school authorities to meet the pleading standard for federal court actions arising under Section 1983 and had also pleaded the requisite bad faith or gross misjudgment necessary to avoid pre-trial dismissal of their claims arising under the ADA and the Rehabilitation Act.** They successfully asserted that the board acted intentionally, recklessly and willfully to deny the student of his right to a FAPE. Therefore, the court dismissed the school board's motion to dismiss the entire case. *R.B. v. Board of Education of City of New York*, 99 F.Supp.2d 411 (S.D.N.Y. 2000).

◆ The District of Columbia Public Schools considered a recommendation to move a 19-year-old student with a serious emotional disturbance into a residential placement, but failed to make any placement decision by the time the 1997-98 school year began. The student's parents unilaterally enrolled him in a Virginia special education school and took personal responsibility for his annual tuition. DCPS orally advised them that it would accept and fund the placement, but never issued a formal placement notice. DCPS paid tuition bills sporadically and incompletely. It also failed to complete an interstate compact placement request form required by Virginia law. The school threatened to reject the student's attendance for the following school year if DCPS did not complete the placement request form. DCPS failed to complete the interstate compact placement request form and the parents sought a temporary restraining order that would require DCPS to do so. **They also sought a declaration that the DCPS violated their rights under the IDEA, permanent injunctive relief requiring compliance with the IDEA and damages under 42 U.S.C. § 1983** for violation of the student's civil rights. The court issued a temporary restraining order requiring DCPS to complete the form. The student's emotional problems forced him to leave the private school, and his parents requested a meeting to revise his IEP in view of his worsening condition. DCPS failed to schedule a meeting and moved the court to dismiss the action, arguing that its completion of the placement form made the case moot.

The court observed that a case becomes moot when the issues presented are no longer live or the parties lack a true interest in the outcome of the case. Because the student remained eligible for special education placements until his 21st birthday, and DCPS had a history of noncompliance with the parents' requests, the case was not moot. There was evidence that DCPS failed to: (1) comply with IDEA procedures; (2) timely provide the student with a placement for the 1997-98 school year; and (3) perform basic administrative tasks. It failed to satisfy his IEP requirements, and the sporadic tuition payments threatened his placement. The parents were entitled to summary judgment on their IDEA claims. **The court held that DCPS could be held liable for an award of damages under Section 1983 for IDEA violations**. It held that an implied right of action exists for monetary damages in a Section 1983 action under *Franklin v. Gwinnett County Public Schools*, 503 U.S. 60 (1992). DCPS had a longstanding history of delinquent payment practices that amounted to official acquiescence in the violation of student civil rights. The court denied its motion for summary judgment on the Section 1983 claim. *Zearley v. Ackerman*, 116 F.Supp.2d 109 (D.D.C. 2000).

◆ A student with Asperger's Syndrome attended a public school during the first grade under an IEP. Two different IEPs for that year had a goal of improving the student's classroom behavior and authorized physical restraint when necessary for the safety of the student and others. That school year, **the student told his mother that his teacher and an aide used a restraint hold that suffocated him or caused a choking sensation on many occasions** when he was being placed in time-out, to make him stop crying or for bad behavior. He stated that school employees held his wrists, crossed his arms in front of his body and pushed his head into his chest so that he could not breathe. The parents did not take the student to a doctor to determine if he had suffered any physical injury from the classroom restraints, but took him to a psychotherapist almost two years later for emotional problems. The psychotherapist diagnosed the student as having post-traumatic stress disorder. The family sued school officials and employees, including the teacher and aide, in a federal district court for civil rights violations, including claims arising under 42 U.S.C. § 1983.

The court referred the case to a magistrate judge, who issued a lengthy report recommending that the court grant the school employees' motion for summary judgment. The court affirmed the magistrate's report except for the Section 1983 claims against the teacher and aide. The teacher and aide then moved the court for summary judgment. The court emphasized that Section 1983 applied only to violations of federal law and did not serve as a vehicle for redressing state law violations and personal injury claims. The U.S. Supreme Court has limited the scope of federal civil rights actions in cases alleging corporal punishment where state law civil and criminal remedies exist to vindicate student rights. The leading case concerning Section 1983 claims arising from excessive corporal punishment is *Hall v. Tawney*, 621 F.2d 607 (4th Cir. 1980), which established a test for official liability in such cases that considers whether force applied by a school employee caused severe injury, was disproportionate to the need presented, and was so inspired by malice or sadism or an unwise excess of zeal as to be a brutal and inhumane abuse of official power that literally shocks the conscience. Under the circumstances of this case, the court determined that the student failed to meet this high standard for liability. Applying the *Hall* factors, the court granted the teachers' motion for summary judgment, finding that **no reasonable jury could find that the student's injuries were severe or that the alleged abuse rose to the level of a constitutional rights violation. The method of restraint was not disproportionate to the student's behavior and was not shocking to the conscience**. The court noted the teacher and aide both testified that they only restrained the student when necessary because he was a danger to himself or others and that they did not act with malice when restraining him. *Brown v. Ramsey*, 121 F.Supp.2d (E.D. Va. 2000).

◆ When a student with congenital hydrocephalus for which she received medication three times daily was nine years old, **a substitute school nurse gave her an overdose of the medication**. A month later, the student's parents contended that the district performed an unauthorized medical inspection on her. The next school year, the student was transferred to another classroom due to the extensive time she was spending in her special education program. **She then refused to stand and recite the Pledge of Allegiance** or participate in other aspects of her class's morning routine. Her teacher scolded her in front of other students, took her to the principal's office as punishment, and allegedly imposed other sanctions such as removing her from art, recess and music periods and segregating her in the classroom and at lunch. The family sued the school district, teacher, principal and other school officials in a federal district court for civil rights violations arising under 42 U.S.C. § 1983.

The court considered the district's summary judgment motion and agreed with the district that **there could be no liability for the overdose or unauthorized medical examination. There was no evidence that the district had a policy or custom of overmedicating students or subjecting them to unauthorized examinations**. In the absence of such a practice or custom, there could be no liability. The court also agreed with the district that any claims arising from alleged violations of the IDEA must be dismissed, since the family had failed to exhaust available administrative proceedings as required. This included the claim that the district had improperly moved the student to another classroom without the family's consent. However, the court refused to dismiss the student's First Amendment claims based on the allegation that she was forced to stand and say the Pledge of Allegiance and was subjected to punishment. According to the court, **it is well established that a school may not require students to stand and recite the Pledge of Allegiance or punish any student for not doing so**. Because there was evidence that the student's teacher compelled her to stand and recite the Pledge of Allegiance against her will, the court denied the district's summary judgment motion on the First Amendment claims. The principal's consent to discipline for this behavior created potential liability for the district because she was the highest-ranking person in the school and was directly responsible for school discipline. The principal's behavior and acquiescence to the special education teacher's conduct was attributable to the district, and the court denied summary judgment on the First Amendment claims. *Rabideau v. Beekmantown Central School District*, 89 F.Supp.2d 263 (N.D.N.Y. 2000).

◆ A student claimed that a teacher mocked him, that the school refused to provide him with his standardized test scores and that he was publicly humiliated by a school employee in his eighth-grade graduation ceremony. He also stated that the school's principal created an "isolation chamber" for him out of bookcases and placed him there for several weeks. As a result, **the student filed a lawsuit against the school board and certain board employees, alleging negligent supervision, negligence, conspiracy to inflict emotional distress, and violations of 42 U.S.C. 1983, the IDEA and the ADA**. The court considered a motion by the school board and employees to dismiss the case. It held that the Illinois Tort Immunity Act did not require pretrial dismissal of the case, but found that each of the student's claims related to his opportunity to receive a free appropriate public education under the IDEA. Thus, **he was required to exhaust his IDEA administrative remedies even though he sought relief under other statutes and requested monetary damages that were unavailable in an IDEA action**. Contrary to the court in the *Padilla* case, above, the Illinois court held that "the IDEA does not allow for money damages." It nonetheless found no merit to the student's claim that exhaustion of his administrative remedies was futile. The court also dismissed the state-law negligent supervision and intentional infliction of emotional distress claims. *Kubistal v. Hirsch*, 1999 WL 90625 (N.D.Ill.1999).

◆ A student with disabilities challenged a district's decision to allow him to graduate. An administrative review officer held that the student's IEP was adequate and denied his claim for compensatory education. **He then sued the district and certain district officials in a federal district court, alleging IDEA procedural due process claims** for allowing him to graduate. In addition to the wrongful graduation claim, the former student sought monetary damages for IDEA violations under 42 U.S.C. § 1983.

The court considered a motion by the district and officials to dismiss the claims for monetary damages and observed that four federal circuit courts have held that monetary damages are unavailable under the IDEA. The court observed that the U.S. Court of Appeals for the Third Circuit has interpreted the IDEA as allowing compensatory damage claims. See *W.B. v. Matula*, 67 F.3d 484 (3d Cir.1995). The Third Circuit encompasses Pennsylvania, New Jersey, Delaware and the Virgin Islands, and while the New York court was not bound to follow the Third Circuit, it found the *W.B. v. Matula* case persuasive. According to the court, **the 1986 amendments to the IDEA do not limit a student's right to seek monetary damages. The court found this particularly true in this case, since the former student had graduated some time ago and claimed to be struggling from the effects of the earlier deprivation of services**. The court held that "it is entirely possible that his earning capacity since graduation was diminished, and that such diminution may only be remediable via damages…." Finding that nothing in the IDEA limited a claim for damages under 42 U.S.C. § 1983, the court denied the school district's summary judgment motion. *Cappillino v. Hyde Park Central School Dist.*, 40 F.Supp.2d 513 (S.D.N.Y. 1999).

◆ A Minnesota student with achondroplasia and a central auditory processing dysfunction received special education services from her public school. The school district provided her with access to an elevator, but she had to inform an adult when she needed to use it. The student's parents disagreed with the district's refusal to provide her with an elevator key and disputed her IEP. They requested a due process hearing. A hearing officer determined that the district had not violated the IDEA. However, the decision was reversed by a hearing review officer who held that the district had to provide the student 108 hours of compensatory tutoring. The district provided most of the required tutoring, but the parents refused the district's offer to furnish the remaining tutoring the following school year. **They filed a lawsuit against the district in a federal district court, asserting IDEA violations that created liability under 42 U.S.C. § 1983 as a deliberate deprivation of civil rights.** They also asserted that the refusal to provide an elevator key discriminated against the student in violation of the ADA. The court granted the district's summary judgment motion and the parents appealed to the U.S. Court of Appeals, Eighth Circuit.

The court affirmed dismissal of the IDEA-based § 1983 claims, stating that a general damage award for emotional injuries based upon an IDEA violation is impermissible. The family had refused the remaining hours of compensatory tutoring, the only remedy allowed under the IDEA for failure to provide a free appropriate public education. There was no evidence that the district had denied the student access to the elevator based upon her disability. Contrary evidence indicated that a key had been provided to her after the district established student elevator operation safety criteria. The district court had properly denied relief under the ADA, using a bad faith standard, which was necessary to avoid general liability for educational malpractice by a school district. The court affirmed the dismissal of the lawsuit. *Hoekstra v. Indep. School Dist., No. 283*, 103 F.3d 624 (8th Cir.1996).

◆ An Ohio student with a heart condition known as Q.T. syndrome collapsed on her school bus while being driven home. The driver was unable to contact the garage because of a radio malfunction. **She believed that the student was having a seizure that did not require medical attention and she continued taking students home.** By the time the bus arrived at the student's home, she was not breathing. She fell into a coma and died three days later. The student's estate filed a lawsuit against the school board and some of its employees in the U.S. District Court for the Northern District of Ohio, asserting violations of the U.S. Constitution and Ohio law. The court granted summary judgment to the school district and employees, and the estate appealed to the U.S. Court of Appeals, Sixth Circuit.

The court observed that in order to find a government entity liable for constitutional violations under 42 U.S.C. § 1983, the complaining party must demonstrate a special relationship with the government entity. To date, courts have found a special relationship only where the government entity deprives the complaining party of freedom, as in the case of involuntary commitment or incarceration. **Because compulsory attendance laws did not create a special relationship for § 1983 purposes, the district had no constitutional duty to protect the student from the consequences of a seizure while on her school**

bus. The court found that the district had not adopted a custom, practice or policy of failing to train school bus drivers or institute emergency policies that caused the student's death. The school district had not created a dangerous condition resulting in a risk of harm to students and was not liable for any constitutional violation. The court also affirmed the dismissal of the state law claims. *Sargi v. Kent City Bd. of Educ.*, 70 F.3d 907 (6th Cir.1995).

◆ Parents of two 13-year-old special education students in Maine claimed that their children were "subjected to physical and emotional assaults" from placement in their school district's regional special services behavior program. Both children were identified as educationally handicapped and behaviorally impaired. The parents sued the school district and individual school district employees for violating their children's substantive due process rights under the "State Created Danger" theory of liability. **This theory was based on the claim that the school district had affirmatively acted to create a danger to the students and placed them in a position of harm due to a policy, practice, or custom of deliberate indifference**. The district filed a motion for summary judgment in the U.S. District Court for the District of Maine. The court relied on the U.S. Supreme Court's decision in *DeShaney v. Winnebago County Dept. of Social Servs.*, 489 U.S. 189, 109 S.Ct. 998, 103 L.Ed.2d 249 (1989) in consideration of the school district's summary judgment motion.

According to the court, under *DeShaney*, **there was no special relationship between the state and the students that was sufficient to create a special custodial relationship. Therefore, the school district was under no constitutional duty to protect its students**. Without a showing that the school district had affirmatively acted to create a danger, it could not be held liable. Because the students had not demonstrated that the school district and its employees had acted with deliberate indifference to their rights by establishing or maintaining practices or customs which directly inflicted physical or emotional injury, the court granted the school district's summary judgment motion. Contrary to the students' argument, the school district had maintained a policy of adequate supervision. The court granted the school district's motion for summary judgment and denied the motion of one of the students to submit additional evidence. *Robbins v. Maine School Administrative Dist. No. 56,* 807 F.Supp. 11 (D.Me.1992).

APPENDIX A

Chapter 33—Education of Individuals with Disabilities

The statutory text of the Individuals with Disabilities Education Act Amendments of 1997 is reproduced below. The 1997 amendments were enacted to replace the previous statutory text. Among the changes in the amendments are provisions allowing the removal of a student from class in certain circumstances (§ 1415(k)). The amendments also change reimbursement requirements where parents unilaterally place their children in private schools (§ 1412(a)).

(g) Subgrants to local educational agencies.
(h) Definitions.
(i) Use of amounts by Secretary of the Interior.
(j) Authorization of appropriations.

Sec. 1412. State eligibility.
(a) In general.
(b) State educational agency as provider of free appropriate public education or direct services.
(c) Exception for prior State plans.
(d) Approval by the Secretary.
(e) Assistance under other Federal programs.
(f) By-pass for children in private schools.

Sec. 1413. Local educational agency eligibility.
(a) In general.
(b) Exception for prior local plans.
(c) Notification of local educational agency or State agency in case of ineligibility.
(d) Local educational agency compliance.
(e) Joint establishment of eligibility.
(f) Coordinated services system.
(g) School-based improvement plan.
(h) Direct services by the State educational agency.
(i) State agency eligibility.
(j) Disciplinary information.

Sec. 1414. Evaluations, eligibility determinations, individualized education programs, and educational placements.
(a) Evaluations and reevaluations.
(b) Evaluation procedures.
(c) Additional requirements for evaluation and reevaluations.
(d) Construction.
(f) Educational placements.

Sec. 1415. Procedural safeguards.
(a) Establishment of procedures.
(b) Types of procedures.
(c) Content of prior written notice.
(d) Procedural safeguards notice.
(e) Mediation.
(f) Impartial due process hearing.
(g) Appeal.
(h) Safeguards.
(i) Administrative procedures.
(j) Maintenance of current educational placement.
(k) Placement in alternative educational setting.
(l) Rule of construction.
(m) Transfer of parental rights at age of majority.

Sec. 1416. Withholding and judicial review.
(a) Withholding of payments.
(b) Judicial review.
(c) Divided State agency responsibility.

Sec. 1417. Administration.
(a) Responsibilities of Secretary.
(b) Rules and regulations.
(c) Confidentiality.
(d) Personnel.

Sec. 1418. Program information.
(a) In general.
(b) Sampling.
(c) Disproportionality.

Sec. 1419. Preschool grants.
(a) In general.

SUBCHAPTER I—GENERAL PROVISIONS

§ 1400. Congressional statements and declarations

(a) Short title

This Act may be cited as the 'Individuals with Disabilities Education Act'.

(b) [Omitted]

(c) Findings

The Congress finds the following:

(1) Disability is a natural part of the human experience and in no way diminishes the right of individuals to participate in or contribute to society. Improving educational results for children with disabilities is an essential element of our national policy of ensuring equality of opportunity, full participation, independent living, and economic self-sufficiency for individuals with disabilities.

(2) Before the date of the enactment of the Education for All Handicapped Children Act of 1975 (Public Law 94–142)—

(A) the special educational needs of children with disabilities were not being fully met;

(B) more than one-half of the children with disabilities in the United States did not receive appropriate educational services that would enable such children to have full equality of opportunity;

(C) 1,000,000 of the children with disabilities in the United States were excluded entirely from the public school system and did not go through the educational process with their peers;

(D) there were many children with disabilities throughout the United States participating in regular school programs whose disabilities prevented such children from having a successful educational experience because their disabilities were undetected; and

(E) because of the lack of adequate services within the public school system, families were often forced to find services outside the public school system, often at great distance from their residence and at their own expense.

(3) Since the enactment and implementation of the Education for All Handicapped Children Act of 1975, this Act has been successful in ensuring children with disabilities and the families of such children access to a free appropriate public education and in improving educational results for children with disabilities.

(4) However, the implementation of this Act has been impeded by low expectations, and an insufficient focus on applying replicable research on proven methods of teaching and learning for children with disabilities.

(5) Over 20 years of research and experience has demonstrated that the education of children with disabilities can be made more effective by—

(A) having high expectations for such children and ensuring their access in the general curriculum to the maximum extent possible;

(B) strengthening the role of parents and ensuring that families of such children have meaningful opportunities to participate in the education of their children at school and at home;

(C) coordinating this Act with other local, educational service agency, State, and Federal school improvement efforts in order to ensure that such children benefit from such efforts and that special education can become a service for such children rather than a place where they are sent;

(D) providing appropriate special education and related services and aids and supports in the regular classroom to such children, whenever appropriate;

(E) supporting high-quality, intensive professional development for all personnel who work with such children in order to ensure that they have the skills and knowledge necessary to enable them—

(i) to meet developmental goals and, to the maximum extent possible, those challenging expectations that have been established for all children; and

(ii) to be prepared to lead productive, independent, adult lives, to the maximum extent possible;

(F) providing incentives for whole-school approaches and pre-referral intervention to reduce the need to label children as disabled in order to address their learning needs; and

(G) focusing resources on teaching and learning while reducing paperwork and requirements that do not assist in improving educational results.

(6) While States, local educational agencies, and educational service agencies are responsible for providing an education for all children with disabilities, it is in the national interest that the Federal Government have a role in assisting State and local efforts to educate children with disabilities in order to improve results for such children and to ensure equal protection of the law.

(7)(A) The Federal Government must be responsive to the growing needs of an increasingly more diverse society. A more equitable allocation of resources is essential for the Federal Government to meet its responsibility to provide an equal educational opportunity for all individuals.

(B) America's racial profile is rapidly changing. Between 1980 and 1990, the rate of increase in the population for white Americans was 6 percent, while the rate of increase for racial and ethnic minorities was much higher: 53 percent for Hispanics, 13.2 percent for African-Americans, and 107.8 percent for Asians.

(C) By the year 2000, this Nation will have 275,000,000 people, nearly one of every three of whom will be either African-American, Hispanic, Asian-American, or American Indian.

(D) Taken together as a group, minority children are comprising an ever larger percentage of public school students. Large-city school populations are overwhelmingly minority, for example: for fall 1993, the figure for Miami was 84 percent; Chicago, 89 percent; Philadelphia, 78 percent; Baltimore, 84 percent; Houston, 88 percent; and Los Angeles, 88 percent.

(E) Recruitment efforts within special education must focus on bringing larger numbers of minorities into the profession in order to provide appropriate practitioner knowledge, role models, and sufficient manpower to address the clearly changing demography of special education.

(F) The limited English proficient population is the fastest growing in our Nation, and the growth is occurring in many parts of our Nation. In the Nation's 2 largest school districts, limited English proficient students make up almost half of all students initially entering school at the kindergarten level. Studies have documented apparent discrepancies in the levels of referral and placement of limited English proficient children in special education. The Department of Education has found that services provided to limited English proficient students often do not respond primarily to the pupil's academic needs. These trends pose special challenges for special education in the referral, assessment, and services for our Nation's students from non-English language backgrounds.

(8)(A) Greater efforts are needed to prevent the intensification of problems connected with mislabeling and high dropout rates among minority children with disabilities.

(B) More minority children continue to be served in special education than would be expected from the percentage of minority students in the general school population.

(C) Poor African-American children are 2.3 times more likely to be identified by their teacher as having mental retardation than their white counterpart.

(D) Although African-Americans represent 16 percent of elementary and secondary enrollments, they constitute 21 percent of total enrollments in special education.

(E) The drop-out rate is 68 percent higher for minorities than for whites.

(F) More than 50 percent of minority students in large cities drop out of school.

(9)(A) The opportunity for full participation in awards for grants and contracts; boards of organizations receiving funds under this Act; and peer review panels; and training of professionals in the area of special education by minority individuals, organizations, and historically black colleges and universities is essential if we are to obtain greater success in the education of minority children with disabilities.

(B) In 1993, of the 915,000 college and university professors, 4.9 percent were African-American and 2.4 percent were Hispanic. Of the 2,940,000 teachers, prekindergarten through high school, 6.8 percent were African-American and 4.1 percent were Hispanic.

(C) Students from minority groups comprise more than 50 percent of K–12 public school enrollment in seven States yet minority enrollment in teacher training programs is less than 15 percent in all but six States.

(D) As the number of African-American and Hispanic students in special education increases, the number of minority teachers and related service personnel produced in our colleges and universities continues to decrease.

(E) Ten years ago, 12 percent of the United States teaching force in public elementary and secondary schools were members of a minority group. Minorities comprised 21 percent of the national population at that time and were clearly underrepresented then among employed teachers. Today, the elementary and secondary teaching force is 13 percent minority, while one-third of the students in public schools are minority children.

(F) As recently as 1991, historically black colleges and universities enrolled 44 percent of the African-American teacher trainees in the Nation. However, in 1993, historically black colleges and universities received only 4 percent of the discretionary funds for special education and related services personnel training under this Act.

(G) While African-American students constitute 28 percent of total enrollment in special education, only 11.2 percent of individuals enrolled in preservice training programs for special education are African-American.

(H) In 1986-87, of the degrees conferred in education at the B.A., M.A., and Ph.D. levels, only 6, 8, and 8 percent, respectively, were awarded to African-American or Hispanic students.

(10) Minorities and underserved persons are socially disadvantaged because of the lack of opportunities in training and educational programs, undergirded by the practices in the private sector that impede their full participation in the mainstream of society.

(d) Purposes

The purposes of this title are—

(1)(A) to ensure that all children with disabilities have available to them a free appropriate public education that emphasizes special education and related services designed to meet their unique needs and prepare them for employment and independent living;

(B) to ensure that the rights of children with disabilities and parents of such children are protected; and

(C) to assist States, localities, educational service agencies, and Federal agencies to provide for the education of all children with disabilities;

(2) to assist States in the implementation of a statewide, comprehensive, coordinated, multidisciplinary, interagency system of early intervention services for infants and toddlers with disabilities and their families;

(3) to ensure that educators and parents have the necessary tools to improve educational results for children with disabilities by supporting systemic-change activities; coordinated research and personnel preparation; coordinated technical assistance, dissemination, and support; and technology development and media services; and

(4) to assess, and ensure the effectiveness of, efforts to educate children with disabilities.

§ 1401. Definitions

Except as otherwise provided, as used in this Act:

(1) Assistive technology device—The term 'assistive technology device' means any item, piece of equipment, or product system, whether acquired commercially off the shelf, modified, or customized, that is used to increase, maintain, or improve functional capabilities of a child with a disability.

(2) Assistive technology service—The term 'assistive technology service' means any service that directly assists a child with a disability in the selection, acquisition, or use of an assistive technology device. Such term includes—

(A) the evaluation of the needs of such child, including a functional evaluation of the child in the child's customary environment;

(B) purchasing, leasing, or otherwise providing for the acquisition of assistive technology devices by such child;

(C) selecting, designing, fitting, customizing, adapting, applying, maintaining, repairing, or replacing of assistive technology devices;

(D) coordinating and using other therapies, interventions, or services with assistive technology devices, such as those associated with existing education and rehabilitation plans and programs;

(E) training or technical assistance for such child, or, where appropriate, the family of such child; and

(F) training or technical assistance for professionals (including individuals providing education and rehabilitation services), employers, or other individuals who provide services to, employ, or are otherwise substantially involved in the major life functions of such child.

(3) Child with a disability

(A) In general—The term 'child with a disability' means a child—

(i) with mental retardation, hearing impairments (including deafness), speech or language impairments, visual impairments (including blindness), serious emotional disturbance (hereinafter referred to as 'emotional disturbance'), orthopedic impairments, autism, traumatic brain injury, other health impairments, or specific learning disabilities; and

(ii) who, by reason thereof, needs special education and related services.

(B) Child aged 3 through 9—The term 'child with a disability' for a child aged 3 through 9 may, at the discretion of the State and the local educational agency, include a child—

(i) experiencing developmental delays, as defined by the State and as measured by appropriate diagnostic instruments and procedures, in one or more of the following areas: physical development, cognitive development, communication development, social or emotional development, or adaptive development; and

(ii) who, by reason thereof, needs special education and related services.

(4) Educational service agency—The term 'educational service agency'—

(A) means a regional public multiservice agency—

(i) authorized by State law to develop, manage, and provide services or programs to local educational agencies; and

(ii) recognized as an administrative agency for purposes of the provision of special education and related services provided within public elementary and secondary schools of the State; and

(B) includes any other public institution or agency having administrative control and direction over a public elementary or secondary school.

(5) Elementary school—The term 'elementary school' means a nonprofit institutional day or residential school that provides elementary education, as determined under State law.

(6) Equipment—The term 'equipment' includes—

(A) machinery, utilities, and built-in equipment and any necessary enclosures or structures to house such machinery, utilities, or equipment; and

(B) all other items necessary for the functioning of a particular facility as a facility for the provision of educational services, including items such as instructional equipment and necessary furniture; printed, published, and audiovisual instructional materials; telecommunications, sensory, and other technological aids and devices; and books, periodicals, documents, and other related materials.

(7) Excess costs—The term 'excess costs' means those costs that are in excess of the average annual per-student expenditure in a local educational agency during the preceding school year for an elementary or secondary school student, as may be appropriate, and which shall be computed after deducting—

(A) amounts received—

(i) under part B of this title;

(ii) under part A of title I of the Elementary and Secondary Education Act of 1965; or

(iii) under part A of title VII of that Act; and

(B) any State or local funds expended for programs that would qualify for assistance under any of those parts.

(8) Free appropriate public education—The term 'free appropriate public education' means special education and related services that—

(A) have been provided at public expense, under public supervision and direction, and without charge;

(B) meet the standards of the State educational agency;

(C) include an appropriate preschool, elementary, or secondary school education in the State involved; and

(D) are provided in conformity with the individualized education program required under section 1414(d) of this title.

(9) Indian—The term 'Indian' means an individual who is a member of an Indian tribe.

(10) Indian tribe—The term 'Indian tribe' means any Federal or State Indian tribe, band, rancheria, pueblo, colony, or community, including any Alaska Native village or regional village corporation (as defined in or established under the Alaska Native Claims Settlement Act).

(11) Individualized education program—The term 'individualized education program' or 'IEP' means a written statement for each child with a disability that is developed, reviewed, and revised in accordance with section 1414(d) of this title.

(12) Individualized family service plan—The term 'individualized family service plan' has the meaning given such term in section 1436 of this title.

(13) Infant or toddler with a disability—The term 'infant or toddler with a disability' has the meaning given such term in section 1432 of this title.

(14) Institution of higher education—The term 'institution of higher education'—

(A) has the meaning given that term in section 1141(a) of this title; and

(B) also includes any community college receiving funding from the Secretary of the Interior under the Tribally Controlled Community College Assistance Act of 1978.

(15) Local educational agency

(A) The term 'local educational agency' means a public board of education or other public authority legally constituted within a State for either administrative control or direction of, or to perform a service function for, public elementary or secondary schools in a city, county, township, school district, or other political subdivision of a State, or for such combination of school districts or counties as are recognized in a State as an administrative agency for its public elementary or secondary schools.

(B) The term includes—

(i) an educational service agency, as defined in paragraph (4); and

(ii) any other public institution or agency having administrative control and direction of a public elementary or secondary school.

(C) The term includes an elementary or secondary school funded by the Bureau of Indian Affairs, but only to the extent that such inclusion makes the school eligible for programs for which specific eligibility is not provided to the school in another provision of law and the school does not have a student population that is smaller than the student population of the local educational agency receiving assistance under this Act with the smallest student population, except that the school shall not be subject to the jurisdiction of any State educational agency other than the Bureau of Indian Affairs.

(16) Native language—The term 'native language', when used with reference to an individual of limited English proficiency, means the language normally used by the individual, or in the case of a child, the language normally used by the parents of the child.

(17) Nonprofit—The term 'nonprofit', as applied to a school, agency, organization, or institution, means a school, agency, organization, or institution owned and operated by one or more nonprofit corporations or associations no part of the net earnings of which inures, or may lawfully inure, to the benefit of any private shareholder or individual.

(18) Outlying area—The term 'outlying area' means the United States Virgin Islands, Guam, American Samoa, and the Commonwealth of the Northern Mariana Islands.

(19) Parent—The term 'parent'—

(A) includes a legal guardian; and

(B) except as used in sections 1415(b)(2) and 1439(a)(5) of this title, includes an individual assigned under either of those sections to be a surrogate parent.

(20) Parent organization—The term 'parent organization' has the meaning given that term in section 1482(g) of this title.

(21) Parent training and information center—The term 'parent training and information center' means a center assisted under section 1482 or 1483 of this title.

(22) Related services—The term 'related services' means transportation, and such developmental, corrective, and other supportive services (including speech-language pathology and audiology services, psychological services, physical and occupational therapy, recreation, including therapeutic recreation, social work services, counseling services, including rehabilitation counseling, orientation and mobility services, and medical services, except that such medical services shall be for diagnostic and evaluation purposes only) as may be required to assist a child with a disability to benefit from special education, and includes the early identification and assessment of disabling conditions in children.

(23) Secondary school—The term 'secondary school' means a nonprofit institutional day or residential school that provides secondary education, as determined under State law, except that it does not include any education beyond grade 12.

(24) Secretary—The term 'Secretary' means the Secretary of Education.

(25) Special education—The term 'special education' means specially designed instruction, at no cost to parents, to meet the unique needs of a child with a disability, including—

(A) instruction conducted in the classroom, in the home, in hospitals and institutions, and in other settings; and

(B) instruction in physical education.

(26) Specific learning disability

(A) In general—The term 'specific learning disability' means a disorder in one or more of the basic psychological processes involved in understanding or in using language, spoken or written, which disorder may manifest itself in imperfect ability to listen, think, speak, read, write, spell, or do mathematical calculations.

(B) Disorders included—Such term includes such conditions as perceptual disabilities, brain injury, minimal brain dysfunction, dyslexia, and developmental aphasia.

(C) Disorders not included—Such term does not include a learning problem that is primarily the result of visual, hearing, or motor disabilities, of mental retardation, of emotional disturbance, or of environmental, cultural, or economic disadvantage.

(27) State—The term 'State' means each of the 50 States, the District of Columbia, the Commonwealth of Puerto Rico, and each of the outlying areas.

(28) State educational agency—The term 'State educational agency' means the State board of education or other agency or officer primarily responsible for the State supervision of public elementary and secondary schools, or, if there is no such officer or agency, an officer or agency designated by the Governor or by State law.

(29) Supplementary aids and services—The term 'supplementary aids and services' means, aids, services, and other supports that are provided in regular education classes or other education-related settings to enable children with disabilities to be educated with nondisabled children to the maximum extent appropriate in accordance with section 1412(a)(5) of this title.

(30) Transition services—The term 'transition services' means a coordinated set of activities for a student with a disability that—

(A) is designed within an outcome-oriented process, which promotes movement from school to post-school activities, including post-secondary education, vocational training, integrated employment (including supported employment), continuing and adult education, adult services, independent living, or community participation;

(B) is based upon the individual student's needs, taking into account the student's preferences and interests; and

(C) includes instruction, related services, community experiences, the development of employment and other post-school adult living objectives, and, when appropriate, acquisition of daily living skills and functional vocational evaluation.

§ 1402. Office of special education programs

(a) Establishment

There shall be, within the Office of Special Education and Rehabilitative Services in the Department of Education, an Office of Special Education Programs, which shall be the principal agency in such Department for administering and carrying out this chapter and other programs and activities concerning the education of children with disabilities.

(b) Director

The Office established under subsection (a) shall be headed by a Director who shall be selected by the Secretary and shall report directly to the Assistant Secretary for Special Education and Rehabilitative Services.

(c) Voluntary and uncompensated services

Notwithstanding section 1342 of title 31, the Secretary is authorized to accept voluntary and uncompensated services in furtherance of the purposes of this chapter.

§ 1403. Abrogation of state sovereign immunity

(a) In general

A State shall not be immune under the eleventh amendment to the Constitution of the United States from suit in Federal court for a violation of this chapter.

(b) Remedies

In a suit against a State for a violation of this chapter, remedies (including remedies both at law and in equity) are available for such a violation to the same extent as those remedies are available for such a violation in the suit against any public entity other than a State.

(c) Effective date

Subsections (a) and (b) of this section apply with respect to violations that occur in whole or part after October 30, 1990.

§ 1404. Acquisition of equipment; construction or alteration of facilities

(a) In general

If the Secretary determines that a program authorized under this chapter would be improved by permitting program funds to be used to acquire appropriate equipment, or to construct new facilities or alter existing facilities, the Secretary is authorized to allow the use of those funds for those purposes.

(b) Compliance with certain regulations

Any construction of new facilities or alteration of existing facilities under subsection (a) of this section shall comply with the requirements of—

(1) appendix A of part 36 of title 28, Code of Federal Regulations (commonly known as the 'Americans with Disabilities Accessibility Guidelines for Buildings and Facilities'); or

(2) appendix A of part 101–19.6 of title 41, Code of Federal Regulations (commonly known as the 'Uniform Federal Accessibility Standards').

§ 1405. Employment of individuals with disabilities

The Secretary shall ensure that each recipient of assistance under this chapter makes positive efforts to employ and advance in employment qualified individuals with disabilities in programs assisted under this chapter.

§ 1406. Requirements for prescribing regulations

(a) Public comment period

The Secretary shall provide a public comment period of at least 90 days on any regulation proposed under subchapters II or III of this chapter on which an opportunity for public comment is otherwise required by law.

(b) Protections provided to children

The Secretary may not implement, or publish in final form, any regulation prescribed pursuant to this chapter that would procedurally or substantively lessen the protections provided to children with disabilities under this chapter, as embodied in regulations in effect on July 20, 1983 (particularly as such protections relate to parental consent to initial evaluation or initial placement in special education, least restrictive environment, related services, timelines, attendance of evaluation personnel at individualized education program meetings, or qualifications of personnel), except to the extent that such regulation reflects the clear and unequivocal intent of the Congress in legislation.

(c) Policy letters and statements

The Secretary may not, through policy letters or other statements, establish a rule that is required for compliance with, and eligibility under, this part without following the requirements of section 553 of Title 5.

(d) Correspondence from Department of Education describing interpretations of this part

(1) In general—The Secretary shall, on a quarterly basis, publish in the Federal Register, and widely disseminate to interested entities through various additional forms of communication, a list of correspondence from the Department of Education received by individuals during the previous quarter that describes the interpretations of the Department of Education of this chapter or the regulations implemented pursuant to this chapter.

(2) Additional information—For each item of correspondence published in a list under paragraph (1), the Secretary shall identify the topic addressed by the correspondence and shall include such other summary information as the Secretary determines to be appropriate.

(e) Issues of national significance

If the Secretary receives a written request regarding a policy, question, or interpretation under part B of this Act, and determines that it raises an issue of general interest or applicability of national significance to the implementation of part B, the Secretary shall—

(1) include a statement to that effect in any written response;

(2) widely disseminate that response to State educational agencies, local educational agencies, parent and advocacy organizations, and other interested organizations, subject to applicable laws relating to confidentiality of information; and

(3) not later than one year after the date on which the Secretary responds to the written request, issue written guidance on such policy, question, or interpretation through such means as the Secretary determines to be appropriate and consistent with law, such as a policy memorandum, notice of interpretation, or notice of proposed rulemaking.

(f) Explanation

Any written response by the Secretary under subsection (e) regarding a policy, question, or interpretation under part B of this Act shall include an explanation that the written response—

(1) is provided as informal guidance and is not legally binding; and

(2) represents the interpretation by the Department of Education of the applicable statutory or regulatory requirements in the context of the specific facts presented.

SUBCHAPTER II—ASSISTANCE FOR EDUCATION OF ALL CHILDREN WITH DISABILITIES

§ 1411. Authorization; allotment; use of funds; authorization of appropriations

(a) Grants to states

(1) Purpose of grants—The Secretary shall make grants to States and the outlying areas, and provide funds to the Secretary of the Interior, to assist them to provide special education and related services to children with disabilities in accordance with this subchapter.

(2) Maximum amounts—The maximum amount of the grant a State may receive under this section for any fiscal year is—

(A) the number of children with disabilities in the State who are receiving special education and related services—

(i) aged 3 through 5 if the State is eligible for a grant under section 1419 of this title; and

(ii) aged 6 through 21; multiplied by

(B) 40 percent of the average per-pupil expenditure in public elementary and secondary schools in the United States.

(b) Outlying areas and freely associated states

(1) Funds reserved—From the amount appropriated for any fiscal year under subsection (j) of this section, the Secretary shall reserve not more than one percent, which shall be used—

(A) to provide assistance to the outlying areas in accordance with their respective populations of individuals aged 3 through 21; and

(B) for fiscal years 1998 through 2001, to carry out the competition described in paragraph (2), except that the amount reserved to carry out that competition shall not exceed the amount reserved for fiscal year 1996 for the competition under part B of this Act described under the heading 'SPECIAL EDUCATION' in Public Law 104–134.

(2) Limitation for freely associated states

(A) Competitive grants—The Secretary shall use funds described in paragraph (1)(B) to award grants, on a competitive basis, to Guam, American Samoa, the Commonwealth of the Northern Mariana Islands, and the freely associated States to carry out the purposes of this part.

(B) Award basis—The Secretary shall award grants under subparagraph (A) on a competitive basis, pursuant to the recommendations of the Pacific Region Educational Laboratory in Honolulu, Hawaii. Those recommendations shall be made by experts in the field of special education and related services.

(C) Assistance requirements—Any freely associated State that wishes to receive funds under this part shall include, in its application for assistance—

(i) information demonstrating that it will meet all conditions that apply to States under this subchapter;

(ii) an assurance that, notwithstanding any other provision of this part, it will use those funds only for the direct provision of special education and related services to children with disabilities and to enhance its capacity to make a free appropriate public education available to all children with disabilities;

(iii) the identity of the source and amount of funds, in addition to funds under this part, that it will make available to ensure that a free appropriate public education is available to all children with disabilities within its jurisdiction; and

(iv) such other information and assurances as the Secretary may require.

(D) Termination of eligibility—Notwithstanding any other provision of law, the freely associated States shall not receive any funds under this subchapter for any program year that begins after September 30, 2001.

(E) Administrative costs—The Secretary may provide not more than five percent of the amount reserved for grants under this paragraph to pay the administrative costs of the Pacific Region Educational Laboratory under subparagraph (B).

(3) Limitation—An outlying area is not eligible for a competitive award under paragraph (2) unless it receives assistance under paragraph (1)(A).

(4) Special rule—The provisions of Public Law 95–134, permitting the consolidation of grants by the outlying areas, shall not apply to funds provided to those areas or to the freely associated States under this section.

(5) Eligibility for discretionary programs—The freely associated States shall be eligible to receive assistance under part B 2 of subchapter IV of this chapter until September 30, 2001.

(6) Definition—As used in this subsection, the term 'freely associated States' means the Republic of the Marshall Islands, the Federated States of Micronesia, and the Republic of Palau.

(c) Secretary of the Interior

From the amount appropriated for any fiscal year under subsection (j) of this section, the Secretary shall reserve 1.226 percent to provide assistance to the Secretary of the Interior in accordance with subsection (i) of this section.

(d) Allocations to states

(1) In general—After reserving funds for studies and evaluations under section 1474(e) of this title, and for payments to the outlying areas and the Secretary of the Interior under subsections (b) and (c), the Secretary shall allocate the remaining amount among the States in accordance with paragraph (2) or subsection (e), as the case may be.

(2) Interim formula—Except as provided in subsection (e) of this section, the Secretary shall allocate the amount described in paragraph (1) among the States in accordance with section 1411(a)(3), (4), and (5) and (b)(1), (2), and (3) of this title, as in effect prior to the enactment of the Individuals with Disabilities Education Act Amendments of 1997, except that the determination of the number of children with disabilities receiving special education and related services under such section 1411(a)(3) may, at the State's discretion, be calculated as of the last Friday in October or as of December 1 of the fiscal year for which the funds are appropriated.

(e) Permanent formula

(1) Establishment of base year—The Secretary shall allocate the amount described in subsection (d)(1) of this section among the States in accordance with this subsection for each fiscal year beginning with the first fiscal year for which the amount appropriated under subsection (j) of this section is more than $4,924,672,200.

(2) Use of base year

(A) Definition—As used in this subsection, the term 'base year' means the fiscal year preceding the first fiscal year in which this subsection applies.

(B) Special rule for use of base year amount—If a State received any funds under this section for the base year on the basis of children aged 3 through 5, but does not make a free appropriate public education available to all children with disabilities aged 3 through 5 in the State in any subsequent fiscal year, the Secretary shall compute the State's base year amount, solely for the purpose of calculating the State's allocation in that subsequent year under paragraph (3) or (4), by subtracting the amount allocated to the State for the base year on the basis of those children.

(3) Increase in funds—If the amount available for allocations to States under paragraph (1) is equal to or greater than the amount allocated to the States under this paragraph for the preceding fiscal year, those allocations shall be calculated as follows:

(A)(i) Except as provided in subparagraph (B), the Secretary shall—

(I) allocate to each State the amount it received for the base year;

(II) allocate 85 percent of any remaining funds to States on the basis of their relative populations of children aged 3 through 21 who are of the same age as children with disabilities for whom the State ensures the availability of a free appropriate public education under this subchapter; and

(III) allocate 15 percent of those remaining funds to States on the basis of their relative populations of children described in subclause (II) who are living in poverty.

(ii) For the purpose of making grants under this paragraph, the Secretary shall use the most recent population data, including data on children living in poverty, that are available and satisfactory to the Secretary.

(B) Notwithstanding subparagraph (A), allocations under this paragraph shall be subject to the following:

(i) No State's allocation shall be less than its allocation for the preceding fiscal year.

(ii) No State's allocation shall be less than the greatest of—

(I) the sum of—

(aa) the amount it received for the base year; and

(bb) one third of one percent of the amount by which the amount appropriated under subsection (j) of this section exceeds the amount appropriated under this section for the base year;

(II) the sum of—

(aa) the amount it received for the preceding fiscal year; and

(bb) that amount multiplied by the percentage by which the increase in the funds appropriated from the preceding fiscal year exceeds 1.5 percent; or

(III) the sum of—

(aa) the amount it received for the preceding fiscal year; and

(bb) that amount multiplied by 90 percent of the percentage increase in the amount appropriated from the preceding fiscal year.

(iii) Notwithstanding clause (ii), no State's allocation under this paragraph shall exceed the sum of—

(I) the amount it received for the preceding fiscal year; and

(II) that amount multiplied by the sum of 1.5 percent and the percentage increase in the amount appropriated.

(C) If the amount available for allocations under this paragraph is insufficient to pay those allocations in full, those allocations shall be ratably reduced, subject to subparagraph (B)(i).

(4) Decrease in funds—If the amount available for allocations to States under paragraph (1) is less than the amount allocated to the States under this section for the preceding fiscal year, those allocations shall be calculated as follows:

(A) If the amount available for allocations is greater than the amount allocated to the States for the base year, each State shall be allocated the sum of—

(i) the amount it received for the base year; and

(ii) an amount that bears the same relation to any remaining funds as the increase the State received for the preceding fiscal year over the base year bears to the total of all such increases for all States.

(B)(i) If the amount available for allocations is equal to or less than the amount allocated to the States for the base year, each State shall be allocated the amount it received for the base year.

(ii) If the amount available is insufficient to make the allocations described in clause (i), those allocations shall be ratably reduced.

(f) State-level activities

(1) General

(A) Each State may retain not more than the amount described in subpara-

Secretary of the Interior. The Secretary of the Interior shall be responsible for meeting all of the requirements of this part for these children, in accordance with paragraph (2).

(C) Additional requirement—With respect to all other children aged 3 to 21, inclusive, on reservations, the State educational agency shall be responsible for ensuring that all of the requirements of this part are implemented.

(2) Submission of information—The Secretary of Education may provide the Secretary of the Interior amounts under paragraph (1) for a fiscal year only if the Secretary of the Interior submits to the Secretary of Education information that—

(A) demonstrates that the Department of the Interior meets the appropriate requirements, as determined by the Secretary of Education, of sections 1412 of this title (including monitoring and evaluation activities) and 1413 of this title;

(B) includes a description of how the Secretary of the Interior will coordinate the provision of services under this part with local educational agencies, tribes and tribal organizations, and other private and Federal service providers;

(C) includes an assurance that there are public hearings, adequate notice of such hearings, and an opportunity for comment afforded to members of tribes, tribal governing bodies, and affected local school boards before the adoption of the policies, programs, and procedures described in subparagraph (A);

(D) includes an assurance that the Secretary of the Interior will provide such information as the Secretary of Education may require to comply with section 1418 of this title;

(E) includes an assurance that the Secretary of the Interior and the Secretary of Health and Human Services have entered into a memorandum of agreement, to be provided to the Secretary of Education, for the coordination of services, resources, and personnel between their respective Federal, State, and local offices and with State and local educational agencies and other entities to facilitate the provision of services to Indian children with disabilities residing on or near reservations (such agreement shall provide for the apportionment of responsibilities and costs including, but not limited to, child find, evaluation, diagnosis, remediation or therapeutic measures, and (where appropriate) equipment and medical or personal supplies as needed for a child to remain in school or a program); and

(F) includes an assurance that the Department of the Interior will cooperate with the Department of Education in its exercise of monitoring and oversight of this application, and any agreements entered into between the Secretary of the Interior and other entities under this subchapter, and will fulfill its duties under this subchapter.

Section 1416(a) of this title shall apply to the information described in this paragraph.

(3) Payments for education and services for Indian children with disabilities aged 3 through 5

(A) In general—With funds appropriated under subsection (j) of this section, the Secretary of Education shall make payments to the Secretary of the Interior to be distributed to tribes or tribal organizations (as defined under section 4 of the Indian Self-Determination and Education Assistance Act) or consortia of the above to provide for the coordination of assistance for special education and related services for children with disabilities aged 3 through 5 on reservations served by elementary and secondary schools for Indian children operated or funded by the Department of the Interior. The amount of such payments under subparagraph (B) for any fiscal year shall be equal to 20 percent of the amount allotted under subsection (c) of this section.

(B) Distribution of funds—The Secretary of the Interior shall distribute the total amount of the payment under subparagraph (A) by allocating to each tribe or tribal organization an amount based on the number of children with disabilities ages 3 through 5 residing on reservations as reported annually, divided by the total of those children served by all tribes or tribal organizations.

(C) Submission of information—To receive a payment under this paragraph, the tribe or tribal organization shall submit such figures to the Secretary of the Interior as required to determine the amounts to be allocated under subparagraph (B). This information shall be compiled and submitted to the Secretary of Education.

(D) Use of funds—The funds received by a tribe or tribal organization shall be used to assist in child find, screening, and other procedures for the early identification of children aged 3 through 5, parent training, and the provision of direct services. These activities may be carried out directly or through contracts or cooperative agreements with the BIA, local educational agencies, and other public or private nonprofit organizations. The tribe or tribal organization is encouraged to involve Indian parents in the development and implementation of these activities. The above entities shall, as appropriate, make referrals to local, State, or Federal entities for the provision of services or further diagnosis.

(E) Biennial report—To be eligible to receive a grant pursuant to subparagraph (A), the tribe or tribal organization shall provide to the Secretary of the Interior a biennial report of activities undertaken under this paragraph, including the number of contracts and cooperative agreements entered into, the number of children contacted and receiving services for each year, and the estimated number of children needing services during the 2 years following the one in which the report is made. The Secretary of the Interior shall include a summary of this information on a biennial basis in the report to the Secretary of Education required under this subsection. The Secretary of Education may require any additional information from the Secretary of the Interior.

(F) Prohibitions—None of the funds allocated under this paragraph may be used by the Secretary of the Interior for administrative purposes, including child count and the provision of technical assistance.

(4) Plan for coordination of services—The Secretary of the Interior shall develop and implement a plan for the coordination of services for all Indian children with disabilities residing on reservations covered under this chapter. Such plan shall provide for the coordination of services benefiting these children from whatever source, including tribes, the Indian Health Service, other BIA divisions, and other Federal agencies. In developing the plan, the Secretary of the Interior shall consult with all interested and involved parties. It shall be based on the needs of the children and the system best suited for meeting those needs, and may involve the establishment of cooperative agreements between the BIA, other Federal agencies, and other entities. The plan shall also be distributed upon request to States, State and local educational agencies, and other agencies providing services to infants, toddlers, and children with disabilities, to tribes, and to other interested parties.

(5) Establishment of advisory board—To meet the requirements of section 1412(a)(21) of this title, the Secretary of the Interior shall establish, not later than 6 months after June 4, 1997, under the BIA, an advisory board composed of individuals involved in or concerned with the education and provision of services to Indian infants, toddlers, children, and youth with disabilities, including Indians with disabilities, Indian parents or guardians of such children, teachers, service providers, State and local educational officials, representatives of tribes or tribal organizations, representatives from State Interagency Coordinating Councils under section 1441 of this title in States having reservations, and other members representing the various divisions and entities of the BIA. The chairperson shall be selected by the Secretary of the Interior. The advisory board shall—

(A) assist in the coordination of services within the BIA and with other local, State, and Federal agencies in the provision of education for infants, toddlers, and children with disabilities;

(B) advise and assist the Secretary of the Interior in the performance of the Secretary's responsibilities described in this subsection;

(C) develop and recommend policies concerning effective inter- and intra-agency collaboration, including modifications to regulations, and the elimination of barriers to inter- and intra-agency programs and activities;

(D) provide assistance and disseminate information on best practices, effective program coordination strategies, and recommendations for improved educational programming for Indian infants, toddlers, and children with disabilities; and

(E) provide assistance in the preparation of information required under paragraph (2)(D).

(6) Annual reports

(A) In general—The advisory board established under paragraph (5) shall prepare and submit to the Secretary of the Interior and to the Congress an annual report containing a description of the activities of the advisory board for the preceding year.

(B) Availability—The Secretary of the Interior shall make available to the Secretary of Education the report described in subparagraph (A).

(j) Authorization of appropriations

For the purpose of carrying out this part, other than section 1419 of this title, there are authorized to be appropriated such sums as may be necessary.

§ 1412. State eligibility

(a) In general

A State is eligible for assistance under this part for a fiscal year if the State demonstrates to the satisfaction of the Secretary that the State has in effect policies and procedures to ensure that it meets each of the following conditions:

(1) Free appropriate public education

(A) In general—A free appropriate public education is available to all children with disabilities residing in the State between the ages of 3 and 21, inclusive, including children with disabilities who have been suspended or expelled from school.

(B) Limitation—The obligation to make a free appropriate public education available to all children with disabilities does not apply with respect to children:

(i) aged 3 through 5 and 18 through 21 in a State to the extent that its application to those children would be inconsistent with State law or practice, or the order of any court, respecting the provision of public education to children in those age ranges; and

(ii) aged 18 through 21 to the extent that State law does not require that special education and related services under this part be provided to children with disabilities who, in the educational placement prior to their incarceration in an adult correctional facility:

(I) were not actually identified as being a child with a disability under section 1401(3) of this title; or

(II) did not have an individualized education program under this part.

(2) Full educational opportunity goal—The State has established a goal of providing full educational opportunity to all children with disabilities and a detailed timetable for accomplishing that goal.

(3) Child find

(A) In general—All children with disabilities residing in the State, including children with disabilities attending private schools, regardless of the severity of their disabilities, and who are in need of special education and related services, are identified, located, and evaluated and a practical method is developed and implemented to determine which children with disabilities are currently receiving needed special education and related services.

(B) Construction—Nothing in this Act requires that children be classified by their disability so long as each child who has a disability listed in section 1401 of this title and who, by reason of that disability, needs special education and related services is regarded as a child with a disability under this subchapter.

(4) Individualized education program—An individualized education program, or an individualized family service plan that meets the requirements of section 1436(d) of this title, is developed, reviewed, and revised for each child with a disability in accordance with section 1414(d) of this title.

(5) Least restrictive environment

(A) In general—To the maximum extent appropriate, children with disabilities, including children in public or private institutions or other care facilities, are educated with children who are not disabled, and special classes, separate schooling, or other removal of children with disabilities from the regular educational environment occurs only when the nature or severity of the disability of a child is such that education in regular classes with the use of supplementary aids and services cannot be achieved satisfactorily.

(B) Additional requirement

(i) In general—If the State uses a funding mechanism by which the State distributes State funds on the basis of the type of setting in which a child is served, the funding mechanism does not result in placements that violate the requirements of subparagraph (A).

(ii) Assurance—If the State does not have policies and procedures to ensure compliance with clause (i), the State shall provide the Secretary an assurance that it will revise the funding mechanism as soon as feasible to ensure that such mechanism does not result in such placements.

(6) Procedural safeguards

(A) In general—Children with disabilities and their parents are afforded the procedural safeguards required by section 1415 of this title.

(B) Additional procedural safeguards—Procedures to ensure that testing and evaluation materials and procedures utilized for the purposes of evaluation and placement of children with disabilities will be selected and administered so as not to be racially or culturally discriminatory. Such materials or procedures shall be provided and administered in the child's native language or mode of communication, unless it clearly is not feasible to do so, and no single procedure shall be the sole criterion for determining an appropriate educational program for a child.

(7) Evaluation—Children with disabilities are evaluated in accordance with subsections (a) through (c) of section 1414 of this title.

(8) Confidentiality—Agencies in the State comply with section 1417(c) of this title (relating to the confidentiality of records and information).

(9) Transition from subchapter III to preschool programs—Children participating in early-intervention programs assisted under subchapter III of this chapter, and who will participate in preschool programs assisted under this part, experience a smooth and effective transition to those preschool programs in a manner consistent with section 1437(a)(8) of this title. By the third birthday of such a child, an individualized education program or, if consistent with sections 1414(d)(2)(B) and 1436(d) of this title, an individualized family service plan, has been developed and is being implemented for the child. The local educational agency will participate in transition planning conferences arranged by the designated lead agency under section 1437(a)(8) of this title.

(10) Children in private schools

(A) Children enrolled in private schools by their parents

(i) In general—To the extent consistent with the number and location of children with disabilities in the State who are enrolled by their parents in private elementary and secondary schools, provision is made for the participation of those children in the program assisted or carried out under this part by providing for such children special education and related services in accordance with the following requirements, unless the Secretary has arranged for services to those children under subsection (f) of this section:

(I) Amounts expended for the provision of those services by a local educational agency shall be equal to a proportionate amount of Federal funds made available under this part.

(II) Such services may be provided to children with disabilities on the premises of private, including parochial, schools, to the extent consistent with law.

(ii) Child-find requirement—The requirements of paragraph (3) of this subsection (relating to child find) shall apply with respect to children with disabilities in the State who are enrolled in private, including parochial, elementary and secondary schools.

(B) Children placed in, or referred to, private schools by public agencies

(i) In general—Children with disabilities in private schools and facilities are provided special education and related services, in accordance with an individualized education program, at no cost to their parents, if such children are placed in, or referred to, such schools or facilities by the State or appropriate local educational agency as the means of carrying out the requirements of this part or any other applicable law requiring the provision of special education and related services to all children with disabilities within such State.

(ii) Standards—In all cases described in clause (i), the State educational agency shall determine whether such schools and facilities meet standards that apply to State and local educational agencies and that children so served have all the rights they would have if served by such agencies.

(C) Payment for education of children enrolled in private schools without consent of or referral by the public agency

(i) In general—Subject to subparagraph (A), this subchapter does not require a local educational agency to pay for the cost of education, including special education and related services, of a child with a disability at a private school or facility if that agency made a free appropriate public education available to the child and the parents elected to place the child in such private school or facility.

(ii) Reimbursement for private school placement—If the parents of a child with a disability, who previously received special education and related services under the authority of a public agency, enroll the child in a private elementary or secondary school without the consent of or referral by the public agency, a court or a hearing officer may require the agency to reimburse the parents for the cost of that enrollment if the court or hearing officer finds that the agency had not made a free appropriate public education available to the child in a timely manner prior to that enrollment.

(iii) Limitation on reimbursement—The cost of reimbursement described in clause (ii) may be reduced or denied—

(I) if—

(aa) at the most recent IEP meeting that the parents attended prior to removal of the child from the public school, the parents did not inform the IEP Team that they were rejecting the placement proposed by the public agency to provide a free appropriate public education to their child, including stating their concerns and their intent to enroll their child in a private school at public expense; or

(bb) 10 business days (including any holidays that occur on a business day) prior to the removal of the child from the public school, the parents did not give written notice to the public agency of the information described in division (aa);

(II) if, prior to the parents' removal of the child from the public school, the public agency informed the parents, through the notice requirements described in section 1415(b)(7) of this title, of its intent to evaluate the child (including a statement of the purpose of the evaluation that was appropriate and reasonable), but the parents did not make the child available for such evaluation; or

(III) upon a judicial finding of unreasonableness with respect to actions taken by the parents.

(iv) Exception—Notwithstanding the notice requirement in clause (iii)(I), the cost of reimbursement may not be reduced or denied for failure to provide such notice if—

(I) the parent is illiterate and cannot write in English;

(II) compliance with clause (iii)(I) would likely result in physical or serious emotional harm to the child;

(III) the school prevented the parent from providing such notice; or

(IV) the parents had not received notice, pursuant to section 1415 of this title, of the notice requirement in clause (iii)(I).

(11) State educational agency responsible for general supervision

(A) In general—The State educational agency is responsible for

received under this subchapter.

(D) Subsequent years—If, for any year, a State fails to meet the requirement of subparagraph (A), including any year for which the State is granted a waiver under subparagraph (C), the financial support required of the State in future years under subparagraph (A) shall be the amount that would have been required in the absence of that failure and not the reduced level of the State's support.

(E) Regulations

(i) The Secretary shall, by regulation, establish procedures (including objective criteria and consideration of the results of compliance reviews of the State conducted by the Secretary) for determining whether to grant a waiver under subparagraph (C)(ii).

(ii) The Secretary shall publish proposed regulations under clause (i) not later than 6 months after June 4, 1997, and shall issue final regulations under clause (i) not later than 1 year after such date.

(20) Public participation—Prior to the adoption of any policies and procedures needed to comply with this section (including any amendments to such policies and procedures), the State ensures that there are public hearings, adequate notice of the hearings, and an opportunity for comment available to the general public, including individuals with disabilities and parents of children with disabilities.

(21) State advisory panel

(A) In general—The State has established and maintains an advisory panel for the purpose of providing policy guidance with respect to special education and related services for children with disabilities in the State.

(B) Membership—Such advisory panel shall consist of members appointed by the Governor, or any other official authorized under State law to make such appointments, that is representative of the State population and that is composed of individuals involved in, or concerned with, the education of children with disabilities, including—

(i) parents of children with disabilities;

(ii) individuals with disabilities;

(iii) teachers;

(iv) representatives of institutions of higher education that prepare special education and related services personnel;

(v) State and local education officials;

(vi) administrators of programs for children with disabilities;

(vii) representatives of other State agencies involved in the financing or delivery of related services to children with disabilities;

(viii) representatives of private schools and public charter schools;

(ix) at least one representative of a vocational, community, or business organization concerned with the provision of transition services to children with disabilities; and

(x) representatives from the State juvenile and adult corrections agencies.

(C) Special rule—A majority of the members of the panel shall be individuals with disabilities or parents of children with disabilities.

(D) Duties—The advisory panel shall—

(i) advise the State educational agency of unmet needs within the State in the education of children with disabilities;

(ii) comment publicly on any rules or regulations proposed by the State regarding the education of children with disabilities;

(iii) advise the State educational agency in developing evaluations and reporting on data to the Secretary under section 1418 of this title;

(iv) advise the State educational agency in developing corrective action plans to address findings identified in Federal monitoring reports under this part; and

(v) advise the State educational agency in developing and implementing policies relating to the coordination of services for children with disabilities.

(22) Suspension and expulsion rates

(A) In general—The State educational agency examines data to determine if significant discrepancies are occurring in the rate of long-term suspensions and expulsions of children with disabilities—

(i) among local educational agencies in the State; or

(ii) compared to such rates for nondisabled children within such agencies.

(B) Review and revision of policies—If such discrepancies are occurring, the State educational agency reviews and, if appropriate, revises (or requires the affected State or local educational agency to revise) its policies, procedures, and practices relating to the development and implementation of IEPs, the use of behavioral interventions, and procedural safeguards, to ensure that such policies, procedures, and practices comply with this chapter.

(b) State educational agency as provider of free appropriate public education or direct services

If the State educational agency provides free appropriate public education to children with disabilities, or provides direct services to such children, such agency—

(1) shall comply with any additional requirements of section 1413(a) of this title, as if such agency were a local educational agency; and

(2) may use amounts that are otherwise available to such agency under this part to serve those children without regard to section 1413(a)(2)(A)(i) of this title (relating to excess costs).

(c) Exception for prior state plans

(1) In general—If a State has on file with the Secretary policies and procedures that demonstrate that such State meets any requirement of subsection (a), including any policies and procedures filed under this part as in effect before the effective date of the Individuals with Disabilities Education Act Amendments of 1997, the Secretary shall consider such State to have met such requirement for purposes of receiving a grant under this subchapter.

(2) Modifications made by state—Subject to paragraph (3), an application submitted by a State in accordance with this section shall remain in effect until the State submits to the Secretary such modifications as the State deems necessary. This section shall apply to a modification to an application to the same extent and in the same manner as this section applies to the original plan.

(3) Modifications required by the Secretary—If, after the effective date of the Individuals with Disabilities Education Act Amendments of 1997, the provisions of this chapter are amended (or the regulations developed to carry out this Act are amended), or there is a new interpretation of this chapter by a Federal court or a State's highest court, or there is an official finding of noncompliance with Federal law or regulations, the Secretary may require a State to modify its application only to the extent necessary to ensure the State's compliance with this subchapter.

(d) Approval by the Secretary

(1) In general—If the Secretary determines that a State is eligible to receive a grant under this subchapter, the Secretary shall notify the State of that determination.

(2) Notice and hearing—The Secretary shall not make a final determination that a State is not eligible to receive a grant under this subchapter until after providing the State—

(A) with reasonable notice; and

(B) with an opportunity for a hearing.

(e) Assistance under other federal programs

Nothing in this title permits a State to reduce medical and other assistance available, or to alter eligibility, under titles V and XIX of the Social Security Act with respect to the provision of a free appropriate public education for children with disabilities in the State.

(f) By-pass for children in private schools

(1) In general—If, on December 2, 1983, a State educational agency is prohibited by law from providing for the participation in special programs of children with disabilities enrolled in private elementary and secondary schools as required by subsection (a)(10)(A) of this section, the Secretary shall, notwithstanding such provision of law, arrange for the provision of services to such children through arrangements which shall be subject to the requirements of such subsection.

(2) Payments

(A) Determination of amounts—If the Secretary arranges for services pursuant to this subsection, the Secretary, after consultation with the appropriate public and private school officials, shall pay to the provider of such services for a fiscal year an amount per child that does not exceed the amount determined by dividing—

(i) the total amount received by the State under this subchapter for such fiscal year; by

(ii) the number of children with disabilities served in the prior year, as reported to the Secretary by the State under section 1418 of this title.

(B) Withholding of certain amounts—Pending final resolution of any investigation or complaint that could result in a determination under this subsection, the Secretary may withhold from the allocation of the affected State educational agency the amount the Secretary estimates would be necessary to pay the cost of services described in subparagraph (A).

(C) Period of payments—The period under which payments are made under subparagraph (A) shall continue until the Secretary determines that there will no longer be any failure or inability on the part of the State educational agency to meet the requirements of subsection (a)(10)(A) of this section.

(3) Notice and hearing

(A) In general—The Secretary shall not take any final action under this subsection until the State educational agency affected by such action has had an opportunity, for at least 45 days after receiving written notice thereof, to submit written objections and to appear before the Secretary or the Secretary's designee to show cause why such action should not be taken.

(B) Review of action—If a State educational agency is dissatisfied with the Secretary's final action after a proceeding under subparagraph (A), such agency may, not later than 60 days after notice of such action, file with the United States court of appeals for the circuit in which such State is located a petition for review of that action. A copy of the petition shall be forthwith transmitted by the clerk of the court to the Secretary. The Secretary thereupon shall file in the court the record of the proceedings on which the Secretary based the Secretary's action, as provided in section 2112 of Title 28.

(C) Review of findings of fact—The findings of fact by the Secretary, if supported by substantial evidence, shall be conclusive, but the court, for good cause shown, may remand the case to the Secretary to take further evidence, and the Secretary may thereupon make new or modified findings of fact and may modify the Secretary's previous action, and shall file in the court the record of the further proceedings. Such new or modified findings of fact shall likewise be conclusive if supported by substantial evidence.

(D) Jurisdiction of court of appeals; review by United States Supreme Court—Upon the filing of a petition under subparagraph (B), the United States court of appeals shall have jurisdiction to affirm the action of the Secretary or to set it aside, in whole or in part. The judgment of the court shall be subject to review by the Supreme Court of the United States upon certiorari or certification as provided in section 1254 of Title 28.

§ 1413. Local educational agency eligibility

(a) In general

A local educational agency is eligible for assistance under this part for a fiscal year if such agency demonstrates to the satisfaction of the State educational agency that it meets each of the following conditions:

(1) Consistency with state policies—The local educational agency, in providing for the education of children with disabilities within its jurisdiction, has in effect policies, procedures, and programs that are consistent with the State policies and procedures established under section 1412 of this title.

(2) Use of amounts

(A) In general—Amounts provided to the local educational agency under this part shall be expended in accordance with the applicable provisions of this subchapter and—

(i) shall be used only to pay the excess costs of providing special education and related services to children with disabilities;

(ii) shall be used to supplement State, local, and other Federal funds and not to supplant such funds; and

(iii) shall not be used, except as provided in subparagraphs (B) and (C), to reduce the level of expenditures for the education of children with disabilities made by the local educational agency from local funds below the level of those expenditures for the preceding fiscal year.

(B) Exception—Notwithstanding the restriction in subparagraph (A)(iii), a local educational agency may reduce the level of expenditures where such reduction is attributable to—

(i) the voluntary departure, by retirement or otherwise, or departure for just cause, of special education personnel;

(ii) a decrease in the enrollment of children with disabilities;

(iii) the termination of the obligation of the agency, consistent with this subchapter, to provide a program of special education to a particular child with a disability that is an exceptionally costly program, as determined by the State educational agency, because the child—

(I) has left the jurisdiction of the agency;

(II) has reached the age at which the obligation of the agency to provide a free appropriate public education to the child has terminated; or

(III) no longer needs such program of special education; or

(iv) the termination of costly expenditures for long-term purchases, such as the acquisition of equipment or the construction of school facilities.

(C) Treatment of federal funds in certain fiscal years

(i) Notwithstanding clauses (ii) and (iii) of subparagraph (A), for any fiscal year for which amounts appropriated to carry out section 1411 of this title exceeds $4,100,000,000, a local educational agency may treat as local funds, for the purpose of such clauses, up to 20 percent of the amount of funds it receives under this subchapter that exceeds the amount it received under this subchapter for the previous fiscal year.

(ii) Notwithstanding clause (i), if a State educational agency determines that a local educational agency is not meeting the requirements of this subchapter, the State educational agency may prohibit the local educational agency from treating funds received under this subchapter as local funds under clause (i) for any fiscal year, only if it is authorized to do so by the State constitution or a State statute.

(D) Schoolwide programs under title I of the ESEA—Notwithstanding subparagraph (A) or any other provision of this subchapter, a local educational agency may use funds received under this part for any fiscal year to carry out a schoolwide program under section 1114 of the Elementary and Secondary Education Act of 1965, except that the amount so used in any such program shall not exceed—

(i) the number of children with disabilities participating in the schoolwide program; multiplied by

(ii)(I) the amount received by the local educational agency under this subchapter for that fiscal year, divided by

(II) the number of children with disabilities in the jurisdiction of that agency.

(3) Personnel development—The local educational agency—

(A) shall ensure that all personnel necessary to carry out this subchapter are appropriately and adequately prepared, consistent with the requirements of section 1453(c)(3)(D) of this title; and

(B) to the extent such agency determines appropriate, shall contribute to and use the comprehensive system of personnel development of the State established under section 1412(a)(14) of this title.

(4) Permissive use of funds—Notwithstanding paragraph (2)(A) or section 1412(a)(18)(B) of this title (relating to commingled funds), funds provided to the local educational agency under this subchapter may be used for the following activities:

(A) Services and aids that also benefit nondisabled children—For the costs of special education and related services and supplementary aids and services provided in a regular class or other education-related setting to a child with a disability in accordance with the individualized education program of the child, even if one or more nondisabled children benefit from such services.

(B) Integrated and coordinated services system—To develop and implement a fully integrated and coordinated services system in accordance with subsection (f) of this section.

(5) Treatment of charter schools and their students—In carrying out this subchapter with respect to charter schools that are public schools of the local educational agency, the local educational agency—

(A) serves children with disabilities attending those schools in the same manner as it serves children with disabilities in its other schools; and

(B) provides funds under this subchapter to those schools in the same manner as it provides those funds to its other schools.

(6) Information for state educational agency—The local educational agency shall provide the State educational agency with information necessary to enable the State educational agency to carry out its duties under this subchapter, including, with respect to paragraphs (16) and (17) of section 1412(a) of this title, information relating to the performance of children with disabilities participating in programs carried out under this subchapter.

(7) Public information—The local educational agency shall make available to parents of children with disabilities and to the general public all documents relating to the eligibility of such agency under this subchapter.

(b) Exception for prior local plans

(1) In general—If a local educational agency or State agency has on file with the State educational agency policies and procedures that demonstrate that such local educational agency, or such State agency, as the case may be, meets any requirement of subsection (a) of this section, including any policies and procedures filed under this part as in effect before the effective date of the Individuals with Disabilities Education Act Amendments of 1997, the State educational agency shall consider such local educational agency or State agency, as the case may be, to have met such requirement for purposes of receiving assistance under this subchapter.

(2) Modification made by local educational agency—Subject to paragraph (3), an application submitted by a local educational agency in accordance with this section shall remain in effect until it submits to the State educational agency such modifications as the local educational agency deems necessary.

(3) Modifications required by state educational agency—If, after the effective date of the Individuals with Disabilities Education Act Amendments of 1997, the provisions of this chapter are amended (or the regulations developed to carry out this chapter are amended), or there is a new interpretation of this Act by Federal or State courts, or there is an official finding of noncompliance with Federal or State law or regulations, the State educational agency may require a local educational agency to modify its application only to the extent necessary to ensure the local educational agency's compliance with this subchapter or State law.

(c) Notification of local educational agency or state agency in case of ineligibility

If the State educational agency determines that a local educational agency or State agency is not eligible under this section, the State educational agency shall notify the local educational agency or State agency, as the case may be, of that determination and shall provide such local educational agency or State agency with reasonable notice and an opportunity for a hearing.

(d) Local educational agency compliance

(1) In general—If the State educational agency, after reasonable notice and an opportunity for a hearing, finds that a local educational agency or State agency that has been determined to be eligible under this section is failing to comply with any requirement described in subsection (a) of this section, the State educational agency shall reduce or shall not provide any further payments to the local educational agency or State agency until the State educational agency is satisfied that the local educational agency or State agency, as the case may be, is complying with that requirement.

(2) Additional requirement—Any State agency or local educational agency in receipt of a notice described in paragraph (1) shall, by means of public notice, take such measures as may be necessary to bring the pendency of an action pursuant to this subsection to the attention of the public within the jurisdiction of such agency.

(3) Consideration—In carrying out its responsibilities under paragraph (1), the State educational agency shall consider any decision made in a hearing held under section 1415 of this title that is adverse to the local educational agency or State agency involved in that decision.

(e) Joint establishment of eligibility

(1) Joint establishment

(A) In general—A State educational agency may require a local educational agency to establish its eligibility jointly with another local educational agency if the State educational agency determines that the local educational agency would be ineligible under this section because the local educational agency would not be able to establish and maintain programs of sufficient size and scope to effectively meet the needs of children with disabilities.

(B) Charter school exception—A State educational agency may not require a charter school that is a local educational agency to jointly establish its eligibility under subparagraph (A) unless it is explicitly permitted to do so under the State's charter school statute.

(2) Amount of payments—If a State educational agency requires the joint establishment of eligibility under paragraph (1), the total amount of funds made available to the affected local educational agencies shall be equal to the sum of the payments that each such local educational agency would have received under section 1411(g) of this title if such agencies were eligible for such payments.

(3) Requirements—Local educational agencies that establish joint eligibility under this subsection shall—

(A) adopt policies and procedures that are consistent with the State's policies and procedures under section 1412(a) of this title; and

(B) be jointly responsible for implementing programs that receive assistance under this subchapter.

(4) Requirements for educational service agencies

(A) In general—If an educational service agency is required by State law to carry out programs under this subchapter, the joint responsibilities given to local educational agencies under this subsection shall—

(i) not apply to the administration and disbursement of any payments received by that educational service agency; and

(ii) be carried out only by that educational service agency.

(B) Additional requirement—Notwithstanding any other provision of this subsection, an educational service agency shall provide for the education of children with disabilities in the least restrictive environment, as required by section 1412(a)(5) of this title.

(f) Coordinated services system

(1) In general—A local educational agency may not use more than 5 percent of the amount such agency receives under this subchapter for any fiscal year, in combination with other amounts (which shall include amounts other than education funds), to develop and implement a coordinated services system designed to improve results for children and families, including children with disabilities and their families.

(2) Activities—In implementing a coordinated services system under this subsection, a local educational agency may carry out activities that include—

(A) improving the effectiveness and efficiency of service delivery, including developing strategies that promote accountability for results;

(B) service coordination and case management that facilitates the linkage of individualized education programs under this part and individualized family service plans under subchapter III of this chapter with individualized service plans under multiple Federal and State programs, such as title I of the Rehabilitation Act of 1973 (vocational rehabilitation), title XIX of the Social Security Act (Medicaid), and title XVI of the Social Security Act (supplemental security income);

(C) developing and implementing interagency financing strategies for the provision of education, health, mental health, and social services, including transition services and related services under this chapter; and

(D) interagency personnel development for individuals working on coordinated services.

(3) Coordination with certain projects under Elementary and Secondary Education Act of 1965—If a local educational agency is carrying out a coordinated services project under title XI of the Elementary and Secondary Education Act of 1965 and a coordinated services project under this subchapter in the same schools, such agency shall use amounts under this subsection in accordance with the requirements of that title.

(g) School-based improvement plan

(1) In general—Each local educational agency may, in accordance with paragraph (2), use funds made available under this subchapter to permit a public school within the jurisdiction of the local educational agency to design, implement, and evaluate a school-based improvement plan that is consistent with the purposes described in section 1451(b) of this title and that is designed to improve educational and transitional results for all children with disabilities and, as appropriate, for other children consistent with subparagraphs (A) and (B) of subsection (a)(4) of this section in that public school.

(2) Authority

(A) In general—A State educational agency may grant authority to a local educational agency to permit a public school described in paragraph (1) (through a school-based standing panel established under paragraph (4)(B)) to design, implement, and evaluate a school-based improvement plan described in paragraph (1) for a period not to exceed 3 years.

(B) Responsibility of local educational agency—If a State educational agency grants the authority described in subparagraph (A), a local educational agency that is granted such authority shall have the sole responsibility of oversight of all activities relating to the design, implementation, and evaluation of any school-based improvement plan that a public school is permitted to design under this subsection.

(3) Plan requirements—A school-based improvement plan described in paragraph (1) shall—

(A) be designed to be consistent with the purposes described in section 1451(b) of this title and to improve educational and transitional results for all children with disabilities and, as appropriate, for other children consistent with subparagraphs (A) and (B) of subsection (a)(4) of this section, who attend the school for which the plan is designed and implemented;

(B) be designed, evaluated, and, as appropriate, implemented by a school-based standing panel established in accordance with paragraph (4)(B);

(C) include goals and measurable indicators to assess the progress of the public school in meeting such goals; and

(D) ensure that all children with disabilities receive the services described in the individualized education programs of such children.

(4) Responsibilities of the local educational agency—A local educational agency that is granted authority under paragraph (2) to permit a public school to design, implement, and evaluate a school-based improvement plan shall—

(A) select each school under the jurisdiction of such agency that is eligible to design, implement, and evaluate such a plan;

(B) require each school selected under subparagraph (A), in accordance with criteria established by such local educational agency under subparagraph (C), to establish a school-based standing panel to carry out the duties described in paragraph (3)(B);

(C) establish—

(i) criteria that shall be used by such local educational agency in the selection of an eligible school under subparagraph (A);

(ii) criteria that shall be used by a public school selected under subparagraph (A) in the establishment of a school-based standing panel to carry out the duties described in paragraph (3)(B) and that shall ensure that the membership of such panel reflects the diversity of the community in which the public school is located and includes, at a minimum—

(I) parents of children with disabilities who attend such public school, including parents of children with disabilities from unserved and underserved populations, as appropriate;

(II) special education and general education teachers of such public school;

(III) special education and general education administrators, or the designee of such administrators, of such public school; and

(IV) related services providers who are responsible for providing services to the children with disabilities who attend such public school; and

(iii) criteria that shall be used by such local educational agency with respect to the distribution of funds under this part to carry out this subsection;

(D) disseminate the criteria established under subparagraph (C) to local school district personnel and local parent organizations within the jurisdiction of such local educational agency;

(E) require a public school that desires to design, implement, and evaluate a school-based improvement plan to submit an application at such time, in such manner, and accompanied by such information as such local educational agency shall reasonably require; and

(F) establish procedures for approval by such local educational agency of a school-based improvement plan designed under this subsection.

(5) Limitation—A school-based improvement plan described in paragraph (1) may be submitted to a local educational agency for approval only if a consensus with respect to any matter relating to the design, implementation, or evaluation of the goals of such plan is reached by the school-based standing panel that designed such plan.

(6) Additional requirements

(A) Parental involvement—In carrying out the requirements of this subsection, a local educational agency shall ensure that the parents of children with disabilities are involved in the design, evaluation, and, where appropriate, implementation of school-based improvement plans in accordance with this subsection.

(B) Plan approval—A local educational agency may approve a school-based improvement plan of a public school within the jurisdiction of such agency for a period of 3 years, if—

(i) the approval is consistent with the policies, procedures, and practices established by such local educational agency and in accordance with this subsection; and

(ii) a majority of parents of children who are members of the school-based standing panel, and a majority of other members of the school-based standing panel, that designed such plan agree in writing to such plan.

(7) Extension of plan—If a public school within the jurisdiction of a local educational agency meets the applicable requirements and criteria described in paragraphs (3) and (4) at the expiration of the 3-year approval period described in paragraph (6)(B), such agency may approve a school-based improvement plan of such school for an additional 3-year period.

(h) Direct services by the state educational agency

(1) In general—A State educational agency shall use the payments that would otherwise have been available to a local educational agency or to a State agency to provide special education and related services directly to children with disabilities residing in the area served by that local agency, or for whom that State agency is responsible, if the State educational agency determines that the local education agency or State agency, as the case may be—

(A) has not provided the information needed to establish the eligibility of such agency under this section;

(B) is unable to establish and maintain programs of free appropriate public education that meet the requirements of subsection (a) of this section;

(C) is unable or unwilling to be consolidated with one or more local educational agencies in order to establish and maintain such programs; or

(D) has one or more children with disabilities who can best be served by a regional or State program or service-delivery system designed to meet the needs of such children.

(2) Manner and location of education and services—The State educational agency may provide special education and related services under paragraph (1) in such manner and at such locations (including regional or State centers) as the State agency considers appropriate. Such education and services shall be provided in accordance with this part.

(i) State agency eligibility

Any State agency that desires to receive a subgrant for any fiscal year under section 1411(g) of this title shall demonstrate to the satisfaction of the State educational agency that—

(1) all children with disabilities who are participating in programs and projects funded under this subchapter receive a free appropriate public education, and that those children and their parents are provided all the rights and procedural safeguards described in this subchapter; and

(2) the agency meets such other conditions of this section as the Secretary determines to be appropriate.

(j) Disciplinary information

The State may require that a local educational agency include in the records of a child with a disability a statement of any current or previous disciplinary action that has been taken against the child and transmit such statement to the same extent that such disciplinary information is included in, and transmitted with, the student records of nondisabled children. The statement may include a description of any behavior engaged in by the child that required disciplinary action, a description of the disciplinary action taken, and any other information that is relevant to the safety of the child and other individuals involved with the child. If the State adopts such a policy, and the child transfers from one school to another, the transmission of any of the child's records must include both the child's current individualized education program and any such statement of current or previous disciplinary action that has been taken against the child.

§ 1414. Evaluations, eligibility determinations, individualized education programs, and educational placements

(a) Evaluations and reevaluations

(1) Initial evaluations

(A) In general—A State educational agency, other State agency, or local educational agency shall conduct a full and individual initial evaluation, in accordance with this paragraph and subsection (b) of this section, before the initial provision of special education and related services to a child with a disability under this subchapter.

(B) Procedures—Such initial evaluation shall consist of procedures—

(i) to determine whether a child is a child with a disability (as defined in section 1401(3) of this title); and

(ii) to determine the educational needs of such child.

(C) Parental consent

(i) In general—The agency proposing to conduct an initial evaluation to determine if the child qualifies as a child with a disability as defined in section 1401(3)(A) or 1401(3)(B) of this title shall obtain an informed consent from the parent of such child before the evaluation is conducted. Parental consent for evaluation shall not be construed as consent for placement for receipt of special education and related services.

(ii) Refusal—If the parents of such child refuse consent for the evaluation, the agency may continue to pursue an evaluation by utilizing the mediation and due process procedures under section 1415 of this title, except to the extent inconsistent with State law relating to parental consent.

(2) Reevaluations—A local educational agency shall ensure that a reevaluation of each child with a disability is conducted—

(A) if conditions warrant a reevaluation or if the child's parent or teacher requests a reevaluation, but at least once every 3 years; and

(B) in accordance with subsections (b) and (c) of this section.

(b) Evaluation procedures

(1) Notice—The local educational agency shall provide notice to the parents of a child with a disability, in accordance with subsections (b)(3), (b)(4), and (c) of section 1415 of this title, that describes any evaluation procedures such agency proposes to conduct.

(2) Conduct of evaluation—In conducting the evaluation, the local educational agency shall—

(A) use a variety of assessment tools and strategies to gather relevant functional and developmental information, including information provided by the parent, that may assist in determining whether the child is a child with a disability and the content of the child's individualized education program, including information related to enabling the child to be involved in and progress in the general curriculum or, for preschool children, to participate in appropriate activities;

(B) not use any single procedure as the sole criterion for determining whether a child is a child with a disability or determining an appropriate educational program for the child; and

(C) use technically sound instruments that may assess the relative contribution of cognitive and behavioral factors, in addition to physical or developmental factors.

(3) Additional requirements—Each local educational agency shall ensure that—

(A) tests and other evaluation materials used to assess a child under this section—

(i) are selected and administered so as not to be discriminatory on a racial or cultural basis, and

(ii) are provided and administered in the child's native language or other mode of communication, unless it is clearly not feasible to do so; and

(B) any standardized tests that are given to the child—

(i) have been validated for the specific purpose for which they are used;

(ii) are administered by trained and knowledgeable personnel; and

(iii) are administered in accordance with any instructions provided by the producer of such tests;

(C) the child is assessed in all areas of suspected disability; and

(D) assessment tools and strategies that provide relevant information that directly assists persons in determining the educational needs of the child are provided.

(4) Determination of eligibility—Upon completion of administration of tests and other evaluation materials—

(A) the determination of whether the child is a child with a disability as defined in section 1401(3) of this title shall be made by a team of qualified professionals and the parent of the child in accordance with paragraph (5); and

(B) a copy of the evaluation report and the documentation of determination of eligibility will be given to the parent.

(5) Special rule for eligibility determination—In making a determination of eligibility under paragraph (4)(A), a child shall not be determined to be a child with a disability if the determinant factor for such determination is lack of instruction in reading or math or limited English proficiency.

(c) Additional requirements for evaluation and reevaluations

(1) Review of existing evaluation data—As part of an initial evaluation (if appropriate) and as part of any reevaluation under this section, the IEP Team described in subsection (d)(1)(B) of this section and other qualified professionals, as appropriate, shall—

(A) review existing evaluation data on the child, including evaluations and information provided by the parents of the child, current classroom-based assessments and observations, and teacher and related services providers observation; and

(B) on the basis of that review, and input from the child's parents, identify what additional data, if any, are needed to determine—

(i) whether the child has a particular category of disability, as described in section 1401(3) of this title, or, in case of a reevaluation of a child, whether the child continues to have such a disability;

(ii) the present levels of performance and educational needs of the child;

(iii) whether the child needs special education and related services, or in the case of a reevaluation of a child, whether the child continues to need special education and related services; and

(iv) whether any additions or modifications to the special education and related services are needed to enable the child to meet the measurable annual goals set out in the individualized education program of the child and to participate, as appropriate, in the general curriculum.

(2) Source of data—The local educational agency shall administer such tests and other evaluation materials as may be needed to produce the data identified by the IEP Team under paragraph (1)(B).

(3) Parental consent—Each local educational agency shall obtain informed parental consent, in accordance with subsection (a)(1)(C) of this section, prior to conducting any reevaluation of a child with a disability, except that such informed parent consent need not be obtained if the local educational agency can demonstrate that it had taken reasonable measures to obtain such consent and the child's parent has failed to respond.

(4) Requirements if additional data are not needed—If the IEP Team and other qualified professionals, as appropriate, determine that no additional data are needed to determine whether the child continues to be a child with a disability, the local educational agency—

(A) shall notify the child's parents of—

(i) that determination and the reasons for it; and

(ii) the right of such parents to request an assessment to determine whether the child continues to be a child with a disability; and

(B) shall not be required to conduct such an assessment unless requested to by the child's parents.

(5) Evaluations before change in eligibility—A local educational agency shall evaluate a child with a disability in accordance with this section before determining that the child is no longer a child with a disability.

(d) Individualized education programs

(1) Definitions—As used in this title:

(A) Individualized education program—The term 'individualized education program' or 'IEP' means a written statement for each child with a disability that is developed, reviewed, and revised in accordance with this section and that includes—

(i) a statement of the child's present levels of educational performance, including—

(I) how the child's disability affects the child's involvement and progress in the general curriculum; or

(II) for preschool children, as appropriate, how the disability affects the child's participation in appropriate activities;

(ii) a statement of measurable annual goals, including benchmarks or short-term objectives, related to—

(I) meeting the child's needs that result from the child's disability to enable the child to be involved in and progress in the general curriculum; and

(II) meeting each of the child's other educational needs that result from the child's disability;

(iii) a statement of the special education and related services and supplementary aids and services to be provided to the child, or on behalf of the child, and a statement of the program modifications or supports for school personnel that will be provided for the child—

(I) to advance appropriately toward attaining the annual goals;

(II) to be involved and progress in the general curriculum in accordance with clause (i) and to participate in extracurricular and other nonacademic activities; and

(III) to be educated and participate with other children with disabilities and nondisabled children in the activities described in this paragraph;

(iv) an explanation of the extent, if any, to which the child will not participate with nondisabled children in the regular class and in the activities described in clause (iii);

(v)(I) a statement of any individual modifications in the administration of State or districtwide assessments of student achievement that are needed in order for the child to participate in such assessment; and

(II) if the IEP Team determines that the child will not participate in a particular State or districtwide assessment of student achievement (or part of such an assessment), a statement of—

(aa) why that assessment is not appropriate for the child; and

(bb) how the child will be assessed;

(vi) the projected date for the beginning of the services and modifications described in clause (iii), and the anticipated frequency, location, and duration of those services and modifications;

(vii)(I) beginning at age 14, and updated annually, a statement of the transition service needs of the child under the applicable components of the child's IEP that focuses on the child's courses of study (such as participation in advanced-placement courses or a vocational education program);

(II) beginning at age 16 (or younger, if determined appropriate by the IEP Team), a statement of needed transition services for the child, including, when appropriate, a statement of the interagency responsibilities or any needed linkages; and

(III) beginning at least one year before the child reaches the age of majority under State law, a statement that the child has been informed of his or her rights under this title, if any, that will transfer to the child on reaching the age of majority under section 1415(m) of this title; and

(viii) a statement of—

(I) how the child's progress toward the annual goals described in clause (ii) will be measured; and

(II) how the child's parents will be regularly informed (by such means as periodic report cards), at least as often as parents are informed of their nondisabled children's progress, of—

(aa) their child's progress toward the annual goals described in clause (ii); and

(bb) the extent to which that progress is sufficient to enable the child to achieve the goals by the end of the year.

(B) Individualized education program team—The term 'individualized education program team' or 'IEP Team' means a group of individuals composed of—

(i) the parents of a child with a disability;

(ii) at least one regular education teacher of such child (if the child is, or may be, participating in the regular education environment);

(iii) at least one special education teacher, or where appropriate, at least one special education provider of such child;

(iv) a representative of the local educational agency who—

(I) is qualified to provide, or supervise the provision of, specially designed instruction to meet the unique needs of children with disabilities;

(II) is knowledgeable about the general curriculum; and

(III) is knowledgeable about the availability of resources of the local educational agency;

(v) an individual who can interpret the instructional implications of evaluation results, who may be a member of the team described in clauses (ii) through (vi);

(vi) at the discretion of the parent or the agency, other individuals who have knowledge or special expertise regarding the child, including related services personnel as appropriate; and

(vii) whenever appropriate, the child with a disability.

(2) Requirement that program be in effect

(A) In general—At the beginning of each school year, each local educational agency, State educational agency, or other State agency, as the case may be, shall have in effect, for each child with a disability in its jurisdiction, an individualized education program, as defined in paragraph (1)(A).

(B) Program for child aged 3 through 5—In the case of a child with a disability aged 3 through 5 (or, at the discretion of the State educational agency, a 2 year-old child with a disability who will turn age 3 during the school year), an individualized family service plan that contains the material described in section 1436 of this title, and that is developed in accordance with this section, may serve as the IEP of the child if using that plan as the IEP is—

(i) consistent with State policy; and

(ii) agreed to by the agency and the child's parents.

(3) Development of IEP

(A) In general—In developing each child's IEP, the IEP Team, subject to subparagraph (C), shall consider—

(i) the strengths of the child and the concerns of the parents for enhancing the education of their child; and

(ii) the results of the initial evaluation or most recent evaluation of the child.

(B) Consideration of special factors—The IEP Team shall—

(i) in the case of a child whose behavior impedes his or her learning or that of others, consider, when appropriate, strategies, including positive behavioral interventions, strategies, and supports to address that behavior;

(ii) in the case of a child with limited English proficiency, consider the language needs of the child as such needs relate to the child's IEP;

(iii) in the case of a child who is blind or visually impaired, provide for instruction in Braille and the use of Braille unless the IEP Team determines, after an evaluation of the child's reading and writing skills, needs, and appropriate reading and writing media (including an evaluation of the child's future needs for instruction in Braille or the use of Braille), that instruction in Braille or the use of Braille is not appropriate for the child;

(iv) consider the communication needs of the child, and in the case of a child who is deaf or hard of hearing, consider the child's language and communication needs, opportunities for direct communications with peers and professional personnel in the child's language and communication mode, academic level, and full range of needs, including opportunities for direct instruction in the child's language and communication mode; and

(v) consider whether the child requires assistive technology devices and services.

(C) Requirement with respect to regular education teacher—The regular education teacher of the child, as a member of the IEP Team, shall, to the extent appropriate, participate in the development of the IEP of the child, including the determination of appropriate positive behavioral interventions and strategies and the determination of supplementary aids and services, program modifications, and support for school personnel consistent with paragraph (1)(A)(iii).

(4) Review and revision of IEP

(A) In general—The local educational agency shall ensure that, subject to subparagraph (B), the IEP Team—

(i) reviews the child's IEP periodically, but not less than annually to determine whether the annual goals for the child are being achieved; and

(ii) revises the IEP as appropriate to address—

(I) any lack of expected progress toward the annual goals and in the general curriculum, where appropriate;

(II) the results of any reevaluation conducted under this section;

(III) information about the child provided to, or by, the parents, as described in subsection (c)(1)(B) of this section;

(IV) the child's anticipated needs; or

(V) other matters.

(B) Requirement with respect to regular education teacher—The regular education teacher of the child, as a member of the IEP Team, shall, to the extent appropriate, participate in the review and revision of the IEP of the child.

(5) Failure to meet transition objectives—If a participating agency, other than the local educational agency, fails to provide the transition services described in the IEP in accordance with paragraph (1)(A)(vii), the local educational agency shall reconvene the IEP Team to identify alternative strategies to meet the transition objectives for the child set out in that program.

(6) Children with disabilities in adult prisons

(A) In general—The following requirements do not apply to children with disabilities who are convicted as adults under State law and incarcerated in adult prisons:

(i) The requirements contained in section 1412(a)(17) of this title and paragraph (1)(A)(v) of this subsection (relating to participation of children with disabilities in general assessments).

(ii) The requirements of subclauses (I) and (II) of paragraph (1)(A)(vii) of this subsection (relating to transition planning and transition services), do not apply with respect to such children whose eligibility under this part will end, because of their age, before they will be released from prison.

(B) Additional requirement—If a child with a disability is convicted as an adult under State law and incarcerated in an adult prison, the child's IEP Team may modify the child's IEP or placement notwithstanding the requirements of sections 1412(a)(5)(A) and 1414(d)(1)(A) of this title if the State has demonstrated a bona fide security or compelling penological interest that cannot otherwise be accommodated.

(e) Construction

Nothing in this section shall be construed to require the IEP Team to include information under one component of a child's IEP that is already contained under another component of such IEP.

(f) Educational placements

Each local educational agency or State educational agency shall ensure that the parents of each child with a disability are members of any group that makes decisions on the educational placement of their child.

§ 1415. Procedural safeguards

(a) Establishment of procedures

Any State educational agency, State agency, or local educational agency that receives assistance under this subchapter shall establish and maintain procedures in accordance with this section to ensure that children with disabilities and their parents are guaranteed procedural safeguards with respect to the provision of free appropriate public education by such agencies.

(b) Types of procedures

The procedures required by this section shall include—

(1) an opportunity for the parents of a child with a disability to examine all records relating to such child and to participate in meetings with respect to the identification, evaluation, and educational placement of the child, and the provision of a free appropriate public education to such child, and to obtain an independent educational evaluation of the child;

(2) procedures to protect the rights of the child whenever the parents of the child are not known, the agency cannot, after reasonable efforts, locate the parents, or the child is a ward of the State, including the assignment of an individual (who shall not be an employee of the State educational agency, the local educational agency, or any other agency that is involved in the education or care of the child) to act as a surrogate for the parents;

(3) written prior notice to the parents of the child whenever such agency—

(A) proposes to initiate or change; or

(B) refuses to initiate or change;

the identification, evaluation, or educational placement of the child, in accordance with subsection (c) of this section, or the provision of a free appropriate public education to the child;

(4) procedures designed to ensure that the notice required by paragraph (3) is in the native language of the parents, unless it clearly is not feasible to do so;

(5) an opportunity for mediation in accordance with subsection (e) of this section;

(6) an opportunity to present complaints with respect to any matter relating to the identification, evaluation, or educational placement of the child, or the provision of a free appropriate public education to such child;

(7) procedures that require the parent of a child with a disability, or the attorney representing the child, to provide notice (which shall remain confidential)—

(A) to the State educational agency or local educational agency, as the case may be, in the complaint filed under paragraph (6); and

(B) that shall include—

(i) the name of the child, the address of the residence of the child, and the name of the school the child is attending;

(ii) a description of the nature of the problem of the child relating to such proposed initiation or change, including facts relating to such problem; and

(iii) a proposed resolution of the problem to the extent known and available to the parents at the time; and

(8) procedures that require the State educational agency to develop a model form to assist parents in filing a complaint in accordance with paragraph (7).

(c) Content of prior written notice

The notice required by subsection (b)(3) of this section shall include—

(1) a description of the action proposed or refused by the agency;

(2) an explanation of why the agency proposes or refuses to take the action;

(3) a description of any other options that the agency considered and the reasons why those options were rejected;

(4) a description of each evaluation procedure, test, record, or report the agency used as a basis for the proposed or refused action;

(5) a description of any other factors that are relevant to the agency's proposal or refusal;

(6) a statement that the parents of a child with a disability have protection under the procedural safeguards of this part and, if this notice is not an initial referral for evaluation, the means by which a copy of a description of the procedural safeguards can be obtained; and

(7) sources for parents to contact to obtain assistance in understanding the provisions of this subchapter.

(d) Procedural safeguards notice

(1) In general—A copy of the procedural safeguards available to the parents of a child with a disability shall be given to the parents, at a minimum—

(A) upon initial referral for evaluation;

(B) upon each notification of an individualized education program meeting and upon reevaluation of the child; and

(C) upon registration of a complaint under subsection (b)(6) of this section.

(2) Contents—The procedural safeguards notice shall include a full explanation of the procedural safeguards, written in the native language of the parents, unless it clearly is not feasible to do so, and written in an easily understandable manner, available under this section and under regulations promulgated by the Secretary relating to—

(A) independent educational evaluation;

(B) prior written notice;

(C) parental consent;

(D) access to educational records;

(E) opportunity to present complaints;

(F) the child's placement during pendency of due process proceedings;

(G) procedures for students who are subject to placement in an interim alternative educational setting;

(H) requirements for unilateral placement by parents of children in private schools at public expense;

(I) mediation;

(J) due process hearings, including requirements for disclosure of evaluation results and recommendations;

(K) State-level appeals (if applicable in that State);

(L) civil actions; and

(M) attorneys' fees.

(e) Mediation

(1) In general—Any State educational agency or local educational agency that receives assistance under this subchapter shall ensure that procedures are established and implemented to allow parties to disputes involving any matter described in subsection (b)(6) of this section to resolve such disputes through a mediation process which, at a minimum, shall be available whenever a hearing is requested under subsection (f) or (k) of this section.

(2) Requirements—Such procedures shall meet the following requirements:

(A) The procedures shall ensure that the mediation process—

(i) is voluntary on the part of the parties;

(ii) is not used to deny or delay a parent's right to a due process hearing under subsection (f) of this section, or to deny any other rights afforded under this subchapter; and

(iii) is conducted by a qualified and impartial mediator who is trained in effective mediation techniques.

(B) A local educational agency or a State agency may establish procedures to require parents who choose not to use the mediation process to meet, at a time and location convenient to the parents, with a disinterested party who is under contract with—

(i) a parent training and information center or community parent resource center in the State established under section 1482 or 1483 of this title; or

(ii) an appropriate alternative dispute resolution entity; to encourage the use, and explain the benefits, of the mediation process to the parents.

(C) The State shall maintain a list of individuals who are qualified mediators and knowledgeable in laws and regulations relating to the provision of special education and related services.

(D) The State shall bear the cost of the mediation process, including the costs of meetings described in subparagraph (B).

(E) Each session in the mediation process shall be scheduled in a timely manner and shall be held in a location that is convenient to the parties to the dispute.

(F) An agreement reached by the parties to the dispute in the mediation process shall be set forth in a written mediation agreement.

(G) Discussions that occur during the mediation process shall be confidential and may not be used as evidence in any subsequent due process hearings or civil proceedings and the parties to the mediation process may be required to sign a confidentiality pledge prior to the commencement of such process.

(f) Impartial due process hearing

(1) In general—Whenever a complaint has been received under subsection (b)(6) or (k) of this section, the parents involved in such complaint shall have an opportunity for an impartial due process hearing, which shall be conducted by the State educational agency or by the local educational agency, as determined by State law or by the State educational agency.

(2) Disclosure of evaluations and recommendations

(A) In general—At least 5 business days prior to a hearing conducted pursuant to paragraph (1), each party shall disclose to all other parties all evaluations completed by that date and recommendations based on the offering party's evaluations that the party intends to use at the hearing.

(B) Failure to disclose—A hearing officer may bar any party that fails to comply with subparagraph (A) from introducing the relevant evaluation or recommendation at the hearing without the consent of the other party.

(3) Limitation on conduct of hearing—A hearing conducted pursuant to paragraph (1) may not be conducted by an employee of the State educational agency or the local educational agency involved in the education or care of the child.

(g) Appeal

If the hearing required by subsection (f) of this section is conducted by a local educational agency, any party aggrieved by the findings and decision rendered in such a hearing may appeal such findings and decision to the State educational agency. Such agency shall conduct an impartial review of such decision. The officer conducting such review shall make an independent decision upon completion of such review.

(h) Safeguards

Any party to a hearing conducted pursuant to subsection (f) or (k) of this section, or an appeal conducted pursuant to subsection (g) of this section, shall be accorded—

(1) the right to be accompanied and advised by counsel and by individuals with special knowledge or training with respect to the problems of children with disabilities;

(2) the right to present evidence and confront, cross-examine, and compel the attendance of witnesses;

(3) the right to a written, or, at the option of the parents, electronic verbatim record of such hearing; and

(4) the right to written, or, at the option of the parents, electronic findings of fact and decisions (which findings and decisions shall be made available to the public consistent with the requirements of section 1417(c) of this title (relating to the confidentiality of data, information, and records) and shall also be transmitted

to the advisory panel established pursuant to section 1412(a)(21) of this title).

(i) Administrative procedures

(1) In general

(A) Decision made in hearing—A decision made in a hearing conducted pursuant to subsection (f) or (k) of this section shall be final, except that any party involved in such hearing may appeal such decision under the provisions of subsection (g) of this section and paragraph (2) of this subsection.

(B) Decision made at appeal—A decision made under subsection (g) of this section shall be final, except that any party may bring an action under paragraph (2) of this subsection.

(2) Right to bring civil action

(A) In general—Any party aggrieved by the findings and decision made under subsection (f) or (k) of this section who does not have the right to an appeal under subsection (g) of this section, and any party aggrieved by the findings and decision under this subsection, shall have the right to bring a civil action with respect to the complaint presented pursuant to this section, which action may be brought in any State court of competent jurisdiction or in a district court of the United States without regard to the amount in controversy.

(B) Additional requirements—In any action brought under this paragraph, the court—

(i) shall receive the records of the administrative proceedings;

(ii) shall hear additional evidence at the request of a party; and

(iii) basing its decision on the preponderance of the evidence, shall grant such relief as the court determines is appropriate.

(3) Jurisdiction of district courts; attorneys' fees

(A) In general—The district courts of the United States shall have jurisdiction of actions brought under this section without regard to the amount in controversy.

(B) Award of attorneys' fees—In any action or proceeding brought under this section, the court, in its discretion, may award reasonable attorneys' fees as part of the costs to the parents of a child with a disability who is the prevailing party.

(C) Determination of amount of attorneys' fees—Fees awarded under this paragraph shall be based on rates prevailing in the community in which the action or proceeding arose for the kind and quality of services furnished. No bonus or multiplier may be used in calculating the fees awarded under this subsection.

(D) Prohibition of attorneys' fees and related costs for certain services

(i) Attorneys' fees may not be awarded and related costs may not be reimbursed in any action or proceeding under this section for services performed subsequent to the time of a written offer of settlement to a parent if—

(I) the offer is made within the time prescribed by Rule 68 of the Federal Rules of Civil Procedure or, in the case of an administrative proceeding, at any time more than 10 days before the proceeding begins;

(II) the offer is not accepted within 10 days; and

(III) the court or administrative hearing officer finds that the relief finally obtained by the parents is not more favorable to the parents than the offer of settlement.

(ii) Attorneys' fees may not be awarded relating to any meeting of the IEP Team unless such meeting is convened as a result of an administrative proceeding or judicial action, or, at the discretion of the State, for a mediation described in subsection (e) of this section that is conducted prior to the filing of a complaint under subsection (b)(6) or (k) of this section.

(E) Exception to prohibition on attorneys' fees and related costs—Notwithstanding subparagraph (D), an award of attorneys' fees and related costs may be made to a parent who is the prevailing party and who was substantially justified in rejecting the settlement offer.

(F) Reduction in amount of attorneys' fees—Except as provided in subparagraph (G), whenever the court finds that—

(i) the parent, during the course of the action or proceeding, unreasonably protracted the final resolution of the controversy;

(ii) the amount of the attorneys' fees otherwise authorized to be awarded unreasonably exceeds the hourly rate prevailing in the community for similar services by attorneys of reasonably comparable skill, reputation, and experience;

(iii) the time spent and legal services furnished were excessive considering the nature of the action or proceeding; or

(iv) the attorney representing the parent did not provide to the school district the appropriate information in the due process complaint in accordance with subsection (b)(7) of this section;

the court shall reduce, accordingly, the amount of the attorneys' fees awarded under this section.

(G) Exception to reduction in amount of attorneys' fees—The provisions of subparagraph (F) shall not apply in any action or proceeding if the court finds that the State or local educational agency unreasonably protracted the final resolution of the action or proceeding or there was a violation of this section.

(j) Maintenance of current educational placement

Except as provided in subsection (k)(7) of this section, during the pendency of any proceedings conducted pursuant to this section, unless the State or local educational agency and the parents otherwise agree, the child shall remain in the then-current educational placement of such child, or, if applying for initial admission to a public school, shall, with the consent of the parents, be placed in the public school program until all such proceedings have been completed.

(k) Placement in alternative educational setting

(1) Authority of school personnel

(A) School personnel under this section may order a change in the placement of a child with a disability—

(i) to an appropriate interim alternative educational setting, another setting, or suspension, for not more than 10 school days (to the extent such alternatives would be applied to children without disabilities); and

(ii) to an appropriate interim alternative educational setting for the same amount of time that a child without a disability would be subject to discipline, but for not more than 45 days if—

(I) the child carries or possesses a weapon to or at school, on school premises, or to or at a school function under the jurisdiction of a State or a local educational agency; or

(II) the child knowingly possesses or uses illegal drugs or sells or solicits the sale of a controlled substance while at school or a school function under the jurisdiction of a State or local educational agency.

(B) Either before or not later than 10 days after taking a disciplinary action described in subparagraph (A)—

(i) if the local educational agency did not conduct a functional behavioral assessment and implement a behavioral intervention plan for such child before the behavior that resulted in the suspension described in subparagraph (A), the agency shall convene an IEP meeting to develop an assessment plan to address that behavior; or

(ii) if the child already has a behavioral intervention plan, the IEP Team shall review the plan and modify it, as necessary, to address the behavior.

(2) Authority of hearing officer—A hearing officer under this section may order a change in the placement of a child with a disability to an appropriate interim alternative educational setting for not more than 45 days if the hearing officer—

(A) determines that the public agency has demonstrated by substantial evidence that maintaining the current placement of such child is substantially likely to result in injury to the child or to others;

(B) considers the appropriateness of the child's current placement;

(C) considers whether the public agency has made reasonable efforts to minimize the risk of harm in the child's current placement, including the use of supplementary aids and services; and

(D) determines that the interim alternative educational setting meets the requirements of paragraph (3)(B).

(3) Determination of setting

(A) In general—The alternative educational setting described in paragraph (1)(A)(ii) shall be determined by the IEP Team.

(B) Additional requirements—Any interim alternative educational setting in which a child is placed under paragraph (1) or (2) shall—

(i) be selected so as to enable the child to continue to participate in the general curriculum, although in another setting, and to continue to receive those services and modifications, including those described in the child's current IEP, that will enable the child to meet the goals set out in that IEP; and

(ii) include services and modifications designed to address the behavior described in paragraph (1) or paragraph (2) so that it does not recur.

(4) Manifestation determination review

(A) In general—If a disciplinary action is contemplated as described in paragraph (1) or paragraph (2) for a behavior of a child with a disability described in either of those paragraphs, or if a disciplinary action involving a change of placement for more than 10 days is contemplated for a child with a disability who has engaged in other behavior that violated any rule or code of conduct of the local educational agency that applies to all children—

(i) not later than the date on which the decision to take that action is made, the parents shall be notified of that decision and of all procedural safeguards accorded under this section; and

(ii) immediately, if possible, but in no case later than 10 school days after the date on which the decision to take that action is made, a review shall be conducted of the relationship between the child's disability and the behavior subject to the disciplinary action.

(B) Individuals to carry out review—A review described in subparagraph (A) shall be conducted by the IEP Team and other qualified personnel.

(C) Conduct of review—In carrying out a review described in subparagraph (A), the IEP Team may determine that the behavior of the child was not a manifestation of such child's disability only if the IEP Team—

(i) first considers, in terms of the behavior subject to disciplinary action, all relevant information, including—

(I) evaluation and diagnostic results, including such results or other relevant information supplied by the parents of the child;

(II) observations of the child; and

(III) the child's IEP and placement; and

(ii) then determines that—

(I) in relationship to the behavior subject to disciplinary action, the child's IEP and placement were appropriate and the special education services, supplementary aids and services, and behavior intervention strategies were provided consistent with the child's IEP and placement;

(II) the child's disability did not impair the ability of the child to understand the impact and consequences of the behavior subject to disciplinary action; and

(III) the child's disability did not impair the ability of the child to control the behavior subject to disciplinary action.

(5) Determination that behavior was not manifestation of disability

(A) In general—If the result of the review described in paragraph (4) is a determination, consistent with paragraph (4)(C), that the behavior of the child with a disability was not a manifestation of the child's disability, the relevant disciplinary procedures applicable to children without disabilities may be applied to the child in the same manner in which they would be applied to children without disabilities, except as provided in section 1412(a)(1) of this title.

(B) Additional requirement—If the public agency initiates disciplinary procedures applicable to all children, the agency shall ensure that the special education and disciplinary records of the child with a disability are transmitted for consideration by the person or persons making the final determination regarding the disciplinary action.

(6) Parent appeal

(A) In general

(i) If the child's parent disagrees with a determination that the child's behavior was not a manifestation of the child's disability or with any decision regarding placement, the parent may request a hearing.

(ii) The State or local educational agency shall arrange for an expedited hearing in any case described in this subsection when requested by a parent.

(B) Review of decision

(i) In reviewing a decision with respect to the manifestation determination, the hearing officer shall determine whether the public agency has demonstrated that the child's behavior was not a manifestation of such child's disability consistent with the requirements of paragraph (4)(C).

(ii) In reviewing a decision under paragraph (1)(A)(ii) to place the child in an interim alternative educational setting, the hearing officer shall apply the standards set out in paragraph (2).

(7) Placement during appeals

(A) In general—When a parent requests a hearing regarding a disciplinary action described in paragraph (1)(A)(ii) or paragraph (2) to challenge the interim alternative educational setting or the manifestation determination, the child shall remain in the interim alternative educational setting pending the decision of the hearing officer or until the expiration of the time period provided for in paragraph (1)(A)(ii) or paragraph (2), whichever occurs first, unless the parent and the State or local educational agency agree otherwise.

(B) Current placement—If a child is placed in an interim alternative educational setting pursuant to paragraph (1)(A)(ii) or paragraph (2) and school personnel propose to change the child's placement after expiration of the interim alternative placement, during the pendency of any proceeding to challenge the proposed change in placement, the child shall remain in the current placement (the child's placement prior to the interim alternative educational setting), except as provided in subparagraph (C).

(C) Expedited hearing

(i) If school personnel maintain that it is dangerous for the child to be in the current placement (placement prior to removal to the interim alternative education setting) during the pendency of the due process proceedings, the local educational agency may request an expedited hearing.

(ii) In determining whether the child may be placed in the alternative educational setting or in another appropriate placement ordered by the hearing officer, the hearing officer shall apply the standards set out in paragraph (2).

(8) Protections for children not yet eligible for special education and related services

(A) In general—A child who has not been determined to be eligible for special education and related services under this subchapter and who has engaged in behavior that violated any rule or code of conduct of the local educational agency, including any behavior described in paragraph (1), may assert any of the protections provided for in this subchapter if the local educational agency had knowledge (as determined in accordance with this paragraph) that the child was a child with a disability before the behavior that precipitated the disciplinary action occurred.

(B) Basis of knowledge—A local educational agency shall be deemed to have knowledge that a child is a child with a disability if—

(i) the parent of the child has expressed concern in writing (unless the parent is illiterate or has a disability that prevents compliance with the requirements contained in this clause) to personnel of the appropriate educational agency that the child is in need of special education and related services;

(ii) the behavior or performance of the child demonstrates the need for such services;

(iii) the parent of the child has requested an evaluation of the child pursuant to section 1414 of this title; or

(iv) the teacher of the child, or other personnel of the local educational agency, has expressed concern about the behavior or performance of the child to the director of special education of such agency or to other personnel of the agency.

(C) Conditions that apply if no basis of knowledge

(i) In general—If a local educational agency does not have knowledge that a child is a child with a disability (in accordance with subparagraph (B)) prior to taking disciplinary measures against the child, the child may be subjected to the same disciplinary measures as measures applied to children without disabilities who engaged in comparable behaviors consistent with clause (ii).

(ii) Limitations—If a request is made for an evaluation of a child during the time period in which the child is subjected to disciplinary measures under paragraph (1) or (2), the evaluation shall be conducted in an expedited manner. If the child is determined to be a child with a disability, taking into consideration information from the evaluation conducted by the agency and information provided by the parents, the agency shall provide special education and related services in accordance with the provisions of this subchapter, except that, pending the results of the evaluation, the child shall remain in the educational placement determined by school authorities.

(9) Referral to and action by law enforcement and judicial authorities—

(A) Nothing in this part shall be construed to prohibit an agency from reporting a crime committed by a child with a disability to appropriate authorities or to prevent State law enforcement and judicial authorities from exercising their responsibilities with regard to the application of Federal and State law to crimes committed by a child with a disability.

(B) An agency reporting a crime committed by a child with a disability shall ensure that copies of the special education and disciplinary records of the child are transmitted for consideration by the appropriate authorities to whom it reports the crime.

(10) Definitions—For purposes of this subsection, the following definitions apply:

(A) Controlled substance—The term 'controlled substance' means a drug or other substance identified under schedules I, II, III, IV, or V in section 812(c) of Title 21.

(B) Illegal drug—The term 'illegal drug'—

(i) means a controlled substance; but

(ii) does not include such a substance that is legally possessed or used under the supervision of a licensed health-care professional or that is legally possessed or used under any other authority under that Act or under any other provision of Federal law.

(C) Substantial evidence—The term 'substantial evidence' means beyond a preponderance of the evidence.

(D) Weapon—The term 'weapon' has the meaning given the term 'dangerous weapon' under paragraph (2) of the first subsection (g) of section 930 of Title 18.

(*l*) Rule of construction

Nothing in this chapter shall be construed to restrict or limit the rights, procedures, and remedies available under the Constitution, the Americans with Disabilities Act of 1990, title V of the Rehabilitation Act of 1973, or other Federal laws protecting the rights of children with disabilities, except that before the filing of a civil action under such laws seeking relief that is also available under this subchapter, the procedures under subsections (f) and (g) of this section shall be exhausted to the same extent as would be required had the action been brought under this subchapter.

(m) Transfer of parental rights at age of majority

(1) In general—A State that receives amounts from a grant under this subchapter may provide that, when a child with a disability reaches the age of majority under State law (except for a child with a disability who has been determined to be incompetent under State law)—

(A) the public agency shall provide any notice required by this section to both the individual and the parents;

(B) all other rights accorded to parents under this subchapter transfer to the child;

(C) the agency shall notify the individual and the parents of the transfer of rights; and

(D) all rights accorded to parents under this subchapter transfer to children who are incarcerated in an adult or juvenile Federal, State, or local correctional institution.

(2) Special rule—If, under State law, a child with a disability who has reached the age of majority under State law, who has not been determined to be incompetent, but who is determined not to have the ability to provide informed consent with respect to the educational program of the child, the State shall establish procedures for appointing the parent of the child, or if the parent is not available, another appropriate individual, to represent the educational interests of the child throughout the period of eligibility of the child under this subchapter.

§ 1416. Withholding and judicial review

(a) Withholding of payments

(1) In general—Whenever the Secretary, after reasonable notice and opportunity for hearing to the State educational agency involved (and to any local educational agency or State agency affected by any failure described in subparagraph (B)), finds—

(A) that there has been a failure by the State to comply substantially with any provision of this subchapter; or

(B) that there is a failure to comply with any condition of a local educational agency's or State agency's eligibility under this subchapter, including the terms of any agreement to achieve compliance with this subchapter within the timelines specified in the agreement;

the Secretary shall, after notifying the State educational agency, withhold, in whole or in part, any further payments to the State under this subchapter, or refer the matter for appropriate enforcement action, which may include referral to the Department of Justice.

(2) Nature of withholding—If the Secretary withholds further payments under paragraph (1), the Secretary may determine that such withholding will be limited to programs or projects, or portions thereof, affected by the failure, or that the State educational agency shall not make further payments under this subchapter to specified local educational agencies or State agencies affected by the failure. Until the Secretary is satisfied that there is no longer any failure to comply with the provisions of this subchapter, as specified in subparagraph (A) or (B) of paragraph (1), payments to the State under this subchapter shall be withheld in whole or in part, or payments by the State educational agency under this subchapter shall be limited to local educational agencies and State agencies whose actions did not cause or were not involved in the failure, as the case may be. Any State educational agency, State agency, or local educational agency that has received notice under paragraph (1) shall, by means of a public notice, take such measures as may be necessary to bring the pendency of an action pursuant to this subsection to the attention of the public within the jurisdiction of such agency.

(b) Judicial review

(1) In general—If any State is dissatisfied with the Secretary's final action with respect to the eligibility of the State under section 1412 of this title, such State may, not later than 60 days after notice of such action, file with the United States court of appeals for the circuit in which such State is located a petition for review of that action. A copy of the petition shall be forthwith transmitted by the clerk of the court to the Secretary. The Secretary thereupon shall file in the court the record of the proceedings upon which the Secretary's action was based, as provided in section 2112 of Title 28.

(2) Jurisdiction; review by United States Supreme Court—Upon the filing of such petition, the court shall have jurisdiction to affirm the action of the Secretary or to set it aside, in whole or in part. The judgment of the court shall be subject to review by the Supreme Court of the United States upon certiorari or certification as provided in section 1254 of Title 28.

(3) Standard of review—The findings of fact by the Secretary, if supported by substantial evidence, shall be conclusive, but the court, for good cause shown, may remand the case to the Secretary to take further evidence, and the Secretary may thereupon make new or modified findings of fact and may modify the Secretary's previous action, and shall file in the court the record of the further proceedings. Such new or modified findings of fact shall likewise be conclusive if supported by substantial evidence.

(c) Divided state agency responsibility

For purposes of this section, where responsibility for ensuring that the requirements of this subchapter are met with respect to children with disabilities who are convicted as adults under State law and incarcerated in adult prisons is assigned to a public agency other than the State educational agency pursuant to section 1412(a)(11)(C) of this title, the Secretary, in instances where the Secretary finds that the failure to comply substantially with the provisions of this subchapter are related to a failure by the public agency, shall take appropriate corrective action to ensure compliance with this subchapter, except—

(1) any reduction or withholding of payments to the State is proportionate to the total funds allotted under section 1411 of this title to the State as the number of eligible children with disabilities in adult prisons under the supervision of the other public agency is proportionate to the number of eligible individuals with disabilities in the State under the supervision of the State educational agency; and

(2) any withholding of funds under paragraph (1) shall be limited to the specific agency responsible for the failure to comply with this part.

§ 1417. Administration

(a) Responsibilities of Secretary

In carrying out this subchapter, the Secretary shall—

(1) cooperate with, and (directly or by grant or contract) furnish technical assistance necessary to, the State in matters relating to—

(A) the education of children with disabilities; and

(B) carrying out this subchapter; and

(2) provide short-term training programs and institutes.

(b) Rules and regulations

In carrying out the provisions of this subchapter, the Secretary shall issue regulations under this chapter only to the extent that such regulations are necessary to ensure that there is compliance with the specific requirements of this chapter.

(c) Confidentiality

The Secretary shall take appropriate action, in accordance with the provisions of section 1232g of this title, to assure the protection of the confidentiality of any personally identifiable data, information, and records collected or maintained by the Secretary and by State and local educational agencies pursuant to the provisions of this part.

(d) Personnel

The Secretary is authorized to hire qualified personnel necessary to carry out the Secretary's duties under subsection (a) of this section and under sections 1418, 1461, and 1473 of this title (or their predecessor authorities through October 1, 1997) without regard to the provisions of Title 5, relating to appointments in the competitive service and without regard to chapter 51 and subchapter III of chapter 53 of Title 5 relating to classification and general schedule pay rates, except that no more than twenty such personnel shall be employed at any time.

§ 1418. Program information

(a) In general

Each State that receives assistance under this subchapter, and the Secretary of the Interior, shall provide data each year to the Secretary—

(1)(A) on—

(i) the number of children with disabilities, by race, ethnicity, and disability category, who are receiving a free appropriate public education;

(ii) the number of children with disabilities, by race and ethnicity, who are receiving early intervention services;

(iii) the number of children with disabilities, by race, ethnicity, and disability category, who are participating in regular education;

(iv) the number of children with disabilities, by race, ethnicity, and disability category, who are in separate classes, separate schools or facilities, or public or private residential facilities;

(v) the number of children with disabilities, by race, ethnicity, and disability category, who, for each year of age from age 14 to 21, stopped receiving special education and related services because of program completion or other reasons and the reasons why those children stopped receiving special education and related services;

(vi) the number of children with disabilities, by race and ethnicity, who, from birth through age 2, stopped receiving early intervention services because of program completion or for other reasons; and

(vii)(I) the number of children with disabilities, by race, ethnicity, and disability category, who under subparagraphs (A)(ii) and (B) of section 1415(k)(1) of this title, are removed to an interim alternative educational setting;

(II) the acts or items precipitating those removals; and

(III) the number of children with disabilities who are subject to long-term suspensions or expulsions; and

(B) on the number of infants and toddlers, by race and ethnicity, who are at risk of having substantial developmental delays (as described in section 1432 of this title), and who are receiving early intervention services under subchapter III of this chapter; and

(2) on any other information that may be required by the Secretary.

(b) Sampling

The Secretary may permit States and the Secretary of the Interior to obtain the data described in subsection (a) of this section through sampling.

(c) Disproportionality

(1) In general—Each State that receives assistance under this subchapter, and the Secretary of the Interior, shall provide for the collection and examination of data to determine if significant disproportionality based on race is occurring in the State with respect to—

(A) the identification of children as children with disabilities, including the identification of children as children with disabilities in accordance with a particular impairment described in section 1401(3) of this title; and

(B) the placement in particular educational settings of such children.

(2) Review and revision of policies, practices, and procedures—In the case of a determination of significant disproportionality with respect to the identification of children as children with disabilities, or the placement in particular educational settings of such children, in accordance with paragraph (1), the State or the Secretary of the Interior, as the case may be, shall provide for the review and, if appropriate, revision of the policies, procedures, and practices used in such identification or placement to ensure that such policies, procedures, and practices comply with the requirements of this chapter.

§ 1419. Preschool grants

(a) In general

The Secretary shall provide grants under this section to assist States to provide special education and related services, in accordance with this subchapter—

(1) to children with disabilities aged 3 through 5, inclusive; and

(2) at the State's discretion, to 2-year-old children with disabilities who will turn 3 during the school year.

(b) Eligibility

A State shall be eligible for a grant under this section if such State—

(1) is eligible under section 1412 of this title to receive a grant under this subchapter; and

(2) makes a free appropriate public education available to all children with disabilities, aged 3 through 5, residing in the State.

(c) Allocations to states

(1) In general—After reserving funds for studies and evaluations under section 1474(e) of this title, the Secretary shall allocate the remaining amount among the States in accordance with paragraph (2) or (3), as the case may be.

(2) Increase in funds—If the amount available for allocations to States under paragraph (1) is equal to or greater than the amount allocated to the States under this section for the preceding fiscal year, those allocations shall be calculated as follows:

(A)(i) Except as provided in subparagraph (B), the Secretary shall—

(I) allocate to each State the amount it received for fiscal year 1997;

(II) allocate 85 percent of any remaining funds to States on the basis of their relative populations of children aged 3 through 5; and

(III) allocate 15 percent of those remaining funds to States on the basis of their relative populations of all children aged 3 through 5 who are living in poverty.

(ii) For the purpose of making grants under this paragraph, the Secretary shall use the most recent population data, including data on children living in poverty, that are available and satisfactory to the Secretary.

(B) Notwithstanding subparagraph (A), allocations under this paragraph shall be subject to the following:

(i) No State's allocation shall be less than its allocation for the preceding fiscal year.

(ii) No State's allocation shall be less than the greatest of—

(I) the sum of—

(aa) the amount it received for fiscal year 1997; and

(bb) one third of one percent of the amount by which the amount appropriated under subsection (j) of this section exceeds the amount appropriated under this section for fiscal year 1997;

(II) the sum of—

(aa) the amount it received for the preceding fiscal year; and

(bb) that amount multiplied by the percentage by which the increase in the funds appropriated from the preceding fiscal year exceeds 1.5 percent; or

(III) the sum of—

(aa) the amount it received for the preceding fiscal year; and

(bb) that amount multiplied by 90 percent of the percentage increase in the amount appropriated from the preceding fiscal year.

(iii) Notwithstanding clause (ii), no State's allocation under this paragraph shall exceed the sum of—

(I) the amount it received for the preceding fiscal year; and

(II) that amount multiplied by the sum of 1.5 percent and the percentage increase in the amount appropriated.

(C) If the amount available for allocations under this paragraph is insufficient to pay those allocations in full, those allocations shall be ratably reduced, subject to subparagraph (B)(i).

(3) Decrease in funds—If the amount available for allocations to States under paragraph (1) is less than the amount allocated to the States under this section for the preceding fiscal year, those allocations shall be calculated as follows:

(A) If the amount available for allocations is greater than the amount allocated to the States for fiscal year 1997, each State shall be allocated the sum of—

(i) the amount it received for fiscal year 1997; and

(ii) an amount that bears the same relation to any remaining funds as the increase the State received for the preceding fiscal year over fiscal year 1997 bears to the total of all such increases for all States.

(B) If the amount available for allocations is equal to or less than the amount allocated to the States for fiscal year 1997, each State shall be allocated the amount it received for that year, ratably reduced, if necessary.

(4) Outlying areas—The Secretary shall increase the fiscal year 1998 allotment of each outlying area under section 1411 of this title by at least the amount that the area received under this section for fiscal year 1997.

(d) Reservation for state activities

(1) In general—Each State may retain not more than the amount described in paragraph (2) for administration and other State-level activities in accordance with subsections (e) and (f) of this section.

(2) Amount described—For each fiscal year, the Secretary shall determine and report to the State educational agency an amount that is 25 percent of the amount the State received under this section for fiscal year 1997, cumulatively adjusted by the Secretary for each succeeding fiscal year by the lesser of—

(A) the percentage increase, if any, from the preceding fiscal year in the State's allocation under this section; or

(B) the percentage increase, if any, from the preceding fiscal year in the Consumer Price Index For All Urban Consumers published by the Bureau of Labor Statistics of the Department of Labor.

(e) State administration

(1) In general—For the purpose of administering this section (including the coordination of activities under this subchapter with, and providing technical assistance to, other programs that provide services to children with disabilities) a State may use not more than 20 percent of the maximum amount it may retain under subsection (d) of this section for any fiscal year.

(2) Administration of subchapter III of this chapter—Funds described in paragraph (1) may also be used for the administration of subchapter III of this chapter, if the State educational agency is the lead agency for the State under that subchapter.

(f) Other state-level activities

Each State shall use any funds it retains under subsection (d) of this section and does not use for administration under subsection (e) of this section—

(1) for support services (including establishing and implementing the mediation process required by section 1415(e) of this title), which may benefit children with disabilities younger than 3 or older than 5 as long as those services also benefit children with disabilities aged 3 through 5;

(2) for direct services for children eligible for services under this section;

(3) to develop a State improvement plan under part A of subchapter IV of this chapter;

(4) for activities at the State and local levels to meet the performance goals established by the State under section 1412(a)(16) of this title and to support implementation of the State improvement plan under part A of subchapter IV of this chapter if the State receives funds under that part; or

(5) to supplement other funds used to develop and implement a Statewide coordinated services system designed to improve results for children and families, including children with disabilities and their families, but not to exceed one percent of the amount received by the State under this section for a fiscal year.

(g) Subgrants to local educational agencies

(1) Subgrants required—Each State that receives a grant under this section for any fiscal year shall distribute any of the grant funds that it does not reserve under subsection (d) of this section to local educational agencies in the State that have established their eligibility under section 1413 of this title, as follows:

(A) Base payments—The State shall first award each agency described in paragraph (1) the amount that agency would have received under this section for fiscal year 1997 if the State had distributed 75 percent of its grant for that year under section 1419(c)(3) of this title, as then in effect.

(B) Allocation of remaining funds—After making allocations under subparagraph (A), the State shall—

(i) allocate 85 percent of any remaining funds to those agencies on the basis of the relative numbers of children enrolled in public and private elementary and secondary schools within the agency's jurisdiction; and

(ii) allocate 15 percent of those remaining funds to those agencies in accordance with their relative numbers of children living in poverty, as determined by the State educational agency.

(2) Reallocation of funds—If a State educational agency determines that a local educational agency is adequately providing a free appropriate public education to all children with disabilities aged 3 through 5 residing in the area served by that agency with State and local funds, the State educational agency may reallocate any portion of the funds under this section that are not needed by that local agency to provide a free appropriate public education to other local educational agencies in the State that are not adequately providing special education and related services to all children with disabilities aged 3 through 5 residing in the areas they serve.

(h) Subchapter III inapplicable

Subchapter III of this chapter does not apply to any child with a disability receiving a free appropriate public education, in accordance with this subchapter, with funds received under this section.

(i) Definition

For the purpose of this section, the term 'State' means each of the 50 States, the District of Columbia, and the Commonwealth of Puerto Rico.

(j) Authorization of appropriations

For the purpose of carrying out this section, there are authorized to be appropriated to the Secretary $500,000,000 for fiscal year 1998 and such sums as may be necessary for each subsequent fiscal year.

SUBCHAPTER III—INFANTS AND TODDLERS WITH DISABILITIES

§ 1431. Findings and policy

(a) Findings

The Congress finds that there is an urgent and substantial need—

(1) to enhance the development of infants and toddlers with disabilities and to minimize their potential for developmental delay;

(2) to reduce the educational costs to our society, including our Nation's schools, by minimizing the need for special education and related services after infants and toddlers with disabilities reach school age;

(3) to minimize the likelihood of institutionalization of individuals with disabilities and maximize the potential for their independently living in society;

(4) to enhance the capacity of families to meet the special needs of their infants and toddlers with disabilities; and

(5) to enhance the capacity of State and local agencies and service providers

to identify, evaluate, and meet the needs of historically underrepresented populations, particularly minority, low-income, inner-city, and rural populations.

(b) Policy

It is therefore the policy of the United States to provide financial assistance to States—

(1) to develop and implement a statewide, comprehensive, coordinated, multidisciplinary, interagency system that provides early intervention services for infants and toddlers with disabilities and their families;

(2) to facilitate the coordination of payment for early intervention services from Federal, State, local, and private sources (including public and private insurance coverage);

(3) to enhance their capacity to provide quality early intervention services and expand and improve existing early intervention services being provided to infants and toddlers with disabilities and their families; and

(4) to encourage States to expand opportunities for children under 3 years of age who would be at risk of having substantial developmental delay if they did not receive early intervention services.

§ 1432. Definitions

As used in this subchapter:

(1) at-risk infant or toddler—The term 'at-risk infant or toddler' means an individual under 3 years of age who would be at risk of experiencing a substantial developmental delay if early intervention services were not provided to the individual.

(2) Council—The term 'council' means a State interagency coordinating council established under section 1441 of this title.

(3) Developmental delay—The term 'developmental delay', when used with respect to an individual residing in a State, has the meaning given such term by the State under section 1435(a)(1) of this title.

(4) Early intervention services—The term 'early intervention services' means developmental services that—

(A) are provided under public supervision;

(B) are provided at no cost except where Federal or State law provides for a system of payments by families, including a schedule of sliding fees;

(C) are designed to meet the developmental needs of an infant or toddler with a disability in any one or more of the following areas—

(i) physical development;

(ii) cognitive development;

(iii) communication development;

(iv) social or emotional development; or

(v) adaptive development;

(D) meet the standards of the State in which they are provided, including the requirements of this subchapter;

(E) include—

(i) family training, counseling, and home visits;

(ii) special instruction;

(iii) speech-language pathology and audiology services;

(iv) occupational therapy;

(v) physical therapy;

(vi) psychological services;

(vii) service coordination services;

(viii) medical services only for diagnostic or evaluation purposes;

(ix) early identification, screening, and assessment services;

(x) health services necessary to enable the infant or toddler to benefit from the other early intervention services;

(xi) social work services;

(xii) vision services;

(xiii) assistive technology devices and assistive technology services; and

(xiv) transportation and related costs that are necessary to enable an infant or toddler and the infant's or toddler's family to receive another service described in this paragraph;

(F) are provided by qualified personnel, including—

(i) special educators;

(ii) speech-language pathologists and audiologists;

(iii) occupational therapists;

(iv) physical therapists;

(v) psychologists;

(vi) social workers;

(vii) nurses;

(viii) nutritionists;

(ix) family therapists;

(x) orientation and mobility specialists; and

(xi) pediatricians and other physicians;

(G) to the maximum extent appropriate, are provided in natural environments, including the home, and community settings in which children without disabilities participate; and

(H) are provided in conformity with an individualized family service plan adopted in accordance with section 1436 of this title.

(5) Infant or toddler with a disability—The term 'infant or toddler with a disability'—

(A) means an individual under 3 years of age who needs early intervention services because the individual—

(i) is experiencing developmental delays, as measured by appropriate diagnostic instruments and procedures in one or more of the areas of cognitive development, physical development, communication development, social or emotional development, and adaptive development; or

(ii) has a diagnosed physical or mental condition which has a high probability of resulting in developmental delay; and

(B) may also include, at a State's discretion, at-risk infants and toddlers.

§ 1433. General authority

The Secretary shall, in accordance with this subchapter, make grants to States (from their allotments under section 1443 of this title) to assist each State to maintain and implement a statewide, comprehensive, coordinated, multidisciplinary, interagency system to provide early intervention services for infants and toddlers with disabilities and their families.

§ 1434. Eligibility

In order to be eligible for a grant under section 1433 of this title, a State shall demonstrate to the Secretary that the State—

(1) has adopted a policy that appropriate early intervention services are available to all infants and toddlers with disabilities in the State and their families, including Indian infants and toddlers with disabilities and their families residing on a reservation geographically located in the State; and

(2) has in effect a statewide system that meets the requirements of section 1435 of this title.

§ 1435. Requirements for statewide system

(a) In general

A statewide system described in section 1433 of this title shall include, at a minimum, the following components:

(1) A definition of the term 'developmental delay' that will be used by the State in carrying out programs under this subchapter.

(2) A State policy that is in effect and that ensures that appropriate early intervention services are available to all infants and toddlers with disabilities and their families, including Indian infants and toddlers and their families residing on a reservation geographically located in the State.

(3) A timely, comprehensive, multidisciplinary evaluation of the functioning of each infant or toddler with a disability in the State, and a family-directed identification of the needs of each family of such an infant or toddler, to appropriately assist in the development of the infant or toddler.

(4) For each infant or toddler with a disability in the State, an individualized family service plan in accordance with section 1436 of this title, including service coordination services in accordance with such service plan.

(5) A comprehensive child find system, consistent with part B, including a system for making referrals to service providers that includes timelines and provides for participation by primary referral sources.

(6) A public awareness program focusing on early identification of infants and toddlers with disabilities, including the preparation and dissemination by the lead agency designated or established under paragraph (10) to all primary referral sources, especially hospitals and physicians, of information for parents on the availability of early intervention services, and procedures for determining the extent to which such sources disseminate such information to parents of infants and toddlers.

(7) A central directory which includes information on early intervention services, resources, and experts available in the State and research and demonstration projects being conducted in the State.

(8) A comprehensive system of personnel development, including the training of paraprofessionals and the training of primary referral sources respecting the basic components of early intervention services available in the State, that is consistent with the comprehensive system of personnel development described in section 1412(a)(14) of this title and may include—

(A) implementing innovative strategies and activities for the recruitment and retention of early education service providers;

(B) promoting the preparation of early intervention providers who are fully and appropriately qualified to provide early intervention services under this subchapter;

(C) training personnel to work in rural and inner-city areas; and

(D) training personnel to coordinate transition services for infants and toddlers served under this subchapter from an early intervention program under this subchapter to preschool or other appropriate services.

(9) Subject to subsection (b), policies and procedures relating to the establishment and maintenance of standards to ensure that personnel necessary to carry out this subchapter are appropriately and adequately prepared and trained, including—

(A) the establishment and maintenance of standards which are consistent with any State-approved or recognized certification, licensing, registration, or other comparable requirements which apply to the area in which such personnel are providing early intervention services; and

(B) to the extent such standards are not based on the highest requirements in the State applicable to a specific profession or discipline, the steps the State is taking to require the retraining or hiring of personnel that meet appropriate professional requirements in the State;

except that nothing in this subchapter, including this paragraph, prohibits the use of paraprofessionals and assistants who are appropriately trained and supervised, in accordance with State law, regulations, or written policy, to assist in the provision of early intervention services to infants and toddlers with disabilities under this subchapter.

(10) A single line of responsibility in a lead agency designated or established by the Governor for carrying out—

(A) the general administration and supervision of programs and activities receiving assistance under section 1433 of this title, and the monitoring of programs and activities used by the State to carry out this subchapter, whether or not such programs or activities are receiving assistance made available under section 1433 of this title, to ensure that the State complies with this subchapter;

(B) the identification and coordination of all available resources within the State from Federal, State, local, and private sources;

(C) the assignment of financial responsibility in accordance with section 1437(a)(2) of this title to the appropriate agencies;

(D) the development of procedures to ensure that services are provided to infants and toddlers with disabilities and their families under this subchapter in a timely manner pending the resolution of any disputes among public agencies or service providers;

(E) the resolution of intra- and interagency disputes; and

(F) the entry into formal interagency agreements that define the financial responsibility of each agency for paying for early intervention services (consistent with State law) and procedures for resolving disputes and that include all additional components necessary to ensure meaningful cooperation and coordination.

(11) A policy pertaining to the contracting or making of other arrangements with service providers to provide early intervention services in the State, consistent with the provisions of this subchapter, including the contents of the application used and the conditions of the contract or other arrangements.

(12) A procedure for securing timely reimbursements of funds used under this subchapter in accordance with section 1440(a) of this title.

(13) Procedural safeguards with respect to programs under this subchapter, as required by section 1439 of this title.

(14) A system for compiling data requested by the Secretary under section 1418 of this title that relates to this subchapter.

(15) A State interagency coordinating council that meets the requirements of section 1441 of this title.

(16) Policies and procedures to ensure that, consistent with section 1436(d)(5) of this title—

(A) to the maximum extent appropriate, early intervention services are provided in natural environments; and

(B) the provision of early intervention services for any infant or toddler occurs in a setting other than a natural environment only when early intervention cannot be achieved satisfactorily for the infant or toddler in a natural environment.

(b) Policy

In implementing subsection (a)(9) of this section, a State may adopt a policy that includes making ongoing good-faith efforts to recruit and hire appropriately and adequately trained personnel to provide early intervention services to infants and toddlers with disabilities, including, in a geographic area of the State where there is a shortage of such personnel, the most qualified individuals available who are making satisfactory progress toward completing applicable course work necessary to meet the standards described in subsection (a)(9) of this section, consistent with State law within 3 years.

§ 1436. Individualized family service plan

(a) Assessment and program development

A statewide system described in section 1433 of this title shall provide, at a minimum, for each infant or toddler with a disability, and the infant's or toddler's family, to receive—

(1) a multidisciplinary assessment of the unique strengths and needs of the infant or toddler and the identification of services appropriate to meet such needs;

(2) a family-directed assessment of the resources, priorities, and concerns of the family and the identification of the supports and services necessary to enhance the family's capacity to meet the developmental needs of the infant or toddler; and

(3) a written individualized family service plan developed by a multidisciplinary team, including the parents, as required by subsection (e) of this section.

(b) Periodic review

The individualized family service plan shall be evaluated once a year and the family shall be provided a review of the plan at 6-month intervals (or more often where appropriate based on infant or toddler and family needs).

(c) Promptness after assessment

The individualized family service plan shall be developed within a reasonable time after the assessment required by subsection (a)(1) of this section is completed. With the parents' consent, early intervention services may commence prior to the completion of the assessment.

(d) Content of plan

The individualized family service plan shall be in writing and contain—

(1) a statement of the infant's or toddler's present levels of physical develop-

ment, cognitive development, communication development, social or emotional development, and adaptive development, based on objective criteria;

(2) a statement of the family's resources, priorities, and concerns relating to enhancing the development of the family's infant or toddler with a disability;

(3) a statement of the major outcomes expected to be achieved for the infant or toddler and the family, and the criteria, procedures, and timelines used to determine the degree to which progress toward achieving the outcomes is being made and whether modifications or revisions of the outcomes or services are necessary;

(4) a statement of specific early intervention services necessary to meet the unique needs of the infant or toddler and the family, including the frequency, intensity, and method of delivering services;

(5) a statement of the natural environments in which early intervention services shall appropriately be provided, including a justification of the extent, if any, to which the services will not be provided in a natural environment;

(6) the projected dates for initiation of services and the anticipated duration of the services;

(7) the identification of the service coordinator from the profession most immediately relevant to the infant's or toddler's or family's needs (or who is otherwise qualified to carry out all applicable responsibilities under this subchapter) who will be responsible for the implementation of the plan and coordination with other agencies and persons; and

(8) the steps to be taken to support the transition of the toddler with a disability to preschool or other appropriate services.

(e) Parental consent

The contents of the individualized family service plan shall be fully explained to the parents and informed written consent from the parents shall be obtained prior to the provision of early intervention services described in such plan. If the parents do not provide consent with respect to a particular early intervention service, then the early intervention services to which consent is obtained shall be provided.

§ 1437. State application and assurances

(a) Application

A State desiring to receive a grant under section 1433 of this title shall submit an application to the Secretary at such time and in such manner as the Secretary may reasonably require. The application shall contain—

(1) a designation of the lead agency in the State that will be responsible for the administration of funds provided under section 1433 of this title;

(2) a designation of an individual or entity responsible for assigning financial responsibility among appropriate agencies;

(3) information demonstrating eligibility of the State under section 1434 of this title, including—

(A) information demonstrating to the Secretary's satisfaction that the State has in effect the statewide system required by section 1433 of this title; and

(B) a description of services to be provided to infants and toddlers with disabilities and their families through the system;

(4) if the State provides services to at-risk infants and toddlers through the system, a description of such services;

(5) a description of the uses for which funds will be expended in accordance

with this subchapter;

(6) a description of the procedure used to ensure that resources are made available under this subchapter for all geographic areas within the State;

(7) a description of State policies and procedures that ensure that, prior to the adoption by the State of any other policy or procedure necessary to meet the requirements of this subchapter, there are public hearings, adequate notice of the hearings, and an opportunity for comment available to the general public, including individuals with disabilities and parents of infants and toddlers with disabilities;

(8) a description of the policies and procedures to be used—

(A) to ensure a smooth transition for toddlers receiving early intervention services under this subchapter to preschool or other appropriate services, including a description of how—

(i) the families of such toddlers will be included in the transition plans required by subparagraph (C); and

(ii) the lead agency designated or established under section 1435(a)(10) of this title will—

(I) notify the local educational agency for the area in which such a child resides that the child will shortly reach the age of eligibility for preschool services under subchapter II of this chapter, as determined in accordance with State law;

(II) in the case of a child who may be eligible for such preschool services, with the approval of the family of the child, convene a conference among the lead agency, the family, and the local educational agency at least 90 days (and at the discretion of all such parties, up to 6 months) before the child is eligible for the preschool services, to discuss any such services that the child may receive; and

(III) in the case of a child who may not be eligible for such preschool services, with the approval of the family, make reasonable efforts to convene a conference among the lead agency, the family, and providers of other appropriate services for children who are not eligible for preschool services under subchapter II of this chapter, to discuss the appropriate services that the child may receive;

(B) to review the child's program options for the period from the child's third birthday through the remainder of the school year; and

(C) to establish a transition plan; and

(9) such other information and assurances as the Secretary may reasonably require.

(b) Assurances

The application described in subsection (a) of this section—

(1) shall provide satisfactory assurance that Federal funds made available under section 1443 of this title to the State will be expended in accordance with this subchapter;

(2) shall contain an assurance that the State will comply with the requirements of section 1440 of this title;

(3) shall provide satisfactory assurance that the control of funds provided under section 1443 of this title, and title to property derived from those funds, will be in a public agency for the uses and purposes provided in this subchapter and that a public agency will administer such funds and property;

(4) shall provide for—

(A) making such reports in such form and containing such information as the Secretary may require to carry out the Secretary's functions under this subchapter; and

(B) keeping such records and affording such access to them as the Secretary may find necessary to ensure the correctness and verification of those reports and proper disbursement of Federal funds under this subchapter;

(5) provide satisfactory assurance that Federal funds made available under section 1443 of this title to the State—

(A) will not be commingled with State funds; and

(B) will be used so as to supplement the level of State and local funds expended for infants and toddlers with disabilities and their families and in no case to supplant those State and local funds;

(6) shall provide satisfactory assurance that such fiscal control and fund accounting procedures will be adopted as may be necessary to ensure proper disbursement of, and accounting for, Federal funds paid under section 1443 of this title to the State;

(7) shall provide satisfactory assurance that policies and procedures have been adopted to ensure meaningful involvement of underserved groups, including minority, low-income, and rural families, in the planning and implementation of all the requirements of this subchapter; and

(8) shall contain such other information and assurances as the Secretary may reasonably require by regulation.

(c) Standard for disapproval of application

The Secretary may not disapprove such an application unless the Secretary determines, after notice and opportunity for a hearing, that the application fails to comply with the requirements of this section.

(d) Subsequent state application

If a State has on file with the Secretary a policy, procedure, or assurance that demonstrates that the State meets a requirement of this section, including any policy or procedure filed under subchapter VIII (as in effect before July 1, 1998), the Secretary shall consider the State to have met the requirement for purposes of receiving a grant under this subchapter.

(e) Modification of application

An application submitted by a State in accordance with this section shall remain in effect until the State submits to the Secretary such modifications as the State determines necessary. This section shall apply to a modification of an application to the same extent and in the same manner as this section applies to the original application.

(f) Modifications required by the Secretary

The Secretary may require a State to modify its application under this section, but only to the extent necessary to ensure the State's compliance with this subchapter, if—

(1) an amendment is made to this chapter, or a Federal regulation issued under this chapter;

(2) a new interpretation of this chapter is made by a Federal court or the State's highest court; or

(3) an official finding of noncompliance with Federal law or regulations is made with respect to the State.

§ 1438. Uses of funds

In addition to using funds provided under section 1433 of this title to maintain and implement the statewide system required by such section, a State may use such funds—

(1) for direct early intervention services for infants and toddlers with disabilities, and their families, under this subchapter that are not otherwise funded through other public or private sources;

(2) to expand and improve on services for infants and toddlers and their families under this subchapter that are otherwise available;

(3) to provide a free appropriate public education, in accordance with subchapter II of this chapter, to children with disabilities from their third birthday to the beginning of the following school year; and

(4) in any State that does not provide services for at-risk infants and toddlers under section 1437(a)(4) of this title, to strengthen the statewide system by initiating, expanding, or improving collaborative efforts related to at-risk infants and toddlers, including establishing linkages with appropriate public or private community-based organizations, services, and personnel for the purposes of—

(A) identifying and evaluating at-risk infants and toddlers;

(B) making referrals of the infants and toddlers identified and evaluated under subparagraph (A); and

(C) conducting periodic follow-up on each such referral to determine if the status of the infant or toddler involved has changed with respect to the eligibility of the infant or toddler for services under this subchapter.

§ 1439. Procedural safeguards

(a) Minimum procedures

The procedural safeguards required to be included in a statewide system under section 1435(a)(13) of this title shall provide, at a minimum, the following:

(1) The timely administrative resolution of complaints by parents. Any party aggrieved by the findings and decision regarding an administrative complaint shall have the right to bring a civil action with respect to the complaint in any State court of competent jurisdiction or in a district court of the United States without regard to the amount in controversy. In any action brought under this paragraph, the court shall receive the records of the administrative proceedings, shall hear additional evidence at the request of a party, and, basing its decision on the preponderance of the evidence, shall grant such relief as the court determines is appropriate.

(2) The right to confidentiality of personally identifiable information, including the right of parents to written notice of and written consent to the exchange of such information among agencies consistent with Federal and State law.

(3) The right of the parents to determine whether they, their infant or toddler, or other family members will accept or decline any early intervention service under this subchapter in accordance with State law without jeopardizing other early intervention services under this subchapter.

(4) The opportunity for parents to examine records relating to assessment, screening, eligibility determinations, and the development and implementation of the individualized family service plan.

(5) Procedures to protect the rights of the infant or toddler whenever the parents of the infant or toddler are not known or cannot be found or the infant or

toddler is a ward of the State, including the assignment of an individual (who shall not be an employee of the State lead agency, or other State agency, and who shall not be any person, or any employee of a person, providing early intervention services to the infant or toddler or any family member of the infant or toddler) to act as a surrogate for the parents.

(6) Written prior notice to the parents of the infant or toddler with a disability whenever the State agency or service provider proposes to initiate or change or refuses to initiate or change the identification, evaluation, or placement of the infant or toddler with a disability, or the provision of appropriate early intervention services to the infant or toddler.

(7) Procedures designed to ensure that the notice required by paragraph (6) fully informs the parents, in the parents' native language, unless it clearly is not feasible to do so, of all procedures available pursuant to this section.

(8) The right of parents to use mediation in accordance with section 1415(e) of this title, except that—

(A) any reference in the section to a State educational agency shall be considered to be a reference to a State's lead agency established or designated under section 1435(a)(10) of this title;

(B) any reference in the section to a local educational agency shall be considered to be a reference to a local service provider or the State's lead agency under this subchapter, as the case may be; and

(C) any reference in the section to the provision of free appropriate public education to children with disabilities shall be considered to be a reference to the provision of appropriate early intervention services to infants and toddlers with disabilities.

(b) Services during pendency of proceedings

During the pendency of any proceeding or action involving a complaint by the parents of an infant or toddler with a disability, unless the State agency and the parents otherwise agree, the infant or toddler shall continue to receive the appropriate early intervention services currently being provided or, if applying for initial services, shall receive the services not in dispute.

§ 1440. Payor of last resort

(a) Nonsubstitution

Funds provided under section 1443 of this title may not be used to satisfy a financial commitment for services that would have been paid for from another public or private source, including any medical program administered by the Secretary of Defense, but for the enactment of this subchapter, except that whenever considered necessary to prevent a delay in the receipt of appropriate early intervention services by an infant, toddler, or family in a timely fashion, funds provided under section 1443 of this title may be used to pay the provider of services pending reimbursement from the agency that has ultimate responsibility for the payment.

(b) Reduction of other benefits

Nothing in this subchapter shall be construed to permit the State to reduce medical or other assistance available or to alter eligibility under title V of the Social Security Act (relating to maternal and child health) or title XIX of the Social Security Act (relating to Medicaid for infants or toddlers with disabilities) within the State.

§ 1441. State interagency coordinating council

(a) Establishment

(1) In general—State that desires to receive financial assistance under this subchapter shall establish a State interagency coordinating council.

(2) Appointment—The council shall be appointed by the Governor. In making appointments to the council, the Governor shall ensure that the membership of the council reasonably represents the population of the State.

(3) Chairperson—The Governor shall designate a member of the council to serve as the chairperson of the council, or shall require the council to so designate such a member. Any member of the council who is a representative of the lead agency designated under section 1435(a)(10) of this title may not serve as the chairperson of the council.

(b) Composition

(1) In general—The council shall be composed as follows:

(A) Parents—At least 20 percent of the members shall be parents of infants or toddlers with disabilities or children with disabilities aged 12 or younger, with knowledge of, or experience with, programs for infants and toddlers with disabilities. At least one such member shall be a parent of an infant or toddler with a disability or a child with a disability aged 6 or younger.

(B) Service providers—At least 20 percent of the members shall be public or private providers of early intervention services.

(C) State legislature—At least one member shall be from the State legislature.

(D) Personnel preparation—At least one member shall be involved in personnel preparation.

(E) Agency for early intervention services—At least one member shall be from each of the State agencies involved in the provision of, or payment for, early intervention services to infants and toddlers with disabilities and their families and shall have sufficient authority to engage in policy planning and implementation on behalf of such agencies.

(F) Agency for preschool services—At least one member shall be from the State educational agency responsible for preschool services to children with disabilities and shall have sufficient authority to engage in policy planning and implementation on behalf of such agency.

(G) Agency for health insurance—At least one member shall be from the agency responsible for the State governance of health insurance.

(H) Head start agency—At least one representative from a Head Start agency or program in the State.

(I) Child care agency—At least one representative from a State agency responsible for child care.

(2) Other members—The council may include other members selected by the Governor, including a representative from the Bureau of Indian Affairs, or where there is no BIA-operated or BIA-funded school, from the Indian Health Service or the tribe or tribal council.

(c) Meetings

The council shall meet at least quarterly and in such places as it deems necessary. The meetings shall be publicly announced, and, to the extent appropriate, open and accessible to the general public.

(d) Management authority

Subject to the approval of the Governor, the council may prepare and approve a budget using funds under this subchapter to conduct hearings and forums, to reimburse members of the council for reasonable and necessary expenses for attending council meetings and performing council duties (including child care for parent representatives), to pay compensation to a member of the council if the member is not employed or must forfeit wages from other employment when performing official council business, to hire staff, and to obtain the services of such professional, technical, and clerical personnel as may be necessary to carry out its functions under this subchapter.

(e) Functions of council

(1) Duties—The council shall—

(A) advise and assist the lead agency designated or established under section 1435(a)(10) of this title in the performance of the responsibilities set forth in such section, particularly the identification of the sources of fiscal and other support for services for early intervention programs, assignment of financial responsibility to the appropriate agency, and the promotion of the interagency agreements;

(B) advise and assist the lead agency in the preparation of applications and amendments thereto;

(C) advise and assist the State educational agency regarding the transition of toddlers with disabilities to preschool and other appropriate services, and

(D) prepare and submit an annual report to the Governor and to the Secretary on the status of early intervention programs for infants and toddlers with disabilities and their families operated within the State.

(2) Authorized activity—The council may advise and assist the lead agency and the State educational agency regarding the provision of appropriate services for children from birth through age 5. The council may advise appropriate agencies in the State with respect to the integration of services for infants and toddlers with disabilities and at-risk infants and toddlers and their families, regardless of whether at-risk infants and toddlers are eligible for early intervention services in the State.

(f) Conflict of interest

No member of the council shall cast a vote on any matter that would provide direct financial benefit to that member or otherwise give the appearance of a conflict of interest under State law.

§ 1442. Federal administration

Sections 1416, 1417, and 1418 of this title shall, to the extent not inconsistent with this subchapter, apply to the program authorized by this subchapter, except that—

(1) any reference in such sections to a State educational agency shall be considered to be a reference to a State's lead agency established or designated under section 1435(a)(10) of this title;

(2) any reference in such sections to a local educational agency, educational service agency, or a State agency shall be considered to be a reference to an early intervention service provider under this subchapter; and

(3) any reference to the education of children with disabilities or the education of all children with disabilities shall be considered to be a reference to the

provision of appropriate early intervention services to infants and toddlers with disabilities.

§ 1443. Allocation of funds

(a) Reservation of funds for outlying areas

(1) In general—From the sums appropriated to carry out this subchapter for any fiscal year, the Secretary may reserve up to one percent for payments to Guam, American Samoa, the Virgin Islands, and the Commonwealth of the Northern Mariana Islands in accordance with their respective needs.

(2) Consolidation of funds—The provisions of Public Law 95–134, permitting the consolidation of grants to the outlying areas, shall not apply to funds those areas receive under this subchapter.

(b) Payments to Indians

(1) In general—The Secretary shall, subject to this subsection, make payments to the Secretary of the Interior to be distributed to tribes, tribal organizations (as defined under section 450b of Title 25), or consortia of the above entities for the coordination of assistance in the provision of early intervention services by the States to infants and toddlers with disabilities and their families on reservations served by elementary and secondary schools for Indian children operated or funded by the Department of the Interior. The amount of such payment for any fiscal year shall be 1.25 percent of the aggregate of the amount available to all States under this subchapter for such fiscal year.

(2) Allocation—For each fiscal year, the Secretary of the Interior shall distribute the entire payment received under paragraph (1) by providing to each tribe, tribal organization, or consortium an amount based on the number of infants and toddlers residing on the reservation, as determined annually, divided by the total of such children served by all tribes, tribal organizations, or consortia.

(3) Information—To receive a payment under this subsection, the tribe, tribal organization, or consortium shall submit such information to the Secretary of the Interior as is needed to determine the amounts to be distributed under paragraph (2).

(4) Use of funds—The funds received by a tribe, tribal organization, or consortium shall be used to assist States in child find, screening, and other procedures for the early identification of Indian children under 3 years of age and for parent training. Such funds may also be used to provide early intervention services in accordance with this subchapter. Such activities may be carried out directly or through contracts or cooperative agreements with the BIA, local educational agencies, and other public or private nonprofit organizations. The tribe, tribal organization, or consortium is encouraged to involve Indian parents in the development and implementation of these activities. The above entities shall, as appropriate, make referrals to local, State, or Federal entities for the provision of services or further diagnosis.

(5) Reports—To be eligible to receive a grant under paragraph (2), a tribe, tribal organization, or consortium shall make a biennial report to the Secretary of the Interior of activities undertaken under this subsection, including the number of contracts and cooperative agreements entered into, the number of children contacted and receiving services for each year, and the estimated number of children needing services during the 2 years following the year in which the report is made. The

Secretary of the Interior shall include a summary of this information on a biennial basis to the Secretary of Education along with such other information as required under section 1411(i)(3)(E) of this title. The Secretary of Education may require any additional information from the Secretary of the Interior.

(6) Prohibited uses of funds—None of the funds under this subsection may be used by the Secretary of the Interior for administrative purposes, including child count, and the provision of technical assistance.

(c) State allotments

(1) In general—Except as provided in paragraphs (2), (3), and (4), from the funds remaining for each fiscal year after the reservation and payments under subsections (a) and (b), the Secretary shall first allot to each State an amount that bears the same ratio to the amount of such remainder as the number of infants and toddlers in the State bears to the number of infants and toddlers in all States.

(2) Minimum allotments—Except as provided in paragraphs (3) and (4), no State shall receive an amount under this section for any fiscal year that is less than the greatest of—

(A) one-half of one percent of the remaining amount described in paragraph (1); or

(B) $500,000.

(3) Special rule for 1998 and 1999

(A) In general—Except as provided in paragraph (4), no State may receive an amount under this section for either fiscal year 1998 or 1999 that is less than the sum of the amounts such State received for fiscal year 1994 under—

(i) subchapter VIII (as in effect for such fiscal year); and

(ii) subpart 2 of part D of chapter 1 of title I of the Elementary and Secondary Education Act of 1965 (as in effect on the day before the date of the enactment of the Improving America's Schools Act of 1994) for children with disabilities under 3 years of age.

(B) Exception—If, for fiscal year 1998 or 1999, the number of infants and toddlers in a State, as determined under paragraph (1), is less than the number of infants and toddlers so determined for fiscal year 1994, the amount determined under subparagraph (A) for the State shall be reduced by the same percentage by which the number of such infants and toddlers so declined.

(4) Ratable reduction

(A) In general—If the sums made available under this subchapter for any fiscal year are insufficient to pay the full amounts that all States are eligible to receive under this subsection for such year, the Secretary shall ratably reduce the allotments to such States for such year.

(B) Additional funds—If additional funds become available for making payments under this subsection for a fiscal year, allotments that were reduced under subparagraph (A) shall be increased on the same basis they were reduced.

(5) Definitions—For the purpose of this subsection—

(A) the terms 'infants' and 'toddlers' mean children under 3 years of age; and

(B) the term 'State' means each of the 50 States, the District of Columbia, and the Commonwealth of Puerto Rico.

(d) Reallotment of funds

If a State elects not to receive its allotment under subsection (c) of this section, the

Secretary shall reallot, among the remaining States, amounts from such State in accordance with such subsection.

§ 1444. Federal interagency coordinating council

(a) Establishment and purpose

(1) In general—The Secretary shall establish a Federal Interagency Coordinating Council in order to—

(A) minimize duplication of programs and activities across Federal, State, and local agencies, relating to—

(i) early intervention services for infants and toddlers with disabilities (including at-risk infants and toddlers) and their families; and

(ii) preschool or other appropriate services for children with disabilities;

(B) ensure the effective coordination of Federal early intervention and preschool programs and policies across Federal agencies;

(C) coordinate the provision of Federal technical assistance and support activities to States;

(D) identify gaps in Federal agency programs and services; and

(E) identify barriers to Federal interagency cooperation.

(2) Appointments—The council established under paragraph (1) (hereafter in this section referred to as the 'Council') and the chairperson of the Council shall be appointed by the Secretary in consultation with other appropriate Federal agencies. In making the appointments, the Secretary shall ensure that each member has sufficient authority to engage in policy planning and implementation on behalf of the department, agency, or program that the member represents.

(b) Composition

The Council shall be composed of—

(1) a representative of the Office of Special Education Programs;

(2) a representative of the National Institute on Disability and Rehabilitation Research and a representative of the Office of Educational Research and Improvement;

(3) a representative of the Maternal and Child Health Services Block Grant Program;

(4) a representative of programs administered under the Developmental Disabilities Assistance and Bill of Rights Act;

(5) a representative of the Health Care Financing Administration;

(6) a representative of the Division of Birth Defects and Developmental Disabilities of the Centers for Disease Control;

(7) a representative of the Social Security Administration;

(8) a representative of the special supplemental nutrition program for women, infants, and children of the Department of Agriculture;

(9) a representative of the National Institute of Mental Health;

(10) a representative of the National Institute of Child Health and Human Development;

(11) a representative of the Bureau of Indian Affairs of the Department of the Interior;

(12) a representative of the Indian Health Service;

(13) a representative of the Surgeon General;

(14) a representative of the Department of Defense;

(15) a representative of the Children's Bureau, and a representative of the Head Start Bureau, of the Administration for Children and Families;

(16) a representative of the Substance Abuse and Mental Health Services Administration;

(17) a representative of the Pediatric AIDS Health Care Demonstration Program in the Public Health Service;

(18) parents of children with disabilities age 12 or under (who shall constitute at least 20 percent of the members of the Council), of whom at least one must have a child with a disability under the age of 6;

(19) at least two representatives of State lead agencies for early intervention services to infants and toddlers, one of whom must be a representative of a State educational agency and the other a representative of a non-educational agency;

(20) other members representing appropriate agencies involved in the provision of, or payment for, early intervention services and special education and related services to infants and toddlers with disabilities and their families and preschool children with disabilities; and

(21) other persons appointed by the Secretary.

(c) Meetings

The Council shall meet at least quarterly and in such places as the Council deems necessary. The meetings shall be publicly announced, and, to the extent appropriate, open and accessible to the general public.

(d) Functions of the council

The Council shall—

(1) advise and assist the Secretary of Education, the Secretary of Health and Human Services, the Secretary of Defense, the Secretary of the Interior, the Secretary of Agriculture, and the Commissioner of Social Security in the performance of their responsibilities related to serving children from birth through age 5 who are eligible for services under this subchapter or under subchapter II of this chapter;

(2) conduct policy analyses of Federal programs related to the provision of early intervention services and special educational and related services to infants and toddlers with disabilities and their families, and preschool children with disabilities, in order to determine areas of conflict, overlap, duplication, or inappropriate omission;

(3) identify strategies to address issues described in paragraph (2);

(4) develop and recommend joint policy memoranda concerning effective interagency collaboration, including modifications to regulations, and the elimination of barriers to interagency programs and activities;

(5) coordinate technical assistance and disseminate information on best practices, effective program coordination strategies, and recommendations for improved early intervention programming for infants and toddlers with disabilities and their families and preschool children with disabilities; and

(6) facilitate activities in support of States' interagency coordination efforts.

(e) Conflict of interest

No member of the Council shall cast a vote on any matter that would provide direct financial benefit to that member or otherwise give the appearance of a conflict of interest under Federal law.

(f) Federal advisory committee act

The Federal Advisory Committee Act (5 U.S.C. App.) shall not apply to the establishment or operation of the Council.

§ 1445. Authorization of appropriations

For the purpose of carrying out this subchapter, there are authorized to be appropriated $400,000,000 for fiscal year 1998 and such sums as may be necessary for each of the fiscal years 1999 through 2002.

SUBCHAPTER IV—NATIONAL ACTIVITIES TO IMPROVE EDUCATION OF CHILDREN WITH DISABILITIES

PART A—STATE PROGRAM IMPROVEMENT GRANTS FOR CHILDREN WITH DISABILITIES

§ 1451. Findings and purpose

(a) Findings

The Congress finds the following:

(1) States are responding with some success to multiple pressures to improve educational and transitional services and results for children with disabilities in response to growing demands imposed by ever-changing factors, such as demographics, social policies, and labor and economic markets.

(2) In order for States to address such demands and to facilitate lasting systemic change that is of benefit to all students, including children with disabilities, States must involve local educational agencies, parents, individuals with disabilities and their families, teachers and other service providers, and other interested individuals and organizations in carrying out comprehensive strategies to improve educational results for children with disabilities.

(3) Targeted Federal financial resources are needed to assist States, working in partnership with others, to identify and make needed changes to address the needs of children with disabilities into the next century.

(4) State educational agencies, in partnership with local educational agencies and other individuals and organizations, are in the best position to identify and design ways to meet emerging and expanding demands to improve education for children with disabilities and to address their special needs.

(5) Research, demonstration, and practice over the past 20 years in special education and related disciplines have built a foundation of knowledge on which State and local systemic-change activities can now be based.

(6) Such research, demonstration, and practice in special education and related disciplines have demonstrated that an effective educational system now and in the future must—

(A) maintain high academic standards and clear performance goals for children with disabilities, consistent with the standards and expectations for all students in the educational system, and provide for appropriate and effective strategies and methods to ensure that students who are children with disabilities have maximum opportunities to achieve those standards and goals;

(B) create a system that fully addresses the needs of all students, including children with disabilities, by addressing the needs of children with disabilities in carrying out educational reform activities;

(C) clearly define, in measurable terms, the school and post-school results that children with disabilities are expected to achieve;

(D) promote service integration, and the coordination of State and local education, social, health, mental health, and other services, in addressing the full range of student needs, particularly the needs of children with disabilities who require significant levels of support to maximize their participation and learning in school and the community;

(E) ensure that children with disabilities are provided assistance and support in making transitions as described in section 1474(b)(3)(C) of this title;

(F) promote comprehensive programs of professional development to ensure that the persons responsible for the education or a transition of children with disabilities possess the skills and knowledge necessary to address the educational and related needs of those children;

(G) disseminate to teachers and other personnel serving children with disabilities research-based knowledge about successful teaching practices and models and provide technical assistance to local educational agencies and schools on how to improve results for children with disabilities;

(H) create school-based disciplinary strategies that will be used to reduce or eliminate the need to use suspension and expulsion as disciplinary options for children with disabilities;

(I) establish placement-neutral funding formulas and cost-effective strategies for meeting the needs of children with disabilities; and

(J) involve individuals with disabilities and parents of children with disabilities in planning, implementing, and evaluating systemic-change activities and educational reforms.

(b) Purpose

The purpose of this subpart is to assist State educational agencies, and their partners referred to in section 1452(b) of this title, in reforming and improving their systems for providing educational, early intervention, and transitional services, including their systems for professional development, technical assistance, and dissemination of knowledge about best practices, to improve results for children with disabilities.

§ 1452. Eligibility and collaborative process

(a) Eligible applicants

A State educational agency may apply for a grant under this part for a grant period of not less than 1 year and not more than 5 years.

(b) Partners

(1) Required partners

(A) Contractual partners—In order to be considered for a grant under this part, a State educational agency shall establish a partnership with local educational agencies and other State agencies involved in, or concerned with, the education of children with disabilities.

(B) Other partners—In order to be considered for a grant under this part, a State educational agency shall work in partnership with other persons and organizations involved in, and concerned with, the education of children with disabilities, including—

(i) the Governor;

(ii) parents of children with disabilities;

(iii) parents of nondisabled children;

(iv) individuals with disabilities;

(v) organizations representing individuals with disabilities and their parents, such as parent training and information centers;

(vi) community-based and other nonprofit organizations involved in the education and employment of individuals with disabilities;

(vii) the lead State agency for subchapter III of this chapter;

(viii) general and special education teachers, and early intervention personnel;

(ix) the State advisory panel established under subchapter III of this chapter;

(x) the State interagency coordinating council established under subchapter III of this chapter; and

(xi) institutions of higher education within the State.

(2) Optional partners—A partnership under subparagraph (A) or (B) of paragraph (1) may also include—

(A) individuals knowledgeable about vocational education;

(B) the State agency for higher education;

(C) the State vocational rehabilitation agency;

(D) public agencies with jurisdiction in the areas of health, mental health, social services, and juvenile justice; and

(E) other individuals.

§ 1453. Applications

(a) In general

(1) Submission—A State educational agency that desires to receive a grant under this subpart shall submit to the Secretary an application at such time, in such manner, and including such information as the Secretary may require.

(2) State improvement plan—The application shall include a State improvement plan that—

(A) is integrated, to the maximum extent possible, with State plans under the Elementary and Secondary Education Act of 1965 and the Rehabilitation Act of 1973, as appropriate; and

(B) meets the requirements of this section.

(b) Determining child and program needs

(1) In general—Each State improvement plan shall identify those critical aspects of early intervention, general education, and special education programs (including professional development, based on an assessment of State and local needs) that must be improved to enable children with disabilities to meet the goals established by the State under section 1412(a)(16) of this title.

(2) Required analyses—To meet the requirement of paragraph (1), the State improvement plan shall include at least—

(A) an analysis of all information, reasonably available to the State educational agency, on the performance of children with disabilities in the State, including—

(i) their performance on State assessments and other performance indicators established for all children, including drop-out rates and graduation rates;

(ii) their participation in postsecondary education and employment; and

(iii) how their performance on the assessments and indicators described in clause (i) compares to that of non-disabled children;

(B) an analysis of State and local needs for professional development for personnel to serve children with disabilities that includes, at a minimum—

(i) the number of personnel providing special education and related services; and

(ii) relevant information on current and anticipated personnel vacancies and shortages (including the number of individuals described in clause (i) with temporary certification), and on the extent of certification or retraining necessary to eliminate such shortages, that is based, to the maximum extent possible, on existing assessments of personnel needs;

(C) an analysis of the major findings of the Secretary's most recent reviews of State compliance, as they relate to improving results for children with disabilities) and

(D) an analysis of other information, reasonably available to the State, on the effectiveness of the State's systems of early intervention, special education, and general education in meeting the needs of children with disabilities.

(c) Improvement strategies

Each State improvement plan shall—

(1) describe a partnership agreement that—

(A) specifies—

(i) the nature and extent of the partnership among the State educational agency, local educational agencies, and other State agencies involved in, or concerned with, the education of children with disabilities, and the respective roles of each member of the partnership; and

(ii) how such agencies will work in partnership with other persons and organizations involved in, and concerned with, the education of children with disabilities, including the respective roles of each of these persons and organizations; and

(B) is in effect for the period of the grant;

(2) describe how grant funds will be used in undertaking the systemic-change activities, and the amount and nature of funds from any other sources, including funds under subchapter II of this chapter retained for use at the State level under sections 1411(f) and 1419(d) of this title, that will be committed to the systemic-change activities;

(3) describe the strategies the State will use to address the needs identified under subsection (b) of this section, including—

(A) how the State will change State policies and procedures to address systemic barriers to improving results for children with disabilities;

(B) how the State will hold local educational agencies and schools accountable for educational progress of children with disabilities;

(C) how the State will provide technical assistance to local educational agencies and schools to improve results for children with disabilities;

(D) how the State will address the identified needs for in-service and pre-service preparation to ensure that all personnel who work with children with disabilities (including both professional and paraprofessional personnel who provide special education, general education, related services, or early intervention services) have the skills and knowledge necessary to meet the needs of children with disabilities, including a description of how—

(i) the State will prepare general and special education personnel with the content knowledge and collaborative skills needed to meet the needs of children with disabilities, including how the State will work with other States on common certification criteria;

(ii) the State will prepare professionals and paraprofessionals in the area of early intervention with the content knowledge and collaborative skills needed to meet the needs of infants and toddlers with disabilities;

(iii) the State will work with institutions of higher education and other entities that (on both a pre-service and an in-service basis) prepare personnel who work with children with disabilities to ensure that those institutions and entities develop the capacity to support quality professional development programs that meet State and local needs;

(iv) the State will work to develop collaborative agreements with other States for the joint support and development of programs to prepare personnel for which there is not sufficient demand within a single State to justify support or development of such a program of preparation;

(v) the State will work in collaboration with other States, particularly neighboring States, to address the lack of uniformity and reciprocity in the credentialing of teachers and other personnel;

(vi) the State will enhance the ability of teachers and others to use strategies, such as behavioral interventions, to address the conduct of children with disabilities that impedes the learning of children with disabilities and others;

(vii) the State will acquire and disseminate, to teachers, administrators, school board members, and related services personnel, significant knowledge derived from educational research and other sources, and how the State will, when appropriate, adopt promising practices, materials, and technology;

(viii) the State will recruit, prepare, and retain qualified personnel, including personnel with disabilities and personnel from groups that are underrepresented in the fields of regular education, special education, and related services;

(ix) the plan is integrated, to the maximum extent possible, with other professional development plans and activities, including plans and activities developed and carried out under other Federal and State laws that address personnel recruitment and training; and

(x) the State will provide for the joint training of parents and special education, related services, and general education personnel;

(E) strategies that will address systemic problems identified in Federal compliance reviews, including shortages of qualified personnel;

(F) how the State will disseminate results of the local capacity-building and improvement projects funded under section 1411(f)(4) of this title;

(G) how the State will address improving results for children with disabilities in the geographic areas of greatest need; and

(H) how the State will assess, on a regular basis, the extent to which the strategies implemented under this part have been effective; and

(4) describe how the improvement strategies described in paragraph (3) will be coordinated with public and private sector resources.

(d) Competitive awards

(1) In general—The Secretary shall make grants under this part on a competitive basis.

(2) Priority—The Secretary may give priority to applications on the basis of need, as indicated by such information as the findings of Federal compliance reviews.

(e) Peer review

(1) In general—The Secretary shall use a panel of experts who are competent, by virtue of their training, expertise, or experience, to evaluate applications under this part.

(2) Composition of panel—A majority of a panel described in paragraph (1) shall be composed of individuals who are not employees of the Federal Government.

(3) Payment of fees and expenses of certain members—The Secretary may use available funds appropriated to carry out this part to pay the expenses and fees of panel members who are not employees of the Federal Government.

(f) Reporting procedures

Each State educational agency that receives a grant under this part shall submit performance reports to the Secretary pursuant to a schedule to be determined by the Secretary, but not more frequently than annually. The reports shall describe the progress of the State in meeting the performance goals established under section 1412(a)(16) of this title, analyze the effectiveness of the State's strategies in meeting those goals, and identify any changes in the strategies needed to improve its performance.

§ 1454. Use of funds

(a) In general

(1) Activities—A State educational agency that receives a grant under this part may use the grant to carry out any activities that are described in the State's application and that are consistent with the purpose of this part.

(2) Contracts and subgrants—Each such State educational agency—

(A) shall, consistent with its partnership agreement under section 1452(b) of this title, award contracts or subgrants to local educational agencies, institutions of higher education, and parent training and information centers, as appropriate, to carry out its State improvement plan under this part; and

(B) may award contracts and subgrants to other public and private entities, including the lead agency under subchapter III of this chapter, to carry out such plan.

(b) Use of funds for professional development

A State educational agency that receives a grant under this part—

(1) shall use not less than 75 percent of the funds it receives under the grant for any fiscal year—

(A) to ensure that there are sufficient regular education, special education, and related services personnel who have the skills and knowledge necessary to meet the needs of children with disabilities and developmental goals of young children; or

(B) to work with other States on common certification criteria; or

(2) shall use not less than 50 percent of such funds for such purposes, if the State demonstrates to the Secretary's satisfaction that it has the personnel described in paragraph (1)(A).

(c) Grants to outlying areas

Public Law 95–134, permitting the consolidation of grants to the outlying areas, shall not apply to funds received under this part.

§ 1455. Minimum state grant amounts

(a) In general

The Secretary shall make a grant to each State educational agency whose application the Secretary has selected for funding under this part in an amount for each fiscal year that is—

(1) not less than $500,000, nor more than $2,000,000, in the case of the 50 States, the District of Columbia, and the Commonwealth of Puerto Rico; and

(2) not less than $80,000, in the case of an outlying area.

(b) Inflation adjustment

Beginning with fiscal year 1999, the Secretary may increase the maximum amount described in subsection (a)(1) to account for inflation.

(c) Factors

The Secretary shall set the amount of each grant under subsection (a) of this section after considering—

(1) the amount of funds available for making the grants;

(2) the relative population of the State or outlying area; and

(3) the types of activities proposed by the State or outlying area.

§ 1456. Authorization of appropriations

There are authorized to be appropriated to carry out this part such sums as may be necessary for each of the fiscal years 1998 through 2002.

PART B—COORDINATED RESEARCH, PERSONNEL PREPARATION, TECHNICAL ASSISTANCE, SUPPORT, AND DISSEMINATION OF INFORMATION

§ 1461. Administrative provisions

(a) Comprehensive plan

(1) In general—The Secretary shall develop and implement a comprehensive plan for activities carried out under this part in order to enhance the provision of educational, related, transitional, and early intervention services to children with disabilities under subchapters II and III of this chapter. The plan shall include mechanisms to address educational, related services, transitional, and early intervention needs identified by State educational agencies in applications submitted for State program improvement grants under part A of this subchapter.

(2) Participants in plan development—In developing the plan described in paragraph (1), the Secretary shall consult with—

(A) individuals with disabilities;

(B) parents of children with disabilities

(C) appropriate professionals; and

(D) representatives of State and local educational agencies, private schools, institutions of higher education, other Federal agencies, the National Council on Disability, and national organizations with an interest in, and expertise in, providing services to children with disabilities and their families.

(3) Public comment—The Secretary shall take public comment on the plan.

(4) Distribution of funds—In implementing the plan, the Secretary shall, to the extent appropriate, ensure that funds are awarded to recipients under this part to carry out activities that benefit, directly or indirectly, children with disabilities of all ages.

(5) Reports to Congress—The Secretary shall periodically report to the Congress on the Secretary's activities under this subsection, including an initial report not later than the date that is 18 months after June 4, 1997.

(b) Eligible applicants

(1) In general—Except as otherwise provided in this part, the following entities are eligible to apply for a grant, contract, or cooperative agreement under this part:

(A) A State educational agency.

(B) A local educational agency.

(C) An institution of higher education.

(D) Any other public agency.

(E) A private nonprofit organization.

(F) An outlying area.

(G) An Indian tribe or a tribal organization (as defined under section 450b of Title 25).

(H) A for-profit organization, if the Secretary finds it appropriate in light of the purposes of a particular competition for a grant, contract, or cooperative agreement under this part.

(2) Special rule—The Secretary may limit the entities eligible for an award of a grant, contract, or cooperative agreement to one or more categories of eligible entities described in paragraph (1).

(c) Use of funds by Secretary

Notwithstanding any other provision of law, and in addition to any authority granted the Secretary under subpart 1 or subpart 2 of this part, the Secretary may use up to 20 percent of the funds available under either subpart 1 or subpart 2 of this part for any fiscal year to carry out any activity, or combination of activities, subject to such conditions as the Secretary determines are appropriate effectively to carry out the purposes of such subparts, that—

(1) is consistent with the purposes of subpart 1, subpart 2 of this part, or both; and

(2) involves—

(A) research;

(B) personnel preparation;

(C) parent training and information;

(D) technical assistance and dissemination;

(E) technology development, demonstration, and utilization; or

(F) media services.

(d) Special populations

(1) Application requirement—In making an award of a grant, contract, or cooperative agreement under this part, the Secretary shall, as appropriate, require an applicant to demonstrate how the applicant will address the needs of children with disabilities from minority backgrounds.

(2) Outreach and technical assistance—

(A) Requirement—Notwithstanding any other provision of this chapter, the Secretary shall ensure that at least one percent of the total amount of funds appropriated to carry out this part is used for either or both of the following activities:

(i) To provide outreach and technical assistance to Historically Black Colleges and Universities, and to institutions of higher education with minority enrollments of at least 25 percent, to promote the participation of such colleges, universities, and institutions in activities under this part.

(ii) To enable Historically Black Colleges and Universities, and the institutions described in clause (i), to assist other colleges, universities, institutions, and agencies in improving educational and transitional results for children with disabilities.

(B) Reservation of funds—The Secretary may reserve funds appropriated under this part to satisfy the requirement of subparagraph (A).

(e) Priorities

(1) In general—Except as otherwise explicitly authorized in this part, the Secretary shall ensure that a grant, contract, or cooperative agreement under subpart 1 or subpart 2 of this part is awarded only—

(A) for activities that are designed to benefit children with disabilities, their families, or the personnel employed to work with such children or their families; or

(B) to benefit other individuals with disabilities that such subpart is intended to benefit.

(2) Priority for particular activities—Subject to paragraph (1), the Secretary, in making an award of a grant, contract, or cooperative agreement under this part, may, without regard to the rule making procedures under section 553 of Title 5, limit competitions to, or otherwise give priority to—

(A) projects that address one or more—

(i) age ranges;

(ii) disabilities;

(iii) school grades;

(iv) types of educational placements or early intervention environments;

(v) types of services;

(vi) content areas, such as reading; or

(vii) effective strategies for helping children with disabilities learn appropriate behavior in the school and other community-based educational settings;

(B) projects that address the needs of children based on the severity of their disability;

(C) projects that address the needs of—

(i) low-achieving students;

(ii) underserved populations;

(iii) children from low-income families;

(iv) children with limited English proficiency;

(v) unserved and underserved areas;

(vi) particular types of geographic areas; or

(vii) children whose behavior interferes with their learning and socialization;

(D) projects to reduce inappropriate identification of children as children with disabilities, particularly among minority children;

(E) projects that are carried out in particular areas of the country, to ensure broad geographic coverage; and

(F) any activity that is expressly authorized in subpart 1 or 2 of this part.

(f) Applicant and recipient responsibilities

(1) Development and assessment of projects—The Secretary shall require that an applicant for, and a recipient of, a grant, contract, or cooperative agreement for a project under this part—

(A) involve individuals with disabilities or parents of individuals with disabilities in planning, implementing, and evaluating the project; and

(B) where appropriate, determine whether the project has any potential for replication and adoption by other entities.

(2) Additional responsibilities—The Secretary may require a recipient of a grant, contract, or cooperative agreement for a project under this part—

(A) to share in the cost of the project;

(B) to prepare the research and evaluation findings and products from the project in formats that are useful for specific audiences, including parents, administrators, teachers, early intervention personnel, related services personnel, and individuals with disabilities;

(C) to disseminate such findings and products; and

(D) to collaborate with other such recipients in carrying out subparagraphs (B) and (C).

(g) Application management

(1) Standing panel

(A) In general—The Secretary shall establish and use a standing panel of experts who are competent, by virtue of their training, expertise, or experience, to evaluate applications under this subpart that, individually, request more than $75,000 per year in Federal financial assistance.

(B) Membership—The standing panel shall include, at a minimum—

(i) individuals who are representatives of institutions of higher education that plan, develop, and carry out programs of personnel preparation;

(ii) individuals who design and carry out programs of research targeted to the improvement of special education programs and services;

(iii) individuals who have recognized experience and knowledge necessary to integrate and apply research findings to improve educational and transitional results for children with disabilities;

(iv) individuals who administer programs at the State or local level in which children with disabilities participate;

(v) individuals who prepare parents of children with disabilities to participate in making decisions about the education of their children;

(vi) individuals who establish policies that affect the delivery of services to children with disabilities;

(vii) individuals who are parents of children with disabilities who are benefiting, or have benefited, from coordinated research, personnel preparation, and technical assistance; and

(viii) individuals with disabilities.

(C) Training—The Secretary shall provide training to the individuals who are selected as members of the standing panel under this paragraph.

(D) Term—No individual shall serve on the standing panel for more than 3 consecutive years, unless the Secretary determines that the individual's continued participation is necessary for the sound administration of this part.

(2) Peer-review panels for particular competitions

(A) Composition—The Secretary shall ensure that each sub-panel selected from the standing panel that reviews applications under this part includes—

(i) individuals with knowledge and expertise on the issues addressed by the activities authorized by the part; and

(ii) to the extent practicable, parents of children with disabilities, individuals with disabilities, and persons from diverse backgrounds.

(B) Federal employment limitation—A majority of the individuals on each sub-panel that reviews an application under this part shall be individuals who are not employees of the Federal Government.

(3) Use of discretionary funds for administrative purposes

(A) Expenses and fees of non-federal panel members—The Secretary may use funds available under this part to pay the expenses and fees of the panel members who are not officers or employees of the Federal Government.

(B) Administrative support—The Secretary may use not more than 1 percent of the funds appropriated to carry out this part to pay non-Federal entities for administrative support related to management of applications submitted under this part.

(C) Monitoring—The Secretary may use funds available under this part to pay the expenses of Federal employees to conduct on-site monitoring of projects receiving $500,000 or more for any fiscal year under this part.

(h) Program evaluation

The Secretary may use funds appropriated to carry out this part to evaluate activities carried out under the part.

(i) Minimum funding required

(1) In general—Subject to paragraph (2), the Secretary shall ensure that, for each fiscal year, at least the following amounts are provided under this part to address the following needs:

(A) $12,832,000 to address the educational, related services, transitional, and early intervention needs of children with deaf-blindness.

(B) $4,000,000 to address the postsecondary, vocational, technical, continuing, and adult education needs of individuals with deafness.

(C) $4,000,000 to address the educational, related services, and transitional needs of children with an emotional disturbance and those who are at risk of developing an emotional disturbance.

(2) Ratable reduction—If the total amount appropriated to carry out sections 1472, 1473, and 1485 of this title for any fiscal year is less than $130,000,000, the amounts listed in paragraph (1) shall be ratably reduced.

(j) Eligibility for financial assistance

Effective for fiscal years for which the Secretary may make grants under section 1419(b) of this title, no State or local educational agency or educational service agency or other public institution or agency may receive a grant under this part which relates exclusively to programs, projects, and activities pertaining to children aged 3 through 5, inclusive, unless the State is eligible to receive a grant under section 1419(b) of this title.

Subpart 1—Improving Early Intervention, Educational, and Transitional Services and Results for Children With Disabilities Through Coordinated Research and Personnel Preparation

§ 1471. Findings and purpose

(a) Findings

The Congress finds the following:

(1) The Federal Government has an ongoing obligation to support programs, projects, and activities that contribute to positive results for children with disabilities, enabling them—

(A) to meet their early intervention, educational, and transitional goals and, to the maximum extent possible, educational standards that have been established for all children; and

(B) to acquire the skills that will empower them to lead productive and independent adult lives.

(2)(A) As a result of more than 20 years of Federal support for research, demonstration projects, and personnel preparation, there is an important knowledge base for improving results for children with disabilities.

(B) Such knowledge should be used by States and local educational agencies to design and implement state-of-the-art educational systems that consider the needs of, and include, children with disabilities, especially in environments in which they can learn along with their peers and achieve results measured by the same standards as the results of their peers.

(3)(A) Continued Federal support is essential for the development and maintenance of a coordinated and high-quality program of research, demonstration projects, dissemination of information, and personnel preparation.

(B) Such support—

(i) enables State educational agencies and local educational agencies to improve their educational systems and results for children with disabilities;

(ii) enables State and local agencies to improve early intervention services and results for infants and toddlers with disabilities and their families; and

(iii) enhances the opportunities for general and special education personnel, related services personnel, parents, and paraprofessionals to participate in pre-service and in-service training, to collaborate, and to improve results for children with disabilities and their families.

(4) The Federal Government plays a critical role in facilitating the availability of an adequate number of Qualified personnel—

(A) to serve effectively the over 5,000,000 children with disabilities;

(B) to assume leadership positions in administrative and direct-service capacities related to teacher training and research concerning the provision of early intervention services, special education, and related services; and

(C) to work with children with low-incidence disabilities and their families.

(5) The Federal Government performs the role described in Paragraph (4)—

(A) by supporting models of personnel development that reflect successful practice, including strategies for recruiting, preparing, and retaining personnel;

(B) by promoting the coordination and integration of—

(i) personnel-development activities for teachers of children with disabilities; and

(ii) other personnel-development activities supported under Federal law, including this subpart;

(C) by supporting the development and dissemination of information about teaching standards; and

(D) by promoting the coordination and integration of personnel-development activities through linkage with systemic-change activities within States and nationally.

(b) Purpose

The purpose of this subpart is to provide Federal funding for coordinated research, demonstration projects, outreach, and personnel-preparation activities that—

(1) are described in sections 1472 through 1474 of this title;

(2) are linked with, and promote, systemic change; and

(3) improve early intervention, educational, and transitional results for children with disabilities.

§ 1472. Research and innovation to improve services and results for children with disabilities

(a) In general

The Secretary shall make competitive grants to, or enter into contracts or cooperative agreements with, eligible entities to produce, and advance the use of, knowledge—

(1) to improve—

(A) services provided under this chapter, including the practices of professionals and others involved in providing such services to children with disabilities; and

(B) educational results for children with disabilities;

(2) to address the special needs of preschool-aged children and infants and toddlers with disabilities, including infants and toddlers who would be at risk of having substantial developmental delays if early intervention services were not provided to them;

(3) to address the specific problems of over-identification and under-identification of children with disabilities;

(4) to develop and implement effective strategies for addressing inappropriate behavior of students with disabilities in schools, including strategies to prevent children with emotional and behavioral problems from developing emotional

disturbances that require the provision of special education and related services;

(5) to improve secondary and postsecondary education and transitional services for children with disabilities; and

(6) to address the range of special education, related services, and early intervention needs of children with disabilities who need significant levels of support to maximize their participation and learning in school and in the community.

(b) New knowledge production; authorized activities

(1) In general—In carrying out this section, the Secretary shall support activities, consistent with the objectives described in subsection (a) of this section, that lead to the production of new knowledge.

(2) Authorized activities—Activities that may be carried out under this subsection include activities such as the following:

(A) Expanding understanding of the relationships between learning characteristics of children with disabilities and the diverse ethnic, cultural, linguistic, social, and economic backgrounds of children with disabilities and their families.

(B) Developing or identifying innovative, effective, and efficient curricula designs, instructional approaches, and strategies, and developing or identifying positive academic and social learning opportunities, that—

(i) enable children with disabilities to make effective transitions described in section 1474(b)(3)(C) of this title or transitions between educational settings; and

(ii) improve educational and transitional results for children with disabilities at all levels of the educational system in which the activities are carried out and, in particular, that improve the progress of the children, as measured by assessments within the general education curriculum involved.

(C) Advancing the design of assessment tools and procedures that will accurately and efficiently determine the special instructional, learning, and behavioral needs of children with disabilities, especially within the context of general education.

(D) Studying and promoting improved alignment and compatibility of general and special education reforms concerned with curricular and instructional reform, evaluation and accountability of such reforms, and administrative procedures.

(E) Advancing the design, development, and integration of technology, assistive technology devices, media, and materials, to improve early intervention, educational, and transitional services and results for children with disabilities.

(F) Improving designs, processes, and results of personnel preparation for personnel who provide services to children with disabilities through the acquisition of information on, and implementation of, research-based practices.

(G) Advancing knowledge about the coordination of education with health and social services.

(H) Producing information on the long-term impact of early intervention and education on results for individuals with disabilities through large-scale longitudinal studies.

(c) Integration of research and practice, authorized activities

(1) In general—In carrying out this section, the Secretary shall support activities, consistent with the objectives described in subsection (a) of this section, that integrate research and practice, including activities that support State systemic-change and local capacity-building and improvement efforts.

(2) Authorized activities—Activities that may be carried out under this subsection include activities such as the following:

(A) Model demonstration projects to apply and test research findings in typical service settings to determine the usability, effectiveness, and general applicability of such research findings in such areas as improving instructional methods, curricula, and tools, such as textbooks and media.

(B) Demonstrating and applying research-based findings to facilitate systemic changes, related to the provision of services to children with disabilities, in policy, procedure, practice, and the training and use of personnel.

(C) Promoting and demonstrating the coordination of early intervention and educational services for children with disabilities with services provided by health, rehabilitation, and social service agencies.

(D) Identifying and disseminating solutions that overcome systemic barriers to the effective and efficient delivery of early intervention, educational, and transitional services to children with disabilities.

(d) Improving the use of professional knowledge; authorized activities

(1) In general—In carrying out this section, the Secretary shall support activities, consistent with the objectives described in subsection (a) of this section, that improve the use of professional knowledge, including activities that support State systemic-change and local capacity-building and improvement efforts.

(2) Authorized activities—Activities that may be carried out under this subsection include activities such as the following:

(A) Synthesizing useful research and other information relating to the provision of services to children with disabilities, including effective practices.

(B) Analyzing professional knowledge bases to advance an understanding of the relationships, and the effectiveness of practices, relating to the provision of services to children with disabilities.

(C) Ensuring that research and related products are in appropriate formats for distribution to teachers, parents, and individuals with disabilities.

(D) Enabling professionals, parents of children with disabilities, and other persons, to learn about, and implement, the findings of research, and successful practices developed in model demonstration projects, relating to the provision of services to children with disabilities.

(E) Conducting outreach, and disseminating information relating to successful approaches to overcoming systemic barriers to the effective and efficient delivery of early intervention, educational, and transitional services, to personnel who provide services to children with disabilities.

(e) Balance among activities and age ranges

In carrying out this section, the Secretary shall ensure that there is an appropriate balance—

(1) among knowledge production, integration of research and practice, and use of professional knowledge; and

(2) across all age ranges of children with disabilities.

(f) Applications

An eligible entity that wishes to receive a grant, or enter into a contract or cooperative agreement, under this section shall submit an application to the Secretary at such time, in such manner, and containing such information as the Secretary may require.

(g) Authorization of appropriations

There are authorized to be appropriated to carry out this section such sums as may be necessary for each of the fiscal years 1998 through 2002.

§ 1473. Personnel preparation to improve services and results for children with disabilities

(a) In general

The Secretary shall, on a competitive basis, make grants to, or enter into contracts or cooperative agreements with, eligible entities—

(1) to help address State-identified needs for qualified personnel in special education, related services, early intervention, and regular education, to work with children with disabilities; and

(2) to ensure that those personnel have the skills and knowledge, derived from practices that have been determined, through research and experience, to be successful, that are needed to serve those children.

(b) Low-incidence disabilities; authorized activities

(1) In general—In carrying out this section, the Secretary shall support activities, consistent with the objectives described in subsection (a) of this section, that benefit children with low-incidence disabilities.

(2) Authorized activities—Activities that may be carried out under this subsection include activities such as the following:

(A) Preparing persons who—

(i) have prior training in educational and other related service fields; and

(ii) are studying to obtain degrees, certificates, or licensure that will enable them to assist children with disabilities to achieve the objectives set out in their individualized education programs described in section 1414(d) of this title, or to assist infants and toddlers with disabilities to achieve the outcomes described in their individualized family service plans described in section 1436 of this title.

(B) Providing personnel from various disciplines with interdisciplinary training that will contribute to improvement in early intervention, educational, and transitional results for children with disabilities.

(C) Preparing personnel in the innovative uses and application of technology to enhance learning by children with disabilities through early intervention, educational, and transitional services.

(D) Preparing personnel who provide services to visually impaired or blind children to teach and use Braille in the provision of services to such children.

(E) Preparing personnel to be qualified educational interpreters, to assist children with disabilities, particularly deaf and hard-of-hearing children in school and school-related activities and deaf and hard-of-hearing infants and toddlers and preschool children in early intervention and preschool programs.

(F) Preparing personnel who provide services to children with significant cognitive disabilities and children with multiple disabilities.

(3) Definition—As used in this section, the term 'low-incidence disability' means—

(A) a visual or hearing impairment, or simultaneous visual and hearing impairments;

(B) a significant cognitive impairment; or

(C) any impairment for which a small number of personnel with highly specialized skills and knowledge are needed in order for children with that impairment to receive early intervention services or a free appropriate public education.

(4) Selection of recipients—In selecting recipients under this subsection, the Secretary may give preference to applications that propose to prepare personnel in more than one low-incidence disability, such as deafness and blindness.

(5) Preparation in use of Braille—The Secretary shall ensure that all recipients of assistance under this subsection who will use that assistance to prepare personnel to provide services to visually impaired or blind children that can appropriately be provided in Braille will prepare those individuals to provide those services in Braille.

(c) Leadership preparation; authorized activities

(1) In general—In carrying out this section, the Secretary shall support leadership preparation activities that are consistent with the objectives described in subsection (a) of this section.

(2) Authorized activities—Activities that may be carried out under this subsection include activities such as the following:

(A) Preparing personnel at the advanced graduate, doctoral, and postdoctoral levels of training to administer, enhance, or provide services for children with disabilities.

(B) Providing interdisciplinary training for various types of leadership personnel, including teacher preparation faculty, administrators, researchers, supervisors, principals, and other persons whose work affects early intervention, educational, and transitional services for children with disabilities.

(d) Projects of national significance; authorized activities

(1) In general—In carrying out this section, the Secretary shall support activities, consistent with the objectives described in subsection (a), that are of national significance and have broad applicability.

(2) Authorized activities—Activities that may be carried out under this subsection include activities such as the following:

(A) Developing and demonstrating effective and efficient practices for preparing personnel to provide services to children with disabilities, including practices that address any needs identified in the State's improvement plan under subchapter III of this chapter;

(B) Demonstrating the application of significant knowledge derived from research and other sources in the development of programs to prepare personnel to provide services to children with disabilities.

(C) Demonstrating models for the preparation of, and interdisciplinary training of, early intervention, special education, and general education personnel, to enable the personnel—

(i) to acquire the collaboration skills necessary to work within teams to assist children with disabilities; and

(ii) to achieve results that meet challenging standards, particularly within the general education curriculum.

(D) Demonstrating models that reduce shortages of teachers, and personnel from other relevant disciplines, who serve children with disabilities, through reciprocity arrangements between States that are related to licensure and certification.

(E) Developing, evaluating, and disseminating model teaching standards for persons working with children with disabilities.

(F) Promoting the transferability, across State and local jurisdictions, of licensure and certification of teachers and administrators working with such children.

(G) Developing and disseminating models that prepare teachers with strategies, including behavioral interventions, for addressing the conduct of children with disabilities that impedes their learning and that of others in the classroom.

(H) Institutes that provide professional development that addresses the needs of children with disabilities to teachers or teams of teachers, and where appropriate, to school board members, administrators, principals, pupil-service personnel, and other staff from individual schools.

(I) Projects to improve the ability of general education teachers, principals, and other administrators to meet the needs of children with disabilities.

(J) Developing, evaluating, and disseminating innovative models for the recruitment, induction, retention, and assessment of new, qualified teachers, especially from groups that are underrepresented in the teaching profession, including individuals with disabilities.

(K) Supporting institutions of higher education with minority enrollments of at least 25 percent for the purpose of preparing personnel to work with children with disabilities.

(e) High-incidence disabilities; authorized activities

(1) In general—In carrying out this section, the Secretary shall support activities, consistent with the objectives described in subsection (a) of this section, to benefit children with high-incidence disabilities, such as children with specific learning disabilities, speech or language impairment, or mental retardation.

(2) Authorized activities—Activities that may be carried out under this subsection include the following:

(A) Activities undertaken by institutions of higher education, local educational agencies, and other local entities—

(i) to improve and reform their existing programs to prepare teachers and related services personnel—

(I) to meet the diverse needs of children with disabilities for early intervention, educational, and transitional services; and

(II) to work collaboratively in regular classroom settings; and

(ii) to incorporate best practices and research-based knowledge about preparing personnel so they will have the knowledge and skills to improve educational results for children with disabilities.

(B) Activities incorporating innovative strategies to recruit and prepare teachers and other personnel to meet the needs of areas in which there are acute and persistent shortages of personnel.

(C) Developing career opportunities for paraprofessionals to receive training as special education teachers, related services personnel, and early intervention personnel, including interdisciplinary training to enable them to improve early intervention, educational, and transitional results for children with disabilities.

(f) Applications

(1) In general—Any eligible entity that wishes to receive a grant, or enter into a contract or cooperative agreement, under this section shall submit an application to the Secretary at such time, in such manner, and containing such information as the Secretary may require.

(2) Identified state needs

(A) Requirement to address identified needs—Any application under subsection (b), (c), or (e) of this section shall include information demonstrating to the satisfaction of the Secretary that the activities described in the application will address needs identified by the State or States the applicant proposes to serve.

(B) Cooperation with State educational agencies—Any applicant that is not a local educational agency or a State educational agency shall include information demonstrating to the satisfaction of the Secretary that the applicant and one or more State educational agencies have engaged in a cooperative effort to plan the project to which the application pertains, and will cooperate in carrying out and monitoring the project.

(3) Acceptance by States of personnel preparation requirements—The Secretary may require applicants to provide letters from one or more States stating that the States—

(A) intend to accept successful completion of the proposed personnel preparation program as meeting State personnel standards for serving children with disabilities or serving infants and toddlers with disabilities; and

(B) need personnel in the area or areas in which the applicant proposes to provide preparation, as identified in the States' comprehensive systems of personnel development under subchapters II and III of this chapter.

(g) Selection of recipients

(1) Impact of project—In selecting recipients under this section, the Secretary may consider the impact of the project proposed in the application in meeting the need for personnel identified by the States.

(2) Requirement on applicants to meet State and professional standards—The Secretary shall make grants under this section only to eligible applicants that meet State and professionally-recognized standards for the preparation of special education and related services personnel, if the purpose of the project is to assist personnel in obtaining degrees.

(3) Preferences—In selecting recipients under this section, the Secretary may—

(A) give preference to institutions of higher education that are educating regular education personnel to meet the needs of children with disabilities in integrated settings and educating special education personnel to work in collaboration with regular educators in integrated settings; and

(B) give preference to institutions of higher education that are successfully recruiting and preparing individuals with disabilities and individuals from groups that are underrepresented in the profession for which they are preparing individuals.

(h) Service obligation

(1) In general—Each application for funds under subsections (b) and (e) of this section, and to the extent appropriate subsection (d) of this section, shall include an assurance that the applicant will ensure that individuals who receive a scholarship under the proposed project will subsequently provide special education and related services to children with disabilities for a period of 2 years for every year for which assistance was received or repay all or part of the cost of that assistance, in accordance with regulations issued by the Secretary.

(2) Leadership preparation—Each application for funds under subsection (c) of this section shall include an assurance that the applicant will ensure that individuals who receive a scholarship under the proposed project will subsequently perform work related to their preparation for a period of 2 years for every year for which assistance was received or repay all or part of such costs, in accordance with regulations issued by the Secretary.

(i) Scholarships

The Secretary may include funds for scholarships, with necessary stipends and allowances, in awards under subsections (b), (c), (d), and (e) of this section.

(j) Authorization of appropriations

There are authorized to be appropriated to carry out this section such sums as may be necessary for each of the fiscal years 1998 through 2002.

§ 1474. Studies and evaluations

(a) Studies and evaluations

(1) In general—The Secretary shall, directly or through grants, contracts, or cooperative agreements, assess the progress in the implementation of this chapter, including the effectiveness of State and local efforts to provide—

(A) a free appropriate public education to children with disabilities; and

(B) early intervention services to infants and toddlers with disabilities and infants and toddlers who would be at risk of having substantial developmental delays if early intervention services were not provided to them.

(2) Authorized activities—In carrying out this subsection, the Secretary may support studies, evaluations, and assessments, including studies that—

(A) analyze measurable impact, outcomes, and results achieved by State educational agencies and local educational agencies through their activities to reform policies, procedures, and practices designed to improve educational and transitional services and results for children with disabilities;

(B) analyze State and local needs for professional development, parent training, and other appropriate activities that can reduce the need for disciplinary actions involving children with disabilities;

(C) assess educational and transitional services and results for children with disabilities from minority backgrounds, including—

(i) data on—

(I) the number of minority children who are referred for special education evaluation;

(II) the number of minority children who are receiving special education and related services and their educational or other service placement; and

(III) the number of minority children who graduated from secondary and postsecondary education programs; and

(ii) the performance of children with disabilities from minority backgrounds on State assessments and other performance indicators established for all students;

(D) measure educational and transitional services and results of children with disabilities under this chapter, including longitudinal studies that—

(i) examine educational and transitional services and results for children with disabilities who are 3 through 17 years of age and are receiving special education and related services under this chapter, using a national, representative sample of distinct age cohorts and disability categories; and

(ii) examine educational results, postsecondary placement, and employment status of individuals with disabilities, 18 through 21 years of age, who are receiving or have received special education and related services under this chapter; and

(E) identify and report on the placement of children with disabilities by disability category.

(b) National assessment

(1) In general—The Secretary shall carry out a national assessment of activities carried out with Federal funds under this chapter in order—

(A) to determine the effectiveness of this chapter in achieving its purposes;

(B) to provide information to the President, the Congress, the States, local educational agencies, and the public on how to implement the chapter more effectively; and

(C) to provide the President and the Congress with information that will be useful in developing legislation to achieve the purposes of this chapter more effectively.

(2) Consultation—The Secretary shall plan, review, and conduct the national assessment under this subsection in consultation with researchers, State practitioners, local practitioners, parents of children with disabilities, individuals with disabilities, and other appropriate individuals.

(3) Scope of assessment—The national assessment shall examine how well schools, local educational agencies, States, other recipients of assistance under this chapter, and the Secretary are achieving the purposes of this chapter, including—

(A) improving the performance of children with disabilities in general scholastic activities and assessments as compared to nondisabled children;

(B) providing for the participation of children with disabilities in the general curriculum;

(C) helping children with disabilities make successful transitions from—

(i) early intervention services to preschool education;

(ii) preschool education to elementary school; and

(iii) secondary school to adult life;

(D) placing and serving children with disabilities, including minority children, in the least restrictive environment appropriate;

(E) preventing children with disabilities, especially children with emotional disturbances and specific learning disabilities, from dropping out of school;

(F) addressing behavioral problems of children with disabilities as compared to nondisabled children;

(G) coordinating services provided under this chapter with each other, with other educational and pupil services (including preschool services), and with health and social services funded from other sources;

(H) providing for the participation of parents of children with disabilities in the education of their children; and

(I) resolving disagreements between education personnel and parents through activities such as mediation.

(4) Interim and final reports—The Secretary shall submit to the President and the Congress—

(A) an interim report that summarizes the preliminary findings of the assessment not later than October 1, 1999; and

(B) a final report of the findings of the assessment not later than October 1, 2001.

(c) Annual report

The Secretary shall report annually to the Congress on—

(1) an analysis and summary of the data reported by the States and the Secretary of the Interior under section 1418 of this title;

(2) the results of activities conducted under subsection (a) of this section;

(3) the findings and determinations resulting from reviews of State implementation of this chapter.

(d) Technical assistance to LEAs

The Secretary shall provide directly, or through grants, contracts, or cooperative agreements, technical assistance to local educational agencies to assist them in carrying out local capacity-building and improvement projects under section 1411(f)(4) of this title and other LEA systemic improvement activities under this chapter.

(e) Reservation for studies and technical assistance

(1) In general—Except as provided in paragraph (2) and notwithstanding any other provision of this chapter, the Secretary may reserve up to one-half of one percent of the amount appropriated under subchapters II and III of this chapter for each fiscal year to carry out this section.

(2) Maximum amount—For the first fiscal year in which the amount described in paragraph (1) is at least $20,000,000, the maximum amount the Secretary may reserve under paragraph (1) is $20,000,000. For each subsequent fiscal year, the maximum amount the Secretary may reserve under paragraph (1) is $20,000,000, increased by the cumulative rate of inflation since the fiscal year described in the previous sentence.

(3) Use of maximum amount—In any fiscal year described in paragraph (2) for which the Secretary reserves the maximum amount described in that paragraph, the Secretary shall use at least half of the reserved amount for activities under subsection (d).

Subpart 2—Improving Early Intervention, Educational, and Transitional Services and Results for Children With Disabilities Through Coordinated Technical Assistance, Support, and Dissemination of Information

§ 1481. Findings and purposes

(a) In general

The Congress finds as follows:

(1) National technical assistance, support, and dissemination activities are necessary to ensure that subchapters II and III of this chapter are fully implemented and achieve quality early intervention, educational, and transitional results for children with disabilities and their families.

(2) Parents, teachers, administrators, and related services personnel need technical assistance and information in a timely, coordinated, and accessible manner in order to improve early intervention, educational, and transitional services and results at the State and local levels for children with disabilities and their families.

(3) Parent training and information activities have taken on increased importance in efforts to assist parents of a child with a disability in dealing with the multiple pressures of rearing such a child and are of particular importance in—

(A) ensuring the involvement of such parents in planning and decisionmaking with respect to early intervention, educational, and transitional services;

(B) achieving quality early intervention, educational, and transitional results for children with disabilities;

(C) providing such parents information on their rights and protections under this Act to ensure improved early intervention, educational, and transitional results for children with disabilities;

(D) assisting such parents in the development of skills to participate effectively in the education and development of their children and in the transitions described in section 1474(b)(3)(C) of this title; and

(E) supporting the roles of such parents as participants within partnerships seeking to improve early intervention, educational, and transitional services and results for children with disabilities and their families.

(4) Providers of parent training and information activities need to ensure that such parents who have limited access to services and supports, due to economic, cultural, or linguistic barriers, are provided with access to appropriate parent training and information activities.

(5) Parents of children with disabilities need information that helps the parents to understand the rights and responsibilities of their children under subchapter II of this chapter.

(6) The provision of coordinated technical assistance and dissemination of information to State and local agencies, institutions of higher education, and other providers of services to children with disabilities is essential in—

(A) supporting the process of achieving systemic change;

(B) supporting actions in areas of priority specific to the improvement of early intervention, educational, and transitional results for children with disabilities;

(C) conveying information and assistance that are—

(i) based on current research (as of the date the information and assistance are conveyed);

(ii) accessible and meaningful for use in supporting systemic-change activities of State and local partnerships; and

(iii) linked directly to improving early intervention, educational, and transitional services and results for children with disabilities and their families; and

(D) organizing systems and information networks for such information, based on modern technology related to—

(i) storing and gaining access to information; and

(ii) distributing information in a systematic manner to parents, students, professionals, and policymakers.

(7) Federal support for carrying out technology research, technology development, and educational media services and activities has resulted in major innovations that have significantly improved early intervention, educational, and transitional services and results for children with disabilities and their families.

(8) Such Federal support is needed—

(A) to stimulate the development of software, interactive learning tools, and devices to address early intervention, educational, and transitional needs of children with disabilities who have certain disabilities;

(B) to make information available on technology research, technology development, and educational media services and activities to individuals involved in the provision of early intervention, educational, and transitional services to children with disabilities;

(C) to promote the integration of technology into curricula to improve early intervention, educational, and transitional results for children with disabilities;

(D) to provide incentives for the development of technology and media devices and tools that are not readily found or available because of the small size of potential markets;

(E) to make resources available to pay for such devices and tools and educational media services and activities;

(F) to promote the training of personnel—

(i) to provide such devices, tools, services, and activities in a competent manner; and

(ii) to assist children with disabilities and their families in using such devices, tools, services, and activities; and

(G) to coordinate the provision of such devices, tools, services, and activities—

(i) among State human services programs; and

(ii) between such programs and private agencies.

(b) Purposes

The purposes of this subpart are to ensure that—

(1) children with disabilities, and their parents, receive training and information on their rights and protections under this chapter, in order to develop the skills necessary to effectively participate in planning and decisionmaking relating to early intervention, educational, and transitional services and in systemic-change activities;

(2) parents, teachers, administrators, early intervention personnel, related services personnel, and transition personnel receive coordinated and accessible technical assistance and information to assist such persons, through systemic-change activities and other efforts, to improve early intervention, educational, and transitional services and results for children with disabilities and their families;

(3) appropriate technology and media are researched, developed, demonstrated, and made available in timely and accessible formats to parents, teachers, and all types of personnel providing services to children with disabilities to support their roles as partners in the improvement and implementation of early intervention, educational, and transitional services and results for children with disabilities and their families;

(4) on reaching the age of majority under State law, children with disabilities understand their rights and responsibilities under subchapter II of this chapter, if the State provides for the transfer of parental rights under section 1415(m) of this title; and

(5) the general welfare of deaf and hard-of-hearing individuals is promoted by—

(A) bringing to such individuals understanding and appreciation of the films and television programs that play an important part in the general and cultural advancement of hearing individuals;

(B) providing, through those films and television programs, enriched educational and cultural experiences through which deaf and hard-of-hearing individuals can better understand the realities of their environment; and

(C) providing wholesome and rewarding experiences that deaf and hard-of-hearing individuals may share.

§ 1482. Parent training and information centers

(a) Program authorized

The Secretary may make grants to, and enter into contracts and cooperative agreements with, parent organizations to support parent training and information centers to carry out activities under this section.

(b) Required activities

Each parent training and information center that receives assistance under this section shall—

(1) provide training and information that meets the training and information needs of parents of children with disabilities living in the area served by the center, particularly underserved parents and parents of children who may be inappropriately identified;

(2) assist parents to understand the availability of, and how to effectively use, procedural safeguards under this chapter, including encouraging the use, and explaining the benefits, of alternative methods of dispute resolution, such as the mediation process described in section 1415(e) of this title;

(3) serve the parents of infants, toddlers, and children with the full range of disabilities;

(4) assist parents to—

(A) better understand the nature of their children's disabilities and their educational and developmental needs;

(B) communicate effectively with personnel responsible for providing special education, early intervention, and related services;

(C) participate in decisionmaking processes and the development of individualized education programs under subchapter II of this chapter and individualized family service plans under subchapter III of this chapter;

(D) obtain appropriate information about the range of options, programs, services, and resources available to assist children with disabilities and their families;

(E) understand the provisions of this chapter for the education of, and the provision of early intervention services to, children with disabilities; and

(F) participate in school reform activities;

(5) in States where the State elects to contract with the parent training and information center, contract with State educational agencies to provide, consistent with subparagraphs (B) and (D) of section 1415(e)(2) of this title, individuals who meet with parents to explain the mediation process to them;

(6) network with appropriate clearinghouses, including organizations conducting national dissemination activities under section 1485(d) of this title, and with other national, State, and local organizations and agencies, such as protection and advocacy agencies, that serve parents and families of children with the full range of disabilities; and

(7) annually report to the Secretary on—

(A) the number of parents to whom it provided information and training in the most recently concluded fiscal year; and

(B) the effectiveness of strategies used to reach and serve parents, including underserved parents of children with disabilities.

(c) Optional activities

A parent training and information center that receives assistance under this section may—

(1) provide information to teachers and other professionals who provide special education and related services to children with disabilities;

(2) assist students with disabilities to understand their rights and responsibilities under section 1415(m) of this title on reaching the age of majority; and

(3) assist parents of children with disabilities to be informed participants in the development and implementation of the State's State improvement plan under part A of this subchapter.

(d) Application requirements

Each application for assistance under this section shall identify with specificity the special efforts that the applicant will undertake—

(1) to ensure that the needs for training and information of underserved parents of children with disabilities in the area to be served are effectively met; and

(2) to work with community-based organizations.

(e) Distribution of funds

(1) In general—The Secretary shall make at least 1 award to a parent organization in each State, unless the Secretary does not receive an application from such an organization in each State of sufficient quality to warrant approval.

(2) Selection requirement—The Secretary shall select among applications submitted by parent organizations in a State in a manner that ensures the most effective assistance to parents, including parents in urban and rural areas, in the State.

(f) Quarterly review

(1) Requirements

(A) Meetings—The board of directors or special governing committee of each organization that receives an award under this section shall meet at least once in each calendar quarter to review the activities for which the award was made.

(B) Advising board—Each special governing committee shall directly advise the organization's governing board of its views and recommendations.

(2) Continuation award—When an organization requests a continuation award under this section, the board of directors or special governing committee shall submit to the Secretary a written review of the parent training and information program conducted by the organization during the preceding fiscal year.

(g) Definition of parent organization

As used in this section, the term 'parent organization' means a private nonprofit organization (other than an institution of higher education) that—

(1) has a board of directors—

(A) the majority of whom are parents of children with disabilities;

(B) that includes—

(i) individuals working in the fields of special education, related services, and early intervention; and

(ii) individuals with disabilities; and

(C) the parent and professional members of which are broadly representative of the population to be served; or

(2) has—

(A) a membership that represents the interests of individuals with disabilities and has established a special governing committee that meets the requirements of paragraph (1); and

(B) a memorandum of understanding between the special governing committee and the board of directors of the organization that clearly outlines the relationship between the board and the committee and the decisionmaking responsibilities and authority of each.

§ 1483. Community parent resource centers

(a) In general

The Secretary may make grants to, and enter into contracts and cooperative agreements with, local parent organizations to support parent training and information centers that will help ensure that underserved parents of children with disabilities, including low-income parents, parents of children with limited English proficiency, and parents with disabilities, have the training and information they need to enable them to participate effectively in helping their children with disabilities—

(1) to meet developmental goals and, to the maximum extent possible, those challenging standards that have been established for all children; and

(2) to be prepared to lead productive independent adult lives, to the maximum extent possible.

(b) Required activities

Each parent training and information center assisted under this section shall—

(1) provide training and information that meets the training and information needs of parents of children with disabilities proposed to be served by the grant, contract, or cooperative agreement;

(2) carry out the activities required of parent training and information centers under paragraphs (2) through (7) of section 1482(b) of this title;

(3) establish cooperative partnerships with the parent training and information centers funded under section 1482 of this title; and

(4) be designed to meet the specific needs of families who experience significant isolation from available sources of information and support.

(c) Definition

As used is this section, the term 'local parent organization' means a parent organization, as defined in section 1482(g) of this title, that either—

(1) has a board of directors the majority of whom are from the community to be served; or

(2) has—

(A) as a part of its mission, serving the interests of individuals with disabilities from such community; and

(B) a special governing committee to administer the grant, contract, or cooperative agreement, a majority of the members of which are individuals from such community.

§ 1484. Technical assistance for parent training and information centers

(a) In general

The Secretary may, directly or through awards to eligible entities, provide technical assistance for developing, assisting, and coordinating parent training and information programs carried out by parent training and information centers receiving assistance under sections 1482 and 1483 of this title.

(b) Authorized activities

The Secretary may provide technical assistance to a parent training and information center under this section in areas such as—

(1) effective coordination of parent training efforts;

(2) dissemination of information;

(3) evaluation by the center of itself;

(4) promotion of the use of technology, including assistive technology devices and assistive technology services;

(5) reaching underserved populations;

(6) including children with disabilities in general education programs;

(7) facilitation of transitions from—

(A) early intervention services to preschool;

(B) preschool to school; and

(C) secondary school to postsecondary environments; and

(8) promotion of alternative methods of dispute resolution.

§ 1485. Coordinated technical assistance and dissemination

(a) In general

The Secretary shall, by competitively making grants or entering into contracts and cooperative agreements with eligible entities, provide technical assistance and information, through such mechanisms as institutes, Regional Resource Centers, clearinghouses, and programs that support States and local entities in building capacity, to improve early intervention, educational, and transitional services and results for children with disabilities and their families, and address systemic-change goals and priorities.

(b) Systemic technical assistance; authorized activities

(1) In general—In carrying out this section, the Secretary shall carry out or support technical assistance activities, consistent with the objectives described in subsection (a) of this section, relating to systemic change.

(2) Authorized activities—Activities that may be carried out under this subsection include activities such as the following:

(A) Assisting States, local educational agencies, and other participants in partnerships established under part A of this subchapter with the process of planning systemic changes that will promote improved early intervention, educational, and transitional results for children with disabilities.

(B) Promoting change through a multistate or regional framework that benefits States, local educational agencies, and other participants in partnerships that are in the process of achieving systemic-change outcomes.

(C) Increasing the depth and utility of information in ongoing and emerging areas of priority need identified by States, local educational agencies, and other participants in partnerships that are in the process of achieving systemic-change outcomes.

(D) Promoting communication and information exchange among States, local educational agencies, and other participants in partnerships, based on the needs and concerns identified by the participants in the partnerships, rather than on externally imposed criteria or topics, regarding—

(i) the practices, procedures, and policies of the States, local educational agencies, and other participants in partnerships; and

(ii) accountability of the States, local educational agencies, and other participants in partnerships for improved early intervention, educational, and transitional results for children with disabilities.

(c) Specialized technical assistance; authorized activities

(1) In general—In carrying out this section, the Secretary shall carry out or support activities, consistent with the objectives described in subsection (a) of this section, relating to areas of priority or specific populations.

(2) Authorized activities—Examples of activities that may be carried out under this subsection include activities that—

(A) focus on specific areas of high-priority need that—

(i) are identified by States, local educational agencies, and other participants in partnerships;

(ii) require the development of new knowledge, or the analysis and synthesis of substantial bodies of information not readily available to the States, agencies, and other participants in partnerships; and

(iii) will contribute significantly to the improvement of early intervention, educational, and transitional services and results for children with disabilities and their families;

(B) focus on needs and issues that are specific to a population of children with disabilities, such as the provision of single-State and multi-State technical assistance and in-service training—

(i) to schools and agencies serving deaf-blind children and their families; and

(ii) to programs and agencies serving other groups of children with low-incidence disabilities and their families; or

(C) address the postsecondary education needs of individuals who are deaf or hard-of-hearing.

(d) National information dissemination; authorized activities

(1) In general—In carrying out this section, the Secretary shall carry out or support information dissemination activities that are consistent with the objectives described in subsection (a) of this section, including activities that address national needs for the preparation and dissemination of information relating to eliminating barriers to systemic-change and improving early intervention, educational, and transitional results for children with disabilities.

(2) Authorized activities—Examples of activities that may be carried out under this subsection include activities relating to—

(A) infants and toddlers with disabilities and their families, and children with disabilities and their families;

(B) services for populations of children with low-incidence disabilities, including deaf-blind children, and targeted age groupings;

(C) the provision of postsecondary services to individuals with disabilities;

(D) the need for and use of personnel to provide services to children with disabilities, and personnel recruitment, retention, and preparation;

(E) issues that are of critical interest to State educational agencies and local educational agencies, other agency personnel, parents of children with disabilities, and individuals with disabilities;

(F) educational reform and systemic change within States; and

(G) promoting schools that are safe and conducive to learning.

(3) Linking States to information sources—In carrying out this subsection, the Secretary may support projects that link States to technical assistance resources, including special education and general education resources, and may make research and related products available through libraries, electronic networks, parent training projects, and other information sources.

(e) Applications

An eligible entity that wishes to receive a grant, or enter into a contract or cooperative agreement, under this section shall submit an application to the Secretary at such time, in such manner, and containing such information as the Secretary may require.

§ 1486. Authorization of appropriations

There are authorized to be appropriated to carry out sections 1481 through 1485 of this title such sums as may be necessary for each of the fiscal years 1998 through 2002.

§ 1487. Technology development, demonstration, and utilization; and media services

(a) In general

The Secretary shall competitively make grants to, and enter into contracts and cooperative agreements with, eligible entities to support activities described in subsections (b) and (c) of this section.

(b) Technology development, demonstration, and utilization; authorized activities

(1) In general—In carrying out this section, the Secretary shall support activities to promote the development, demonstration, and utilization of technology.

(2) Authorized activities—Activities that may be carried out under this subsection include activities such as the following:

(A) Conducting research and development activities on the use of innovative and emerging technologies for children with disabilities.

(B) Promoting the demonstration and use of innovative and emerging technologies for children with disabilities by improving and expanding the transfer of technology from research and development to practice.

(C) Providing technical assistance to recipients of other assistance under this section, concerning the development of accessible, effective, and usable products.

(D) Communicating information on available technology and the uses of such technology to assist children with disabilities.

(E) Supporting the implementation of research programs on captioning or video description.

(F) Supporting research, development, and dissemination of technology with universal-design features, so that the technology is accessible to individuals with disabilities without further modification or adaptation.

(G) Demonstrating the use of publicly-funded telecommunications systems to provide parents and teachers with information and training concerning early diagnosis of, intervention for, and effective teaching strategies for, young children with reading disabilities.

(c) Educational media services; authorized activities

In carrying out this section, the Secretary shall support—

(1) educational media activities that are designed to be of educational value to children with disabilities;

(2) providing video description, open captioning, or closed captioning of television programs, videos, or educational materials through September 30, 2001; and after fiscal year 2001, providing video description, open captioning, or closed captioning of educational, news, and informational television, videos, or materials;

(3) distributing captioned and described videos or educational materials through such mechanisms as a loan service;

(4) providing free educational materials, including textbooks, in accessible media for visually impaired and print-disabled students in elementary, secondary, postsecondary, and graduate schools;

(5) providing cultural experiences through appropriate nonprofit organizations, such as the National Theater of the Deaf, that—

(A) enrich the lives of deaf and hard-of-hearing children and adults;

(B) increase public awareness and understanding of deafness and of the artistic and intellectual achievements of deaf and hard-of-hearing persons; or

(C) promote the integration of hearing, deaf, and hard-of-hearing persons through shared cultural, educational, and social experiences; and

(6) compiling and analyzing appropriate data relating to the activities described in paragraphs (1) through (5).

(d) Applications

Any eligible entity that wishes to receive a grant, or enter into a contract or cooperative agreement, under this section shall submit an application to the Secretary at such time, in such manner, and containing such information as the Secretary may require.

(e) Authorization of appropriations

There are authorized to be appropriated to carry out this section such sums as may be necessary for each of the fiscal years 1998 through 2002.

TITLE II—MISCELLANEOUS PROVISIONS

§ 201. Effective dates

(a) Parts A and B

(1) IN GENERAL—Except as provided in paragraph (2), parts A and B of the Individuals with Disabilities Education Act, as amended by title I, shall take effect upon the enactment of this Act.

(2) EXCEPTIONS—

(A) IN GENERAL—Sections 612(a)(4), 612(a)(14), 612 (a)(16), 614(d) (except for paragraph (6)), and 618 of the Individuals with Disabilities Education Act, as amended by title I, shall take effect on July 1, 1998.

(B) SECTION 617—Section 617 of the Individuals with Disabilities Education

Act, as amended by title I, shall take effect on October 1, 1997.

(C) INDIVIDUALIZED EDUCATION PROGRAMS AND COMPREHENSIVE SYSTEM OF PERSONNEL DEVELOPMENT—Section 618 of the Individuals with Disabilities Education Act, as in effect on the day before the date of the enactment of this Act, and the provisions of parts A and B of the Individuals with Disabilities Education Act relating to individualized education programs and the State's comprehensive system of personnel development, as so in effect, shall remain in effect until July 1, 1998.

(D) SECTIONS 611 AND 619—Sections 611 and 619, as amended by title I, shall take effect beginning with funds appropriated for fiscal year 1998.

(b) Part C

Part C of the Individuals with Disabilities Education Act, as amended by title I, shall take effect on July 1, 1998.

(c) Part D

(1) IN GENERAL—Except as provided in paragraph (2), part D of the Individuals with Disabilities Education Act, as amended by title I, shall take effect on October 1, 1997.

(2) EXCEPTION—Paragraphs (1) and (2) of section 661(g) of the Individuals with Disabilities Education Act, as amended by title I, shall take effect on January 1, 1998.

§ 202. Transition

Notwithstanding any other provision of law, beginning on October 1, 1997, the Secretary of Education may use funds appropriated under part D of the Individuals with Disabilities Education Act to make continuation awards for projects that were funded under section 618 and parts C through G of such Act (as in effect on September 30, 1997).

§ 203. Repealers

(a) Part I

Effective October 1, 1998, part I of the Individuals with Disabilities Education Act is hereby repealed.

(b) Part H

Effective July 1, 1998, part H of such Act is hereby repealed.

(c) Parts C, E, F and G

Effective October 1, 1997, parts C, E, F, and G of such Act are hereby repealed.

APPENDIX B

Federal Regulations Implementing The 1997 IDEA Amendments

[The most important federal regulations affecting the education of children with disabilities, Parts 300 and 104 of Title 34 of the Code of Federal Regulations, as well as sections 76.532 and 76.654, have been reproduced here in their entirety as promulgated by the U.S. Department of Education.]

PART 300—ASSISTANCE TO STATES FOR THE EDUCATION OF CHILDREN WITH DISABILITIES

Subpart A—General

Purposes, Applicability, and Regulations That Apply to This Program

Sec.
300.1 Purposes.
300.2 Applicability of this part to State, local, and private agencies.

Definitions Used in This Part

300.3 Regulations that apply.
300.4 Act.
300.5 Assistive technology device.
300.6 Assistive technology service.
300.7 Child with a disability.
300.8 Consent.
300.9 Day; business day; school day.
300.10 Educational service agency.
300.11 Equipment.
300.12 Evaluation.
300.13 Free appropriate public education.
300.14 Include.
300.15 Individualized education program.
300.16 Individualized education program team.
300.17 Individualized family service plan.
300.18 Local educational agency.
300.19 Native language.
300.20 Parent.
300.21 Personally identifiable.
300.22 Public agency.
300.23 Qualified personnel.
300.24 Related services.
300.25 Secondary school.
300.26 Special education.
300.27 State.
300.28 Supplementary aids and services.
300.29 Transition services.
300.30 Definitions in EDGAR.

Subpart B—State and Local Eligibility

State Eligibility—General

300.110 Condition of assistance.
300.111 Exception for prior State policies

State Eligibility—Specific Conditions

LEA and State Agency Eligibility—General

LEA and State Agency Eligibility—Specific Conditions

School-Based Improvement Plan

Secretary of the Interior—Eligibility

300.577 Department use of personally identifiable information.

Department Procedures

300.580 Determination by the Secretary that a State is eligible.
300.581 Notice and hearing before determining that a State is not eligible.
300.582 Hearing official or panel.
300.583 Hearing procedures.
300.584 Initial decision; final decision.
300.585 Filing requirements.
300.586 Judicial review.
300.587 Enforcement.
300.588 [Reserved]
300.589 Waiver of requirement regarding supplementing and not supplanting with Part B funds.

Subpart F—State Administration

General

300.600 Responsibility for all educational programs.
300.601 Relation of Part B to other Federal programs.
300.602 State-level activities.

Use of Funds

300.620 Use of funds for State administration.
300.621 Allowable costs.
300.622 Subgrants to LEAs for capacity-building and improvement.
300.623 Amount required for subgrants to LEAs.
300.624 State discretion in awarding subgrants.

State Advisory Panel

300.650 Establishment of advisory panels.
300.651 Membership.
300.652 Advisory panel functions.
300.653 Advisory panel procedures.

State Complaint Procedures

300.660 Adoption of State complaint procedures.
300.661 Minimum State complaint procedures.
300.662 Filing a complaint.

Subpart G—Allocation of Funds; Reports

Allocations

300.700 Special definition of the term "State."
300.701 Grants to States.
300.702 Definition.
300.703 Allocations to States.
300.704—300.705 [Reserved]
300.706 Permanent formula.
300.707 Increase in funds.
300.708 Limitation.
300.709 Decrease in funds.
300.710 Allocation for State in which by-pass is implemented for private school children with disabilities.
300.711 Subgrants to LEAs.
300.712 Allocations to LEAs.
300.713 Former Chapter 1 State agencies.
300.714 Reallocation of LEA funds.
300.715 Payments to the Secretary of the Interior for the education of Indian children.
300.716 Payments for education and services for Indian children with disabilities aged 3 through 5.
300.717 Outlying areas and freely associated States.
300.718 Outlying area—definition.
300.719 Limitation for freely associated States.
300.720 Special rule.
300.721 [Reserved]
300.722 Definition.

Reports

300.750 Annual report of children served report requirement.
300.751 Annual report of children served information required in the report.
300.752 Annual report of children served certification.
300.753 Annual report of children served criteria for counting children.
300.754 Annual report of children served other responsibilities of the SEA.
300.755 Disproportionality.
300.756 Acquisition of equipment; construction or alteration of facilities.

Appendix A to Part 300—
Notice of Interpretation

Appendix B to Part 300—
Index for IDEA—Part B Regulations

Authority: 20 U.S.C. 1411–1420, unless otherwise noted.

Subpart A—General

Purposes, Applicability, and Regulations That Apply to This Program

§ 300.1 Purposes.

The purposes of this part are—

(a) To ensure that all children with disabilities have available to them a free appropriate public education that emphasizes special education and related services designed to meet their unique needs and prepare them for employment and independent living;

(b) To ensure that the rights of children with disabilities and their parents are protected;

(c) To assist States, localities, educational service agencies, and Federal agencies to provide for the education of all children with disabilities; and

(d) To assess and ensure the effectiveness of efforts to educate children with disabilities.

(Authority: 20 U.S.C. 1400 note)

§ 300.2 Applicability of this part to State, local, and private agencies.

(a) *States.* This part applies to each State that receives payments under Part B of the Act.

(b) *Public agencies within the State.* The provisions of this part—

(1) Apply to all political subdivisions of the State that are involved in the education of children with disabilities, including—

(i) The State educational agency (SEA);

(ii) Local educational agencies (LEAs), educational service agencies (ESAs), and public charter schools that are not otherwise included as LEAs or ESAs and are not a school of an LEA or ESA;

(iii) Other State agencies and schools (such as Departments of Mental Health and Welfare and State schools for children with deafness or children with blindness); and

(iv) State and local juvenile and adult correctional facilities; and

(2) Are binding on each public agency in the State that provides special education and related services to children with disabilities, regardless of whether that agency is receiving funds under Part B.

(c) *Private schools and facilities.* Each public agency in the State is responsible for ensuring that the rights and protections under Part B of the Act are given to children with disabilities—

(1) Referred to or placed in private schools and facilities by that public agency; or

(2) Placed in private schools by their parents under the provisions of § 300.403(c).

(Authority: 20 U.S.C. 1412)

§ 300.3 Regulations that apply.

The following regulations apply to this program:

(a) 34 CFR part 76 (State-Administered Programs) except for §§ 76.125–76.137 and 76.650–76.662.

(b) 34 CFR part 77 (Definitions).

(c) 34 CFR part 79 (Intergovernmental Review of Department of Education Programs and Activities).

(d) 34 CFR part 80 (Uniform Administrative Requirements for Grants and Cooperative Agreements to State and Local Governments).

(e) 34 CFR part 81 (General Education Provisions Act—Enforcement).

(f) 34 CFR part 82 (New Restrictions on Lobbying).

(g) 34 CFR part 85 (Government-wide Debarment and Suspension (Nonprocurement) and Government-wide Requirements for Drug-Free Workplace (Grants)).

(h) The regulations in this part—34 CFR part 300 (Assistance for Education of Children with Disabilities).

(Authority: 20 U.S.C. 1221e-3(a)(1))

Definitions Used in This Part

§ 300.4 Act.

As used in this part, *Act* means the Individuals with Disabilities Education Act (IDEA), as amended.

(Authority: 20 U.S.C. 1400(a))

§ 300.5 Assistive technology device.

As used in this part, *Assistive technology device* means any item, piece of equipment, or product system, whether acquired commercially off the shelf, modified, or customized, that is used to increase, maintain, or improve the functional capabilities of a child with a disability.

(Authority: 20 U.S.C. 1401(1))

§ 300.6 Assistive technology service.

As used in this part, *Assistive technology service* means any service that directly assists a child with a disability in the selection, acquisition, or use of an assistive technology device. The term includes—

(a) The evaluation of the needs of a child with a disability, including a functional evaluation of the child in the child's customary environment;

(b) Purchasing, leasing, or otherwise providing for the acquisition of assistive technology devices by children with disabilities;

(c) Selecting, designing, fitting, customizing, adapting, applying, maintaining, repairing, or replacing assistive technology devices;

(d) Coordinating and using other therapies, interventions, or services with assistive technology devices, such as those associated with existing education and rehabilitation plans and programs;

(e) Training or technical assistance for a child with a disability or, if appropriate, that child's family; and

(f) Training or technical assistance for professionals (including individuals providing education or rehabilitation services), employers, or other individuals who provide services to, employ, or are otherwise substantially involved in the major life functions of that child.

(Authority: 20 U.S.C. 1401(2))

§ 300.7 Child with a disability.

(a) *General.* (1) As used in this part, the term *child with a disability* means a child evaluated in accordance with §§ 300.530–300.536 as having mental retardation, a hearing impairment including deafness, a speech or language impairment, a visual impairment including blindness, serious emotional disturbance (hereafter referred to as emotional disturbance), an orthopedic impairment, autism, traumatic brain injury, an other health impairment, a specific learning disability, deaf-blindness, or multiple disabilities, and who, by reason thereof, needs special education and related services.

(2)(i) Subject to paragraph (a)(2)(ii) of this section, if it is determined, through an appropriate evaluation under §§ 300.530–300.536, that a child has one of the disabilities identified in paragraph (a)(1) of this section, but only needs a related service and not special education, the child is not a *child with a disability* under this part.

(ii) If, consistent with § 300.26(a)(2), the related service required by the child is considered special education rather than a related service under State standards, the child would be determined to be a *child with a disability* under paragraph (a)(1) of this section.

(b) *Children aged 3 through 9 experiencing developmental delays.* The term *child with a disability* for children aged 3 through 9 may, at the discretion of the State and LEA and in accordance with § 300.313, include a child—

(1) Who is experiencing developmental delays, as defined by the State and as measured by appropriate diagnostic instruments and procedures, in one or more of the following areas: physical development, cognitive development, communication development, social or emotional development, or adaptive development; and

(2) Who, by reason thereof, needs special education and related services.

(c) *Definitions of disability terms.* The terms used in this definition are defined as follows:

(1)(i) *Autism* means a developmental disability significantly affecting verbal and nonverbal communication and social interaction, generally evident before age 3, that adversely affects a child's educational performance. Other characteristics often associated with autism are engagement in repetitive activities and stereotyped movements, resistance to environmental change or change in daily routines, and unusual responses to sensory experiences. The term does not apply if a child's educational performance is adversely affected primarily because the child has an emotional disturbance, as defined in paragraph (b)(4) of this section.

(ii) A child who manifests the characteristics of "autism" after age 3 could be diagnosed as having "autism" if the criteria in paragraph (c)(1)(i) of this section are satisfied.

(2) *Deaf-blindness* means concomitant hearing and visual impairments, the combination of which causes such severe communication and other developmental and educational needs that they cannot be accommodated in special education programs solely for children with deafness or children with blindness.

(3) *Deafness* means a hearing impairment that is so severe that the child is impaired in processing linguistic information through hearing, with or without amplification, that adversely affects a child's educational performance.

(4) *Emotional disturbance* is defined as follows:

(i) The term means a condition exhibiting one or more of the following characteristics over a long period of time and to a marked degree that adversely affects a child's educational performance:

(A) An inability to learn that cannot be explained by intellectual, sensory, or health factors.

(B) An inability to build or maintain satisfactory interpersonal relationships with peers and teachers.

(C) Inappropriate types of behavior or feelings under normal circumstances.

(D) A general pervasive mood of unhappiness or depression.

(E) A tendency to develop physical symptoms or fears associated with personal or school problems.

(ii) The term includes schizophrenia. The term does not apply to children who are socially maladjusted, unless it is determined that they have an emotional disturbance.

(5) *Hearing impairment* means an impairment in hearing, whether permanent or fluctuating, that adversely affects a child's educational performance but that is not included under the definition of deafness in this section.

(6) *Mental retardation* means significantly subaverage general intellectual functioning, existing concurrently with deficits in adaptive behavior

and manifested during the developmental period, that adversely affects a child's educational performance.

(7) *Multiple disabilities* means concomitant impairments (such as mental retardation-blindness, mental retardation-orthopedic impairment, etc.), the combination of which causes such severe educational needs that they cannot be accommodated in special education programs solely for one of the impairments. The term does not include deaf-blindness.

(8) *Orthopedic impairment* means a severe orthopedic impairment that adversely affects a child's educational performance. The term includes impairments caused by congenital anomaly (e.g., clubfoot, absence of some member, etc.), impairments caused by disease (e.g., poliomyelitis, bone tuberculosis, etc.), and impairments from other causes (e.g., cerebral palsy, amputations, and fractures or burns that cause contractures).

(9) *Other health impairment* means having limited strength, vitality or alertness, including a heightened alertness to environmental stimuli, that results in limited alertness with respect to the educational environment, that—

(i) Is due to chronic or acute health problems such as asthma, attention deficit disorder or attention deficit hyperactivity disorder, diabetes, epilepsy, a heart condition, hemophilia, lead poisoning, leukemia, nephritis, rheumatic fever, and sickle cell anemia; and

(ii) Adversely affects a child's educational performance.

(10) *Specific learning disability* is defined as follows:

(i) *General.* The term means a disorder in one or more of the basic psychological processes involved in understanding or in using language, spoken or written, that may manifest itself in an imperfect ability to listen, think, speak, read, write, spell, or to do mathematical calculations, including conditions such as perceptual disabilities, brain injury, minimal brain dysfunction, dyslexia, and developmental aphasia.

(ii) *Disorders not included.* The term does not include learning problems that are primarily the result of visual, hearing, or motor disabilities, of mental retardation, of emotional disturbance, or of environmental, cultural, or economic disadvantage.

(11) *Speech or language impairment* means a communication disorder, such as stuttering, impaired articulation, a language impairment, or a voice impairment, that adversely affects a child's educational performance.

(12) *Traumatic brain injury* means an acquired injury to the brain caused by an external physical force, resulting in total or partial functional disability or psychosocial impairment, or both, that adversely affects a child's educational performance. The term applies to open or closed head injuries resulting in impairments in one or more areas, such as cognition; language; memory; attention; reasoning; abstract thinking; judgment; problem-solving; sensory, perceptual, and motor abilities; psychosocial behavior; physical functions; information processing; and speech. The term does not apply to brain injuries that are congenital or degenerative, or to brain injuries induced by birth trauma.

(13) *Visual impairment including blindness* means an impairment in vision that, even with correction, adversely affects a child's educational performance. The term includes both partial sight and blindness.

(Authority: 20 U.S.C. 1401(3)(A) and (B); 1401(26))

§ 300.8 Consent.

As used in this part, the term *consent* has the meaning given that term in § 300.500(b)(1).

(Authority: 20 U.S.C. 1415(a))

§ 300.9 Day; business day; school day.

As used in this part, the term—

(a) *Day* means calendar day unless otherwise indicated as business day or school day;

(b) *Business day* means Monday through Friday, except for Federal and State holidays (unless holidays are specifically included in the designation of business day, as in § 300.403(d)(1)(ii)); and

(c)(1) *School day* means any day, including a partial day, that children are in attendance at school for instructional purposes.

(2) The term *school day* has the same meaning for all children in school, including children with and without disabilities.

(Authority: 20 U.S.C. 1221e-3)

§ 300.10 Educational service agency.

As used in this part, the term *educational service agency*—

(a) Means a regional public multiservice agency—

(1) Authorized by State law to develop, manage, and provide services or programs to LEAs; and

(2) Recognized as an administrative agency for purposes of the provision of special education and related services provided within public elementary and secondary schools of the State;

(b) Includes any other public institution or agency having administrative control and direction over a public elementary or secondary school; and

(c) Includes entities that meet the definition of *intermediate educational unit* in section 602(23) of IDEA as in effect prior to June 4, 1997.

(Authority: 20 U.S.C. 1401(4))

§ 300.11 Equipment.

As used in this part, the term *equipment* means—

(a) Machinery, utilities, and built-in equipment and any necessary enclosures or structures to house the machinery, utilities, or equipment; and

(b) All other items necessary for the functioning of a particular facility as a facility for the provision of educational services, including items such as instructional equipment and necessary furniture; printed, published and audio-visual instructional materials; telecommunications, sensory, and other technological aids and devices; and books, periodicals, documents, and other related materials.

(Authority: 20 U.S.C. 1401(6))

§ 300.12 Evaluation.

As used in this part, the term *evaluation* has the meaning given that term in § 300.500(b)(2).

(Authority: 20 U.S.C. 1415(a))

§ 300.13 Free appropriate public education.

As used in this part, the term *free appropriate public education* or *FAPE* means special education and related services that—

(a) Are provided at public expense, under public supervision and direction, and without charge;

(b) Meet the standards of the SEA, including the requirements of this part;

(c) Include preschool, elementary school, or secondary school education in the State; and

(d) Are provided in conformity with an individualized education program (IEP) that meets the requirements of §§ 300.340-300.350.

(Authority: 20 U.S.C. 1401(8))

§ 300.14 Include.

As used in this part, the term *include* means that the items named are not all of the possible items that are covered, whether like or unlike the ones named.

(Authority: 20 U.S.C. 1221e-3)

§ 300.15 Individualized education program.

As used in this part, the term *individualized education program* or *IEP* has the meaning given the term in § 300.340(a).

(Authority: 20 U.S.C. 1401(11))

§ 300.16 Individualized education program team.

As used in this part, the term *individualized education program team* or *IEP team* means a group of individuals described in § 300.344 that is responsible for developing, reviewing, or revising an IEP for a child with a disability.

(Authority: 20 U.S.C. 1221e-3)

§ 300.17 Individualized family service plan.

As used in this part, the term *individualized family service plan* or *IFSP* has the meaning given the term in 34 CFR 303.340(b).

(Authority: 20 U.S.C. 1401(12))

§ 300.18 Local educational agency.

(a) As used in this part, the term *local educational agency* means a public board of education or other public authority legally constituted within a State for either administrative control or direction of, or to perform a service function for, public elementary or secondary schools in a city, county, township, school district, or other political subdivision of a State, or for a combination of school districts or counties as are recognized in a State as an administrative agency for its public elementary or secondary schools.

(b) The term includes—

(1) An educational service agency, as defined in § 300.10;

(2) Any other public institution or agency having administrative control and direction of a public elementary or secondary school, including a public charter school that is established as an LEA under State law; and

(3) An elementary or secondary school funded by the Bureau of Indian Affairs, and not subject to the jurisdiction of any SEA other than the Bureau of Indian Affairs, but only to the extent that the inclusion makes the school eligible for programs for which specific eligibility is not provided to the school in another provision of law and the school does not have a student population that is smaller than the student population of the LEA receiving assistance under this Act with the smallest student population.

(Authority: 20 U.S.C. 1401(15))

§ 300.19 Native language.

(a) As used in this part, the term *native language*, if used with reference to an individual of limited English proficiency, means the following:

(1) The language normally used by that individual, or, in the case of a child, the language normally used by the parents of the child, except as provided in paragraph (a)(2) of this section.

(2) In all direct contact with a child (including evaluation of the child), the language normally used by the child in the home or learning environment.

(b) For an individual with deafness or blindness, or for an individual with no written language, the mode of communication is that normally used by the individual (such as sign language, braille, or oral communication).

(Authority: 20 U.S.C. 1401(16))

§ 300.20 Parent.

(a) *General.* As used in this part, the term parent means—

(1) A natural or adoptive parent of a child;

(2) A guardian but not the State if the child is a ward of the State;

(3) A person acting in the place of a parent (such as a grandparent or stepparent with whom the child lives, or a person who is legally responsible for the child's welfare); or

(4) A surrogate parent who has been appointed in accordance with § 300.515.

(b) *Foster parent.* Unless State law prohibits a foster parent from acting as a parent, a State may allow a foster parent to act as a parent under Part B of the Act if—

(1) The natural parents' authority to make educational decisions on the child's behalf has been extinguished under State law; and

(2) The foster parent—

(i) Has an ongoing, long-term parental relationship with the child;

(ii) Is willing to make the educational decisions required of parents under the Act; and

(iii) Has no interest that would conflict with the interests of the child.

(Authority: 20 U.S.C. 1401(19))

§ 300.21 Personally identifiable

As used in this part, the term *personally identifiable* has the meaning given that term in § 300.500(b)(3).

(Authority: 20 U.S.C. 1415(a))

§ 300.22 Public agency.

As used in this part, the term *public agency* includes the SEA, LEAs, ESAs, public charter schools that are not otherwise included as LEAs or ESAs and are not a school of an LEA or ESA, and any other political subdivisions of the State that are responsible for providing education to children with disabilities.

(Authority: 20 U.S.C. 1412(a)(1)(A), (a)(11))

§ 300.23 Qualified personnel.

As used in this part, the term *qualified personnel* means personnel who have met SEA-approved or SEA-recognized certification, licensing, registration, or other comparable requirements that apply to the area in which the individuals are providing special education or related services.

(Authority: 20 U.S.C. 1221e-3)

§ 300.24 Related services.

(a) *General.* As used in this part, the term *related services* means transportation and such developmental, corrective, and other supportive services as are required to assist a child with a disability to benefit from special education, and includes speech-language pathology and audiology services, psychological services, physical and occupational therapy, recreation, including therapeutic recreation, early identification and assessment of disabilities in children, counseling services, including rehabilitation counseling, orientation and mobility services, and medical services for diagnostic or evaluation purposes. The term also includes school health services, social work services in schools, and parent counseling and training.

(b) *Individual terms defined.* The terms used in this definition are defined as follows:

(1) *Audiology* includes—

(i) Identification of children with hearing loss;

(ii) Determination of the range, nature, and degree of hearing loss, including referral for medical or other professional attention for the habilitation of hearing;

(iii) Provision of habilitative activities, such as language habilitation, auditory training, speech reading (lip-reading), hearing evaluation, and speech conservation;

(iv) Creation and administration of programs for prevention of hearing loss;

(v) Counseling and guidance of children, parents, and teachers regarding hearing loss; and

(vi) Determination of children's needs for group and individual amplification, selecting and fitting an appropriate aid, and evaluating the effectiveness of amplification.

(2) *Counseling services* means services provided by qualified social workers, psychologists, guidance counselors, or other qualified personnel.

(3) *Early identification and assessment of disabilities in children* means the implementation of a formal plan for identifying a disability as early as possible in a child's life.

(4) *Medical services* means services provided by a licensed physician to determine a child's medically related disability that results in the child's need for special education and related services.

(5) *Occupational therapy*—

(i) Means services provided by a qualified occupational therapist; and

(ii) Includes—

(A) Improving, developing or restoring functions impaired or lost through illness, injury, or deprivation;

(B) Improving ability to perform tasks for independent functioning if functions are impaired or lost; and

(C) Preventing, through early intervention, initial or further impairment or loss of function.

(6) *Orientation and mobility services*—

(i) Means services provided to blind or visually impaired students by qualified personnel to enable those students to attain systematic orientation to and safe movement within their environments in school, home, and community; and

(ii) Includes teaching students the following, as appropriate:

(A) Spatial and environmental concepts and use of information received by the senses (such as sound, temperature and vibrations) to establish, maintain, or regain orientation and line of travel (e.g., using sound at a traffic light to cross the street);

(B) To use the long cane to supplement visual travel skills or as a tool for safely negotiating the environment for students with no available travel vision;

(C) To understand and use remaining vision and distance low vision aids; and

(D) Other concepts, techniques, and tools.

(7) *Parent counseling and training* means—

(i) Assisting parents in understanding the special needs of their child;

(ii) Providing parents with information about child development; and

(iii) Helping parents to acquire the necessary skills that will allow them to support the implementation of their child's IEP or IFSP.

(8) *Physical therapy* means services provided by a qualified physical therapist.

(9) *Psychological services* includes—

(i) Administering psychological and educational tests, and other assessment procedures;

(ii) Interpreting assessment results;

(iii) Obtaining, integrating, and interpreting information about child behavior and conditions relating to learning;

(iv) Consulting with other staff members in planning school programs to meet the special needs of children as indicated by psychological tests, interviews, and behavioral evaluations;

(v) Planning and managing a program of psychological services, including psychological counseling for children and parents; and

(vi) Assisting in developing positive behavioral intervention strategies.

(10) *Recreation* includes—

(i) Assessment of leisure function;

(ii) Therapeutic recreation services;

(iii) Recreation programs in schools and community agencies; and

(iv) Leisure education.

(11) *Rehabilitation counseling services* means services provided by qualified personnel in individual or group sessions that focus specifically on career development, employment preparation, achieving independence, and integration in the workplace and community of a student with a disability. The term also includes vocational rehabilitation services provided to a student with disabilities by vocational rehabilitation programs funded under the Rehabilitation Act of 1973, as amended.

(12) *School health services* means services provided by a qualified school nurse or other qualified person.

(13) *Social work services in schools* includes—

(i) Preparing a social or developmental history on a child with a disability;

(ii) Group and individual counseling with the child and family;

(iii) Working in partnership with parents and others on those problems in a child's living situation (home, school, and community) that affect the child's adjustment in school;

(iv) Mobilizing school and community resources to enable the child to learn as effectively as possible in his or her educational program; and

(v) Assisting in developing positive behavioral intervention strategies.

(14) *Speech-language pathology services* includes—

(i) Identification of children with speech or language impairments;

(ii) Diagnosis and appraisal of specific speech or language impairments;

(iii) Referral for medical or other professional attention necessary for the habilitation of speech or language impairments;

(iv) Provision of speech and language services for the habilitation or prevention of communicative impairments; and

(v) Counseling and guidance of parents, children, and teachers regarding speech and language impairments.

(15) *Transportation* includes—

(i) Travel to and from school and between schools;

(ii) Travel in and around school buildings; and

(iii) Specialized equipment (such as special or adapted buses, lifts, and ramps), if required to provide special transportation for a child with a disability.

(Authority: 20 U.S.C. 1401(22))

§ 300.25 Secondary school.

As used in this part, the term *secondary school* means a nonprofit institutional day or residential school that provides secondary education, as determined under State law, except that it does not include any education beyond grade 12.

(Authority: 20 U.S.C. 1401(23))

§ 300.26 Special education.

(a) *General.* (1) As used in this part, the term *special education* means specially designed instruction, at no cost to the parents, to meet the unique needs of a child with a disability, including—

(i) Instruction conducted in the classroom, in the home, in hospitals and institutions, and in other settings; and

(ii) Instruction in physical education.

(2) The term includes each of the following, if it meets the requirements of paragraph (a)(1) of this section:

(i) Speech-language pathology services, or any other related service, if the service is considered special education rather than a related service under State standards;

(ii) Travel training; and

(iii) Vocational education.

(b) *Individual terms defined.* The terms in this definition are defined as follows:

(1) *At no cost* means that all specially-designed instruction is provided without charge, but does not preclude incidental fees that are normally charged to nondisabled students or their parents as a part of the regular education program.

(2) *Physical education*—

(i) Means the development of—

(A) Physical and motor fitness;

(B) Fundamental motor skills and patterns; and

(C) Skills in aquatics, dance, and individual and group games and sports (including intramural and lifetime sports); and

(ii) Includes special physical education, adapted physical education, movement education, and motor development.

(3) *Specially-designed instruction* means adapting, as appropriate to the needs of an eligible child under this part, the content, methodology, or delivery of instruction—

(i) To address the unique needs of the child that result from the child's disability; and

(ii) To ensure access of the child to the general curriculum, so that he or she can meet the educational standards within the jurisdiction of the public agency that apply to all children.

(4) *Travel training* means providing instruction, as appropriate, to children with significant cognitive disabilities, and any other children with disabilities who require this instruction, to enable them to—

(i) Develop an awareness of the environment in which they live; and

(ii) Learn the skills necessary to move effectively and safely from place to place within that environment (e.g., in school, in the home, at work, and in the community).

(5) *Vocational education* means organized educational programs that are directly related to the preparation of individuals for paid or unpaid employment, or for additional preparation for a career requiring other than a baccalaureate or advanced degree.

(Authority: 20 U.S.C. 1401(25))

§ 300.27 State.

As used in this part, the term *State* means each of the 50 States, the District of Columbia, the Commonwealth of Puerto Rico, and each of the outlying areas.

(Authority: 20 U.S.C. 1401(27))

§ 300.28 Supplementary aids and services.

As used in this part, the term *supplementary aids and services* means, aids, services, and other supports that are provided in regular education classes or other education-related settings to enable children with disabilities to be educated with nondisabled children to the maximum extent appropriate in accordance with §§ 300.550-300.556.

(Authority: 20 U.S.C. 1401(29))

§ 300.29 Transition services.

(a) As used in this part, *transition services* means a coordinated set of activities for a student with a disability that—

(1) Is designed within an outcome-oriented process, that promotes movement from school to post-school activities, including postsecondary education, vocational training, integrated employment (including supported employment), continuing and adult education, adult services, independent living, or community participation;

(2) Is based on the individual student's needs, taking into account the student's preferences and interests; and

(3) Includes—

(i) Instruction;

(ii) Related services;

(iii) Community experiences;

(iv) The development of employment and other post-school adult living objectives; and

(v) If appropriate, acquisition of daily living skills and functional vocational evaluation.

(b) Transition services for students with disabilities may be special education, if provided as specially designed instruction, or related services, if required to assist a student with a disability to benefit from special education.

(Authority: 20 U.S.C. 1401(30))

§ 300.30 Definitions in EDGAR.

The following terms used in this part are defined in 34 CFR 77.1:

Application
Award
Contract
Department
EDGAR
Elementary school
Fiscal year
Grant
Nonprofit
Project
Secretary
Subgrant
State educational agency

(Authority: 20 U.S.C. 1221e-3(a)(1))

Subpart B—State and Local Eligibility

State Eligibility—General

§ 300.110 Condition of assistance.

(a) A State is eligible for assistance under Part B of the Act for a fiscal year if the State demonstrates to the satisfaction of the Secretary that the State has in effect policies and procedures to ensure that it meets the conditions in §§ 300.121–300.156.

(b) To meet the requirement of paragraph (a) of this section, the State must have on file with the Secretary—

(1) The information specified in §§ 300.121–300.156 that the State uses to implement the requirements of this part; and

(2) Copies of all applicable State statutes, regulations, and other State documents that show the basis of that information.

(Authority: 20 U.S.C. 1412(a))

§ 300.111 Exception for prior State policies and procedures on file with the Secretary.

If a State has on file with the Secretary policies and procedures approved by the Secretary that demonstrate that the State meets any requirement of § 300.110, including any policies and procedures filed under Part B of the Act as in effect before June 4, 1997, the Secretary considers the State to have met the requirement for purposes of receiving a grant under Part B of the Act.

(Authority: 20 U.S.C. 1412(c)(1))

§ 300.112 Amendments to State policies and procedures.

(a) *Modifications made by a State.* (1) Subject to paragraph (b) of this section, policies and procedures submitted by a State in accordance with this subpart remain in effect until the State submits to the Secretary the modifications that the State decides are necessary.

(2) The provisions of this subpart apply to a modification to a State's policies and procedures in the same manner and to the same extent that they apply to the State's original policies and procedures.

(b) *Modifications required by the Secretary.* The Secretary may require a State to modify its policies and procedures, but only to the extent necessary to ensure the State's compliance with this part, if—

(1) After June 4, 1997, the provisions of the Act or the regulations in this part are amended;

(2) There is a new interpretation of this Act or regulations by a Federal court or a State's highest court; or

(3) There is an official finding of noncompliance with Federal law or regulations.

(Authority: 20 U.S.C. 1412(c)(2) and (3))

§ 300.113 Approval by the Secretary.

(a) *General.* If the Secretary determines that a State is eligible to receive a grant under Part B of the Act, the Secretary notifies the State of that determination.

(b) *Notice and hearing before determining a State is not eligible.* The Secretary does not make a final determination that a State is not eligible to receive a grant under Part B of the Act until after providing the State reasonable notice and an opportunity for a hearing in accordance with the procedures in §§ 300.581–300.586.

(Authority: 20 U.S.C. 1412(d))

§§ 300.114—300.120 [Reserved]

State Eligibility—Specific Conditions

§ 300.121 Free appropriate public education (FAPE).

(a) *General.* Each State must have on file with the Secretary information that shows that, subject to § 300.122, the State has in effect a policy that ensures that all children with disabilities aged 3 through 21 residing in the State have the right to FAPE, including children with disabilities who have been suspended or expelled from school.

(b) *Required information.* The information described in paragraph (a) of this section must—

(1) Include a copy of each State statute, court order, State Attorney General opinion, and other State documents that show the source of the State's policy relating to FAPE; and

(2) Show that the policy—

(i)(A) Applies to all public agencies in the State; and

(B) Is consistent with the requirements of §§ 300.300–300.313; and

(ii) Applies to all children with disabilities, including children who have been suspended or expelled from school.

(c) *FAPE for children beginning at age 3.* (1) Each State shall ensure that—

(i) The obligation to make FAPE available to each eligible child residing in the State begins no later than the child's third birthday; and

(ii) An IEP or an IFSP is in effect for the child by that date, in accordance with § 300.342(c).

(2) If a child's third birthday occurs during the summer, the child's IEP team shall determine the date when services under the IEP or IFSP will begin.

(d) *FAPE for children suspended or expelled from school.* (1) A public agency need not provide services during periods of removal under § 300.520(a)(1) to a child with a disability who has been removed from his or her current placement for 10 school days or less in that school year, if services are not provided to a child without disabilities who has been similarly removed.

(2) In the case of a child with a disability who has been removed from his or her current placement for more than 10 school days in that school year, the public agency, for the remainder of the removals, must—

(i) Provide services to the extent necessary to enable the child to appropriately progress in the general curriculum and appropriately advance toward achieving the goals set out in the child's IEP, if the removal is—

(A) Under the school personnel's authority to remove for not more than 10 consecutive school days as long as that removal does not constitute a change of placement under § 300.519(b) (§ 300.520((a)(1)); or

(B) For behavior that is not a manifestation of the child's disability, consistent with § 300.524; and

(ii) Provide services consistent with § 300.522, regarding determination of the appropriate interim alternative educational setting, if the removal is—

(A) For drug or weapons offenses under § 300.520(a)(2); or

(B) Based on a hearing officer determination that maintaining the current placement of the child is substantially likely to result in injury to the child or to others if he or she remains in the current placement, consistent with § 300.521.

(3)(i) School personnel, in consultation with the child's special education teacher, determine the extent to which services are necessary to enable the child to appropriately progress in the general curriculum and appropriately advance toward achieving the goals set out in the child's IEP if the child is removed under the authority of school personnel to remove for not more than 10 consecutive school days as long as that removal does not constitute a change of placement under § 300.519 (§ 300.520(a)(1)).

(ii) The child's IEP team determines the extent to which services are necessary to enable the child to appropriately progress in the general curriculum and appropriately advance toward achieving the goals set out in the child's IEP if the child is removed because of behavior that has been determined not to be a manifestation of the child's disability, consistent with § 300.524.

(e) *Children advancing from grade to grade.* (1) Each State shall ensure that FAPE is available to any individual child with a disability who needs special education and related services, even though the child is advancing from grade to grade.

(2) The determination that a child described in paragraph (a)(1) of this section is eligible under this part, must be made on an individual basis by the group responsible within the child's LEA for making those determinations.

(Authority: 20 U.S.C. 1412(a)(1))

§ 300.122 Exception to FAPE for certain ages.

(a) *General.* The obligation to make FAPE available to all children with disabilities does not apply with respect to the following:

(1) Children aged 3, 4, 5, 18, 19, 20, or 21 in a State to the extent that its application to those children would be inconsistent with State law or practice, or the order of any court, respecting the provision of public education to children in one or more of those age groups.

(2)(i) Students aged 18 through 21 to the extent that State law does not require that special education and related services under Part B of the Act be provided to students with disabilities who, in the last educational placement prior to their incarceration in an adult correctional facility—

(A) Were not actually identified as being a child with a disability under § 300.7; and

(B) Did not have an IEP under Part B of the Act.

(ii) The exception in paragraph (a)(2)(i) of this section does not apply to students with disabilities, aged 18 through 21, who—

(A) Had been identified as a child with disability and had received services in accordance with an IEP, but who left school prior to their incarceration; or

(B) Did not have an IEP in their last educational setting, but who had actually been identified as a "child with a disability" under § 300.7.

(3)(i) Students with disabilities who have graduated from high school with a regular high school diploma.

(ii) The exception in paragraph (a)(3)(i) of this section does not apply to students who have graduated but have not been awarded a regular high school diploma.

(iii) Graduation from high school with a regular diploma constitutes a change in placement, requiring written prior notice in accordance with § 300.503.

(b) *Documents relating to exceptions.* The State must have on file with the Secretary—

(1)(i) Information that describes in detail the extent to which the exception in paragraph (a)(1) of this section applies to the State; and

(ii) A copy of each State law, court order, and other documents that provide a basis for the exception; and

(2) With respect to paragraph (a)(2) of this section, a copy of the State law that excludes from services under Part B of the Act certain students who are incarcerated in an adult correctional facility.

(Authority: 20 U.S.C. 1412(a)(1)(B))

§ 300.123 Full educational opportunity goal (FEOG).

The State must have on file with the Secretary detailed policies and procedures through which the State has established a goal of providing full educational opportunity to all children with disabilities aged birth through 21.

(Authority: 20 U.S.C. 1412(a)(2))

§ 300.124 FEOG—timetable.

The State must have on file with the Secretary a detailed timetable for accomplishing the goal of providing full educational opportunity for all children with disabilities.

(Authority: 20 U.S.C. 1412(a)(2))

§ 300.125 Child find.

(a) *General requirement.* (1) The State must have in effect policies and procedures to ensure that—

(i) All children with disabilities residing in the State, including children with disabilities attending private schools, regardless of the severity of their disability, and who are in need of special education and related services, are identified, located, and evaluated; and

(ii) A practical method is developed and implemented to determine which children are currently receiving needed special education and related services.

(2) The requirements of paragraph (a)(1) of this section apply to—

(i) Highly mobile children with disabilities (such as migrant and homeless children); and

(ii) Children who are suspected of being a child with a disability under § 300.7 and in need of special education, even though they are advancing from grade to grade.

(b) *Documents relating to child find.* The State must have on file with the Secretary the policies and procedures described in paragraph (a) of this section, including—

(1) The name of the State agency (if other than the SEA) responsible for coordinating the planning and implementation of the policies and procedures under paragraph (a) of this section;

(2) The name of each agency that participates in the planning and implementation of the child find activities and a description of the nature and extent of its participation;

(3) A description of how the policies and procedures under paragraph (a) of this section will be monitored to ensure that the SEA obtains—

(i) The number of children with disabilities within each disability category that have been identified, located, and evaluated; and

(ii) Information adequate to evaluate the effectiveness of those policies and procedures; and

(4) A description of the method the State uses to determine which children are currently receiving special education and related services.

(c) *Child find for children from birth through age 2 when the SEA and lead agency for the Part C program are different.* (1) In States where the SEA and the State's lead agency for the Part C program are different and the Part C lead agency will be participating in the child find activities described in paragraph (a) of this section, a description of the nature and extent of the Part C lead agency's participation must be included under paragraph (b)(2) of this section.

(2) With the SEA's agreement, the Part C lead agency's participation may include the actual implementation of child find activities for infants and toddlers with disabilities.

(3) The use of an interagency agreement or other mechanism for providing for the Part C lead

agency's participation does not alter or diminish the responsibility of the SEA to ensure compliance with the requirements of this section.

(d) *Construction*. Nothing in the Act requires that children be classified by their disability so long as each child who has a disability listed in § 300.7 and who, by reason of that disability, needs special education and related services is regarded as a child with a disability under Part B of the Act.

(e) *Confidentiality of child find data*. The collection and use of data to meet the requirements of this section are subject to the confidentiality requirements of §§ 300.560–300.577.

(Authority: 20 U.S.C. 1412 (a)(3)(A) and (B))

§ 300.126 Procedures for evaluation and determination of eligibility.

The State must have on file with the Secretary policies and procedures that ensure that the requirements of §§ 300.530–300.536 are met.

(Authority: 20 U.S.C. 1412(a)(6)(B), (7))

§ 300.127 Confidentiality of personally identifiable information.

(a) The State must have on file in detail the policies and procedures that the State has undertaken to ensure protection of the confidentiality of any personally identifiable information, collected, used, or maintained under Part B of the Act.

(b) The Secretary uses the criteria in §§ 300.560–300.576 to evaluate the policies and procedures of the State under paragraph (a) of this section.

(Authority: 20 U.S.C. 1412(a)(8))

§ 300.128 Individualized education programs.

(a) *General*. The State must have on file with the Secretary information that shows that an IEP, or an IFSP that meets the requirements of section 636(d) of the Act, is developed, reviewed, and revised for each child with a disability in accordance with §§ 300.340–300.350.

(b) *Required information*. The information described in paragraph (a) of this section must include—

(1) A copy of each State statute, policy, and standard that regulates the manner in which IEPs are developed, implemented, reviewed, and revised; and

(2) The procedures that the SEA follows in monitoring and evaluating those IEPs or IFSPs.

(Authority: 20 U.S.C. 1412(a)(4))

§ 300.129 Procedural safeguards.

(a) The State must have on file with the Secretary procedural safeguards that ensure that the requirements of §§ 300.500–300.529 are met.

(b) Children with disabilities and their parents must be afforded the procedural safeguards identified in paragraph (a) of this section.

(Authority: 20 U.S.C. 1412(a)(6)(A))

§ 300.130 Least restrictive environment.

(a) *General*. The State must have on file with the Secretary procedures that ensure that the requirements of §§ 300.550–300.556 are met, including the provision in § 300.551 requiring a continuum of alternative placements to meet the unique needs of each child with a disability.

(b) *Additional requirement*. (1) If the State uses a funding mechanism by which the State distributes State funds on the basis of the type of setting where a child is served, the funding mechanism may not result in placements that violate the requirements of paragraph (a) of this section.

(2) If the State does not have policies and procedures to ensure compliance with paragraph (b)(1) of this section, the State must provide the Secretary an assurance that the State will revise the funding mechanism as soon as feasible to ensure that the mechanism does not result in placements that violate that paragraph.

(Authority: 20 U.S.C. 1412(a)(5))

§ 300.131 [Reserved]

§ 300.132 Transition of children from Part C to preschool programs.

The State must have on file with the Secretary policies and procedures to ensure that—

(a) Children participating in early-intervention programs assisted under Part C of the Act, and who will participate in preschool programs assisted under Part B of the Act, experience a smooth and effective transition to those preschool programs in a manner consistent with section 637(a)(8) of the Act;

(b) By the third birthday of a child described in paragraph (a) of this section, an IEP or, if consistent with § 300.342(c) and section 636(d) of the Act, an IFSP, has been developed and is being implemented for the child consistent with § 300.121(c); and

(c) Each LEA will participate in transition planning conferences arranged by the designated lead agency under section 637(a)(8) of the Act.

(Authority: 20 U.S.C. 1412(a)(9))

§ 300.133 Children in private schools.

The State must have on file with the Secretary policies and procedures that ensure that the requirements of §§ 300.400–300.403 and §§ 300.450-300.462 are met.

(Authority: 20 U.S.C. 1413(a)(4))

§ 300.134 [Reserved]

§ 300.135 Comprehensive system of personnel development.

(a) *General.* The State must have in effect, consistent with the purposes of this part and with section 635(a)(8) of the Act, a comprehensive system of personnel development that—

(1) Is designed to ensure an adequate supply of qualified special education, regular education, and related services personnel; and

(2) Meets the requirements for a State improvement plan relating to personnel development in section 653(b)(2)(B) and (c)(3)(D) of the Act.

(b) *Information.* The State must have on file with the Secretary information that shows that the requirements of paragraph (a) of this section are met.

(Authority: 20 U.S.C. 1412(a)(14))

§ 300.136 Personnel standards.

(a) *Definitions.* As used in this part—

(1) *Appropriate professional requirements in the State* means entry level requirements that—

(i) Are based on the highest requirements in the State applicable to the profession or discipline in which a person is providing special education or related services; and

(ii) Establish suitable qualifications for personnel providing special education and related services under Part B of the Act to children with disabilities who are served by State, local, and private agencies (see § 300.2);

(2) *Highest requirements in the State applicable to a specific profession or discipline* means the highest entry-level academic degree needed for any State-approved or -recognized certification, licensing, registration, or other comparable requirements that apply to that profession or discipline;

(3) *Profession or discipline* means a specific occupational category that—

(i) Provides special education and related services to children with disabilities under Part B of the Act;

(ii) Has been established or designated by the State;

(iii) Has a required scope of responsibility and degree of supervision; and

(iv) Is not limited to traditional occupational categories; and

(4) *State-approved or -recognized certification, licensing, registration, or other comparable requirements* means the requirements that a State legislature either has enacted or has authorized a State agency to promulgate through rules to establish the entry-level standards for employment in a specific profession or discipline in that State.

(b) *Policies and procedures.* (1)(i) The State must have on file with the Secretary policies and procedures relating to the establishment and maintenance of standards to ensure that personnel necessary to carry out the purposes of this part are appropriately and adequately prepared and trained.

(ii) The policies and procedures required in paragraph (b)(1)(i) of this section must provide for the establishment and maintenance of standards that are consistent with any State-approved or -recognized certification, licensing, registration, or other comparable requirements that apply to the profession or discipline in which a person is providing special education or related services.

(2) Each State may—

(i) Determine the specific occupational categories required to provide special education and related services within the State; and

(ii) Revise or expand those categories as needed.

(3) Nothing in this part requires a State to establish a specified training standard (e.g., a masters degree) for personnel who provide special education and related services under Part B of the Act.

(4) A State with only one entry-level academic degree for employment of personnel in a specific profession or discipline may modify that standard as necessary to ensure the provision of FAPE to all children with disabilities in the State without violating the requirements of this section.

(c) *Steps for retraining or hiring personnel.* To the extent that a State's standards for a profession or discipline, including standards for temporary or emergency certification, are not based on the highest requirements in the State applicable to a specific profession or discipline, the State must provide the steps the State is taking and the procedures for notifying public agencies and personnel of those steps and the timelines it has established for the retraining or hiring of personnel to meet appropriate professional requirements in the State.

(d) *Status of personnel standards in the State.* (1) In meeting the requirements in paragraphs (b) and (c) of this section, a determination must be made about the status of personnel standards in the State. That determination must be based on current information that accurately describes, for each profession or discipline in which personnel are providing special education or related services, whether the applicable standards are consistent with the highest requirements in the State for that profession or discipline.

(2) The information required in paragraph (d)(1) of this section must be on file in the SEA and available to the public.

(e) *Applicability of State statutes and agency rules*. In identifying the highest requirements in the State for purposes of this section, the requirements of all State statutes and the rules of all State agencies applicable to serving children with disabilities must be considered.

(f) *Use of paraprofessionals and assistants.* A State may allow paraprofessionals and assistants who are appropriately trained and supervised, in accordance with State law, regulations, or written policy, in meeting the requirements of this part to be used to assist in the provision of special education and related services to children with disabilities under Part B of the Act.

(g) *Policy to address shortage of personnel.* (1) In implementing this section, a State may adopt a policy that includes a requirement that LEAs in the State make an ongoing good faith effort to recruit and hire appropriately and adequately trained personnel to provide special education and related services to children with disabilities, including, in a geographic area of the State where there is a shortage of personnel that meet these qualifications, the most qualified individuals available who are making satisfactory progress toward completing applicable course work necessary to meet the standards described in paragraph (b)(2) of this section, consistent with State law and the steps described in paragraph (c) of this section, within three years.

(2) If a State has reached its established date under paragraph (c) of this section, the State may still exercise the option under paragraph (g)(1) of this section for training or hiring all personnel in a specific profession or discipline to meet appropriate professional requirements in the State.

(3)(i) Each State must have a mechanism for serving children with disabilities if instructional needs exceed available personnel who meet appropriate professional requirements in the State for a specific profession or discipline.

(ii) A State that continues to experience shortages of qualified personnel must address those shortages in its comprehensive system of personnel development under § 300.135.

(Authority: 20 U.S.C. 1412(a)(15))

§ 300.137 Performance goals and indicators.

The State must have on file with the Secretary information to demonstrate that the State—

(a) Has established goals for the performance of children with disabilities in the State that—

(1) Will promote the purposes of this part, as stated in § 300.1; and

(2) Are consistent, to the maximum extent appropriate, with other goals and standards for all children established by the State;

(b) Has established performance indicators that the State will use to assess progress toward achieving those goals that, at a minimum, address the performance of children with disabilities on assessments, drop-out rates, and graduation rates;

(c) Every two years, will report to the Secretary and the public on the progress of the State, and of children with disabilities in the State, toward meeting the goals established under paragraph (a) of this section; and

(d) Based on its assessment of that progress, will revise its State improvement plan under subpart 1 of Part D of the Act as may be needed to improve its performance, if the State receives assistance under that subpart.

(Authority: 20 U.S.C. 1412(a)(16))

§ 300.138 Participation in assessments.

The State must have on file with the Secretary information to demonstrate that—

(a) Children with disabilities are included in general State and district-wide assessment programs, with appropriate accommodations and modifications in administration, if necessary;

(b) As appropriate, the State or LEA—

(1) Develops guidelines for the participation of children with disabilities in alternate assessments for those children who cannot participate in State and district-wide assessment programs;

(2) Develops alternate assessments in accordance with paragraph (b)(1) of this section; and

(3) Beginning not later than, July 1, 2000, conducts the alternate assessments described in paragraph (b)(2) of this section.

(Authority: 20 U.S.C. 1412(a)(17)(A))

§ 300.139 Reports relating to assessments.

(a) *General.* In implementing the requirements of § 300.138, the SEA shall make available to the public, and report to the public with the same frequency and in the same detail as it reports on the assessment of nondisabled children, the following information:

(1) The number of children with disabilities participating—

(i) In regular assessments; and

(ii) In alternate assessments.

(2) The performance results of the children described in paragraph (a)(1) of this section if doing so would be statistically sound and would not result in the disclosure of performance results identifiable to individual children—

(i) On regular assessments (beginning not later than July 1, 1998); and

(ii) On alternate assessments (not later than July 1, 2000).

(b) *Combined reports*. Reports to the public under paragraph (a) of this section must include—

(1) Aggregated data that include the performance of children with disabilities together with all other children; and

(2) Disaggregated data on the performance of children with disabilities.

(c) *Timeline for disaggregation of data*. Data relating to the performance of children described under paragraph (a)(2) of this section must be disaggregated—

(1) For assessments conducted after July 1, 1998; and

(2) For assessments conducted before July 1, 1998, if the State is required to disaggregate the data prior to July 1, 1998.

(Authority: 20 U.S.C. 612(a)(17)(B))

§ 300.140 [Reserved]

§ 300.141 SEA responsibility for general supervision.

(a) The State must have on file with the Secretary information that shows that the requirements of § 300.600 are met.

(b) The information described under paragraph (a) of this section must include a copy of each State statute, State regulation, signed agreement between respective agency officials, and any other documents that show compliance with that paragraph.

(Authority: 20 U.S.C. 1412(a)(11))

§ 300.142 Methods of ensuring services.

(a) *Establishing responsibility for services*. The Chief Executive Officer or designee of that officer shall ensure that an interagency agreement or other mechanism for interagency coordination is in effect between each noneducational public agency described in paragraph (b) of this section and the SEA, in order to ensure that all services described in paragraph (b)(1) of this section that are needed to ensure FAPE are provided, including the provision of these services during the pendency of any dispute under paragraph (a)(3) of this section. The agreement or mechanism must include the following:

(1) *Agency financial responsibility*. An identification of, or a method for defining, the financial responsibility of each agency for providing services described in paragraph (b)(1) of this section to ensure FAPE to children with disabilities. The financial responsibility of each noneducational public agency described in paragraph (b) of this section, including the State Medicaid agency and other public insurers of children with disabilities, must precede the financial responsibility of the LEA (or the State agency responsible for developing the child's IEP).

(2) *Conditions and terms of reimbursement*. The conditions, terms, and procedures under which an LEA must be reimbursed by other agencies.

(3) *Interagency disputes*. Procedures for resolving interagency disputes (including procedures under which LEAs may initiate proceedings) under the agreement or other mechanism to secure reimbursement from other agencies or otherwise implement the provisions of the agreement or mechanism.

(4) *Coordination of services procedures*. Policies and procedures for agencies to determine and identify the interagency coordination responsibilities of each agency to promote the coordination and timely and appropriate delivery of services described in paragraph (b)(1) of this section.

(b) *Obligation of noneducational public agencies*. (1) *General*. (i) If any public agency other than an educational agency is otherwise obligated under Federal or State law, or assigned responsibility under State policy or pursuant to paragraph (a) of this section, to provide or pay for any services that are also considered special education or related services (such as, but not limited to, services described in § 300.5 relating to assistive technology devices, § 300.6 relating to assistive technology services, § 300.24 relating to related services, § 300.28 relating to supplementary aids and services, and § 300.29 relating to transition services) that are necessary for ensuring FAPE to children with disabilities within the State, the public agency shall fulfill that obligation or responsibility, either directly or through contract or other arrangement.

(ii) A noneducational public agency described in paragraph (b)(1)(i) of this section may not disqualify an eligible service for Medicaid reimbursement because that service is provided in a school context.

(2) Reimbursement for services by noneducational public agency. If a public agency other than an educational agency fails to provide or pay for the special education and related services described in paragraph (b)(1) of this section, the LEA (or State agency responsible for developing the child's IEP) shall provide or pay for these services to the child in a timely manner. The LEA or State agency may then claim reimbursement for the services from the noneducational public agency that failed to provide or pay for these services and that agency shall reimburse the LEA or State agency in accordance with the terms of the interagency agreement or other mechanism described in paragraph (a)(1) of this section, and the agreement described in paragraph (a)(2) of this section.

(c) *Special rule*. The requirements of paragraph (a) of this section may be met through—

(1) State statute or regulation;

(2) Signed agreements between respective agency officials that clearly identify the responsibilities of each agency relating to the provision of services; or

(3) Other appropriate written methods as determined by the Chief Executive Officer of the State or designee of that officer.

(d) *Information.* The State must have on file with the Secretary information to demonstrate that the requirements of paragraphs (a) through (c) of this section are met.

(e) *Children with disabilities who are covered by public insurance.* (1) A public agency may use the Medicaid or other public insurance benefits programs in which a child participates to provide or pay for services required under this part, as permitted under the public insurance program, except as provided in paragraph (e)(2) of this section.

(2) With regard to services required to provide FAPE to an eligible child under this part, the public agency—

(i) May not require parents to sign up for or enroll in public insurance programs in order for their child to receive FAPE under Part B of the Act;

(ii) May not require parents to incur an out-of-pocket expense such as the payment of a deductible or co-pay amount incurred in filing a claim for services provided pursuant to this part, but pursuant to paragraph (g)(2) of this section, may pay the cost that the parent otherwise would be required to pay; and

(iii) May not use a child's benefits under a public insurance program if that use would—

(A) Decrease available lifetime coverage or any other insured benefit;

(B) Result in the family paying for services that would otherwise be covered by the public insurance program and that are required for the child outside of the time the child is in school;

(C) Increase premiums or lead to the discontinuation of insurance; or

(D) Risk loss of eligibility for home and community-based waivers, based on aggregate health-related expenditures.

(f) *Children with disabilities who are covered by private insurance.* (1) With regard to services required to provide FAPE to an eligible child under this part, a public agency may access a parent's private insurance proceeds only if the parent provides informed consent consistent with § 300.500(b)(1).

(2) Each time the public agency proposes to access the parent's private insurance proceeds, it must—

(i) Obtain parent consent in accordance with paragraph (f)(1) of this section; and

(ii) Inform the parents that their refusal to permit the public agency to access their private insurance does not relieve the public agency of its responsibility to ensure that all required services are provided at no cost to the parents.

(g) *Use of Part B funds.* (1) If a public agency is unable to obtain parental consent to use the parent's private insurance, or public insurance when the parent would incur a cost for a specified service required under this part, to ensure FAPE the public agency may use its Part B funds to pay for the service.

(2) To avoid financial cost to parents who otherwise would consent to use private insurance, or public insurance if the parent would incur a cost, the public agency may use its Part B funds to pay the cost the parents otherwise would have to pay to use the parent's insurance (e.g., the deductible or co-pay amounts).

(h) *Proceeds from public or private insurance.* (1) Proceeds from public or private insurance will not be treated as program income for purposes of 34 CFR 80.25.

(2) If a public agency spends reimbursements from Federal funds (e.g., Medicaid) for services under this part, those funds will not be considered "State or local" funds for purposes of the maintenance of effort provisions in §§ 300.154 and 300.231.

(i) *Construction.* Nothing in this part should be construed to alter the requirements imposed on a State Medicaid agency, or any other agency administering a public insurance program by Federal statute, regulations or policy under title XIX, or title XXI of the Social Security Act, or any other public insurance program.

(Authority: 20 U.S.C. 1412(a)(12)(A), (B), and (C); 1401(8))

§ 300.143 SEA implementation of procedural safeguards.

The State must have on file with the Secretary the procedures that the SEA (and any agency assigned responsibility pursuant to § 300.600(d)) follows to inform each public agency of its responsibility for ensuring effective implementation of procedural safeguards for the children with disabilities served by that public agency.

(Authority: 20 U.S.C. 1412(a)(11); 1415(a))

§ 300.144 Hearings relating to LEA eligibility.

The State must have on file with the Secretary procedures to ensure that the SEA does not make any final determination that an LEA is not eligible for assistance under Part B of the Act without first giving the LEA reasonable notice and an opportunity for a hearing under 34 CFR 76.401(d).

(Authority: 20 U.S.C. 1412(a)(13))

§ 300.145 Recovery of funds for misclassified children.

The State must have on file with the Secretary policies and procedures that ensure that the State seeks to recover any funds provided under Part B of the Act for services to a child who is determined to be erroneously classified as eligible to be counted under section 611(a) or (d) of the Act.

(Authority: 20 U.S.C. 1221e-3(a)(1))

§ 300.146 Suspension and expulsion rates.

The State must have on file with the Secretary information to demonstrate that the following requirements are met:

(a) *General.* The SEA examines data to determine if significant discrepancies are occurring in the rate of long-term suspensions and expulsions of children with disabilities—

(1) Among LEAs in the State; or

(2) Compared to the rates for nondisabled children within the agencies.

(b) *Review and revision of policies.* If the discrepancies described in paragraph (a) of this section are occurring, the SEA reviews and, if appropriate, revises (or requires the affected State agency or LEA to revise) its policies, procedures, and practices relating to the development and implementation of IEPs, the use of behavioral interventions, and procedural safeguards, to ensure that these policies, procedures, and practices comply with the Act.

(Authority: 20 U.S.C. 612(a)(22))

§ 300.147 Additional information if SEA provides direct services.

(a) If the SEA provides FAPE to children with disabilities, or provides direct services to these children, the agency—

(1) Shall comply with any additional requirements of §§ 300.220-300.230(a) and 300.234-300.250 as if the agency were an LEA; and

(2) May use amounts that are otherwise available to the agency under Part B of the Act to serve those children without regard to § 300.184 (relating to excess costs).

(b) The SEA must have on file with the Secretary information to demonstrate that it meets the requirements of paragraph (a)(1) of this section.

(Authority: 20 U.S.C. 1412(b))

§ 300.148 Public participation.

(a) *General; exception.* (1) Subject to paragraph (a)(2) of this section, each State must ensure that, prior to the adoption of any policies and procedures needed to comply with this part, there are public hearings, adequate notice of the hearings, and an opportunity for comment available to the general public, including individuals with disabilities and parents of children with disabilities consistent with §§ 300.280–300.284.

(2) A State will be considered to have met paragraph (a)(1) of this section with regard to a policy or procedure needed to comply with this part if it can demonstrate that prior to the adoption of that policy or procedure, the policy or procedure was subjected to a public review and comment process that is required by the State for other purposes and is comparable to and consistent with the requirements of §§ 300.280–300.284.

(b) *Documentation.* The State must have on file with the Secretary information to demonstrate that the requirements of paragraph (a) of this section are met.

(Authority: 20 U.S.C. 1412(a)(20))

§ 300.149 [Reserved]

§ 300.150 State advisory panel.

The State must have on file with the Secretary information to demonstrate that the State has established and maintains an advisory panel for the purpose of providing policy guidance with respect to special education and related services for children with disabilities in the State in accordance with the requirements of §§ 300.650–300.653.

(Authority: 20 U.S.C. 1412(a)(21)(A))

§ 300.151 [Reserved]

§ 300.152 Prohibition against commingling.

(a) The State must have on file with the Secretary an assurance satisfactory to the Secretary that the funds under Part B of the Act are not commingled with State funds.

(b) The assurance in paragraph (a) of this section is satisfied by the use of a separate accounting system that includes an audit trail of the expenditure of the Part B funds. Separate bank accounts are not required. (See 34 CFR 76.702 (Fiscal control and fund accounting procedures).)

(Authority: 20 U.S.C. 1412(a)(18)(B))

§ 300.153 State-level nonsupplanting.

(a) *General.* (1) Except as provided in § 300.230, funds paid to a State under Part B of the Act must be used to supplement the level of Federal, State, and local funds (including funds that are not under the direct control of the SEA or LEAs) expended for special education and related services provided to children with disabilities under Part B of the Act and in no case to supplant these Federal, State, and local funds.

(2) The State must have on file with the Secretary information to demonstrate to the satisfaction of the Secretary that the requirements of paragraph (a)(1) of this section are met.

(b) *Waiver*. If the State provides clear and convincing evidence that all children with disabilities have available to them FAPE, the Secretary may waive, in whole or in part, the requirements of paragraph (a) of this section if the Secretary concurs with the evidence provided by the State under § 300.589.

(Authority: 20 U.S.C. 1412(a)(18)(c))

§ 300.154 Maintenance of State financial support.

(a) *General*. The State must have on file with the Secretary information to demonstrate, on either a total or per-capita basis, that the State will not reduce the amount of State financial support for special education and related services for children with disabilities, or otherwise made available because of the excess costs of educating those children, below the amount of that support for the preceding fiscal year.

(b) *Reduction of funds for failure to maintain support*. The Secretary reduces the allocation of funds under section 611 of the Act for any fiscal year following the fiscal year in which the State fails to comply with the requirement of paragraph (a) of this section by the same amount by which the State fails to meet the requirement.

(c) *Waivers for exceptional or uncontrollable circumstances*. The Secretary may waive the requirement of paragraph (a) of this section for a State, for one fiscal year at a time, if the Secretary determines that—

(1) Granting a waiver would be equitable due to exceptional or uncontrollable circumstances such as a natural disaster or a precipitous and unforeseen decline in the financial resources of the State; or

(2) The State meets the standard in § 300.589 for a waiver of the requirement to supplement, and not to supplant, funds received under Part B of the Act.

(d) *Subsequent years*. If, for any fiscal year, a State fails to meet the requirement of paragraph (a) of this section, including any year for which the State is granted a waiver under paragraph (c) of this section, the financial support required of the State in future years under paragraph (a) of this section must be the amount that would have been required in the absence of that failure and not the reduced level of the State's support.

(Authority: 20 U.S.C. 1412(a)(19))

§ 300.155 Policies and procedures for use of Part B funds.

The State must have on file with the Secretary policies and procedures designed to ensure that funds paid to the State under Part B of the Act are spent in accordance with the provisions of Part B.

(Authority: 20 U.S.C. 1412(a)(18)(A))

§ 300.156 Annual description of use of Part B funds.

(a) In order to receive a grant in any fiscal year a State must annually describe—

(1) How amounts retained for State-level activities under § 300.602 will be used to meet the requirements of this part;

(2) How those amounts will be allocated among the activities described in §§ 300.621 and 300.370 to meet State priorities based on input from LEAs; and

(3) The percentage of those amounts, if any, that will be distributed to LEAs by formula.

(b) If a State's plans for use of its funds under §§ 300.370 and 300.620 for the forthcoming year do not change from the prior year, the State may submit a letter to that effect to meet the requirement in paragraph (a) of this section.

(Authority: 20 U.S.C. 1411(f)(5))

LEA and State Agency Eligibility—General

§ 300.180 Condition of assistance.

An LEA or State agency is eligible for assistance under Part B of the Act for a fiscal year if the agency demonstrates to the satisfaction of the SEA that it meets the conditions in §§ 300.220–300.250.

(Authority: 20 U.S.C. 1413(a))

§ 300.181 Exception for prior LEA or State agency policies and procedures on file with the SEA.

If an LEA or a State agency described in § 300.194 has on file with the SEA policies and procedures that demonstrate that the LEA or State agency meets any requirement of § 300.180, including any policies and procedures filed under Part B of the Act as in effect before June 4, 1997, the SEA shall consider the LEA or State agency to have met the requirement for purposes of receiving assistance under Part B of the Act.

(Authority: 20 U.S.C. 1413(b)(1))

§ 300.182 Amendments to LEA policies and procedures.

(a) *Modification made by an LEA or a State agency.* (1) Subject to paragraph (b) of this section, policies and procedures submitted by an LEA or a State agency in accordance with this subpart remain in effect until it submits to the SEA the modifications that the LEA or State agency decides are necessary.

(2) The provisions of this subpart apply to a modification to an LEA's or State agency's policies and procedures in the same manner and to the same extent that they apply to the LEA's or State agency's original policies and procedures.

(b) *Modifications required by the SEA.* The SEA may require an LEA or a State agency to modify its policies and procedures, but only to the extent necessary to ensure the LEA's or State agency's compliance with this part, if—

(1) After June 4, 1997, the provisions of the Act or the regulations in this part are amended;

(2) There is a new interpretation of the Act by Federal or State courts; or

(3) There is an official finding of noncompliance with Federal or State law or regulations.

(Authority: 20 U.S.C. 1413(b))

§ 300.183 [Reserved]

§ 300.184 Excess cost requirement.

(a) *General.* Amounts provided to an LEA under Part B of the Act may be used only to pay the excess costs of providing special education and related services to children with disabilities.

(b) *Definition.* As used in this part, the term excess costs means those costs that are in excess of the average annual per-student expenditure in an LEA during the preceding school year for an elementary or secondary school student, as may be appropriate. Excess costs must be computed after deducting—

(1) Amounts received—

(i) Under Part B of the Act;

(ii) Under Part A of title I of the Elementary and Secondary Education Act of 1965; or

(iii) Under Part A of title VII of that Act; and

(2) Any State or local funds expended for programs that would qualify for assistance under any of those parts.

(c) *Limitation on use of Part B funds.* (1) The excess cost requirement prevents an LEA from using funds provided under Part B of the Act to pay for all of the costs directly attributable to the education of a child with a disability, subject to paragraph (c)(2) of this section.

(2) The excess cost requirement does not prevent an LEA from using Part B funds to pay for all of the costs directly attributable to the education of a child with a disability in any of the ages 3, 4, 5, 18, 19, 20, or 21, if no local or State funds are available for nondisabled children in that age range. However, the LEA must comply with the nonsupplanting and other requirements of this part in providing the education and services for these children.

(Authority: 20 U.S.C. 1401(7), 1413(a)(2)(A))

§ 300.185 Meeting the excess cost requirement.

(a)(1) *General.* An LEA meets the excess cost requirement if it has spent at least a minimum average amount for the education of its children with disabilities before funds under Part B of the Act are used.

(2) The amount described in paragraph (a)(1) of this section is determined using the formula in § 300.184(b). This amount may not include capital outlay or debt service.

(b) *Joint establishment of eligibility.* If two or more LEAs jointly establish eligibility in accordance with § 300.190, the minimum average amount is the average of the combined minimum average amounts determined under § 300.184 in those agencies for elementary or secondary school students, as the case may be.

(Authority: 20 U.S.C. 1413(a)(2)(A))

§§ 300.186-300.189 [Reserved]

§ 300.190 Joint establishment of eligibility.

(a) *General.* An SEA may require an LEA to establish its eligibility jointly with another LEA if the SEA determines that the LEA would be ineligible under this section because the agency would not be able to establish and maintain programs of sufficient size and scope to effectively meet the needs of children with disabilities.

(b) *Charter school exception.* An SEA may not require a charter school that is an LEA to jointly establish its eligibility under paragraph (a) of this section unless it is explicitly permitted to do so under the State's charter school statute.

(c) *Amount of payments.* If an SEA requires the joint establishment of eligibility under paragraph (a) of this section, the total amount of funds made available to the affected LEAs must be equal to the sum of the payments that each LEA would have received under §§ 300.711-300.714 if the agencies were eligible for these payments.

(Authority: 20 U.S.C. 1413(e)(1), and (2))

§ 300.191 [Reserved]

§ 300.192 Requirements for establishing eligibility.

(a) *Requirements for LEAs in general.* LEAs that establish joint eligibility under this section must—

(1) Adopt policies and procedures that are consistent with the State's policies and procedures under §§ 300.121–300.156; and

(2) Be jointly responsible for implementing programs that receive assistance under Part B of the Act.

(b) *Requirements for educational service agencies in general.* If an educational service agency is required by State law to carry out programs under Part B of the Act, the joint responsibilities given to LEAs under Part B of the Act—

(1) Do not apply to the administration and disbursement of any payments received by that educational service agency; and

(2) Must be carried out only by that educational service agency.

(c) *Additional requirement.* Notwithstanding any other provision of §§ 300.190–300.192, an educational service agency shall provide for the education of children with disabilities in the least restrictive environment, as required by § 300.130.

(Authority: 20 U.S.C. 1413(e)(3), and (4))

§ 300.193 [Reserved]

§ 300.194 State agency eligibility.

Any State agency that desires to receive a subgrant for any fiscal year under §§ 300.711-300.714 must demonstrate to the satisfaction of the SEA that—

(a) All children with disabilities who are participating in programs and projects funded under Part B of the Act receive FAPE, and that those children and their parents are provided all the rights and procedural safeguards described in this part; and

(b) The agency meets the other conditions of this subpart that apply to LEAs.

(Authority: 20 U.S.C. 1413(i))

§ 300.195 [Reserved]

§ 300.196 Notification of LEA or State agency in case of ineligibility.

If the SEA determines that an LEA or State agency is not eligible under Part B of the Act, the SEA shall—

(a) Notify the LEA or State agency of that determination; and

(b) Provide the LEA or State agency with reasonable notice and an opportunity for a hearing.

(Authority: 20 U.S.C. 1413(c))

§ 300.197 LEA and State agency compliance.

(a) *General.* If the SEA, after reasonable notice and an opportunity for a hearing, finds that an LEA or State agency that has been determined to be eligible under this section is failing to comply with any requirement described in §§ 300.220-300.250, the SEA shall reduce or may not provide any further payments to the LEA or State agency until the SEA is satisfied that the LEA or State agency is complying with that requirement.

(b) *Notice requirement.* Any State agency or LEA in receipt of a notice described in paragraph (a) of this section shall, by means of public notice, take the measures necessary to bring the pendency of an action pursuant to this section to the attention of the public within the jurisdiction of the agency.

(c) In carrying out its functions under this section, each SEA shall consider any decision resulting from a hearing under §§ 300.507-300.528 that is adverse to the LEA or State agency involved in the decision.

(Authority: 20 U.S.C. 1413(d))

LEA and State Agency Eligibility—Specific Conditions

§ 300.220 Consistency with State policies.

(a) *General.* The LEA, in providing for the education of children with disabilities within its jurisdiction, must have in effect policies, procedures, and programs that are consistent with the State policies and procedures established under §§ 300.121-300.156.

(b) *Policies on file with SEA.* The LEA must have on file with the SEA the policies and procedures described in paragraph (a) of this section.

(Authority: 20 U.S.C. 1413(a)(1))

§ 300.221 Implementation of CSPD.

The LEA must have on file with the SEA information to demonstrate that—

(a) All personnel necessary to carry out Part B of the Act within the jurisdiction of the agency are appropriately and adequately prepared, consistent with the requirements of §§ 300.380-300.382; and

(b) To the extent the LEA determines appropriate, it shall contribute to and use the comprehensive system of personnel development of the State established under § 300.135.

(Authority: 20 U.S.C. 1413(a)(3))

§§ 300.222-300.229 [Reserved]

§ 300.230 Use of amounts.

The LEA must have on file with the SEA information to demonstrate that amounts provided to the LEA under Part B of the Act—

(a) Will be expended in accordance with the applicable provisions of this part;

(b) Will be used only to pay the excess costs of providing special education and related services to children with disabilities, consistent with §§ 300.184-300.185; and

(c) Will be used to supplement State, local, and other Federal funds and not to supplant those funds.

(Authority: 20 U.S.C. 1413(a)(2)(A))

§ 300.231 Maintenance of effort.

(a) *General.* Except as provided in §§ 300.232 and 300.233, funds provided to an LEA under Part B of the Act may not be used to reduce the level of expenditures for the education of children with disabilities made by the LEA from local funds below the level of those expenditures for the preceding fiscal year.

(b) *Information.* The LEA must have on file with the SEA information to demonstrate that the requirements of paragraph (a) of this section are met.

(c) *Standard.* (1) Except as provided in paragraph (c)(2) of this section, the SEA determines that an LEA complies with paragraph (a) of this section for purposes of establishing the LEA's eligibility for an award for a fiscal year if the LEA budgets, for the education of children with disabilities, at least the same total or per-capita amount from either of the following sources as the LEA spent for that purpose from the same source for the most recent prior year for which information is available:

(i) Local funds only.

(ii) The combination of State and local funds.

(2) An LEA that relies on paragraph (c)(1)(i) of this section for any fiscal year must ensure that the amount of local funds it budgets for the education of children with disabilities in that year is at least the same, either in total or per capita, as the amount it spent for that purpose in—

(i) The most recent fiscal year for which information is available, if that year is, or is before, the first fiscal year beginning on or after July 1, 1997; or

(ii) If later, the most recent fiscal year for which information is available and the standard in paragraph (c)(1)(i) of this section was used to establish its compliance with this section.

(3) The SEA may not consider any expenditures made from funds provided by the Federal Government for which the SEA is required to account to the Federal Government or for which the LEA is required to account to the Federal Government directly or through the SEA in determining an LEA's compliance with the requirement in paragraph (a) of this section.

(Authority: 20 U.S.C. 1413(a)(2)(A))

§ 300.232 Exception to maintenance of effort.

An LEA may reduce the level of expenditures by the LEA under Part B of the Act below the level of those expenditures for the preceding fiscal year if the reduction is attributable to the following:

(a)(1) The voluntary departure, by retirement or otherwise, or departure for just cause, of special education or related services personnel, who are replaced by qualified, lower-salaried staff.

(2) In order for an LEA to invoke the exception in paragraph (a)(1) of this section, the LEA must ensure that those voluntary retirements or resignations and replacements are in full conformity with:

(i) Existing school board policies in the agency;

(ii) The applicable collective bargaining agreement in effect at that time; and

(iii) Applicable State statutes.

(b) A decrease in the enrollment of children with disabilities.

(c) The termination of the obligation of the agency, consistent with this part, to provide a program of special education to a particular child with a disability that is an exceptionally costly program, as determined by the SEA, because the child—

(1) Has left the jurisdiction of the agency;

(2) Has reached the age at which the obligation of the agency to provide FAPE to the child has terminated; or

(3) No longer needs the program of special education.

(d) The termination of costly expenditures for long-term purchases, such as the acquisition of equipment or the construction of school facilities.

(Authority: 20 U.S.C. 1413(a)(2)(B))

§ 300.233 Treatment of federal funds in certain fiscal years.

(a)(1) Subject to paragraphs (a)(2), (a)(3), and (b) of this section, for any fiscal year for which amounts appropriated to carry out section 611 of the Act exceed $4.1 billion, an LEA may treat as local funds up to 20 percent of the amount of funds it is eligible to receive under § 300.712 from that appropriation that exceeds the amount from funds appropriated for the previous fiscal year that the LEA was eligible to receive under § 300.712.

(2) The requirements of §§ 300.230(c) and 300.231 do not apply with respect to the

amount that may be treated as local funds under paragraph (a)(1) of this section.

(3) For purposes of this section:

(i)(A) An LEA is not eligible to receive funds during any period in which those funds under this part are withheld from the LEA because of a finding of noncompliance under § 300.197 or § 300.587.

(B) An LEA is eligible to receive funds that have been withheld under § 300.197 or § 300.587 but are subsequently released to the LEA within the period of the funds availability.

(ii) An LEA is not eligible to receive funds that have been reallocated to other LEAs under § 300.714.

(b) If an SEA determines that an LEA is not meeting the requirements of this part, the SEA may prohibit the LEA from treating funds received under Part B of the Act as local funds under paragraph (a)(1) of this section for any fiscal year, but only if it is authorized to do so by the State constitution or a State statute.

(Authority: 20 U.S.C. 1413(a)(2)(C))

§ 300.234 Schoolwide programs under title I of the ESEA.

(a) *General; limitation on amount of Part B funds used.* An LEA may use funds received under Part B of the Act for any fiscal year to carry out a schoolwide program under section 1114 of the Elementary and Secondary Education Act of 1965, except that the amount used in any schoolwide program may not exceed—

(1)(i) The amount received by the LEA under Part B for that fiscal year; divided by

(ii) The number of children with disabilities in the jurisdiction of the LEA; and multiplied by

(2) The number of children with disabilities participating in the schoolwide program.

(b) *Funding conditions.* The funds described in paragraph (a) of this section are subject to the following conditions:

(1) The funds must be considered as Federal Part B funds for purposes of the calculations required by §§ 300.230(b) and (c).

(2) The funds may be used without regard to the requirements of § 300.230(a).

(c) *Meeting other Part B requirements.* Except as provided in paragraph (b) of this section, all other requirements of Part B must be met by an LEA using Part B funds in accordance with paragraph (a) of this section, including ensuring that children with disabilities in schoolwide program schools—

(1) Receive services in accordance with a properly developed IEP; and

(2) Are afforded all of the rights and services guaranteed to children with disabilities under the IDEA.

(Authority: 20 U.S.C. 1413(a)(2)(D))

§ 300.235 Permissive use of funds.

(a) *General.* Subject to paragraph (b) of this section, funds provided to an LEA under Part B of the Act may be used for the following activities:

(1) Services and aids that also benefit nondisabled children. For the costs of special education and related services and supplementary aids and services provided in a regular class or other education-related setting to a child with a disability in accordance with the IEP of the child, even if one or more nondisabled children benefit from these services.

(2) Integrated and coordinated services system. To develop and implement a fully integrated and coordinated services system in accordance with § 300.244.

(b) *Non-applicability of certain provisions.* An LEA does not violate §§ 300.152, 300.230, and 300.231 based on its use of funds provided under Part B of the Act in accordance with paragraphs (a)(1) and (a)(2) of this section.

(Authority: 20 U.S.C. 1413(a)(4))

§§ 300.236-300.239 [Reserved]

§ 300.240 Information for SEA.

(a) The LEA shall provide the SEA with information necessary to enable the SEA to carry out its duties under Part B of the Act, including, with respect to §§ 300.137 and 300.138, information relating to the performance of children with disabilities participating in programs carried out under Part B of the Act.

(b) The LEA must have on file with the SEA an assurance satisfactory to the SEA that the LEA will comply with the requirements of paragraph (a) of this section.

(Authority: 20 U.S.C. 1413(a)(6))

§ 300.241 Treatment of charter schools and their students.

The LEA must have on file with the SEA information to demonstrate that in carrying out this part with respect to charter schools that are public schools of the LEA, the LEA will—

(a) Serve children with disabilities attending those schools in the same manner as it serves children with disabilities in its other schools; and

(b) Provide funds under Part B of the Act to those schools in the same manner as it provides those funds to its other schools.

(Authority: 20 U.S.C. 1413(a)(5))

§ 300.242 Public information.

The LEA must have on file with the SEA information to demonstrate to the satisfaction of the SEA that it will make available to parents of children with disabilities and to the general public all documents relating to the eligibility of the agency under Part B of the Act.

(Authority: 20 U.S.C. 1413(a)(7))

§ 300.243 [Reserved]

§ 300.244 Coordinated services system.

(a) *General.* An LEA may not use more than 5 percent of the amount the agency receives under Part B of the Act for any fiscal year, in combination with other amounts (which must include amounts other than education funds), to develop and implement a coordinated services system designed to improve results for children and families, including children with disabilities and their families.

(b) *Activities.* In implementing a coordinated services system under this section, an LEA may carry out activities that include—

(1) Improving the effectiveness and efficiency of service delivery, including developing strategies that promote accountability for results;

(2) Service coordination and case management that facilitate the linkage of IEPs under Part B of the Act and IFSPs under Part C of the Act with individualized service plans under multiple Federal and State programs, such as title I of the Rehabilitation Act of 1973 (vocational rehabilitation), title XIX of the Social Security Act (Medicaid), and title XVI of the Social Security Act (supplemental security income);

(3) Developing and implementing interagency financing strategies for the provision of education, health, mental health, and social services, including transition services and related services under the Act; and

(4) Interagency personnel development for individuals working on coordinated services.

(c) *Coordination with certain projects under Elementary and Secondary Education Act of 1965.* If an LEA is carrying out a coordinated services project under title XI of the Elementary and Secondary Education Act of 1965 and a coordinated services project under Part B of the Act in the same schools, the agency shall use the amounts under § 300.244 in accordance with the requirements of that title.

(Authority: 20 U.S.C. 1413(f))

School-Based Improvement Plan

§ 300.245 School-based improvement plan.

(a) *General.* Each LEA may, in accordance with paragraph (b) of this section, use funds made available under Part B of the Act to permit a public school within the jurisdiction of the LEA to design, implement, and evaluate a school-based improvement plan that—

(1) Is consistent with the purposes described in section 651(b) of the Act; and

(2) Is designed to improve educational and transitional results for all children with disabilities and, as appropriate, for other children consistent with § 300.235(a) and (b) in that public school.

(b) *Authority.* (1) General. An SEA may grant authority to an LEA to permit a public school described in § 300.245 (through a school-based standing panel established under § 300.247(b)) to design, implement, and evaluate a school-based improvement plan described in § 300.245 for a period not to exceed 3 years.

(2) Responsibility of LEA. If an SEA grants the authority described in paragraph (b)(1) of this section, an LEA that is granted this authority must have the sole responsibility of oversight of all activities relating to the design, implementation, and evaluation of any school-based improvement plan that a public school is permitted to design under this section.

(Authority: 20 U.S.C. 1413(g)(1) and (g)(2)).

§ 300.246 Plan requirements.

A school-based improvement plan described in § 300.245 must—

(a) Be designed to be consistent with the purposes described in section 651(b) of the Act and to improve educational and transitional results for all children with disabilities and, as appropriate, for other children consistent with § 300.235(a) and (b), who attend the school for which the plan is designed and implemented;

(b) Be designed, evaluated, and, as appropriate, implemented by a school-based standing panel established in accordance with § 300.247(b);

(c) Include goals and measurable indicators to assess the progress of the public school in meeting these goals; and

(d) Ensure that all children with disabilities receive the services described in their IEPs.

(Authority: 20 U.S.C. 1413(g)(3))

§ 300.247 Responsibilities of the LEA.

An LEA that is granted authority under § 300.245(b) to permit a public school to design, implement, and evaluate a school-based improvement plan shall—

(a) Select each school under the jurisdiction of the agency that is eligible to design, implement, and evaluate the plan;

(b) Require each school selected under paragraph (a) of this section, in accordance with criteria established by the LEA under paragraph (c) of this section, to establish a school-based standing panel to carry out the duties described in § 300.246(b);

(c) Establish—

(1) Criteria that must be used by the LEA in the selection of an eligible school under paragraph (a) of this section;

(2) Criteria that must be used by a public school selected under paragraph (a) of this section in the establishment of a school-based standing panel to carry out the duties described in § 300.246(b) and that ensure that the membership of the panel reflects the diversity of the community in which the public school is located and includes, at a minimum—

(i) Parents of children with disabilities who attend a public school, including parents of children with disabilities from unserved and underserved populations, as appropriate;

(ii) Special education and general education teachers of public schools;

(iii) Special education and general education administrators, or the designee of those administrators, of those public schools; and

(iv) Related services providers who are responsible for providing services to the children with disabilities who attend those public schools; and

(3) Criteria that must be used by the LEA with respect to the distribution of funds under Part B of the Act to carry out this section;

(d) Disseminate the criteria established under paragraph (c) of this section to local school district personnel and local parent organizations within the jurisdiction of the LEA;

(e) Require a public school that desires to design, implement, and evaluate a school-based improvement plan to submit an application at the time, in the manner and accompanied by the information, that the LEA shall reasonably require; and

(f) Establish procedures for approval by the LEA of a school-based improvement plan designed under Part B of the Act.

(Authority: 20 U.S.C. 1413(g)(4))

§ 300.248 Limitation.

A school-based improvement plan described in § 300.245(a) may be submitted to an LEA for approval only if a consensus with respect to any matter relating to the design, implementation, or evaluation of the goals of the plan is reached by the school-based standing panel that designed the plan.

(Authority: 20 U.S.C. 1413(g)(5))

§ 300.249 Additional requirements.

(a) *Parental involvement*. In carrying out the requirements of §§ 300.245-300.250, an LEA shall ensure that the parents of children with disabilities are involved in the design, evaluation, and, if appropriate, implementation of school-based improvement plans in accordance with this section.

(b) *Plan approval*. An LEA may approve a school-based improvement plan of a public school within the jurisdiction of the agency for a period of 3 years, if—

(1) The approval is consistent with the policies, procedures, and practices established by the LEA and in accordance with §§ 300.245-300.250; and

(2) A majority of parents of children who are members of the school-based standing panel, and a majority of other members of the school-based standing panel that designed the plan, agree in writing to the plan.

(Authority: 20 U.S.C. 1413(g)(6))

§ 300.250 Extension of plan.

If a public school within the jurisdiction of an LEA meets the applicable requirements and criteria described in §§ 300.246 and 300.247 at the expiration of the 3-year approval period described § 300.249(b), the agency may approve a school-based improvement plan of the school for an additional 3-year period.

(Authority: 20 U.S.C. 1413(g)(7))

Secretary of the Interior—Eligibility

§ 300.260 Submission of information.

The Secretary may provide the Secretary of the Interior amounts under § 300.715(b) and (c) for a fiscal year only if the Secretary of the Interior submits to the Secretary information that—

(a) Meets the requirements of section 612(a)(1), (3)–(9), (10)(B), (C), (11)–(12), (14)–(17), (20), (21) and (22) of the Act (including monitoring and evaluation activities);

(b) Meets the requirements of section 612(b) and (e) of the Act;

(c) Meets the requirements of section 613(a)(1), (2)(A)(i), (6), and (7) of the Act;

(d) Meets the requirements of this part that implement the sections of the Act listed in paragraphs (a)–(c) of this section;

(e) Includes a description of how the Secretary of the Interior will coordinate the provision of services under Part B of the Act with LEAs, tribes and tribal organizations, and other private and Federal service providers;

(f) Includes an assurance that there are public hearings, adequate notice of the hearings, and an opportunity for comment afforded to members of tribes, tribal governing bodies, and affected local school boards before the adoption of the policies, programs, and procedures described in paragraph (a) of this section;

(g) Includes an assurance that the Secretary of the Interior will provide the information that the Secretary may require to comply with section 618 of the Act, including data on the number of children with disabilities served and the types and amounts of services provided and needed;

(h)(1) Includes an assurance that the Secretary of the Interior and the Secretary of Health and Human Services have entered into a memorandum of agreement, to be provided to the Secretary, for the coordination of services, resources, and personnel between their respective Federal, State, and local offices and with the SEAs and LEAs and other entities to facilitate the provision of services to Indian children with disabilities residing on or near reservations.

(2) The agreement must provide for the apportionment of responsibilities and costs, including child find, evaluation, diagnosis, remediation or therapeutic measures, and (if appropriate) equipment and medical or personal supplies, as needed for a child with a disability to remain in a school or program; and

(i) Includes an assurance that the Department of the Interior will cooperate with the Department in its exercise of monitoring and oversight of the requirements in this section and §§ 300.261–300.267, and any agreements entered into between the Secretary of the Interior and other entities under Part B of the Act, and will fulfill its duties under Part B of the Act. Section 616(a) of the Act applies to the information described in this section.

(Authority: 20 U.S.C. 1411(i)(2))

§ 300.261 Public participation.

In fulfilling the requirements of § 300.260 the Secretary of the Interior shall provide for public participation consistent with §§ 300.280–300.284.

(Authority: 20 U.S.C. 1411(i))

§ 300.262 Use of Part B funds.

(a) The Department of the Interior may use five percent of its payment under § 300.715(b) and (c) in any fiscal year, or $500,000, whichever is greater, for administrative costs in carrying out the provisions of this part.

(b) Payments to the Secretary of the Interior under § 300.716 must be used in accordance with that section.

(Authority: 20 U.S.C. 1411(i))

§ 300.263 Plan for coordination of services.

(a) The Secretary of the Interior shall develop and implement a plan for the coordination of services for all Indian children with disabilities residing on reservations covered under Part B of the Act.

(b) The plan must provide for the coordination of services benefiting these children from whatever source, including tribes, the Indian Health Service, other BIA divisions, and other Federal agencies.

(c) In developing the plan, the Secretary of the Interior shall consult with all interested and involved parties.

(d) The plan must be based on the needs of the children and the system best suited for meeting those needs, and may involve the establishment of cooperative agreements between the BIA, other Federal agencies, and other entities.

(e) The plan also must be distributed upon request to States, SEAs and LEAs, and other agencies providing services to infants, toddlers, and children with disabilities, to tribes, and to other interested parties.

(Authority: 20 U.S.C. 1411(i)(4))

§ 300.264 Definitions.

(a) *Indian*. As used in this part, the term *Indian* means an individual who is a member of an Indian tribe.

(b) *Indian tribe*. As used in this part, the term *Indian tribe* means any Federal or State Indian tribe, band, rancheria, pueblo, colony, or community, including any Alaska Native village or regional village corporation (as defined in or established under the Alaska Native Claims Settlement Act).

(Authority: 20 U.S.C. 1401(9) and (10))

§ 300.265 Establishment of advisory board.

(a) To meet the requirements of section 612(a)(21) of the Act, the Secretary of the Interior shall establish, not later than December 4, 1997 under the BIA, an advisory board composed of individuals involved in or concerned with the education and provision of services to Indian infants, toddlers, and children with disabilities, including Indians with disabilities, Indian parents of the children, teachers, service providers, State and local educational officials, representatives of tribes or tribal organizations, representatives from State Interagency Coordinating Councils under section 641 of the Act in States having reservations, and other members representing the various divisions and entities of the BIA. The chairperson must be selected by the Secretary of the Interior.

(b) The advisory board shall—

(1) Assist in the coordination of services within the BIA and with other local, State, and Federal agencies in the provision of education for infants, toddlers, and children with disabilities;

(2) Advise and assist the Secretary of the Interior in the performance of the Secretary's responsibilities described in section 611(i) of the Act;

(3) Develop and recommend policies concerning effective inter- and intra-agency collaboration, including modifications to regulations, and the elimination of barriers to inter- and intra-agency programs and activities;

(4) Provide assistance and disseminate information on best practices, effective program coordination strategies, and recommendations for improved educational programming for Indian infants, toddlers, and children with disabilities; and

(5) Provide assistance in the preparation of information required under § 300.260(g).

(Authority: 20 U.S.C. 1411(i)(5))

§ 300.266 Annual report by advisory board.

(a) *General.* The advisory board established under § 300.265 shall prepare and submit to the Secretary of the Interior and to the Congress an annual report containing a description of the activities of the advisory board for the preceding year.

(b) *Report to the Secretary.* The Secretary of the Interior shall make available to the Secretary the report described in paragraph (a) of this section.

(Authority: 20 U.S.C. 1411(i)(6)(A))

§ 300.267 Applicable regulations.

The Secretary of the Interior shall comply with the requirements of §§ 300.301-300.303, 300.305-300.309, 300.340-300.348, 300.351, 300.360-300.382, 300.400-300.402, 300.500-300.586, 300.600-300.621, and 300.660-300.662.

(Authority: 20 U.S.C. 1411(i)(2)(A))

Public Participation

§ 300.280 Public hearings before adopting State policies and procedures.

Prior to its adoption of State policies and procedures related to this part, the SEA shall—

(a) Make the policies and procedures available to the general public;

(b) Hold public hearings; and

(c) Provide an opportunity for comment by the general public on the policies and procedures.

(Authority: 20 U.S.C. 1412(a)(20))

§ 300.281 Notice.

(a) The SEA shall provide adequate notice to the general public of the public hearings.

(b) The notice must be in sufficient detail to inform the general public about—

(1) The purpose and scope of the State policies and procedures and their relation to Part B of the Act;

(2) The availability of the State policies and procedures;

(3) The date, time, and location of each public hearing;

(4) The procedures for submitting written comments about the policies and procedures; and

(5) The timetable for submitting the policies and procedures to the Secretary for approval.

(c) The notice must be published or announced—

(1) In newspapers or other media, or both, with circulation adequate to notify the general public about the hearings; and

(2) Enough in advance of the date of the hearings to afford interested parties throughout the State a reasonable opportunity to participate.

(Authority: 20 U.S.C. 1412(a)(20))

§ 300.282 Opportunity to participate; comment period.

(a) The SEA shall conduct the public hearings at times and places that afford interested parties throughout the State a reasonable opportunity to participate.

(b) The policies and procedures must be available for comment for a period of at least 30 days following the date of the notice under § 300.281.

(Authority: 20 U.S.C. 1412(a)(20))

§ 300.283 Review of public comments before adopting policies and procedures.

Before adopting the policies and procedures, the SEA shall—

(a) Review and consider all public comments; and

(b) Make any necessary modifications in those policies and procedures.

(Authority: 20 U.S.C. 1412(a)(20))

§ 300.284 Publication and availability of approved policies and procedures.

After the Secretary approves a State's policies and procedures, the SEA shall give notice in newspapers or other media, or both, that the policies and procedures are approved. The notice must name places throughout the State where the policies and procedures are available for access by any interested person.

(Authority: 20 U.S.C. 1412(a)(20))

Subpart C—Services

Free Appropriate Public Education

§ 300.300 Provision of FAPE.

(a) *General.* (1) Subject to paragraphs (b) and (c) of this section and § 300.311, each State receiving assistance under this part shall ensure that FAPE is available to all children with disabilities, aged 3 through 21, residing in the State, including children with disabilities who have been suspended or expelled from school.

(2) As a part of its obligation under paragraph (a)(1) of this section, each State must ensure that the requirements of § 300.125 (to identify, locate, and evaluate all children with disabilities) are implemented by public agencies throughout the State.

(3)(i) The services provided to the child under this part address all of the child's identified special education and related services needs described in paragraph (a) of this section.

(ii) The services and placement needed by each child with a disability to receive FAPE must be based on the child's unique needs and not on the child's disability.

(b) *Exception for age ranges 3-5 and 18-21.* This paragraph provides the rules for applying the requirements in paragraph (a) of this section to children with disabilities aged 3, 4, 5, 18, 19, 20, and 21 within the State:

(1) If State law or a court order requires the State to provide education for children with disabilities in any disability category in any of these age groups, the State must make FAPE available to all children with disabilities of the same age who have that disability.

(2) If a public agency provides education to nondisabled children in any of these age groups, it must make FAPE available to at least a proportionate number of children with disabilities of the same age.

(3) If a public agency provides education to 50 percent or more of its children with disabilities in any disability category in any of these age groups, it must make FAPE available to all its children with disabilities of the same age who have that disability. This provision does not apply to children aged 3 through 5 for any fiscal year for which the State receives a grant under section 619(a)(1) of the Act.

(4) If a public agency provides education to a child with a disability in any of these age groups, it must make FAPE available to that child and provide that child and his or her parents all of the rights under Part B of the Act and this part.

(5) A State is not required to make FAPE available to a child with a disability in one of these age groups if—

(i) State law expressly prohibits, or does not authorize, the expenditure of public funds to provide education to nondisabled children in that age group; or

(ii) The requirement is inconsistent with a court order that governs the provision of free public education to children with disabilities in that State.

(c) *Children aged 3 through 21 on Indian reservations.* With the exception of children identified in § 300.715(b) and (c), the SEA shall ensure that all of the requirements of Part B of the Act are implemented for all children with disabilities aged 3 through 21 on reservations.

(Authority: 20 U.S.C. 1412(a)(1), 1411(i)(1)(C), S. Rep. No. 94—168, p. 19 (1975))

§ 300.301 FAPE—methods and payments.

(a) Each State may use whatever State, local, Federal, and private sources of support are available in the State to meet the requirements of this part. For example, if it is necessary to place a child with a disability in a residential facility, a State could use joint agreements between the agencies involved for sharing the cost of that placement.

(b) Nothing in this part relieves an insurer or similar third party from an otherwise valid obligation to provide or to pay for services provided to a child with a disability.

(c) Consistent with §§ 300.342(b)(2) and 300.343(b), the State must ensure that there is no delay in implementing a child's IEP, including any case in which the payment source for providing or paying for special education and related services to the child is being determined.

(Authority: 20 U.S.C. 1401(8), 1412(a)(1))

§ 300.302 Residential placement.

If placement in a public or private residential program is necessary to provide special education and related services to a child with a disability, the program, including non-medical care and room and board, must be at no cost to the parents of the child.

(Authority: 20 U.S.C. 1412(a)(1), 1412(a)(10)(B))

§ 300.303 Proper functioning of hearing aids.

Each public agency shall ensure that the hearing aids worn in school by children with hearing impairments, including deafness, are functioning properly.

(Authority: 20 U.S.C. 1412(a)(1))

§ 300.304 Full educational opportunity goal.

Each SEA shall ensure that each public agency establishes and implements a goal of providing full educational opportunity to all children with disabilities in the area served by the public agency.

(Authority: 20 U.S.C. 1412(a)(2)

§ 300.305 Program options.

Each public agency shall take steps to ensure that its children with disabilities have available to them the variety of educational programs and services available to nondisabled children in the area served by the agency, including art, music, industrial arts, consumer and homemaking education, and vocational education.

(Authority: 20 U.S.C. 1412(a)(2), 1413(a)(1))

§ 300.306 Nonacademic services.

(a) Each public agency shall take steps to provide nonacademic and extracurricular services and activities in the manner necessary to afford children with disabilities an equal opportunity for participation in those services and activities.

(b) Nonacademic and extracurricular services and activities may include counseling services, athletics, transportation, health services, recreational activities, special interest groups or clubs sponsored by the public agency, referrals to agencies that provide assistance to individuals with disabilities, and employment of students, including both employment by the public agency and assistance in making outside employment available.

(Authority: 20 U.S.C. 1412(a)(1))

§ 300.307 Physical education.

(a) *General.* Physical education services, specially designed if necessary, must be made available to every child with a disability receiving FAPE.

(b) *Regular physical education.* Each child with a disability must be afforded the opportunity to participate in the regular physical education program available to nondisabled children unless—

(1) The child is enrolled full time in a separate facility; or

(2) The child needs specially designed physical education, as prescribed in the child's IEP.

(c) *Special physical education.* If specially designed physical education is prescribed in a child's IEP, the public agency responsible for the education of that child shall provide the services directly or make arrangements for those services to be provided through other public or private programs.

(d) *Education in separate facilities.* The public agency responsible for the education of a child with a disability who is enrolled in a separate facility shall ensure that the child receives appropriate physical education services in compliance with paragraphs (a) and (c) of this section.

(Authority: 20 U.S.C. 1412(a)(25), 1412(a)(5)(A))

§ 300.308 Assistive technology.

(a) Each public agency shall ensure that assistive technology devices or assistive technology services, or both, as those terms are defined in §§ 300.5-300.6, are made available to a child with a disability if required as a part of the child's—

(1) Special education under § 300.26;

(2) Related services under § 300.24; or

(3) Supplementary aids and services under §§ 300.28 and 300.550(b)(2).

(b) On a case-by-case basis, the use of school-purchased assistive technology devices in a child's home or in other settings is required if the child's IEP team determines that the child needs access to those devices in order to receive FAPE.

(Authority: 20 U.S.C. 1412(a)(12)(B)(i))

§ 300.309 Extended school year services.

(a) *General.* (1) Each public agency shall ensure that extended school year services are available as necessary to provide FAPE, consistent with paragraph (a)(2) of this section.

(2) Extended school year services must be provided only if a child's IEP team determines, on an individual basis, in accordance with §§ 300.340–300.350, that the services are necessary for the provision of FAPE to the child.

(3) In implementing the requirements of this section, a public agency may not—

(i) Limit extended school year services to particular categories of disability; or

(ii) Unilaterally limit the type, amount, or duration of those services.

(b) *Definition.* As used in this section, the term extended school year services means special education and related services that—

(1) Are provided to a child with a disability—

(i) Beyond the normal school year of the public agency;

(ii) In accordance with the child's IEP; and

(iii) At no cost to the parents of the child; and

(2) Meet the standards of the SEA.

(Authority: 20 U.S.C. 1412(a)(1))

§ 300.310 [Reserved]

§ 300.311 FAPE requirements for students with disabilities in adult prisons.

(a) *Exception to FAPE for certain students.* Except as provided in § 300.122(a)(2)(ii), the obligation to make FAPE available to all children with disabilities does not apply with respect to students aged 18 through 21 to the extent that State law does not require that special education and related services under Part B of the Act be provided to students with disabilities who, in the last educational placement prior to their incarceration in an adult correctional facility—

(1) Were not actually identified as being a child with a disability under § 300.7; and

(2) Did not have an IEP under Part B of the Act.

(b) *Requirements that do not apply.* The following requirements do not apply to students with disabilities who are convicted as adults under State law and incarcerated in adult prisons:

(1) The requirements contained in § 300.138 and § 300.347(a)(5)(i) (relating to participation of children with disabilities in general assessments).

(2) The requirements in § 300.347(b) (relating to transition planning and transition services), with respect to the students whose eligibility under Part B of the Act will end, because of their age, before they will be eligible to be released from prison based on consideration of their sentence and eligibility for early release.

(c) *Modifications of IEP or placement.* (1) Subject to paragraph (c)(2) of this section, the IEP team of a student with a disability, who is convicted as an adult under State law and incarcerated in an adult prison, may modify the student's IEP or placement if the State has demonstrated a bona fide security or compelling penological interest that cannot otherwise be accommodated.

(2) The requirements of §§ 300.340(a) and 300.347(a) relating to IEPs, and 300.550(b) relating to LRE, do not apply with respect to the modifications described in paragraph (c)(1) of this section.

(Authority: 20 U.S.C. 1412(a)(1), 1414(d)(6))

§ 300.312 Children with disabilities in public charter schools.

(a) Children with disabilities who attend public charter schools and their parents retain all rights under this part.

(b) If the public charter school is an LEA, consistent with § 300.17, that receives funding under §§ 300.711-300.714, that charter school is responsible for ensuring that the requirements of this part are met, unless State law assigns that responsibility to some other entity.

(c) If the public charter school is a school of an LEA that receives funding under §§ 300.711-300.714 and includes other public schools—

(1) The LEA is responsible for ensuring that the requirements of this part are met, unless State law assigns that responsibility to some other entity; and

(2) The LEA must meet the requirements of § 300.241.

(d)(1) If the public charter school is not an LEA receiving funding under §§ 300.711–300.714, or a school that is part of an LEA receiving funding under §§ 300.711–300.714, the SEA is responsible for ensuring that the requirements of this part are met.

(2) Paragraph (d)(1) of this section does not preclude a State from assigning initial responsibility for ensuring the requirements of this part are met to another entity; however, the SEA must maintain the ultimate responsibility for ensuring compliance with this part, consistent with § 300.600.

(Authority: 20 U.S.C. 1413(a)(5))

§ 300.313 Children experiencing developmental delays.

(a) *Use of term developmental delay.* (1) A State that adopts the term *developmental delay* under § 300.7(b) determines whether it applies to children aged 3 through 9, or to a subset of that age range (e.g., ages 3 through 5).

(2) A State may not require an LEA to adopt and use the term *developmental delay* for any children within its jurisdiction.

(3) If an LEA uses the term *developmental delay* for children described in § 300.7(b), the LEA must conform to both the State's definition of that term and to the age range that has been adopted by the State.

(4) If a State does not adopt the term *developmental delay*, an LEA may not independently use that term as a basis for establishing a child's eligibility under this part.

(b) *Use of individual disability categories.* (1) Any State or LEA that elects to use the term developmental delay for children aged 3 through 9 may also use one or more of the disability categories described in § 300.7 for any child within that age range if it is determined, through the evaluation conducted under §§ 300.53–300.536, that the child has an impairment described in § 300.7, and because of that impairment needs special education and related services.

(2) The State or LEA shall ensure that all of the child's special education and related services needs that have been identified through the

evaluation described in paragraph (b)(1) of this section are appropriately addressed.

(c) *Common definition of developmental delay.* A State may adopt a common definition of developmental delay for use in programs under Parts B and C of the Act.

(Authority: 20 U.S.C. 1401(3)(A) and (B))

Evaluations and Reevaluations

§ 300.320 Initial evaluations.

(a) Each public agency shall ensure that a full and individual evaluation is conducted for each child being considered for special education and related services under Part B of the Act—

(1) To determine if the child is a "child with a disability" under § 300.7; and

(2) To determine the educational needs of the child.

(b) In implementing the requirements of paragraph (a) of this section, the public agency shall ensure that—

(1) The evaluation is conducted in accordance with the procedures described in §§ 300.53–300.535; and

(2) The results of the evaluation are used by the child's IEP team in meeting the requirements of §§ 300.34–300.350.

(Authority: 20 U.S.C. 1414(a), (b), and (c))

§ 300.321 Reevaluations.

Each public agency shall ensure that—

(a) A reevaluation of each child with a disability is conducted in accordance with § 300.536; and

(b) The results of any reevaluations are addressed by the child's IEP team under §§ 300.34–300.349 in reviewing and, as appropriate, revising the child's IEP.

(Authority: 20 U.S.C. 1414(a)(2))

§§ 300.322-300.324 [Reserved]

Individualized Education Programs

§ 300.340 Definitions related to IEPs.

(a) *Individualized education program.* As used in this part, the term *individualized education program* or *IEP* means a written statement for a child with a disability that is developed, reviewed, and revised in a meeting in accordance with §§ 300.341–300.350.

(b) *Participating agency.* As used in § 300.348, *participating agency* means a State or local agency, other than the public agency responsible for a student's education, that is financially and legally responsible for providing transition services to the student.

(Authority: 20 U.S.C. 1401(11), 1412(a)(10)(B))

§ 300.341 Responsibility of SEA and other public agencies for IEPs.

(a) The SEA shall ensure that each public agency—

(1) Except as provided in §§ 300.450-300.462, develops and implements an IEP for each child with a disability served by that agency; and

(2) Ensures that an IEP is developed and implemented for each eligible child placed in or referred to a private school or facility by the public agency.

(b) Paragraph (a) of this section applies to—

(1) The SEA, if it is involved in providing direct services to children with disabilities, in accordance with § 300.370(a) and (b)(1); and

(2) Except as provided in § 300.600(d), the other public agencies described in § 300.2, including LEAs and other State agencies that provide special education and related services either directly, by contract, or through other arrangements.

(Authority: 20 U.S.C. 1412(a)(4), (a)(10)(B))

§ 300.342 When IEPs must be in effect.

(a) *General.* At the beginning of each school year, each public agency shall have an IEP in effect for each child with a disability within its jurisdiction.

(b) *Implementation of IEPs.* Each public agency shall ensure that—

(1) An IEP—

(i) Is in effect before special education and related services are provided to an eligible child under this part; and

(ii) Is implemented as soon as possible following the meetings described under § 300.343;

(2) The child's IEP is accessible to each regular education teacher, special education teacher, related service provider, and other service provider who is responsible for its implementation; and

(3) Each teacher and provider described in paragraph (b)(2) of this section is informed of—

(i) His or her specific responsibilities related to implementing the child's IEP; and

(ii) The specific accommodations, modifications, and supports that must be provided for the child in accordance with the IEP.

(c) *IEP or IFSP for children aged 3 through 5.* (1) In the case of a child with a disability aged 3 through 5 (or, at the discretion of the SEA a 2-year-old child with a disability who will turn age 3 during the school year), an IFSP that contains the material described in section 636 of the Act, and that is developed in accordance with §§ 300.341–

300.346 and §§ 300.349–300.350, may serve as the IEP of the child if using that plan as the IEP is—

(i) Consistent with State policy; and

(ii) Agreed to by the agency and the child's parents.

(2) In implementing the requirements of paragraph (c)(1) of this section, the public agency shall—

(i) Provide to the child's parents a detailed explanation of the differences between an IFSP and an IEP; and

(ii) If the parents choose an IFSP, obtain written informed consent from the parents.

(d) *Effective date for new requirements.* All IEPs developed, reviewed, or revised on or after July 1, 1998 must meet the requirements of §§ 300.34–300.350.

(Authority: 20 U.S.C. 1414(d)(2)(A) and (B), Pub. L. 105–17, § 201(a)(2)(A), (C)

§ 300.343 IEP meetings.

(a) *General.* Each public agency is responsible for initiating and conducting meetings for the purpose of developing, reviewing, and revising the IEP of a child with a disability (or, if consistent with § 300.342(c), an IFSP).

(b) *Initial IEPs; provision of services.* (1) Each public agency shall ensure that within a reasonable period of time following the agency's receipt of parent consent to an initial evaluation of a child—

(i) The child is evaluated; and

(ii) If determined eligible under this part, special education and related services are made available to the child in accordance with an IEP.

(2) In meeting the requirement in paragraph (b)(1) of this section, a meeting to develop an IEP for the child must be conducted within 30-days of a determination that the child needs special education and related services.

(c) *Review and revision of IEPs.* Each public agency shall ensure that the IEP team—

(1) Reviews the child's IEP periodically, but not less than annually, to determine whether the annual goals for the child are being achieved; and

(2) Revises the IEP as appropriate to address—

(i) Any lack of expected progress toward the annual goals described in § 300.347(a), and in the general curriculum, if appropriate;

(ii) The results of any reevaluation conducted under § 300.536;

(iii) Information about the child provided to, or by, the parents, as described in § 300.533(a)(1);

(iv) The child's anticipated needs; or

(v) Other matters.

(Authority: 20 U.S.C. 1413(a)(1), 1414(d)(4)(A))

§ 300.344 IEP team.

(a) *General.* The public agency shall ensure that the IEP team for each child with a disability includes—

(1) The parents of the child;

(2) At least one regular education teacher of the child (if the child is, or may be, participating in the regular education environment);

(3) At least one special education teacher of the child, or if appropriate, at least one special education provider of the child;

(4) A representative of the public agency who—

(i) Is qualified to provide, or supervise the provision of, specially designed instruction to meet the unique needs of children with disabilities;

(ii) Is knowledgeable about the general curriculum; and

(iii) Is knowledgeable about the availability of resources of the public agency;

(5) An individual who can interpret the instructional implications of evaluation results, who may be a member of the team described in paragraphs (a)(2) through (6) of this section;

(6) At the discretion of the parent or the agency, other individuals who have knowledge or special expertise regarding the child, including related services personnel as appropriate; and

(7) If appropriate, the child.

(b) *Transition services participants.* (1) Under paragraph (a)(7) of this section, the public agency shall invite a student with a disability of any age to attend his or her IEP meeting if a purpose of the meeting will be the consideration of—

(i) The student's transition services needs under § 300.347(b)(1);

(ii) The needed transition services for the student under § 300.347(b)(2); or

(iii) Both.

(2) If the student does not attend the IEP meeting, the public agency shall take other steps to ensure that the student's preferences and interests are considered.

(3)(i) In implementing the requirements of § 300.347(b)(2), the public agency also shall invite a representative of any other agency that is likely to be responsible for providing or paying for transition services.

(ii) If an agency invited to send a representative to a meeting does not do so, the public agency shall take other steps to obtain participation of the other agency in the planning of any transition services.

(c) *Determination of knowledge and special expertise.* The determination of the knowledge or special expertise of any individual described in paragraph (a)(6) of this section shall be made by the party (parents or public agency) who invited the individual to be a member of the IEP.

(d) *Designating a public agency representative.* A public agency may designate another public agency member of the IEP team to also serve as the agency representative, if the criteria in paragraph (a)(4) of this section are satisfied.

(Authority: 20 U.S.C. 1401(30), 1414(d)(1)(A)(7), (B))

§ 300.345 Parent participation.

(a) *Public agency responsibility—general.* Each public agency shall take steps to ensure that one or both of the parents of a child with a disability are present at each IEP meeting or are afforded the opportunity to participate, including—

(1) Notifying parents of the meeting early enough to ensure that they will have an opportunity to attend; and

(2) Scheduling the meeting at a mutually agreed on time and place.

(b) *Information provided to parents.* (1) The notice required under paragraph (a)(1) of this section must—

(i) Indicate the purpose, time, and location of the meeting and who will be in attendance; and

(ii) Inform the parents of the provisions in § 300.344(a)(6) and (c) (relating to the participation of other individuals on the IEP team who have knowledge or special expertise about the child).

(2) For a student with a disability beginning at age 14, or younger, if appropriate, the notice must also—

(i) Indicate that a purpose of the meeting will be the development of a statement of the transition services needs of the student required in § 300.347(b)(1); and

(ii) Indicate that the agency will invite the student.

(3) For a student with a disability beginning at age 16, or younger, if appropriate, the notice must—

(i) Indicate that a purpose of the meeting is the consideration of needed transition services for the student required in § 300.347(b)(2);

(ii) Indicate that the agency will invite the student; and

(iii) Identify any other agency that will be invited to send a representative.

(c) *Other methods to ensure parent participation.* If neither parent can attend, the public agency shall use other methods to ensure parent participation, including individual or conference telephone calls.

(d) *Conducting an IEP meeting without a parent in attendance.* A meeting may be conducted without a parent in attendance if the public agency is unable to convince the parents that they should attend. In this case the public agency must have a record of its attempts to arrange a mutually agreed on time and place, such as—

(1) Detailed records of telephone calls made or attempted and the results of those calls;

(2) Copies of correspondence sent to the parents and any responses received; and

(3) Detailed records of visits made to the parent's home or place of employment and the results of those visits.

(e) *Use of interpreters or other action, as appropriate.* The public agency shall take whatever action is necessary to ensure that the parent understands the proceedings at the IEP meeting, including arranging for an interpreter for parents with deafness or whose native language is other than English.

(f) *Parent copy of child's IEP.* The public agency shall give the parent a copy of the child's IEP at no cost to the parent.

(Authority: 20 U.S.C. 1414(d)(1)(B)(i))

§ 300.346 Development, review, and revision of IEP.

(a) *Development of IEP.* (1) *General.* In developing each child's IEP, the IEP team, shall consider—

(i) The strengths of the child and the concerns of the parents for enhancing the education of their child;

(ii) The results of the initial or most recent evaluation of the child; and

(iii) As appropriate, the results of the child's performance on any general State or district-wide assessment programs.

(2) *Consideration of special factors.* The IEP team also shall—

(i) In the case of a child whose behavior impedes his or her learning or that of others, consider, if appropriate, strategies, including positive behavioral interventions, strategies, and supports to address that behavior;

(ii) In the case of a child with limited English proficiency, consider the language needs of the child as those needs relate to the child's IEP;

(iii) In the case of a child who is blind or visually impaired, provide for instruction in Braille and the use of Braille unless the IEP team determines, after an evaluation of the child's reading and writing skills, needs, and appropriate reading and writing media (including an evaluation of the child's future needs for instruction in Braille or the use of Braille), that instruction in Braille or the use of Braille is not appropriate for the child;

(iv) Consider the communication needs of the child, and in the case of a child who is deaf or hard of hearing, consider the child's language and communication needs, opportunities for direct communications with peers and professional personnel in the child's language and communication mode, academic level, and full range of needs, including opportunities for direct instruction in the child's language and communication mode; and

(v) Consider whether the child requires assistive technology devices and services.

(b) *Review and Revision of IEP*. In conducting a meeting to review, and, if appropriate, revise a child's IEP, the IEP team shall consider the factors described in paragraph (a) of this section.

(c) *Statement in IEP*. If, in considering the special factors described in paragraphs (a)(1) and (2) of this section, the IEP team determines that a child needs a particular device or service (including an intervention, accommodation, or other program modification) in order for the child to receive FAPE, the IEP team must include a statement to that effect in the child's IEP.

(d) *Requirement with respect to regular education teacher*. The regular education teacher of a child with a disability, as a member of the IEP team, must, to the extent appropriate, participate in the development, review, and revision of the child's IEP, including assisting in the determination of—

(1) Appropriate positive behavioral interventions and strategies for the child; and

(2) Supplementary aids and services, program modifications or supports for school personnel that will be provided for the child, consistent with § 300.347(a)(3).

(e) *Construction*. Nothing in this section shall be construed to require the IEP team to include information under one component of a child's IEP that is already contained under another component of the child's IEP.

(Authority: 20 U.S.C. 1414(d)(3) and (4)(B) and (e))

§ 300.347 Content of IEP.

(a) *General*. The IEP for each child with a disability must include—

(1) A statement of the child's present levels of educational performance, including—

(i) How the child's disability affects the child's involvement and progress in the general curriculum (i.e., the same curriculum as for nondisabled children); or

(ii) For preschool children, as appropriate, how the disability affects the child's participation in appropriate activities;

(2) A statement of measurable annual goals, including benchmarks or short-term objectives, related to—

(i) Meeting the child's needs that result from the child's disability to enable the child to be involved in and progress in the general curriculum (i.e., the same curriculum as for nondisabled children), or for preschool children, as appropriate, to participate in appropriate activities; and

(ii) Meeting each of the child's other educational needs that result from the child's disability;

(3) A statement of the special education and related services and supplementary aids and services to be provided to the child, or on behalf of the child, and a statement of the program modifications or supports for school personnel that will be provided for the child—

(i) To advance appropriately toward attaining the annual goals;

(ii) To be involved and progress in the general curriculum in accordance with paragraph (a)(1) of this section and to participate in extracurricular and other nonacademic activities; and

(iii) To be educated and participate with other children with disabilities and nondisabled children in the activities described in this section;

(4) An explanation of the extent, if any, to which the child will not participate with nondisabled children in the regular class and in the activities described in paragraph (a)(3) of this section;

(5)(i) A statement of any individual modifications in the administration of State or district-wide assessments of student achievement that are needed in order for the child to participate in the assessment; and

(ii) If the IEP team determines that the child will not participate in a particular State or district-wide assessment of student achievement (or part of an assessment), a statement of—

(A) Why that assessment is not appropriate for the child; and

(B) How the child will be assessed;

(6) The projected date for the beginning of the services and modifications described in paragraph (a)(3) of this section, and the anticipated frequency, location, and duration of those services and modifications; and

(7) A statement of—

(i) How the child's progress toward the annual goals described in paragraph (a)(2) of this section will be measured; and

(ii) How the child's parents will be regularly informed (through such means as periodic report cards), at least as often as parents are informed of their nondisabled children's progress, of—

(A) Their child's progress toward the annual goals; and

(B) The extent to which that progress is sufficient to enable the child to achieve the goals by the end of the year.

(b) *Transition services*. The IEP must include—

(1) For each student with a disability beginning at age 14 (or younger, if determined appropriate by the IEP team), and updated annually, a statement of the transition service needs of the student under the applicable components of the student's IEP that focuses on the student's courses of study (such as participation in advanced-placement courses or a vocational education program); and

(2) For each student beginning at age 16 (or younger, if determined appropriate by the IEP

team), a statement of needed transition services for the student, including, if appropriate, a statement of the interagency responsibilities or any needed linkages.

(c) *Transfer of rights*. In a State that transfers rights at the age majority, beginning at least one year before a student reaches the age of majority under State law, the student's IEP must include a statement that the student has been informed of his or her rights under Part B of the Act, if any, that will transfer to the student on reaching the age of majority, consistent with § 300.517.

(d) *Students with disabilities convicted as adults and incarcerated in adult prisons*. Special rules concerning the content of IEPs for students with disabilities convicted as adults and incarcerated in adult prisons are contained in § 300.311(b) and (c).

(Authority: 20 U.S.C. 1414(d)(1)(A) and (d)(6)(A)(ii))

§ 300.348 Agency responsibilities for transition services.

(a) If a participating agency, other than the public agency, fails to provide the transition services described in the IEP in accordance with § 300.347(b)(1), the public agency shall reconvene the IEP team to identify alternative strategies to meet the transition objectives for the student set out in the IEP.

(b) Nothing in this part relieves any participating agency, including a State vocational rehabilitation agency, of the responsibility to provide or pay for any transition service that the agency would otherwise provide to students with disabilities who meet the eligibility criteria of that agency.

(Authority: 20 U.S.C. 1414(d)(5); 1414(d)(1)(A)(vii))

§ 300.349 Private school placements by public agencies.

(a) *Developing IEPs*. (1) Before a public agency places a child with a disability in, or refers a child to, a private school or facility, the agency shall initiate and conduct a meeting to develop an IEP for the child in accordance with §§ 300.346 and 300.347.

(2) The agency shall ensure that a representative of the private school or facility attends the meeting. If the representative cannot attend, the agency shall use other methods to ensure participation by the private school or facility, including individual or conference telephone calls.

(b) *Reviewing and revising IEPs*. (1) After a child with a disability enters a private school or facility, any meetings to review and revise the child's IEP may be initiated and conducted by the private school or facility at the discretion of the public agency.

(2) If the private school or facility initiates and conducts these meetings, the public agency shall ensure that the parents and an agency representative—

(i) Are involved in any decision about the child's IEP; and

(ii) Agree to any proposed changes in the IEP before those changes are implemented.

(c) *Responsibility*. Even if a private school or facility implements a child's IEP, responsibility for compliance with this part remains with the public agency and the SEA.

(Authority: 20 U.S.C. 1412(a)(10)(B))

§ 300.350 IEP—accountability.

(a) *Provision of services*. Subject to paragraph (b) of this section, each public agency must—

(1) Provide special education and related services to a child with a disability in accordance with the child's IEP; and

(2) Make a good faith effort to assist the child to achieve the goals and objectives or benchmarks listed in the IEP.

(b) *Accountability*. Part B of the Act does not require that any agency, teacher, or other person be held accountable if a child does not achieve the growth projected in the annual goals and benchmarks or objectives. However, the Act does not prohibit a State or public agency from establishing its own accountability systems regarding teacher, school, or agency performance.

(c) *Construction—parent rights*. Nothing in this section limits a parent's right to ask for revisions of the child's IEP or to invoke due process procedures if the parent feels that the efforts required in paragraph (a) of this section are not being made.

(Authority: 20 U.S.C. 1414(d)); Cong. Rec. at H7152 (daily ed., July 21, 1975))

Direct Services by the SEA

§ 300.360 Use of LEA allocation for direct services.

(a) *General*. An SEA shall use the payments that would otherwise have been available to an LEA or to a State agency to provide special education and related services directly to children with disabilities residing in the area served by that local agency, or for whom that State agency is responsible, if the SEA determines that the LEA or State agency—

(1) Has not provided the information needed to establish the eligibility of the agency under Part B of the Act;

(2) Is unable to establish and maintain programs of FAPE that meet the requirements of this part;

(3) Is unable or unwilling to be consolidated with one or more LEAs in order to establish and maintain the programs; or

(4) Has one or more children with disabilities who can best be served by a regional or State program or service-delivery system designed to meet the needs of these children.

(b) *SEA responsibility if an LEA does not apply for Part B funds.* (1) If an LEA elects not to apply for its Part B allotment, the SEA must use those funds to ensure that FAPE is available to all eligible children residing in the jurisdiction of the LEA.

(2)(i) If the local allotment is not sufficient to meet the purpose described in paragraph (b)(1) of this section, the SEA must ensure compliance with §§ 300.121(a) and 300.300(a).

(ii) Consistent with § 300.301(a), the [State; SEA] may use whatever funding sources are available in the State to implement paragraph (b)(2)(i) of this section.

(c) *SEA administrative procedures.* (1) In meeting the requirements in paragraph (a) of this section, the SEA may provide special education and related services directly, by contract, or through other arrangements.

(2) The excess cost requirements of §§ 300.184 and 300.185 do not apply to the SEA.

(Authority: 20 U.S.C. 1413(h)(1))

§ 300.361 Nature and location of services.

The SEA may provide special education and related services under § 300.360(a) in the manner and at the location it considers appropriate (including regional and State centers). However, the manner in which the education and services are provided must be consistent with the requirements of this part (including the LRE provisions of §§ 300.550-300.556).

(Authority: 20 U.S.C. 1413(h)(2))

§§ 300.362-300.369 [Reserved]

§ 300.370 Use of SEA allocations.

(a) Each State shall use any funds it retains under § 300.602 and does not use for administration under § 300.620 for any of the following:

(1) Support and direct services, including technical assistance and personnel development and training.

(2) Administrative costs of monitoring and complaint investigation, but only to the extent that those costs exceed the costs incurred for those activities during fiscal year 1985.

(3) To establish and implement the mediation process required by § 300.506, including providing for the costs of mediators and support personnel.

(4) To assist LEAs in meeting personnel shortages.

(5) To develop a State Improvement Plan under subpart 1 of Part D of the Act.

(6) Activities at the State and local levels to meet the performance goals established by the State under § 300.137 and to support implementation of the State Improvement Plan under subpart 1 of Part D of the Act if the State receives funds under that subpart.

(7) To supplement other amounts used to develop and implement a Statewide coordinated services system designed to improve results for children and families, including children with disabilities and their families, but not to exceed one percent of the amount received by the State under section 611 of the Act. This system must be coordinated with and, to the extent appropriate, build on the system of coordinated services developed by the State under Part C of the Act.

(8) For subgrants to LEAs for the purposes described in § 300.622 (local capacity building).

(b) For the purposes of paragraph (a) of this section—

(1) *Direct services* means services provided to a child with a disability by the State directly, by contract, or through other arrangements; and

(2) *Support services* includes implementing the comprehensive system of personnel development under §§ 300.380-300.382, recruitment and training of mediators, hearing officers, and surrogate parents, and public information and parent training activities relating to FAPE for children with disabilities.

(c) Of the funds an SEA retains under paragraph (a) of this section, the SEA may use the funds directly, or distribute them to LEAs on a competitive, targeted, or formula basis.

(Authority: 20 U.S.C. 1411(f)(3))

§ 300.371 [Reserved]

§ 300.372 Nonapplicability of requirements that prohibit commingling and supplanting of funds.

A State may use funds it retains under § 300.602 without regard to—

(a) The prohibition on commingling of funds in § 300.152; and

(b) The prohibition on supplanting other funds in § 300.153.

(Authority: 20 U.S.C. 1411(f)(1)(C))

Comprehensive System of Personnel Development (CSPD)

§ 300.380 General CSPD requirements.

(a) Each State shall develop and implement a comprehensive system of personnel development that—

(1) Is consistent with the purposes of this part and with section 635(a)(8) of the Act;

(2) Is designed to ensure an adequate supply of qualified special education, regular education, and related services personnel;

(3) Meets the requirements of §§ 300.381 and 300.382; and

(4) Is updated at least every five years.

(b) A State that has a State improvement grant has met the requirements of paragraph (a) of this section.

(Authority: 20 U.S.C. 1412(a)(14))

§ 300.381 Adequate supply of qualified personnel.

Each State must include, at least, an analysis of State and local needs for professional development for personnel to serve children with disabilities that includes, at a minimum—

(a) The number of personnel providing special education and related services; and

(b) Relevant information on current and anticipated personnel vacancies and shortages (including the number of individuals described in paragraph (a) of this section with temporary certification), and on the extent of certification or retraining necessary to eliminate these shortages, that is based, to the maximum extent possible, on existing assessments of personnel needs.

(Authority: 20 U.S.C. 1453(b)(2)(B))

§ 300.382 Improvement strategies.

Each State must describe the strategies the State will use to address the needs identified under § 300.381. These strategies must include how the State will address the identified needs for in-service and pre-service preparation to ensure that all personnel who work with children with disabilities (including both professional and paraprofessional personnel who provide special education, general education, related services, or early intervention services) have the skills and knowledge necessary to meet the needs of children with disabilities. The plan must include a description of how the State will—

(a) Prepare general and special education personnel with the content knowledge and collaborative skills needed to meet the needs of children with disabilities including how the State will work with other States on common certification criteria;

(b) Prepare professionals and paraprofessionals in the area of early intervention with the content knowledge and collaborative skills needed to meet the needs of infants and toddlers with disabilities;

(c) Work with institutions of higher education and other entities that (on both a pre-service and an in-service basis) prepare personnel who work with children with disabilities to ensure that those institutions and entities develop the capacity to support quality professional development programs that meet State and local needs;

(d) Work to develop collaborative agreements with other States for the joint support and development of programs to prepare personnel for which there is not sufficient demand within a single State to justify support or development of a program of preparation;

(e) Work in collaboration with other States, particularly neighboring States, to address the lack of uniformity and reciprocity in credentialing of teachers and other personnel;

(f) Enhance the ability of teachers and others to use strategies, such as behavioral interventions, to address the conduct of children with disabilities that impedes the learning of children with disabilities and others;

(g) Acquire and disseminate, to teachers, administrators, school board members, and related services personnel, significant knowledge derived from educational research and other sources, and how the State will, if appropriate, adopt promising practices, materials, and technology;

(h) Recruit, prepare, and retain qualified personnel, including personnel with disabilities and personnel from groups that are under-represented in the fields of regular education, special education, and related services;

(i) Insure that the plan is integrated, to the maximum extent possible, with other professional development plans and activities, including plans and activities developed and carried out under other Federal and State laws that address personnel recruitment and training; and

(j) Provide for the joint training of parents and special education, related services, and general education personnel.

(Authority: 20 U.S.C. 1453 (c)(3)(D))

§§ 300.383–300.387 [Reserved]

Subpart D—Children in Private Schools

Children With Disabilities in Private Schools Placed or Referred by Public Agencies

§ 300.400 Applicability of §§ 300.400–300.402.

Sections 300.401-300.402 apply only to children with disabilities who are or have been placed in or referred to a private school or facility by a public agency as a means of providing special education and related services.

(Authority: 20 U.S.C. 1412(a)(10)(B))

§ 300.401 Responsibility of State educational agency.

Each SEA shall ensure that a child with a disability who is placed in or referred to a private school or facility by a public agency—

(a) Is provided special education and related services—

(1) In conformance with an IEP that meets the requirements of §§ 300.340-300.350; and

(2) At no cost to the parents;

(b) Is provided an education that meets the standards that apply to education provided by the SEA and LEAs (including the requirements of this part); and

(c) Has all of the rights of a child with a disability who is served by a public agency.

(Authority: 20 U.S.C. 1412(a)(10)(B))

§ 300.402 Implementation by State educational agency.

In implementing § 300.401, the SEA shall—

(a) Monitor compliance through procedures such as written reports, on-site visits, and parent questionnaires;

(b) Disseminate copies of applicable standards to each private school and facility to which a public agency has referred or placed a child with a disability; and

(c) Provide an opportunity for those private schools and facilities to participate in the development and revision of State standards that apply to them.

(Authority: 20 U.S.C. 1412(a)(10)(B))

Children With Disabilities Enrolled by Their Parents in Private Schools When FAPE Is at Issue

§ 300.403 Placement of children by parents if FAPE is at issue.

(a) *General.* This part does not require an LEA to pay for the cost of education, including special education and related services, of a child with a disability at a private school or facility if that agency made FAPE available to the child and the parents elected to place the child in a private school or facility. However, the public agency shall include that child in the population whose needs are addressed consistent with §§ 300.450–300.462.

(b) *Disagreements about FAPE.* Disagreements between a parent and a public agency regarding the availability of a program appropriate for the child, and the question of financial responsibility, are subject to the due process procedures of §§ 300.500–300.517.

(c) *Reimbursement for private school placement.* If the parents of a child with a disability, who previously received special education and related services under the authority of a public agency, enroll the child in a private preschool, elementary, or secondary school without the consent of or referral by the public agency, a court or a hearing officer may require the agency to reimburse the parents for the cost of that enrollment if the court or hearing officer finds that the agency had not made FAPE available to the child in a timely manner prior to that enrollment and that the private placement is appropriate. A parental placement may be found to be appropriate by a hearing officer or a court even if it does not meet the State standards that apply to education provided by the SEA and LEAs.

(d) *Limitation on reimbursement.* The cost of reimbursement described in paragraph (c) of this section may be reduced or denied—

(1) If—

(i) At the most recent IEP meeting that the parents attended prior to removal of the child from the public school, the parents did not inform the IEP team that they were rejecting the placement proposed by the public agency to provide FAPE to their child, including stating their concerns and their intent to enroll their child in a private school at public expense; or

(ii) At least ten (10) business days (including any holidays that occur on a business day) prior to the removal of the child from the public school, the parents did not give written notice to the public agency of the information described in paragraph (d)(1)(i) of this section;

(2) If, prior to the parents' removal of the child from the public school, the public agency informed the parents, through the notice requirements described in § 300.503(a)(1), of its intent to evaluate the child (including a statement of the purpose of the evaluation that was appropriate and reasonable), but the parents did not make the child available for the evaluation; or

(3) Upon a judicial finding of unreasonableness with respect to actions taken by the parents.

(e) *Exception.* Notwithstanding the notice requirement in paragraph (d)(1) of this section, the cost of reimbursement may not be reduced or denied for failure to provide the notice if—

(1) The parent is illiterate and cannot write in English;

(2) Compliance with paragraph (d)(1) of this section would likely result in physical or serious emotional harm to the child;

(3) The school prevented the parent from providing the notice; or

(4) The parents had not received notice, pursuant to section 615 of the Act, of the notice

requirement in paragraph (d)(1) of this section.

(Authority: 20 U.S.C. 1412(a)(10)(C))

Children With Disabilities Enrolled by Their Parents in Private Schools

§ 300.450 Definition of "private school children with disabilities."

As used in this part, *private school children with disabilities* means children with disabilities enrolled by their parents in private schools or facilities other than children with disabilities covered under §§ 300.400-300.402.

(Authority: 20 U.S.C. 1412(a)(10)(A))

§ 300.451 Child find for private school children with disabilities.

(a) Each LEA shall locate, identify, and evaluate all private school children with disabilities, including religious-school children residing in the jurisdiction of the LEA, in accordance with §§ 300.125 and 300.220. The activities undertaken to carry out this responsibility for private school children with disabilities must be comparable to activities undertaken for children with disabilities in public schools.

(b) Each LEA shall consult with appropriate representatives of private school children with disabilities on how to carry out the activities described in paragraph (a) of this section.

(Authority: 20 U.S.C. 1412(a)(10)(A)(ii))

§ 300.452 Provision of services—basic requirement.

(a) *General.* To the extent consistent with their number and location in the State, provision must be made for the participation of private school children with disabilities in the program assisted or carried out under Part B of the Act by providing them with special education and related services in accordance with §§ 300.453-300.462.

(b) *SEA Responsibility—services plan.* Each SEA shall ensure that, in accordance with paragraph (a) of this section and §§ 300.454-300.456, a services plan is developed and implemented for each private school child with a disability who has been designated to receive special education and related services under this part.

(Authority: 20 U.S.C. 1412(a)(10)(A)(i))

§ 300.453 Expenditures.

(a) *Formula.* To meet the requirement of § 300.452(a), each LEA must spend on providing special education and related services to private school children with disabilities—

(1) For children aged 3 through 21, an amount that is the same proportion of the LEA's total subgrant under section 611(g) of the Act as the number of private school children with disabilities aged 3 through 21 residing in its jurisdiction is to the total number of children with disabilities in its jurisdiction aged 3 through 21; and

(2) For children aged 3 through 5, an amount that is the same proportion of the LEA's total subgrant under section 619(g) of the Act as the number of private school children with disabilities aged 3 through 5 residing in its jurisdiction is to the total number of children with disabilities in its jurisdiction aged 3 through 5.

(b) *Child count.* (1) Each LEA shall—

(i) Consult with representatives of private school children in deciding how to conduct the annual count of the number of private school children with disabilities; and

(ii) Ensure that the count is conducted on December 1 or the last Friday of October of each year.

(2) The child count must be used to determine the amount that the LEA must spend on providing special education and related services to private school children with disabilities in the next subsequent fiscal year.

(c) *Expenditures for child find may not be considered.* Expenditures for child find activities described in § 300.451 may not be considered in determining whether the LEA has met the requirements of paragraph (a) of this section.

(d) *Additional services permissible.* State and local educational agencies are not prohibited from providing services to private school children with disabilities in excess of those required by this part, consistent with State law or local policy.

(Authority: 20 U.S.C. 1412(a)(10)(A))

§ 300.454 Services determined.

(a) *No individual right to special education and related services.* (1) No private school child with a disability has an individual right to receive some or all of the special education and related services that the child would receive if enrolled in a public school.

(2) Decisions about the services that will be provided to private school children with disabilities under §§ 300.452-300.462, must be made in accordance with paragraphs (b), and (c) of this section.

(b) *Consultation with representatives of private school children with disabilities.* (1) *General.* Each LEA shall consult, in a timely and meaningful way, with appropriate representatives of private school children with disabilities in light of the funding under § 300.453, the number of private school children with disabilities, the needs of private school children with disabilities, and their location to decide—

(i) Which children will receive services under § 300.452;

(ii) What services will be provided;

(iii) How and where the services will be provided; and

(iv) How the services provided will be evaluated.

(2) *Genuine opportunity*. Each LEA shall give appropriate representatives of private school children with disabilities a genuine opportunity to express their views regarding each matter that is subject to the consultation requirements in this section.

(3) *Timing*. The consultation required by paragraph (b)(1) of this section must occur before the LEA makes any decision that affects the opportunities of private school children with disabilities to participate in services under §§ 300.452-300.462.

(4) *Decisions*. The LEA shall make the final decisions with respect to the services to be provided to eligible private school children.

(c) *Services plan for each child served under §§ 300.450-300.462*. If a child with a disability is enrolled in a religious or other private school and will receive special education or related services from an LEA, the LEA shall—

(1) Initiate and conduct meetings to develop, review, and revise a services plan for the child, in accordance with § 300.455(b); and

(2) Ensure that a representative of the religious or other private school attends each meeting. If the representative cannot attend, the LEA shall use other methods to ensure participation by the private school, including individual or conference telephone calls.

(Authority: 1412(a)(10)(A))

§ 300.455 Services provided.

(a) *General*. (1) The services provided to private school children with disabilities must be provided by personnel meeting the same standards as personnel providing services in the public schools.

(2) Private school children with disabilities may receive a different amount of services than children with disabilities in public schools.

(3) No private school child with a disability is entitled to any service or to any amount of a service the child would receive if enrolled in a public school.

(b) *Services provided in accordance with a services plan*. (1) Each private school child with a disability who has been designated to receive services under § 300.452 must have a services plan that describes the specific special education and related services that the LEA will provide to the child in light of the services that the LEA has determined, through the process described in §§ 300.453-300.454, it will make available to private school children with disabilities.

(2) The services plan must, to the extent appropriate—

(i) Meet the requirements of § 300.347, with respect to the services provided; and

(ii) Be developed, reviewed, and revised consistent with §§ 300.342–300.346.

(Authority: 20 U.S.C. 1412(a)(10)(A))

§ 300.456 Location of services; transportation.

(a) *On-site*. Services provided to private school children with disabilities may be provided on-site at a child's private school, including a religious school, to the extent consistent with law.

(b) *Transportation*. (1) General. (i) If necessary for the child to benefit from or participate in the services provided under this part, a private school child with a disability must be provided transportation—

(A) From the child's school or the child's home to a site other than the private school; and

(B) From the service site to the private school, or to the child's home, depending on the timing of the services.

(ii) LEAs are not required to provide transportation from the child's home to the private school.

(2) *Cost of transportation*. The cost of the transportation described in paragraph (b)(1)(i) of this section may be included in calculating whether the LEA has met the requirement of § 300.453.

(Authority: 20 U.S.C. 1412(a)(10)(A))

§ 300.457 Complaints.

(a) *Due process inapplicable*. The procedures in §§ 300.504–300.515 do not apply to complaints that an LEA has failed to meet the requirements of §§ 300.452–300.462, including the provision of services indicated on the child's services plan.

(b) *Due process applicable*. The procedures in §§ 300.504–300.515 do apply to complaints that an LEA has failed to meet the requirements of § 300.451, including the requirements of §§ 300.53–300.543.

(c) *State complaints*. Complaints that an SEA or LEA has failed to meet the requirements of §§ 300.451–300.462 may be filed under the procedures in §§ 300.66–300.662.

(Authority: 20 U.S.C. 1412(a)(10)(A))

§ 300.458 Separate classes prohibited.

An LEA may not use funds available under section 611 or 619 of the Act for classes that are organized separately on the basis of school enrollment or religion of the students if—

(a) The classes are at the same site; and

(b) The classes include students enrolled in public schools and students enrolled in private schools.

(Authority: 20 U.S.C. 1412(a)(10)(A))

§ 300.459 Requirement that funds not benefit a private school.

(a) An LEA may not use funds provided under section 611 or 619 of the Act to finance the existing level of instruction in a private school or to otherwise benefit the private school.

(b) The LEA shall use funds provided under Part B of the Act to meet the special education and related services needs of students enrolled in private schools, but not for—

(1) The needs of a private school; or

(2) The general needs of the students enrolled in the private school.

(Authority: 20 U.S.C. 1412(a)(10)(A))

§ 300.460 Use of public school personnel.

An LEA may use funds available under sections 611 and 619 of the Act to make public school personnel available in other than public facilities—

(a) To the extent necessary to provide services under §§ 300.450-300.462 for private school children with disabilities; and

(b) If those services are not normally provided by the private school.

(Authority: 20 U.S.C. 1412(a)(10)(A))

§ 300.461 Use of private school personnel.

An LEA may use funds available under section 611 or 619 of the Act to pay for the services of an employee of a private school to provide services under §§ 300.450-300.462 if—

(a) The employee performs the services outside of his or her regular hours of duty; and

(b) The employee performs the services under public supervision and control.

(Authority: 20 U.S.C. 1412(a)(10)(A))

§ 300.462 Requirements concerning property, equipment, and supplies for the benefit of private school children with disabilities.

(a) A public agency must keep title to and exercise continuing administrative control of all property, equipment, and supplies that the public agency acquires with funds under section 611 or 619 of the Act for the benefit of private school children with disabilities.

(b) The public agency may place equipment and supplies in a private school for the period of time needed for the program.

(c) The public agency shall ensure that the equipment and supplies placed in a private school—

(1) Are used only for Part B purposes; and

(2) Can be removed from the private school without remodeling the private school facility.

(d) The public agency shall remove equipment and supplies from a private school if—

(1) The equipment and supplies are no longer needed for Part B purposes; or

(2) Removal is necessary to avoid unauthorized use of the equipment and supplies for other than Part B purposes.

(e) No funds under Part B of the Act may be used for repairs, minor remodeling, or construction of private school facilities.

(Authority: 20 U.S.C. 1412(a)(10)(A))

Procedures for By-Pass

§ 300.480 By-pass—general.

(a) The Secretary implements a by-pass if an SEA is, and was on December 2, 1983, prohibited by law from providing for the participation of private school children with disabilities in the program assisted or carried out under Part B of the Act, as required by section 612(a)(10)(A) of the Act and by §§ 300.452-300.462.

(b) The Secretary waives the requirement of section 612(a)(10)(A) of the Act and of §§ 300.452-300.462 if the Secretary implements a by-pass.

(Authority: 20 U.S.C. 1412(f)(1))

§ 300.481 Provisions for services under a by-pass.

(a) Before implementing a by-pass, the Secretary consults with appropriate public and private school officials, including SEA officials, in the affected State to consider matters such as—

(1) The prohibition imposed by State law that results in the need for a by-pass;

(2) The scope and nature of the services required by private school children with disabilities

in the State, and the number of children to be served under the by-pass; and

(3) The establishment of policies and procedures to ensure that private school children with disabilities receive services consistent with the requirements of section 612(a)(10)(A) of the Act and §§ 300.452–300.462.

(b) After determining that a by-pass is required, the Secretary arranges for the provision of services to private school children with disabilities in the State in a manner consistent with the requirements of section 612(a)(10)(A) of the Act and §§ 300.452–300.462 by providing services through one or more agreements with appropriate parties.

(c) For any fiscal year that a by-pass is implemented, the Secretary determines the maximum amount to be paid to the providers of services by multiplying—

(1) A per child amount that may not exceed the amount per child provided by the Secretary under Part B of the Act for all children with disabilities in the State for the preceding fiscal year; by

(2) The number of private school children with disabilities (as defined by §§ 300.7(a) and 300.450) in the State, as determined by the Secretary on the basis of the most recent satisfactory data available, which may include an estimate of the number of those children with disabilities.

(d) The Secretary deducts from the State's allocation under Part B of the Act the amount the Secretary determines is necessary to implement a by-pass and pays that amount to the provider of services. The Secretary may withhold this amount from the State's allocation pending final resolution of any investigation or complaint that could result in a determination that a by-pass must be implemented.

(Authority: 20 U.S.C. 1412(f)(2))

§ 300.482 Notice of intent to implement a by-pass.

(a) Before taking any final action to implement a by-pass, the Secretary provides the affected SEA with written notice.

(b) In the written notice, the Secretary—

(1) States the reasons for the proposed by-pass in sufficient detail to allow the SEA to respond; and

(2) Advises the SEA that it has a specific period of time (at least 45 days) from receipt of the written notice to submit written objections to the proposed by-pass and that it may request in writing the opportunity for a hearing to show cause why a by-pass should not be implemented.

(c) The Secretary sends the notice to the SEA by certified mail with return receipt requested.

(Authority: 20 U.S.C. 1412(f)(3)(A))

§ 300.483 Request to show cause.

An SEA seeking an opportunity to show cause why a by-pass should not be implemented shall submit a written request for a show cause hearing to the Secretary.

(Authority: 20 U.S.C. 1412(f)(3))

§ 300.484 Show cause hearing.

(a) If a show cause hearing is requested, the Secretary—

(1) Notifies the SEA and other appropriate public and private school officials of the time and place for the hearing; and

(2) Designates a person to conduct the show cause hearing. The designee must not have had any responsibility for the matter brought for a hearing.

(b) At the show cause hearing, the designee considers matters such as—

(1) The necessity for implementing a by-pass;

(2) Possible factual errors in the written notice of intent to implement a by-pass; and

(3) The objections raised by public and private school representatives.

(c) The designee may regulate the course of the proceedings and the conduct of parties during the pendency of the proceedings. The designee takes all steps necessary to conduct a fair and impartial proceeding, to avoid delay, and to maintain order.

(d) The designee may interpret applicable statutes and regulations, but may not waive them or rule on their validity.

(e) The designee arranges for the preparation, retention, and, if appropriate, dissemination of the record of the hearing.

(Authority: 20 U.S.C. 1412(f)(3))

§ 300.485 Decision.

(a) The designee who conducts the show cause hearing—

(1) Issues a written decision that includes a statement of findings; and

(2) Submits a copy of the decision to the Secretary and sends a copy to each party by certified mail with return receipt requested.

(b) Each party may submit comments and recommendations on the designee's decision to the Secretary within 15 days of the date the party receives the designee's decision.

(c) The Secretary adopts, reverses, or modifies the designee's decision and notifies the SEA of the Secretary's final action. That notice is sent by certified mail with return receipt requested.

(Authority: 20 U.S.C. 1412(f)(3))

§ 300.486 Filing requirements.

(a) Any written submission under §§ 300.482-300.485 must be filed by hand-delivery, by mail, or by facsimile transmission. The Secretary discourages the use of facsimile transmission for documents longer than five pages.

(b) The filing date under paragraph (a) of this section is the date the document is—

(1) Hand-delivered;

(2) Mailed; or

(3) Sent by facsimile transmission.

(c) A party filing by facsimile transmission is responsible for confirming that a complete and legible copy of the document was received by the Department.

(d) If a document is filed by facsimile transmission, the Secretary or the hearing officer, as applicable, may require the filing of a follow-up hard copy by hand-delivery or by mail within a reasonable period of time.

(e) If agreed upon by the parties, service of a document may be made upon the other party by facsimile transmission.

(Authority: 20 U.S.C. 1412(f)(3))

§ 300.487 Judicial review.

If dissatisfied with the Secretary's final action, the SEA may, within 60 days after notice of that action, file a petition for review with the United States Court of Appeals for the circuit in which the State is located. The procedures for judicial review are described in section 612(f)(3)(B)–(D) of the Act.

(Authority: 20 U.S.C. 1412(f)(3)(B)-(D))

Subpart E—Procedural Safeguards

Due Process Procedures for Parents and Children

§ 300.500 General responsibility of public agencies; definitions.

(a) *Responsibility of SEA and other public agencies*. Each SEA shall ensure that each public agency establishes, maintains, and implements procedural safeguards that meet the requirements of §§ 300.500-300.529.

(b) *Definitions of "consent," "evaluation," and "personally identifiable."* As used in this part—

(1) *Consent* means that—

(i) The parent has been fully informed of all information relevant to the activity for which consent is sought, in his or her native language, or other mode of communication;

(ii) The parent understands and agrees in writing to the carrying out of the activity for which his or her consent is sought, and the consent describes that activity and lists the records (if any) that will be released and to whom; and

(iii)(A) The parent understands that the granting of consent is voluntary on the part of the parent and may be revoked at anytime.

(B) If a parent revokes consent, that revocation is not retroactive (i.e., it does not negate an action that has occurred after the consent was given and before the consent was revoked).

(2) *Evaluation* means procedures used in accordance with §§ 300.53–300.536 to determine whether a child has a disability and the nature and extent of the special education and related services that the child needs; and

(3) *Personally identifiable* means that information includes—

(i) The name of the child, the child's parent, or other family member;

(ii) The address of the child;

(iii) A personal identifier, such as the child's social security number or student number; or

(iv) A list of personal characteristics or other information that would make it possible to identify the child with reasonable certainty.

(Authority: 20 U.S.C. 1415(a))

§ 300.501 Opportunity to examine records; parent participation in meetings.

(a) *General*. The parents of a child with a disability must be afforded, in accordance with the procedures of §§ 300.562-300.569, an opportunity to—

(1) Inspect and review all education records with respect to—

(i) The identification, evaluation, and educational placement of the child; and

(ii) The provision of FAPE to the child; and

(2) Participate in meetings with respect to—

(i) The identification, evaluation, and educational placement of the child; and

(ii) The provision of FAPE to the child.

(b) *Parent participation in meetings*. (1) Each public agency shall provide notice consistent with § 300.345(a)(1) and (b)(1) to ensure that parents of children with disabilities have the opportunity to participate in meetings described in paragraph (a)(2) of this section.

(2) A meeting does not include informal or unscheduled conversations involving public agency personnel and conversations on issues such as teaching methodology, lesson plans, or coordination of service provision if those issues are not addressed in the child's IEP. A meeting also does not include preparatory activities that public agency personnel engage in to develop a proposal or response to a parent proposal that will be discussed at a later meeting.

(c) *Parent involvement in placement decisions.* (1) Each public agency shall ensure that the parents of each child with a disability are members of any group that makes decisions on the educational placement of their child.

(2) In implementing the requirements of paragraph (c)(1) of this section, the public agency shall use procedures consistent with the procedures described in § 300.345(a) through (b)(1).

(3) If neither parent can participate in a meeting in which a decision is to be made relating to the educational placement of their child, the public agency shall use other methods to ensure their participation, including individual or conference telephone calls, or video conferencing.

(4) A placement decision may be made by a group without the involvement of the parents, if the public agency is unable to obtain the parents' participation in the decision. In this case, the public agency must have a record of its attempt to ensure their involvement, including information that is consistent with the requirements of § 300.345(d).

(5) The public agency shall make reasonable efforts to ensure that the parents understand, and are able to participate in, any group discussions relating to the educational placement of their child, including arranging for an interpreter for parents with deafness, or whose native language is other than English.

(Authority: 20 U.S.C. 1414(f), 1415(b)(1))

§ 300.502 Independent educational evaluation.

(a) *General.* (1) The parents of a child with a disability have the right under this part to obtain an independent educational evaluation of the child, subject to paragraphs (b) through (e) of this section.

(2) Each public agency shall provide to parents, upon request for an independent educational evaluation, information about where an independent educational evaluation may be obtained, and the agency criteria applicable for independent educational evaluations as set forth in paragraph (e) of this section.

(3) For the purposes of this part—

(i) *Independent educational evaluation* means an evaluation conducted by a qualified examiner who is not employed by the public agency responsible for the education of the child in question; and

(ii) *Public expense* means that the public agency either pays for the full cost of the evaluation or ensures that the evaluation is otherwise provided at no cost to the parent, consistent with § 300.301.

(b) *Parent right to evaluation at public expense.* (1) A parent has the right to an independent educational evaluation at public expense if the parent disagrees with an evaluation obtained by the public agency.

(2) If a parent requests an independent educational evaluation at public expense, the public agency must, without unnecessary delay, either—

(i) Initiate a hearing under § 300.507 to show that its evaluation is appropriate; or

(ii) Ensure that an independent educational evaluation is provided at public expense, unless the agency demonstrates in a hearing under § 300.507 that the evaluation obtained by the parent did not meet agency criteria.

(3) If the public agency initiates a hearing and the final decision is that the agency's evaluation is appropriate, the parent still has the right to an independent educational evaluation, but not at public expense.

(4) If a parent requests an independent educational evaluation, the public agency may ask for the parent's reason why he or she objects to the public evaluation. However, the explanation by the parent may not be required and the public agency may not unreasonably delay either providing the independent educational evaluation at public expense or initiating a due process hearing to defend the public evaluation.

(c) *Parent-initiated evaluations.* If the parent obtains an independent educational evaluation at private expense, the results of the evaluation—

(1) Must be considered by the public agency, if it meets agency criteria, in any decision made with respect to the provision of FAPE to the child; and

(2) May be presented as evidence at a hearing under this subpart regarding that child.

(d) *Requests for evaluations by hearing officers.* If a hearing officer requests an independent educational evaluation as part of a hearing, the cost of the evaluation must be at public expense.

(e) *Agency criteria.* (1) If an independent educational evaluation is at public expense, the criteria under which the evaluation is obtained, including the location of the evaluation and the qualifications of the examiner, must be the same as the criteria that the public agency uses when it initiates an evaluation, to the extent those criteria are consistent with the parent's right to an independent educational evaluation.

(2) Except for the criteria described in paragraph (e)(1) of this section, a public agency may not impose conditions or timelines related to obtaining an independent educational evaluation at public expense.

(Authority: 20 U.S.C. 1415(b)(1))

§ 300.503 Prior notice by the public agency; content of notice.

(a) *Notice.* (1) Written notice that meets the requirements of paragraph (b) of this section must be given to the parents of a child with a disability a reasonable time before the public agency—

(i) Proposes to initiate or change the identification, evaluation, or educational placement of the child or the provision of FAPE to the child; or

(ii) Refuses to initiate or change the identification, evaluation, or educational placement of the child or the provision of FAPE to the child.

(2) If the notice described under paragraph (a)(1) of this section relates to an action proposed by the public agency that also requires parental consent under § 300.505, the agency may give notice at the same time it requests parent consent.

(b) *Content of notice.* The notice required under paragraph (a) of this section must include—

(1) A description of the action proposed or refused by the agency;

(2) An explanation of why the agency proposes or refuses to take the action;

(3) A description of any other options that the agency considered and the reasons why those options were rejected;

(4) A description of each evaluation procedure, test, record, or report the agency used as a basis for the proposed or refused action;

(5) A description of any other factors that are relevant to the agency's proposal or refusal;

(6) A statement that the parents of a child with a disability have protection under the procedural safeguards of this part and, if this notice is not an initial referral for evaluation, the means by which a copy of a description of the procedural safeguards can be obtained; and

(7) Sources for parents to contact to obtain assistance in understanding the provisions of this part.

(c) *Notice in understandable language.* (1) The notice required under paragraph (a) of this section must be—

(i) Written in language understandable to the general public; and

(ii) Provided in the native language of the parent or other mode of communication used by the parent, unless it is clearly not feasible to do so.

(2) If the native language or other mode of communication of the parent is not a written language, the public agency shall take steps to ensure—

(i) That the notice is translated orally or by other means to the parent in his or her native language or other mode of communication;

(ii) That the parent understands the content of the notice; and

(iii) That there is written evidence that the requirements in paragraphs (c)(2) (i) and (ii) of this section have been met.

(Authority: 20 U.S.C. 1415(b)(3), (4) and (c), 1414(b)(1))

§ 300.504 Procedural safeguards notice.

(a) *General.* A copy of the procedural safeguards available to the parents of a child with a disability must be given to the parents, at a minimum—

(1) Upon initial referral for evaluation;

(2) Upon each notification of an IEP meeting;

(3) Upon reevaluation of the child; and

(4) Upon receipt of a request for due process under § 300.507.

(b) *Contents.* The procedural safeguards notice must include a full explanation of all of the procedural safeguards available under §§ 300.403, 300.50–300.529, and 300.56–300.577, and the State complaint procedures available under §§ 300.660-300.662 relating to—

(1) Independent educational evaluation;

(2) Prior written notice;

(3) Parental consent;

(4) Access to educational records;

(5) Opportunity to present complaints to initiate due process hearings;

(6) The child's placement during pendency of due process proceedings;

(7) Procedures for students who are subject to placement in an interim alternative educational setting;

(8) Requirements for unilateral placement by parents of children in private schools at public expense;

(9) Mediation;

(10) Due process hearings, including requirements for disclosure of evaluation results and recommendations;

(11) State-level appeals (if applicable in that State);

(12) Civil actions;

(13) Attorneys' fees; and

(14) The State complaint procedures under §§ 300.66–300.662, including a description of how to file a complaint and the timelines under those procedures.

(c) *Notice in understandable language.* The notice required under paragraph (a) of this section must meet the requirements of § 300.503(c).

(Authority: 20 U.S.C. 1415(d))

§ 300.505 Parental consent.

(a) *General.* (1) Subject to paragraphs (a)(3), (b) and (c) of this section, informed parent consent must be obtained before—

(i) Conducting an initial evaluation or reevaluation; and

(ii) Initial provision of special education and related services to a child with a disability.

(2) Consent for initial evaluation may not be construed as consent for initial placement described in paragraph (a)(1)(ii) of this section.

(3) Parental consent is not required before—

(i) Reviewing existing data as part of an evaluation or a reevaluation; or

(ii) Administering a test or other evaluation that is administered to all children unless, before administration of that test or evaluation, consent is required of parents of all children.

(b) *Refusal*. If the parents of a child with a disability refuse consent for initial evaluation or a reevaluation, the agency may continue to pursue those evaluations by using the due process procedures under §§ 300.507-300.509, or the mediation procedures under § 300.506 if appropriate, except to the extent inconsistent with State law relating to parental consent.

(c) *Failure to respond to request for reevaluation*. (1) Informed parental consent need not be obtained for reevaluation if the public agency can demonstrate that it has taken reasonable measures to obtain that consent, and the child's parent has failed to respond.

(2) To meet the reasonable measures requirement in paragraph (c)(1) of this section, the public agency must use procedures consistent with those in § 300.345(d).

(d) *Additional State consent requirements*. In addition to the parental consent requirements described in paragraph (a) of this section, a State may require parental consent for other services and activities under this part if it ensures that each public agency in the State establishes and implements effective procedures to ensure that a parent's refusal to consent does not result in a failure to provide the child with FAPE.

(e) *Limitation*. A public agency may not use a parent's refusal to consent to one service or activity under paragraphs (a) and (d) of this section to deny the parent or child any other service, benefit, or activity of the public agency, except as required by this part.

(Authority: 20 U.S.C. 1415(b)(3); 1414(a)(1)(C) and (c)(3))

§ 300.506 Mediation.

(a) *General*. Each public agency shall ensure that procedures are established and implemented to allow parties to disputes involving any matter described in § 300.503(a)(1) to resolve the disputes through a mediation process that, at a minimum, must be available whenever a hearing is requested under §§ 300.507 or 300.520-300.528.

(b) *Requirements*. The procedures must meet the following requirements:

(1) The procedures must ensure that the mediation process—

(i) Is voluntary on the part of the parties;

(ii) Is not used to deny or delay a parent's right to a due process hearing under § 300.507, or to deny any other rights afforded under Part B of the Act; and

(iii) Is conducted by a qualified and impartial mediator who is trained in effective mediation techniques.

(2)(i) The State shall maintain a list of individuals who are qualified mediators and knowledgeable in laws and regulations relating to the provision of special education and related services.

(ii) If a mediator is not selected on a random (e.g., a rotation) basis from the list described in paragraph (b)(2)(i) of this section, both parties must be involved in selecting the mediator and agree with the selection of the individual who will mediate.

(3) The State shall bear the cost of the mediation process, including the costs of meetings described in paragraph (d) of this section.

(4) Each session in the mediation process must be scheduled in a timely manner and must be held in a location that is convenient to the parties to the dispute.

(5) An agreement reached by the parties to the dispute in the mediation process must be set forth in a written mediation agreement.

(6) Discussions that occur during the mediation process must be confidential and may not be used as evidence in any subsequent due process hearings or civil proceedings, and the parties to the mediation process may be required to sign a confidentiality pledge prior to the commencement of the process.

(c) *Impartiality of mediator*. (1) An individual who serves as a mediator under this part—

(i) May not be an employee of—

(A) Any LEA or any State agency described under § 300.194; or

(B) An SEA that is providing direct services to a child who is the subject of the mediation process; and

(ii) Must not have a personal or professional conflict of interest.

(2) A person who otherwise qualifies as a mediator is not an employee of an LEA or State agency described under § 300.194 solely because he or she is paid by the agency to serve as a mediator.

(d) *Meeting to encourage mediation*. (1) A public agency may establish procedures to require parents who elect not to use the mediation process to meet, at a time and location convenient to the parents, with a disinterested party—

(i) Who is under contract with a parent training and information center or community parent resource center in the State established under section 682 or 683 of the Act, or an appropriate alternative dispute resolution entity; and

(ii) Who would explain the benefits of the mediation process, and encourage the parents to use the process.

(2) A public agency may not deny or delay a parent's right to a due process hearing under § 300.507 if the parent fails to participate in the meeting described in paragraph (d)(1) of this section.

(Authority: 20 U.S.C. 1415(e))

§ 300.507 Impartial due process hearing; parent notice.

(a) *General.* (1) A parent or a public agency may initiate a hearing on any of the matters described in § 300.503(a)(1) and (2) (relating to the identification, evaluation or educational placement of a child with a disability, or the provision of FAPE to the child).

(2) When a hearing is initiated under paragraph (a)(1) of this section, the public agency shall inform the parents of the availability of mediation described in § 300.506.

(3) The public agency shall inform the parent of any free or low-cost legal and other relevant services available in the area if—

(i) The parent requests the information; or

(ii) The parent or the agency initiates a hearing under this section.

(b) *Agency responsible for conducting hearing.* The hearing described in paragraph (a) of this section must be conducted by the SEA or the public agency directly responsible for the education of the child, as determined under State statute, State regulation, or a written policy of the SEA.

(c) *Parent notice to the public agency.* (1) *General.* The public agency must have procedures that require the parent of a child with a disability or the attorney representing the child, to provide notice (which must remain confidential) to the public agency in a request for a hearing under paragraph (a)(1) of this section.

(2) *Content of parent notice.* The notice required in paragraph (c)(1) of this section must include—

(i) The name of the child;

(ii) The address of the residence of the child;

(iii) The name of the school the child is attending;

(iv) A description of the nature of the problem of the child relating to the proposed or refused initiation or change, including facts relating to the problem; and

(v) A proposed resolution of the problem to the extent known and available to the parents at the time.

(3) *Model form to assist parents.* Each SEA shall develop a model form to assist parents in filing a request for due process that includes the information required in paragraphs (c)(1) and (2) of this section.

(4) *Right to due process hearing.* A public agency may not deny or delay a parent's right to a due process hearing for failure to provide the notice required in paragraphs (c)(1) and (2) of this section.

(Authority: 20 U.S.C. 1415(b)(5), (b)(6), (b)(7), (b)(8), (e)(1) and (f)(1))

§ 300.508 Impartial hearing officer.

(a) A hearing may not be conducted—

(1) By a person who is an employee of the State agency or the LEA that is involved in the education or care of the child; or

(2) By any person having a personal or professional interest that would conflict with his or her objectivity in the hearing.

(b) A person who otherwise qualifies to conduct a hearing under paragraph (a) of this section is not an employee of the agency solely because he or she is paid by the agency to serve as a hearing officer.

(c) Each public agency shall keep a list of the persons who serve as hearing officers. The list must include a statement of the qualifications of each of those persons.

(Authority: 20 U.S.C. 1415(f)(3))

§ 300.509 Hearing rights.

(a) *General.* Any party to a hearing conducted pursuant to §§ 300.507 or 300.520-300.528, or an appeal conducted pursuant to § 300.510, has the right to—

(1) Be accompanied and advised by counsel and by individuals with special knowledge or training with respect to the problems of children with disabilities;

(2) Present evidence and confront, cross-examine, and compel the attendance of witnesses;

(3) Prohibit the introduction of any evidence at the hearing that has not been disclosed to that party at least 5 business days before the hearing;

(4) Obtain a written, or, at the option of the parents, electronic, verbatim record of the hearing; and

(5) Obtain written, or, at the option of the parents, electronic findings of fact and decisions.

(b) *Additional disclosure of information.* (1) At least 5 business days prior to a hearing conducted pursuant to § 300.507(a), each party shall disclose to all other parties all evaluations completed by that date and recommendations based on the offering party's evaluations that the party intends to use at the hearing.

(2) A hearing officer may bar any party that fails to comply with paragraph (b)(1) of this section from introducing the relevant evaluation or recommendation at the hearing without the consent of the other party.

(c) *Parental rights at hearings.* (1) Parents involved in hearings must be given the right to—

(i) Have the child who is the subject of the hearing present; and

(ii) Open the hearing to the public.

(2) The record of the hearing and the findings of fact and decisions described in paragraphs (a)(4) and (a)(5) of this section must be provided at no cost to parents.

(d) *Findings and decision to advisory panel and general public.* The public agency, after deleting any personally identifiable information, shall—

(1) Transmit the findings and decisions referred to in paragraph (a)(5) of this section to the State advisory panel established under § 300.650; and

(2) Make those findings and decisions available to the public.

(Authority: 20 U.S.C. 1415(f)(2) and (h))

§ 300.510 Finality of decision; appeal; impartial review.

(a) *Finality of decision.* A decision made in a hearing conducted pursuant to §§ 300.507 or 300.520-300.528 is final, except that any party involved in the hearing may appeal the decision under the provisions of paragraph (b) of this section and § 300.512.

(Authority: 20 U.S.C. 1415(i)(1)(A))

(b) *Appeal of decisions; impartial review.* (1) *General.* If the hearing required by § 300.507 is conducted by a public agency other than the SEA, any party aggrieved by the findings and decision in the hearing may appeal to the SEA.

(2) *SEA responsibility for review.* If there is an appeal, the SEA shall conduct an impartial review of the hearing. The official conducting the review shall—

(i) Examine the entire hearing record;

(ii) Ensure that the procedures at the hearing were consistent with the requirements of due process;

(iii) Seek additional evidence if necessary. If a hearing is held to receive additional evidence, the rights in § 300.509 apply;

(iv) Afford the parties an opportunity for oral or written argument, or both, at the discretion of the reviewing official;

(v) Make an independent decision on completion of the review; and

(vi) Give a copy of the written, or, at the option of the parents, electronic findings of fact and decisions to the parties.

(c) *Findings and decision to advisory panel and general public.* The SEA, after deleting any personally identifiable information, shall—

(1) Transmit the findings and decisions referred to in paragraph (b)(2)(vi) of this section to the State advisory panel established under § 300.650; and

(2) Make those findings and decisions available to the public.

(d) *Finality of review decision.* The decision made by the reviewing official is final unless a party brings a civil action under § 300.512.

(Authority: 20 U.S.C. 1415(g); H. R. Rep. No. 94-664, at p. 49 (1975))

§ 300.511 Timelines and convenience of hearings and reviews.

(a) The public agency shall ensure that not later than 45 days after the receipt of a request for a hearing—

(1) A final decision is reached in the hearing; and

(2) A copy of the decision is mailed to each of the parties.

(b) The SEA shall ensure that not later than 30 days after the receipt of a request for a review—

(1) A final decision is reached in the review; and

(2) A copy of the decision is mailed to each of the parties.

(c) A hearing or reviewing officer may grant specific extensions of time beyond the periods set out in paragraphs (a) and (b) of this section at the request of either party.

(d) Each hearing and each review involving oral arguments must be conducted at a time and place that is reasonably convenient to the parents and child involved.

(Authority: 20 U.S.C. 1415)

§ 300.512 Civil action.

(a) *General.* Any party aggrieved by the findings and decision made under §§ 300.507 or 300.520–300.528 who does not have the right to an appeal under § 300.510(b), and any party aggrieved by the findings and decision under § 300.510(b), has the right to bring a civil action with respect to the complaint presented pursuant to § 300.507. The action may be brought in any State court of competent jurisdiction or in a district court of the United States without regard to the amount in controversy.

(b) *Additional requirements.* In any action brought under paragraph (a) of this section, the court—

(1) Shall receive the records of the administrative proceedings;

(2) Shall hear additional evidence at the request of a party; and

(3) Basing its decision on the preponderance of the evidence, shall grant the relief that the court determines to be appropriate.

(c) *Jurisdiction of district courts.* The district courts of the United States have jurisdiction of actions brought under section 615 of the

Act without regard to the amount in controversy.

(d) *Rule of construction*. Nothing in this part restricts or limits the rights, procedures, and remedies available under the Constitution, the Americans with Disabilities Act of 1990, title V of the Rehabilitation Act of 1973, or other Federal laws protecting the rights of children with disabilities, except that before the filing of a civil action under these laws seeking relief that is also available under section 615 of the Act, the procedures under §§ 300.507 and 300.510 must be exhausted to the same extent as would be required had the action been brought under section 615 of the Act.

(Authority: 20 U.S.C. 1415(i)(2), (i)(3)(A), and 1415(l))

§ 300.513 Attorneys' fees.

(a) In any action or proceeding brought under section 615 of the Act, the court, in its discretion, may award reasonable attorneys' fees as part of the costs to the parents of a child with a disability who is the prevailing party.

(b)(1) Funds under Part B of the Act may not be used to pay attorneys' fees or costs of a party related to an action or proceeding under section 615 of the Act and subpart E of this part.

(2) Paragraph (b)(1) of this section does not preclude a public agency from using funds under Part B of the Act for conducting an action or proceeding under section 615 of the Act.

(c) A court awards reasonable attorney's fees under section 615(i)(3) of the Act consistent with the following:

(1) *Determination of amount of attorneys' fees*. Fees awarded under section 615(i)(3) of the Act must be based on rates prevailing in the community in which the action or proceeding arose for the kind and quality of services furnished. No bonus or multiplier may be used in calculating the fees awarded under this subsection.

(2) *Prohibition of attorneys' fees and related costs for certain services*. (i) Attorneys' fees may not be awarded and related costs may not be reimbursed in any action or proceeding under section 615 of the Act for services performed subsequent to the time of a written offer of settlement to a parent if—

(A) The offer is made within the time prescribed by Rule 68 of the Federal Rules of Civil Procedure or, in the case of an administrative proceeding, at any time more than 10 days before the proceeding begins;

(B) The offer is not accepted within 10 days; and

(C) The court or administrative hearing officer finds that the relief finally obtained by the parents is not more favorable to the parents than the offer of settlement.

(ii) Attorneys' fees may not be awarded relating to any meeting of the IEP team unless the meeting is convened as a result of an administrative proceeding or judicial action, or at the discretion of the State, for a mediation described in § 300.506 that is conducted prior to the filing of a request for due process under §§ 300.507 or 300.520-300.528.

(3) *Exception to prohibition on attorneys' fees and related costs*. Notwithstanding paragraph (c)(2) of this section, an award of attorneys' fees and related costs may be made to a parent who is the prevailing party and who was substantially justified in rejecting the settlement offer.

(4) *Reduction of amount of attorneys' fees*. Except as provided in paragraph (c)(5) of this section, the court reduces, accordingly, the amount of the attorneys' fees awarded under section 615 of the Act, if the court finds that—

(i) The parent, during the course of the action or proceeding, unreasonably protracted the final resolution of the controversy;

(ii) The amount of the attorneys' fees otherwise authorized to be awarded unreasonably exceeds the hourly rate prevailing in the community for similar services by attorneys of reasonably comparable skill, reputation, and experience;

(iii) The time spent and legal services furnished were excessive considering the nature of the action or proceeding; or

(iv) The attorney representing the parent did not provide to the school district the appropriate information in the due process complaint in accordance with § 300.507(c).

(5) *Exception to reduction in amount of attorneys' fees*. The provisions of paragraph (c)(4) of this section do not apply in any action or proceeding if the court finds that the State or local agency unreasonably protracted the final resolution of the action or proceeding or there was a violation of section 615 of the Act.

(Authority: 20 U.S.C. 1415(i)(3)(B)-(G))

§ 300.514 Child's status during proceedings.

(a) Except as provided in § 300.526, during the pendency of any administrative or judicial proceeding regarding a complaint under § 300.507, unless the State or local agency and the parents of the child agree otherwise, the child involved in the complaint must remain in his or her current educational placement.

(b) If the complaint involves an application for initial admission to public school, the child, with the consent of the parents, must be placed in the public school until the completion of all the proceedings.

(c) If the decision of a hearing officer in a due process hearing conducted by the SEA or a State review official in an administrative appeal agrees with the child's parents that a change of placement is appropriate, that placement must be treated as an agreement between the State or local agency and the parents for purposes of paragraph (a) of this section.

(Authority: 20 U.S.C. 1415(j))

§ 300.515 Surrogate parents.

(a) *General.* Each public agency shall ensure that the rights of a child are protected if—

(1) No parent (as defined in § 300.20) can be identified;

(2) The public agency, after reasonable efforts, cannot discover the whereabouts of a parent; or

(3) The child is a ward of the State under the laws of that State.

(b) *Duty of public agency.* The duty of a public agency under paragraph (a) of this section includes the assignment of an individual to act as a surrogate for the parents. This must include a method—

(1) For determining whether a child needs a surrogate parent; and

(2) For assigning a surrogate parent to the child.

(c) *Criteria for selection of surrogates.* (1) The public agency may select a surrogate parent in any way permitted under State law.

(2) Except as provided in paragraph (c)(3) of this section, public agencies shall ensure that a person selected as a surrogate—

(i) Is not an employee of the SEA, the LEA, or any other agency that is involved in the education or care of the child;

(ii) Has no interest that conflicts with the interest of the child he or she represents; and

(iii) Has knowledge and skills that ensure adequate representation of the child.

(3) A public agency may select as a surrogate a person who is an employee of a nonpublic agency that only provides non-educational care for the child and who meets the standards in paragraphs (c)(2)(ii) and (iii) of this section.

(d) *Non-employee requirement; compensation.* A person who otherwise qualifies to be a surrogate parent under paragraph (c) of this section is not an employee of the agency solely because he or she is paid by the agency to serve as a surrogate parent.

(e) *Responsibilities.* The surrogate parent may represent the child in all matters relating to—

(1) The identification, evaluation, and educational placement of the child; and

(2) The provision of FAPE to the child.

(Authority: 20 U.S.C. 1415(b)(2))

§ 300.516 [Reserved].

§ 300.517 Transfer of parental rights at age of majority.

(a) *General.* A State may provide that, when a student with a disability reaches the age of majority under State law that applies to all students (except for a student with a disability who has been determined to be incompetent under State law)—

(1)(i) The public agency shall provide any notice required by this part to both the individual and the parents; and

(ii) All other rights accorded to parents under Part B of the Act transfer to the student; and

(2) All rights accorded to parents under Part B of the Act transfer to students who are incarcerated in an adult or juvenile, State or local correctional institution.

(3) Whenever a State transfers rights under this part pursuant to paragraph (a)(1) or (a)(2) of this section, the agency shall notify the individual and the parents of the transfer of rights.

(b) *Special rule.* If, under State law, a State has a mechanism to determine that a student with a disability, who has reached the age of majority under State law that applies to all children and has not been determined incompetent under State law, does not have the ability to provide informed consent with respect to his or her educational program, the State shall establish procedures for appointing the parent, or, if the parent is not available another appropriate individual, to represent the educational interests of the student throughout the student's eligibility under Part B of the Act.

(Authority: 20 U.S.C. 1415(m))

Discipline Procedures

§ 300.519 Change of placement for disciplinary removals.

For purposes of removals of a child with a disability from the child's current educational placement under §§ 300.520-300.529, a change of placement occurs if—

(a) The removal is for more than 10 consecutive school days; or

(b) The child is subjected to a series of removals that constitute a pattern because they cumulate to more than 10 school days in a school year, and because of factors such as the length of each removal, the total amount of time the child is removed, and the proximity of the removals to one another.

(Authority: 20 U.S.C. 1415(k))

§ 300.520 Authority of school personnel.

(a) School personnel may order—

(1)(i) To the extent removal would be applied to children without disabilities, the removal of a child with a disability from the child's current placement for not more than 10 consecutive school days for any violation of school rules, and additional removals of not more than 10 consecutive school days in that same school year for separate incidents of misconduct (as long as those removals do not constitute a change of placement under § 300.519(b));

(ii) After a child with a disability has been removed from his or her current placement for more than 10 school days in the same school year, during any subsequent days of removal the public agency must provide services to the extent required under § 300.121(d); and

(2) A change in placement of a child with a disability to an appropriate interim alternative educational setting for the same amount of time that a child without a disability would be subject to discipline, but for not more than 45 days, if—

(i) The child carries a weapon to school or to a school function under the jurisdiction of a State or a local educational agency; or

(ii) The child knowingly possesses or uses illegal drugs or sells or solicits the sale of a controlled substance while at school or a school function under the jurisdiction of a State or local educational agency.

(b)(1) Either before or not later than 10 business days after either first removing the child for more than 10 school days in a school year or commencing a removal that constitutes a change of placement under § 300.519, including the action described in paragraph (a)(2) of this section—

(i) If the LEA did not conduct a functional behavioral assessment and implement a behavioral intervention plan for the child before the behavior that resulted in the removal described in paragraph (a) of this section, the agency shall convene an IEP meeting to develop an assessment plan.

(ii) If the child already has a behavioral intervention plan, the IEP team shall meet to review the plan and its implementation, and, modify the plan and its implementation as necessary, to address the behavior.

(2) As soon as practicable after developing the plan described in paragraph (b)(1)(i) of this section, and completing the assessments required by the plan, the LEA shall convene an IEP meeting to develop appropriate behavioral interventions to address that behavior and shall implement those interventions.

(c)(1) If subsequently, a child with a disability who has a behavioral intervention plan and who has been removed from the child's current educational placement for more than 10 school days in a school year is subjected to a removal that does not constitute a change of placement under § 300.519, the IEP team members shall review the behavioral intervention plan and its implementation to determine if modifications are necessary.

(2) If one or more of the team members believe that modifications are needed, the team shall meet to modify the plan and its implementation, to the extent the team determines necessary.

(d) For purposes of this section, the following definitions apply:

(1) *Controlled substance* means a drug or other substance identified under schedules I, II, III, IV, or V in section 202(c) of the Controlled Substances Act (21 U.S.C. 812(c)).

(2) *Illegal drug*—

(i) Means a controlled substance; but

(ii) Does not include a substance that is legally possessed or used under the supervision of a licensed health-care professional or that is legally possessed or used under any other authority under that Act or under any other provision of Federal law.

(3) *Weapon* has the meaning given the term "dangerous weapon" under paragraph (2) of the first subsection (g) of section 930 of title 18, United States Code.

(Authority: 20 U.S.C. 1415(k)(1), (10))

§ 300.521 Authority of hearing officer.

A hearing officer under section 615 of the Act may order a change in the placement of a child with a disability to an appropriate interim alternative educational setting for not more than 45 days if the hearing officer, in an expedited due process hearing—

(a) Determines that the public agency has demonstrated by substantial evidence that maintaining the current placement of the child is substantially likely to result in injury to the child or to others;

(b) Considers the appropriateness of the child's current placement;

(c) Considers whether the public agency has made reasonable efforts to minimize the risk of harm in the child's current placement, including the use of supplementary aids and services; and

(d) Determines that the interim alternative educational setting that is proposed by school personnel who have consulted with the child's special education teacher, meets the requirements of § 300.522(b).

(e) As used in this section, the term substantial evidence means beyond a preponderance of the evidence.

(Authority: 20 U.S.C. 1415(k)(2), (10))

§ 300.522 Determination of setting.

(a) *General.* The interim alternative educational setting referred to in § 300.520(a)(2) must be determined by the IEP team.

(b) *Additional requirements.* Any interim alternative educational setting in which a child is placed under §§ 300.520(a)(2) or 300.521 must—

(1) Be selected so as to enable the child to continue to progress in the general curriculum, although in another setting, and to continue to receive those services and modifications, including those described in the child's current IEP, that will enable the child to meet the goals set out in that IEP; and

(2) Include services and modifications to address the behavior described in §§ 300.520(a)(2) or 300.521, that are designed to prevent the behavior from recurring.

(Authority: 20 U.S.C. 1415(k)(3))

§ 300.523 Manifestation determination review.

(a) *General.* If an action is contemplated regarding behavior described in §§ 300.520(a)(2) or 300.521, or involving a removal that constitutes a change of placement under § 300.519 for a child with a disability who has engaged in other behavior that violated any rule or code of conduct of the LEA that applies to all children—

(1) Not later than the date on which the decision to take that action is made, the parents must be notified of that decision and provided the procedural safeguards notice described in § 300.504; and

(2) Immediately, if possible, but in no case later than 10 school days after the date on which the decision to take that action is made, a review must be conducted of the relationship between the child's disability and the behavior subject to the disciplinary action.

(b) *Individuals to carry out review.* A review described in paragraph (a) of this section must be conducted by the IEP team and other qualified personnel in a meeting.

(c) *Conduct of review.* In carrying out a review described in paragraph (a) of this section, the IEP team and other qualified personnel may determine that the behavior of the child was not a manifestation of the child's disability only if the IEP team and other qualified personnel—

(1) First consider, in terms of the behavior subject to disciplinary action, all relevant information, including—

(i) Evaluation and diagnostic results, including the results or other relevant information supplied by the parents of the child;

(ii) Observations of the child; and

(iii) The child's IEP and placement; and

(2) Then determine that—

(i) In relationship to the behavior subject to disciplinary action, the child's IEP and placement were appropriate and the special education services, supplementary aids and services, and behavior intervention strategies were provided consistent with the child's IEP and placement;

(ii) The child's disability did not impair the ability of the child to understand the impact and consequences of the behavior subject to disciplinary action; and

(iii) The child's disability did not impair the ability of the child to control the behavior subject to disciplinary action.

(d) *Decision.* If the IEP team and other qualified personnel determine that any of the standards in paragraph (c)(2) of this section were not met, the behavior must be considered a manifestation of the child's disability.

(e) *Meeting.* The review described in paragraph (a) of this section may be conducted at the same IEP meeting that is convened under § 300.520(b).

(f) *Deficiencies in IEP or placement.* If, in the review in paragraphs (b) and (c) of this section, a public agency identifies deficiencies in the child's IEP or placement or in their implementation, it must take immediate steps to remedy those deficiencies.

(Authority: 20 U.S.C. 1415(k)(4))

§ 300.524 Determination that behavior was not manifestation of disability.

(a) *General.* If the result of the review described in § 300.523 is a determination, consistent with § 300.523(d), that the behavior of the child with a disability was not a manifestation of the child's disability, the relevant disciplinary procedures applicable to children without disabilities may be applied to the child in the same manner in which they would be applied to children without disabilities, except as provided in § 300.121(d).

(b) *Additional requirement.* If the public agency initiates disciplinary procedures applicable to all children, the agency shall ensure that the special education and disciplinary records of the child with a disability are transmitted for consideration by the person or persons making the final determination regarding the disciplinary action.

(c) *Child's status during due process proceedings.* Except as provided in § 300.526, § 300.514 applies if a parent requests a hearing to challenge a determination, made through the review described in § 300.523, that the behavior of the child was not a manifestation of the child's disability.

(Authority: 20 U.S.C. 1415(k)(5))

§ 300.525 Parent appeal.

(a) *General.* (1) If the child's parent disagrees with a determination that the child's behavior was not a manifestation of the child's disability or with any decision regarding placement under §§ 300.520-300.528, the parent may request a hearing.

(2) The State or local educational agency shall arrange for an expedited hearing in any case described in paragraph (a)(1) of this section if a hearing is requested by a parent.

(b) *Review of decision.* (1) In reviewing a decision with respect to the manifestation determination, the hearing officer shall determine whether the public agency has demonstrated that the child's behavior was not a manifestation of the child's disability consistent with the requirements of § 300.523(d).

(2) In reviewing a decision under § 300.520(a)(2) to place the child in an interim alternative educational setting, the hearing officer shall apply the standards in § 300.521.

(Authority: 20 U.S.C. 1415(k)(6))

§ 300.526 Placement during appeals.

(a) *General.* If a parent requests a hearing or an appeal regarding a disciplinary action described in § 300.520(a)(2) or 300.521 to challenge the interim alternative educational setting or the manifestation determination, the child must remain in the interim alternative educational setting pending the decision of the hearing officer or until the expiration of the time period provided for in § 300.520(a)(2) or 300.521, whichever occurs first, unless the parent and the State agency or local educational agency agree otherwise.

(b) *Current placement.* If a child is placed in an interim alternative educational setting pursuant to § 300.520(a)(2) or 300.521 and school personnel propose to change the child's placement after expiration of the interim alternative placement, during the pendency of any proceeding to challenge the proposed change in placement the child must remain in the current placement (the child's placement prior to the interim alternative educational setting), except as provided in paragraph (c) of this section.

(c) *Expedited hearing.* (1) If school personnel maintain that it is dangerous for the child to be in the current placement (placement prior to removal to the interim alternative education setting) during the pendency of the due process proceedings, the LEA may request an expedited due process hearing.

(2) In determining whether the child may be placed in the alternative educational setting or in another appropriate placement ordered by the hearing officer, the hearing officer shall apply the standards in § 300.521.

(3) A placement ordered pursuant to paragraph (c)(2) of this section may not be longer than 45 days.

(4) The procedure in paragraph (c) of this section may be repeated, as necessary.

(Authority: 20 U.S.C. 1415(k)(7))

§ 300.527 Protections for children not yet eligible for special education and related services.

(a) *General.* A child who has not been determined to be eligible for special education and related services under this part and who has engaged in behavior that violated any rule or code of conduct of the local educational agency, including any behavior described in §§ 300.520 or 300.521, may assert any of the protections provided or in this part if the LEA had knowledge (as determined in accordance with paragraph (b) of this section) that the child was a child with a disability before the behavior that precipitated the disciplinary action occurred.

(b) *Basis of knowledge.* An LEA must be deemed to have knowledge that a child is a child with a disability if—

(1) The parent of the child has expressed concern in writing (or orally if the parent does not know how to write or has a disability that prevents a written statement) to personnel of the appropriate educational agency that the child is in need of special education and related services;

(2) The behavior or performance of the child demonstrates the need for these services, in accordance with § 300.7;

(3) The parent of the child has requested an evaluation of the child pursuant to §§ 300.530-300.536; or

(4) The teacher of the child, or other personnel of the local educational agency, has expressed concern about the behavior or performance of the child to the director of special education of the agency or to other personnel in accordance with the agency's established child find or special education referral system.

(c) *Exception.* A public agency would not be deemed to have knowledge under paragraph (b) of this section if, as a result of receiving the information specified in that paragraph, the agency—

(1) Either—

(i) Conducted an evaluation under §§ 300.530-300.536, and determined that the child was not a child with a disability under this part; or

(ii) Determined that an evaluation was not necessary; and

(2) Provided notice to the child's parents of its determination under paragraph (c)(1) of this section, consistent with § 300.503.

(d) *Conditions that apply if no basis of knowledge.* (1) *General.* If an LEA does not have knowledge that a child is a child with a disability (in accordance with paragraphs (b) and (c) of this section) prior to taking disciplinary measures against the child, the child may be subjected to the same disciplinary measures as measures applied to children without disabilities who engaged in comparable behaviors consistent with paragraph (d)(2) of this section.

(2) *Limitations*. (i) If a request is made for an evaluation of a child during the time period in which the child is subjected to disciplinary measures under § 300.520 or 300.521, the evaluation must be conducted in an expedited manner.

(ii) Until the evaluation is completed, the child remains in the educational placement determined by school authorities, which can include suspension or expulsion without educational services.

(iii) If the child is determined to be a child with a disability, taking into consideration information from the evaluation conducted by the agency and information provided by the parents, the agency shall provide special education and related services in accordance with the provisions of this part, including the requirements of §§ 300.520-300.529 and section 612(a)(1)(A) of the Act.

(Authority: 20 U.S.C. 1415(k)(8))

§ 300.528 Expedited due process hearings.

(a) Expedited due process hearings under §§ 300.521-300.526 must—

(1) Meet the requirements of § 300.509, except that a State may provide that the time periods identified in §§ 300.509(a)(3) and § 300.509(b) for purposes of expedited due process hearings under §§ 300.521-300.526 are not less than two business days; and

(2) Be conducted by a due process hearing officer who satisfies the requirements of § 300.508.

(b)(1) Each State shall establish a timeline for expedited due process hearings that results in a written decision being mailed to the parties within 45 days of the public agency's receipt of the request for the hearing, without exceptions or extensions.

(2) The timeline established under paragraph (b)(1) of this section must be the same for hearings requested by parents or public agencies.

(c) A State may establish different procedural rules for expedited hearings under §§ 300.521-300.526 than it has established for due process hearings under § 300.507.

(d) The decisions on expedited due process hearings are appealable consistent with § 300.510.

(Authority: 20 U.S.C. 1415(k)(2), (6), (7))

§ 300.529 Referral to and action by law enforcement and judicial authorities.

(a) Nothing in this part prohibits an agency from reporting a crime committed by a child with a disability to appropriate authorities or to prevent State law enforcement and judicial authorities from exercising their responsibilities with regard to the application of Federal and State law to crimes committed by a child with a disability.

(b)(1) An agency reporting a crime committed by a child with a disability shall ensure that copies of the special education and disciplinary records of the child are transmitted for consideration by the appropriate authorities to whom it reports the crime.

(2) An agency reporting a crime under this section may transmit copies of the child's special education and disciplinary records only to the extent that the transmission is permitted by the Family Educational Rights and Privacy Act.

(Authority: 20 U.S.C. 1415(k)(9))

Procedures for Evaluation and Determination of Eligibility

§ 300.530 General.

Each SEA shall ensure that each public agency establishes and implements procedures that meet the requirements of §§ 300.531-300.536.

(Authority: 20 U.S.C. 1414(b)(3); 1412(a)(7))

§ 300.531 Initial evaluation.

Each public agency shall conduct a full and individual initial evaluation, in accordance with §§ 300.532 and 300.533, before the initial provision of special education and related services to a child with a disability under Part B of the Act.

(Authority: 20 U.S.C. 1414(a)(1))

§ 300.532 Evaluation procedures.

Each public agency shall ensure, at a minimum, that the following requirements are met:

(a)(1) Tests and other evaluation materials used to assess a child under Part B of the Act—

(i) Are selected and administered so as not to be discriminatory on a racial or cultural basis; and

(ii) Are provided and administered in the child's native language or other mode of communication, unless it is clearly not feasible to do so; and

(2) Materials and procedures used to assess a child with limited English proficiency are selected and administered to ensure that they measure the extent to which the child has a disability and needs special education, rather than measuring the child's English language skills.

(b) A variety of assessment tools and strategies are used to gather relevant functional and developmental information about the child, including information provided by the parent, and information related to enabling the child to be involved in and progress in the general curriculum (or for a preschool child, to participate in appropriate activities), that may assist in determining—

(1) Whether the child is a child with a disability under § 300.7; and

(2) The content of the child's IEP.

(c)(1) Any standardized tests that are given to a child—

(i) Have been validated for the specific purpose for which they are used; and

(ii) Are administered by trained and knowledgeable personnel in accordance with any instructions provided by the producer of the tests.

(2) If an assessment is not conducted under standard conditions, a description of the extent to which it varied from standard conditions (e.g., the qualifications of the person administering the test, or the method of test administration) must be included in the evaluation report.

(d) Tests and other evaluation materials include those tailored to assess specific areas of educational need and not merely those that are designed to provide a single general intelligence quotient.

(e) Tests are selected and administered so as best to ensure that if a test is administered to a child with impaired sensory, manual, or speaking skills, the test results accurately reflect the child's aptitude or achievement level or whatever other factors the test purports to measure, rather than reflecting the child's impaired sensory, manual, or speaking skills (unless those skills are the factors that the test purports to measure).

(f) No single procedure is used as the sole criterion for determining whether a child is a child with a disability and for determining an appropriate educational program for the child.

(g) The child is assessed in all areas related to the suspected disability, including, if appropriate, health, vision, hearing, social and emotional status, general intelligence, academic performance, communicative status, and motor abilities.

(h) In evaluating each child with a disability under §§ 300.531-300.536, the evaluation is sufficiently comprehensive to identify all of the child's special education and related services needs, whether or not commonly linked to the disability category in which the child has been classified.

(i) The public agency uses technically sound instruments that may assess the relative contribution of cognitive and behavioral factors, in addition to physical or developmental factors.

(j) The public agency uses assessment tools and strategies that provide relevant information that directly assists persons in determining the educational needs of the child.

(Authority: 20 U.S.C. 1412(a)(6)(B), 1414(b)(2) and (3))

§ 300.533 Determination of needed evaluation data.

(a) *Review of existing evaluation data.* As part of an initial evaluation (if appropriate) and as part of any reevaluation under Part B of the Act, a group that includes the individuals described in § 300.344, and other qualified professionals, as appropriate, shall—

(1) Review existing evaluation data on the child, including—

(i) Evaluations and information provided by the parents of the child;

(ii) Current classroom-based assessments and observations; and

(iii) Observations by teachers and related services providers; and

(2) On the basis of that review, and input from the child's parents, identify what additional data, if any, are needed to determine—

(i) Whether the child has a particular category of disability, as described in § 300.7, or, in case of a reevaluation of a child, whether the child continues to have such a disability;

(ii) The present levels of performance and educational needs of the child;

(iii) Whether the child needs special education and related services, or in the case of a reevaluation of a child, whether the child continues to need special education and related services; and

(iv) Whether any additions or modifications to the special education and related services are needed to enable the child to meet the measurable annual goals set out in the IEP of the child and to participate, as appropriate, in the general curriculum.

(b) *Conduct of review.* The group described in paragraph (a) of this section may conduct its review without a meeting.

(c) *Need for additional data.* The public agency shall administer tests and other evaluation materials as may be needed to produce the data identified under paragraph (a) of this section.

(d) *Requirements if additional data are not needed.* (1) If the determination under paragraph (a) of this section is that no additional data are needed to determine whether the child continues to be a child with a disability, the public agency shall notify the child's parents—

(i) Of that determination and the reasons for it; and

(ii) Of the right of the parents to request an assessment to determine whether, for purposes of services under this part, the child continues to be a child with a disability.

(2) The public agency is not required to conduct the assessment described in paragraph

(d)(1)(ii) of this section unless requested to do so by the child's parents.

(Authority: 20 U.S.C. 1414(c)(1), (2) and (4))

§ 300.534 Determination of eligibility

(a) Upon completing the administration of tests and other evaluation materials—

(1) A group of qualified professionals and the parent of the child must determine whether the child is a child with a disability, as defined in § 300.7; and

(2) The public agency must provide a copy of the evaluation report and the documentation of determination of eligibility to the parent.

(b) A child may not be determined to be eligible under this part if—

(1) The determinant factor for that eligibility determination is—

(i) Lack of instruction in reading or math; or

(ii) Limited English proficiency; and

(2) The child does not otherwise meet the eligibility criteria under § 300.7(a).

(c)(1) A public agency must evaluate a child with a disability in accordance with §§ 300.532 and 300.533 before determining that the child is no longer a child with a disability.

(2) The evaluation described in paragraph (c)(1) of this section is not required before the termination of a student's eligibility under Part B of the Act due to graduation with a regular high school diploma, or exceeding the age eligibility for FAPE under State law.

(Authority: 20 U.S.C. 1414(b)(4) and (5), (c)(5))

§ 300.535 Procedures for determining eligibility and placement.

(a) In interpreting evaluation data for the purpose of determining if a child is a child with a disability under § 300.7, and the educational needs of the child, each public agency shall—

(1) Draw upon information from a variety of sources, including aptitude and achievement tests, parent input, teacher recommendations, physical condition, social or cultural background, and adaptive behavior; and

(2) Ensure that information obtained from all of these sources is documented and carefully considered.

(b) If a determination is made that a child has a disability and needs special education and related services, an IEP must be developed for the child in accordance with §§ 300.340-300.350.

(Authority: 20 U.S.C. 1412(a)(6), 1414(b)(4))

§ 300.536 Reevaluation.

Each public agency shall ensure—

(a) That the IEP of each child with a disability is reviewed in accordance with §§ 300.340–300.350; and

(b) That a reevaluation of each child, in accordance with §§ 300.532–300.535, is conducted if conditions warrant a reevaluation, or if the child's parent or teacher requests a reevaluation, but at least once every three years.

(Authority: 20 U.S.C. 1414(a)(2))

Additional Procedures for Evaluating Children With Specific Learning Disabilities

§ 300.540 Additional team members.

The determination of whether a child suspected of having a specific learning disability is a child with a disability as defined in § 300.7, must be made by the child's parents and a team of qualified professionals which must include—

(a)(1) The child's regular teacher; or

(2) If the child does not have a regular teacher, a regular classroom teacher qualified to teach a child of his or her age; or

(3) For a child of less than school age, an individual qualified by the SEA to teach a child of his or her age; and

(b) At least one person qualified to conduct individual diagnostic examinations of children, such as a school psychologist, speech-language pathologist, or remedial reading teacher.

(Authority: § 5(b), Pub. L. 94-142)

§ 300.541 Criteria for determining the existence of a specific learning disability.

(a) A team may determine that a child has a specific learning disability if—

(1) The child does not achieve commensurate with his or her age and ability levels in one or more of the areas listed in paragraph (a)(2) of this section, if provided with learning experiences appropriate for the child's age and ability levels; and

(2) The team finds that a child has a severe discrepancy between achievement and intellectual ability in one or more of the following areas:

(i) Oral expression.

(ii) Listening comprehension.

(iii) Written expression.

(iv) Basic reading skill.

(v) Reading comprehension.

(vi) Mathematics calculation.

(vii) Mathematics reasoning.

(b) The team may not identify a child as having a specific learning disability if the severe discrepancy between ability and achievement is primarily the result of—

(1) A visual, hearing, or motor impairment;

(2) Mental retardation;
(3) Emotional disturbance; or
(4) Environmental, cultural or economic disadvantage.

(Authority: § 5(b), Pub. L. 94–142)

§ 300.542 Observation.

(a) At least one team member other than the child's regular teacher shall observe the child's academic performance in the regular classroom setting.
(b) In the case of a child of less than school age or out of school, a team member shall observe the child in an environment appropriate for a child of that age.

(Authority: § 5(b), Pub. L. 94-142)

§ 300.543 Written report.

(a) For a child suspected of having a specific learning disability, the documentation of the team's determination of eligibility, as required by § 300.534(a)(2), must include a statement of—
(1) Whether the child has a specific learning disability;
(2) The basis for making the determination;
(3) The relevant behavior noted during the observation of the child;
(4) The relationship of that behavior to the child's academic functioning;
(5) The educationally relevant medical findings, if any;
(6) Whether there is a severe discrepancy between achievement and ability that is not correctable without special education and related services; and
(7) The determination of the team concerning the effects of environmental, cultural, or economic disadvantage.
(b) Each team member shall certify in writing whether the report reflects his or her conclusion. If it does not reflect his or her conclusion, the team member must submit a separate statement presenting his or her conclusions.

(Authority: § 5(b), Pub. L. 94-142)

Least Restrictive Environment (LRE)

§ 300.550 General LRE requirements.

(a) Except as provided in § 300.311(b) and (c), a State shall demonstrate to the satisfaction of the Secretary that the State has in effect policies and procedures to ensure that it meets the requirements of §§ 300.550-300.556.
(b) Each public agency shall ensure—
(1) That to the maximum extent appropriate, children with disabilities, including children in public or private institutions or other care facilities, are educated with children who are nondisabled; and
(2) That special classes, separate schooling or other removal of children with disabilities from the regular educational environment occurs only if the nature or severity of the disability is such that education in regular classes with the use of supplementary aids and services cannot be achieved satisfactorily.

(Authority: 20 U.S.C. 1412(a)(5))

§ 300.551 Continuum of alternative placements.

(a) Each public agency shall ensure that a continuum of alternative placements is available to meet the needs of children with disabilities for special education and related services.
(b) The continuum required in paragraph (a) of this section must—
(1) Include the alternative placements listed in the definition of special education under § 300.26 (instruction in regular classes, special classes, special schools, home instruction, and instruction in hospitals and institutions); and
(2) Make provision for supplementary services (such as resource room or itinerant instruction) to be provided in conjunction with regular class placement.

(Authority: 20 U.S.C. 1412(a)(5))

§ 300.552 Placements.

In determining the educational placement of a child with a disability, including a preschool child with a disability, each public agency shall ensure that—
(a) The placement decision—
(1) Is made by a group of persons, including the parents, and other persons knowledgeable about the child, the meaning of the evaluation data, and the placement options; and
(2) Is made in conformity with the LRE provisions of this subpart, including §§ 300.550–300.554;
(b) The child's placement—
(1) Is determined at least annually;
(2) Is based on the child's IEP; and
(3) Is as close as possible to the child's home;
(c) Unless the IEP of a child with a disability requires some other arrangement, the child is educated in the school that he or she would attend if nondisabled;
(d) In selecting the LRE, consideration is given to any potential harmful effect on the child or on the quality of services that he or she needs; and
(e) A child with a disability is not removed from education in age-appropriate regular class-

rooms solely because of needed modifications in the general curriculum.

(Authority: 20 U.S.C. 1412(a)(5))

§ 300.553 Nonacademic settings.

In providing or arranging for the provision of nonacademic and extracurricular services and activities, including meals, recess periods, and the services and activities set forth in § 300.306, each public agency shall ensure that each child with a disability participates with nondisabled children in those services and activities to the maximum extent appropriate to the needs of that child.

(Authority: 20 U.S.C. 1412(a)(5))

§ 300.554 Children in public or private institutions.

Except as provided in § 300.600(d), an SEA must ensure that § 300.550 is effectively implemented, including, if necessary, making arrangements with public and private institutions (such as a memorandum of agreement or special implementation procedures).

(Authority: 20 U.S.C. 1412(a)(5))

§ 300.555 Technical assistance and training activities.

Each SEA shall carry out activities to ensure that teachers and administrators in all public agencies—

(a) Are fully informed about their responsibilities for implementing § 300.550; and

(b) Are provided with technical assistance and training necessary to assist them in this effort.

(Authority: 20 U.S.C. 1412(a)(5))

§ 300.556 Monitoring activities.

(a) The SEA shall carry out activities to ensure that § 300.550 is implemented by each public agency.

(b) If there is evidence that a public agency makes placements that are inconsistent with § 300.550, the SEA shall—

(1) Review the public agency's justification for its actions; and

(2) Assist in planning and implementing any necessary corrective action.

(Authority: 20 U.S.C. 1412(a)(5))

Confidentiality of Information

§ 300.560 Definitions.

As used in §§ 300.560–300.577—

(a) *Destruction* means physical destruction or removal of personal identifiers from information so that the information is no longer personally identifiable.

(b) *Education records* means the type of records covered under the definition of "education records" in 34 CFR part 99 (the regulations implementing the Family Educational Rights and Privacy Act of 1974).

(c) *Participating agency* means any agency or institution that collects, maintains, or uses personally identifiable information, or from which information is obtained, under Part B of the Act.

(Authority: 20 U.S.C. 1221e-3, 1412(a)(8), 1417(c))

§ 300.561 Notice to parents.

(a) The SEA shall give notice that is adequate to fully inform parents about the requirements of § 300.127, including—

(1) A description of the extent that the notice is given in the native languages of the various population groups in the State;

(2) A description of the children on whom personally identifiable information is maintained, the types of information sought, the methods the State intends to use in gathering the information (including the sources from whom information is gathered), and the uses to be made of the information;

(3) A summary of the policies and procedures that participating agencies must follow regarding storage, disclosure to third parties, retention, and destruction of personally identifiable information; and

(4) A description of all of the rights of parents and children regarding this information, including the rights under the Family Educational Rights and Privacy Act of 1974 and implementing regulations in 34 CFR part 99.

(b) Before any major identification, location, or evaluation activity, the notice must be published or announced in newspapers or other media, or both, with circulation adequate to notify parents throughout the State of the activity.

(Authority: 20 U.S.C. 1412(a)(8), 1417(c))

§ 300.562 Access rights.

(a) Each participating agency shall permit parents to inspect and review any education records relating to their children that are collected, maintained, or used by the agency under this part. The agency shall comply with a request without unnecessary delay and before any meeting regarding an IEP, or any hearing pursuant to §§ 300.507 and 300.521–300.528, and in no case more than 45 days after the request has been made.

(b) The right to inspect and review education records under this section includes—

(1) The right to a response from the participating agency to reasonable requests for explanations and interpretations of the records;

(2) The right to request that the agency provide copies of the records containing the information if failure to provide those copies would effectively prevent the parent from exercising the right to inspect and review the records; and

(3) The right to have a representative of the parent inspect and review the records.

(c) An agency may presume that the parent has authority to inspect and review records relating to his or her child unless the agency has been advised that the parent does not have the authority under applicable State law governing such matters as guardianship, separation, and divorce.

(Authority: 20 U.S.C. 1412(a)(8), 1417(c))

§ 300.563 Record of access.

Each participating agency shall keep a record of parties obtaining access to education records collected, maintained, or used under Part B of the Act (except access by parents and authorized employees of the participating agency), including the name of the party, the date access was given, and the purpose for which the party is authorized to use the records.

(Authority: 20 U.S.C. 1412(a)(8), 1417(c))

§ 300.564 Records on more than one child.

If any education record includes information on more than one child, the parents of those children have the right to inspect and review only the information relating to their child or to be informed of that specific information.

(Authority: 20 U.S.C. 1412(a)(8), 1417(c))

§ 300.565 List of types and locations of information.

Each participating agency shall provide parents on request a list of the types and locations of education records collected, maintained, or used by the agency.

(Authority: 20 U.S.C. 1412(a)(8), 1417(c))

§ 300.566 Fees.

(a) Each participating agency may charge a fee for copies of records that are made for parents under this part if the fee does not effectively prevent the parents from exercising their right to inspect and review those records.

(b) A participating agency may not charge a fee to search for or to retrieve information under this part.

(Authority: 20 U.S.C. 1412(a)(8), 1417(c))

§ 300.567 Amendment of records at parent's request.

(a) A parent who believes that information in the education records collected, maintained, or used under this part is inaccurate or misleading or violates the privacy or other rights of the child may request the participating agency that maintains the information to amend the information.

(b) The agency shall decide whether to amend the information in accordance with the request within a reasonable period of time of receipt of the request.

(c) If the agency decides to refuse to amend the information in accordance with the request, it shall inform the parent of the refusal and advise the parent of the right to a hearing under § 300.568.

(Authority: 20 U.S.C. 1412(a)(8); 1417(c))

§ 300.568 Opportunity for a hearing.

The agency shall, on request, provide an opportunity for a hearing to challenge information in education records to ensure that it is not inaccurate, misleading, or otherwise in violation of the privacy or other rights of the child.

(Authority: 20 U.S.C. 1412(a)(8), 1417(c))

§ 300.569 Result of hearing.

(a) If, as a result of the hearing, the agency decides that the information is inaccurate, misleading or otherwise in violation of the privacy or other rights of the child, it shall amend the information accordingly and so inform the parent in writing.

(b) If, as a result of the hearing, the agency decides that the information is not inaccurate, misleading, or otherwise in violation of the privacy or other rights of the child, it shall inform the parent of the right to place in the records it maintains on the child a statement commenting on the information or setting forth any reasons for disagreeing with the decision of the agency.

(c) Any explanation placed in the records of the child under this section must—

(1) Be maintained by the agency as part of the records of the child as long as the record or contested portion is maintained by the agency; and

(2) If the records of the child or the contested portion is disclosed by the agency to any party, the explanation must also be disclosed to the party.

(Authority: 20 U.S.C. 1412(a)(8), 1417(c))

§ 300.570 Hearing procedures.

A hearing held under § 300.568 must be conducted according to the procedures under 34 CFR 99.22.

(Authority: 20 U.S.C. 1412(a)(8), 1417(c))

§ 300.571 Consent.

(a) Except as to disclosures addressed in § 300.529(b) for which parental consent is not required by Part 99, parental consent must be obtained before personally identifiable information is—

(1) Disclosed to anyone other than officials of participating agencies collecting or using the information under this part, subject to paragraph (b) of this section; or

(2) Used for any purpose other than meeting a requirement of this part.

(b) An educational agency or institution subject to 34 CFR part 99 may not release information from education records to participating agencies without parental consent unless authorized to do so under part 99.

(c) The SEA shall provide policies and procedures that are used in the event that a parent refuses to provide consent under this section.

(Authority: 20 U.S.C. 1412(a)(8), 1417(c))

§ 300.572 Safeguards.

(a) Each participating agency shall protect the confidentiality of personally identifiable information at collection, storage, disclosure, and destruction stages.

(b) One official at each participating agency shall assume responsibility for ensuring the confidentiality of any personally identifiable information.

(c) All persons collecting or using personally identifiable information must receive training or instruction regarding the State's policies and procedures under § 300.127 and 34 CFR part 99.

(d) Each participating agency shall maintain, for public inspection, a current listing of the names and positions of those employees within the agency who may have access to personally identifiable information.

(Authority: 20 U.S.C. 1412(a)(8), 1417(c))

§ 300.573 Destruction of information.

(a) The public agency shall inform parents when personally identifiable information collected, maintained, or used under this part is no longer needed to provide educational services to the child.

(b) The information must be destroyed at the request of the parents. However, a permanent record of a student's name, address, and phone number, his or her grades, attendance record, classes attended, grade level completed, and year completed may be maintained without time limitation.

(Authority: 20 U.S.C. 1412(a)(8), 1417(c))

§ 300.574 Children's rights.

(a) The SEA shall provide policies and procedures regarding the extent to which children are afforded rights of privacy similar to those afforded to parents, taking into consideration the age of the child and type or severity of disability.

(b) Under the regulations for the Family Educational Rights and Privacy Act of 1974 (34 CFR 99.5(a)), the rights of parents regarding education records are transferred to the student at age 18.

(c) If the rights accorded to parents under Part B of the Act are transferred to a student who reaches the age of majority, consistent with § 300.517, the rights regarding educational records in §§ 300.562–300.573 must also be transferred to the student. However, the public agency must provide any notice required under section 615 of the Act to the student and the parents.

(Authority: 20 U.S.C. 1412(a)(8), 1417(c))

§ 300.575 Enforcement.

The SEA shall provide the policies and procedures, including sanctions, that the State uses to ensure that its policies and procedures are followed and that the requirements of the Act and the regulations in this part are met.

(Authority: 20 U.S.C. 1412(a)(8), 1417(c))

§ 300.576 Disciplinary information.

(a) The State may require that a public agency include in the records of a child with a disability a statement of any current or previous disciplinary action that has been taken against the child and transmit the statement to the same extent that the disciplinary information is included in, and transmitted with, the student records of nondisabled children.

(b) The statement may include a description of any behavior engaged in by the child that required disciplinary action, a description of the disciplinary action taken, and any other information that is relevant to the safety of the child and other individuals involved with the child.

(c) If the State adopts such a policy, and the child transfers from one school to another, the transmission of any of the child's records must include both the child's current individualized education program and any statement of current or previous disciplinary action that has been taken against the child.

(Authority: 20 U.S.C. 1413(j))

§ 300.577 Department use of personally identifiable information.

If the Department or its authorized representatives collect any personally identifiable information regarding children with disabilities that is not subject to 5 U.S.C. 552a (the Privacy Act of 1974), the Secretary applies the requirements of 5 U.S.C. 552a (b)(1)-(2), (4)-(11); (c); (d); (e)(1), (2), (3)(A), (B), and (D), (5)-(10); (h); (m); and (n); and the regulations implementing those provisions in 34 CFR part 5b.

(Authority: 20 U.S.C. 1412(a)(8), 1417(c))

Department Procedures

§ 300.580 Determination by the Secretary that a State is eligible.

If the Secretary determines that a State is eligible to receive a grant under Part B of the Act, the Secretary notifies the State of that determination.

(Authority: 20 U.S.C. 1412(d))

§ 300.581 Notice and hearing before determining that a State is not eligible.

(a) *General.* (1) The Secretary does not make a final determination that a State is not eligible to receive a grant under Part B of the Act until providing the State—

(i) With reasonable notice; and

(ii) With an opportunity for a hearing.

(2) In implementing paragraph (a)(1)(i) of this section, the Secretary sends a written notice to the SEA by certified mail with return receipt requested.

(b) *Content of notice.* In the written notice described in paragraph (a)(2) of this section, the Secretary—

(1) States the basis on which the Secretary proposes to make a final determination that the State is not eligible;

(2) May describe possible options for resolving the issues;

(3) Advises the SEA that it may request a hearing and that the request for a hearing must be made not later than 30 days after it receives the notice of the proposed final determination that the State is not eligible; and

(4) Provides information about the procedures followed for a hearing.

(Authority: 20 U.S.C. (1412(d)(2))

§ 300.582 Hearing official or panel.

(a) If the SEA requests a hearing, the Secretary designates one or more individuals, either from the Department or elsewhere, not responsible for or connected with the administration of this program, to conduct a hearing.

(b) If more than one individual is designated, the Secretary designates one of those individuals as the Chief Hearing Official of the Hearing Panel. If one individual is designated, that individual is the Hearing Official.

(Authority: 20 U.S.C. (1412(d)(2))

§ 300.583 Hearing procedures.

(a) As used in §§ 300.581–300.586 the term *party* or *parties* means the following:

(1) An SEA that requests a hearing regarding the proposed disapproval of the State's eligibility under this part.

(2) The Department official who administers the program of financial assistance under this part.

(3) A person, group or agency with an interest in and having relevant information about the case that has applied for and been granted leave to intervene by the Hearing Official or Panel.

(b) Within 15 days after receiving a request for a hearing, the Secretary designates a Hearing Official or Panel and notifies the parties.

(c) The Hearing Official or Panel may regulate the course of proceedings and the conduct of the parties during the proceedings. The Hearing Official or Panel takes all steps necessary to conduct a fair and impartial proceeding, to avoid delay, and to maintain order, including the following:

(1) The Hearing Official or Panel may hold conferences or other types of appropriate proceedings to clarify, simplify, or define the issues or to consider other matters that may aid in the disposition of the case.

(2) The Hearing Official or Panel may schedule a prehearing conference of the Hearing Official or Panel and parties.

(3) Any party may request the Hearing Official or Panel to schedule a prehearing or other conference. The Hearing Official or Panel decides whether a conference is necessary and notifies all parties.

(4) At a prehearing or other conference, the Hearing Official or Panel and the parties may consider subjects such a—

(i) Narrowing and clarifying issues;

(ii) Assisting the parties in reaching agreements and stipulations;

(iii) Clarifying the positions of the parties;

(iv) Determining whether an evidentiary hearing or oral argument should be held; and

(v) Setting dates for—

(A) The exchange of written documents;

(B) The receipt of comments from the parties on the need for oral argument or evidentiary hearing;

(C) Further proceedings before the Hearing Official or Panel (including an evidentiary hearing or oral argument, if either is scheduled);

(D) Requesting the names of witnesses each party wishes to present at an evidentiary hearing and estimation of time for each presentation; or

(E) Completion of the review and the initial decision of the Hearing Official or Panel.

(5) A prehearing or other conference held under paragraph (b)(4) of this section may be conducted by telephone conference call.

(6) At a prehearing or other conference, the parties shall be prepared to discuss the subjects listed in paragraph (b)(4) of this section.

(7) Following a prehearing or other conference the Hearing Official or Panel may issue a written statement describing the issues raised, the action taken, and the stipulations and agreements reached by the parties.

(d) The Hearing Official or Panel may require parties to state their positions and to provide all or part of the evidence in writing.

(e) The Hearing Official or Panel may require parties to present testimony through affidavits and to conduct cross-examination through interrogatories.

(f) The Hearing Official or Panel may direct the parties to exchange relevant documents or information and lists of witnesses, and to send copies to the Hearing Official or Panel.

(g) The Hearing Official or Panel may receive, rule on, exclude, or limit evidence at any stage of the proceedings.

(h) The Hearing Official or Panel may rule on motions and other issues at any stage of the proceedings.

(i) The Hearing Official or Panel may examine witnesses.

(j) The Hearing Official or Panel may set reasonable time limits for submission of written documents.

(k) The Hearing Official or Panel may refuse to consider documents or other submissions if they are not submitted in a timely manner unless good cause is shown.

(l) The Hearing Official or Panel may interpret applicable statutes and regulations but may not waive them or rule on their validity.

(m)(1) The parties shall present their positions through briefs and the submission of other documents and may request an oral argument or evidentiary hearing. The Hearing Official or Panel shall determine whether an oral argument or an evidentiary hearing is needed to clarify the positions of the parties.

(2) The Hearing Official or Panel gives each party an opportunity to be represented by counsel.

(n) If the Hearing Official or Panel determines that an evidentiary hearing would materially assist the resolution of the matter, the Hearing Official or Panel gives each party, in addition to the opportunity to be represented by counsel—

(1) An opportunity to present witnesses on the party's behalf; and

(2) An opportunity to cross-examine witnesses either orally or with written questions.

(o) The Hearing Official or Panel accepts any evidence that it finds is relevant and material to the proceedings and is not unduly repetitious.

(p)(1) The Hearing Official or Panel—

(i) Arranges for the preparation of a transcript of each hearing;

(ii) Retains the original transcript as part of the record of the hearing; and

(iii) Provides one copy of the transcript to each party.

(2) Additional copies of the transcript are available on request and with payment of the reproduction fee.

(q) Each party shall file with the Hearing Official or Panel all written motions, briefs, and other documents and shall at the same time provide a copy to the other parties to the proceedings.

(Authority: 20 U.S.C. (1412(d)(2))

§ 300.584 Initial decision; final decision.

(a) The Hearing Official or Panel prepares an initial written decision that addresses each of the points in the notice sent by the Secretary to the SEA under § 300.581.

(b) The initial decision of a Panel is made by a majority of Panel members.

(c) The Hearing Official or Panel mails by certified mail with return receipt requested a copy of the initial decision to each party (or to the party's counsel) and to the Secretary, with a notice stating that each party has an opportunity to submit written comments regarding the decision to the Secretary.

(d) Each party may file comments and recommendations on the initial decision with the Hearing Official or Panel within 15 days of the date the party receives the Panel's decision.

(e) The Hearing Official or Panel sends a copy of a party's initial comments and recommendations to the other parties by certified mail with return receipt requested. Each party may file responsive comments and recommendations with the Hearing Official or Panel within seven days of the date the party receives the initial comments and recommendations.

(f) The Hearing Official or Panel forwards the parties' initial and responsive comments on the initial decision to the Secretary who reviews the initial decision and issues a final decision.

(g) The initial decision of the Hearing Official or Panel becomes the final decision of the Secretary unless, within 25 days after the end of the time for receipt of written comments, the Secretary informs the Hearing Official or Panel and the parties to a hearing in writing that the decision is being further reviewed for possible modification.

(h) The Secretary may reject or modify the initial decision of the Hearing Official or Panel if the Secretary finds that it is clearly erroneous.

(i) The Secretary conducts the review based on the initial decision, the written record, the Hearing Official's or Panel's proceedings, and written comments. The Secretary may remand the matter for further proceedings.

(j) The Secretary issues the final decision within 30 days after notifying the Hearing Official or Panel that the initial decision is being further reviewed.

(Authority: 20 U.S.C. (1412(d)(2))

§ 300.585 Filing requirements.

(a) Any written submission under §§ 300.581–300.585 must be filed by hand-delivery, by mail, or by facsimile transmission. The Secretary discourages the use of facsimile transmission for documents longer than five pages.

(b) The filing date under paragraph (a) of this section is the date the document is—

(1) Hand-delivered;

(2) Mailed; or (3) Sent by facsimile transmission.

(c) A party filing by facsimile transmission is responsible for confirming that a complete and legible copy of the document was received by the Department.

(d) If a document is filed by facsimile transmission, the Secretary, the Hearing Official, or the Panel, as applicable, may require the filing of a follow-up hard copy by hand-delivery or by mail within a reasonable period of time.

(e) If agreed upon by the parties, service of a document may be made upon the other party by facsimile transmission.

(Authority: 20 U.S.C. 1413(c))

§ 300.586 Judicial review.

If a State is dissatisfied with the Secretary's final action with respect to the eligibility of the State under section 612 of the Act, the State may, not later than 60 days after notice of that action, file with the United States Court of Appeals for the circuit in which that State is located a petition for review of that action. A copy of the petition must be forthwith transmitted by the clerk of the court to the Secretary. The Secretary then files in the court the record of the proceedings upon which the Secretary's action was based, as provided in section 2112 of title 28, United States Code.

(Authority: 20 U.S.C. 1416(b))

§ 300.587 Enforcement.

(a) *General.* The Secretary initiates an action described in paragraph (b) of this section if the Secretary finds—

(1) That there has been a failure by the State to comply substantially with any provision of Part B of the Act, this part, or 34 CFR part 301; or

(2) That there is a failure to comply with any condition of an LEA's or SEA's eligibility under Part B of the Act, this part or 34 CFR part 301, including the terms of any agreement to achieve compliance with Part B of the Act, this part, or Part 301 within the timelines specified in the agreement.

(b) *Types of action.* The Secretary, after notifying the SEA (and any LEA or State agency affected by a failure described in paragraph (a)(2) of this section)—

(1) Withholds in whole or in part any further payments to the State under Part B of the Act;

(2) Refers the matter to the Department of Justice for enforcement; or

(3) Takes any other enforcement action authorized by law.

(c) *Nature of withholding.* (1) If the Secretary determines that it is appropriate to withhold further payments under paragraph (b)(1) of this section, the Secretary may determine that the withholding will be limited to programs or projects, or portions thereof, affected by the failure, or that the SEA shall not make further payments under Part B of the Act to specified LEA or State agencies affected by the failure.

(2) Until the Secretary is satisfied that there is no longer any failure to comply with the provisions of Part B of the Act, this part, or 34 CFR part 301, as specified in paragraph (a) of this section, payments to the State under Part B of the Act are withheld in whole or in part, or payments by the SEA under Part B of the Act are limited to local educational agencies and State agencies whose actions did not cause or were not involved in the failure, as the case may be.

(3) Any SEA, LEA, or other State agency that has received notice under paragraph (a) of this section shall, by means of a public notice, take such measures as may be necessary to bring the pendency of an action pursuant to this subsection to the attention of the public within the jurisdiction of that agency.

(4) Before withholding under paragraph (b)(1) of this section, the Secretary provides notice and a hearing pursuant to the procedures in §§ 300.581–300.586.

(d) *Referral for appropriate enforcement.* (1) Before the Secretary makes a referral under paragraph (b)(2) of this section for enforcement, or takes any other enforcement action authorized by law under paragraph (b)(3), the Secretary provides the State—

(i) With reasonable notice; and

(ii) With an opportunity for a hearing.

(2) The hearing described in paragraph (d)(1)(ii) of this section consists of an opportunity to meet with the Assistant Secretary for the Office of Special Education and Rehabilitative Services to demonstrate why the Department should not make a referral for enforcement.

(e) *Divided State agency responsibility.* For purposes of this part, if responsibility for ensuring that the requirements of this part are met with respect to children with disabilities who are convicted as adults under State law and incarcerated in adult prisons is assigned to a public agency other than the SEA pursuant to § 300.600(d), and if the Secretary finds that the failure to comply substantially with the provisions of Part B of the Act or this part are related to a failure by the public agency, the Secretary takes one of the enforcement actions described in paragraph (b) of this section to ensure compliance with Part B of the Act and this part, except—

(1) Any reduction or withholding of payments to the State under paragraph (b)(1) of this section is proportionate to the total funds allotted under section 611 of the Act to the State as the number of eligible children with disabilities in adult prisons under the supervision of the other public agency is proportionate to the number of eligible individuals with disabilities in the State under the supervision of the State educational agency; and

(2) Any withholding of funds under paragraph (e)(1) of this section is limited to the specific agency responsible for the failure to comply with Part B of the Act or this part.

(Authority: 20 U.S.C. 1416)

§§ 300.588 [Reserved]

§ 300.589 Waiver of requirement regarding supplementing and not supplanting with Part B funds.

(a) Except as provided under §§ 300.232–300.235, funds paid to a State under Part B of the Act must be used to supplement and increase the level of Federal, State, and local funds (including funds that are not under the direct control of SEAs or LEAs) expended for special education and related services provided to children with disabilities under Part B of the Act and in no case to supplant those Federal, State, and local funds. A State may use funds it retains under § 300.602 without regard to the prohibition on supplanting other funds (see § 300.372).

(b) If a State provides clear and convincing evidence that all eligible children with disabilities throughout the State have FAPE available to them, the Secretary may waive for a period of one year in whole or in part the requirement under § 300.153 (regarding State-level nonsupplanting) if the Secretary concurs with the evidence provided by the State.

(c) If a State wishes to request a waiver under this section, it must submit to the Secretary a written request that includes—

(1) An assurance that FAPE is currently available, and will remain available throughout the period that a waiver would be in effect, to all eligible children with disabilities throughout the State, regardless of the public agency that is responsible for providing FAPE to them. The assurance must be signed by an official who has the authority to provide that assurance as it applies to all eligible children with disabilities in the State;

(2) All evidence that the State wishes the Secretary to consider in determining whether all eligible children with disabilities have FAPE available to them, setting forth in detail—

(i) The basis on which the State has concluded that FAPE is available to all eligible children in the State; and

(ii) The procedures that the State will implement to ensure that FAPE remains available to all eligible children in the State, which must include—

(A) The State's procedures under § 300.125 for ensuring that all eligible children are identified, located and evaluated;

(B) The State's procedures for monitoring public agencies to ensure that they comply with all requirements of this part;

(C) The State's complaint procedures under §§ 300.660–300.662; and

(D) The State's hearing procedures under §§ 300.507–300.511 and 300.520–300.528;

(3) A summary of all State and Federal monitoring reports, and State complaint decisions (see §§ 300.660–300.662) and hearing decisions (see §§ 300.507–300.511 and

300.520–300.528), issued within three years prior to the date of the State's request for a waiver under this section, that includes any finding that FAPE has not been available to one or more eligible children, and evidence that FAPE is now available to all children addressed in those reports or decisions; and

(4) Evidence that the State, in determining that FAPE is currently available to all eligible children with disabilities in the State, has consulted with the State advisory panel under § 300.650, the State's parent training and information center or centers, the State's protection and advocacy organization, and other organizations representing the interests of children with disabilities and their parents, and a summary of the input of these organizations.

(d) If the Secretary determines that the request and supporting evidence submitted by the State makes a prima facie showing that FAPE is, and will remain, available to all eligible children with disabilities in the State, the Secretary, after notice to the public throughout the State, conducts a public hearing at which all interested persons and organizations may present evidence regarding the following issues:

(1) Whether FAPE is currently available to all eligible children with disabilities in the State.

(2) Whether the State will be able to ensure that FAPE remains available to all eligible children with disabilities in the State if the Secretary provides the requested waiver.

(e) Following the hearing, the Secretary, based on all submitted evidence, will provide a waiver, in whole or in part, for a period of one year if the Secretary finds that the State has provided clear and convincing evidence that FAPE is currently available to all eligible children with disabilities in the State, and the State will be able to ensure that FAPE remains available to all eligible children with disabilities in the State if the Secretary provides the requested waiver.

(f) A State may receive a waiver of the requirement of section 612(a)(19)(A) and § 300.154(a) if it satisfies the requirements of paragraphs (b) through (e) of this section.

(g) The Secretary may grant subsequent waivers for a period of one year each, if the Secretary determines that the State has provided clear and convincing evidence that all eligible children with disabilities throughout the State have, and will continue to have throughout the one-year period of the waiver, FAPE available to them.

(Authority: 20 U.S.C. 1412(a)(18)(C), (19)(C)(ii) and (E))

Subpart F—State Administration

General

§ 300.600 Responsibility for all educational programs.

(a) The SEA is responsible for ensuring—

(1) That the requirements of this part are carried out; and

(2) That each educational program for children with disabilities administered within the State, including each program administered by any other State or local agency—

(i) Is under the general supervision of the persons responsible for educational programs for children with disabilities in the SEA; and

(ii) Meets the education standards of the SEA (including the requirements of this part).

(b) The State must comply with paragraph (a) of this section through State statute, State regulation, signed agreement between respective agency officials, or other documents.

(c) Part B of the Act does not limit the responsibility of agencies other than educational agencies for providing or paying some or all of the costs of FAPE to children with disabilities in the State.

(d) Notwithstanding paragraph (a) of this section, the Governor (or another individual pursuant to State law) may assign to any public agency in the State the responsibility of ensuring that the requirements of Part B of the Act are met with respect to students with disabilities who are convicted as adults under State law and incarcerated in adult prisons.

(Authority: 20 U.S.C. 1412(a)(11))

§ 300.601 Relation of Part B to other Federal programs.

Part B of the Act may not be construed to permit a State to reduce medical and other assistance available to children with disabilities, or to alter the eligibility of a child with a disability, under title V (Maternal and Child Health) or title XIX (Medicaid) of the Social Security Act, to receive services that are also part of FAPE.

(Authority: 20 U.S.C. 1412(e))

§ 300.602 State-level activities.

(a) Each State may retain not more than the amount described in paragraph (b) of this section for administration in accordance with §§ 300.620 and 300.621 and other State-level activities in accordance with § 300.370.

(b) For each fiscal year, the Secretary determines and reports to the SEA an amount that is 25 percent of the amount the State received under this section for fiscal year 1997, cumulatively adjusted by the Secretary for each succeeding fiscal year by the lesser of—

(1) The percentage increase, if any, from the preceding fiscal year in the State's allocation under section 611 of the Act; or

(2) The rate of inflation, as measured by the percentage increase, if any, from the preceding fiscal year in the Consumer Price Index For All Urban Consumers, published by the Bureau of Labor Statistics of the Department of Labor.

(Authority: 20 U.S.C. 1411(f)(1)(A) and (B))

Use of Funds

§ 300.620 Use of funds for State administration.

(a) For the purpose of administering Part B of the Act, including section 619 of the Act (including the coordination of activities under Part B of the Act with, and providing technical assistance to, other programs that provide services to children with disabilities)—

(1) Each State may use not more than twenty percent of the maximum amount it may retain under § 300.602(a) for any fiscal year or $500,000 (adjusted by the cumulative rate of inflation since fiscal year 1998, as measured by the percentage increase, if any, in the Consumer Price Index For All Urban Consumers, published by the Bureau of Labor Statistics of the Department of Labor), whichever is greater; and

(2) Each outlying area may use up to five percent of the amount it receives under this section for any fiscal year or $35,000, whichever is greater.

(b) Funds described in paragraph (a) of this section may also be used for the administration of Part C of the Act, if the SEA is the lead agency for the State under that part.

(Authority: 20 U.S.C. 1411(f)(2))

§ 300.621 Allowable costs.

(a) The SEA may use funds under § 300.620 for—

(1) Administration of State activities under Part B of the Act and for planning at the State level, including planning, or assisting in the planning, of programs or projects for the education of children with disabilities;

(2) Approval, supervision, monitoring, and evaluation of the effectiveness of local programs and projects for the education of children with disabilities;

(3) Technical assistance to LEAs with respect to the requirements of Part B of the Act;

(4) Leadership services for the program supervision and management of special education activities for children with disabilities; and

(5) Other State leadership activities and consultative services.

(b) The SEA shall use the remainder of its funds under § 300.620 in accordance with § 300.370.

(Authority: 20 U.S.C. 1411(f)(2))

§ 300.622 Subgrants to LEAs for capacity-building and improvement.

In any fiscal year in which the percentage increase in the State's allocation under 611 of the Act exceeds the rate of inflation (as measured by the percentage increase, if any, from the preceding fiscal year in the Consumer Price Index For All Urban Consumers, published by the Bureau of Labor Statistics of the Department of Labor), each State shall reserve, from its allocation under 611 of the Act, the amount described in § 300.623 to make subgrants to LEAs, unless that amount is less than $100,000, to assist them in providing direct services and in making systemic change to improve results for children with disabilities through one or more of the following:

(a) Direct services, including alternative programming for children who have been expelled from school, and services for children in correctional facilities, children enrolled in State-operated or State- supported schools, and children in charter schools.

(b) Addressing needs or carrying out improvement strategies identified in the State's Improvement Plan under subpart 1 of Part D of the Act.

(c) Adopting promising practices, materials, and technology, based on knowledge derived from education research and other sources.

(d) Establishing, expanding, or implementing interagency agreements and arrangements between LEAs and other agencies or organizations concerning the provision of services to children with disabilities and their families.

(e) Increasing cooperative problem-solving between parents and school personnel and promoting the use of alternative dispute resolution.

(Authority: 20 U.S.C. 1411(f)(4)(A))

§ 300.623 Amount required for subgrants to LEAs.

For each fiscal year, the amount referred to in § 300.622 is—

(a) The maximum amount the State was allowed to retain under § 300.602(a) for the prior fiscal year, or, for fiscal year 1998, 25 percent of the State's allocation for fiscal year 1997 under section 611; multiplied by

(b) The difference between the percentage increase in the State's allocation under this section and the rate of inflation, as measured by the percentage increase, if any, from the preceding fiscal year in the Consumer Price Index For All Urban Consumers, published by the Bureau of Labor Statistics of the Department of Labor.

(Authority: 20 U.S.C. 1411(f)(4)(B))

§ 300.624 State discretion in awarding subgrants.

The State may establish priorities in awarding subgrants under § 300.622 to LEAs competitively or on a targeted basis.

(Authority: 20 U.S.C. 1411(f)(4)(A))

State Advisory Panel

§ 300.650 Establishment of advisory panels.

(a) Each State shall establish and maintain, in accordance with §§ 300.650–300.653, a State advisory panel on the education of children with disabilities.

(b) The advisory panel must be appointed by the Governor or any other official authorized under State law to make those appointments.

(c) If a State has an existing advisory panel that can perform the functions in § 300.652, the State may modify the existing panel so that it fulfills all of the requirements of §§ 300.650-300.653, instead of establishing a new advisory panel.

(Authority: 20 U.S.C. 1412(a)(21)(A))

§ 300.651 Membership.

(a) *General.* The membership of the State advisory panel must consist of members appointed by the Governor, or any other official authorized under State law to make these appointments, that is representative of the State population and that is composed of individuals involved in, or concerned with the education of children with disabilities, including—

(1) Parents of children with disabilities;

(2) Individuals with disabilities;

(3) Teachers;

(4) Representatives of institutions of higher education that prepare special education and related services personnel;

(5) State and local education officials;

(6) Administrators of programs for children with disabilities;

(7) Representatives of other State agencies involved in the financing or delivery of related services to children with disabilities;

(8) Representatives of private schools and public charter schools;

(9) At least one representative of a vocational, community, or business organization concerned with the provision of transition services to children with disabilities; and

(10) Representatives from the State juvenile and adult corrections agencies.

(b) *Special rule.* A majority of the members of the panel must be individuals with disabilities or parents of children with disabilities.

(Authority: 20 U.S.C. 1412(a)(21)(B) and (C))

§ 300.652 Advisory panel functions.

(a) *General.* The State advisory panel shall—

(1) Advise the SEA of unmet needs within the State in the education of children with disabilities;

(2) Comment publicly on any rules or regulations proposed by the State regarding the education of children with disabilities;

(3) Advise the SEA in developing evaluations and reporting on data to the Secretary under section 618 of the Act;

(4) Advise the SEA in developing corrective action plans to address findings identified in Federal monitoring reports under Part B of the Act; and

(5) Advise the SEA in developing and implementing policies relating to the coordination of services for children with disabilities.

(b) *Advising on eligible students with disabilities in adult prisons.* The advisory panel also shall advise on the education of eligible students with disabilities who have been convicted as adults and incarcerated in adult prisons, even if, consistent with § 300.600(d), a State assigns general supervision responsibility for those students to a public agency other than an SEA.

(Authority: 20 U.S.C. 1412(a)(21)(D))

§ 300.653 Advisory panel procedures.

(a) The advisory panel shall meet as often as necessary to conduct its business.

(b) By July 1 of each year, the advisory panel shall submit an annual report of panel activities and suggestions to the SEA. This report must be made available to the public in a manner consistent with other public reporting requirements of Part B of the Act.

(c) Official minutes must be kept on all panel meetings and must be made available to the public on request.

(d) All advisory panel meetings and agenda items must be announced enough in advance of the meeting to afford interested parties a reasonable opportunity to attend. Meetings must be open to the public.

(e) Interpreters and other necessary services must be provided at panel meetings for panel members or participants. The State may pay for these services from funds under § 300.620.

(f) The advisory panel shall serve without compensation but the State must reimburse the panel for reasonable and necessary expenses for attending meetings and performing duties. The State may use funds under § 300.620 for this purpose.

(Authority: 20 U.S.C. 1412(a)(21))

State Complaint Procedures

§ 300.660 Adoption of State complaint procedures.

(a) *General.* Each SEA shall adopt written procedures for—

(1) Resolving any complaint, including a complaint filed by an organization or individual from another State, that meets the requirements of § 300.662 by—

(i) Providing for the filing of a complaint with the SEA; and

(ii) At the SEA's discretion, providing for the filing of a complaint with a public agency and the right to have the SEA review the public agency's decision on the complaint; and

(2) Widely disseminating to parents and other interested individuals, including parent training and information centers, protection and advocacy agencies, independent living centers, and other appropriate entities, the State's procedures under §§ 300.660–300.662.

(b) *Remedies for denial of appropriate services.* In resolving a complaint in which it has found a failure to provide appropriate services, an SEA, pursuant to its general supervisory authority under Part B of the Act, must address:

(1) How to remediate the denial of those services, including, as appropriate, the awarding of monetary reimbursement or other corrective action appropriate to the needs of the child; and

(2) Appropriate future provision of services for all children with disabilities.

(Authority: 20 U.S.C. 1221e-3)

§ 300.661 Minimum State complaint procedures.

(a) *Time limit; minimum procedures.* Each SEA shall include in its complaint procedures a time limit of 60 days after a complaint is filed under § 300.660(a) to—

(1) Carry out an independent on-site investigation, if the SEA determines that an investigation is necessary;

(2) Give the complainant the opportunity to submit additional information, either orally or in writing, about the allegations in the complaint;

(3) Review all relevant information and make an independent determination as to whether the public agency is violating a requirement of Part B of the Act or of this part; and

(4) Issue a written decision to the complainant that addresses each allegation in the complaint and contains—

(i) Findings of fact and conclusions; and

(ii) The reasons for the SEA's final decision.

(b) *Time extension; final decision; implementation.* The SEA's procedures described in paragraph (a) of this section also must—

(1) Permit an extension of the time limit under paragraph (a) of this section only if exceptional circumstances exist with respect to a particular complaint; and

(2) Include procedures for effective implementation of the SEA's final decision, if needed, including—

(i) Technical assistance activities;

(ii) Negotiations; and

(iii) Corrective actions to achieve compliance.

(c) *Complaints filed under this section, and due process hearings under §§ 300.507 and 300.520–300.528.* (1) If a written complaint is received that is also the subject of a due process hearing under § 300.507 or §§ 300.520–300.528, or contains multiple issues, of which one or more are part of that hearing, the State must set aside any part of the complaint that is being addressed in the due process hearing, until the conclusion of the hearing. However, any issue in the complaint that is not a part of the due process action must be resolved using the time limit and procedures described in paragraphs (a) and (b) of this section.

(2) If an issue is raised in a complaint filed under this section that has previously been decided in a due process hearing involving the same parties—

(i) The hearing decision is binding; and

(ii) The SEA must inform the complainant to that effect.

(3) A complaint alleging a public agency's failure to implement a due process decision must be resolved by the SEA.

(Authority: 20 U.S.C. 1221e-3)

§ 300.662 Filing a complaint.

(a) An organization or individual may file a signed written complaint under the procedures described in §§ 300.660-300.661.

(b) The complaint must include—

(1) A statement that a public agency has violated a requirement of Part B of the Act or of this part; and

(2) The facts on which the statement is based.

(c) The complaint must allege a violation that occurred not more than one year prior to the date that the complaint is received in accordance with § 300.660(a) unless a longer period is reasonable because the violation is continuing, or the complainant is requesting compensatory services for a violation that occurred not more than three years prior to the date the complaint is received under § 300.660(a).

(Authority: 20 U.S.C. 1221e-3)

Subpart G—Allocation of Funds; Reports

Allocations

§ 300.700 Special definition of the term "State".

For the purposes of §§ 300.701, and 300.703–300.714, the term *State* means each of the 50 States, the District of Columbia, and the Commonwealth of Puerto Rico.

(Authority: 20 U.S.C. 1411(h)(2))

§ 300.701 Grants to States.

(a) *Purpose of grants*. The Secretary makes grants to States and the outlying areas and provides funds to the Secretary of the Interior, to assist them to provide special education and related services to children with disabilities in accordance with Part B of the Act.

(b) *Maximum amounts*. The maximum amount of the grant a State may receive under section 611 of the Act for any fiscal year is—

(1) The number of children with disabilities in the State who are receiving special education and related services—

(i) Aged 3 through 5 if the State is eligible for a grant under section 619 of the Act; and

(ii) Aged 6 through 21; multiplied by—

(2) Forty (40) percent of the average per-pupil expenditure in public elementary and secondary schools in the United States.

(Authority: 20 U.S.C. 1411(a))

§ 300.702 Definition.

For the purposes of this section the term *average per-pupil expenditure in public elementary and secondary schools in the United States* means—

(a) Without regard to the source of funds—

(1) The aggregate current expenditures, during the second fiscal year preceding the fiscal year for which the determination is made (or, if satisfactory data for that year are not available, during the most recent preceding fiscal year for which satisfactory data are available) of all LEAs in the 50 States and the District of Columbia); plus

(2) Any direct expenditures by the State for the operation of those agencies; divided by

(b) The aggregate number of children in average daily attendance to whom those agencies provided free public education during that preceding year.

(Authority: 20 U.S.C. 1411(h)(1))

§ 300.703 Allocations to States.

(a) *General*. After reserving funds for studies and evaluations under section 674(e) of the Act, and for payments to the outlying areas, the freely associated States, and the Secretary of the Interior under §§ 300.715 and 300.717-300.719, the Secretary allocates the remaining amount among the States in accordance with paragraph (b) of this section and §§ 300.706-300.709.

(b) *Interim formula*. Except as provided in §§ 300.706-300.709, the Secretary allocates the amount described in paragraph (a) of this section among the States in accordance with section 611(a)(3), (4), (5) and (b)(1), (2) and (3) of the Act, as in effect prior to June 4, 1997, except that the determination of the number of children with disabilities receiving special education and related services under section 611(a)(3) of the Act (as then in effect) may be calculated as of December 1, or, at the State's discretion, the last Friday in October, of the fiscal year for which the funds were appropriated.

(Authority: 20 U.S.C. 1411(d))

§§ 300.704-300.705 [Reserved]

§ 300.706 Permanent formula.

(a) *Establishment of base year*. The Secretary allocates the amount described in § 300.703(a) among the States in accordance with §§ 300.706–300.709 for each fiscal year beginning with the first fiscal year for which the amount appropriated under 611(j) of the Act is more than $4,924,672,200.

(b) *Use of base year*. (1) *Definition*. As used in this section, the term *base year* means the fiscal year preceding the first fiscal year in which this section applies.

(2) *Special rule for use of base year amount*. If a State received any funds under section 611 of the Act for the base year on the basis of children aged 3 through 5, but does not make FAPE available to all children with disabilities aged 3 through 5 in the State in any subsequent fiscal year, the Secretary computes the State's base year amount, solely for the purpose of calculating the State's allocation in that subsequent year under §§ 300.707–300.709, by subtracting the amount allocated to the State for the base year on the basis of those children.

(Authority: 20 U.S.C. 1411(e)(1) and (2))

§ 300.707 Increase in funds.

If the amount available for allocations to States under § 300.706 is equal to or greater than the amount allocated to the States under section 611 of the Act for the preceding fiscal year, those allocations are calculated as follows:

(a) Except as provided in § 300.708, the Secretary—

(1) Allocates to each State the amount it received for the base year;

(2) Allocates 85 percent of any remaining funds to States on the basis of their relative populations of children aged 3 through 21 who are of the same age as children with disabilities for whom the State ensures the availability of FAPE under Part B of the Act; and

(3) Allocates 15 percent of those remaining funds to States on the basis of their relative populations of children described in paragraph (a)(2) of this section who are living in poverty.

(b) For the purpose of making grants under this section, the Secretary uses the most recent population data, including data on children living in poverty, that are available and satisfactory to the Secretary.

(Authority: 20 U.S.C. 1411(e)(3))

§ 300.708 Limitation.

(a) Allocations under § 300.707 are subject to the following:

(1) No State's allocation may be less than its allocation for the preceding fiscal year.

(2) No State's allocation may be less than the greatest of—

(i) The sum of—

(A) The amount it received for the base year; and

(B) One-third of one percent of the amount by which the amount appropriated under section 611(j) of the Act exceeds the amount appropriated under section 611 of the Act for the base year; or

(ii) The sum of—

(A) The amount it received for the preceding fiscal year; and

(B) That amount multiplied by the percentage by which the increase in the funds appropriated from the preceding fiscal year exceeds 1.5 percent; or

(iii) The sum of—

(A) The amount it received for the preceding fiscal year; and

(B) That amount multiplied by 90 percent of the percentage increase in the amount appropriated from the preceding fiscal year.

(b) Notwithstanding paragraph (a)(2) of this section, no State's allocation under § 300.707 may exceed the sum of—

(1) The amount it received for the preceding fiscal year; and

(2) That amount multiplied by the sum of 1.5 percent and the percentage increase in the amount appropriated.

(c) If the amount available for allocations to States under § 300.703 and paragraphs (a) and (b) of this section is insufficient to pay those allocations in full those allocations are ratably reduced, subject to paragraph (a)(1) of this section.

(Authority: 20 U.S.C. 1411(e)(3)(B) and (C))

§ 300.709 Decrease in funds.

If the amount available for allocations to States under § 300.706 is less than the amount allocated to the States under section 611 of the Act for the preceding fiscal year, those allocations are calculated as follows:

(a) If the amount available for allocations is greater than the amount allocated to the States for the base year, each State is allocated the sum of—

(1) The amount it received for the base year; and

(2) An amount that bears the same relation to any remaining funds as the increase the State received for the preceding fiscal year over the base year bears to the total of those increases for all States.

(b)(1) If the amount available for allocations is equal to or less than the amount allocated to the States for the base year, each State is allocated the amount it received for the base year.

(2) If the amount available is insufficient to make the allocations described in paragraph (b)(1) of this section, those allocations are ratably reduced.

(Authority: 20 U.S.C. 1411(e)(4))

§ 300.710 Allocation for State in which by-pass is implemented for private school children with disabilities.

In determining the allocation under §§ 300.700–300.709 of a State in which the Secretary will implement a by-pass for private school children with disabilities under §§ 300.451–300.487, the Secretary includes in the State's child count—

(a) For the first year of a by-pass, the actual or estimated number of private school children with disabilities (as defined in §§ 300.7(a) and 300.450) in the State, as of the preceding December 1; and

(b) For succeeding years of a by-pass, the number of private school children with disabilities who received special education and related services under the by-pass in the preceding year.

(Authority: 20 U.S.C. 1412(f)(2))

§ 300.711 Subgrants to LEAs.

Each State that receives a grant under section 611 of the Act for any fiscal year shall distribute in accordance with § 300.712 any funds it does not retain under § 300.602 and is not required to distribute under §§ 300.622 and 300.623 to LEAs in the State that have established their eligibility under section 613 of the Act, and to State agencies that received funds under section 614A(a) of the Act for fiscal year 1997, as then in effect, and have established their eligibility under section 613 of the Act, for use in accordance with Part B of the Act.

(Authority: 20 U.S.C. 1411(g)(1))

§ 300.712 Allocations to LEAs.

(a) *Interim procedure*. For each fiscal year for which funds are allocated to States under § 300.703(b) each State shall allocate funds under § 300.711 in accordance with section 611(d) of the Act, as in effect prior to June 4, 1997.

(b) *Permanent procedure*. For each fiscal year for which funds are allocated to States under §§ 300.706–300.709, each State shall allocate funds under § 300.711 as follows:

(1) *Base payments*. The State first shall award each agency described in § 300.711 the amount that agency would have received under this section for the base year, as defined in § 300.706(b)(1), if the State had distributed 75 percent of its grant for that year under section § 300.703(b).

(2) *Base payment adjustments*. For any fiscal year after the base year fiscal year—

(i) If a new LEA is created, the State shall divide the base allocation determined under paragraph (b)(1) of this section for the LEAs that would have been responsible for serving children with disabilities now being served by the new LEA, among the new LEA and affected LEAs based on the relative numbers of children with disabilities ages 3 through 21, or ages 6 through 21 if a State has had its payment reduced under § 300.706(b)(2), currently provided special education by each of the LEAs;

(ii) If one or more LEAs are combined into a single new LEA, the State shall combine the base allocations of the merged LEAs; and

(iii) If, for two or more LEAs, geographic boundaries or administrative responsibility for providing services to children with disabilities ages 3 through 21 change, the base allocations of affected LEAs shall be redistributed among affected LEAs based on the relative numbers of children with disabilities ages 3 through 21, or ages 6 through 21 if a State has had its payment reduced under § 300.706(b)(2), currently provided special education by each affected LEA.

(3) *Allocation of remaining funds*. The State then shall—

(i) Allocate 85 percent of any remaining funds to those agencies on the basis of the relative numbers of children enrolled in public and private elementary and secondary schools within each agency's jurisdiction; and

(ii) Allocate 15 percent of those remaining funds to those agencies in accordance with their relative numbers of children living in poverty, as determined by the SEA.

(iii) For the purposes of making grants under this section, States must apply on a uniform basis across all LEAs the best data that are available to them on the numbers of children enrolled in public and private elementary and secondary schools and the numbers of children living in poverty.

(Authority: 20 U.S.C. 1411(g)(2))

§ 300.713 Former Chapter 1 State agencies.

(a) To the extent necessary, the State—

(1) Shall use funds that are available under § 300.602(a) to ensure that each State agency that received fiscal year 1994 funds under subpart 2 of Part D of chapter 1 of title I of the Elementary and Secondary Education Act of 1965 (as in effect in fiscal year 1994) receives, from the combination of funds under § 300.602(a) and funds provided under § 300.711, an amount no less than—

(i) The number of children with disabilities, aged 6 through 21, to whom the agency was providing special education and related services on December 1, or, at the State's discretion, the last Friday in October, of the fiscal year for which the funds were appropriated, subject to the limitation in paragraph (b) of this section; multiplied by

(ii) The per-child amount provided under that subpart for fiscal year 1994; and

(2) May use funds under § 300.602(a) to ensure that each LEA that received fiscal year 1994 funds under that subpart for children who had transferred from a State-operated or State-supported school or program assisted under that subpart receives, from the combination of funds available under § 300.602(a) and funds provided under § 300.711, an amount for each child, aged 3 through 21 to whom the agency was providing special education and related services on December 1, or, at the State's discretion, the last Friday in October, of the fiscal year for which the funds were appropriated, equal to the per-child amount the agency received under that subpart for fiscal year 1994.

(b) The number of children counted under paragraph (a)(1)(i) of this section may not exceed the number of children aged 3 through 21 for whom the agency received fiscal year 1994 funds under subpart 2 of Part D of chapter 1 of title I of the Elementary and Secondary Education Act of 1965 (as in effect in fiscal year 1994).

(Authority: 20 U.S.C. 1411(g)(3))

§ 300.714 Reallocation of LEA funds.

If an SEA determines that an LEA is adequately providing FAPE to all children with disabilities residing in the area served by that agency with State and local funds, the SEA may reallocate any portion of the funds under Part B of the Act that are not needed by that local agency to provide FAPE to other LEAs in the State that are not adequately providing special education and related services to all children with disabilities residing in the areas they serve.

(Authority: 20 U.S.C. 1411(g)(4))

§ 300.715 Payments to the Secretary of the Interior for the education of Indian children.

(a) *Reserved amounts for Secretary of Interior.* From the amount appropriated for any fiscal year under 611(j) of the Act, the Secretary reserves 1.226 percent to provide assistance to the Secretary of the Interior in accordance with this section and § 300.716.

(b) *Provision of amounts for assistance.* The Secretary provides amounts to the Secretary of the Interior to meet the need for assistance for the education of children with disabilities on reservations aged 5 to 21, inclusive, enrolled in elementary and secondary schools for Indian children operated or funded by the Secretary of the Interior. The amount of the payment for any fiscal year is equal to 80 percent of the amount allotted under paragraph (a) of this section for that fiscal year.

(c) *Calculation of number of children.* In the case of Indian students aged 3 to 5, inclusive, who are enrolled in programs affiliated with the Bureau of Indian Affairs (BIA) schools and that are required by the States in which these schools are located to attain or maintain State accreditation, and which schools have this accreditation prior to the date of enactment of the Individuals with Disabilities Education Act Amendments of 1991, the school may count those children for the purpose of distribution of the funds provided under this section to the Secretary of the Interior.

(d) *Responsibility for meeting the requirements of Part B.* The Secretary of the Interior shall meet all of the requirements of Part B of the Act for the children described in paragraphs (b) and (c) of this section, in accordance with § 300.260.

(Authority: 20 U.S.C. 1411(c); 1411(i)(1)(A) and (B))

§ 300.716 Payments for education and services for Indian children with disabilities aged 3 through 5.

(a) *General.* With funds appropriated under 611(j) of the Act, the Secretary makes payments to the Secretary of the Interior to be distributed to tribes or tribal organizations (as defined under section 4 of the Indian Self-Determination and Education Assistance Act) or consortia of those tribes or tribal organizations to provide for the coordination of assistance for special education and related services for children with disabilities aged 3 through 5 on reservations served by elementary and secondary schools for Indian children operated or funded by the Department of the Interior. The amount of the payments under paragraph (b) of this section for any fiscal year is equal to 20 percent of the amount allotted under § 300.715(a).

(b) *Distribution of funds.* The Secretary of the Interior shall distribute the total amount of the payment under paragraph (a) of this section by allocating to each tribe or tribal organization an amount based on the number of children with disabilities ages 3 through 5 residing on reservations as reported annually, divided by the total of those children served by all tribes or tribal organizations.

(c) *Submission of information.* To receive a payment under this section, the tribe or tribal organization shall submit the figures to the Secretary of the Interior as required to determine the amounts to be allocated under paragraph (b) of this section. This information must be compiled and submitted to the Secretary.

(d) *Use of funds.* (1) The funds received by a tribe or tribal organization must be used to assist in child find, screening, and other procedures for the early identification of children aged 3 through 5, parent training, and the provision of direct services. These activities may be carried out directly or through contracts or cooperative agreements with the BIA, LEAs, and other public or private nonprofit organizations. The tribe or tribal organization is encouraged to involve Indian parents in the development and implementation of these activities.

(2) The entities shall, as appropriate, make referrals to local, State, or Federal entities for the provision of services or further diagnosis.

(e) *Biennial report.* To be eligible to receive a grant pursuant to paragraph (a) of this section, the tribe or tribal organization shall provide to the Secretary of the Interior a biennial report of activities undertaken under this paragraph, including the number of contracts and cooperative agreements entered into, the number of children contacted and receiving services for each year, and the estimated number of children needing services during the two years following the one in which the report is made. The

Secretary of the Interior shall include a summary of this information on a biennial basis in the report to the Secretary required under section 611(i) of the Act. The Secretary may require any additional information from the Secretary of the Interior.

(f) *Prohibitions*. None of the funds allocated under this section may be used by the Secretary of the Interior for administrative purposes, including child count and the provision of technical assistance.

(Authority: 20 U.S.C. 1411(i)(3))

§ 300.717 Outlying areas and freely associated States.

From the amount appropriated for any fiscal year under section 611(j) of the Act, the Secretary reserves not more than one percent, which must be used—

(a) To provide assistance to the outlying areas in accordance with their respective populations of individuals aged 3 through 21; and

(b) For fiscal years 1998 through 2001, to carry out the competition described in § 300.719, except that the amount reserved to carry out that competition may not exceed the amount reserved for fiscal year 1996 for the competition under Part B of the Act described under the heading "SPECIAL EDUCATION" in Public Law 104–134.

(Authority: 20 U.S.C. 1411(b)(1))

§ 300.718 Outlying area—definition.

As used in this part, the term *outlying area* means the United States Virgin Islands, Guam, American Samoa, and the Commonwealth of the Northern Mariana Islands.

(Authority: 20 U.S.C. 1402(18))

§ 300.719 Limitation for freely associated States.

(a) *Competitive grants*. The Secretary uses funds described in § 300.717(b) to award grants, on a competitive basis, to Guam, American Samoa, the Commonwealth of the Northern Mariana Islands, and the freely associated States to carry out the purposes of this part.

(b) *Award basis*. The Secretary awards grants under paragraph (a) of this section on a competitive basis, pursuant to the recommendations of the Pacific Region Educational Laboratory in Honolulu, Hawaii. Those recommendations must be made by experts in the field of special education and related services.

(c) *Assistance requirements*. Any freely associated State that wishes to receive funds under Part B of the Act shall include, in its application for assistance—

(1) Information demonstrating that it will meet all conditions that apply to States under Part B of the Act;

(2) An assurance that, notwithstanding any other provision of Part B of the Act, it will use those funds only for the direct provision of special education and related services to children with disabilities and to enhance its capacity to make FAPE available to all children with disabilities;

(3) The identity of the source and amount of funds, in addition to funds under Part B of the Act, that it will make available to ensure that FAPE is available to all children with disabilities within its jurisdiction; and

(4) Such other information and assurances as the Secretary may require.

(d) *Termination of eligibility*. Notwithstanding any other provision of law, the freely associated States may not receive any funds under Part B of the Act for any program year that begins after September 30, 2001.

(e) *Administrative costs*. The Secretary may provide not more than five percent of the amount reserved for grants under this section to pay the administrative costs of the Pacific Region Educational Laboratory under paragraph (b) of this section.

(f) *Eligibility for award*. An outlying area is not eligible for a competitive award under § 300.719 unless it receives assistance under § 300.717(a).

(Authority: 20 U.S.C. 1411(b)(2) and (3))

§ 300.720 Special rule.

The provisions of Public Law 95-134, permitting the consolidation of grants by the outlying areas, do not apply to funds provided to those areas or to the freely associated States under Part B of the Act.

(Authority: 20 U.S.C. 1411(b)(4))

§ 300.721 [Reserved]

§ 300.722 Definition.

As used in this part, the term *freely associated States* means the Republic of the Marshall Islands, the Federated States of Micronesia, and the Republic of Palau.

(Authority: 20 U.S.C. 1411(b)(6))

Reports

§ 300.750 Annual report of children served—report requirement.

(a) The SEA shall report to the Secretary no later than February 1 of each year the number of children with disabilities aged 3 through 21 residing in the State who are receiving special education and related services.

(b) The SEA shall submit the report on forms provided by the Secretary.

(Authority: 20 U.S.C. 1411(d)(2); 1418(a))

§ 300.751 Annual report of children served—information required in the report.

(a) For any year the SEA shall include in its report a table that shows the number of children with disabilities receiving special education and related services on December 1, or at the State's discretion on the last Friday in October, of that school year—

(1) Aged 3 through 5;

(2) Aged 6 through 17; and

(3) Aged 18 through 21.

(b) For the purpose of this part, a child's age is the child's actual age on the date of the child count: December 1, or, at the State's discretion, the last Friday in October.

(c) Reports must also include the number of those children with disabilities aged 3 through 21 for each year of age (3, 4, 5, etc.) within each disability category, as defined in the definition of "children with disabilities" in § 300.7; and

(d) The Secretary may permit the collection of the data in paragraph (c) of this section through sampling.

(e) The SEA may not report a child under paragraph (c) of this section under more than one disability category.

(f) If a child with a disability has more than one disability, the SEA shall report that child under paragraph (c) of this section in accordance with the following procedure:

(1) If a child has only two disabilities and those disabilities are deafness and blindness, and the child is not reported as having a developmental delay, that child must be reported under the category "deaf-blindness".

(2) A child who has more than one disability and is not reported as having deaf-blindness or as having a developmental delay must be reported under the category "multiple disabilities".

(Authority: 20 U.S.C. 1411(d)(2); 1418(a) and (b))

§ 300.752 Annual report of children served—certification.

The SEA shall include in its report a certification signed by an authorized official of the agency that the information provided under § 300.751(a) is an accurate and unduplicated count of children with disabilities receiving special education and related services on the dates in question.

(Authority: 20 U.S.C. 1411(d)(2); 1417(b))

§ 300.753 Annual report of children served—criteria for counting children.

(a) The SEA may include in its report children with disabilities who are enrolled in a school or program that is operated or supported by a public agency, and that—

(1) Provides them with both special education and related services that meet State standards;

(2) Provides them only with special education, if a related service is not required, that meets State standards; or

(3) In the case of children with disabilities enrolled by their parents in private schools, provides them with special education or related services under §§ 300.452-300.462 that meet State standards.

(b) The SEA may not include children with disabilities in its report who are receiving special education funded solely by the Federal Government, including children served by the Department of Interior, the Department of Defense, or the Department of Education. However, the State may count children covered under § 300.184(c)(2).

(Authority: 20 U.S.C. 1411(d)(2); 1417(b))

§ 300.754 Annual report of children served—other responsibilities of the SEA.

In addition to meeting the other requirements of §§ 300.750-300.753, the SEA shall—

(a) Establish procedures to be used by LEAs and other educational institutions in counting the number of children with disabilities receiving special education and related services;

(b) Set dates by which those agencies and institutions must report to the SEA to ensure that the State complies with § 300.750(a);

(c) Obtain certification from each agency and institution that an unduplicated and accurate count has been made;

(d) Aggregate the data from the count obtained from each agency and institution, and prepare the reports required under §§ 300.750-300.753; and

(e) Ensure that documentation is maintained that enables the State and the Secretary to audit the accuracy of the count.

(Authority: 20 U.S.C. 1411(d)(2); 1417(b))

§ 300.755 Disproportionality.

(a) *General.* Each State that receives assistance under Part B of the Act, and the Secretary of the Interior, shall provide for the collection and examination of data to determine if significant disproportionality based on race is occurring in the State or in the schools operated by the Secretary of the Interior with respect to—

(1) The identification of children as children with disabilities, including the identification of children as children with disabilities in accordance with a particular impairment described in section 602(3) of the Act; and

(2) The placement in particular educational settings of these children.

(b) *Review and revision of policies, practices, and procedures.* In the case of a determination of significant disproportionality with respect to the identification of children as children with disabilities, or the placement in particular educational settings of these children, in accordance with paragraph (a) of this section, the State or the Secretary of the Interior shall provide for the review and, if appropriate revision of the policies, procedures, and practices used in the identification or placement to ensure that the policies, procedures, and practices comply with the requirements of Part B of the Act.

(Authority: 20 U.S.C. 1418(c))

§ 300.756 Acquisition of equipment; construction or alteration of facilities.

(a) *General.* If the Secretary determines that a program authorized under Part B of the Act would be improved by permitting program funds to be used to acquire appropriate equipment, or to construct new facilities or alter existing facilities, the Secretary may allow the use of those funds for those purposes.

(b) *Compliance with certain regulations.* Any construction of new facilities or alteration of existing facilities under paragraph (a) of this section must comply with the requirements of—

(1) Appendix A of part 36 of title 28, Code of Federal Regulations (commonly known as the "Americans with Disabilities Accessibility Guidelines for Buildings and Facilities"); or

(2) Appendix A of part 101-19.6 of title 41, Code of Federal Regulations (commonly known as the "Uniform Federal Accessibility Standards").

(Authority: 20 U.S.C. 1405)

Appendix A to Part 300—Notice of Interpretation

I. Involvement and Progress of Each Child With a Disability in the General Curriculum

1. What are the major Part B IEP requirements that govern the involvement and progress of children with disabilities in the general curriculum?

2. Must a child's IEP address his or her involvement in the general curriculum, regardless of the nature and severity of the child's disability and the setting in which the child is educated?

3. What must public agencies do to meet the requirements at §§ 300.344(a)(2) and 300.346(d) regarding the participation of a "regular education teacher" in the development review, and revision of the IEPs, for children age 3 through 5 who are receiving special education and related services?

4. Must the measurable annual goals in a child's IEP address all areas of the general curriculum, or only those areas in which the child's involvement and progress are affected by the child's disability?

II. Involvement of Parents and Students

5. What is the role of the parents, including surrogate parents, in decisions regarding the educational program of their children?

6. What are the Part B requirements regarding the participation of a student (child) with a disability in an IEP meeting?

7. Must the public agency inform the parents of who will be at the IEP meeting?

8. Do parents have the right to a copy of their child's IEP?

9. What is a public agency's responsibility if it is not possible to reach consensus on what services should be included in a child's IEP?

10. Does Part B require that public agencies inform parents regarding the educational progress of their children with disabilities?

III. Preparing Students With Disabilities for Employment and Other Post-School Experiences

11. What must the IEP team do to meet the requirements that the IEP include a statement of "transition service needs" beginning at age 14 (§ 300.347(b)(1), and a statement of "needed transition services" beginning at age 16 (§ 300.347(b)(2)?

12. Must the IEP for each student with a disability, beginning no later than age 16, include all "needed transition services," as identified by the IEP team and consistent with the definition at § 300.29, even if an agency other than the public agency will provide those services? What is the public agency's responsibility if another agency fails to provide agreed-upon transition services?

13. Under what circumstances must a public agency invite representatives from other agencies to an IEP meeting at which a child's need for transition services will be considered?

IV. Other Questions Regarding Implementation of Idea

14. For a child with a disability receiving special education for the first time, when must an IEP be developed—before placement or after placement?

15. Who is responsible for ensuring the development of IEPs for children with disabilities served by a public agency other than an LEA?

16. For a child placed out of State by an educational or non-educational State or local agency, is the placing or receiving State responsible for the child's IEP?

17. If a disabled child has been receiving special education from one public agency and transfers to another public agency in the same State, must the new public agency develop an IEP before the child can be placed in a special education program?

18. What timelines apply to the development and implementation of an initial IEP for a child with a disability?

19. Must a public agency hold separate meetings to determine a child's eligibility for special education and related services, develop the child's IEP, and determine the child's placement, or may the agency meet all of these requirements in a single meeting?

20. How frequently must a public agency conduct meetings to review, and if appropriate revise, the IEP for each child with a disability?

21. May IEP meetings be audio or video-tape-recorded?

22. Who can serve as the representative of the public agency at an IEP meeting?

23. For a child with a disability being considered for initial placement in special education, which teacher or teachers should attend the IEP meeting?

24. What is the role of a regular education teacher in the development, review, and revision of the IEP for a child who is, or may be, participating in the regular education environment?

25. If a child with a disability attends several regular classes, must all of the child's regular education teachers be members of the child's IEP team?

26. How should a public agency determine which regular education teacher and special education teacher will members of the IEP team for a particular child with a disability?

27. For a child whose primary disability is a speech impairment, may a public agency meet its responsibility under § 300.344(a)(3) to ensure that the IEP team includes "at least one special education teacher, or, if appropriate, at least one special education provider of the child" by including a speech-language pathologist on the IEP team?

28. Do public agencies and parents have the option of having any individual of their choice attend a child's IEP meeting as participants on their child's IEP team?

29. Can parents or public agencies bring their attorneys to IEP meetings, and, if so under what circumstances? Are attorney's fees available for parents' attorneys if the parents are prevailing parties in actions or proceedings brought under Part B?

30. Must related services personnel attend IEP meetings?

31. Must the public agency ensure that all services specified in a child's IEP are provided?

32. Is it permissible for an agency to have the IEP completed before the IEP meeting begins?

33. Must a public agency include transportation in a child's IEP as a related service?

34. Must a public agency provide related services that are required to assist a child with a disability to benefit from special education, whether or not those services are included in the list of related services in § 300.24?

35. Must the IEP specify the amount of services or may it simply list the services to be provided?

36. Under what circumstances is a public agency required to permit a child with a disability to use a school-purchased assistive technology device in the child's home or in another setting?

37. Can the IEP team also function as the group making the placement decision for a child with a disability?

38. If a child's IEP includes behavioral strategies to address a particular behavior, can a child ever be suspended for engaging in that behavior?

39. If a child's behavior in the regular classroom, even with appropriate interventions, would significantly impair the learning of others, can the group that makes the placement decision determine that placement in the regular classroom is inappropriate for that child?

40. May school personnel during a school year implement more than one short-term removal of a child with disabilities from his or her classroom or school for misconduct?

Authority: Part B of the Individuals with Disabilities Education Act (20 U.S.C. 1401, et seq.), unless otherwise noted.

Individualized Education Programs (IEPS) and Other Selected ImplementatioN Issues

Interpretation of IEP and Other selected Requirements under Part B of the Individuals with Disabilities Education Act (IDEA; Part B)

Introduction

The IEP requirements under Part B of the IDEA emphasize the importance of three core concepts: (1) the involvement and progress of each child with a disability in the general curriculum including addressing the unique needs that arise out of the child's disability; (2) the involvement of parents and students, together with regular and special education personnel, in making individual decisions to support each student's (child's) educational success, and (3) the preparation of students with disabilities for employment and other post-school activities.

The first three sections of this Appendix (I-III) provide guidance regarding the IEP requirements as they relate to the three core concepts described above. Section IV addresses other questions regarding the development and content of IEPs, including questions about the timelines and responsibility for developing and implementing IEPs, participation in IEP meetings, and IEP content. Section IV also addresses questions on other selected requirements under IDEA.

I. Involvement and Progress of Each Child With a Disability in the General Curriculum

In enacting the IDEA Amendments of 1997, the Congress found that research, demonstration, and practice over the past 20 years in special education and related disciplines have demonstrated that an effective educational system now and in the future must maintain high academic standards and clear performance goals for children with disabilities, consistent with the standards and expectations for all students in the educational system, and provide for appropriate and effective strategies and methods to ensure that students who are children with disabilities have maximum opportunities to achieve those standards and goals. [Section 651(a)(6)(A) of the Act.]

Accordingly, the evaluation and IEP provisions of Part B place great emphasis on the involvement and progress of children with disabilities in the general curriculum. (The term "general curriculum,'' as used in these regulations, including this Appendix, refers to the curriculum that is used with nondisabled children.)

While the Act and regulations recognize that IEP teams must make individualized decisions about the special education and related services, and supplementary aids and services, provided to each child with a disability, they are driven by IDEA's strong preference that, to the maximum extent appropriate, children with disabilities be educated in regular classes with their nondisabled peers with appropriate supplementary aids and services.

In many cases, children with disabilities will need appropriate supports in order to successfully progress in the general curriculum, participate in State and district-wide assessment programs, achieve the measurable goals in their IEPs, and be educated together with their nondisabled peers. Accordingly, the Act requires the IEP team to determine, and the public agency to provide, the accommodations, modifications, supports, and supplementary aids and services, needed by each child with a disability to successfully be involved in and progress in the general curriculum achieve the goals of the IEP, and successfully demonstrate his or her competencies in State and district-wide assessments.

1. What are the major Part B IEP requirements that govern the involvement and progress of children with disabilities in the general curriculum?

Present Levels of Educational Performance

Section 300.347(a)(1) requires that the IEP for each child with a disability include "* * * a statement of the child's present levels of educational performance, including—(i) *how the child's disability affects the child's involvement and progress in the general curriculum; or (ii) for preschool children, as appropriate, how the child's disability affects the child's participation in appropriate activities* * * *'' ("Appropriate activities" in this context refers to age-relevant developmental abilities or milestones that typically developing children of the same age would be performing or would have achieved.)

The IEP team's determination of how each child's disability affects the child's involvement and progress in the general curriculum is a primary consideration in the development of the child's IEP. In assessing children with disabilities, school districts may use a variety of assessment techniques to determine the extent to which these children can be involved and progress in the general curriculum, such as criterion-referenced tests, standard achievement tests, diagnostic tests, other tests, or any combination of the above.

The purpose of using these assessments is to determine the child's present levels of educational performance and areas of need arising from the child's disability so that approaches for ensuring the child's involvement and progress in the general curriculum and any needed adaptations or modifications to that curriculum can be identified.

Measurable Annual Goals, including Benchmarks or Short-term ojectives

Measurable annual goals, including benchmarks or short-term objectives, are critical to the strategic planning process used to develop and implement the IEP for each child with a disability. Once the IEP team has developed measurable annual goals for a child, the team (1) can develop strategies that will be most effective in realizing those goals and (2) must develop either measurable, intermediate steps (short-term objectives) or major milestones (benchmarks) that will enable parents, students, and educators to monitor progress during the year, and, if appropriate, to revise the IEP consistent with the student's instructional needs.

The strong emphasis in Part B on linking the educational program of children with disabilities to the general curriculum is reflected in § 300.347(a)(2), which requires that the IEP include:

a statement of measurable annual goals, including benchmarks or short-term objectives, related to—(i) *meeting the child's needs that result from the child's disability to enable the child to be involved in and progress in the general curriculum;* and (ii) meeting each of the child's other educational needs that result from the child's disability.

As noted above, each annual goal must include either short-term objectives or benchmarks. The purpose of both is to enable a child's teacher(s), parents, and others involved in developing and implementing the child's IEP, to gauge, at intermediate times during the year, how well the child is progressing toward achievement of the annual goal. IEP teams may continue to develop short-term instructional objectives, that generally break the skills described in the annual goal down into discrete components. The revised statute and regulations also provide that, as an alternative, IEP teams may develop benchmarks, which can be thought of as describing the amount of progress the child is expected to make within specified segments of the year. Generally, benchmarks establish expected performance levels that allow for regular checks of progress that coincide with the reporting periods for informing parents of their child's progress toward achieving the annual goals. An IEP team may use either short term objectives or benchmarks or a combination of the two depending on the nature of the annual goals and the needs of the child.

Special Education and Related Services and Supplementary Aids and Services

The requirements regarding services provided to address a child's present levels of educational performance and to make progress toward the identified goals reinforce the emphasis on progress in the general curriculum, as well as maximizing the extent to which children with disabilities are educated with nondisabled children. Section 300.347(a)(3) requires that the IEP include:

a statement of the special education and related services and supplementary aids and services to be provided to the child, or on behalf of the child, and a statement of the program modifications or supports for school personnel that will be provided for the child—
(i) to advance appropriately toward attaining the annual goals; (ii) *to be involved and progress in the general curriculum* * * * and to participate in extracurricular and other nonacademic activities; and (iii) *to be educated and participate with other children with disabilities and nondisabled children in [extracurricular and other nonacademic activities]* * * * [Italics added.]

Extent to Which Child Will Participate With Nondisabled Children

Section 300.347(a)(4) requires that each child's IEP include "An explanation of the extent, if any, to which the child will not participate with nondisabled children in the regular class and in [extracurricular and other nonacademic] activities * * *" This is consistent with the least restrictive environment (LRE) provisions at §§ 300.550–300.553, which include requirements that:

(1) each child with a disability be educated with nondisabled children to the maximum extent appropriate (§ 300.550(b)(1));

(2) each child with a disability be removed from the regular educational environment only when the nature or severity of the child's disability is such that education in regular classes with the use of supplementary aids and services cannot be achieved satisfactorily (§ 300.550(b)(1)); and

(3) to the maximum extent appropriate to the child's needs, each child with a disability participates with nondisabled children in nonacademic and extracurricular services and activities (§ 300.553).

All services and educational placements under Part B must be individually determined in light of each child's unique abilities and needs, to reasonably promote the child's educational success. Placing children with disabilities in this manner should enable each disabled child to meet high expectations in the future.

Although Part B requires that a child with a disability not be removed from the regular educational environment if the child's education can be achieved satisfactorily in regular classes with the use of supplementary aids and services, Part B's LRE principle is intended to ensure that a child with a disability is served in a setting where the child can be educated successfully. Even though IDEA does not mandate regular class placement for every disabled student, IDEA presumes that the first placement option considered for each disabled student by the student's placement team, which must include the parent, is the school the child would attend if not disabled, with appropriate supplementary aids and services to facilitate such placement. Thus, before a disabled child can be placed outside of the regular educational environment, the full range of supplementary aids and services that if provided would facilitate the student's placement in the regular classroom setting must be considered. Following that consideration, if a determination is made that particular disabled student cannot be educated satisfactorily in the regular educational environment, even with the provision of appropriate supplementary aids and services, that student then could be placed in a setting other than the regular classroom. Later, if it becomes apparent that the child's IEP can be carried out in a less restrictive setting, with the provision of appropriate supplementary aids and services, if needed, Part B would require that the child's placement be changed from the more restrictive setting to a less restrictive setting. In all cases, placement decisions must be individually determined on the basis of each child's abilities and needs, and not solely on factors such as category of disability, significance of disability, availability of special education and related services, configuration of the service delivery system, availability of space, or administrative convenience. Rather, each student's IEP forms the basis for the placement decision.

Further, a student need not fail in the regular classroom before another placement can be considered. Conversely, IDEA does not require that a student demonstrate achievement of a specific performance level as a prerequisite for placement into a regular classroom.

Participation in State or District-Wide Assessments of Student Achievement

Consistent with § 300.138(a), which sets forth a presumption that children with disabilities will be included in general State and district-wide assessment programs, and provided with appropriate accommodations if necessary, § 300.347(a)(5) requires that the IEP for each student with a disability include: "(i) a statement of any individual modifications in the administration of State or district-wide assessments of student achievement that are needed in order for the child to participate in the assessment; and (ii) if the IEP team determines that the child will not participate in a particular State or district-wide assessment of student achievement (or part of an assessment of student achievement), a statement of—(A) Why that assessment is not appropriate for the child; and (B) How the child will be assessed."

Regular Education Teacher Participation in the Development, Review, and Revision of IEPs

Very often, regular education teachers play a central role in the education of children with disabilities (H. Rep. No. 105-95, p. 103 (1997); S. Rep. No. 105-17, p. 23 (1997)) and have important expertise regarding the general curriculum and the general education environment. Further, with the emphasis on involvement and progress in the general curriculum added by the IDEA Amendments of 1997, regular education teachers have an increasingly critical role (together with special education and related services personnel) in implementing the program of FAPE for most children with disabilities, as described in their IEPs.

Accordingly, the IDEA Amendments of 1997 added a requirement that each child's IEP team must include at least one regular education teacher of the child, if the child is, or may be, participating in the regular education environment (see § 300.344(a)(2)). (See also §§ 300.346(d) on the role of a regular education teacher in the development, review and revision of IEPs.)

2. Must a child's IEP address his or her involvement in the general curriculum, regardless of the nature and severity of the child's disability and the setting in which the child is educated?

Yes. The IEP for each child with a disability (including children who are educated in separate classrooms or schools) must address how the child will be involved and progress in the general curriculum. However, the Part B regulations recognize that some children have other educational needs resulting from their disability that also must be met, even though those needs are not directly linked to participation in the general curriculum.

Accordingly, § 300.347(a)(1)(2) requires that each child's IEP include:

A statement of measurable annual goals, including benchmarks or short-term objectives related to—(i) Meeting the child's needs that result from the child's disability to enable the child to be involved in and progress in the general curriculum; and (ii) meeting each of the child's other educational needs that result from the child's disability. [Italics added.]

Thus, the IEP team for each child with a disability must make an individualized determination regarding (1) how the child will be involved and progress in the general curriculum and what needs that result from the child's disability must be met to facilitate that participation; (2) whether the child has any other educational needs resulting from his or her disability that also must be met; and (3) what special education and other services and supports must be described in the child's IEP to address both sets of needs (consistent with § 300.347(a)). For example, if the IEP team determines that in order for a child who is deaf to participate in the general curriculum he or she needs sign language and materials which reflect his or her language development, those needs (relating to the child's participation in the general curriculum) must be addressed in the child's IEP. In addition, if the team determines that the child also needs to expand his or her vocabulary in sign language that service must also be addressed in the applicable components of the child's IEP. The IEP team may also wish to consider whether there is a need for members of the child's family to receive training in sign language in order for the child to receive FAPE.

3. What must public agencies do to meet the requirements at §§ 300.344(a)(2) and 300.346(d) regarding the participation of a "regular education teacher" in the development, review, and revision of IEPs, for children aged 3 through 5 who are receiving preschool special education services?

If a public agency provides "regular education" preschool services to non-disabled children, then the requirements of §§ 300.344(a)(2) and 300.346(d) apply as they do in the case of older children with disabilities. If a public agency makes kindergarten available to nondisabled children, then a regular education kindergarten teacher could appropriately be the regular education teacher who would be a member of the IEP team, and, as appropriate, participate in IEP meetings, for a kindergarten-aged child who is, or may be, participating in the regular education environment.

If a public agency does not provide regular preschool education services to nondisabled children, the agency could designate an individual who, under State standards, is qualified to serve nondisabled children of the same age.

4. Must the measurable annual goals in a child's IEP address all areas of the general curriculum, or only those areas in which the child's involvement and progress are affected by the child's disability?

Section 300.347(a)(2) requires that each child's IEP include "A statement of measurable annual goals, including benchmarks or short-term objectives, related to—(i) *meeting the child's needs that result from the child's disability to enable the child to be involved in and progress in the general curriculum* * * *; and (ii) meeting each of the child's other educational needs that result from the child's disability. . . ." (Italics added).

Thus, a public agency is not required to include in an IEP annual goals that relate to areas of the general curriculum in which the child's disability does not affect the child's ability to be involved in and progress in the general curriculum. If a child with a disability needs only modifications or accommodations in order to progress in an area of the general curriculum, the IEP does not need to include a goal for that area; however, the IEP would need to specify those modifications or accommodations.

Public agencies often require all children, including children with disabilities, to demonstrate mastery in a given area of the general curriculum before allowing them to progress to the next level or grade in that area. Thus, in order to ensure that each child with a disability can effectively demonstrate competencies in an applicable area of the general curriculum, it is important for the IEP team to consider the accommodations and modifications that the child needs to assist him or her in demonstrating progress in that area.

II. Involvement of Parents and Students

The Congressional Committee Reports on the IDEA Amendments of 1997 express the view that the Amendments provide an opportunity for strengthening the role of parents, and emphasize that one of the purposes of the Amendments is to expand opportunities for parents and key public agency staff (e.g., special education, related services, regular education, and early intervention service providers, and other personnel) to work in new partnerships at both the State and local levels (H. Rep. 105-95, p. 82 (1997); S. Rep. No. 105-17, p. 4 and 5 (1997)). Accordingly, the IDEA Amendments of 1997 require that parents have an opportunity to participate in meetings with respect to the identification, evaluation, and educational placement of the child, and the provision of FAPE to the child. (§ 300.501(a)(2)). Thus, parents must now be part of: (1) the group that determines what additional data are needed as part of an evaluation of their child (§ 300.533(a)(1)); (2) the team that determines their child's eligibility (§ 300.534(a)(1)); and (3) the group that makes decisions on the educational placement of their child (§ 300.501(c)).

In addition, the concerns of parents and the information that they provide regarding their children must be considered in developing and reviewing their children's IEPs (§§ 300.343(c)(iii) and 300.346(a)(1)(i) and (b)); and the requirements for keeping parents informed about the educational progress of their children, particularly as it relates to their progress in the general curriculum, have been strengthened (§ 300.347(a)(7)).

The IDEA Amendments of 1997 also contain provisions that greatly strengthen the involvement of students with disabilities in decisions regarding their own futures, to facilitate movement from school to post-school activities. For example, those amendments (1) retained, essentially verbatim, the "transition services" requirements from the IDEA Amendments of 1990 (which provide that a statement of needed transition services must be in the IEP of each student with a disability, beginning no later than age 16); and (2) significantly expanded those provisions by adding a new annual requirement for the IEP to include "transition planning" activities for students beginning at age 14. (See section IV of this appendix for a description of the transition services requirements and definition.)

With respect to student involvement in decisions regarding transition services, § 300.344(b) provides that (1) "the public agency shall invite a student with a disability of any age to attend his or her IEP meeting if a purpose of the meeting will be the consideration of—(i) The student's transition services needs under § 300.347(b)(1); or (ii) The needed transition services for the student under § 300.347(b)(2); or (iii) Both;'' and (2) "If the student does not attend the IEP meeting, the public agency shall take other steps to ensure that the student's preferences and interests are considered.'' (§ 300.344(b)(2)).

The IDEA Amendments of 1997 also give States the authority to elect to transfer the rights accorded to parents under Part B to each student with a disability upon reaching the age of majority under State law (if the student has not been determined incompetent under State law) (§ 300.517). (Part B requires that if the rights transfer to the student, the public agency must provide any notice required under Part B to both the student and the parents.) If the State elects to provide for the transfer of rights from the parents to the student at the age of majority, the IEP must, beginning at least one year before a student reaches the age of majority under State law, include a statement that the student has been informed of any rights that will transfer to him or her upon reaching the age of majority. (§ 300.347(c)).

The IDEA Amendments of 1997 also permit, but do not require, States to establish a procedure for appointing the parent, or another appropriate individual if the parent is not available, to represent the educational interests of a student with a disability who has reached the age of majority under State law and has not been determined to be incompetent, but who is determined not to have the ability to provide informed consent with respect to his or her educational program.

5. What is the role of the parents, including surrogate parents, in decisions regarding the educational program of their children?

The parents of a child with a disability are expected to be equal participants along with school personnel, in developing, reviewing, and revising the IEP for their child. This is an active role in which the parents (1) provide critical information regarding the strengths of their child and express their concerns for enhancing the education of their child; (2) participate in discussions about the child's need for special education and related services and supplementary aids and services; and (3) join with the other participants in deciding how the child will be involved and progress in the general curriculum and participate in State and district-wide assessments, and what services the agency will provide to the child and in what setting.

As previously noted in the introduction to section II of this Appendix, Part B specifically provides that parents of children with disabilities—

- Have an opportunity to participate in meetings with respect to the identification, evaluation, and educational placement of their child, and the provision of FAPE to the child (including IEP meetings) (§§ 300.501(b), 300.344(a)(1), and 300.517;
- Be part of the groups that determine what additional data are needed as part of an evaluation of their child (§ 300.533(a)(1)), and determine their child's eligibility (§ 300.534(a)(1)) and educational placement (§ 300.501(c));
- Have their concerns and the information that they provide regarding their child considered in developing and reviewing their child's IEPs (§§ 300.343(c)(iii) and 300.346(a)(1)(i) and (b)); and
- Be regularly informed (by such means as periodic report cards), as specified in their child's IEP, at least as often as parents are informed of their nondisabled children's progress, of their child's progress toward the annual goals in the IEP and the extent to which that progress is sufficient to enable the child to achieve the goals by the end of the year (§ 300.347(a)(7)).

A surrogate parent is a person appointed to represent the interests of a child with a disability in the educational decision-making process when no parent (as defined at § 300.20) is known, the agency, after reasonable efforts, cannot locate the child's parents, or the child is a ward of the State under the laws of the State. A surrogate parent has all of the rights and responsibilities of a parent under Part B (§ 300.515.)

6. What are the Part B requirements regarding the participation of a student (child) with a disability in an IEP meeting?

If a purpose of an IEP meeting for a student with a disability will be the consideration of the student's transition services needs or needed transition services under § 300.347(b)(1) or (2), or both, the public agency must invite the student and, as part of the notification to the parents of the IEP meeting, inform the parents that the agency will invite the student to the IEP meeting.

If the student does not attend, the public agency must take other steps to ensure that the student's preferences and interests are considered. (See § 300.344(b)).

Section § 300.517 permits, but does not require, States to transfer procedural rights under Part B from the parents to students with disabilities who reach the age of majority under State law, if they have not been determined to be incompetent under State law. If those rights are to be transferred from the parents to the student, the public agency would be required to ensure that the student has the right to participate in IEP meetings set forth for parents in § 300.345. However, at the discretion of the student or the public agency, the parents also could attend IEP meetings as "* * * individuals who have knowledge or special expertise regarding the child * * *'' (see § 300.344(a)(6)).

In other circumstances, a child with a disability may attend "if appropriate." (§ 300.344(a)(7)). Generally, a child with a disability should attend the IEP meeting if the parent decides that it is appropriate for the child to do so. If possible, the agency and parents should discuss the appropriateness of the child's participation before a decision is made, in order to help the parents determine whether or not the child's attendance would be (1) helpful in developing the IEP or (2) directly beneficial to the child or both. The agency should inform the parents before each IEP meeting—as part of notification under § 300.345(a)(1)—that they may invite their child to participate.

7. Must the public agency inform the parents of who will be at the IEP meeting?

Yes. In notifying parents about the meeting, the agency "must indicate the purpose, time, and location of the meeting, and who will be in attendance." (§ 300.345(b), italics added.) In addition, if a purpose of the IEP meeting will be the consideration of a student's transition services needs or needed transition services under § 300.347(b)(1) or (2) or both, the notice must also inform the parents that the agency is inviting the student, and identify any other agency that will be invited to send a representative.

The public agency also must inform the parents of the right of the parents and the agency to invite other individuals who have knowledge or special expertise regarding the child, including related services personnel as appropriate to be members of the IEP team. (§ 300.345(b)(1)(ii).)

It also may be appropriate for the agency to ask the parents to inform the agency of any individuals the parents will be bringing to the meeting. Parents are encouraged to let the agency know whom they intend to bring. Such cooperation can facilitate arrangements for the meeting, and help ensure a productive, child-centered meeting.

8. Do parents have the right to a copy of their child's IEP?

Yes. Section 300.345(f) states that the public agency shall give the parent a copy of the IEP at no cost to the parent.

9. What is a public agency's responsibility if it is not possible to reach consensus on what services should be included in a child's IEP?

The IEP meeting serves as a communication vehicle between parents and school personnel, and enables them, as equal participants, to make joint, informed decisions regarding the (1) child's needs and appropriate goals; (2) extent to which the child will be involved in the general curriculum and participate in the regular education environment and State and district-wide assessments; and (3) services needed to support that involvement and participation and to achieve agreed-upon goals. Parents are considered equal partners with school personnel in making these decisions, and the IEP team must consider the parents' concerns and the information that they provide regarding their child in developing, reviewing, and revising IEPs (§§ 300.343(c)(iii) and 300.346(a)(1) and (b)).

The IEP team should work toward consensus, but the public agency has ultimate responsibility to ensure that the IEP includes the services that the child needs in order to receive FAPE. It is not appropriate to make IEP decisions based upon a majority "vote." If the team cannot reach consensus, the public agency must provide the parents with prior written notice of the agency's proposals or refusals, or both, regarding the child's educational program, and the parents have the right to seek resolution of any disagreements by initiating an impartial due process hearing.

Every effort should be made to resolve differences between parents and school staff through voluntary mediation or some other informal step, without resort to a due process hearing. However, mediation or other informal procedures may not be used to deny or delay a parent's right to a due process hearing, or to deny any other rights afforded under Part B.

10. Does Part B require that public agencies inform parents regarding the educational progress of their children with disabilities?

Yes. The Part B statute and regulations include a number of provisions to help ensure that parents are involved in decisions regarding, and are informed about, their child's educational progress, including the child's progress in the general curriculum. First, the parents will be informed regarding their child's present levels of educational performance through the development of the IEP. Section 300.347(a)(1) requires that each IEP include:

* * * A statement of the child's present levels of educational performance, including—(i) how the child's disability affects the child's involvement and progress in the general curriculum; or (ii) for preschool children, as appropriate, how the disability affects the child's participation in appropriate activities * * *

Further, § 300.347(a)(7) sets forth new requirements for regularly informing parents about their child's educational progress, as regularly as parents of nondisabled children are informed of their child's progress. That section requires that the IEP include:

A statement of—(i) How the child's progress toward the annual goals * * * will be measured; and (ii) how the child's parents will be regularly informed (by such means as periodic report cards), at least as often as parents are informed of their nondisabled children's progress, of—(A) their child's progress toward the annual goals; and (B) the extent to which that progress is sufficient to enable the child to achieve the goals by the end of the year.

One method that public agencies could use in meeting this requirement would be to provide periodic report cards to the parents of students with disabilities that include both (1) the grading information provided for all children in the agency at the same intervals; and (2) the specific information required by § 300.347(a)(7)(ii)(A) and (B).

Finally, the parents, as part of the IEP team, will participate at least once every 12 months in a review of their child's educational progress. Section 300.343(c) requires that a public agency initiate and conduct a meeting, at which the IEP team:

* * * (1) Reviews the child's IEP periodically, but not less than annually to determine whether the annual goals for the child are being achieved; and (2) revises the IEP as appropriate to address—(i) any lack of expected progress toward the annual goals * * * and in the general curriculum, if appropriate; (ii) The results of any reevaluation * * *; (iii) Information about the child provided to, or by, the parents * * *; (iv) The child's anticipated needs; or (v) Other matters.

III. Preparing Students With Disabilities for Employment and Other Post-School Experiences

One of the primary purposes of the IDEA is to "* * * ensure that all children with disabilities have available to them a free appropriate public education that emphasizes special education and related services designed to meet their unique needs and prepare them for employment and independent living * * *'' (§ 300.1(a)). Section 701 of the Rehabilitation Act of 1973 describes the philosophy of independent living as including a philosophy of consumer control, peer support, self-help, self-determination, equal access, and individual and system advocacy, in order to maximize the leadership, empowerment, independence, and productivity of individuals with disabilities, and the integration and full inclusion of individuals with disabilities into the mainstream of American society. Because many students receiving services under IDEA will also receive services under the Rehabilitation Act, it is important, in planning for their future, to consider the impact of both statutes.

Similarly, one of the key purposes of the IDEA Amendments of 1997 was to "promote improved educational results for children with disabilities through early intervention, preschool, and educational experiences that prepare them for later educational challenges and employment.'' (H. Rep. No. 105-95, p. 82 (1997); S. Rep. No. 105-17, p. 4 (1997)).

Thus, throughout their preschool, elementary, and secondary education, the IEPs for children with disabilities must, to the extent appropriate for each individual child, focus on providing instruction and experiences that enable the child to prepare himself or herself for later educational experiences and for post-school activities, including formal education, if appropriate, employment, and independent living. Many students with disabilities will obtain services through State vocational rehabilitation programs to ensure that their educational goals are effectively implemented in post-school activities. Services available through rehabilitation programs are consistent with the underlying purpose of IDEA.

Although preparation for adult life is a key component of FAPE throughout the educational experiences of students with disabilities, Part B sets forth specific requirements related to transition planning and transition services that must be implemented no later than ages 14 and 16, respectively, and which require an intensified focus on that preparation as these students begin and prepare to complete their secondary education.

11. What must the IEP team do to meet the requirements that the IEP include "a statement of * * * transition service needs" beginning at age 14 (§ 300.347(b)(1)(i)),'' and a statement of needed transition services'' no later than age 16 (§ 300.347(b)(2)?

Section 300.347(b)(1) requires that, beginning no later than age 14, each student's IEP include specific transition-related content, and, beginning no later than age 16, a statement of needed transition services:

Beginning at age 14 and younger if appropriate, and updated annually, each student's IEP must include:

"* * * a statement of the transition service needs of the student under the applicable components of the student's IEP that focuses on the student's courses of study (such as participation in advanced-placement courses or a vocational education program)'' (§ 300.347(b)(1)(i)).

Beginning at age 16 (or younger, if determined appropriate by the IEP team), each student's IEP must include:

"* * * a statement of needed transition services for the student, including, if appropriate, a statement of the interagency responsibilities or any needed linkages.'' (§ 300.347(b)(2)).

The Committee Reports on the IDEA Amendments of 1997 make clear that the requirement added to the statute in 1997 that beginning at age 14, and updated annually, the IEP include "a statement of the transition service needs'' is "* * * designed to augment, and not replace,'' the separate, preexisting requirement that the IEP include, "* * * beginning at age 16 (or younger, if determined appropriate by the IEP team), a statement of needed transition services * * *'' (H. Rep. No. 105-95, p. 102 (1997); S. Rep. No. 105-17, p. 22 (1997)). As clarified by the Reports, "The purpose of [the requirement in § 300.347(b)(1)(i)] is to focus attention on how the child's educational program can be planned to help the child make a successful transition to his or her goals for life after secondary school.'' (H. Rep. No. 105-95, pp. 101-102 (1997); S.

Rep. No. 105-17, p. 22 (1997)). The Reports further explain that "[F]or example, for a child whose transition goal is a job, a transition service could be teaching the child how to get to the job site on public transportation.'' (H. Rep. No. 105-95, p. 102 (1997); S. Rep. No. 105-17, p. 22 (1997)).

Thus, beginning at age 14, the IEP team, in determining appropriate measurable annual goals (including benchmarks or short-term objectives) and services for a student, must determine what instruction and educational experiences will assist the student to prepare for transition from secondary education to post-secondary life.

The statement of transition service needs should relate directly to the student's goals beyond secondary education, and show how planned studies are linked to these goals. For example, a student interested in exploring a career in computer science may have a statement of transition services needs connected to technology course work, while another student's statement of transition services needs could describe why public bus transportation training is important for future independence in the community.

Although the focus of the transition planning process may shift as the student approaches graduation, the IEP team must discuss specific areas beginning at least at the age of 14 years and review these areas annually. As noted in the Committee Reports, a disproportionate number of students with disabilities drop out of school before they complete their secondary education: "Too many students with disabilities are failing courses and dropping out of school. Almost twice as many students with disabilities drop out as compared to students without disabilities.'' (H. Rep. No. 105-95, p. 85 (1997),
S. Rep. No. 105-17, p. 5 (1997).)

To help reduce the number of students with disabilities that drop out, it is important that the IEP team work with each student with a disability and the student's family to select courses of study that will be meaningful to the student's future and motivate the student to complete his or her education.

This requirement is distinct from the requirement, at § 300.347(b)(2), that the IEP include:

> * * * beginning at age 16 (or younger, if determined appropriate by the IEP team), a statement of needed transition services for the child, including, if appropriate, a statement of the interagency responsibilities or any needed linkages.

The term "transition services" is defined at § 300.29 to mean:

> * * * a coordinated set of activities for a student with a disability that—(1) Is designed within an outcome-oriented process, that promotes movement from school to post-school activities, including postsecondary education, vocational training, integrated employment (including supported employment), continuing and adult education, adult services, independent living, or community participation; (2) Is based on the individual student's needs, taking into account the student's preferences and interests; and (3) Includes—(i) Instruction; (ii) Related services; (iii) Community experiences; (iv) The development of employment and other post-school adult living objectives; and (v) If appropriate, acquisition of daily living skills and functional vocational evaluation.

Thus, while § 300.347(b)(1) requires that the IEP team begin by age 14 to address the student's need for instruction that will assist the student to prepare for transition, the IEP must include by age 16 a statement of needed transition services under § 300.347(b)(2) that includes a "coordinated set of activities * * *, designed within an outcome-oriented process, that promotes movement from school to post-school activities * * *.'' (§ 300.29) Section 300.344(b)(3) further requires that, in implementing § 300.347(b)(1), public agencies (in addition to required participants for all IEP meetings), must also invite a representative of any other agency that is likely to be responsible for providing or paying for transition services. Thus, § 300.347(b)(2) requires a broader focus on coordination of services across, and linkages between, agencies beyond the SEA and LEA.

12. Must the IEP for each student with a disability, beginning no later than age 16, include all "needed transition services," as identified by the IEP team and consistent with the definition at § 300.29, even if an agency other than the public agency will provide those services? What is the public agency's responsibility if another agency fails to provide agreed-upon transition services?

Section 300.347(b)(2) requires that the IEP for each child with a disability, beginning no later than age 16, or younger if determined appropriate by the IEP team, include all "needed transition services,'' as identified by the IEP team and consistent with the definition at § 300.29, regardless of whether the public agency or some other agency will provide those services. Section 300.347(b)(2) specifically requires that the statement of needed transition services include, "* * * if appropriate, a statement of the interagency responsibilities or any needed linkages.''

Further, the IDEA Amendments of 1997 also permit an LEA to use up to five percent of the Part B funds it receives in any fiscal year in combination with other amounts, which must include amounts other than education funds, to develop and implement a coordinated services system. These funds may be used for activities such as: (1) linking IEPs under Part B and Individualized Family Service Plans (IFSPs) under Part C, with Individualized Service Plans developed under multiple Federal and State programs, such as Title I of the Rehabilitation Act; and (2) developing and implementing interagency financing strategies for the provision of services, including transition services under Part B.

The need to include, as part of a student's IEP, transition services to be provided by agencies other than the public agency is contemplated by § 300.348(a), which specifies what the public agency must do if another agency participating in the development of the statement of needed transition services fails to provide a needed transition service that it had agreed to provide.

If an agreed-upon service by another agency is not provided, the public agency responsible for the student's education must implement alternative strategies to meet the student's needs. This requires that the public agency provide the services, or convene an IEP meeting as soon as possible to identify alternative strategies to meet the transition services objectives, and to revise the IEP accordingly.

Alternative strategies might include the identification of another funding source, referral to another agency, the public agency's identification of other district-wide or community resources that it can use to meet the student's identified needs appropriately, or a combination of these strategies. As emphasized by § 300.348(b), however:

Nothing in [Part B] relieves any participating agency, including a State vocational rehabilitation agency, of the responsibility to provide or pay for any transition service that the agency would otherwise provide to students with disabilities who meet the eligibility criteria of that agency.

However, the fact that an agency other than the public agency does not fulfill its responsibility does not relieve the public agency of its responsibility to ensure that FAPE is available to each student with a disability. (Section 300.142(b)(2) specifically requires that if an agency other than the LEA fails to provide or pay for a special education or related service (which could include a transition service), the LEA must, without delay, provide or pay for the service, and may then claim reimbursement from the agency that failed to provide or pay for the service.)

13. Under what circumstances must a public agency invite representatives from other agencies to an IEP meeting at which a child's need for transition services will be considered?

Section 300.344 requires that, "In implementing the requirements of [§ 300.347(b)(1)(ii) requiring a statement of needed transition services], the public agency shall also invite a representative of any other agency that is likely to be responsible for providing or paying for transition services." To meet this requirement, the public agency must identify all agencies that are "likely to be responsible for providing or paying for transition services" for each student addressed by § 300.347(b)(1), and must invite each of those agencies to the IEP meeting; and if an agency invited to send a representative to a meeting does not do so, the public agency must take other steps to obtain the participation of that agency in the planning of any transition services.

If, during the course of an IEP meeting, the team identifies additional agencies that are "likely to be responsible for providing or paying for transition services" for the student, the public agency must determine how it will meet the requirements of § 300.344.

IV. Other Questions Regarding the Development and Content of IEPS

14. For a child with a disability receiving special education for the first time, when must an IEP be developed—before or after the child begins to receive special education and related services?

Section 300.342(b)(1) requires that an IEP be "*in effect* before special education and related services are provided to an eligible child * * *" (Italics added.)

The appropriate placement for a particular child with a disability cannot be determined until after decisions have been made about the child's needs and the services that the public agency will provide to meet those needs. These decisions must be made at the IEP meeting, and it would not be permissible first to place the child and then develop the IEP. Therefore, the IEP must be developed before placement. (Further, the child's placement must be based, among other factors, on the child's IEP.)

This requirement does not preclude temporarily placing an eligible child with a disability in a program as part of the evaluation process—before the IEP is finalized—to assist a public agency in determining the appropriate placement for the child. However, it is essential that the temporary placement not become the final placement before the IEP is finalized. In order to ensure that this does not happen, the State might consider requiring LEAs to take the following actions:

a. Develop an *interim* IEP for the child that sets out the specific conditions and timelines for the trial placement. (See paragraph c, following.)

b. Ensure that the parents agree to the interim placement before it is carried out, and that they are involved throughout the process of developing, reviewing, and revising the child's IEP.

c. Set a specific timeline (e.g., 30 days) for completing the evaluation, finalizing the IEP, and determining the appropriate placement for the child.

d. Conduct an IEP meeting at the end of the trial period in order to finalize the child's IEP.

15. Who is responsible for ensuring the development of IEPs for children with disabili-

ties served by a public agency other than an LEA?

The answer as to which public agency has direct responsibility for ensuring the development of IEPs for children with disabilities served by a public agency other than an LEA will vary from State to State, depending upon State law, policy, or practice. The SEA is ultimately responsible for ensuring that all Part B requirements, including the IEP requirements, are met for eligible children within the State, including those children served by a public agency other than an LEA. Thus, the SEA must ensure that every eligible child with a disability in the State has FAPE available, regardless of which State or local agency is responsible for educating the child. (The only exception to this responsibility is that the SEA is not responsible for ensuring that FAPE is made available to children with disabilities who are convicted as adults under State law and incarcerated in adult prisons, if the State has assigned that responsibility to a public agency other than the SEA. (See § 300.600(d)).

Although the SEA has flexibility in deciding the best means to meet this obligation (e.g., through interagency agreements), the SEA must ensure that no eligible child with a disability is denied FAPE due to jurisdictional disputes among agencies.

When an LEA is responsible for the education of a child with a disability, the LEA remains responsible for developing the child's IEP, regardless of the public or private school setting into which it places the child.

16. For a child placed out of State by an educational or non-educational State or local agency, is the placing or receiving State responsible for the child's IEP?

Regardless of the reason for the placement, the "placing" State is responsible for ensuring that the child's IEP is developed and that it is implemented. The determination of the specific agency in the placing State that is responsible for the child's IEP would be based on State law, policy, or practice. However, the SEA in the placing State is ultimately responsible for ensuring that the child has FAPE available.

17. If a disabled child has been receiving special education from one public agency and transfers to another public agency in the same State, must the new public agency develop an IEP before the child can be placed in a special education program?

If a child with a disability moves from one public agency to another in the same State, the State and its public agencies have an ongoing responsibility to ensure that FAPE is made available to that child. This means that if a child moves to another public agency the new agency is responsible for ensuring that the child has available special education and related services in conformity with an IEP.

The new public agency must ensure that the child has an IEP in effect before the agency can provide special education and related services. The new public agency may meet this responsibility by either adopting the IEP the former public agency developed for the child or by developing a new IEP for the child. (The new public agency is strongly encouraged to continue implementing the IEP developed by the former public agency, if appropriate, especially if the parents believe their child was progressing appropriately under that IEP.)

Before the child's IEP is finalized, the new public agency may provide interim services agreed to by both the parents and the new public agency. If the parents and the new public agency are unable to agree on an interim IEP and placement, the new public agency must implement the old IEP to the extent possible until a new IEP is developed and implemented.

In general, while the new public agency must conduct an IEP meeting, it would not be necessary if: (1) A copy of the child's current IEP is available; (2) the parents indicate that they are satisfied with the current IEP; and (3) the new public agency determines that the current IEP is appropriate and can be implemented as written.

If the child's current IEP is not available, or if either the new public agency or the parent believes that it is not appropriate, the new public agency must develop a new IEP through appropriate procedures within a short time after the child enrolls in the new public agency (normally, within one week).

18. What timelines apply to the development and implementation of an initial IEP for a child with a disability?

Section 300.343(b) requires each public agency to ensure that within a reasonable period of time following the agency's receipt of parent consent to an initial evaluation of a child, the child is evaluated and, if determined eligible, special education and related services are made available to the child in accordance with an IEP. The section further requires the agency to conduct a meeting to develop an IEP for the child within 30 days of determining that the child needs special education and related services.

Section 300.342(b)(2) provides that an IEP must be implemented as soon as possible following the meeting in which the IEP is developed.

19. Must a public agency hold separate meetings to determine a child's eligibility for special education and related services, develop the child's IEP, and determine the child's placement, or may the agency meet all of these requirements in a single meeting?

A public agency may, after a child is determined by "a group of qualified professionals and the parent" (see § 300.534(a)(1)) to be a child with a disability, continue in the same meeting to develop an IEP for the child and then to determine the child's placement. However, the public agency must ensure that it meets: (1) the requirements of § 300.535 regarding eligibility decisions; (2) all of the Part B requirements regarding meetings to develop IEPs (including providing appropriate notification to the parents, consistent with the requirements of §§ 300.345, 300.503, and 300.504, and ensuring that all the required team members participate in the development of the IEP, consistent with the requirements of § 300.344;) and (3) ensuring that the placement is made by the required individuals, including the parent, as required by §§ 300.552 and 300.501(c).

20. How frequently must a public agency conduct meetings to review, and, if appropriate, revise the IEP for each child with a disability?

A public agency must initiate and conduct meetings periodically, but at least once every twelve months, to review each child's IEP, in order to determine whether the annual goals for the child are being achieved, and to revise the IEP, as appropriate, to address: (a) Any lack of expected progress toward the annual goals and in the general curriculum, if appropriate; (b) the results of any reevaluation; (c) information about the child provided to, or by, the parents; (d) the child's anticipated needs; or (e) other matters (§ 300.343(c)).

A public agency also must ensure that an IEP is in effect for each child at the beginning of each school year (§ 300.342(a)). It may conduct IEP meetings at any time during the year. However, if the agency conducts the IEP meeting prior to the beginning of the next school year, it must ensure that the IEP contains the necessary special education and related services and supplementary aids and services to ensure that the student's IEP can be appropriately implemented during the next school year. Otherwise, it would be necessary for the public agency to conduct another IEP meeting.

Although the public agency is responsible for determining when it is necessary to conduct an IEP meeting, the parents of a child with a disability have the right to request an IEP meeting at any time. For example, if the parents believe that the child is not progressing satisfactorily or that there is a problem with the child's current IEP, it would be appropriate for the parents to request an IEP meeting.

If a child's teacher feels that the child's IEP or placement is not appropriate for the child, the teacher should follow agency procedures with respect to: (1) calling or meeting with the parents or (2) requesting the agency to hold another IEP meeting to review the child's IEP.

The legislative history of Public Law 94-142 makes it clear that there should be as many meetings a year as any one child may need (121 Cong. Rec. S20428-29 (Nov. 19, 1975) (remarks of Senator Stafford)). Public agencies should grant any reasonable parent request for an IEP meeting. For example, if the parents question the adequacy of services that are provided while their child is suspended for short periods of time, it would be appropriate to convene an IEP meeting.

In general, if either a parent or a public agency believes that a required component of the student's IEP should be changed, the public agency must conduct an IEP meeting if it believes that a change in the IEP may be necessary to ensure the provision of FAPE.

If a parent requests an IEP meeting because the parent believes that a change is needed in the provision of FAPE to the child or the educational placement of the child, and the agency refuses to convene an IEP meeting to determine whether such a change is needed, the agency must provide written notice to the parents of the refusal, including an explanation of why the agency has determined that conducting the meeting is not necessary to ensure the provision of FAPE to the student.

Under § 300.507(a), the parents or agency may initiate a due process hearing at any time regarding any proposal or refusal regarding the identification, evaluation, or educational placement of the child, or the provision of FAPE to the child, and the public agency must inform parents about the availability of mediation.

21. May IEP meetings be audio- or video-tape-recorded?

Part B does not address the use of audio or video recording devices at IEP meetings, and no other Federal statute either authorizes or prohibits the recording of an IEP meeting by either a parent or a school official. Therefore, an SEA or public agency has the option to require, prohibit, limit, or otherwise regulate the use of recording devices at IEP meetings.

If a public agency has a policy that prohibits or limits the use of recording devices at IEP meetings, that policy must provide for exceptions if they are necessary to ensure that the parent understands the IEP or the IEP process or to implement other parental rights guaranteed under Part B. An SEA or school district that adopts a rule regulating the tape recording of IEP meetings also should ensure that it is uniformly applied.

Any recording of an IEP meeting that is maintained by the public agency is an "education record," within the meaning of the Family Educational Rights and Privacy Act ("FERPA"; 20 U.S.C. 1232g), and would, therefore, be subject to the confidentiality requirements of the regulations under both FERPA (34 CFR part 99) and part B (§§ 300.560-300.575).

Parents wishing to use audio or video recording devices at IEP meetings should consult State or local policies for further guidance.

22. Who can serve as the representative of the public agency at an IEP meeting?

The IEP team must include a representative of the public agency who: (a) Is qualified to provide, or supervise the provision of, specially designed instruction to meet the unique needs of children with disabilities; (b) is knowledgeable about the general curriculum; and (c) is knowledgeable about the availability of resources of the public agency (§ 300.344(a)(4)).

Each public agency may determine which specific staff member will serve as the agency representative in a particular IEP meeting, so long as the individual meets these requirements. It is important, however, that the agency representative have the authority to commit agency resources and be able to ensure that whatever services are set out in the IEP will actually be provided.

A public agency may designate another public agency member of the IEP team to also serve as the agency representative, so long as that individual meets the requirements of § 300.344(a)(4).

23. For a child with a disability being considered for initial provision of special education and related services, which teacher or teachers should attend the IEP meeting?

A child's IEP team must include at least one of the child's regular education teachers (if the child is, or may be participating in the regular education environment) and at least one of the child's special education teachers, or, if appropriate, at least one of the child's special education providers (§ 300.344(a)(2) and (3)).

Each IEP must include a statement of the present levels of educational performance, including a statement of how the child's disability affects the child's involvement and progress in the general curriculum (§ 300.347(a)(1)). At least one regular education teacher is a required member of the IEP team of a child who is, or may be, participating in the regular educational environment, regardless of the extent of that participation.

The requirements of § 300.344(a)(3) can be met by either: (1) a special education teacher of the child; or (2) another special education provider of the child, such as a speech pathologist, physical or occupational therapist, etc., if the related service consists of specially designed instruction and is considered special education under applicable State standards.

Sometimes more than one meeting is necessary in order to finalize a child's IEP. In this process, if the special education teacher or special education provider who will be working with the child is identified, it would be useful to have that teacher or provider participate in the meeting with the parents and other members of the IEP team in finalizing the IEP. If this is not possible, the public agency must ensure that the teacher or provider has access to the child's IEP as soon as possible after it is finalized and before beginning to work with the child.

Further, (consistent with § 300.342(b)), the public agency must ensure that each regular education teacher, special education teacher, related services provider and other service provider of an eligible child under this part (1) has access to the child's IEP, and (2) is informed of his or her specific responsibilities related to implementing the IEP, and of the specific accommodations, modifications, and supports that must be provided to the child in accordance with the IEP. This requirement is crucial to ensuring that each child receives FAPE in accordance with his or her IEP, and that the IEP is appropriately and effectively implemented.

24. What is the role of a regular education teacher in the development, review and revision of the IEP for a child who is, or may be, participating in the regular education environment?

As required by § 300.344(a)(2), the IEP team for a child with a disability must include at least one regular education teacher of the child if the child is, or may be, participating in the regular education environment. Section 300.346(d) further specifies that the regular education teacher of a child with a disability, as a member of the IEP team, must, to the extent appropriate, participate in the development, review, and revision of the child's IEP, including assisting in—(1) the determination of appropriate positive behavioral interventions and strategies for the child; and (2) the determination of supplementary aids and services, program modifications, and supports for school personnel that will be provided for the child, consistent with 300.347(a)(3) (§ 300.344(d)).

Thus, while a regular education teacher must be a member of the IEP team if the child is, or may be, participating in the regular education environment, the teacher need not (depending upon the child's needs and the purpose of the specific IEP team meeting) be required to participate in all decisions made as part of the meeting or to be present throughout the entire meeting or attend every meeting. For example, the regular education teacher who is a member of the IEP team must participate in discussions and decisions about how to modify the general curriculum in the regular classroom to ensure the child's involvement and progress in the general curriculum and participation in the regular education environment.

Depending upon the specific circumstances, however, it may not be necessary for the regular education teacher to participate in discussions and decisions regarding, for example, the physical therapy needs of the child, if the teacher is not responsible for implementing that portion of the child's IEP.

In determining the extent of the regular education teacher's participation at IEP meetings, public agencies and parents should discuss and try to reach agreement on whether the child's regular education teacher that is a member of the IEP team should be present at a particular IEP meeting and, if so, for what period of time. The extent to which it would be appropriate for the regular education teacher member of the IEP team to participate in IEP meetings must be decided on a case-by-case basis.

25. If a child with a disability attends several regular classes, must all of the child's regular education teachers be members of the child's IEP team?

No. The IEP team need not include more than one regular education teacher of the child. If the participation of more than one regular education teacher would be beneficial to the child's success in school (e.g., in terms of enhancing the child's participation in the general curriculum), it would be appropriate for them to attend the meeting.

26. How should a public agency determine which regular education teacher and special education teacher will be members of the IEP team for a particular child with a disability?

The regular education teacher who serves as a member of a child's IEP team should be a teacher who is, or may be, responsible for implementing a portion of the IEP, so that the teacher can participate in discussions about how best to teach the child.

If the child has more than one regular education teacher responsible for carrying out a portion of the IEP, the LEA may designate which teacher or teachers will serve as IEP team member(s), taking into account the best interest of the child.

In a situation in which not all of the child's regular education teachers are members of the child's IEP team, the LEA is strongly encouraged to seek input from the teachers who will not be attending. In addition, (consistent with § 300.342(b)), the LEA must ensure that each regular education teacher (as well as each special education teacher, related services provider, and other service provider) of an eligible child under this part (1) has access to the child's IEP, and (2) is informed of his or her specific responsibilities related to implementing the IEP, and of the specific accommodations, modifications and supports that must be provided to the child in accordance with the IEP.

In the case of a child whose behavior impedes the learning of the child or others, the LEA is encouraged to have a regular education teacher or other person knowledgeable about positive behavior strategies at the IEP meeting. This is especially important if the regular education teacher is expected to carry out portions of the IEP.

Similarly, the special education teacher or provider of the child who is a member of the child's IEP team should be the person who is, or will be, responsible for implementing the IEP. If, for example, the child's disability is a speech impairment, the special education teacher on the IEP team could be the speech-language pathologist.

27. For a child whose primary disability is a speech impairment, may a public agency meet its responsibility under § 300.344(a)(3) to ensure that the IEP team includes "at least one special education teacher, or, if appropriate, at least one special education provider of the child" by including a speech-language pathologist on the IEP team?

Yes, if speech is considered special education under State standards. As with other children with disabilities, the IEP team must also include at least one of the child's *regular education* teachers if the child is, or may be, participating in the regular education environment.

28. Do parents and public agencies have the option of inviting any individual of their choice be participants on their child's IEP team?

The IEP team may, at the discretion of the parent or the agency, include "other individuals *who have knowledge or special expertise regarding the child* * * *" (§ 300.344(a)(6), italics added). Under § 300.344(a)(6), these individuals are members of the IEP team. This is a change from prior law, which provided, without qualification, that parents or agencies could have other individuals as members of the IEP team at the discretion of the parents or agency.

Under § 300.344(c), the determination as to whether an individual has knowledge or special expertise, within the meaning of § 300.344(a)(6), shall be made by the parent or public agency who has invited the individual to be a member of the IEP team.

Part B does not provide for including individuals such as representatives of teacher organizations as part of an IEP team, unless they are included because of knowledge or special expertise regarding the child. (Because a representative of a teacher organization would generally be concerned with the interests of the teacher rather than the interests of the child, and generally would not possess knowledge or expertise regarding the child, it generally would be inappropriate for such an official to be a member of the IEP team or to otherwise participate in an IEP meeting.)

29. Can parents or public agencies bring their attorneys to IEP meetings, and, if so under what circumstances? Are attorney's fees available for parents' attorneys if the parents are prevailing parties in actions or proceedings brought under Part B?

Section 300.344(a)(6) authorizes the addition to the IEP team of other individuals at the discretion of the parent or the public agency only if those other individuals have knowledge or special expertise regarding the child. The determination of whether an attorney possesses knowledge or special expertise regarding the child would have to be made on a case-by-case basis by the parent or public agency inviting the attorney to be a member of the team.

The presence of the agency's attorney could contribute to a potentially adversarial atmosphere at the meeting. The same is true with regard to the presence of an attorney accompanying the parents at the IEP meeting. Even if the attorney possessed knowledge or special expertise regarding the child (§ 300.344(a)(6)), an attorney's presence would have the potential for creating an adversarial atmosphere that would not necessarily be in the best interests of the child.

Therefore, the attendance of attorneys at IEP meetings should be strongly discouraged. Further, as specified in Section 615(i)(3)(D)(ii) of the Act and § 300.513(c)(2)(ii), Attorneys' fees may not be awarded relating to any meeting of the IEP team unless the meeting is convened as a result of an administrative proceeding or judicial action, or, at the discretion of the State, for a mediation conducted prior to the request for a due process hearing.

30. Must related services personnel attend IEP meetings?

Although Part B does not expressly require that the IEP team include related services personnel as part of the IEP team (§ 300.344(a)), it is appropriate for those persons to be included if a particular related service is to be discussed as part of the IEP meeting. Section 300.344(a)(6) provides that the IEP team also includes "at the discretion of the parent or the agency, other individuals who have knowledge or special expertise regarding the child, *including related services personnel as appropriate.* * * *" (Italics added.)

Further, § 300.344(a)(3) requires that the IEP team for each child with a disability include "at least one special education teacher, or, if appropriate, at least one special education provider of the child * * *" This requirement can be met by the participation of either (1) a special education teacher of the child, or (2) another special education provider such as a speech-language pathologist, physical or occupational therapist, etc., if the related service consists of specially designed instruction and is considered special education under the applicable State standard.

If a child with a disability has an identified need for related services, it would be appropriate for the related services personnel to attend the meeting or otherwise be involved in developing the IEP. As explained in the Committee Reports on the IDEA Amendments of 1997, "Related services personnel should be included on the team when a particular related service will be discussed at the request of the child's parents or the school." (H. Rep. No. 105-95, p. 103 (1997); S. Rep. No. 105-17, p. 23 (1997)). For example, if the child's evaluation indicates the need for a specific related service (e.g., physical therapy, occupational therapy, special transportation services, school social work services, school health services, or counseling), the agency should ensure that a qualified provider of that service either (1) attends the IEP meeting, or (2) provides a written recommendation concerning the nature, frequency, and amount of service to be provided to the child. This written recommendation could be a part of the evaluation report.

A public agency must ensure that all individuals who are necessary to develop an IEP that will meet the child's unique needs, and ensure the provision of FAPE to the child, participate in the child's IEP meeting.

31. Must the public agency ensure that all services specified in a child's IEP are provided?

Yes. The public agency must ensure that all services set forth in the child's IEP are provided, consistent with the child's needs as identified in the IEP. The agency may provide each of those services directly, through its own staff resources; indirectly, by contracting with another public or private agency; or through other arrangements. In providing the services, the agency may use whatever State, local, Federal, and private sources of support are available for those purposes (see § 300.301(a)); but the services must be at no cost to the parents, and the public agency remains responsible for ensuring that the IEP services are provided in a manner that appropriately meets the student's needs as specified in the IEP. The SEA and responsible public agency may not allow the failure of another agency to provide service(s) described in the child's IEP to deny or delay the provision of FAPE to the child. (See § 300.142, Methods of ensuring services.)

32. Is it permissible for an agency to have the IEP completed before the IEP meeting begins?

No. Agency staff may come to an IEP meeting prepared with evaluation findings and proposed recommendations regarding IEP content, but the agency must make it clear to the parents at the outset of the meeting that the services proposed by the agency are only recommendations for review and discussion with the parents. Parents have the right to bring questions, concerns, and recommendations to an IEP meeting as part of a full discussion, of the child's needs and the services to be provided to meet those needs before the IEP is finalized.

Public agencies must ensure that, if agency personnel bring drafts of some or all of the IEP content to the IEP meeting, there is a full discussion with the child's parents, before the child's IEP is finalized, regarding drafted content and the child's needs and the services to be provided to meet those needs.

33. Must a public agency include transportation in a child's IEP as a related service?

As with other related services, a public agency must provide transportation as a related service if it is required to assist the disabled child to benefit from special education. (This includes transporting a preschool-aged child to the site at which the public agency provides special education and related services to the child, if that site is different from the site at which the child receives other preschool or day care services.)

In determining whether to include transportation in a child's IEP, and whether the child needs to receive transportation as a related service, it would be appropriate to have at the IEP meeting a person with expertise in that area. In making this determination, the IEP team must consider how the child's disability affects the child's need for transportation, including determining whether the child's disability prevents the child from using the same transportation provided to nondisabled children, or from getting to school in the same manner as nondisabled children.

The public agency must ensure that any transportation service included in a child's IEP as a related service is provided at public expense and at no cost to the parents, and that the child's IEP describes the transportation arrangement.

Even if a child's IEP team determines that the child does not require transportation as a related service, Section 504 of the Rehabilitation Act of 1973, as amended, requires that the child receive the same transportation provided to nondisabled children. If a public agency transports nondisabled children, it must transport disabled children under the same terms and conditions. However, if a child's IEP team determines that the child does not need transportation as a related service, and the public agency transports only those children whose IEPs specify transportation as a related service, and does not transport nondisabled children, the public agency would not be required to provide transportation to a disabled child.

It should be assumed that most children with disabilities receive the same transportation services as nondisabled children. For some children with disabilities, integrated transportation may be achieved by providing needed accommodations such as lifts and other equipment adaptations on regular school transportation vehicles.

34. Must a public agency provide related services that are required to assist a child with a disability to benefit from special education, whether or not those services are included in the list of related services in § 300.24?

The list of related services is not exhaustive and may include other developmental, corrective, or supportive services if they are required to assist a child with a disability to benefit from special education. This could, depending upon the unique needs of a child, include such services as nutritional services or service coordination.

These determinations must be made on an individual basis by each child's IEP team.

35. Must the IEP specify the amount of services or may it simply list the services to be provided?

The amount of services to be provided must be stated in the IEP, so that the level of the agency's commitment of resources will be clear to parents and other IEP team members (§ 300.347(a)(6)). The amount of time to be committed to each of the various services to be provided must be (1) appropriate to the specific service, and (2) stated in the IEP in a manner that is clear to all who are involved in both the development and implementation of the IEP.

The amount of a special education or related service to be provided to a child may be stated in the IEP as a range (e.g., speech therapy to be provided three times per week for 30-45 minutes per session) only if the IEP team determines that stating the amount of services as a range is necessary to meet the unique needs of the child. For example, it would be appropriate for the IEP to specify, based upon the IEP team's determination of the student's unique needs, that particular services are needed only under specific circumstances, such as the occurrence of a seizure or of a particular behavior. A range may not be used because of personnel shortages or uncertainty regarding the availability of staff.

36. Under what circumstances is a public agency required to permit a child with a disability to use a school-purchased assistive technology device in the child's home or in another setting?

Each child's IEP team must consider the child's need for assistive technology (AT) in the development of the child's IEP (§ 300.346(a)(2)(v)); and the nature and extent of the AT devices and services to be provided to the child must be reflected in the child's IEP (§ 300.346(c)).

A public agency must permit a child to use school-purchased assistive technology devices at home or in other settings, if the IEP team determines that the child needs access to those devices in nonschool settings in order to receive FAPE (to complete homework, for example).

Any assistive technology devices that are necessary to ensure FAPE must be provided at no cost to the parents, and the parents cannot be charged for normal use, wear and tear. However, while ownership of the devices in these circumstances would remain with the public agency, State law, rather than Part B, generally would govern whether parents are liable for loss, theft, or damage due to negligence or misuse of publicly owned equipment used at home or in other settings in accordance with a child's IEP.

37. Can the IEP team also function as the group making the placement decision for a child with a disability?

Yes, a public agency may use the IEP team to make the placement decision for a child, so long as the group making the placement decision meets the requirements of §§ 300.552 and 300.501(c), which requires that the placement decision be made by a group of persons, including the parents, and other persons knowledgeable about the child, the meaning of the evaluation data, and the placement options.

38. If a child's IEP includes behavioral strategies to address a particular behavior, can a child ever be suspended for engaging in that behavior?

If a child's behavior impedes his or her learning or that of others, the IEP team, in developing the child's IEP, must consider, if appropriate, development of strategies, including positive behavioral interventions, strategies and supports to address that behavior, consistent with § 300.346(a)(2)(i). This means that in most cases in which a child's behavior that impedes his or her learning or that of others is, or can be readily anticipated to be, repetitive, proper development of the child's IEP will include the development of strategies, including positive behavioral interventions, strategies and supports to address that behavior. See § 300.346(c). This includes behavior that could violate a school code of conduct. A failure to, if appropriate, consider and address these behaviors in developing and implementing the child's IEP would constitute a denial of FAPE to the child. Of course, in appropriate circumstances, the IEP team, which includes the child's parents, might determine that the child's behavioral intervention plan includes specific regular or alternative disciplinary measures, such as denial of certain privileges or short suspensions, that would result from particular infractions of school rules, along with positive behavior intervention strategies and supports, as a part of a comprehensive plan to address the child's behavior. Of course, if short suspensions that are included in a child's IEP are being implemented in a manner that denies the child access to the ability to progress in the educational program, the child would be denied FAPE.

Whether other disciplinary measures, including suspension, are ever appropriate for behavior that is addressed in a child's IEP will have to be determined on a case by case basis in light of the particular circumstances of that incident. However, school personnel may not use their ability to suspend a child for 10 days or less at a time on multiple occasions in a school year as a means of avoiding appropriately considering and addressing the child's behavior as a part of providing FAPE to the child.

39. If a child's behavior in the regular classroom, even with appropriate interventions, would significantly impair the learning of others, can the group that makes the placement decision determine that placement in the regular classroom is inappropriate for that child?

The IEP team, in developing the IEP, is required to consider, when appropriate, strategies, including positive behavioral interventions, strategies and supports to address the behavior of a child with a disability whose behavior impedes his or her learning or that of others. If the IEP team determines that such supports, strategies or interventions are necessary to address the behavior of the child, those services must be included in the child's IEP. These provisions are designed to foster increased participation of children with disabilities in regular education environments or other less restrictive environments, not to serve as a basis for placing children with disabilities in more restrictive settings.

The determination of appropriate placement for a child whose behavior is interfering with the education of others requires careful consideration of whether the child can appropriately function in the regular classroom if provided appropriate behavioral supports, strategies and interventions. If the child can appropriately function in the regular classroom with appropriate behavioral supports, strategies or interventions, placement in a more restrictive environment would be inconsistent with the least restrictive environment provisions of the IDEA. If the child's behavior in the regular classroom, even with the provision of appropriate behavioral supports, strategies or interventions, would significantly impair the learning of others, that placement would not meet his or her needs and would not be appropriate for that child.

40. May school personnel during a school year implement more than one short-term removal of a child with disabilities from his or her classroom or school for misconduct?

Yes. Under § 300.520(a)(1), school personnel may order removal of a child with a disability from the child's current placement for not more than 10 consecutive school days for any violation of school rules, and additional removals of not more than 10 consecutive school days in that same school year for separate incidents of misconduct, as long as these removals do not constitute a change of placement under § 300.519(b). However, these removals are permitted only to the extent they are consistent with discipline that is applied to children without disabilities. Also, school personnel should be aware of constitutional due process protections that apply to suspensions of all children. Goss v. Lopez, 419 U.S. 565 (1975). Section 300.121(d) addresses the extent of the obligation to provide services after a child with a disability has been removed from his or her current placement for more than 10 school days in the same school year.

APPENDIX B to Part 300
INDEX FOR IDEA—PART B REGULATIONS

(34 CFR PART 300)

Appendix C to Part 300—Implementation of the 20 Percent Rule Under § 300.233

This appendix is intended to assist States and LEAs to implement the "20 percent rule" under Part B (section 613(a)(2)(C)) of the Individuals with Disabilities Education Act (IDEA), and, specifically, the regulation implementing that provision in § 300.233. The purposes of the appendix are to—(1) provide background information about the 20 percent rule and its intended effect, including specifying which funds under Part B of the Act are covered by the provision (as described in § 300.233), and the basis for the Department's decision regarding those funds; and (2) include examples showing how the 20 percent rule would apply in several situations.

A. Background

1. Purpose of 20 Percent Rule. The IDEA Amendments of 1997 (Pub. L. 105-17) added a provision related to the permissive treatment of a portion of Part B funds by LEAs for maintenance of effort and non-supplanting purposes in certain fiscal years (see section 613(a)(2)(C) of the Act and § 300.233). Under that provision, for any fiscal year (FY) for which the appropriation for section 611 of IDEA exceeds $4.1 billion, an LEA may treat as local funds, for maintenance of effort and non-supplanting purposes, up to 20 percent of the amount it receives that exceeds the amount it received under Part B during the prior year.

Thus, under § 300.233, an LEA is able to meet the maintenance of effort requirement of § 300.231 and the non-supplanting requirement of § 300.230(c) even though it reduces the amount it spends of other local or local and State funds, as the case may be, by an amount equal to the amount of Federal funds that may be treated as local funds.

2. 20 Percent Rule Applies Only to LEA Subgrants. Following enactment of the IDEA Amendments of 1997 (and publication of Part B regulations on March 12, 1999), State and local educational agency officials stated that it is not clear from the Act and regulations whether the funds affected by the 20 percent rule are only those that an LEA receives through statutory subgrants under section 611(g), or whether the provision also applies to other Part B funding sources (i.e., subgrants to LEAs for capacity-building and improvement under section 611(f)(4); other funds the SEA may provide to LEAs under section 611(f); or funds provided under section 619 (Preschool Grants program)).

Further, because section 613(a)(2)(C) refers to an amount of funds that an LEA "receives" in one fiscal year compared to the amount it "received" in the prior fiscal year (and because agencies may, at any one point in time, be using funds appropriated in several Federal fiscal years), agency officials were uncertain as to how to determine that an LEA had "received" Federal funds.

Because the statute and regulations were not sufficiently clear with respect to which precise funds are affected by the 20 percent rule, this could have resulted in the provision being interpreted and applied differently from LEA to LEA. If that situation were to occur, it could result in a significant increase in the number of audit exceptions against LEAs.

Given the confusion about which funding sources are affected by the 20 percent rule, there was a critical need to set out in the regulations a clear interpretation of section 613(a)(2)(C) in order to support its consistent application across LEAs and States, and to reduce the potential for audit exceptions. Thus, on June 10, 2000, the Department published a notice of proposed rulemaking (NPRM) regarding this provision (65 FR 30314). The NPRM stated that—

In light of the statutory structure for distribution of Federal funds to LEAs, we believe that the most reasonable interpretation is to apply that provision only to subgrants to LEAs under section 611(g) of the Act (§ 300.712 of the regulations) from funds appropriated from one Federal fiscal year compared to funds appropriated for the prior Federal fiscal year. (Emphasis added.)

Thus, the NPRM proposed to exclude the other Federal funds under Part B of the Act (i.e., Subgrants to LEAs for capacity-building and improvement under section 611(f)(4) (§ 300.622); other funds the SEA may provide to LEAs under section 611(f) (§ 300.602); and preschool grant funds under section 619 (34 CFR part 301)) from the funds that could be treated as local funds. The reasons for excluding these other Part B funds were stated in the NPRM, as follows:

If IDEA funds that States have the authority to provide to LEAs on a discretionary basis (such as those identified in the preceding paragraph) are included in the 20 percent calculation, it would result in some LEAs receiving a proportionately greater benefit from this provision than other LEAs, based on receipt of funds that may be earmarked for a specific, time-limited purpose. This would lead to inequitable results of the § 300.233 exception across LEAs in a State.

Including section 619 formula grant funds (34 CFR part 301) in the calculation does not appear to be justified as the "trigger" appropriation amount applies only with respect to the amount appropriated under section 611.

The Department subsequently determined that the position taken in the NPRM (that the provision under § 300.233 should apply only to LEA subgrant funds under section 611(g) of the Act) is the most appropriate and reasonable position to follow in implementing the 20 percent rule. Therefore, the proposed provision in § 300.233(a)(1) was retained, without change, in the final regulations.

B. Application of the 20 percent rule

1. Examples Related to Implementing the 20 percent rule

The following are examples showing how the 20 percent provision would apply under several situations:

Example 1: An LEA receives $100,000 in Federal LEA Subgrant funds under section 611(g) of the Act from the appropriation for one fiscal year (FY-1), and $120,000 in section 611(g) funds from the appropriation for the following fiscal year (FY-2). The LEA may spend and treat as local funds up to 20 percent of the $20,000 in section 611(g) funds it receives from FY-2 (i.e., up to $4,000), since this is the amount that exceeds the amount it received from the prior year.

Example 1-A: In Example 1, an LEA in FY-2 is uncertain whether to exercise its option to treat as local funds during FY-2 up to $4,000 of its section 611(g) funds received from FY-2, and wishes to wait until the carry-over year to make a decision. If the LEA decides to exercise its option during the carry-over period regarding the $4,000 from the FY-2 appropriation, it could do so as long as those funds are used within the carry-over period for FY-2.

Example 1-B: An LEA receives $100,000 in section 611(g) funds from FY-1, $120,000 from FY-2 and $140,000 from FY-3. The LEA may spend and treat as local funds up to 20 percent of the $20,000 from FY-2 funds and $20,000 of FY-3 funds (i.e., up to $4,000 for each year). Thus, if its FY-2 funds are not used until FY-3, and the LEA so chooses, it may spend and treat as local funds during FY-3 a total of up to $8,000 in section 611(g) funds (i.e., $4,000 from FY-2 and $4,000 from FY-3), provided those funds are obligated by the end of FY-3.

Example 2: An LEA from one fiscal year (FY-1) receives $100,000 in section 611(g) funds and $20,000 in SEA discretionary funds under section 611(f) of the Act; and from the following year (FY-2) receives $120,000 in section 611(g) funds, but does not receive any funds under section 611(f). The LEA may spend and treat up to 20 percent of the $20,000 in section 611(g) funds it receives from FY-2 (i.e. up to $4,000), since $20,000 is the amount of section 611(g) funds that exceeds the amount it received from FY-1.

Example 3: An LEA had all of its section 611(g) funds ($100,000) withheld from one fiscal year (FY-1); but in the next fiscal year (FY-2), the LEA received a total of $220,000 in section 611(g) funds (i.e., $100,000 from FY-1, plus $120,000 from FY-2). Because the LEA would have been entitled to $100,000 in FY-1, the LEA may spend and treat as local funds up to 20 percent of the $20,000 from FY- 2 that exceeded the FY-1 allotment (i.e., up to $4,000).

Example 4: An LEA received $100,000 under section 611(g) from one fiscal year (FY-1), and would have received $120,000 in section 611(g) funds for the next fiscal year (FY-2); but the LEA has had all of its section 611(g) funds withheld in FY-2 because of a finding of noncompliance under § 300.197 or § 300.587. The LEA would have no section 611(g) funds that could be spent or treated as local funds until those funds are released.

Example 4-A: In example 4, the SEA subsequently determines that the LEA is in compliance, and releases the FY-2 funds to the LEA later in that fiscal year. The LEA could then spend and treat as local funds up to 20 percent of the $20,000 that exceeds the amount it received in FY-1 (i.e., up to $4,000). Those funds could be used by the LEA for the remainder of FY-2 and through the end of the carry-over period for FY-2 funding.

2. Auditing for Compliance with § 300.231 and the 20 percent rule in § 300.233

The following provides guidance for use by auditors in determining if LEAs are in compliance with the maintenance of effort requirement in § 300.231 and the 20 percent rule in § 300.233:

a. Meeting the Maintenance of Effort Requirement. In order to be eligible to receive an IDEA-Part B subgrant in any particular fiscal year, an LEA is required to demonstrate that it has budgeted an amount of State and local funds, or just local funds, to be spent on special education and related services that equals or exceeds (on either an aggregate or per capita basis) the amount of those funds spent by the LEA for those purposes in the prior fiscal year, or in the most recent prior fiscal year for which information is available. 34 CFR 300.231.

b. Auditing Compliance with § 300.231. Auditors, in determining if an LEA has complied with § 300.231 in any particular fiscal year, review the actual level of expenditures of State and local funds, or just local funds, on special education and related services for the year in question and the prior year. For example, consider an LEA that, in the LEA's FY-1, spent a total of $1,000,000 of local funds on special education and related services to serve 100 students with disabilities. (For this discussion, assume that the LEA does not receive any State funds for any year for special education and related services.) An auditor, in trying to determine if the LEA, in its FY-2, had complied with § 300.231, would review the LEA's expenditure of local funds on special education and related services. If, in the LEA's FY-2, the LEA served 100 students with disabilities and spent $1,000,000 or more in local funds on special education and related services, it would have met the requirements of § 300.231 for FY-2.

c. Application of the 20 percent rule to § 300.231. If the LEA in the preceding example had spent only $996,000 of local funds on special education and related services for its 100 students with disabilities in its FY-2 (not counting any section 611(g) subgrant funds that could be considered local funds under the 20 percent rule), then it would have failed to meet its obligation under § 300.231, and an auditor would question $4,000 of the LEA's IDEA-Part B subgrant expenditures in that year.

This questioned cost, however, could be avoided, if the LEA had available, and spent, $4,000 of Federal funds under the 20 percent rule during its FY-2. These funds may be available from a variety of sources (see Examples in paragraph 1). If, as described in Example 1 of paragraph 1 the LEA had received from the Federal FY-2 appropriation, a section 611(g) subgrant that was $20,000 greater than the subgrant it received from the Federal FY-1 appropriation, then up to $4,000 of that subgrant could be treated as local funds. The LEA, however, would have to spend at least $4,000 of its Federal FY-2 section 611(g) subgrant during its FY-2 in order for those funds to count as part of its local expenditures for that year for purposes of § 300.231.

In this example, if the LEA had carried over all of its Federal FY-2 section 611(g) subgrant to the LEA's FY-3 (and thus did not spend any of those funds during its FY-2), then none of the section 611(g) subgrant funds subject to the 20 percent rule could be considered as local funds for purposes of determining compliance with § 300.231. (The reason for this is that auditors, in determining an LEA's compliance with § 300.231, examine State and local, or local funds the LEA actually spent on special education and related services, and not those funds that the LEA could, but did not, spend for those purposes.)

If the LEA, in its FY-2, spent $4,000 of its Federal FY-2 section 611(g) subgrant, then the LEA could count those expenditures and bring itself into compliance with § 300.231 (i.e., $996,000 of the LEA's own local funds spent on special education and related services plus the $4,000 of Federal FY-2 section 611(g) funds that can be counted as local funds equals a total of $1,000,000 of local expenditures on special education in its FY-2—the amount of local expenditures needed to comply with § 300.231). However, if the LEA elected to take this step, it could not count any of the Federal FY-2 section 611(g) subgrant funds that it will spend in its FY-3 as local funds.

If the LEA, in its FY-2, spent only $3,000 of its Federal FY-2 section 611(g) subgrant funds, then those funds could be counted by the LEA as local funds in calculating its compliance with § 300.231 for its FY-2. If the remaining $1,000 of Federal FY-2 funds available to be considered local funds were spent in the LEA's FY-3, those funds could be considered in determining the LEA's compliance with § 300.231 for its FY-3. (Note, However, that if in its FY-2 the LEA had only spent $996,000 of local funds and $3,000 of its Federal funds, it would not have met the requirements of § 300.231. In this case the auditor would have $1,000 of questioned costs ($1,000,000 - [$996,000 + $3,000] =$1,000) for FY-2).

PART 104—NONDISCRIMINATION ON THE BASIS OF HANDICAP IN PROGRAMS AND ACTIVITIES RECEIVING OR BENEFITING FROM FEDERAL FINANCIAL ASSISTANCE

AUTHORITY: Sec. 504, Rehabilitation Act of 1973, Pub. L. 93–112, 87 Stat. 394 (29 U.S.C. 794); sec. 111(a), Rehabilitation Act Amendments of 1974, Pub. L 93–516, 88 Stat. 1619 (29 U.S.C. 706); sec. 606, Education of the Handicapped Act (20 U.S.C. 1405), as amended by Pub. L 94–142, 89 Stat. 795.

Subpart A—General Provisions

§ 104.1 Purpose.

The purpose of this part is to effectuate section 504 of the Rehabilitation Act of 1973, which is designed to eliminate discrimination on the basis of handicap in any program or activity receiving Federal financial assistance.

§ 104.2 Application.

This part applies to each recipient of Federal financial assistance from the Department of Education and to each program or activity that receives or benefits from such assistance.

§ 104.3 Definitions.

As used in this part, the term:

(a) *The Act* means the Rehabilitation Act of 1973, Pub. L. 93–112, as amended by the Rehabilitation Act Amendments of 1974, Pub. L. 93–516, 29 U.S.C. 794

(b) *Section 504* means section 504 of the Act.

(c) *Education of the Handicapped Act* means that statute as amended by the Education for all Handicapped Children Act of 1975, Pub. L 94–142, 20 U.S.C. 1401 et seq.

(d) *Department* means the Department of Education.

(e) *Assistant Secretary* means the Assistant Secretary for Civil Rights of the Department of Education.

(f) *Recipient* means any state or its political subdivision, any instrumentality of a state or its political subdivision, any public or private agency, institution, organization, or other entity, or any person to which Federal financial assistance is extended directly or through another recipient, including any successor, assignee, or transferee of a recipient, but excluding the ultimate beneficiary of the assistance.

(g) *Applicant for assistance* means one who submits an application, request, or plan required to be approved by a Department official or by a recipient as a condition to becoming a recipient.

(h) *Federal financial assistance* means any grant, loan, contract (other than a procurement contract or a contract of insurance or guaranty), or any other arrangement by which the Department provides or otherwise makes available assistance in the form of:

(1) Funds;

(2) Services of Federal personnel; or

(3) Real and personal property or any interest in or use of such property, including:

(i) Transfers or leases of such property for less than fair market value or for reduced consideration; and

(ii) Proceeds from a subsequent transfer or lease of such property if the Federal share of its fair market value is not returned to the Federal Government.

(i) *Facility* means all or any portion of buildings, structures, equipment, roads, walks, parking lots, or other real or personal property or interest in such property.

(j) *Handicapped person.* (1) "Handicapped persons" means any person who (i) has a physical or mental impairment which substantially limits one or more major life activities, (ii) has a record of such an impairment, or (iii) is regarded as having such an impairment.

(2) As used in paragraph (j)(1) of this section, the phrase:

(i) Physical or mental impairment means (A) any physiological disorder or condition, cosmetic disfigurement, or anatomical loss affecting one or more of the following body systems: neurological; musculoskeletal: special sense organs; respiratory, including speech organs; cardiovascular, reproductive, digestive, genito-urinary; hemic and lymphatic; skin; and endocrine; or (B) any mental or psychological disorder, such as mental retardation, organic brain syndrome, emotional or mental illness, and specific learning disabilities.

(ii) *Major life activities* means functions such as caring for one's self, performing manual tasks, walking, seeing, hearing, speaking, breathing, learning, and working.

(iii) *Has a record of such an impairment* means has a history of, or has been misclassified as having, a mental or physical impairment that substantially limits one or more major life activities.

(iv) *Is regarded as having an impairment* means (A) has a physical or mental impairment that does not substantially limit major life activities but that is treated by a recipient as constituting such a limitation; (B) has a physical or mental impairment that substantially limits major life activities only as a result of the attitudes of others toward such impairment; or (C) has none of the impairments defined in paragraph (j)(2)(i) of this section but is treated by a recipient as having such an impairment.

(k) *Qualified handicapped person* means:

(1) With respect to employment, a handicapped person who, with reasonable accommodation, can perform the essential functions of the job in question;

(2) With respect to public preschool elementary, secondary, or adult educational services, a handicapped person (i) of an age during which nonhandicapped persons are provided such services, (ii) of any age during which it is mandatory under state law to provide such services to handicapped persons, or (iii) to whom a state is required to provide a free appropriate public education under section 612 of the Education of the Handicapped Act; and

(3) With respect to postsecondary and vocational education services, a handicapped person who meets the academic and technical standards requisite to admission or participation in the recipient's education program or activity;

(4) With respect to other services, a handicapped person who meets the essential eligibility requirements for the receipt of such services.

(l) *Handicap* means any condition or characteristic that renders a person a handicapped person as defined in paragraph (j) of this section.

§ 104.4 Discrimination prohibited.

(a) *General.* No qualified handicapped person shall, on the basis of handicap, be excluded from participation in, be denied the benefits of, or otherwise be subjected to discrimination under any program or activity which receives or benefits from Federal financial assistance.

(b) *Discriminatory actions prohibited.* (1) A recipient, in providing any aid, benefit, or service, may not, directly or through contractual, licensing, or other arrangements, on the basis of handicap:

(i) Deny a qualified handicapped person the opportunity to participate in or benefit from the aid, benefit, or service;

(ii) Afford a qualified handicapped person an opportunity to participate in or benefit from the aid, benefit, or service that is not equal to that afforded others;

(iii) Provide a qualified handicapped person with an aid, benefit, or service that is not as effective as that provided to others;

(iv) Provide different or separate aid, benefits, or services to handicapped persons or to any class of handicapped persons unless such action is necessary to provide qualified handicapped persons with aid, benefits, or services that are as effective as those provided to others;

(v) Aid or perpetuate discrimination against a qualified handicapped person by providing significant assistance to an agency, organization, or person that discriminates on the basis of handicap in providing any aid, benefit, or service to beneficiaries of the recipients program;

(vi) Deny a qualified handicapped person the opportunity to participate as a member of planning or advisory boards; or

(vii) Otherwise limit a qualified handicapped person in the enjoyment of any right, privilege, advantage, or opportunity enjoyed by others receiving an aid, benefit, or service.

(2) For purposes of this part, aids, benefits, and services, to be equally effective, are not required to produce the identical result or level of achievement for handicapped and nonhandicapped persons, but must afford handicapped persons equal opportunity to obtain the same result, to gain the same benefit, or to reach the same level of achievement, in the most integrated setting appropriate to the person's needs.

(3) Despite the existence of separate or different programs or activities provided in accordance with this part, a recipient may not deny a qualified handicapped person the opportunity to participate in such programs or activities that are not separate or different.

(4) A recipient may not, directly or through contractual or other arrangements, utilize criteria or methods of administration (i) that have the effect of subjecting qualified handicapped persons to discrimination on the basis of handicap, (ii) that have the purpose or effect of defeating or substantially impairing accomplishment of the objectives of the recipient's program with respect to handicapped persons, or (iii) that perpetuate the discrimination of another recipient if both recipients are subject to common administrative control or are agencies of the same State.

(5) In determining the site or location of a facility, an applicant for assistance or a recipient may not make selections (i) that have the effect of excluding handicapped persons from, denying them the benefits of, or otherwise subjecting them to discrimination under any program or activity that receives or benefits from Federal financial assistance or (ii) that have the purpose or effect of defeating or substantially impairing the accomplishment of the objectives of the program or activity with respect to handicapped persons.

(6) As used in this section, the aid, benefit, or service provided under a program or activity receiving or benefiting from Federal financial assistance includes any aid, benefit, or service provided in or through a facility that has been constructed, expanded, altered, leased or rented, or otherwise acquired, in whole or in part, with Federal financial assistance.

(c) *Programs limited by Federal law.* The exclusion of nonhandicapped persons from the benefits of a program limited by Federal statute or executive order to handicapped persons or the exclusion of a specific class of handicapped persons from a program limited by Federal statute or executive order to a different class of handicapped persons is not prohibited by this part.

§ 104.5 Assurances required.

(a) *Assurances.* An applicant for Federal financial assistance for a program or activity to which this part applies shall submit an assurance, in a form specified by the Assistant Secretary that the program will be operated in compliance with this part. An applicant may incorporate these assurances by reference in subsequent applications to the Department.

(b) *Duration of Obligation.* (1) In the case of Federal financial assistance extended in the form of real property or to provide real property or structures on the property, the assurances will obligate the recipient or, in the case of a subsequent transfer, the transferee, for the period during which the real property or structures are for the purpose for which Federal financial assistance is extended or for another purpose involving the provision of similar services or benefits.

(2) In the case of Federal financial assistance extended to provide personal property, the assurance will obligate the recipient for the period during which it retains ownership or possession of the property.

(3) In all other cases the assurance will obligate the recipient for the period during which Federal financial assistance is extended.

(c) *Covenants.* (1) Where Federal financial assistance is provided in the form of real property or interest in the property from the Department, the instrument effecting or recording this transfer shall contain a covenant running with the land to assure nondiscrimination for the period during which the real property is used for a purpose for which the Federal financial assistance is extended or for another purpose involving the provision of similar services or benefits.

(2) Where no transfer of property is involved but property is purchased or improved with Federal financial assistance, the recipient shall agree to include the covenant described in paragraph (b)(2) of this section in the instrument effecting or recording any subsequent transfer of the property.

(3) Where Federal financial assistance is provided in the form of real property or interest in the property from the Department, the covenant shall also include a condition coupled with a right to be reserved by the Department to revert title to the property in the event of a breach of the covenant. If a transferee of real property proposes to mortgage or otherwise encumber the real property as security for financing construction of new, or improvement of existing, facilities on the property for the purposes for which the property was transferred, the Assistant Secretary may, upon request of the transferee and if necessary to accomplish

such financing and upon such conditions as he or she deems appropriate, agree to forbear the exercise of such right to revert title for so long as the lien of such mortgage or other encumbrance remains effective.

§ 104.6 Remedial action, voluntary action, and self-evaluation.

(a) *Remedial action.* (1) If the Assistant Secretary finds that a recipient has discriminated against persons on the basis of handicap in violation of section 504 or this part, the recipient shall take such remedial action as the Assistant Secretary deems necessary to overcome the effects of the discrimination.

(2) Where a recipient is found to have discriminated against persons on the basis of handicap in violation of section 504 or this part and where another recipient exercises control over the recipient that has discriminated, the Assistant Secretary, where appropriate, may require either or both recipients to take remedial action.

(3) The Assistant Secretary may, where necessary to overcome the effects of discrimination in violation of section 504 or this part, require a recipient to take remedial action (i) with respect to handicapped persons who are no longer participants in the recipient's program but who were participants in the program when such discrimination occurred or (ii) with respect to handicapped persons who would have been participants in the program had the discrimination not occurred.

(b) *Voluntary action.* A recipient may take steps, in addition to any action that is required by this part, to overcome the effects of conditions that resulted in limited participation in the recipient's program or activity by qualified handicapped persons.

(c) *Self-evaluation.* (1) A recipient shall, within one year of the effective date of this part:

(i) Evaluate, with the assistance of interested persons, including handicapped persons or organizations representing handicapped persons, its current policies and practices and the effects thereof that do not or may not meet the requirements of this part;

(ii) Modify, after consultation with interested persons, including handicapped persons or organizations representing handicapped persons, any policies and practices that do not meet the requirements of this part; and

(iii) Take, after consultation with interested persons, including handicapped persons or organizations representing handicapped persons, appropriate remedial steps to eliminate the effects of any discrimination that resulted from adherence to these policies and practices.

(2) A recipient that employs fifteen or more persons shall, for at least three years following completion of the evaluation required under paragraph (c)(1) of this section, maintain on file, make available for public inspection, and provide to the Assistant Secretary upon request: (i) A list of the interested persons consulted, (ii) a description of areas examined and any problems identified, and (iii) a description of any modifications made and of any remedial steps taken.

§ 104.7 Designation of responsible employee and adoption of grievance procedures.

(a) *Designation of responsible employee.* A recipient that employs fifteen or more persons shall designate at least one person to coordinate its efforts to comply with this part.

(b) *Adoption of grievance procedures.* A recipient that employs fifteen or more persons shall adopt grievance procedures that incorporate appropriate due process standards and that provide for the prompt and equitable resolution of complaints alleging any action prohibited by this part. Such procedures need not be established with respect to complaints from applicants for employment or from applicants for admission to postsecondary educational institutions.

§ 104.8 Notice.

(a) A recipient that employs fifteen or more persons shall take appropriate initial and continuing steps to notify participants, beneficiaries, applicants, and employees, including those with impaired vision or hearing, and unions or professional organizations holding collective bargaining or professional agreements with the recipient that it does not discriminate on the basis of handicap in violation of section 504 and this part. The notification shall state, where appropriate, that the recipient does not discriminate in admission or access to, or treatment or employment in, its programs and activities. The notification shall also include an identification of the responsible employee designated pursuant to § 104.7(a). A recipient shall make the initial notification required by this paragraph within 90 days of the effective date of this part. Methods of initial and continuing notification may include the posting of notices, publication in newspapers and magazines, placement of notices in recipients' publication, and distribution of memoranda or other written communications.

(b) If a recipient publishes or uses recruitment materials or publications containing general information that it makes available to participants, beneficiaries, applicants, or employees, it shall include in those materials or publications a statement of the policy described in paragraph (a) of this section. A recipient may meet the requirement of this paragraph either by including appropriate inserts in existing materials and publications or by revising and reprinting the materials and publications.

§ 104.9 Administrative requirements for small recipients.

The Assistant Secretary may require any recipient with fewer than fifteen employees, or any class of such recipients, to comply with §§ 104.7 and 104.8, in whole or in part, when the Assistant Secretary finds a violation of this part or finds that such compliance will not significantly impair the ability of the recipient or class of recipients to provide benefits or services.

§ 104.10 Effect of state or local law or other requirements and effect of employment opportunities.

(a) The obligation to comply with this part is not obviated or alleviated by the existence of any state or local law or other requirement that, on the basis of handicap, imposes prohibitions or limits upon the eligibility of qualified handicapped persons to receive services or to practice any occupation or profession.

(b) The obligation to comply with this part is not obviated or alleviated because employment opportunities in any occupation or profession are or may be more limited for handicapped persons than for nonhandicapped persons.

Subpart B—Employment Practices

§ 104.11 Discrimination prohibited.

(a) *General.* (1) No qualified handicapped person shall, on the basis of handicap, be subjected to discrimination in employment under any program or activity to which this part applies.

(2) A recipient that receives assistance under the Education of the Handicapped Act shall take positive steps to employ and advance in employment qualified handicapped persons in programs assisted under that Act.

(3) A recipient shall make all decisions concerning employment under any program or activity to which this part applies in a manner which ensures that discrimination on the basis of handicap does not occur and may not limit, segregate, or classify applicants or employees in any way that adversely affects their opportunities or status because of handicap.

(4) A recipient may not participate in a contractual or other relationship that has the effect of subjecting qualified handicapped applicants or employees to discrimination prohibited by this subpart. The relationships referred to in this subparagraph include relationships with employment and referral agencies, with labor unions, with organizations providing or administering fringe benefits to employees of the recipient, and with organizations providing training and apprenticeship programs

(b) *Specific activities.* The provisions of this subpart apply to:

(1) Recruitment, advertising, and the processing of applications for employment;

(2) Hiring, upgrading, promotion, award of tenure, demotion, transfer, layoff, termination, right of return from layoff and rehiring;

(3) Rates of pay or any other form of compensation and changes in compensation;

(4) Job assignments, job classifications, organizational structures, position descriptions, lines of progression, and seniority lists;

(5) Leaves of absence, sick leave, or any other leave;

(6) Fringe benefits available by virtue of employment, whether or not administered by the recipient;

(7) Selection and financial support for training, including apprenticeship, professional meetings, conferences, and other related activities, and selection for leaves of absence to pursue training;

(8) Employer sponsored activities, including social or recreational programs; and

(9) Any other term, condition, or privilege of employment.

(c) A recipient's obligation to comply with this subpart is not affected by any inconsistent term of any collective bargaining agreement to which it is a party.

§ 104.12 Reasonable accommodation.

(a) A recipient shall make reasonable accommodation to the known physical or mental limitations of an otherwise qualified handicapped applicant or employee unless the recipient can demonstrate that the accommodation would impose an undue hardship on the operation of its program.

(b) Reasonable accommodation may include:

(1) Making facilities used by employees readily accessible to and usable by handicapped persons, and

(2) job restructuring, part-time or modified work schedules, acquisition or modification of equipment or devices, the provision of readers or interpreters, and other similar actions.

(c) In determining pursuant to paragraph (a) of this section whether an accommodation would impose an undue hardship on the operation of a recipient's program, factors to be considered include:

(1) The overall size of the recipient's program with respect to number of employees, number and type of facilities, and size of budget;

(2) The type of the recipient's operation, including the composition and structure of the recipient's workforce; and

(3) The nature and cost of the accommodation needed.

(d) A recipient may not deny any employment opportunity to a qualified handicapped employee or applicant if the basis for the denial is the need to make reasonable accommodation to the physical or mental limitations of the employee or applicant.

§ 104.13 Employment criteria.

(a) A recipient may not make use of any employment test or other selection criterion that screens out or tends to screen out handicapped persons or any class of handicapped persons unless: (1) The test score or other selection criterion, as used by the recipient, is shown to be job-related for the position in question, and (2) alternative job-related tests or criteria that do not screen out or tend to screen out as many handicapped persons are not shown by the Assistant Secretary to be available.

(b) A recipient shall select and administer tests concerning employment so as best to ensure that, when administered to an applicant or employee who has a handicap that impairs sensory, manual, or speaking skills, the test results accurately reflect the applicant's or employee's job skills, aptitude, or whatever other factor the test purports to measure, rather than reflecting the applicant's or employee's impaired sensory, manual, or speaking skills (except where those skills are the factors that the test purports to measure).

§ 104.14 Preemployment inquiries.

(a) Except as provided in paragraphs (b) and (c) of this section, a recipient may not conduct a preemployment medical examination or may not make preemployment inquiry of an applicant as to whether the applicant is a handicapped person or as to the nature or severity of a handicap. A recipient may, however, make preemployment inquiry into an applicant's ability to perform job-related functions.

(b) When a recipient is taking remedial action to correct the effects of past discrimination pursuant to 104.6(a), when a recipient is taking voluntary action to overcome the effects of conditions that resulted in limited participation in its federally assisted program or activity pursuant to 104.6(b), or when a recipient is taking affirmative action pursuant to section 503 of the Act, the recipient may invite applicants for employment to indicate whether and to what extent they are handicapped, *Provided*, That:

(1) The recipient states clearly on any written questionnaire used for this purpose or makes clear orally if no written questionnaire is used that the information requested is intended for use solely in connection with its remedial action obligations or its voluntary or affirmative action efforts; and

(2) The recipient states clearly that the information is being requested on a voluntary basis, that it will be kept confidential as provided in paragraph (d) of this section, that refusal to provide it will not subject the applicant or employee to any adverse treatment, and that it will be used only in accordance with this part.

(c) Nothing in this section shall prohibit a recipient from conditioning an offer of employment on the results of a medical examination conducted prior to the employee's entrance on duty, *Provided*, That: (1) All entering employees are subjected to such an examination regardless of handicap, and (2) the results of such an examination are used only in accordance with the requirements of this part.

(d) Information obtained in accordance with this section as to the medical condition or history of the applicant shall be collected and maintained on separate forms that shall be accorded confidentiality as medical records, except that:

(1) Supervisors and managers may be informed regarding restrictions on the work or duties of handicapped persons and regarding necessary accommodations;

(2) First aid and safety personnel may be informed, where appropriate, if the condition might require emergency treatment; and

(3) Government officials investigating compliance with the Act shall be provided relevant information upon request.

Subpart C—Program accessibility

§ 104.21 Discrimination prohibited.

No qualified handicapped person shall, because a recipient's facilities are inaccessible to or unusable by handicapped persons, be denied the benefits of, be excluded from participation in, or otherwise be subjected to discrimination under any program or activity to which this part applies.

§ 104.22 Existing facilities.

(a) *Program accessibility.* A recipient shall operate each program or activity to which this part applies so that the program or activity, when viewed in its entirety, is readily accessible to handicapped persons. This paragraph does not require a recipient to make each of its existing facilities or every part of a facility accessible to and usable by handicapped persons.

(b) *Methods.* A recipient may comply with the requirements of paragraph (a) of this section through such means as redesign of equipment, reassignment of classes or other services to accessible buildings, assignment of aides to beneficiaries, home visits, delivery of health, welfare, or other social services at alternate accessible sites, alteration of existing facilities and construction of new facilities in conformance with the requirements of § 104.23, or any other methods that result in making its program or activity accessible to handicapped persons. A recipient is not required to make structural changes in existing facilities where other methods are effective in achieving compliance with paragraph (a) of this section. In choosing among available methods for meeting the requirement of paragraph (a) of this section, a recipient shall give priority to those methods that offer programs and activities to handicapped persons in the most integrated setting appropriate.

(c) *Small health, welfare, or other social service providers.* If a recipient with fewer than fifteen employees that provides health, welfare, or other social services finds, after consultation with a handicapped person seeking its services, that there is no method of complying with paragraph (a) of this section other than making a significant alteration in its existing facilities, the recipient may, as an alternative, refer the handicapped person to other providers of those services that are accessible.

(d) *Time period.* A recipient shall comply with the requirement of paragraph (a) of this section within sixty days of the effective date of this part except that where structural changes in facilities are necessary, such changes shall be made within three years of the effective date of this part, but in any event as expeditiously as possible.

(e) *Transition plan.* In the event that structural changes to facilities are necessary to meet the requirement of paragraph (a) of this section, a recipient shall develop, within six months of the effective date of this part, a transition plan setting forth the steps necessary to complete such changes. The plan shall be developed with the assistance of interested persons, including handicapped persons or organizations representing handicapped persons. A copy of the transition plan shall be made available for public inspection. The plan shall, at a minimum:

(1) Identify physical obstacles in the recipient's facilities that limit the accessibility of its program or activity to handicappped persons;

(2) Describe in detail the methods that will be used to make the facilities accessible;

(3) Specify the schedule for taking the steps necessary to achieve full program accessibility and, if the time period of the transition plan is longer than one year, identify steps that will be taken during each year of the transition period; and

(4) Indicate the person responsible for implementation of the plan.

(f) *Notice.* The recipient shall adopt and implement procedures to ensure that interested persons, including persons with impaired vision or hearing, can obtain information as to the existence and location of services, activities, and facilities that are accessible to and usable by handicapped persons.

§ 104.23 New construction.

(a) *Design and construction.* Each facility or part of a facility constructed by, on behalf of, or for the use of a recipient shall be designed and constructed in such manner that the facility or part of the facility is readily accessible to and usable by handicapped persons, if the construction was commenced after the effective date of this part.

(b) *Alteration.* Each facility or part of a facility which is altered by, on behalf of, or for the use of a recipient after the effective date of this part in a manner that affects or could affect the usability of the facility or part of the facility shall, to the maximum extent feasible, be altered in such manner that the altered portion of the facility is readily accessible to and usable by handicapped persons.

(c) *Conformance with Uniform Federal Accessibility Standards.* (1) Effective as of January 18, 1991, design, construction, or alteration of buildings in conformance with sections 3-8 of the Uniform Federal Accessibility Standards (UFAS)(Appendix A to 41 CFR subpart 101-19.6) shall be deemed to comply with the requirements of this section with respect to those buildings. Departures from particular technical and scoping requirements of UFAS by the use of other methods are permitted where substantially equivalent or greater access to and usability of the building is provided.

(2) For purposes of this section, section 4.1.6(g) of UFAS shall be interpreted to exempt from the requirements of UFAS only mechanical rooms and other spaces that, because of their intended use, will not require accessibility to the public or beneficiaries or result in the employment or residence therein of persons with physical handicaps.

(3) This section does not require recipients to make building alterations that have little likelihood of being accomplished without removing or altering a load-bearing structural member.

Subpart D—Preschool, Elementary, and Secondary Education

§ 104.31 Application of this subpart.

Subpart D applies to preschool, elementary, secondary, and adult education programs and activities that receive or benefit from Federal financial assistance and to recipients that operate, or that receive or benefit from Federal financial assistance for the operation of, such programs or activities.

§ 104.32 Location and notification.

A recipient that operates a public elementary or secondary education program shall annually:

(a) Undertake to identify and locate every qualified handicapped person residing in the recipient's jurisdiction who is not receiving a public education; and

(b) Take appropriate steps to notify handicapped persons and their parents or guardians of the recipient's duty under this subpart.

§ 104.33 Free appropriate public education.

(a) *General.* A recipient that operates a public elementary or secondary education program shall provide a free appropriate public education to each qualified handicapped person who is in the recipient's jurisdiction, regardless of the nature or severity of the person's handicap.

(b) *Appropriate education.* (1) For the purpose of this subpart, the provision of an appropriate education is the provision of regular or special education and related aids and services that (i) are designed to meet individual educational needs of handicapped persons as adequately as the needs of nonhandicapped persons are met and (ii) are based upon adherence to procedures that satisfy the requirements of §§ 104.34, 104.35, and 104.36.

(2) Implementation of an individualized education program developed in accordance with the Education of the Handicapped Act is one means of meeting the standard established in paragraph (b)(1)(i) of this section.

(3) A recipient may place a handicapped person in or refer such person to a program other than the one that it operates as its means of carrying out the requirements of this subpart. If so, the recipient remains responsible for ensuring that the requirements of this subpart are met with respect to any handicapped person so placed or referred.

(c) *Free education*—(1) *General.* For the purpose of this section, the provision of a free education is the provision of educational and related services without cost to the handicapped person or to his or her parents or guardian, except for those fees that are imposed on nonhandicapped persons or their parents or guardian. It may consist either of the provision of free services or, if a recipient places a handicapped person in or refers such person to a program not operated by the recipient as its means of carrying out the requirements of this subpart, of payment for the costs of the program. Funds available from any public or private agency may be used to meet the requirements of this subpart. Nothing in this section shall be construed to relieve an insurer or similar third party from an otherwise valid obligation to provide or pay for services provided to a handicapped person.

(2) *Transportation.* If a recipient places a handicapped person in or refers such person to a program not operated by the recipient as its means of carrying out the requirements of this subpart, the recipient shall ensure that adequate transportation to and from the program is provided at no greater cost than would be incurred by the person or his or her parents or guardian if the person were placed in the program operated by the recipient.

(3) *Residential placement.* If placement in a public or private residential program is necessary to provide a free appropriate public education to a handicapped person because of his or her handicap, the program, including nonmedical care and room and board, shall be provided at no cost to the person or his or her parents or guardian.

(4) *Placement of handicapped persons by parents.* If a recipient has made available, in conformance with the requirements of this section and § 104.34, a free appropriate public education to a handicapped person and the person's parents or guardian choose to place the person in a private school, the recipient is not required to pay for the person's education in the private school. Disagreements between a parent or guardian and a recipient regarding whether the recipient has made such a program available or otherwise regarding the question of financial responsibility are subject to the due process procedures of § 104.36.

(d) *Compliance.* A recipient may not exclude any qualified handicapped person from a public elementary or secondary education after the effective date of this part. A recipient that is not, on the effective date of this regulation, in full compliance with the other requirements of the preceding paragraphs of this section shall meet such requirements at the earliest practicable time and in no event later than September 1, 1978.

§ 104.34 Educational setting.

(a) *Academic setting.* A recipient to which this subpart applies shall educate, or shall provide for the education of, each qualified handicapped person in its jurisdiction with persons who are not handicapped to the maximum extent appropriate to the needs of the handicapped person. A recipient shall place a handicapped person in the regular educational environment operated by the recipient unless it is demonstrated by the recipient that the education of the person in the regular environment with the use of supplementary aids and services cannot be achieved satisfactorily. Whenever a recipient places a person in a setting other than the regular educational environment pursuant to this paragraph, it shall take into account the proximity of the alternate setting to the person's home.

(b) *Nonacademic settings.* In providing or arranging for the provision of nonacademic and extracurricular services and activities, including meals, recess periods, and the services and activities set forth in § 104.37(a)(2), a recipient shall ensure that handicapped persons participate with nonhandicapped persons in such activities and services to the maximum extent appropriate to the needs of the handicapped person in question.

(c) *Comparable facilities.* If a recipient, in compliance with paragraph (a) of this section, operates a facility that is identifiable as being for handicapped persons, the recipient shall ensure that the facility and the services and activities provided therein are comparable to the other facilities, services, and activities of the recipient.

§ 104.35 Evaluation and placement.

(a) *Preplacement evaluation.* A recipient that operates a public elementary or secondary education program shall conduct an evaluation in accordance with the requirements of paragraph (b) of this section of any person who, because of handicap, needs or is believed to need special education or related services before taking any action with respect to the initial placement of the person in a regular or special education program and any subsequent significant change in placement.

(b) *Evaluation procedures.* A recipient to which this subpart applies shall establish standards and procedures for the evaluation and placement of persons who, because of handicap, need or are believed to need special education or related services which ensure that:

(1) Tests and other evaluation materials have been validated for the specific purpose for which they are used and are administered by trained personnel in conformance with the instructions provided by their producer;

(2) Tests and other evaluation materials include those tailored to assess specific areas of educational need and not merely those which are designed to provide a single general intelligence quotient; and

(3) Tests are selected and administered so as best to ensure that, when a test is administered to a student with impaired sensory, manual, or speaking skills, the test results accurately reflect the student's aptitude or achievement level or whatever other factor the test purports to measure, rather than reflects the student's impaired sensory, manual, or speaking skills (except where those skills are the factors that the test purports to measure).

(c) *Placement procedures.* In interpreting evaluation data and in making placement decisions, a recipient shall (1) draw upon information from a variety of sources, including aptitude and achievement tests, teacher recommendations, physical condition, social or cultural background, and adaptive behavior, (2) establish procedures to ensure that information obtained from all such sources is documented and carefully considered, (3) ensure that the placement decision is made by a group of persons, including persons knowledgeable about the child, the meaning of the evaluation data, and the placement options, and (4) ensure that the placement decision is made in conformity with § 104.34.

(d) *Reevaluation.* A recipient to which this section applies shall establish procedures, in accordance with paragraph (b) of this section, for periodic reevaluation of students who have been provided special education and related services. A reevaluation procedure consistent with the Education of the Handicapped Act is one means of meeting this requirement.

§ 104.36 Procedural safeguards.

A recipient that operates a public elementary or secondary education program shall establish and implement, with respect to actions regarding the identification, evaluation, or educational placement of persons who, because of handicap, need or are believed to need special instruction or related services, a system of procedural safeguards that includes notice, an opportunity for the parents or guardian of the person to examine relevant records, an impartial hearing with opportunity for participation by the person's parents or guardian and representation by counsel, and a review procedure. Compliance with the procedural safeguards of section 615 of the Education of the Handicapped Act is one means of meeting this requirement.

§ 104.37 Nonacademic services.

(a) *General.* (1) A recipient to which this subpart applies shall provide non-academic and extracurricular services and activities in such manner as is necessary to afford handicapped students an equal opportunity for participation in such services and activities.

(2) Nonacademic and extracurricular services and activities may include counseling services, physical recreational athletics, transportation, health services, recreational activities, special interest groups or clubs sponsored by the recipient referrals to agencies which provide assistance to handicapped persons, and employment of students, including both employment by the recipient and assistance in making available outside employment.

(b) *Counseling services.* A recipient to which this subpart applies that provides personal, academic, or vocational counseling, guidance, or placement services to its students shall provide these services without discrimination on the basis of handicap. The recipient shall ensure that qualified handicapped students are not counseled toward more restrictive career objectives than are nonhandicapped students with similar interests and abilities.

(c) *Physical education and athletics.* (1) In providing physical education courses and athletics and similar programs and activities to any of its students, a recipient to which this subpart applies may not discriminate on the basis of handicap. A recipient that offers physical education courses or that operates or sponsors interscholastic, club, or intramural athletics shall provide to qualified handicapped students an equal opportunity for participation in these activities.

(2) A recipient may offer to handicapped students physical education and athletic activities that are separate or different from those offered to nonhandicapped students only if separation or differentiation is consistent with the requirements of § 104.34 and only if no qualified handicapped student is denied the opportunity to compete for teams or to participate in courses that are not separate or different.

§ 104.38 Preschool and adult education programs.

A recipient to which this subpart applies that operates a preschool education or day care program or activity or an adult education program or activity may not, on the basis of handicap, exclude qualified handicapped persons from the program or activity and shall take into account the needs of such persons in determining the aid, benefits, or services to be provided under the program or activity.

§ 104.39 Private education programs.

(a) A recipient that operates a private elementary or secondary education program may not, on the basis of handicap, exclude a qualified handicapped person from such program if the person can, with minor adjustments, be provided an appropriate education, as defined in 104.33(b)(1), within the recipient's program.

(b) A recipient to which this section applies may not charge more for the provision of an appropriate education to handicapped persons than to nonhandicapped persons except to the extent that any additional charge is justified by a substantial increase in cost to the recipient.

(c) A recipient to which this section applies that operates special education programs shall operate such programs in accordance with the provisions of §§ 104.35 and 104.36. Each recipient to which this section applies is subject to the provisions of §§ 104.34, 104.37, and 104.38.

Subpart E—Postsecondary Education

§ 104.41 Application of this subpart.

Subpart E applies to postsecondary education programs and activities, including postsecondary vocational education programs and activities, that receive or benefit from Federal financial assistance and to recipients that operate, or that receive or benefit from Federal financial assistance for the operation of, such programs or activities.

§ 104.42 Admissions and recruitment.

(a) *General.* Qualified handicapped persons may not, on the basis of handicap, be denied admission or be subjected to discrimination in admission or recruitment by a recipient to which this subpart applies.

(b) *Admissions.* In administering its admission policies, a recipient to which this subpart applies:

(1) May not apply limitations upon the number or proportion of handicapped persons who may be admitted;

(2) May not make use of any test or criterion for admission that has a disproportionate, adverse effect on handicapped persons or any class of handicapped persons unless (i) the test or criterion, as used by the recipient, has been validated as a predictor of success in the education program or activity in question and (ii) alternate tests or criteria that have a less disproportionate, adverse effect are not shown by the Assistant Secretary to be available.

(3) Shall assure itself that (i) admissions tests are selected and administered so as best to ensure that, when a test is administered to an applicant who has a handicap that impairs sensory, manual, or speaking skills, the test results accurately reflect the applicant's aptitude or achievement level or whatever other factor the test purports to measure, rather than reflecting the applicant's impaired sensory, manual, or speaking skills (except where those skills are the factors that the test purports to measure); (ii) admissions tests that are designed for persons with impaired sensory, manual, or speaking skills are offered as often and in as timely a manner as are other admissions tests; and (iii) admissions tests are administered in facilities that, on the whole, are accessible to handicapped persons; and

(4) Except as provided in paragraph (c) of this section, may not make preadmission inquiry as to whether an applicant for admission is a handicapped person but, after admission, may make inquiries on a confidential basis as to handicaps that may require accommodation.

(c) *Preadmission inquiry exception.* When a recipient is taking remedial action to correct the effects of past discrimination pursuant to § 104.6(a) or when a recipient is taking voluntary action to overcome the effects of conditions that resulted in limited participation in its federally assisted program or activity pursuant to 104.6(b), the recipient may invite applicants for admission to indicate whether and to what extent they are handicapped, *Provided*, That:

(1) The recipient states clearly on any written questionnaire used for this purpose or makes clear orally if no written questionnaire is used that the information requested is intended for use solely in connection with its remedial action obligations or its voluntary action efforts; and

(2) The recipient states clearly that the information is being requested on a voluntary basis, that it will be kept confidential, that refusal to provide it will not subject the applicant to any adverse treatment, and that it will be used only in accordance with this part.

(d) *Validity studies.* For the purposes of paragraph (b)(2) of this section, a recipient may base prediction equations on first year grades, but shall conduct periodic validity studies against the criterion of overall success in the education program or activity in question in order to monitor the general validity of the test scores.

§ 104.43 Treatment of students; general.

(a) No qualified handicapped student shall, on the basis of handicap, be excluded from participation in, be denied the benefits of, or otherwise be subjected to discrimination under any academic, research, occupational training, housing, health insurance, counseling, financial aid, physical education, athletics, recreation, transportation, other extracurricular, or other postsecondary education program or activity to which this subpart applies.

(b) A recipient to which this subpart applies that considers participation by students in education programs or activities not operated wholly by the recipient as part of, or equivalent to, an education program or activity operated by the recipient shall assure itself that the other education program or activity, as a whole, provides an equal opportunity for the participation of qualified handicapped persons.

(c) A recipient to which this subpart applies may not, on the basis of handicap, exclude any qualified handicapped student from any course, course of study, or other part of its education program or activity.

(d) A recipient to which this subpart applies shall operate its programs and activities in the most integrated setting appropriate.

§ 104.44 Academic adjustments.

(a) *Academic requirements.* A recipient to which this subpart applies shall make such modifications to its academic requirements as are necessary to ensure that such requirements do not discriminate or have the effect of discriminating, on the basis of handicap, against a qualified handicapped applicant or student. Academic requirements that the recipient can demonstrate are essential to the program of instruction being pursued by such student or to any directly related licensing requirement will not be regarded as discriminatory within the meaning of this section. Modifications may include changes in the length of time permitted for the completion of degree requirements, substitution of specific courses required for completion of degree requirements, and adaptation of the manner in which specific courses are conducted.

(b) *Other rules.* A recipient to which this subpart applies may not impose upon handicapped students other rules such as the prohibition of tape recorders in classrooms or of dog guides in campus buildings, that have the effect of limiting the participation of handicapped students in the recipient's education program or activity.

(c) *Course examinations.* In its course examinations or other procedures for evaluating students' academic achievement in its program, a recipient to which this subpart applies shall provide such methods for evaluating the achievement of students who have a handicap that impairs sensory, manual, or speaking skills as will best ensure that the results of the evaluation represents the student's achievement in the course, rather than reflecting the student's impaired sensory, manual, or speaking skills (except where such skills are the factors that the test purports to measure).

(d) *Auxiliary aids.* (1) A recipient to which this subpart applies shall take such steps as are necessary to ensure that no handicapped student is denied the benefits of, excluded from participation in, or otherwise subjected to discrimination under the education program or activity operated by the recipient because of the absence of educational auxiliary aids for students with impaired sensory, manual, or speaking skills.

(2) Auxiliary aids may include taped texts, interpreters or other effective methods of making orally delivered materials available to students with hearing impairments, readers in libraries for students with visual impairments, classroom equipment adapted for use by students with manual impairments, and other similar services and actions. Recipients need not provide attendants, individually prescribed devices, readers for personal use or study, or other devices or services of a personal nature.

§ 104.45 Housing.

(a) *Housing provided by the recipient.* A recipient that provides housing to its nonhandicapped students shall provide comparable, convenient, and accessible housing to handicapped students at the same cost as to others. At the end of the transition period provided for in Subpart C, such housing shall be available in sufficient quantity and variety so that the scope of handicapped students' choice of living accommodations is, as a whole, comparable to that of nonhandicapped students.

(b) *Other housing.* A recipient that assists any agency, organization, or person in making housing available to any of its students shall take such action as may be necessary to assure itself that such house is, as a whole, made available in a manner that does not result in discrimination on the basis of handicap.

§ 104.46 Financial and employment assistance to students.

(a) *Provision of financial assistance.* (1) In providing financial assistance to qualified handicapped persons, a recipient to which this subpart applies may not (i), on the basis of handicap, provide less assistance than is provided to nonhandicapped persons, limit eligibility for assistance, or otherwise discriminate or (ii) assist any entity or person that provides assistance to any of the recipient's students in a manner that discriminates against qualified handicapped persons on the basis of handicap.

(2) A recipient may administer or assist in the administration of scholarships, fellowships, or other forms of financial assistance established under wills, trusts, bequests, or similar legal instruments that require awards to be made on the basis of factors that discriminate or have the effect of discriminating on the basis of handicap only if the overall effect of the award of scholarships, fellowships, and other forms of financial assis-

tance is not discriminatory on the basis of handicap.

(b) *Assistance in making available outside employment.* A recipient that assists any agency, organization, or person in providing employment opportunities to any of its students shall assure itself that such employment opportunities, as a whole, are made available in a manner that would not violate Subpart B if they were provided by the recipient.

(c) *Employment of students by recipients.* A recipient that employs any of its students may not do so in a manner that violates Subpart B.

§ 104.47 Nonacademic services.

(a) *Physical education and athletics.* (1) In providing physical education courses and athletics and similar programs and activities to any of its students, a recipient to which this subpart applies may not discriminate on the basis of handicap. A recipient that offers physical education courses or that operates or sponsors intercollegiate, club, or intramural athletics shall provide to qualified handicapped students an equal opportunity for participation in these activities.

(2) A recipient may offer to handicapped students physical education and athletic activities that are separate or different only if separation or differentiation is consistent with the requirements of § 104.43(d) and only if no qualified handicapped student is denied the opportunity to compete for teams or to participate in courses that are not separate or different.

(b) *Counseling and placement services.* A recipient to which this subpart applies that provides personal, academic, or vocational counseling, guidance, or placement services to its students shall provide these services without discrimination on the basis of handicap. The recipient shall ensure that qualified handicapped students are not counseled toward more restrictive career objectives than are nonhandicapped students with similar interests and abilities. This requirement does not preclude a recipient from providing factual information about licensing and certification requirements that may present obstacles to handicapped persons in their pursuit of particular careers.

(c) *Social organizations.* A recipient that provides significant assistance to fraternities, sororities, or similar organizations shall assure itself that the membership practices of such organizations do not permit discrimination otherwise prohibited by this subpart.

Subpart F—Health, Welfare, and Social Services

§ 104.51 Application of this subpart.

Subpart F applies to health, welfare, and other social service programs and activities that receive or benefit from Federal financial assistance and to recipients that operate, or that receive or benefit from Federal financial assistance for the operation of, such programs or activities.

§ 104.52 Health, welfare, and other social services.

(a) *General.* In providing health, welfare, or other social services or benefits, a recipient may not, on the basis of handicap:

(1) Deny a qualified handicapped person these benefits or services;

(2) Afford a qualified handicapped person an opportunity to receive benefits or services that is not equal to that offered nonhandicapped persons;

(3) Provide a qualified handicapped person with benefits or services that are not as effective (as defined in § 104.4(b)) as the benefits or services provided to others;

(4) Provide benefits or services in a manner that limits or has the effect of limiting the participation of qualified handicapped persons; or

(5) Provide different or separate benefits or services to handicapped persons except where necessary to provide qualified handicapped persons with benefits and services that are as effective as those provided to others.

(b) *Notice.* A recipient that provides notice concerning benefits or services or written material concerning waivers of rights or consent to treatment shall take such steps as are necessary to ensure that qualified handicapped persons, including those with impaired sensory or speaking skills, are not denied effective notice because of their handicap.

(c) *Emergency treatment for the hearing impaired.* A recipient hospital that provides health services or benefits shall establish a procedure for effective communication with persons with impaired hearing for the purpose of providing emergency health care.

(d) *Auxiliary aids.* (1) A recipient to which this subpart applies that employs fifteen or more persons shall provide appropriate auxiliary aids to persons with impaired sensory, manual, or speaking skills, where necessary to afford such persons an equal opportunity to benefit from the service in question.

(2) The Assistant Secretary may require recipients with fewer than fifteen employees to provide auxiliary aids where the provision of aids would not significantly impair the ability of the recipient to provide its benefits or services.

(3) For the purpose of this paragraph, auxiliary aids may include brailled and taped material, interpreters, and other aids for persons with impaired hearing or vision.

§ 104.53 Drug and alcohol addicts.

A recipient to which this subpart applies that operates a general hospital or outpatient facility may not discriminate in admission or treatment against a drug or alcohol abuser or alcoholic who is suffering from a medical condition, because of the person's drug or alcohol abuse or alcoholism.

§ 104.54 Education of institutionalized persons.

A recipient to which this subpart applies and that operates or supervises a program or activity for persons who are institutionalized because of handicap shall ensure that each qualified handicapped person, as defined in § 104.3(k)(2), in its program or activity is provided an appropriate education, as defined in § 104.33(b). Nothing in this section shall be interpreted as altering in any way the obligations of recipients under Subpart D.

Subpart G—Procedures

§ 104.61 Procedures

The procedural provisions applicable to title VI of the Civil Rights Act of 1964 apply to this part. These procedures are found in §§ 100.6—100.10 and Part 101 of this title.

34 CFR § 76.532 Use of funds for religion prohibited.

(a) No state or subgrantee may use its grant or subgrant to pay for any of the following:

(1) Religious worship, instruction, or proselytization.

(2) Equipment or supplies to be used for any for the activities specified in paragraph (a)(1) of this section.

(3) Construction, remodeling, repair, operation, or maintenance of any facility or part of a facility to be used for any of the activities specified in paragraph (a)(1) of this section.

(4) An activity of a school or department of divinity.

(b) As used in this section, *school or department of divinity* means an institution or a component of an institution whose program is specifically for the education of students to:

(1) Prepare them to enter into a religious vocation; or

(2) Prepare them to teach theological subjects.

34 CFR § 76.654 Benefits for private school students.

(a) *Comparable benefits.* The program benefits that a subgrantee provides for students enrolled in private schools must be comparable in quality, scope, and opportunity for participation to the program benefits that the subgrantee provides for students enrolled in public schools.

(b) *Same Benefits.* If a subgrantee uses funds under a program for public school students in a particular attendance area, or grade or age level, the subgrantee shall insure equitable opportunities for participation by students enrolled in private schools who:

(1) Have the same needs as the public school student to be served; and

(2) Are in that group, attendance area, or age or grade level.

(c) *Different benefits.* If the needs of students enrolled in private schools are different from the needs of students enrolled in public schools, a subgrantee shall provide program benefits for the private school students that are different from the benefits the subgrantee provides for the public school students.

APPENDIX C

Table of Special Education Cases Decided by the U.S. Supreme Court

Title and Citation (in chronological order)

Southeastern Community College v. Davis, 442 U.S. 397, 99 S.Ct. 2361, 60 L.Ed.2d 980 (1979).

University of Texas v. Camenisch, 451 U.S. 390, 101 S.Ct. 1830, 68 L.Ed.2d 175 (1981).

Pennhurst State School and Hospital v. Halderman, 451 U.S. 1, 101 S.Ct. 1531, 67 L.Ed.2d 694 (1981).
(*Pennhurst I*)

Pennhurst State School and Hospital v. Halderman, 465 U.S. 89, 104 S.Ct. 900, 79 L.Ed.2d 67 (1984).
(*Pennhurst II*)

Board of Education v. Rowley, 458 U.S. 176, 102 S.Ct. 3034, 73 L.Ed.2d 690 (1982).

Irving Independent School District v. Tatro, 468 U.S. 883, 104 S.Ct. 3371, 82 L.Ed.2d 664 (1984).

Smith v. Robinson, 468 U.S. 992, 104 S.Ct. 3457, 82 L.Ed.2d 746 (1984).

Honig v. Students of California School for the Blind, 471 U.S. 148, 105 S.Ct. 1820, 85 L.Ed.2d 114 (1985).

Burlington School Committee v. Department of Education of Massachusetts, 471 U.S. 359, 105 S.Ct. 1996, 85 L.Ed.2d 385 (1985).

City of Cleburne, Texas v. Cleburne Living Center, 473 U.S. 432, 105 S.Ct. 3249, 87 L.Ed.2d 313 (1985).

Witters v. Washington Department of Services for the Blind, 474 U.S. 481, 106 S.Ct. 748, 88 L.Ed.2d 846 (1986).

School Board of Nassau County v. Arline, 480 U.S. 273, 107 S.Ct. 1123, 94 L.Ed.2d 307 (1987).

Honig v. Doe, 484 U.S. 305, 108 S.Ct. 592, 98 L.Ed.2d 686 (1988).

Traynor v. Turnage, 485 U.S. 535, 108 S.Ct. 1372, 99 L.Ed.2d 618 (1988).

Dellmuth v. Muth, 491 U.S. 223, 109 S.Ct. 2397, 105 L.Ed.2d 181 (1989).

Zobrest v. Catalina Foothills School Dist., 509 U.S. 1, 113 S.Ct. 2462, 125 L.Ed.2d 1 (1993).

Florence County School Dist. Four v. Carter, 510 U.S. 7, 114 S.Ct. 361, 126 L.Ed.2d 284 (1993).

Bd. of Educ. of Kiryas Joel Village School District v. Grumet, 512 U.S. 687, 114 S.Ct. 2481, 129 L.Ed.2d 546 (1994).

Cedar Rapids Community School Dist. v. Garret F., 526 U.S. 66, 119 S.Ct. 992, 143 L.Ed.2d 154 (1999).

The Judicial System

In order to allow you to determine the relative importance of a judicial decision, the cases included in ***Students with Disabilities and Special Education*** identify the particular court from which a decision has been issued. For example, a case decided by a state supreme court generally will be of greater significance than a state circuit court case. Hence a basic knowledge of the structure of our judicial system is important to an understanding of school law.

Almost all the reports in this volume are taken from appellate court decisions. Although most education law decisions occur at trial court and administrative levels, appellate court decisions have the effect of binding lower courts and administrators so that appellate court decisions have the effect of law within their court systems.

State and federal court systems generally function independently of each other. Each court system applies its own law according to statutes and the determinations of its highest court. However, judges at all levels often consider opinions from other court systems to settle issues which are new or arise under unique fact situations. Similarly, lawyers look at the opinions of many courts to locate authority which supports their clients' cases.

Once a lawsuit is filed in a particular court system, that system retains the matter until its conclusion. Unsuccessful parties at the administrative or trial court level generally have the right to appeal unfavorable determinations of law to appellate courts within the system. When federal law issues or Constitutional grounds are present, lawsuits may be appropriately filed in the federal court system. In those cases, the lawsuit is filed initially in the federal district court for that area.

On rare occasions, the U.S. Supreme Court considers appeals from the highest courts of the states if a distinct federal question exists and at least four justices agree on the question's importance. The federal courts occasionally send cases to state courts for application of state law. These situations are infrequent and in general, the state and federal court systems should be considered separate from each other.

The most common system, used by nearly all states and also the federal judiciary, is as follows: a legal action is commenced in district court (sometimes called trial court, county court, common pleas court or superior court) where a decision is initially reached. The case may then be appealed to the court of appeals (or appellate court), and in turn this decision may be appealed to the supreme court.

Several states, however, do not have a court of appeals; lower court decisions are appealed directly to the state's supreme court. Additionally, some states have labeled their courts in a nonstandard fashion.

In Maryland, the highest state court is called the Court of Appeals. In the state of New York, the trial court is called the Supreme Court. Decisions of this court may be appealed to the Supreme Court, Appellate Division. The highest court in New York is the Court of Appeals. Pennsylvania has perhaps the most complex court system. The lowest state court is the Court of Common Pleas. Depending on the circumstances of the case, appeals may be taken to either the Commonwealth Court or the Superior Court. In certain instances the Commonwealth Court functions as a trial court as well as an appellate court. The Superior Court, however, is strictly an intermediate appellate court. The highest court in Pennsylvania is the Supreme Court.

While supreme court decisions are generally regarded as the last word in legal matters, it is important to remember that trial and appeals court decisions also create important legal precedents. For the hierarchy of typical state and federal court systems, please see the diagram below.

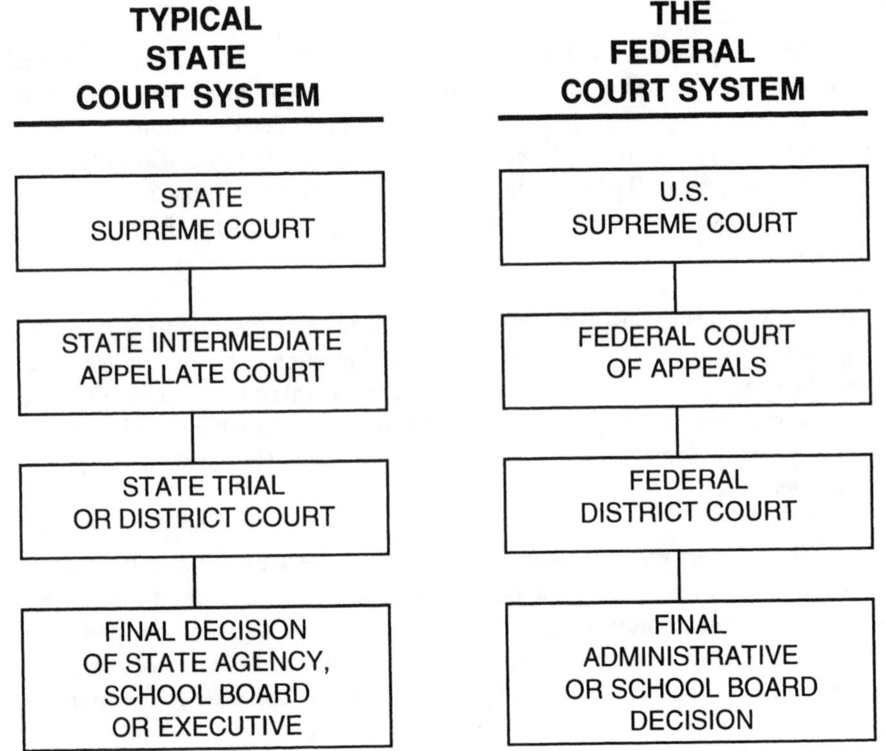

Federal courts of appeals hear appeals from the district courts which are located in their circuits. Below is a list of states matched to the federal circuits in which they are located.

First Circuit	—	Puerto Rico, Maine, New Hampshire, Massachusetts, Rhode Island
Second Circuit	—	New York, Vermont, Connecticut
Third Circuit	—	Pennsylvania, New Jersey, Delaware, Virgin Islands
Fourth Circuit	—	West Virginia, Maryland, Virginia, North Carolina, South Carolina
Fifth Circuit	—	Texas, Louisiana, Mississippi
Sixth Circuit	—	Ohio, Kentucky, Tennessee, Michigan
Seventh Circuit	—	Wisconsin, Indiana, Illinois
Eighth Circuit	—	North Dakota, South Dakota, Nebraska, Arkansas, Missouri, Iowa, Minnesota
Ninth Circuit	—	Alaska, Washington, Oregon, California, Hawaii, Arizona, Nevada, Idaho, Montana, Northern Mariana Islands, Guam
Tenth Circuit	—	Wyoming, Utah, Colorado, Kansas, Oklahoma, New Mexico
Eleventh Circuit	—	Alabama, Georgia, Florida
District of Columbia Circuit	—	Hears cases from the U.S. District Court for the District of Columbia.
Federal Circuit	—	Sitting in Washington, D.C., the U.S. Court of Appeals, Federal Circuit hears patent and trade appeals and certain appeals on claims brought against the federal government and its agencies.

How to Read a Case Citation

Generally, court decisions can be located in case reporters at law school or governmental law libraries. Some cases can also be located on the internet through legal websites or official court websites.

Each case summary contains the citation, or legal reference, to the full text of the case. The diagram below illustrates how to read a case citation.

case name (parties) ↘ — case reporter name and series ↓ — court location ↓

Michael C. v. Radnor Township School Dist., 202 F.3d 642 (3d Cir. 2000).

↗ volume number — ↗ first page — ↑ year of decision

Some cases may have two or three reporter names such as U.S. Supreme Court cases and cases reported in regional case reporters as well as state case reporters. For example, a U.S. Supreme Court case usually contains three case reporter citations.

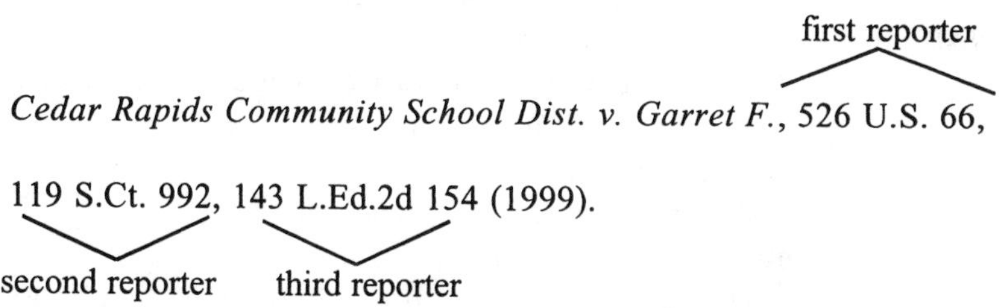

The citations are still read in the same manner as if only one citation has been listed.

Occasionally, a case may contain a citation which does not reference a case reporter. For example, a citation may contain a reference such as:

case name ↓ — year of decision ↓ — first page ↓

Pace v. Bogalusa City Sch. Bd., 2001 WL 258053, No. 99-806 (E.D. La. 2001).

↑ court location — ↖ year of decision — ↑ Westlaw®[1] — ↑ court file number

---

[1] Westlaw® is a computerized database of court cases available for a fee.

The court file number indicates the specific number assigned to a case by the particular court system deciding the case. In our example, the U.S. District Court for the Eastern District of Louisiana has assigned the case of *Pace v. Bogalusa City School Board* the case number of "No. 99-806" which will serve as the reference number for the case and any matter relating to the case. Locating a case on the internet generally requires either the case name and date of the decision, and/or the court file number.

Below, we have listed the full names of the regional reporters. As mentioned previously, many states have individual state reporters. The names of those reporters may be obtained from a reference law librarian.

P. **Pacific Reporter**
Alaska, Arizona, California, Colorado, Hawaii, Idaho, Kansas, Montana, Nevada, New Mexico, Oklahoma, Oregon, Utah, Washington, Wyoming

A. **Atlantic Reporter**
Connecticut, Delaware, District of Columbia, Maine, Maryland, New Hampshire, New Jersey, Pennsylvania, Rhode Island, Vermont

N.E. **Northeastern Reporter**
Illinois, Indiana, Massachusetts, New York, Ohio

N.W. **Northwestern Reporter**
Iowa, Michigan, Minnesota, Nebraska, North Dakota, South Dakota, Wisconsin

S. **Southern Reporter**
Alabama, Florida, Louisiana, Mississippi

S.E. **Southeastern Reporter**
Georgia, North Carolina, South Carolina,Virginia, West Virginia

S.W. **Southwestern Reporter**
Arkansas, Kentucky, Missouri, Tennessee, Texas

F. **Federal Reporter**
The thirteen federal judicial circuits courts of appeals decisions. *See, The Judicial System, p. 665* for specific state circuits.

F.Supp. **Federal Supplement**
The thirteen federal judicial circuits district court decisions.

Fed.Appx. **Federal Appendix**
Contains unpublished opinions of the U.S. Circuit Courts of Appeal.
See, The Judicial System, p. 665 for specific state circuits.

U.S. **United States Reports**
S.Ct. **Supreme Court Reporter** > U.S. Supreme Court Decisions
L.Ed. **Lawyers' Edition**

GLOSSARY

Age Discrimination in Employment Act (ADEA) - The ADEA, 29 U.S.C. § 621 *et seq.*, is part of the Fair Labor Standards Act. It prohibits discrimination against persons who are at least forty years old, and applies to employers which have twenty or more employees and which affect interstate commerce.

Americans With Disabilities Act (ADA) - The ADA, 42 U.S.C. § 12101 *et seq.*, went into effect on July 26, 1992. Among other things, it prohibits discrimination against a qualified individual with a disability because of that person's disability with respect to job application procedures, the hiring, advancement or discharge of employees, employee compensation, job training, and other terms, conditions and privileges of employment.

Bona fide - Latin term meaning "good faith." Generally used to note a party's lack of bad intent or fraudulent purpose.

Class Action Suit - Federal Rule of Civil Procedure 23 allows members of a class to sue as representatives on behalf of the whole class provided that the class is so large that joinder of all parties is impractical, there are questions of law or fact common to the class, the claims or defenses of the representatives are typical of the claims or defenses of the class, and the representative parties will adequately protect the interests of the class. In addition, there must be some danger of inconsistent verdicts or adjudications if the class action were prosecuted as separate actions. Most states also allow class actions under the same or similar circumstances.

Collateral Estoppel - Also known as issue preclusion. The idea that once an issue has been litigated, it may not be re-tried. Similar to the doctrine of *Res Judicata* (see below).

Due Process Clause - The clauses of the Fifth and Fourteenth Amendments to the Constitution which guarantee the citizens of the United States "due process of law" (see below). The Fifth Amendment's Due Process Clause applies to the federal government, and the Fourteenth Amendment's Due Process Clause applies to the states.

Due Process of Law - The idea of "fair play" in the government's application of law to its citizens, guaranteed by the Fifth and Fourteenth Amendments. Substantive due process is just plain *fairness*, and procedural due process is accorded when the government utilizes adequate procedural safeguards for the protection of an individual's liberty or property interests.

Education for All Handicapped Children Act (EAHCA) - [see Individuals with Disabilities Education Act (IDEA).]

Education of the Handicapped Act (EHA) - [see Individuals with Disabilities Education Act (IDEA).]

Enjoin - (see Injunction).

Equal Pay Act - Federal legislation which is part of the Fair Labor Standards Act. It applies to discrimination in wages which is based on gender. For race discrimination, employees paid unequally must utilize Title VII or 42 U.S.C. § 1981. Unlike many labor statutes, there is no minimum number of employees necessary to invoke the act's protection.

Equal Protection Clause - The clause of the Fourteenth Amendment which prohibits a state from denying any person within its jurisdiction equal protection of its laws. Also, the Due Process Clause of the Fifth Amendment which pertains to the federal government. This has been interpreted by the Supreme Court to grant equal protection even though there is no explicit grant in the Constitution.

Establishment Clause - The clause of the First Amendment which prohibits Congress from making "any law respecting an establishment of religion." This clause has been interpreted as creating a "wall of separation" between church and state. The test now used to determine whether government action violates the Establishment Clause, referred to as the *Lemon* test, asks whether the action has a secular purpose, whether its primary effect promotes or inhibits religion, and whether it requires excessive entanglement between church and state.

Fair Labor Standards Act (FLSA) - Federal legislation which mandates the payment of minimum wages and overtime compensation to covered employees. The overtime provisions require employers to pay at least time-and-one-half to employees who work more than 40 hours per week.

Federal Tort Claims Act - Federal legislation which determines the circumstances under which the United States waives its sovereign immunity (see below) and agrees to be sued in court for money damages. The government retains its immunity in cases of intentional torts committed by its employees or agents, and where the tort is the result of a "discretionary function" of a federal employee or agency. Many states have similar acts.

42 U.S.C. §§ 1981, 1983 - Section 1983 of the federal Civil Rights Act prohibits any person acting under color of state law from depriving any other person of rights protected by the Constitution or by federal laws. A vast majority of lawsuits claiming constitutional violations are brought under § 1983. Section 1981 provides that all persons enjoy the same right to make and enforce contracts as "white citizens." Section 1981 applies to employment contracts. Further, unlike § 1983, § 1981 applies even to private actors. It is not limited to those acting under color of state law. These sections do not apply to the federal government, though the government may be sued directly under the Constitution for any violations.

Free Appropriate Public Education (FAPE) - The IDEA requires local educational agencies to provide students with disabilities with a free appropriate public education. Under the federal FAPE standard, a student receives a FAPE through an individually developed education program that allows the student to receive educational benefit. States can enact higher standards under the IDEA, but at a minimum must comply with the federal standard governing the provision of a FAPE.

Free Exercise Clause - The clause of the First Amendment which prohibits Congress from interfering with citizens' rights to the free exercise of their religion. Through the Fourteenth Amendment, it has also been made applicable to the states and their sub-entities. The Supreme Court has held that laws of general applicability which have an incidental effect on persons' free exercise rights are not violative of the Free Exercise Clause.

Handicapped Children's Protection Act (HCPA) - [see also Individuals with Disabilities Education Act (IDEA).] The HCPA, enacted as an amendment to the EHA, provides for the payment of attorney's fees to a prevailing parent or guardian in a lawsuit brought under the EHA (IDEA).

Hearing Officer - Also known as an administrative law judge. The hearing officer decides disputes that arise *at the administrative level*, and has the power to administer oaths, take testimony, rule on evidentiary questions, and make determinations of fact.

Immunity (Sovereign Immunity) - Federal, state and local governments are free from liability for torts committed except in cases in which they have consented to be sued (by statute or by court decisions).

Incorporation Doctrine - By its own terms, the Bill of Rights applies only to the federal government. The Incorporation Doctrine states that the Fourteenth Amendment makes the Bill of Rights applicable to the states.

Individuals with Disabilities Education Act (IDEA) - Also known as the Education of the Handicapped Act (EHA), the Education for All Handicapped Children Act (EAHCA), and the Handicapped Children's Protection Act (HCPA). Originally enacted as the EHA, the IDEA is the federal legislation which provides for the free, appropriate public education of all children with disabilities.

Individualized Education Program (IEP) - The IEP is designed to give children with disabilities a free, appropriate education. It is updated annually, with the participation of the child's parents or guardian.

Injunction - An equitable remedy (see Remedies) wherein a court orders a party to do or refrain from doing some particular action.

Issue Preclusion - Also known as collateral estoppel, the legal rule that prohibits a court from reconsideration of a particular issue in litigation arising from the same set of facts, involving the same parties and requesting similar relief to a matter previously heard by the court.

Jurisdiction - The power of a court to determine cases and controversies. The Supreme Court's jurisdiction extends to cases arising under the Constitution and under federal law. Federal courts have the power to hear cases where there is diversity of citizenship or where a federal question is involved.

Least Restrictive Environment/Mainstreaming - Part of what is required for a free, appropriate education is that each child with a disability be educated in the "least restrictive environment." To the extent that disabled children are educated with nondisabled children in regular education classes, those children are being mainstreamed.

Negligence per se - Negligence on its face. Usually, the violation of an ordinance or statute will be treated as negligence per se because no careful person would have been guilty of it.

Per Curiam - Latin phrase meaning "by the court." Used in court reports to note an opinion written by the court rather than by a single judge or justice.

Placement - A special education student's placement must be appropriate (as well as responsive to the particular child's needs). Under the IDEA's "stay-put" provision, school officials may not remove a special education child from his or her "then current placement" over the parents' objections until the completion of administrative or judicial review proceedings.

Preemption Doctrine - Doctrine which states that when federal and state law attempt to regulate the same subject matter, federal law prevents the state law from operating. Based on the Supremacy Clause of Article VI, Clause 2, of the Constitution.

Pro Se - A party appearing in court, without the benefit of an attorney, is said to be appearing pro se.

Rehabilitation Act - Section 504 of the Rehabilitation Act prohibits employers who receive federal financial assistance from discriminating against otherwise qualified individuals with handicaps solely because of their handicaps. An otherwise qualified individual is one who can perform the "essential functions" of the job with "reasonable accomodation."

Related Services - As part of the free, appropriate education due to children with disabilities, school districts may have to provide related services such as transportation, physical and occupational therapy, and medical services which are for diagnostic or evaluative purposes relating to education.

Remand - The act of an appellate court in returning a case to the court from which it came for further action.

Remedies - There are two general categories of remedies, or relief: legal remedies, which consist of money damages, and equitable remedies, which consist of a court mandate that a specific action be prohibited or required. For example, a claim for compensatory and punitive damages seeks a legal remedy; a claim for an injunction seeks an equitable remedy. Equitable remedies are generally unavailable unless legal remedies are inadequate to address the harm.

Res Judicata - The judicial notion that a claim or action may not be tried twice or relitigated, or that all causes of action arising out of the same set of operative facts should be tried at one time. Also known as claim preclusion.

Section 1981 & Section 1983 - (see 42 U.S.C. §§ 1981, 1983).

Sovereign Immunity - The idea that the government cannot be sued without its consent. It stems from the English notion that the "King could do no wrong." This immunity from suit has been abrogated in most states and by the federal government through legislative acts known as "tort claims acts."

Standing - The judicial doctrine which states that in order to maintain a lawsuit a party must have some real interest at stake in the outcome of the trial.

Statute of Limitations - A statute of limitation provides the time period in which a specific cause of action may be brought.

Summary Judgment - Federal Rule of Civil Procedure 56 provides for the summary adjudication of a case before trial if either party can show that there is no genuine issue as to any material fact and that, given the facts agreed upon, the party is entitled to judgment as a matter of law. In general, summary judgment is used to dispose of claims which do not support a legally recognized claim.

Supremacy Clause - Clause in Article VI of the Constitution which states that federal legislation is the supreme law of the land. This clause is used to support the Preemption Doctrine (see above).

Title VII, Civil Rights Act of 1964 (Title VII) - Title VII prohibits discrimination in employment based upon race, color, sex, national origin, or religion. It applies to any employer having fifteen or more employees. Under Title VII, where an employer intentionally discriminates, employees may obtain money damages unless the claim is for race discrimination. For those claims, monetary relief is available under 42 U.S.C. § 1981.

Tort - A tort is a civil wrong, other than breach of contract. Torts include negligence, assault, battery, trespass, defamation, infliction of emotional distress and wrongful death.

U.S. Equal Employment Opportunity Commission (EEOC) - The EEOC is the government entity which is empowered to enforce Title VII (see above) through investigation and/or lawsuits. Private individuals alleging discrimination must pursue administrative remedies within the EEOC before they are allowed to file suit under Title VII.

Vacate - The act of annulling the judgment of a court either by an appellate court or by the court itself. The Supreme Court will generally vacate a lower court's judgment without deciding the case itself, and remand the case to the lower court for further consideration in light of some recent controlling decision.

Writ of Certiorari - The device used by the Supreme Court to transfer cases from the appellate court's docket to its own. Since the Supreme Court's appellate jurisdiction is largely discretionary, it need only issue such a writ when it desires to rule in the case.

INDEX